ADVANCE PR.

Thinking About Black Education: An Interdisciplinary Reader

"Now this is the book we've been waiting for in educational studies. An ingenious one-stop academic commentary featuring many of the most treasured treatises on historical and contemporary Black education. A must-read!"

—Tondra L. Loder-Jackson, Professor, Educational Foundations,
African American Studies, and History, University of Alabama at Birmingham

"Every so often we need a reminder of the history and hope in Black education. Hilton Kelly and Heather Moore Roberson have put forth a collection that forces us to look back and remember while we question forward and imagine. This volume brings together some of the most brilliant scholars in Black education. Let us listen and learn."

—Donyell L. Roseboro, Professor and Chief Diversity Officer,
University of North Carolina Wilmington

"Black education has been an enduring struggle for freedom, access, equity, and excellence in a world that has largely been systematically and sentimentally anti-black. This wonderfully curated collection reflects how Black scholars have engaged this struggle, transformed the discourse, and emerged as the field of Black educational studies."

—Denise Taliaferro Baszile, Professor and Associate Dean,
Miami University of Ohio

THINKING ABOUT BLACK EDUCATION

Thinking About Black Education

An Interdisciplinary Reader

EDITED BY

Hilton Kelly
and Heather Moore Roberson

Myers
Education
Press

GORHAM, MAINE

Published by Myers Education Press, LLC
P.O. Box 424
Gorham, ME 04038

Myers Education Press is an academic publisher specializing in books, e-books, and digital content in the field of education. All of our books are subjected to a rigorous peer review process and produced in compliance with the standards of the Council on Library and Information Resources.

LIBRARY OF CONGRESS CATALOGING-IN-PUBLICATION DATA AVAILABLE FROM LIBRARY OF CONGRESS.

13-digit ISBN 978-1-9755-0252-2 (paperback)
13-digit ISBN 978-1-9755-0253-9 (library networkable e-edition)
13-digit ISBN 978-1-9755-0254-6 (consumer e-edition)

Printed in the United States of America.

All first editions printed on acid-free paper that meets the American National Standards Institute Z39-48 standard.

Books published by Myers Education Press may be purchased at special quantity discount rates for groups, workshops, training organizations, and classroom usage. Please call our customer service department at 1-800-232-0223 for details.

Cover design by Teresa Lagrange

Visit us on the web at **www.myersedpress.com** to browse our complete list of titles.

Editorial Note to Readers:

Please be aware that there may be typographical errors in some places in the text. The editors of this collection decided to maintain the integrity of the original material, including errors that appeared in those texts. With this acknowledgment, the authors are providing an explanation for what otherwise might be interpreted as carelessness.

Contents

Dedication   xi

Acknowledgments   xiii

Preface   xv

Part I

Introduction: Out From the Gloomy Past   1

Selection 1:

In Secret Places: Acquiring Literacy in Slave Communities   9
   Heather Andrea Williams

Selection 2:

Ex-Slaves and the Rise of Universal Education in the South, 1860–1880   37
   James D. Anderson

Selection 3:

Spreading the Word: The Cultural Work of The Black Press   65
   Elizabeth McHenry

Selection 4:

The Spread of Northern School Segregation, 1890–1940   123
   D. M. Douglas

Selection 5:

Organized Resistance and Black Educators' Quest for School Equality, 1878–1938   163
   Vanessa Siddle Walker

Selection 6:

Patterns of Black Excellence   197
   Thomas Sowell

Selection 7:

The Price of Desegregation   225
   Trudier Harris

Part II

Introduction: A (Black) Nation at Risk?   233

Selection 8:
Black Students' School Success: Coping With the Burden of "Acting White"   241
    Signithia Fordham and John U. Ogbu

Selection 9:
Reexamining Resistance as Oppositional Behavior:
The Nation of Islam and the Creation of a Black Achievement Ideology   273
    A. A. Akom

Selection 10:
The Canary in the Mine: The Achievement Gap Between Black and White Students   303
    Mano Singham

Selection 11: Toward a Theory of Culturally Relevant Pedagogy   317
    Gloria Ladson-Billings

Selection 12:
Introduction: Teaching to Transgress   345
    bell hooks
Feminist Scholarship: Black Scholars   353
    bell hooks

Selection 13:
Toward a Critical Race Theory of Education   359
    Gloria Ladson- Billings and William F. Tate IV

Selection 14:
Early Schooling and Academic Achievement of African American Males   381
    James Earl Davis

Selection 15:
"Those Loud Black Girls": (Black) Women, Silence,
and Gender "Passing" in the Academy   399
    Signithia Fordham

Selection 16: Framing and Reviewing Hip-Hop Educational Research   427
    Emery Petchauer

Selection 17: "Be Real Black for Me": Imagining BlackCrit in Education   463
    Michael J. Dumas and kihana miraya ross

Contributors & Editors   487
Index   493

Dedication

To Mary S. Peake, W. E. B. Du Bois, Booker T. Washington, Carter G. Woodson, Mary McLeod Bethune, Anna Julia Cooper, Septima Clark, Nannie Helen Burroughs, Charlotte Hawkins Brown, and all the other architects of Black education whose thinking and praxes brought monumental changes to the lives and life chances of people of African descent in the United States and the world across many generations.

HK

To Black youth who are eager to learn about the ideas associated with Black education. The future rests with you.

HMR

Acknowledgments

Journal Articles

Adapted from "Organized Resistance and Black Educators' Quest for School Equality, 1878–1938," by V.S. Walker, 2005, *Teachers College Record, Volume 107,* Issue 3, (https://doi.org/10.1111/j.1467-9620.2005.00480.x)

Adapted from "Black students' school success: Coping with the burden of 'Acting White'," by S. Fordham and J.U. Ogbu, 1986, *The Urban Review, Volume 18,* Issue 3, (https://doi.org/10.1007/BF01112192)

Adapted from "Reexamining Resistance as Oppositional Behavior: The Nation of Islam and the Creation of a Black Achievement Ideology," by A. Akom, 2003, *Sociology Of Education, Volume 76,* Issue 4, *(https://doi.org/10.2307/1519868)*

Adapted from "The Canary in the Mine: The Achievement Gap between Black and White Students," by M. Singham, 1998, *Phi Delta Kappan, Volume 80,* Article 1

Adapted from "Toward a Theory of Culturally Relevant Pedagogy," by G. Ladson-Billings, 1995, *American Educational Research Journal, Volume 32,* Issue 3, (https://doi.org/10.2307/1163320)

Adapted from "Toward a Critical Race Theory of Education," by G. Ladson-Billings and W. F. Tate, 1995, *Teachers College Record, Volume 97,* Issue 1, (https://doi.org/10.1177/016146819509700104)

Adapted from "Early Schooling and Academic Achievement of African American Males," by J. E. Davis, 2003, *Urban Education, Volume 38,* Issue 5, (https://doi.org/10.1177/0042085903256)

Adapted from "Those Loud Black Girls: (Black) Women, Silence, and Gender "Passing" in the Academy," by S. Fordham, 1993, *Anthropology & Education Quarterly, Volume 24,* Issue 1, (https://doi.org/10.1525/aeq.1993.24.1.05x1736t)

Adapted from "Framing and reviewing hip-hop educational research," by E. Petchauer, 2009, *Review of Educational Research, Volume 79,* Issue 2, (https://doi.org/10.3102/0034654308330967)

Books

Preface

Education is the one thing that White folk can't take away. This iconic phrase has been spoken, written, remembered, and passed down from generation to generation within Black families, institutions, and communities. Whether used as a motivator to do well in school or as a reminder alongside well-wishes for college graduation, this simple yet powerful phrase links a Black past to a Black present. It communicates, further, the importance of "getting an education" in a White-dominant world. As the editors of *Thinking About Black Education: An Interdisciplinary Reader*, we reminisced about multiple times and situations in which we were told some version of this phrase—from "one thing that a *White man* can't take away" to "one thing that *nobody* can take away." Such sentiments are rooted in a long history of Black people thinking about education as essential to Black liberation (Givens, 2021; Grant et al., 2015).

In this interdisciplinary reader, we provide both content and context for thinking about Black education. We present timeless and contemporary readings from educational anthropology, history, legal studies, literary studies, and sociology to document the foundations and development of Black education in the United States. We highlight scholarship offering historical, conceptual, and pedagogical gems that shine a light on Black people's enduring pursuit of liberatory education. We also extend an invitation to a broad audience, from people with no previous knowledge to published scholars in the field, to think critically about Black education through our carefully selected readings uncovering the dreams, struggles, aspirations, and liberation of Black people over time.

We have compiled these readings into one volume to archive some of the best scholarship on Black education, as well as to inspire future generations to pursue the unfinished business of our ancestors—that is, the business of creating a culturally responsive, democratic, equitable, and just education for all. To this end, any effort to reform or revolutionize the current educational system we inherited demands understanding a nuanced and complex story about Black education in the United States. In the story we tell, Black people are targets of oppression, and they exhibit ingenuity and resilience despite prejudice, discrimination, and violence. Black people are "canaries in the mine," signaling danger for a nation willing to suppress educational attainment and opportunities for marginalized individuals and groups (Singham, 2005). In spite of all the educational progress that Black people have made over centuries, which we cover in this volume, the thoughts and actions presented here are meaningless when readers do not have access to them and when they do not use them for greater purposes.

We hope that *Thinking about Black Education* gives a wider readership access to what ought to be required reading for anyone interested in learning about Black history and culture or working in education-related careers with Black children, educators, and communities. Much of what has been written about Black education is not easily accessible to people outside of college and university settings. Paywalls and subscription costs make it nearly impossible for some people to read many of the articles and book chapters we have provided here. For different reasons, we hope this book will be suitable and useful for our colleagues: K–12 educators in public and private schools; college-level faculty who teach Black education courses in Africana studies, American studies, educational studies, or sociology departments; master's and doctoral students who are writing theses or preparing comprehensive examinations; and education policymakers who need to be informed about Black educational history, theories, and philosophies. After reading the selections in this volume, everyone will understand on a deeper level why it has been important in Black culture to get an education—something White folk can't take away.

Thinking about Black Education reflects our intellectual orientations and academic training. We are both published scholars in the field of Black education with graduate degrees in sociology and in American studies, respectively. We are both social justice–oriented interdisciplinary scholars who read outside of the field of education to understand power, agency, and resistance, which has strongly shaped our approach to the readings selected in this volume. Ultimately, our goal is to contribute to knowledge by identifying and highlighting "essential ideas" that have changed the way we think about Black education. The readings we have selected, then, are somewhat idiosyncratic and, perhaps, surprising to specialists because we are less concerned about including "famous" or "well-known" education scholars. Although we were simply concerned with the ideas, not the person, it is clear that all included in this book are pioneering and well-known scholars in their fields. While there are many brilliant scholars who could have been included, we settled on our personal favorites who we credit with changing the way we think about Black education.

Far from being the last word on Black education, we have provided a bird's-eye view of the field's landscape. For each reading selected, there are many exceptionally good essays, articles, and books that should be read. Our volume is divided into two parts: "Out from a Gloomy Past" and "A (Black) Nation at Risk." The short introductory essays to each part offer a snapshot of the context and content that will be covered. The purpose is to link disparate, groundbreaking, and interdisciplinary research together to tell our story of Black education. *Thinking About Black Education: An Interdisciplinary Reader* is, we believe, effective at bringing together a range of ideas about Black education across and between multiple disciplines in a single volume. We hope the volume urges readers to search for more readings, starting with the ones cited in the references, as well as inspiring others to conduct further research in the areas covered here or in entirely new directions.

The volume has a few limitations that we think are important to address. First, our research focus is on K–12 education in formal and nonformal settings. This is not an oversight—we are limited by our academic training, which was focused on K–12 education, not higher education. An interdisciplinary reader on Black higher education demands a separate volume. Second, Part II is focused entirely on students' experiences inside the classroom or the school. We made the decision to focus on the formal school setting here, because our scholarly interest is in naming and addressing schooling practices in the "afterlife of school segregation" (see ross, 2021). Although we examine Black people's experiences within formal and nonformal educational spaces in Part I, there is much that we left out of the story that could have documented thinking about Black communities, teachers, administrators, and extracurricular activities outside of the school setting. Ultimately, our volume is painted with a broad brush and does not intend to be a history of Black education or a chronicle of every scholarly work that has contributed to Black educational thought.

This volume would not have been possible without the support of many people and institutions. First, we would like to thank the publishers who allowed us to reproduce the writings included here. Without the work of the brilliant contributors, this volume could not exist. More important, without their scholarship, the field of Black education would be lacking some major stories, concepts, and knowledge that have offered a way to freedom and justice for us. Second, we would like to thank the Office of the Vice President of Academic Affairs at Davidson College for its generous investment in and support of the book project with the Faculty of the Future Funds and a Faculty, Study, and Research Publication Grant. Dean Fuji Lozada, who believed in the project from the very beginning, made sure funds were made available. We are grateful to the Office of the Provost at Allegheny College for its professional development funding. Provost Ron Cole, Terry Bensel, and Rachel Weir were extremely supportive and encouraging throughout key moments in the process. Third, we are grateful to our families and colleagues for their listening ears and helpful comments throughout the process.

References

Givens, J. R. (2021). *Fugitive pedagogy: Carter G. Woodson and the art of Black teaching.* Harvard University Press.

Grant, C. A., Brown, K. D., & Brown, A. L. (2015). *Black intellectual thought in education: The missing traditions of Anna Julia Cooper, Carter G. Woodson and Alain Locke*. Routledge.

ross, k. m. (2021). On Black education: Anti-Blackness, refusal, and resistance. In C. A. Grant, A. N. Woodson, & M. J. Dumas (Eds.), *The future is Black: Afropessimism, fugitivity and radical hope in education* (pp. 16–21). Routledge.

Singham, M. (2005). *The achievement gap in U.S. education: Canaries in the mine*. Rowman & Littlefield.

Part I
Out From the Gloomy Past

Out From the Gloomy Past

LIBRARIES ARE FULL of materials that can inform us about the schooling and education of Black people in the United States. An ever-increasing number of books and periodicals have documented Black people's pursuit of education and schooling, the construction of institutions and systems, and the achievements of individuals and groups throughout key historical periods from slavery and Jim Crow to civil rights and the age of Obama. In Part I, we explore readings that provide a historical context and an important corrective to the idea that Black people were merely recipients of education and schooling built by "the White architects of Black education" (see Watkins, 2001). The readings we have selected curate groundbreaking interdisciplinary scholarship that both challenges and revises accepted official stories about the early centuries of Black education. Given the vast literature available, we contend that no one can fully understand and appreciate Black educational experiences in the United States without starting with the scholarship presented here.

The section begins with a reading from Heather Andrea Williams's (2005) *Self-Taught: African American Education in Slavery and Freedom* titled "In Secret Places: Acquiring Literacy in Slave Communities." Here, Williams explains how enslaved people and communities acquired literacy despite enduring and puzzling myths, such as "slaves could not learn to read or write." Williams was not the first to debunk the notion that enslaved people possessed varying levels of literacy and numeracy and that an entire Free Black population forged literate communities. There is mounting evidence uncovering reading and writing practices among enslaved and free Black people that have been lost to history or warehoused in libraries. Williams demonstrates, after masterfully mining numerous archives and old newspapers, "the importance of literacy as an instrument of resistance and for freedom by bringing into clear view the clandestine tactics and strategies that enslaved people employed to gain some control over their own lives" (p. 8). In pursuit of solid evidence to document the world enslaved people created, which included literate individuals, cultures, and subcultures, Williams had to read between the lines and pose different questions to sacred and untapped primary sources.

Once you start thinking about the enslaved and how they were not completely removed from literate culture in the United States, despite antiliteracy statutes and the threat of violence, you have to wonder about the consequences of this new knowledge. James Anderson (1988) covered a great deal of uncharted territory in his pioneering book *The Education of Blacks in the South, 1860–1935*. In the opening chapter "Ex-Slaves and the Rise of Universal Education in the South, 1860–1880," he chronicles, brilliantly, "the ex-slaves' struggle for universal schooling, why they pursued it, how they organized to defend their common interests, how they coped with the resistance of opposing social classes, and finally, how they gained the cooperation of sympathetic social groups" (pp. 4–5). Anderson confirmed a forgotten thesis that it was formerly enslaved people, or freedpeople, who pushed for universal schooling in the United States once they were emancipated (see also Bond, 1934; Du Bois, 1935/1998). Freedpeople embodied the theoretical distinction between education and schooling, as some enslaved people acquired a rudimentary education despite having never stepped one foot inside of a school building. The push for universal schooling signaled freedom and citizenship in the aftermath of the Civil War, and freedpeople led the fight.

In "Spreading the Word: The Cultural Work of the Black Press," Elizabeth McHenry recovers the reading practices and cultures of Free Blacks in the urban North. This reading from McHenry's *Forgotten Readers: Recovering the Lost History of African American Literary Societies* (2002) draws attention to the development in the North of a Black readership outside of formal schooling structures. According to McHenry, she set out to "explore the ways in which and the extent to which the antebellum African American press promoted the development of literary character and extended the formation of literary community among free blacks in the urban North" (p. 86). Thinking beyond the push for universal schooling in the South, which Anderson writes about in this volume, McHenry's recovery project calls attention to not only the pursuit of education by African Americans north of slavery but also the domains outside of formal schooling structures where reading, writing, and thinking happened.

Altogether, Williams, Anderson, and McHenry dispel the notion that abject illiteracy made all African Americans unfit for citizenship after the Civil War ended. Conceding that not everyone read a newspaper, wrote their name, or attended a school, these texts, when read together, explain how people of African descent embraced literacy as freedom and employed "the master's tools" to demand schooling for everyone (Lorde,

2018). Moreover, these readings move us "out from the gloomy past," to borrow words from James Weldon Johnson and J. Rosamond Johnson's "Lift Every Voice and Sing," or what has become known as the Black National Anthem (see I. Perry, 2018). As essential readings for thinking about Black education, they mark both struggle and aspiration during slavery and in emancipation throughout the United States.

The end of slavery should have led to the incorporation of freedpeople and free Blacks—later referred to as Negroes, Coloreds, Blacks, and, much later, African Americans—into the national body politic with full access to social and political institutions, as well as the enjoyment of life, liberty, and the pursuit of happiness. In 1896, however, the *Plessy v. Ferguson* decision choked any dreams or hopes that a constitutionally free Black population could enjoy the rights and privileges of full citizenship. The "separate but equal" principle made it illegal for Blacks and Whites in the South to go to school together, ride on a streetcar or bus side by side, eat in the same restaurants, or watch a movie sitting elbow to elbow. Such examples of everyday racism were rooted in White supremacist logic, practices, and policies that shaped social relations in every town, city, and state in the United States.

The remaining readings focus on the long and historic battle over segregated schooling for Blacks in the United States. Through carefully selected readings, we document how Black people navigated very rough educational terrains in the North and the South and created educational organizations, institutions, and traditions behind the proverbial walls of segregation. Beginning with "The Spread of Northern School Segregation, 1890–1940" in *Jim Crow Moves North: The Battle over Northern School Segregation, 1865–1954*, historian Davison M. Douglas (2005) confirms that school segregation existed in the North, and while it may not have been legal, it was undeniably cultural and political. White people used racial separation as a tool to constrain and control southern Blacks who started moving "up North" for personal freedoms and work opportunities in the late 1800s—decades before the Great Migration. Quite remarkable were the racist justifications by northern White educational authorities—principals, teachers, and school boards—who pushed vehemently for race-based school segregation. One example out of many that Douglas recorded was from a White principal in New Jersey:

> I believe in segregation. . . . [Black children] are like little animals. There is
> no civilization in their homes. They shouldn't hold up white children who
> have had these things for centuries. They are not as clean. They are careless
> about their bodies. Why should we contaminate our race?" (p. 156)

Douglas's work reminds us that common beliefs about a racist legally segregated South obfuscate the origins of segregation in the North and the fact that northern whites disregarded anti-segregation laws when large numbers of Negroes took up residence in their communities (see also Woodward, 1974).

Thinking and writing about the same historical period that Davison covers, Vanessa Siddle Walker's 2005 "Organized Resistance and Black Educators' Quest for School Equality, 1878–1938" uncovers the educational world that Blacks in the South created *because of* segregation and *in spite of* inequalities. While it is important to read Walker's entire body of work on Black educators and segregated schooling, the reading we have selected brings together key aspects of her thinking and writing over time. Here, she interrogates and dispels an enduring belief that "Black educators were sidelined in efforts to achieve equality, and that their primary concern was to protect their own self-centered individual interests" (p. 355). To the contrary, Walker convincingly argues and chronicles the development and organization of teacher associations fighting for pay equity, demanding equal school funding, and acquiring better school facilities, among other things, long before the founding of the National Association for the Advancement of Colored People. Using Georgia as a case study, she demonstrates how educators organized in the segregated South and beyond, eventually establishing a networked umbrella organization—the American Teachers Association, formerly the National Colored Teachers Association (1906–1907) and the National Association of Teachers in Colored Schools (1907–1937). For a full-length study of the American Teachers Association with primary sources, see Thelma Perry's (1975) pioneering work.

In "Patterns of Black Excellence," Thomas Sowell (1976) writes a classic piece that unearthed what he called a long history of Black advancement that complements the research that Douglas and Walker, and so many others, have contributed to the study of "valued segregated schools" in the Age of Segregation (Walker, 2000). Writing against White perceptions and assumptions about Black education before the 1970s, Sowell stated plainly, "the pathology is well known and extensively documented, while the healthy or outstanding functioning is almost totally unknown and unstudied. Yet educational excellence has been achieved by black Americans" (p. 1). Sowell provided six profiles of notable and successful all-Black high schools and elementary schools that exhibited remarkable excellence and high achievement that impacted the world. Sowell's work does not focus on heroic individuals but on the institutions that they built (see also Kelly, 2010). It does, however, highlight a large number of "Black firsts" who share one common denominator—they graduated from one of the all-Black institutions he memorialized in the 1970s.

But why did scholars in this volume across multiple fields think that it was imperative to recall and revise what most people in the 20th century considered to be a gloomy past for Black education? We think the Sowell (1976) reading provides a clue:

> The picture that emerges from these visions is of an inert, fearful, and unconcerned black leadership in the past. . . . This is a libel on the men and women who faced up to far more serious dangers than our generation will ever confront, who took the children of slaves and made them educated men

and women, and who put in the long hours of hard work required to turn a
despised mass into a cohesive community. (p. 58)

Like Sowell, all the scholars in this volume have been engaged in what we call post-
Brown revisionist thinking, research, and writing *against* a shadowy, distorted, and
dismal picture of Black education.

But not everyone swallowed the negative assumptions about Black education
cooked into the *Brown* decision on May 17, 1954. In the last selection in Part I, we revisit
literary scholar Trudier Harris's (2003) "The Price of Desegregation" to remind readers
that many people thought that Zora Neale Hurston had gone mad when she critiqued
Brown fiercely and perceptively in the early days of the ruling. In order to explain Hurston's thinking about *Brown* decades later, mainly that Black children would pay a huge
price for the assumptions of desegregation, Harris "[paints] a picture of the way things
used to be before we decided that so-called integration was better, before our teachers
moved out of our neighborhoods and before disciplining a child became a criminal offense instead of neighborly intervention" (p. 141). In her memoir, Harris recalls thinking
about Black education decades ago that many people overlooked, ignored, or denounced
but proved to be both logical and prophetic.

In *The Promise of Brown: Desegregation, Affirmative Action and the Struggle for Racial
Equality*, which we were unable to include in this volume, the late Manning Marable
(2005) reminisced about a lunch meeting he had once with the late judge Robert Carter,
who was one of the principal attorneys in the famous *Brown v. Board of Education* case.
Like Trudier Harris's reflections, the dialogue between Manning and Carter contextu-
alizes the post-*Brown* thinking and predicament of many scholars of Black education.
From their discussion of the promise and the perils of *Brown*, Manning concluded:

> What remains of the promise of Brown? Separate-but-equal has given way to
> what I have termed in my writings the "New Racial Domain" of color-blind,
> structural racism. In the place of legal segregation and the discrimination
> of Jim Crow laws, we now have a new regime of racial domination, centered
> on three deadly institutional processes: mass unemployment, mass incar-
> ceration, and mass disfranchisement. All three combine to create the new
> enslavement of the African people for the twenty-first century. (p. 39)

Concomitant with the new racial domain that Marable writes about fluently and
coherently, scholars of Black education in this volume demand revision, nuance, and
accuracy.

In the 20th and 21st centuries, there has been a conscious effort among Black ed-
ucation scholars to remember, record, and retell stories about segregated schooling
(Beauboeuf-Lafontant, 1999; Cecelski, 1994; Dempsey & Noblit, 1993; Dougherty, 1998;
Foster, 1993, 1997; Franklin & Savage, 2004; Fultz, 2004; Kelly, 2010; Loder-Jackson,

2015; Perkins, 1989; Ramsey, 2008; Randolph, 2004; Walker, 1996, 2000, 2001, 2005, 2009, 2018). More than anything, they have sought to counter the historical image and humanistic record of Black education. We invite you to think about Black education through the research and writing of the scholars provided here and to read the people whom they have cited as well.

References

Anderson, J. A. (1988). Ex-slaves and the rise of universal education in the South, 1860–1880. In *The education of Blacks in the South, 1860–1935* (pp. 4–32). University of North Carolina Press.

Beauboeuf-Lafontant, T. (1999). A movement against and beyond boundaries: "Politically relevant teaching" among African American teachers. *Teachers College Record, 100*(4), 702–723.

Bond, H. M. (1934). *The education of the Negro in the American social order.* Prentice Hall.

Cecelski, D. (1994). *Along freedom road: Hyde County, North Carolina and the fate of Black schools in the South.* University of North Carolina Press.

Dempsey, V., & Noblit, G. (1993). The demise of caring in an African American community: One consequence of school desegregation. *The Urban Review, 25*(1), 46–61.

Dougherty, J. (1998). "That's when we were marching for jobs": Black teachers and the early civil rights movement in Milwaukee. *History of Education Quarterly, 38*(2), 121–141.

Douglas, D. M. (2005). The spread of northern school segregation, 1890-1940. In *Jim Crow moves North: The battle over northern school segregation, 1865–1954* (pp. 123–166). Cambridge University Press.

Du Bois, W. E. B. (1998). *Black Reconstruction in America, 1860–1880.* The Free Press. (Original work published 1935)

Foster, M. (1993). Educating for competence in community and culture: Exploring the views of exemplary African-American teachers. *Urban Education, 27*(4), 370–394.

Foster, M. (1997). *Black teachers on teaching.* New Press.

Franklin, V. P., & Savage, C. J. (2004). *Cultural capital and Black education: African American communities and the funding of Black schooling, 1865 to the present.* Information Age Publishing.

Fultz, M. (2004). The displacement of Black educators post-*Brown*: An overview and analysis. *History of Education Quarterly, 44*(1), 11–45.

Harris, T. (2003). The price of desegregation. In *Summer snow: Reflections from a Black daughter of the South* (pp. 137–147). Beacon Press.

Kelly, H. (2010). *Race, remembering, and Jim Crow's teachers.* Routledge.

Loder-Jackson, T. (2015). *Schoolhouse activists: African American educators and the long Birmingham civil rights movement.* State University of New York Press.

Lorde, A. (2018). *The master's tools will never dismantle the master's house.* Penguin Classics.

Marable, M. (2005). The promise of *Brown*: Desegregation, affirmative action, and the struggle for racial equality. *Negro Educational Review, 56*(1), 33–41.

McHenry, E. (2002). Spreading the word: The cultural work of the Black press. In *Forgotten readers: Recovering the lost history of African American literary societies* (pp. 81–140). Duke University Press.

Perkins, L. (1989). The history of Blacks in teaching. In D. Warren (Ed.), *American teachers: History of a profession at work* (pp. 344–367). Macmillan.

Perry, I. (2018). *May we forever stand: A history of the Black national anthem*. University of North Carolina Press.

Perry, T. (1975). *History of the American Teachers Association*. National Education Association.

Ramsey, S. (2008). *Reading, writing, and segregation: A century of Black women teachers in Nashville*. University of Illinois Press.

Randolph, A. W. (2004). The memories of an all-Black Northern urban school: Good memories of leadership, teachers, and the curriculum. *Urban Education, 39*(6), 596–620.

Sowell, T. (1976). Patterns of Black excellence. *Public Interest, 43*, 26–58.

Walker, V. S. (1996). *Their highest potential: An African American school community in the segregated South*. University of North Carolina Press.

Walker, V. S. (2000). Valued segregated schools for African American children in the South, 1935–1969: A review of common themes and characteristics. *Review of Educational Research, 70*(3), 253–285.

Walker, V. S. (2001). African American teaching in the South: 1940–1960. *American Educational Research Journal, 38*(4), 751–779.

Walker, V. S. (2005). Organized resistance and Black educators' quest for school equality, 1878–1938. *Teachers College Record, 107*(3), 355–388.

Walker, V. S. (2009). *Hello professor: A Black principal and professional leadership in the segregated South*. University of North Carolina Press.

Walker, V. S. (2018). *The lost education of Horace Tate: Uncovering the hidden heroes who fought for justice in schools*. New Press.

Watkins, W. (2001). *The white architects of Black education: Ideology and power in America, 1865–1954*. Teachers College Press.

Williams, H. A. (2005). In secret places: Acquiring literacy in slave communities. In *Self-taught: African American education in slavery and freedom* (pp. 7–29). UNC Press.

Woodward, C. V. (1974). *The strange career of Jim Crow* (3rd ed.). Oxford University Press. (Original work published 1955)

In Secret Places:
Acquiring Literacy in Slave Communities

Heather Andrea Williams

> *No child, white people never teach colored people nothing, but to be good to dey Master and Mistress. What learning dey would get in dem days, dey been get it at night. Taught demselves.*
>
> LOUISA GAUSE, SOUTH CAROLINA

> *I have seen the Negroes up in the country going away under large oaks, and in secret places, sitting in the woods with spelling books.*
>
> CHARITY BOWERY, NORTH CAROLINA

DESPITE LAWS AND custom in slave states prohibiting enslaved people from learning to read and write, a small percentage managed, through ingenuity and will, to acquire a degree of literacy in the antebellum period.[1] Access to the written word, whether scriptural or political, revealed a world beyond bondage in which African Americans could imagine themselves free to think and behave as they chose. Literacy provided the means to write a pass to freedom, to learn of abolitionist activities, or to read the Bible. Because it most often happened in secret, the very act of learning to read and write subverted the master-slave relationship and created a private life for those who were owned by others. Once literate, many used this hard-won skill to disturb the power relations between master and slave, as they fused their desire for literacy with their desire for freedom.

Placing antiliteracy laws in dialogue with the words of enslaved people enables an examination of the tensions that slave literacy provoked between owned and owner. Masters made every attempt to control their captives' thoughts and imaginations, indeed their hearts and minds. Maintaining a system of bondage in the Age of Enlightenment depended upon the master's being able to speak for the slave, to deny his or her humanity, and to draw a line between slave consciousness and human will. The presence of literate slaves threatened to give lie to the entire system. Reading indicated to the world that this so-called property had a mind, and writing foretold the ability to construct an alternative narrative about bondage itself. Literacy among slaves would expose slavery, and masters knew it.

Understanding how enslaved people learned not only illuminates the importance of literacy as an instrument of resistance and liberation, but also brings into view the clandestine tactics and strategies that enslaved people employed to gain some control over their own lives. While it is common to view Frederick Douglass's antebellum struggle for literacy as exceptional, slave narratives, interviews with former slaves, and other documents offer a view of more widespread communities of learners who also forged the crucial link between literacy and freedom.

The story of Mattie Jackson illustrates the radical potential that enslaved African Americans perceived in literacy. Although Jackson came of age as the institution of slavery faced its final challenge, her personal efforts to free herself are suggestive of other people's experiences in slavery. Once free, Jackson told her story to a more literate black woman who wrote it down. This narrative helps us to understand the key role that literacy—and gender— could play in the crusade for freedom.

As a child in Missouri, Mattie Jackson experienced the family disruptions that so often characterized the experiences of enslaved people. When she was three years old, her father was sold, but he escaped before he could be transferred to his new owner. Months passed before the family received word that he had reached freedom. Two years later, Jackson's mother, Ellen Turner, attempted to escape to Chicago, where her husband now preached. With two children accompanying her, however, Turner was quickly captured and re- turned to her owner, who promptly sold her and the children. It was not unusual that the man would successfully escape while the woman remained behind, as responsibility for childbearing and child-rearing circumscribed slave women's movement. Work assignments also restricted women's mobility. Men were more likely to be hired out or sent on errands into town, thus acquiring greater knowledge of how to move about without detection as well as greater opportunity to meet people who might shield them from discovery. Turner's attempt to leave, then, spoke of her determination to be free even in the face of the discouraging odds against success.[2]

Four years after her initial escape attempt, Turner remarried, and this second husband too escaped, once again to avoid being sold. Now left with four children, Turner went about her job as cook in the household, attending to her domestic duties, even at the expense of caring for her fatally ill son. Her owners, Mr. and Mrs. Lewis, might well have thought that all was in good order with this family of slaves. Turner, it appeared, had been tamed. With the loss of two husbands and a child, she seemed to have given up any hope of ever being free.[3]

In truth, Turner had not surrendered and had in fact managed to pass on some of her resolve to her daughter, Mattie. The coming of the Civil War stirred their hopes to the surface. With Union troops stationed nearby, tension grew in the household. The Lewises' agitation at news of Union victories emboldened Mattie Jackson and her mother in their challenges to being owned. Gathering information through eavesdropping became an important weapon in their private war with their owners. According to Jackson, when husband and wife talked about the war, Mrs. Lewis "cast her eye around to us for fear we might hear her. Her suspicion was correct; there was not a word that passed that escaped our listening ear."[4]

To learn most of their news, the Jackson women had to listen hard and remember well, tasks that slaves had perfected across the South. Such eaves- dropping constituted a vital and accessible component of the intelligence network within slave communities. As important as literacy was to the slaves who employed it in service of their own freedom or for the benefit of others, enslaved African Americans also had other ways of knowing. They relied heavily on oral and aural systems of information. Those with access to white people's conversations listened closely when masters gathered and developed acute skills of perception and memory. As Henry Bibb noted, "slaves were not allowed books, pen, ink, nor paper, to improve their minds. But it seems to me now, that I was particularly observing and apt to retain what came under my observation." Specifically, Bibb recalled, "all that I heard about liberty and freedom to slaves, I never forgot. Among other good trades I learned the art of running away to perfection."[5]

As an enslaved boy in Winchester, Virginia, John Quincy Adams similarly honed his eavesdropping skills. When he learned there was no one to teach him to read and write because whites did not want blacks to become literate, the prohibition only stoked his curiosity. Whenever he heard a white person reading aloud, he lingered to listen, replying "nothing" when asked what he wanted. Then, at the first opportunity, he repeated to his parents everything he had heard. They, in turn, encouraged him to "try to hear all you can, but don't let them know it." By listening in this manner, Adams was able to inform his parents of an impending election that the owners wanted kept from their slaves. His information-gathering skills likely helped the family to escape to Pennsylvania during the Civil War. Other slaves worked as scouts for the one literate person among them. A woman in Beaufort, South Carolina, recalled that her mistress and master spelled out any information they did not want her to understand. As she was unable to read, she memorized the letters and repeated them as soon as she could to her literate uncle. He then decoded her memories into words or scraps of words.[6]

Long after he had transformed himself from enslaved child to prominent African American leader, Booker T. Washington reflected on the eavesdropping that had fed the "grapevine telegraph" among slaves, which had kept them so well informed of the "questions that were agitating the country" leading up to the war. Enslaved people, he recalled, had developed reliable means for acquiring and dispersing information. For example, the man sent to pick up mail at the post office tarried long enough to overhear white men discussing the letters and newspapers they had just received. On the three-mile walk back to the plantation, the mail carrier relayed the news he had gathered. In this way, slaves often heard of important occurrences before the white people at the big house did.[7]

In addition to this traditional and widely available tactic of eavesdropping, Mattie Jackson and her mother had a device that John Quincy Adams would have coveted: they could "read enough to make out the news in the papers." According to Jackson, "The Union soldiers took much delight in tossing a paper over the fence to us. It aggravated my mistress very much." Although the soldiers likely considered the newspapers to be propaganda directed at white residents, Jackson and her mother appropriated them for their own purposes, sitting up late at night to "read and keep posted about the war." They then strategically deployed the information against their owners. During Mrs. Lewis's visits to oversee her slaves in the kitchen, the women taunted her with their knowledge of Union activity. In one kitchen skirmish the infuriated owner declared, "I think it has come to a pretty pass, that old Lincoln, with his long legs, an old rail splitter, wishes to put the Niggers on an equality with the whites." She went on to vow "that her children should never be on an equal footing with a Nigger, she had rather see them dead."[8]

Slave owners grew keenly aware that all around them African Americans were increasingly taking advantage of the Civil War to mount challenges to the institution of slavery. Perhaps spurred on by his wife's diminishing sense of authority over their human property, Mr. Lewis searched Turner's room and, upon finding a newspaper picture of Abraham Lincoln pasted on the wall, angrily demanded an explanation. When Turner, refusing to suppress her own feelings, replied that she had hung the picture because she liked it, a livid Lewis knocked her to the ground and "sent her to the trader's yard for a month as punishment."[9] It must have occurred to Lewis then that Ellen Turner had not been tamed at all; she had merely changed her tactics of resistance. Instead of running away, she now used the newspaper and, by implication, her literacy as a mechanism for destabilizing the master-slave relationship. For her part, Turner fully knew that both she and her room were Lewis's property and that he could enter the space at will. By cutting Lincoln's image from a newspaper and hanging it on a wall in Lewis's house, Turner reinforced for herself the possibility of imminent freedom. At the same time, she issued a challenge to her owner's power by asserting that she and other slaves had allies in high places. In displaying the image of a potential liberator over her bed, she declared that slavery would not last forever and that she fully supported its demise.

In the domestic battle between owners and slaves, literacy persisted as a symbol of resistance. Despite Turner's severe punishment for brandishing Abraham Lincoln's likeness, order in the household continued its decline. While Mrs. Lewis mourned over a Union victory, the enslaved women rejoiced. "The days of sadness for mistress were days of joy for us," Jackson recounted. "We shouted and laughed to the top of our voices. My mistress was more enraged than ever—nothing pleased her." One night, Mrs. Lewis flew into an unprovoked rage. She announced that Jackson would be punished, selected a switch, and placed it in the corner of a room to await her husband's return. Countering

Mrs. Lewis's assertion of power, Jackson proclaimed both her recalcitrance and her literacy by bending the switch into the shape of an "M," the first letter of her name. With this symbolic challenge to her master and mistress, Jackson and another enslaved girl walked away from the house.

Jackson's display of literacy, paired with her departure, telegraphed to her owners the clear message that she refused to acquiesce in her enslavement. She sent them word that despite their prohibitions she had learned to write and was intent on marshaling every means at her disposal to undermine their authority. By asserting that Mr. and Mrs. Lewis could not stop her from learning to write, could not whip her, and could not prevent her from running away, Mattie Jackson utilized at once all the oppositional strategies that her mother had used over a lifetime.

The two girls made their way to the arsenal to find the Union troops, who they believed were a new form of protection. But they could gain neither admission to the arsenal nor the protection they sought. Even so, the girls had made a point. Upon returning to the Lewis household, "not a word was spoken respecting [their] sudden departure."[10]

Silence, however, did not signal peace. Slavery was a negotiated relationship maintained by the power of owners' violence.[11] Sometimes, though, enslaved people overwhelmed shocked owners with displays of their own force. Within weeks the stalemate in the Lewis home erupted into a violent confrontation. Once again the incident began with Mrs. Lewis's complaints. Mr. Lewis intervened, asking Jackson if she had done her work. Jackson said she had, in essence contradicting her mistress, who "flew into a rage and told him I was saucy, and to strike me, and he immediately gave me a severe blow with a stick of wood, which inflicted a deep wound upon my head." When Jackson disobeyed Mr. Lewis's order to change her bloody clothing, he "pulled me into another room and threw me on the floor, placed his knee on my stomach, slapped me on the face and beat me with his fist, and would have punished me more had not my mother interfered." In Jackson's estimation, her mother's refusal to leave the room angered Lewis, but it also intimidated him as he assessed his chances of winning a fight against these two women.

Unlike slave women narrators such as Harriet Jacobs, who felt constrained to present themselves to white northern readers as demure and genteel, Jackson spoke unabashedly of her physical confrontation with her master. "I struggled mightily, and stood him a good test for a while, but he was fast conquering me when my mother came. He was aware my mother could usually defend herself against one man, and both of us would overpower him, so after giving his wife strict orders to take me upstairs and keep me there, he took his carriage and drove away."[12] With his departure Lewis conceded that even the man of the house could no longer control his slaves, which encouraged Jackson to place even more pressure on the weakening slave power. Still wearing her bloody clothing as evidence of her mistreatment, Jackson once again set out for the arsenal to seek protection from the Union army. This time, she was able to convince an officer to hear her complaint and give her shelter.[13]

Mattie Jackson's search for freedom and protection openly asserted her opposition to her owners' control and violence. Her actions were tantamount to a declaration of domestic civil war.[14] By calling on authorities who might exercise some power over her owners, she publicly declared her intention to be free. Certainly Jackson's will to make this declaration gained momentum from the Civil War, yet early in the war, particularly in border states such as Missouri, Union officers refused to interfere in the established relationships of the South. When Jackson turned to Union officers to help execute her private war, they failed to provide long-term protection. Thus, three weeks later when Mr. Lewis appeared to claim his property, the Union troops handed her over. Before long, Lewis sold Jackson, her mother, and her siblings to different owners. Jackson's actions had only served to further infuriate her owners, who retaliated by simultaneously liquidating their investment and disrupting this enslaved family once more.[15]

Like Mattie Jackson and her mother, Ellen Turner, other enslaved people folded literacy into the store of strategies that they called upon both to challenge slavery and make slavery bearable. Becoming literate itself required them to employ creative tactics. Jackson does not reveal how her mother learned to read, but presumably mother taught daughter at night in their room in the Lewis home. Accounts of such efforts make it evident that even in slavery, with its violence, insults, and punishing labor, many African Americans yearned to become literate, to have access to the news and ideas that otherwise would have been beyond their reach. For similar reasons, southern white elites continued their efforts to place literacy itself beyond the reach of African Americans.

Indeed, literacy constituted one of the terrains on which slaves and slave owners waged a perpetual struggle for control.[16] Cognizant of the revolutionary potential of black literacy, white elites enacted laws in slave states to proscribe teaching enslaved and sometimes free blacks to read or write. The timing of these antiliteracy laws often exposed the close association in white minds between black literacy and black resistance. Whether the threat to slavery came in the form of a slave rebellion or talk of abolition, southern law-makers linked black literacy to the institution's demise and invested powers of surveillance and punishment in a host of officials, including justices of the peace, constables, sheriffs, marshals, police officers, and sergeants. Although antiliteracy statutes are often associated with Nat Turner's rebellion in 1831, they in fact had their beginnings a century earlier. In 1739, in an effort to escape to Florida, South Carolina slaves killed more than twenty whites in what became known as the Stono Rebellion. One year later, suspecting that slaves had communicated their insurrectionary plans in writing, the colonial legislature of South Carolina inscribed its fear into a statute that outlawed teaching any slave to write or employing any slave to write. The legislature reasoned that this prohibition was necessary because permitting slaves to engage in writing "may be attended with great inconveniences."[17]

Black people in South Carolina, however, devised methods to circumvent the law, and in 1800 the legislature explicitly acknowledged that earlier laws had been insufficient to keep blacks in "due subordination." Teaching had moved farther underground.

The legislature hoped to root it out by enacting a statute that declared any assembly of "slaves, free negroes, mulattoes and mestizoes," among themselves or with whites, for the purpose of "mental instruction," an unlawful meeting. The new law broadened both the scope of prohibited activity and the categories of individuals covered. Rather than solely criminalizing the teaching of writing, the 1800 statute outlawed "mental instruction," which could include reading, writing, memorization, arithmetic, and much more. Furthermore, while the 1740 statute had only prohibited teaching slaves, the 1800 law prohibited teaching slaves and free blacks. Finally, the 1800 law aimed specifically to prevent African Americans from gathering in secret places to learn "either before the rising of the sun, or after the going down of same." The legislature had undoubtedly become aware of clandestine schools meeting before dawn and late into the night. By way of enforcement, lawmakers required magistrates to enter into such "confined places," to "break down doors," and to disperse such unlawful assemblages. The law subjected each person of color in the group to corporal punishment not to exceed twenty lashes.[18]

In 1829 David Walker's *Appeal to the Coloured Citizens of the World*, with its militant attack on slavery and its call for armed resistance, stirred fears in southern whites that the essay would inspire slaves to rebel. Rebellion, of course, was exactly what Walker hoped to provoke. Born to an enslaved father and a free mother, he had left his home in Wilmington, North Carolina, eventually settling in Boston, where, although free, African Americans led severely circumscribed economic and political lives. In the *Appeal*, Walker declared white Americans the natural enemies of African Americans, and he both predicted and urged warfare that would bring about the destruction of slavery. Moreover, Walker linked literacy to slavery's demise. Powerful whites went to great lengths to deprive blacks of education because, he argued, "for coloured people to acquire learning in this country, makes tyrants quake and tremble on their sandy foundation," knowing that "their infernal deeds of cruelty will be made known to the world." Walker hoped "all coloured men, women and children, of every nation, language and tongue under heaven, [would] try to procure a copy of this Appeal and read it, or get some one to read it to them." Published in September, the pamphlet quickly made its way south.[19]

On December 11, 1829, the Savannah, Georgia, police department seized sixty copies of the Appeal. Walker would no doubt have proposed severe punishment for the black Baptist minister who handed the Appeal over to officials after receiving copies from a ship's steward.[20] The Georgia legislature wasted little time in responding. Ten days following the seizure, the legislature passed a law to quarantine any ship that carried a free black person or a slave into Georgia ports. In addition to outlawing teaching any "slave, negro or free person of colour" to read, the statute provided punishment for blacks or any person bringing into the state and circulating "any printed or written pamphlet, paper or circular, for the purposes of exciting to insurrection, conspiracy or resistance among the slaves, negroes, or free persons of color" of the state.[21] Although a black minister may have betrayed his brethren, white legislators clearly feared that other African Americans would not be so afraid or so loyal.

Louisiana lawmakers were also afraid. In 1830 that state's legislature criminalized teaching slaves to read or write. Sections of the statute resonated with the panic that Walker and other abolitionists had inspired. The law punished with death, or imprisonment at hard labor for life, "whosoever shall write, print, publish or distribute any thing having a tendency to produce discontent among the free coloured population of the state, or insubordination among the slaves therein." Further, the statute specifically targeted anyone who "shall knowingly be instrumental in bringing into this state, any paper, pamphlet or book" that tended to excite insubordination or to cause discontent among African Americans, free or enslaved.[22]

As the northern abolition movement, prodded by African American abolitionists, shifted from a position of gradualism to immediatism, slave states ratcheted up their efforts to sustain a way of life that depended on slavery.[23] In 1830, a critical turning point for the abolition movement, North Carolina enacted a statute that articulated the perceived kinship between slave literacy and slave control. "Whereas the teaching of slaves to read and write, has a tendency to excite dissatisfaction in their minds, and to produce insurrection and rebellion, to the manifest injury of the citizens of the State," the law read, "any free person, who shall hereafter teach, or attempt to teach, any slave within this State to read or write, the use of figures excepted, or shall give or sell to such slave or slaves any books or pamphlets, shall be liable to indictment in any court of record in this State." The law further specifically forbade any slave to teach another slave to read or write. Significantly, North Carolina's antiliteracy stance constituted part of a larger scheme of surveillance and control over African Americans, enslaved and free. In the same legislative session, lawmakers promulgated limiting conditions for the manumission of slaves by owners, targeted runaways and those who harbored them, imposed restrictions on free black peddlers, and sought to exclude northern-produced literature that might "excite insurrection, conspiracy or resistance in the slaves or free negroes."[24] As was often the case, the North Carolina statute punished blacks more harshly than whites. White men and women could be imprisoned or fined between $100 and $200. Free people of color faced fines, imprisonment, or the public humiliation of whipping. Slaves convicted under the statute could be punished with "thirty-nine lashes on [the] bare back."[25]

Notably, North Carolina's antiliteracy law permitted teaching slaves arithmetic, likely because mathematical skill was necessary for trades such as carpentry and would therefore inure to the benefit of slave owners. Writing was strictly forbidden, however, even when a slave might use the skill to benefit his owner. Similarly, an 1833 Georgia statute made it unlawful for any person to "permit a slave, negro or person of colour to transact business for him in writing." Legislators assessed the costs and benefits of having literate slaves in their midst. They concluded that the risk was too high that slaves would use writing skills to subvert owners' power.[26]

A few months after North Carolina did, Virginia moved against African American literacy. In the spring of 1831, Virginia rendered unlawful "all meetings of free negroes or mulattoes, at any school-house, church, meeting- house or other place for teaching them reading or writing, either in the day or night, under whatsoever pretext." The statute also specifically outlawed the compensation of any white person for teaching slaves to read or write.[27] Three months after the August 1831 insurrection in which Nat Turner, a literate slave, and several other slaves killed fifty-five whites in Virginia, Alabama enacted a legislative package intended to severely curtail African American activity.[28] In addition to forbidding any person to teach any free person of color or any slave to spell, read, or write, it forbade slaves to associate with free blacks without permission of their owners, made it unlawful for five or more male slaves to assemble outside of their plantation, and made it unlawful for any person of color to "preach to, exhort, or harangue any slave or slaves, or free persons of color, unless in the presence of five respectable slaveholders." The statute also attempted to legislate paternalism by imposing a duty on all slaveholders to "feed and clothe their slaves with a sufficiency of food and clothing for their comfort." Legislators hoped that satisfying physical needs would stave off insurrectionary fervor.[29]

In 1836 the Alabama legislature voiced its fear that prohibitive laws not-withstanding, some African American slaves were literate and had access to antislavery literature. In a memorial addressed to the legislatures of all other states, Alabama lawmakers condemned the "dark, deep, and malignant designs of the Abolitionists," who were "sending into our country their agents and incendiary pamphlets and publications, lighting up fires of discord in the bosoms of our slave population." The legislators charged that abolitionists "have presses in the various parts of the Union, from which they issue millions of essays, pamphlets and pictures and scatter them amongst our slave population, calculated to urge them to deluge our country in blood." "This cannot be tolerated," Alabama's leaders concluded.[30] As David Walker had urged, some slaves were getting their hands on antislavery writings.

It is clear, too, that enslaved and free black people operated schools, particularly in urban areas.[31] An 1834 South Carolina statute suggests that the state's two earlier attempts to prevent slaves from becoming literate had not succeeded. This third attempt at control punished anyone who taught or assisted any slave in learning to read or write. In a revealing move, the statute added a new level of detail that presumably targeted contemporary practices; it punished by fine, imprisonment, or corporal punishment "any free person of color or a slave [who] shall keep any school or other place of instruction, for teaching any slave or free person of color to read or write." This statute aimed at African Americans who did not rely on sporadic teaching, but who instead established schools to make education more formal and methodical.[32] White Americans' opposition to black education was not limited to the southern states. At the same time that Virginia and Alabama enacted legislation to prohibit African American education in the 1830s, the northern free state of Connecticut used both legal and extralegal means to curtail education options for black people. When the Convention of Colored Men of the United States met in 1831, delegates proposed establishing a college on the manual labor system in New Haven. Following up on a proposal by the convention's education committee, Arthur Tappan, who along with fellow white abolitionists William Lloyd Garrison and Simeon Jocelyn attended the convention, went so far as to purchase several acres of land to house the school. However, the white people of New Haven vehemently opposed any plan to provide higher education for African Americans. Supporters of the school suggested that opponents particularly objected to the impertinent idea of building a college for African Americans. The city's political leaders declared that a college to educate the black population would be "incompatible with the prosperity, if not the existence" of Yale College and the city's other educational institutions. The mayor and city council resolved to "resist the establishment of the proposed college in this place by every lawful means."[33]

Convention delegates abandoned the idea of building a black college in New Haven, but the struggle to provide education for African Americans in Connecticut did not end there. In 1832 Prudence Crandall, a white Quaker schoolteacher, along with black abolitionists James Forten, Reverend Theodore Wright, and Reverend Peter Williams, founded a boarding school for African American girls in Canterbury, Connecticut. In response, in May 1833 the state legislature outlawed the establishment of schools that provided instruction to "colored persons who are not inhabitants of this state." Crandall was prosecuted and convicted for violating the statute, but an appellate court reversed the conviction. Not long after, angry white residents set the occupied school on fire, then vandalized the building with clubs and iron bars, forcing Crandall to close the school.[34]

Back on southern plantations, purveyors of advice warned white masters, or more probably white mistresses, against giving in to any impulse to teach enslaved people to read the Bible to save their own souls. Prizewinning essayist Nathan Bass argued in 1851 that although a literate slave, if provided with appropriate reading material, might learn to "respect and venerate the authority of his owner," the risk was too great. Bass blamed "the spirit of bigotry and fanaticism which are abroad in the country, seeking to disseminate a spirit of insubordination in the bosom of the slave, by the circulation of incendiary publications, inducing him to throw off the authority of those to whom his services are due." Bass thought it wiser for owners to take responsibility for inculcating their own precepts of morality and religion into their slaves. A Mississippi planter also writing on slave management agreed with Bass. "I would gladly learn every negro on the place to read the Bible," he proclaimed, "but for a fanaticism which, while it professes friendship to the negro, is keeping a cloud over his mental vision, and almost crushing out his hopes of salvation."[35] Bass and the Mississippi planter would have considered naive the opinion of a Georgia planter who encouraged teaching slaves to spell and read; he found these skills convenient for slaves engaged in weighing cotton and erecting buildings. "Hurricane," as the planter called himself, saw no danger in the practice because he considered African Americans too stupid to become literate enough to undermine white authority.[36]

Enslaved people realized that those who owned them brought their awe- some and arbitrary power to bear against any effort slaves made to learn to read and write. Interviewed years after slavery had ended, many recalled the barriers that whites had placed between literacy and themselves. Some slaves experienced the threats or punishment directly. Gordon Buford remembered that he and fellow slaves never learned to read and write because their master threatened to "skin them alive" if they tried. Charlie Grant's mistress beat him with a plaited cowhide when she caught him with a book. And Belle Caruthers's master struck her with his muddy boots when he caught her studying a Webster's blue-back speller.[37] Others experienced secondhand the violence that could be visited upon a slave who was caught reading or writing. James Lucas reported that his owner "hung the best slave he had for trying to teach the others how to spell." Literacy could also disrupt a sale. When Lucas's master realized that some of the people he had purchased at auction in Baltimore could read, he sent them back. Similarly, when Tom Hawkins's owner discovered that his carriage driver had learned to read and write while taking the owner's children to and from school, he cut off the driver's thumb and assigned another enslaved man to drive the carriage.[38] Still other former slaves had a broad and daunting sense of the punishment that might be meted out. Charlie Davis believed that he would get one hundred lashes if he so much as picked up a book, and George Washington Albright thought a Mississippi statute provided that if any slave learned to read or write, "he was to be punished with 500 lashes on the naked back, and to have the thumb cut off above the second joint."[39] The Mississippi statute actually prescribed punishment of thirty-nine lashes, but the expectation of even more violent punishment would surely have been enough to terrorize all but the most courageous and persistent.[40]

As slave owners and legislators suspected, African Americans, free and slave, designed all manner of strategies to elude the laws against learning. At about the same time that Virginia first put into writing its prohibition of teaching blacks to read and write, Mary and Thomas Peake, free people in Norfolk, Virginia, sent their six-year-old daughter Mary to live with an aunt in the District of Columbia so that she could attend school. She remained there until, according to Peake, the District of Columbia, too, prohibited teaching blacks. In 1847 she moved to Hampton, Virginia, where she taught black children and adults until the Civil War.[41] In Georgia, Susie King Taylor participated in an intricate web of secrecy to become educated. Born enslaved in Georgia in 1848, Taylor's owner permitted her to live with her free grandmother in Savannah. The port city of Savannah afforded a fair amount of mobility to hired slaves and had a large free black population.[42] Taylor's nominally free status released her from labor and from oversight by an owner, enabling her to pursue an education. Even so, she was constrained to learn in secret and with a patchwork of teachers because both the state of Georgia and the city of Savannah made it illegal to teach slaves or free people of color to read or write.[43] Carrying schoolbooks camouflaged with paper, Taylor and her younger siblings stole, one at a time, into the home of a free black woman each morning, careful not to be spotted by the police or any white person. Twenty-five children studied their lessons in Susan Woodhouse's kitchen each day and slipped out, one at a time, each afternoon. After two years with Mrs. Woodhouse, Taylor went to Mary Beasley, another black woman, who, after teaching everything she knew to Taylor, recommended that Taylor's grandmother find a more advanced teacher. That next teacher was a white playmate, who gave Taylor lessons for four months before joining a convent. Finally, the son of her white landlord gave Taylor lessons for several months until he was conscripted into the Confederate army.[44] Roughly pieced together as it was, Susie King Taylor's education would have appeared veritably formal to many other enslaved people who managed to become literate.

Sometimes masters' wives, inspired by evangelical Christianity, took it upon themselves to teach slaves to read. While some owners turned a blind eye to their wives' efforts, others badgered them into understanding the dangers inherent in teaching slaves. A few owners, however, not only tolerated but even encouraged their slaves' interest in education, particularly when it could benefit the owners. In one unusual instance, Lucy Skipwith in Hopewell, Alabama, kept up a correspondence during the 1850s and 1860s with her absentee owner, John Cocke, in Fluvanna County, Virginia. In her letters she informed Cocke of activities on the plantation, including the progress of her plantation school for other slaves.[45] In Virginia the state legislature passed a special law in 1842 granting permission for an enslaved man, Randolph, to learn to read and write. Randolph's owner, Henry Juett Gray, was blind and wanted to become a teacher of the blind. According to the special act, Gray needed the services of a "servant capable of reading and writing, which object cannot be permanently secured otherwise than by the education of a young slave named Randolph." Despite his usefulness to the young white man, the state considered a literate Randolph a potential danger and required that Henry Gray's father, Robert Gray, "indemnify the public against any possible injury which might be apprehended from the misconduct of said slave."[46]

Most enslaved people were not so fortunate; theirs was a covert mission to become literate. They truly had to "steal" an education. Some slaves hid spelling books under their hats to be ready whenever they could entreat or bribe a literate person to teach them. Some turned to white children, too young to understand that they violated the slave code, or to poor white men who did not care. Former slaves recounted stories of trading food and money for letters and words. In exchange for writing lessons, G. W. Offley fed a white boy whose father had gambled away the family's money. Offley later traded boxing and wrestling lessons with white men for writing instruction. James Fisher gave an old man money to buy whiskey in exchange for his writing lessons. As a young enslaved boy, Richard Parker picked up old nails and traded them for marbles that he then used to pay white boys for reading lessons. He carried a primer under his hat to be ready for class at any time. In addition, he received instruction from his owner's daughter until they were caught. "Uncle" Charles, a former slave in North Carolina, recounted that he also carried a primer under his hat and challenged white boys to tell him what a letter was, until he managed to learn the alphabet. He once traded a knife for a reading lesson from a white boy.[47] These particular means of acquiring literacy had important gender implications, as once again enslaved males tended to have greater mobility than enslaved females. Boys and men were more likely to accompany white children off the property to school and often had wider access to public spaces in which they could convince white males to teach them.

At the same time, women who worked inside the owner's household could entice their young white charges to pass on what they learned in school. Alice Green recalled that her mother had learned to read by keeping a schoolbook in her bosom all the time and asking the white children to tell her everything they had learned in school each day. In this way, she learned enough to teach school once slavery ended. Likewise, Allen Allensworth's mother encouraged him to "play school" with his young master who attended school every day.[48]

Enslaved people put the resources they could garner to maximum use. Mandy Jones knew of a young man who learned to read and write in a cave. She also recalled that there were "pit schools" near her Mississippi plantation. Slaves would dig a pit in the ground way out in the woods, covering the spot with bushes and vines. Runaways sometimes inhabited the pits, but they also housed schools. According to Jones, "slaves would slip out of the Quarters at night, and go to dese pits, an some niggah dat had some learning would have a school."[49] In South Carolina Edmund Carlisle cut blocks from pine bark and smoothed them into slates. He dropped oak into water to make ink, and he used a stick as his pen.[50] Some slaves copied letters and words whose meanings they could not yet decipher onto fences and in the dirt.[51] And, more than one hundred years later, when slave cabins were excavated, archaeologists were surprised to find, along with the predictable shards of colonoware pottery, food bones, and oyster shells, the remains of graphite pencils and writing slates, some with words and numbers still written on them.[52]

Sundays proved to be an important day for enslaved people to learn to read and write. Some slaves took advantage of the opportunity that a few missionaries offered to learn to read. Others relied on their own resources. Since the colonial period, slave management on the Sabbath had presented a vexing challenge to slave owners. Whites struggled to maintain control over black movement on the day when slaves were not required to work, the day when whites attended church and socialized away from their homes. In South Carolina, for example, legislation passed in 1712 aimed to limit the movement of blacks who congregated in Charlestown on Sundays in such great numbers as to "give them opportunity of executing any wicked designs." Twelve years later the colony's assembly directed white men to ride armed on Sundays in order to defend against slaves who congregated in large numbers. Evidently the legislation did not effectively curtail black behavior because over the next thirty years grand juries made several attempts to mandate stricter enforcement. Their concerns were not unfounded; in September 1739 slaves staged the Stono uprising while whites attended "divine service."[53]

In similarly radical fashion, African Americans took advantage of their leisure time and whites' absence on Sundays to become literate. They lurked in their designated places until masters left for Sunday outings, and then they pulled out books and pencils. Former slave Charity Bowery recalled that on Sundays on her Edenton, North Carolina, plantation, she saw "negroes up in the country going away under large oak trees and in secret places, sitting in the woods with spelling books." In Maryland G. W. Offley, who later paid white men and boys for writing lessons, received his first reading lessons at age nineteen from an old black man, who taught him at night and on Sunday mornings. Here were the clandestine schools that legislatures sought to eliminate, schools that convened after dark and on the Sabbath, when masters were likely to be more concerned about their own souls and their own pleasure than about the activities of the people who worked for them on the other six days of the week.[54] In Person County, North Carolina, James Curry began his illegal lessons with his master's son. Curry's mother bought him a spelling book, and the lessons continued until his owner found out and forbade further teaching. According to Curry, though, "when my master's family were all gone away on the Sabbath, I used to go into the house and get down the great Bible, and lie down in the piazza, and read, taking care, however, to put it back before they returned." Just as the slaves who congregated in Charlestown, South Carolina, had used Sundays to resist their owners' control over their bodies, slaves like James Curry took advantage of Sundays to undermine owners' attempts to control their intellect.[55]

But why was literacy so sought after and so forbidden? The motivations on each side were very much the same. Whites feared that literacy would render slaves unmanageable. Blacks wanted access to reading and writing as a way to attain the very information and power that whites strove to withhold from them. Literacy had practical implications for enslaved people. When James Fisher's owner sold him away from his mother in Nashville, Tennessee, Fisher quickly decided that he must learn to write in case he ever had the opportunity to forge a pass and escape. "I copied every scrap of writing I could find, and thus learned to write a tolerable hand before I knew what the words were that I was copying," Fisher recalled. After a while he met the old man who taught him to write in exchange for money to buy whiskey. When his mistress entered his room and discovered his writing materials, she reported him to her father, Captain Davis, who immediately made the same connection between liberty and literacy that Fisher had made. Davis began by threatening Fisher, saying that if Fisher belonged to him he would cut off his right hand. Since he did not have authority to carry out such a threat, Davis attempted instead to convince Fisher to forsake ideas of freedom, arguing that he was better off enslaved than free. Both Davis and Fisher clearly equated wanting to learn to write with wanting to be free. Davis's arguments notwithstanding, Fisher eventually escaped to Canada.[56]

As both James Fisher and Captain Davis understood, African American literacy portended a profound threat to slavery by providing slaves with an advantage for greater movement within a system that relied on individual owners' providing passes for their slaves, rather than on some method of universal registration. Susie King Taylor's clandestine educational efforts in Savannah, for example, provided an immediate reward when she was able to write passes for her grandmother, who, although free, was required to produce a pass from her white guardian in order to move about at night.[57] In Kentucky field hand A. T. Jones cobbled together enough education to write himself a pass to freedom. When Jones learned that his master had sold him instead of allowing him to buy himself as they had previously agreed, he decided to make his way to Canada. "I could hardly put two syllables together grammatically," Jones later confessed, "but in fact, one half the white men there were not much better. I wrote my pass—'Please let the bearer pass and repass, on good behavior, to Cincinnati and return.'" His ability to write, along with the marginal literacy of potential captors, helped Jones to execute the escape.[58]

Figure 1.1.

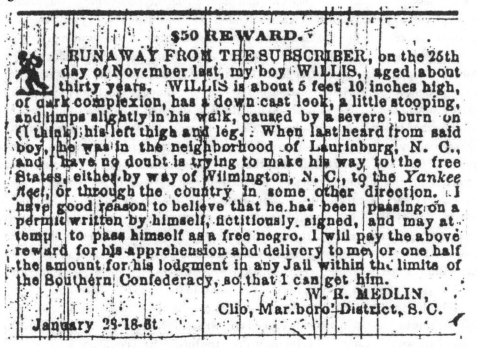

Owners' fears of slave literacy materialized in the loss of their property. In February 1863 a South Carolina slave owner placed a newspaper advertisement in search of an escaped slave. He suspected that Willis, a thirty-year-old man with a "down cast look" and a limp, was making his way north through North Carolina and possibly attempting to enlist with the Union army. He also suspected that Willis was using his literacy to effect his escape. "I have good reason to believe," the advertisement read, "that he has been passing on a permit written by himself, fictitiously signed, and may attempt to pass himself as a free Negro." The erstwhile owner offered a $50 reward for Willis's return.[59]

In addition to providing concrete information about the physical location of freedom and the means to get there, literacy had the potential to help enslaved people articulate intellectual objections to the very existence of the institution of slavery. Reading catapulted some slaves beyond the limited sphere to which owners hoped to keep them restricted and enabled them to engage vicariously in dialogues that raised moral challenges to the enslavement of human beings. When James Curry sneaked into his owner's library on Sunday mornings and carefully took down the family Bible, he somehow made his way to a passage that reinforced the condemnation his slave community had long made of slavery. He "learned that it was contrary to the revealed will of God, that one man should hold another as a slave." Curry recalled that he had always heard it said among the slaves that their ancestors had been stolen from Africa and should never have been enslaved. By reading the Bible, he discerned that "God hath made of one blood all nations of men to dwell on all the face of the earth." Curry interpreted the Apostle Paul's message to mean that since God had made all people, no one group was justified in enslaving another. While his owners attended "divine worship," Curry used the words in their own revered Bible to fashion his own condemnation of their unjust practice.[60]

Another literate slave, C. H. Hall, invoked Patrick Henry, hero of the American Revolution, to support his claim to freedom. Hall's mistress internalized her Baptist teachings of each believer's individual relationship to God and thought it her duty to teach her slaves to read the Bible. Her husband urged her to stop, but she had refused, and thus Hall learned to spell and to read fairly well. As he grew, his master became even more threatened by his literacy and accused Hall of becoming just like his brother, a literate preacher who "was raising the devil on the place." His master's watchful criticism forced Hall to stop reading, but only for a while. When after several years he began reading again, his owner's fears were realized, for according to Hall, "the more I read, the more I fought against slavery. Finally I thought I would make an attempt to get free, and have liberty or death." Hall's invocation of this language suggests that he used the lessons he learned from his mistress to venture beyond the Bible into the writings of American revolutionaries and adapted their language of liberation to his own circumstances. He escaped from his Maryland owners and made his way to Canada in the 1830s.[61]

On the Shelbyville, Kentucky, farm where he was enslaved, Elijah Marrs early in life became interested in learning to read and write. "I was convinced," he later wrote, "that there would be something for me to do in the future that I could not accomplish by remaining in ignorance. I had heard so much about freedom, and of the colored people running off and going to Canada, that my mind was busy with this subject even in my young days."[62] It is perplexing to consider what might cause an enslaved child to think that he would have important things to do, and what propelled him to make the link between education and effectiveness. Nevertheless, as many other slaves did, Marrs "sought the aid of the white boys" to teach him. He then practiced his lessons by reading the newspapers and the addresses on letters that the "white people" sent him to pick up at the post office. After a while, Marrs attended a late-night school that Ham Graves, an old black man, secretly taught. It was Graves who taught Marrs to write, and Marrs, too young to realize that he was leaving evidence of his illicit behavior, practiced his new skill all over the farm: "on every gate-post around the stables, as on the plow-handle, you could see where I had been trying to write."[63]

In the Bible, books, and newspapers, literate slaves found a language of liberation that augmented what they learned in slave quarters.[64] Reading gave a larger voice and conceptualization to ideas they had heard expressed by other slaves. Frederick Douglass, the most famous slave to become literate, demonstrated this progression. In a letter to his former master, Douglass wrote that at the age of six he decided to be free some day. Like James Curry, his first understanding of why he was enslaved came from hearing older black people say that their parents had been stolen from Africa by white men and sold into slavery. These narrations enunciated the community's foundational belief that its enslavement was illegitimate, a belief that was reinforced when Douglass's aunt and uncle escaped to freedom.[65] His desire for freedom grew when his master made a link between literacy and freedom, and the possibility of freedom became real for him when he read a dialogue between a slave and a master. Finally, the idea that all blacks might some day be free took root when he first read a definition of the word "abolition." Reading, then, did not introduce Douglass to the concept of freedom; rather it buttressed and augmented a developing consciousness.

While a boy in Baltimore, Douglass's mistress began teaching him to read, but he had not yet made much progress when Hugh Auld, Douglass's master, forbade his wife to continue. Auld also made the mistake of proclaiming his rationale to Douglass. "If you give a nigger an inch, he will take an ell. A nigger should know nothing but to obey his master—to do as he is told to do," Auld contended. Then he declared that teaching a black person to read would render him forever unfit to be a slave. As Captain Davis had, Auld saw literacy and liberty as indivisible concepts, and he thus considered a literate slave to be an inherent threat. Auld's outburst inspired the young Douglass to make the same transformative link. Taking Auld at his word, Douglass came to see literacy as power and illiteracy as mental darkness. However, convinced by her husband that a literate slave was a dangerous one, Mrs. Auld took up a new mission to keep Douglass from learning. "Nothing seemed to make her more angry than to see me with a newspaper," Douglass recalled. "She seemed to think that here lay the danger." As some other enslaved men and boys did, Douglass adopted a plan in which he befriended every white boy whom he met on the streets and "converted" as many as he could into teachers. He took a book and bread with him on errands, traded the bread for lessons, and so learned to read.[66]

In childhood Douglass may have believed that the mere ability to read would be a magical elixir that would lead to freedom, but in actuality it was the content of the reading material that transformed his life. Caleb Bingham's The Columbian Orator, for example, profoundly influenced Douglass. Originally published in 1810, this palm-sized volume contained speeches and essays intended to "improve the youth and others in the ornamental and useful art of eloquence." Bingham's instructions regarding pronunciation, cadence, pitch, and gesture had been read by thousands of American schoolboys before they found their way into the hands of a slave boy in Maryland.[67] Douglass recalled the particular impact of two items in the book. First, he read a speech delivered in the Irish House of Commons in 1795 in favor of the bill to emancipate the Roman Catholics. The speaker asserted that England could not turn back the tide of the world's movement toward freedom and suggested that England's recent loss in America "should serve as a lasting example to nations, against employing force to subdue the spirit of a people, determined to be free."[68]

Second, in the "Dialogue Between a Master and a Slave," an African American slave who had twice run away challenged his master's right to keep him enslaved. The master, hurt by the slave's desire to be free, questioned whether he had not treated him well, to which the slave responded that no manner of good treatment could ever compensate him for being deprived of his liberty. The slave further contended that as he had been kidnapped and sold into slavery, there could be no moral justification for his enslavement. Finally, he assured his master that as long as he had legs, he would continue trying to escape because "it is impossible to make one, who has felt the value of freedom, acquiesce in being a slave." In the end, the slave's moral argument and his threat of continued resistance, prevailed over the owner's defense of slavery and the owner freed him.[69] Before reading this dialogue, Douglass may never have imagined that a slave and master could speak to each other "man to man," or that their conversation could come to such a positive end. However, Douglass could certainly identify with the slave who had been kidnapped, as his own oral tradition placed him in a genealogy of ancestors who had been kidnapped into slavery. Douglass lived in a world in which members of his slave community, at least among themselves, challenged the legitimacy of their enslavement, and at the same time, his owner expected him to accept enslavement without question. Exposure to the dialogue and speech delivered Douglass intellectually from this restricted, incongruous space to a place where slavery was not only openly challenged but defeated.

Douglass read the speech and the dialogue over and over, finding that they "gave tongue to interesting thoughts of my own soul, which had frequently flashed through my mind and died away for want of utterance." The thoughts, then, were not all new, but seeing them in print provided Douglass with a vocabulary for expressing them, as well as an added confidence derived from the new knowledge that his own thoughts had life and meaning outside of himself and his small community. As he meditated on the readings, he came to "abhor and detest" his enslavers and to experience the torment of hatred. "As I writhed under it," Douglass wrote, "I would at times feel that learning to read had been a curse rather than a blessing. In moments of agony, I envied my fellow-slaves for their stupidity. I have often wished myself a beast. It was the everlasting thinking of my condition that tormented me."[70]

Thus, Douglass suggested that had he not learned to read, he would not have become dissatisfied with slavery. This, of course, contradicted his assertion elsewhere that his initial desire for freedom came at age six when his aunt and uncle escaped. Rather than introducing the idea of freedom, reading, it seems, reinforced an existing desire and expanded his conception of the possible. The possible became even more enticing when Douglass learned the meaning of the word "abolition." He had heard the word and knew that it was significant and somehow opposed to slavery. When he got hold of a newspaper and read about petitions being filed in Washington, D.C., calling for the abolition of slavery, the increased possibility of freedom fired his existing desire to be free. Before he ever mounted a stage to deliver an antislavery speech, Douglass had inserted his consciousness into the national dialogue about the future of slavery.[71]

If legislative proscriptions in tandem with limited resources and the wrath of owners effectively kept most enslaved people from becoming literate, they never fully succeeded in arresting black literacy, as Frederick Douglass, Ellen Turner, and Mattie Jackson could have attested. Indeed, the battle between those who would impede black learning and those who would facilitate it continued right up to the Civil War. In 1853 Margaret Douglass, a southern white woman, was sentenced to one month in jail for teaching free black children in Norfolk, Virginia. Douglass, a seamstress, fell into the role of teacher when a free black barber asked if she would teach his children. She was visiting his shop one day and noticed his two sons reading a spelling book. The boys attended a local Sunday school where they received reading lessons, but they could not advance quickly because Norfolk had no schools for black children. Douglass decided that she and her daughter, Rosa, would teach the barber's children. As it happened, he could not spare the boys from their work, so he sent his three daughters instead, and what began as a private tutorial soon developed into a school with twenty students when other families got wind of the lessons. Douglass excluded enslaved children, but she claimed not to know that the law also prohibited her from teaching free black children. The school continued for several months without disturbance, and the state might have continued to turn a blind eye, as it did regarding the Sunday school, had Douglass not made a public declaration of her association with African Americans.[72]

When one of her students died, the white teacher joined in the funeral procession. Shortly thereafter, constables entered her home and ordered Douglass, her daughter, and the students to report to the mayor's office.[73] Margaret and Rosa Douglass were subsequently indicted by a grand jury on charges that they did "unlawfully assemble with divers negroes, for the purpose of instructing them to read and write, and did instruct them to read and to write, contrary to the Act of the General Assembly." Representing herself before the court, Douglass argued that as a former slaveholder herself, she was no abolitionist or fanatic and was strongly opposed to northern interference with southern institutions. However, she asserted, "I deem it the duty of every Southerner, morally and religiously, to instruct his slaves, that they may know their duties to their masters, and to their common God." She would no longer violate the law, Douglass told the jury, but she would continue her good work by "endeavoring to teach the colored race humility and a prayer- ful spirit, how to bear their sufferings as our Saviour bore his for all of us. I will teach them their duty to their superiors, how to live, and how to die."[74]

Perhaps swayed by Douglass's expression of loyalty to southern values and her sanction of African Americans' subservience to whites, the jury found her guilty but imposed a fine of only $1 instead of the maximum $100. In the two-tiered sentencing structure, however, the judge also had a say, and he imposed an additional sentence of one month in prison. In imposing the sentence, the judge informed Douglass that he had not been convinced by her argument that literacy was vital for religious training. Intellectual and religious instruction often go hand in hand, he wrote, but the fact that in many parts of Virginia, and other parts of the country, more than a quarter of whites

were illiterate and still abided by moral laws proved that literacy was not a prerequisite for understanding moral law.[75] The judge further asserted that the law prohibiting
teaching African Americans was a matter of self-preservation and protection, having
its foundations in Nat Turner's memorable insurrection. He blamed the need for such a
law on "Northern incendiaries" who clogged the mails with "abolition pamphlets and
inflammatory documents, to be distributed among our Southern negroes to induce them
to cut our throats."[76]

As late as 1861, the city of Savannah, Georgia, publicly whipped Reverend James
Simms, a black man, for teaching slaves. A carpenter by trade, Simms purchased his
freedom with money he earned by hiring himself out. Even after being whipped, he
persisted in teaching slaves, and the city fined him $100. Refusing to pay, Simms left
Savannah for Boston, where he remained until after the war.[77]

But what of Mattie Jackson with whom we began? After several escape attempts,
Jackson finally made it to freedom in Indiana through the help of some "colored people"
who "assisted slaves to escape by the Underground Railroad." In 1866, at the age of twenty,
she dictated her narrative, hopeful that its sale would fund her education so that she, in
turn, could teach other former slaves. Where slaves' narratives had previously been sold
to raise funds to get rid of slavery, this narrative, produced in a new time, was sold to
educate those who had outlasted the institution. In a plea to potential readers, Jackson
confided, "I feel it a duty to improve the mind, and have ever had a thirst for education
to fill that vacuum for which the soul has ever yearned since my earliest remembrance."
Jackson believed that she and her race had been oppressed through no fault of their own,
but now that the "links have been broken and the shackles fallen from them" through
the efforts of the "beloved martyr President Lincoln," they needed education to become
full participants in society. "Thus," Jackson implored potential purchasers, "I ask you to
buy my little book to aid me in obtaining an education, that I may be enabled to do some
good in behalf of the elevation of my emancipated brothers and sisters." Jackson had
survived slavery and appealed to "the friends of humanity" to assist her in rendering her
freedom meaningful.[78]

As a free woman, Jackson made a declaration that was arguably as significant as her
earlier determination to end her physical enslavement. She asserted that she would become educated and began the process of making this new goal a reality. In Indianapolis
Jackson boarded with people who became interested in "teaching and encouraging me
in my literary advancement and all other important improvements, which precisely met
the natural desires for which my soul had ever yearned since my earliest recollection. I
could read a little but was not allowed to learn in slavery. I was obliged to pay twenty-five
cents for every letter written for me. I now began to feel that as I was free I could learn
to write, as well as others."[79]

In publishing her plan for education, Jackson made three claims on behalf of African
Americans. First, she challenged notions of black intellectual inferiority by asserting
that she was educable and could learn to write as well as anyone else. Second, she rejected

notions of black degradation and made the radical claim that the soul of an enslaved black child had always yearned for enlightenment. Finally, Jackson sought to eliminate any assumption of exceptionalism by including other former slaves in her claims of intellectual curiosity and capacity. Implicit in her desire to educate other blacks was the confidence that they also wanted to learn, and she encouraged them to do so. "Manage your own secrets, and divulge them by the silent language of your own pen," she counseled. She hinted, too, that once educated, she would write a second book, with her own pen, recounting her experiences in slavery.[80] In Mattie Jackson's view, freedom, combined with education, would empower her to finally take control of her own life, keeping her secrets and speaking her mind.

Endnotes

1   I have identified statutes that prohibited teaching enslaved and/or free black people in the following states: Alabama, Georgia, Louisiana, Mississippi, Missouri, North Carolina, South Carolina, and Virginia. Statutes in Alabama, Georgia, Missouri, South Carolina, and Virginia prohibited teaching any person of color, whether free or enslaved; the others only prohibited teaching slaves. I have not identified such statutes in Kentucky, Maryland, Arkansas, Texas, Florida, Delaware, or Tennessee; however, Maryland, Arkansas, and Florida did specifically legislate that while masters, though obliged to provide some degree of education to white apprentices, had no such duty toward free black apprentices. See the appendix for the full text of the antiliteracy statutes.

2   Mattie J. Jackson, *The Story of Mattie J. Jackson: Her Parentage—Experience of Eighteen Years in Slavery—Incidents During the War—Her Escape from Slavery. A True Story* (Lawrence, Mass.: Printed at Sentinel Office, 1866), 2; Deborah Gray White, *Ar'n't I a Woman? Female Slaves in the Plantation South* (rev. ed.; New York: W. W. Norton, 1999), 70; Michael P. Johnson, "Runaway Slaves and the Slave Communities in South Carolina, 1799 to 1830," *William and Mary Quarterly* 38 (July 1981): 418–41.

3   Jackson, *Story of Mattie J. Jackson*, 3–6.

4   Ibid., 10.

5   Henry Bibb, *Narrative of the Life Adventures of Henry Bibb, an American Slave*, in vol. 2 of *African American Slave Narratives*, editor Sterling Lecatur Bland, Jr. (Westport, Conn.: Greenwood Press, 2001), 355.

6   John Quincy Adams, *Narrative of the Life of John Quincy Adams, When in Slavery and Now as a Freeman* (Harrisburg, Pa.: Sieg, 1872), 6, 36; Elizabeth Hyde Botume, *First Days amongst the Contrabands* (1893; New York: Arno Press, 1968), 6–7.

7   Booker T. Washington, *Up From Slavery* (1901; New York: Doubleday, 1963), 6.

8   Jackson, *Story of Mattie J. Jackson*, 11. Other former slaves also recalled women in their family who could read well enough to gather information about the war from the newspapers. Minnie Davis reported that her mother would "steal the newspapers and read up about the war, and she kept the other slaves posted as to how the war was progressing." Likewise, Chana Littlejohn's aunt was able to keep other slaves updated on the progress of

the war. George P. Rawick, editor, *The American Slave: A Composite Autobiography*, 19 vols. (Westport, Conn.: Greenwood Press, 1972), vol. 12, pt. 1, p. 257, and vol. 15, pt. 2, pp. 57–58.

9   Jackson, *Story of Mattie J. Jackson*, 11.

10 Ibid., 11–12.

11 Regarding the notion of slavery as a negotiated relationship, see Ira Berlin, *Many Thousands Gone: The First Two Generations of Slavery in North America* (Cambridge, Mass.: Harvard University Press, 1998), 2.

12 Jackson, *Story of Mattie J. Jackson*, 12. Regarding slave narrators' "undertelling" the horrors of slavery, see P. Gabrielle Foreman, "Manifest in Signs: The Politics of Sex and Representation in Incidents in the Life of a Slave Girl," 76–99, and Deborah M. Garfield, "Earwitness: Female Abolitionism, Sexuality, and Incidents in the Life of a Slave Girl," 100–130, in *Harriet Jacobs and Incidents in the Life of a Slave Girl: New Critical Essays,* ed. Deborah M. Garfield and Rafia Zafar (New York: Cambridge University Press, 1996).

13 Jackson, *Story of Mattie J. Jackson*, 12. No legal precedent existed in the ante- bellum South for a slave who had escaped from her owners to obtain refuge from a public official. Unlike slave societies such as Cuba, which under Castilian law provided a range of protective legislation placing the state between slave and master, in the slave society of the American South the patriarch of each household reigned all but supreme. Enslaved people sought to transform Union officers into official arbiters in master-slave relationships, ultimately appealing to them for freedom. For a discussion of protections provided by Castilian law, see Herbert Klein, *Slavery in the Americas: A Comparative Study of Virginia and Cuba* (Chicago: University of Chicago Press, 1967), 59–78. See also David Brion Davis, *The Problem of Slavery in Western Culture* (Ithaca, N.Y.: Cornell University Press, 1966), 223–43. Davis argues that these legal protections may have been more theoretical than real, having little if any impact on the brutality of slavery in societies like Brazil and Cuba. For a discussion of master- slave relations and the law, see Peter W. Bardaglio, *Reconstructing the Household: Families, Sex, and the Law in the Nineteenth-Century South* (Chapel Hill: University of North Carolina Press, 1995), 26–31; and Stephanie McCurry, *Masters of Small Worlds: Yeoman Households, Gender Relations, and the Political Culture of the Antebellum South* (New York: Oxford University Press, 1995).

14 James C. Scott, *Domination and the Arts of Resistance: Hidden Transcripts* (New Haven: Yale University Press, 1990), 8.

15 Jackson, *Story of Mattie J. Jackson*, 20.

16 See Bruce Fort, "Reading in the Margins: The Politics and Culture of Literacy in Georgia, 1800–1920" (Ph.D. diss., University of Virginia, 1999).

17 Brevard's Digest 243, in George M. Stroud, editor, *Sketch of the Laws Relating to Slavery in the Several States of the United States* (1856; New York: Negro Universities Press, 1968), 60. Georgia enacted a similar law in 1770 that proscribed reading as well as writing.

18 Acts and Resolutions of the General Assembly of the State of South Carolina, December 1800, in Paul Finkelman, ed., *State Slavery Statutes* (microfiche; Frederick, Md.: University Publications of America, 1989). For a discussion of the Stono Rebellion and its consequences, see Peter Wood, *Black Majority: Negroes in Colonial South Carolina from 1670 through the Stono Rebellion* (New York: Alfred A. Knopf, 1975), 308–26.

19 David Walker, *David Walker's Appeal to the Coloured Citizens of the World*, edited by Peter P. Hinks (University Park: Pennsylvania State University Press, 2000), 34, 2.

20 Peter P. Hinks, *To Awaken My Addicted Brethren: David Walker and the Problem of Antebellum Slave Resistance* (University Park: Pennsylvania State University Press, 1997), 116–18.

21 Georgia Statutes, 1829, in Finkelman, *State Slavery Statutes*.

22 Acts Passed by the Second Session of the Legislature of the State of Louisiana, January 1830, in Stroud, *Sketch of the Laws*, 61.

23 Regarding gradual versus immediate abolition, see David Brion Davis, "The Emergence of Immediatism in British and American Antislavery Thought," in *Antislavery*, edited by Paul Finkelman (New York: Garland Publishing, 1989), 83–104.

24 Acts Passed by the General Assembly of the State of North Carolina, at the Session of 1830–31, in Finkelman, *State Slavery Statutes*.

25 Ibid. Regarding unequal punishment of free blacks, see Ira Berlin, *Slaves without Masters: The Free Negro in the Antebellum South* (New York: Pantheon Books, 1974), 96. Severely imbalanced punishments could be meted out, as in an 1836 Alabama statute that punished with death black people convicted of robbery or burglary but that punished whites convicted of the same crimes with a fine, or two-year sentence, or whipping, at the judge's discretion. Acts Passed at the Annual Session of the General Assembly of the State of Alabama, 1836, Number 48, Sections 2 and 3, in Finkelman, *State Slave Statutes*. Peter Wood suggests that whipping persisted as a punishment for blacks long after it had been eliminated for whites in part because blacks were less likely than whites to be able to afford a fine. Wood, *Black Majority*, 278.

26 Georgia Penal Code, Section 18, 1833, in Stroud, *Sketch of the Laws*, 61.

27 "Acts Passed at the General Assembly of the Commonwealth of Virginia, April 1831, Chapter XXXIX—An Act to amend the act concerning slaves, free negroes and mulattoes," in Finkelman, *State Slavery Statutes*.

28 Approximately twenty-six of fifty-two black people charged with involvement in Turner's insurrection were convicted. The rest were acquitted or had the charges against them dismissed. Many suspected of being participants never made it to court as whites killed them when caught. Kenneth S. Greenberg, editor, *The Confessions of Nat Turner and Related Documents* (New York: Bedford Books of St. Martin's Press, 1996), 57–58.

29 The statute also severely restricted conditions under which slaves could be brought into the state. Acts Passed at the Thirteenth Annual Session of the General Assembly of the State of Alabama, November 1831. In the aftermath of Turner's rebellion the Virginia legislature considered emancipating all slaves in the state. Greenberg, *Confessions of Nat Turner*, 23.

30 "A Memorial of the General Assembly of the State of Alabama to the General Assemblies of the Several States of the Union, January 1836," in Finkelman, *State Slavery Statutes*.

31 Bernard E. Powers Jr., *Black Charlestonians: A Social History, 1822–1885* (Fayetteville: University of Arkansas Press, 1994), 136; Whittington B. Johnson, *Black Savannah, 1788–1864* (Fayetteville: University of Arkansas Press, 1996), 127–29.

32 Acts and Resolutions of the General Assembly of the State of South Carolina, December 1834, in Finkelman, *State Slavery Statutes*.

33 John W. Cromwell, *The Early Negro Convention Movement* (Washington, D.C.: American Negro Academy, 1904), 7.

34 Edmund Fuller, *Prudence Crandall: An Incident of Racism in Nineteenth-Century Connecticut* (Middlebury, Conn.: Wesleyan University Press, 1971), 58, 76–95; Philip S. Foner and Josephine F. Pacheco, eds., *Three Who Dared: Prudence Crandall*, Margaret Douglass, Myrtilla Miner—Champions of Antebellum Black Education (Westport, Conn.: Greenwood Press, 1984), 20–43. I am grateful to Jennifer Rycenga for her insights on the partnership between Prudence Crandall and black abolitionists. Jennifer Rycenga, "Agitation as Education: Race, Class, and Religion in the Pedagogy of the Abolitionist Educator Prudence Crandall (1803–1890)," paper given at the Center for the Study of Religion at Yale University, New Haven, Conn., Spring 2001. Reminiscent of southern laws, though not as restrictive, the Connecticut statute of May 1833 provided, in part: "Whereas, attempts have been made to establish literary institutions in this state for the instruction of colored persons belonging to other states and countries, which would end to the great increase of the colored population of the state, and thereby to the injury of the people[,] . . . no person shall set up or establish in this state any school, academy, or literary institution for the instruction or education of colored persons who are not inhabitants of this state." It went on to prohibit teaching, harboring, or boarding any black person from another state. General Statues of Connecticut, 1835, Title 53—Inhabitants. For a discussion of similar challenges to black education in Illinois during this period, see Robert L. McCaul, *The Black Struggle for Public Schooling in Nineteenth-Century Illinois* (Carbondale: Southern Illinois University Press, 1987).

35 Nathan Bass, "Essay on the Treatment and Management of Slaves," *Transactions of the Southern Central Agricultural Society of Georgia* (1846/1851), in *Advice among Masters: The Ideal in Slave Management in the Old South*, edited by James O. Breeden (Westport, Conn.: Greenwood Press, 1980), 11–16; A Mississippi Planter, "Management of Negroes upon Southern Estates," *DeBow's Review* 10 (June 1851), in *Advice among Masters*, edited by James O. Breeden, 231.

36 Hurricane, "The Negro and His Management," *Southern Cultivator* (September 1860), in *Advice among Masters*, edited by James O. Breeden, 329–32.

37 Rawick, *American Slave*, vol. 2, pt. 1, pp. 63, 176; George P. Rawick, editor, *The American Slave: A Composite Autobiography: Supplement, Series 1*, 12 vols. (Westport, Conn.: Greenwood Press, 1977), vol. 7, pt. 2, p. 365. See also Leonard Black, *The Life and Sufferings of Leonard Black, a Fugitive from Slavery* (New Bedford, Mass.: Benjamin Lindsey, 1847), 19. On Webster's blue-back speller, see below, chap. 7.

38 Rawick, *American Slave . . . Supplement, Series 1*, vol. 8, pt. 3, p. 1329; Rawick, *American Slave*, vol. 12, pt. 1, pp. 130–31.

39 Rawick, *American Slave*, vol. 2, pt. 1, p. 246; Rawick, *American Slave. . . Supplement, Series 1*, vol. 6, pt. 1, pp. 10–11. Albright was elected to the Mississippi state senate in 1874. Many slaves referred to cutting off a hand or thumb as a potential or actual punishment for a slave who was caught reading or writing. See, for example, the statements by William McWhorter and Tom Hawkins in James Mellon, editor, *Bullwhip Days: The Slaves Remember* (New York: Weidenfeld and Nicolson, 1988), 197–98.

40 Code of Mississippi, Article 3, January 16, 1823, in A. Hutchinson, comp., *Code of Mississippi: Being an Analytical Compilation of the Public and General Statutes of the Territory and*

State, with Tabular References to the Local and Private Acts, from 1798–1848 (Jackson, Miss., 1848).

41 Lewis C. Lockwood, "Mary S. Peake: The Colored Teacher at Fortress Monroe," in *Two Black Teachers during the Civil War*, edited by William Loren Katz (New York: Arno Press and the New York Times, 1969), 5–16. See also Robert Francis Engs, *Freedom's First Generation: Black Hampton, Virginia, 1861–1890* (Philadelphia: University of Pennsylvania Press, 1979), 13. Engs suggests that white Hamptonians had an exceptionally lax attitude toward slave control, and therefore Mary Peake may have taught both free blacks and slaves without opposition before the Civil War.

42 For example, in 1788 free and enslaved African Americans had established the first black Baptist church in North America. By 1832, blacks in Savannah supported three independent Baptist churches. James M. Simms, *The First Colored Baptist Church in North America* (1888; New York: Negro Universities Press, 1969), 20–21; Johnson, Black Savannah, 6–15.

43 Stroud, *Sketch of the Laws*, 63.

44 Susie King Taylor, *A Black Woman's Civil War Memoirs: Reminiscences of My Life in Camp with the 33rd U.S. Colored Troops, Late 1st South Carolina Volunteers*, eds. Patricia W. Romero and Willie Lee Rose (New York: M. Wiener Publishing, 1988), 29–30. Taylor's maiden name was Baker; however, in her book she used the surnames of her two husbands, King and Taylor. For convenience, I refer to her as "Taylor" throughout. Ibid., 25–26.

45 Lucy Skipwith to John Cocke, November 1850, August 1854, May 1855, May 1858, October 1859, March, 1862, March 1863, August 1863, March 1864, and May 1864, in John W. Blassingame, ed., *Slave Testimony: Two Centuries of Letters, Speeches, Interviews, and Autobiographies* (Baton Rouge: Louisiana State University Press, 1977), 65–82. According to Blassingame, Cocke supported African colonization, temperance, and popular education. Although Cocke often denounced slavery, he was one of the largest slaveholders in the country, with plantations in Virginia and Alabama. In the 1830s Cocke, a founder of the American Colonization Society, freed one family of slaves and sent them to Liberia in West Africa. See also Randall M. Miller, *"Dear Master": Letters of a Slave Family* (Ithaca, N.Y.: Cornell University Press, 1978), 35.

46 Acts of the General Assembly of Virginia, 1842, in Finkelman, *State Slavery Statutes*.

47 G. W. Offley, *A Narrative of the Life and Labors of the Rev. G. W. Offley, a Colored Man, Local Preacher, and Missionary* (Hartford, Conn., 1859), 9; James Fisher, "Narrative of James Fisher" (originally printed in *National Anti-Slavery Standard*, April 13, 1843), in Blassingame, Slave Testimony, 234; American Missionary, April 1866, 75; *American Missionary*, September 1867, 194.

48 Mellon, *Bullwhip Days*, 200; Charles Alexander, *Battles and Victories of Allen Allensworth, A.M., Ph.D., Lt. Col. Retired U.S. Army* (Boston: Sherman, French and Company, 1914), 8–9.

49 Rawick, *American Slave . . . Supplement*, Series 1, vol. 8, pt. 3, p. 1232.

50 Rawick, *American Slave*, vol. 2, pt. 1, p. 50.

51 Peter Randolph, *From Slave Cabin to the Pulpit: The Autobiography of Rev. Peter Randolph— The Southern Question Illustrated and Sketches of Slave Life* (Boston: James H. Earle Printers, 1893), 11.

52 Theresa A. Singleton, *"The Archaeology of Slave Life,"* in *Before Freedom Came: African-American Life in the Antebellum South,* eds. Edward D. C. Campbell Jr. and Kym S. Rice (Charlottesville: University Press of Virginia, 1991), 171. For a mono- graph on the subject of literacy among slaves, see Janet Duitsman Cornelius, *"When I Can Read My Title Clear": Literacy, Slavery, and Religion in the Antebellum South* (Columbia: University of South Carolina Press, 1991).

53 Wood, *Black Majority,* 278, 314.

54 Interview of Charity Bowery by Lydia Maria Child, 1847–48, in Blassingame, Slave Testimony, 267; Offley, *Narrative,* 9.

55 James Curry, "Narrative of James Curry, a Fugitive Slave" (originally printed in *The Liberator,* January 10, 1840), in Blassingame, *Slave Testimony,* 128–44.

56 Fisher, "Narrative of James Fisher," 230–38.

57 Taylor, *Black Woman's Civil War Memoirs,* 31.

58 A. T. Jones interviewed by the Freedmen's Inquiry Commission in Canada, 1863, in Blassingame, *Slave Testimony,* 430.

59 *Wilmington (N.C.) Journal,* February 12, 1863.

60 Curry, "Narrative of James Curry," 128, 130–31. Curry escaped to Canada. When he returned to North Carolina in 1865, twenty-seven years later, he was attacked by enraged whites. The passage Curry cited is found in Acts 17:26.

61 Freedmen's Inquiry Commission interview of C. H. Hall, 1863, in Blassingame, *Slave Testimony,* 416–18.

62 Elijah Marrs, *Life and History of the Rev. Elijah P. Marrs* (Louisville, Ky.: Bradley and Gilbert Company, 1885), 11–12.

63 Ibid.

64 For a discussion of enslaved people's conceptions of freedom, see Thomas L. Webber, *Deep Like the Rivers: Education in the Slave Quarter Community, 1831–1865* (New York: W. W. Norton, 1978), 139–48.

65 Frederick Douglass to Thomas Auld, September 3, 1848, in Frederick Douglass, *Narrative of the Life of Frederick Douglass, an American Slave,* edited by David W. Blight (New York: Bedford Books, 1993), 135.

66 Ibid., 57–60. An "ell" is an old British measurement roughly equivalent to a yard. *Oxford English Dictionary.*

67 Douglass, *Narrative,* 61; Caleb Bingham, *The Columbian Orator: Containing a Variety of Original and Selected Pieces Together with Rules; Calculated to Improve the Youth and Others in the Ornamental and Useful Art of Eloquence* (Boston: J. H. A. Frost, 1831).

68 Bingham, *Columbian Orator,* 245.

69 Ibid., 240–42.

70 Douglass, *Narrative,* 61.

71 Ibid., 62.

72 Margaret Douglass, *Educational Laws of Virginia: The Personal Narrative of Mrs. Margaret Douglass, a Southern Woman, Who Was Imprisoned for One Month in the Common Jail of Norfolk,*

under the Laws of Virginia, for the Crime of Teaching Free Colored Children to Read (Boston: John P. Jewett and Company, 1854), 7–13; Josephine F. Pacheco, "*Margaret Douglass*," in *Three Who Dared*, edited by Foner and Pacheco, 57–95

73 Douglass, *Educational Laws of Virginia*, 21–22.

74 Ibid., 33–36.

75 Ibid., 44–50.

76 Ibid., 49.

77 Robert E. Perdue, *The Negro in Savannah, 1865–1900* (New York: Exposition Press, 1973), 40, 43, 70.

78 Jackson, *Story of Mattie J. Jackson*, 2.

79 Ibid., 23.

80 Ibid., 31.

Ex-Slaves and The Rise of Universal Education in The South, 1860-1880

James D. Anderson

FORMER SLAVES WERE the first among native southerners to depart from the planters' ideology of education and society and to campaign for universal, state-supported public education. In their movement for universal schooling the ex-slaves welcomed and actively pursued the aid of Republican politicians, the Freedmen's Bureau, northern missionary societies, and the Union army. This uprising among former slaves was the central threat to planter rule and planters' conceptions of the proper roles of state, church, and family in matters of education. The South's landed upper class tolerated the idea of pauper education as a charity to some poor white children, but state-enforced public education was another matter. The planters believed that state government had no right to intervene in the education of children and, by extension, the larger social arrangement. Active intervention in the social hierarchy through public education violated the natural evolution of society, threatened familial authority over children, upset the reciprocal relations and duties of owners to laborers, and usurped the functions of the church. During the period 1860 to 1880, other classes of native white southerners, including small farmers, industrialists, and laborers, showed little inclination to challenge the planters on these questions. Indeed, specific economic, political, social, and psychological relationships bound southern whites in general to the ideological position of the planter regime. The result was a postwar South that was extremely hostile to the idea of universal public education. The ex-slaves broke sharply with this position. With the aid of Republican politicians, they seized significant influence in state governments and laid the first foundation for universal public education in the South. This chapter tells the story of the ex-slaves' struggle for universal schooling, why they pursued it, how they organized to defend their common interests, how they coped with the resistance of opposing social classes, and finally, how they gained the cooperation of sympathetic social groups.

Blacks emerged from slavery with a strong belief in the desirability of learning to read and write. This belief was expressed in the pride with which they talked of other ex-slaves who learned to read or write in slavery and in the esteem in which they held literate blacks. It was expressed in the intensity and the frequency of their anger at slavery for keeping them illiterate. "There is one sin that slavery committed against me," professed one ex-slave, "which I will never forgive. It robbed me of my education." The former slaves' fundamental belief in the value of literate culture was expressed most clearly in their efforts to secure schooling for themselves and their children. Virtually every account by historians or contemporary observers stresses the ex-slaves' demand for universal schooling. In 1879 Harriet Beecher Stowe said of the freedmen's campaign for education: "They rushed not to the grog-shop but to the schoolroom—they cried for the spelling-book as bread, and pleaded for teachers as a necessity of life." Journalist Charles Nordhoff reported that New Orleans's ex-slaves were "almost universally . . . anxious to send their children to school." Booker T. Washington, a part of this movement himself, described most vividly his people's struggle for education: "Few people who were not right in the midst of the scenes can form any exact idea of the intense desire which the people of my race showed for education. It was a whole race trying to go to school. Few were too young, and none too old, to make the attempt to learn." When supervising the first contrabands at Fortress Monroe in 1861, Edward L. Pierce "observed among them a widespread desire to learn to read."[1]

The foundation of the freedmen's educational movement was their self-reliance and deep-seated desire to control and sustain schools for themselves and their children. William Channing Gannett, a white American Missionary Association teacher from New England, reported that "they have a natural praiseworthy pride in keeping their educational institutions in their own hands. There is jealousy of the superintendence of the white man in this matter. What they desire is assistance without control." The values of self-help and self-determination underlay the ex-slaves' educational movement. To be sure, they accepted support from northern missionary societies, the Freedmen's Bureau, and some southern whites, but their own action—class self-activity informed by an ethic of mutuality—was the primary force that brought schools to the children of freed men and women. This underlying force represented the culmination of a process of social class formation and development that started decades before the Civil War. "Emancipation," as Herbert Gutman showed, "transformed an established and developed subordinate class, allowing ex-slave men and women to act on a variety of class beliefs that had developed but been constrained during several generations of enslavement." Hence the South's postbellum movement for universal education is best understood as an expression of the ex-slaves' beliefs and behavior. External assistance notwithstanding, the postwar campaign for free schooling was rooted firmly in the beliefs and behavior of former slaves. W. E. B. DuBois was on the mark when he said: "Public education for all at public expense was, in the South, a Negro idea." Such a view of postbellum southern education acknowledges the important contributions of northerners but recognizes the ex-slaves as the principal challenge to the region's long-standing resistance to free schooling.[2]

Most northern missionaries went south with the preconceived idea that the slave regime was so brutal and dehumanizing that blacks were little more than uncivilized victims who needed to be taught the values and rules of civil society. They were bent on treating the freedmen almost wholly as objects. Many missionaries were astonished, and later chagrined, however, to discover that many ex-slaves had established their own educational collectives and associations, staffed schools entirely with black teachers, and were unwilling to allow their educational movement to be controlled by the "civilized" Yankees. In vital respects, missionary propaganda continued in spite of the social reality that contradicted it, but some of the more insightful Yankees began to appreciate ex-slaves as creative participants in the postbellum social process. John W. Alvord, the national superintendent of schools for the Freedmen's Bureau, was one of those perceptive Yankees. His growing awareness of a distinctly black perspective on educational and social matters was probably a result of his work, which compelled him to travel across the South and thereby afforded him a view of the depth and breadth of ex-slaves' values and behavior.

In September 1865, Alvord was appointed inspector of schools for the bureau. The title was later changed to general superintendent of schools. In July 1865 Alvord appointed a superintendent of schools for each southern state to help compile records on the bureau's educational activities. Alvord had traveled through nearly all the Confederate states by December 1865 and filed his first general report on the Freedmen's Bureau schools in January 1866. In this document he gave special attention to the practice of "self-teaching" and "native schools" among the freed men and women. "Throughout the entire South," Alvord reported, "an effort is being made by the colored people to educate themselves." "In the absence of other teaching they are determined to be self-taught; and everywhere some elementary text-book, or the fragment of one, may be seen in the hands of negroes." Not only were individuals found teaching themselves to read and write, but Alvord also discovered a system of what he chose to call "native schools," one of which he found at Goldsboro, North Carolina: "Two colored young men, who but a little time before commenced to learn themselves, had gathered 150 pupils, all quite orderly and hard at study." Further, Alvord discovered that "no white man, before me, had ever come near them." Hence native schools were common schools founded and maintained exclusively by ex-slaves. Two of Alvord's findings must be heavily emphasized. First, he found "native schools," in his own words, "throughout the entire South." Second, he discovered many of them in places that had not been visited by the Freedmen's Bureau or northern benevolent societies. Alvord, realizing that his findings did not square with existing perceptions of "the character of the Negro," took "special pains" to ascertain the facts on native schools. Such schools were found in "all the large places I visited," and they were "making their appearance through the interior of the entire South." After receiving much testimony from his field agents, "both oral and written," Alvord estimated in 1866 that there were "at least 500 schools of this description . . . already in operation throughout the South." This estimate, he warned his readers, was not an "overstatement." Alvord had little doubt about the significance of his findings: "This educational movement among the freedmen has in it a self-sustaining element." This "self-sustaining" activity was rooted firmly in the slave experience and began to surface before the war's end.[3]

Before northern benevolent societies entered the South in 1862, before President Abraham Lincoln issued the Emancipation Proclamation in 1863, and before Congress created the Bureau of Refugees, Freedmen and Abandoned Lands (Freedmen's Bureau) in 1865, slaves and free persons of color had already begun to make plans for the systematic instruction of their illiterates. Early black schools were established and supported largely through the Afro-Americans' own efforts. The first of these schools, according to current historiography, opened at Fortress Monroe, Virginia, in September 1861, under the leadership of Mary Peake, a black teacher. Primary historical sources, however, demonstrate that slaves and free persons of color started schools even before the Fortress

Figure 2.1.
Zion School in Charleston, South Carolina, established in December 1865, had an entirely black administration and teaching staff. By December 1866 it had 13 teachers, an enrollment of 850 students, and an average daily attendance of 720 pupils. Wood engraving in Harper's Weekly, 15 December 1866.

Monroe venture. In July 1864, for instance, the black New Orleans Union commemorated the founding of the Pioneer School of Freedom, established in New Orleans in 1860, "in the midst of danger and darkness." Some schools predated the Civil War period and simply increased their activities after the war started. A black school in Savannah, Georgia, had existed unknown to the slave regime from 1833 to 1865. Its teacher, a black woman by the name of Deveaux, quickly expanded her literacy campaign during and following the war. It was this type of "self-sustaining" behavior that produced the native schools Alvord observed throughout the South in 1866.[4]

Herbert Gutman's pioneering work on this subject demonstrates further that the native schools of Fortress Monroe, Savannah, and New Orleans were not isolated occurrences. Such schools were also begun among refugees in Alexandria, Virginia. A white teacher did not work with Afro-Americans in Alexandria until October 1862, by which time they had already established several schools. "In April 1863," wrote Gutman, "about four hundred children attended such schools." Likewise, he documented schools for rural ex-slaves in northeastern South Carolina. In 1867 Camden blacks, largely through their own individual and collective efforts, established twenty-two schools in which more than four thousand children were instructed. Schooling also made significant progress among blacks in Sumter, Marion, Darlington, Simmonsville, Florence, Kingstree, Chetau, Bennettsville, and Timonville, South Carolina. Ex-slaves contributed their money and labor to help make these schools possible, and they organized responsible committees to supervise the schools.[5]

What happened in Alexandria, Virginia, before 1865 and in northeastern South Carolina in 1866 and 1867 occurred elsewhere in the South. Afro-Americans over the entire region contributed significantly to the origin and development of universal schooling. Even where the Union army and Freedmen's Bureau were heavily involved in the education of refugees and ex-slaves, the long-term success of schooling depended mainly on Afro-Americans. The activities of Louisiana refugees and ex-slaves illustrate the importance of such involvement. Blacks began establishing small private schools between 1860 and 1862. Though these first schools were inadequately financed and haphazardly run, attempts were made to organize them on a systematic basis. After Union forces occupied New Orleans in 1863, however, the federal Commission of Enrollment presided over blacks' educational activities. According to historian John W. Blassingame, Major General Nathaniel P. Banks "instituted the most thorough of all systems for educating the freedmen in his Department of Gulf (Louisiana, Mississippi, Alabama, and Texas)." In October 1863, Banks authorized the Commission of Enrollment to take a census of Afro-Americans in the Gulf states and to establish schools for blacks in New Orleans. On 22 March 1864, he established a Board of Education to organize and govern the spread of black schools. In September 1864, the black New Orleans Tribune reported that Banks's effort had already resulted in 60 schools with "eight thousand scholars and more than one hundred teachers." By December 1864, the Board of Education was operating 95 schools with 9,571 children and 2,000 adults, instructed by 162 teachers. This system of schooling extended beyond the

New Orleans area. The Tribune reported, in July 1864, that teachers were "sent to instruct black pupils in rural areas." In 1865 the Freedmen's Bureau took control of this school system, which then included iz6 schools, 19,000 pupils, and 100 teachers.[6]

Such historical evidence has been wrongly used to attribute the freedmen's school movement to Yankee benevolence or federal largesse. The events that followed the Freedmen's Bureau takeover, however, underscore Gutman's observation that the ex-slaves' educational movement was rooted deeply within their own communal values. The Board of Education and later the Freedmen's Bureau maintained these schools through federal contributions and by levying a property tax. Jn 1866, allegedly to reduce the financial costs to the bureau, its officials temporarily closed all black schools under their authorization, and the general tax for freedmen's education was suspended by military order. The effect of this change was catastrophic. Alvord recorded the actions of Louisiana ex-slaves: "The consternation of the colored population was intense. . . . They could not consent to have their children sent away from study, and at once expressed willingness to be assessed for the whole expense." Black leaders petitioned Yankee military officers to levy an added tax upon their community to replenish the bureau's school fund. Petitions demanding the continuation of universal schooling poured in from all over Louisiana. As Alvord recounted: "I saw one [petition], from plantations across the river, at least 30 feet in length, representing 10,000 negroes. It was affecting to examine it and note the names and marks (x) of such a long list of parents, ignorant themselves, but begging that their children might be educated, promising that from beneath their present burdens, and out of their extreme poverty, they would pay for it." Such actions reveal the collective effort and shared values of the ex-slaves who built and sustained schools across the postwar South.[7]

Much more than federal largesse made free schooling a reality among Louisiana's ex-slaves. After the bureau withdrew its support, the freedmen took control of the educational system and transformed federal schools into local free schools. The New Orleans Tribune reported that as soon as the bureau's failures were recognized, educational associations "were organized in various parts of the state, at least in its principal cities, to promote the cause of education, and with the particular view of helping the children of parents in reduced circumstances to attend schools." One such association, the Louisiana Educational Relief Association, was organized in June 1866. Its primary aim was to "disseminate the principle of education, by assisting poor children whose friends are unable to do so." The board of trustees could "lease or buy such school property as may be deemed judicious, and examine and employ teachers." Louisiana's freedmen believed themselves primarily responsible for providing education for their children. "Each race of men, each class in society, have [sic] to shape their own destinies themselves," wrote J. Willis Menard, secretary of the Louisiana Educational Relief Association. Although acknowledging the support of the Freedmen's Bureau and northern benevolent societies, Menard maintained that the ex-slaves' survival and development rested largely on their own shoulders: "The colored people are called today to mark out on the map of life with their own hands their future course or locality in the great national body politic. Other hands cannot mark for them; other tongues cannot speak for them; other eyes cannot see for them; they must see and speak for themselves, and make their own characters on the map, however crooked or illegible." That Menard's feelings were not unusual is revealed through the behavior of Louisiana's freedmen from 1866 to 1868. During this period they developed a parallel system of free schools. Even when the bureau reopened its schools, private schools for black pupils continued to spring up outside its control. Enrollment in such schools grew rapidly and actually exceeded the number registered in the bureau's system. In January 1867 there were sixty-five private schools in New Orleans enrolling 2,967 pupils; the bureau maintained fifty-six schools with 2,527 pupils enrolled. Free schooling was sustained in Louisiana largely as a result of the ex-slaves' collective efforts.[8]

The relationship between black self-activity and educational changes in the postwar South is further illustrated by the behavior of Georgia's ex-slaves. In December 1864 a committee of Afro-American leaders in Savannah met with Secretary of War Edwin M. Stanton and General William T. Sherman to request support for the education of Georgia's liberated blacks. Out of this conference evolved a plan for establishing an organized system of free schools. In 1865 Afro-American leaders formed the Georgia Educational Association to supervise schools in districts throughout the state, to establish school policies, and to raise funds to help finance the cost of education. Freedmen's Bureau officials described the aims and structure of this association:

> To associate the efforts of the people, the prominent educators in the State, the agents of northern societies, and such officers of the government as are authorized to aid the work, and to unite in such a manner as shall exclude any subject at all likely to divide their efforts or direct them from their one great and desirable object. To secure this end, subordinate associations are established as far as practicable. By this means a thorough union is formed and a prompt and constant communication with the parent society is had. Connected with the State association is a State board of education, which ... is a general executive committee.

Through this association Georgia's Afro-Americans sustained in full or part the operation of more than two-thirds of their schools. In the fall of 1866, they financed entirely or in part 96 of the 123 day and evening schools. They also owned 57 of the school buildings. Such accomplishments fulfilled the primary purpose of the Georgia Educational Association, "that the freedmen shall establish schools in their own counties and neighborhoods, to be supported entirely by the colored people." In Savannah, for instance, there were z8 schools in 1866, and 16 of them, reported the black Loyal Georgian, were "under the control of an Educational Board of Colored Men, taught by colored teachers, and sustained by the freed people." These beliefs and behavior were consistent with the activities of ex-slaves in Virginia, South Carolina, and Louisiana.[9]

Significantly, Georgia's black educational leaders were critical of popular misconceptions, which attributed the schooling of ex-slaves to Yankee benevolence. The *Loyal Georgian*, official newspaper of the Georgia Educational Association, rejected explicitly the argument that Yankee teachers brought schooling to the freedmen. In February 1866, though defending Yankee teachers against southern white criticism, the *Loyal Georgian* also expressed its hope that missionary teachers were not in the South "in any vain reliance on their superior gifts, either of intelligence or benevolence; or in any foolish self-confidence that they have a special call to this office, or special endowments to meet its demands." Historian Jacqueline Jones has demonstrated that northern teachers in Georgia were "taken aback to discover that some blacks preferred to teach in and operate their own schools without the benefit of northern largesse." Similarly, Ronald E. Butchart has shown that ex-slaves, in general, initiated and supported education for themselves and their children and also resisted external control of their educational institutions. In 1867, for instance, the *Freedmen's Record* complained about the tendency of ex-slaves to prefer sending their children to black-controlled private schools rather than supporting the less expensive northern white-dominated "free" schools. A white observer noted that "in all respects apart from his or her competency to teach—they will keep their children out of school, and go to work, organize and [sic] independent school and send their children to it." It is no wonder, then, that some missionaries complained of the ex-slaves' lack of gratitude "for the charity which northern friends are so graciously bestowing." The ex-slaves' educational movement became a test of their capacity to restructure their lives, to establish their freedom. Although they appreciated northern support, they resisted infringements that threatened to undermine their own initiative and self-reliance.[10]

In other important ways ex-slaves initiated and sustained schools whether or not northern aid was available. The "Sabbath" school system, about which little is known, provides a particularly clear study of educational activities operated largely on the strength of the ex-slave community. Frequently, Sabbath schools were established before "free" or "public" schools. These church-sponsored schools, operated mainly in evenings and on weekends, provided basic literacy instruction. "They reached thousands not able to attend weekday schools," writes historian Samuel L. Horst. In January 1866, in his first report to the Freedmen's Bureau, Alvord commented:

> Sabbath schools among freedmen have opened throughout the entire South; all of them giving elementary instruction, and reaching thousands who cannot attend the week-day teaching. These are not usually included in the regular returns, but are often spoken of with special interest by the superintendents. Indeed, one of the most thrilling spectacles which he who visits the southern country now witnesses in cities, and often upon the plantations, is the large schools gathered upon the Sabbath day, sometimes of many hundreds, dressed in clean Sunday garments, with eyes sparkling, intent upon elementary and Christian instruction. The management of some of these is

admirable, after the fashion of the best Sunday schools of white children, with faithful teachers, the majority of whom it will be noticed are colored.

Some of Alvord's findings are especially worthy of emphasis. Sabbath schools were common in ex-slave communities across the South immediately following the war's end. In 1868 Alvord described the scope of Sabbath schools in North Carolina: "In all the cities of the State, in most of the smaller towns, and in many of the rural districts, Sabbath schools are established and well conducted." Although white religious societies sponsored some Sabbath schools for ex-slaves, the system was largely black-dominated, relied on local black communities for support, and generally had all-black teaching staffs. The importance of the Sabbath schools varied across states and localities. In some areas they constituted the only viable system of free instruction. T. K. Noble, Freedmen's Bureau superintendent of education in Kentucky, said in 1867: "The places of worship owned by the colored people are almost the only available school houses in the State."[11]

It is important, therefore, to emphasize another of Alvord's observations, that the Sabbath schools, often spoken of with special interest by the state superintendents, were not usually included in the regular bureau reports. C. E. Compton, the bureau's superintendent of education in Tennessee, reported in 1870 that "many children attend Sabbath schools at colored churches of which no report is received." The Freedmen's Bureau kept statistics from 1866 to 1870. These records include almost exclusively schools under the auspices of northern societies. Hence, ex-slaves laid a significantly larger foundation for universal education than is accounted for in official reports and in the histories of southern education. James M. McPherson writes, "At no time were more than 10 percent of the freedmen of school age attending the [missionary] societies' schools." Meyer Weinberg concludes that, in 1870, "nine out of ten black children still remained outside any school." These estimates, however accurate for schools reporting to the bureau, do not include data on the black church-operated schools. In 1869 Alvord asked his field agents to estimate numbers of teachers and enrollments in Sabbath schools. These reports,

Figure 2.2

This school on St. Helena Island in South Carolina was typical of the Sabbath and free schools attended by ex-slaves in the period immediately following the Civil War. Courtesy of the National Archives.

admittedly conservative in their estimates, enumerated 1,512 Sabbath schools with 6,146 teachers and 107,109 pupils. Sabbath schools continued to grow in the black community long after Reconstruction. In 1868 the African Methodist Episcopal church (AME), for example, enrolled 40,000 pupils in its Sabbath schools. By 1885, the AME church reported having "200,000 children in Sunday schools" for "intellectual and moral" instruction. These Sunday schools were not devoted entirely to Bible study. As Booker T. Washington recalled from his own experience, "the principal book studied in the Sunday school was the spelling book." The Sabbath schools represent yet another remarkable example of ex-slaves seeking, establishing, and supporting their own schools."[12]

It was such local activities by ex-slaves that spurred the establishment of widespread elementary and literacy education and provided the grassroots foundation for the educational activities of northern missionary societies and the Freedmen's Bureau. To be sure, ex-slaves benefited greatly from the support of northern whites; but they were determined to achieve educational self-sufficiency in the long run with or without the aid of northerners. Their self-determination has escaped the attention of all but a few historians. The larger significance of their behavior, however, did not go unnoticed by Freedmen's Bureau superintendent John Alvord, one of the most perceptive Yankee observers of postwar southern educational changes. As early as January 1866, Alvord noted the "self-sustaining element" in the ex-slaves' educational movement. He quickly recognized the organization and discipline that underlay the school campaign. In July 1866 he reported "that the surprising efforts of our colored population to obtain and [sic] education are not spasmodic." "They are growing to a habit," he continued, "crystalizing into a system, and each succeeding school-term shows their organization more and more complete and permanent." Initially, Alvord did not know what to make of these "surprising efforts." Foreshadowing the interpretations of some later historians, in January 1866 he attributed the ex-slaves' campaign for schooling to "the natural thirst for knowledge common to all men," a desire to imitate educated whites, an attraction to the mystery of literate culture, the practical needs of business life, and the stimulating effects of freedom. By July, however, Alvord pointed to a more fundamental motive for the freedmen's behavior: "They have within themselves . . . a vitality and hope, coupled with patience and willingness to struggle, which foreshadows with certainty their higher education as a people in the coming time." Universal education was certain to become a reality in black society, not because ex-slaves were motivated by childlike, irrational, and primitive drives, but because they were a responsible and politically self-conscious social class. Alvord, therefore, was confident that the ex-slaves' educational movement would not soon fall into decline: "Obstacles are yet to be encountered. Perhaps the most trying period in the freedmen's full emancipation has not yet come. But we can distinctly see that the incipient education universally diffused as it is, has given these whole four millions an impulse onward never to be lost. They are becoming conscious of what they can do, of what they ultimately *can* be. . . . Self-reliance is becoming their pride as it is their responsibility." The great efforts blacks made to establish

schools for their own children soon after the war and to establish state-supported systems of public education for all children reflected both their self-reliance and distinct
educational and social philosophy. These ideals had been cultivated in large part during
their long ordeal of slavery.[13]

Ultimately, the formation and development of the ex-slaves' beliefs and behavior
regarding universal education in the postwar South will have to be understood as part
of a process that started decades before the Civil War. For, as Herbert Gutman has
demonstrated, the choices so many freed men and women made immediately upon their
emancipation, before they had substantial rights by law, had their origins in the ways
their ancestors had adapted to enslavement. Hence, before the reason why Afro-Americans emerged from slavery with a particular desire for literacy can be understood, slavery
and especially slave literacy await refined and detailed study. That is beyond the primary
scope of this chapter, but a few examples might illuminate the social context of slave
literacy and, therefore, black consciousness of literate culture. The way slaves and other
southern social classes thought about literacy and education developed along with the
modes in which they actually learned or experienced it. That experience for slaves was
vastly different in most important respects from the experiences of planters, white small
farmers, industrialists, and poor whites. During the three decades before the Civil War
slaves lived in a society in which for them literacy was forbidden by law and symbolized
as a skill that contradicted the status of slaves. As former slave William Henry Heard
recalled: "We did not learn to read nor write, as it was against the law for any person to
teach any slave to read; and any slave caught writing suffered the penalty of having his
forefinger cut from his right hand; yet there were some who could read and write." Despite
the dangers and difficulties, thousands of slaves learned to read and write. By 1860 about 5
percent of the slaves had learned to read. Many paid a high price for their literacy. Thomas
H. Jones, a slave in mid-nineteenth-century North Carolina, learned how to read while
hiding in the back of his master's store. "It seemed to me that if I could learn to read and
write," said Jones, "this learning might, nay, I really thought it would point out to me the
way to freedom, influence and real secure happiness." As he became more engrossed in
his pursuit of literate culture and careless about concealing it, Jones was surprised one
morning by the sudden appearance of his master. Having only a second to react, Jones
threw his book behind some barrels in the store, but not before his master had seen him
throw something away. The slave owner assumed that Jones had been stealing items from
the stockroom and ordered him to retrieve whatever he had thrown away. "I knew if
my book was discovered that all was lost, and I felt prepared for any hazard or suffering
rather than give up my book and my hopes of improvement," recalled Jones. He endured
three brutal whippings to conceal his pursuit of literacy. In another instance a slave by
the name of Scipio was put to death for teaching a slave child how to read and spell, and
the child was severely beaten to make him "forget what he had learned." The former slave
Ferebe Rogers was married by a slave, Enoch Golden, who persisted throughout his life in
spreading literacy among his fellow slaves. "On his dyin' bed he said he been de death o'

many a nigger 'cause he taught so many to read and write," said Rogers. Elizabeth Sparks was part of a group of rebel slaves who held secret literacy sessions in the slave quarters. The gatherings, known among slaves as "stealin' the meetin'," were attended by free blacks who attempted to teach slaves to read and write. Although slaves became literate in a variety of ways, including at the hands of slaveowners, probably the typical experience was characterized by former slave Louisa Gause: "No child, white people never teach colored people nothin, but to be good to dey massa en mittie, what learnin dey would get in dem days dey been get it at night; taught demselves." No other class of native southerners had experienced literacy in this context. Hence emancipation extruded an ex- slave class with a fundamentally different consciousness of literacy, a class that viewed reading and writing as a contradiction of oppression.[14]

In the history of black education the political significance of slave literacy reaches beyond the antebellum period. Many of the educators and leaders of the postbellum years were men and women who first became literate under slavery. Moreover, many prominent post-Civil War black educators who were not literate as slaves received their initial understanding of the meaning of literacy under slavery. Such black leaders as Frederick Douglass, Bishop Henry M. Turner, Bishop Isaac Lane, Bishop Lucius H. Holsey, and P. B. S. Pinchback and educators Isaac M. Bergman, Bishop John Wesley Gaines, W. S. Scarborough, and Lucy C. Laney are some of the prominent nineteenth-century figures who became literate in the antebellum South. Their ideas about the meaning and purpose of education were shaped partly by the social system of slavery under which they first encountered literacy. After slavery many of the leading black educators emerged from among the rebel literates, those slaves who had sustained their own learning process in defiance of the slaveowners' authority. They viewed literacy and formal education as means to liberation and freedom.

Postslavery experiences continued to reinforce and shape a distinctive Afro-American consciousness of literate culture. "Every little negro in the county is now going to school and the public pays for it," wrote one disgruntled planter. "This is a hell of [a] fix but we can't help it, and the best policy is to conform as far as possible to circumstances." Such responses emphasized the planters' persistent beliefs that literate culture contradicted the status of black southerners. Many postslavery developments provided ex-slaves with compelling reasons to become literate. The uses and abuses of written labor contracts made it worthwhile to be able to read, write, and cipher. Frequently, planters designed labor contracts in ways that would confuse and entrap the ex-slaves. As the Freedmen's Bureau superintendent observed, "I saw one [labor contract] in which it was stipulated that one-third of seven-twelfths of all corn, potatoes, fodder, etc., shall go to the laborers." Hence when a middle-aged black woman was asked why she was so determined to learn to read and write, she replied, "so that the Rebs can't cheat me." The enfranchisement of black males also gave ex-slaves an impulse to become literate. "At the place of voting they look at the ballot-box and then at the printed ticket in their hands, wishing they could read it," reported Alvord in 1867. Education for the freedmen could serve as a safeguard against fraud and manipulation.[15]

More fundamentally, the ex-slaves' struggle for education was an expression of free-dom. It was, as Ronald Butchart maintains, an effort of an oppressed people "to put as great a distance between themselves and bondage as possible." The *New Orleans Black Republican* proclaimed in April 1865: "Freedom and school books and newspapers, go hand in hand. Let us secure the freedom we have received by the intelligence that can maintain it." This proclamation was signed by prominent black leaders of New Orleans, including Thomas S. Isabelle, C. C. Antoine, S. W. Rogers, Professor P. M. Williams, and A. E. Barber. Similarly, in 1867, the black Equal Rights Association of Macon, Georgia, resolved: "That a Free school system is a great need of our state, and that we will do all in our power by voice and by vote to secure adoption of a system." That same year black leaders Henry M. Turner, T. G. Campbell, John T. Costin, and Thomas P. Beard formed the Black Republican party of Georgia. The organization declared that "Free Schools and churches are the guardians of civil and religious liberty." Northern observers quickly noted that education stood as "the token and pledge" of blacks' emancipation. Even adult ex-slaves were, as the Freedmen's Bureau superintendent recorded, "earnestly seeking that instruction which will fit them for their new responsibilities." For the freedmen, universal schooling was a matter of personal liberation and a necessary function of a free society[16]

Thus ex-slaves did much more than establish a tradition of educational self-help that supported most of their schools. They also were the first among native southerners to wage a campaign for universal public education. From its small beginnings in 1860 and with the help of the Freedmen's Bureau and northern benevolent societies, the school system was virtually complete in its institutional form by 1870. According to historian Henry Allen Bullock, fourteen southern states had established 575 schools by 1865, and these schools were employing 1,171 teachers for the 71,779 Negro and white children in regular attendance. School attendance was not uniform across cities and towns, but it was visible in enough places to signal a fundamental shift in southern tradition. In 1866 Alvord reported his findings on the level of ex-slaves' school attendance: "The average attendance is nearly equal to that usually found at the North. For instance, in the District of Columbia, the daily attendance at the public school is but forty-one (41) percent; while at the colored schools of the District it is seventy-five (75) percent. In the State of New York, the daily attendance at the public school averages forty-three (43) percent. At the colored schools in the city of Memphis it is seventy-two (72) percent; and in Virginia eighty-two (82) percent." In Louisiana over 60 percent of all black children from five to twelve years of age were enrolled in school by 1865. The ex-slaves' school enrollment suffered a setback in 1868, rose again in 1869, and leveled off in 1870. In the entire South in 1870, about one-fourth of the school-age ex-slaves attended "public" schools. Reliable data are not available to determine Sabbath school attendance rates, but it seems proba-ble from scattered evidence that Sabbath schools increased their enrollment throughout the 1870s and 1880s. The freedmen's initiative in starting schools and their remarkable attendance rates made it evident that "free" schooling was fast becoming a customary right in the postwar South.[17]

The ex-slaves' most fundamental challenge to the planters' ideology and structure of schooling, however, went beyond the practice of universal schooling as a customary right. They played a central role in etching the idea of universal public education into southern state constitutional law. As DuBois demonstrated, "The first great mass movement for public education at the expense of the state, in the South, came from Negroes." Black politicians played a critical role in establishing universal education as a basic right in southern constitutional conventions during congressional Reconstruction. Under the Military Reconstruction Acts passed in 1867, Congress empowered the generals of the armies of occupation to call for new constitutional conventions in which blacks were to participate along with whites. Black politicians and leaders joined with Republicans in southern constitutional conventions to legalize public education in the constitutions of the former Confederate states. By 1870, every southern state had specific provisions in its constitution to assure a public school system financed by a state fund. And even when white southerners regained control of state governments, they kept the central features of educational governance and finance created by the ex-slave—Republican coalition. Ex-slaves used their resources first in a grass-roots movement to build, fund, and staff schools as a practical right; then they joined with Republicans to incorporate the idea into southern state constitutional law. With these actions they revolutionized the South's position regarding the role of universal public education in society.[18]

The freedmen's educational revolution bred a counterrevolution. Postwar southern economic and social development, including educational reform, was heavily influenced by the persistent domination of the planter class. Traditional historiography has contended that the Civil War and emancipation brought about the downfall of the prewar planter class. The most recent historical scholarship, however, demonstrates convincingly the extent to which wealth and power in the postwar South continued to rest in the planters' hands. What actually occurred was not the downfall or destruction of the old planter class but rather its persistence and metamorphosis. Plantation land tended to remain in the hands of its prewar owners.[19]

The persistence and tenacity of the planter class throughout the war and Reconstruction, contends Jonathan Wiener, laid the basis for its continued domination of the southern political economy in the 1870s and 1880s. As a consequence, the South took the "Prussian road to industrial capitalism—a delayed industrialization under the auspices of a backward agrarian elite, the power of which was based on a repressive system of agricultural labor." In 1880, 75.4 percent of the South's labor force was in agriculture. Black agricultural laborers constituted more than 40 percent of the South's total agricultural labor force and formed a clear majority in several southern states. Agriculture accounted for only 23.3 percent of the work force in the Northeast and 54.5 percent in the North Central region. The planters' approach to labor control posed a formidable threat to the ex-slaves' educational movement. Elsewhere in the nation, particularly the industrial Northeast, dominant classes had already committed themselves to tax-supported public education, partly as a means to train and discipline an industrial work force. Freedmen's

Bureau Superintendent Alvord, echoing the northern idea of universal schooling for the laboring classes, proclaimed to the South in 1866: "Popular education cannot well be opposed; free labor is found to be more contented with its privileges." But southern planters did not share northern ideas on free labor or popular education. Postwar planters complained that their "free" laborers were unreliable, failed to comply with the terms of their labor contracts, and would not obey orders. Most important, schooling most emphatically was not the answer to southern labor problems. "The South could not supply by schools," said one southern writer in 1868, "the restraining, correcting, elevating influences" cultivated and maintained by slavery. When Carl Schurz toured the South in late 1865, he found the planters believing that "learning will spoil the nigger for work." Faced with the possibilities of moving toward a northern-style system of free labor and mass literacy or remaining with their coercive mode of labor allocation and control, the planters chose the labor-repressive system, which rested at least partially on the absence of formal schooling among agricultural and domestic laborers.[20]

Hence at war's end the planters attempted to reestablish the plantation system with only minor modifications. With the overseer renamed "manager" or "agent," the planters tried to force ex-slaves to work the postwar plantation in antebellumlike work gangs. The planters needed above all a resumption of work on the part of black laborers in numbers and involving costs similar to those prevailing in the pre-war era. This desire was thwarted when ex-slaves withdrew a substantial portion of their labor power. By greatly reducing the number of days worked and the number of hours worked each day, they created a serious labor shortage. According to economic historians Roger L. Ransom and Richard Sutch, upon emancipation the supply of black labor fell to two-thirds its pre-war level. This reduced labor supply had a profound impact on the ability of the South to produce cotton. It represented a severe financial blow to the planter class. Therefore, ex-slaves gained some power in the labor market to insist upon educational and economic changes in the South's social hierarchy. Planters, however, generally favored a policy of strict labor control and discouraged the education of freedmen.[21]

In the immediate postwar years, ex-slaves, sometimes assisted by northern troops, were able to use their labor power to give weight to their educational demands. In January 1866 Alvord noted:

> If they are to be retained as laborers in the rural districts, [educational] opportunities must be furnished on the plantations. More than one instance could be already given where a school in the interior has been started from this motive. . . . The head of one of the largest of the timber and turpentine enterprises in South Carolina told me that he formerly had hired only men, but he had now learned that he must have their families too, and that this could only be done by allowing them patches of land, treating them properly, paying them well, and *giving them schools.*

In 1866 and 1867, Freedmen's Bureau officials observed the widespread emergence of the "educational clause" in labor contracts between planters and ex-slaves. In July 1867 Frank R. Chase, the bureau's superintendent of education for Louisiana, reported:

> "Many of the freedmen made it a special clause of their contract this year, that they should have the benefit of schools. But the planter was only willing to have colored teachers employed, thinking that such schools would amount to little or nothing. In this they are mistaken, as many of the most prosperous schools in the State are taught by competent colored teachers."

Such reports from bureau officials throughout the South convinced Alvord that "the educational clause in the contracts . . . is rapidly becoming universal." Hence, he continued, "Schools are everywhere springing up from the soil itself at the demand of those who till it—a state of things which localizes the benefits of education in a fixed, permanent society." Because ex-slaves understood that their labor power was essential for the restoration of southern agriculture to its prewar level of prosperity, they demanded not only fair wages for their work but educational opportunities as well. This practice, at least for a brief period in the postwar years, enabled some plantation ex-slaves to experience the benefits of schooling. Some planters, desiring to secure and stabilize a needed supply of laborers, even shielded freedmen's schools from harassment by white terrorists. Schools on the plantations were usually financed by the ex-slaves, but a few were paid for by planters.[22]

In general, the ex-slaves were unable to reconcile the planters to the idea of black education. It has been argued that the most intelligent and successful planters usually supported Negro education and that the most bitter opposition came from the white lower classes. To be sure, militant opposition did come from lower-class whites, but it came also from planters. A few planters did accept or tolerate the idea of universal education among the ex-slaves, and so did a few poor whites. As a class, however, the planters reacted decisively to the freedmen's educational movement; they were opposed to black education in particular and showed substantial resistance to the very idea of public schooling for the laboring classes. The planters' opposition to black education surfaced early. In 1864 the *New Orleans Tribune* reported that Louisiana planters were strongly opposed to the ex-slaves' educational movement. In the country parishes, white teachers were "condemned and scorned" and landlords "refused to rent buildings for school purposes, and to board the teachers." In 1867 Louisiana's superintendent of education complained that "a large majority of the planters are opposed to the education of the freedmen." An example from 1871 illustrates the point with much greater force. General John Eaton, commissioner of the new Federal Bureau of Education, sent out three thousand questionnaires to laborers and employers regarding the benefits of universal education in the South. Concerning the replies, he wrote: "A large number have been received, and the writers were unanimous in their testimony as to the value of education to every class of laborers, with one striking exception, namely, the southern planters; the majority of whom did not believe in giving the Negro any education." Planters resisted in various ways the ex-slaves' pursuit of universal schooling. Henry Allen Bullock found that Virginia planters in 1865 "were seeking to prevent Negro parents from sending their children to school by threatening to put them out of their houses." Alabama whites who employed ex-slaves as domestics would terminate the employment of servants whose children attended school. Similarly, in 1869 the Freedmen's Bureau school superintendent for northwestern Louisiana and northern Texas discovered that "many of the planters will not allow colored children on their places to go to school at all, even when we have started those which are convenient." The planters, with few exceptions, viewed black education as a distinct threat to the racially qualified form of labor exploitation upon which their agrarian order depended.[23]

The planters' heavy use of child labor contributed significantly to their opposition to black education. During good crop years black school terms were so short and irregular that children hardly had time to learn to read and write. "Owing to unusual employment of children this season in gathering crops, especially cotton, which was very abundant, many schools did not open until December," reported John Alvord in 1870. Many parents fought this infringement upon their children's educational opportunities, but others conceded to the planters' interests.[24]

Figure 2.3.

This Thomas Nast cartoon that appeared in Harper's Weekly, 24 October 1874, depicts the southern white reaction to the ex-slave crusade for universal schooling. Note the fallen school book and the schoolhouse burning in the background while an ex-slave is being lynched. Courtesy of the Library of Congress

Despite the ex-slaves' early success in laying the foundation for universal education in the South, planters presented severe obstacles to those who endeavored to establish an elaborate bureaucratic system of free public schooling. Between 1869 and 1877, the planter-dominated white South regained control of the state governments. The moment of broad retrenchment came with the disputed presidential election of 1876 and the settlement that resulted in the Compromise of 1877. Southerners agreed to the election of Rutherford B. Hayes, and Republicans agreed to remove federal troops from the South. With both state authority and extralegal means of control firmly in their hands, the planters, though unable to eradicate earlier gains, kept universal schooling underdeveloped. They stressed low taxation, opposed compulsory school attendance laws, blocked the passage of new laws that would strengthen the constitutional basis of public education, and generally discouraged the expansion of public school opportunities. The planters' resistance virtually froze the ex-slaves' educational campaign in its mid-1870s position. "At the beginning of the twentieth century," wrote Horace Mann Bond, "the condition of the schools for Negro children in the South was but slightly improved over their condition in 1875." Indeed, between 1880 and 1900, the number of black children of school age increased 2.5 percent, but the proportion attending public school fell.[25]

The planters gained further control over black education as they increased their supervision and control over the ex-slave laboring class. The semiautonomous position and newly acquired economic power of freedmen in the labor market had buttressed their educational movement, but as landlords regained control over black labor, the force and autonomy of the campaign for universal schooling were severely weakened. The planters established a system of coercive labor designed to reduce wages, to restrict labor mobility, to protect individual planters from competition with other employers, and to force blacks to sign repressive labor contracts. Historians William Cohen, Pete Daniel, and Jonathan Wiener discovered a variety of state laws and local customs aimed at helping planters acquire, hold, and exploit black labor virtually at will. Enticement laws passed by ten southern states from 1865 to 1867 were the most common measures aimed at controlling the black labor force. "Enticement statutes," writes Cohen, "established the proprietary claims of employers to 'their' Negroes by making it a crime to hire away a laborer under contract to another man." Many other laws facilitated the recruitment and retention of black labor. Vagrancy laws, passed by all the former Confederate states except Tennessee and Arkansas in 1865 and 1866, gave local authorities a "virtual mandate to arrest any poor man who did not have a labor contract." Such statutes enabled police to round up "idle" blacks in times of labor scarcity, and, except in North Carolina, they provided for the hiring out of convicted offenders. Those jailed on charges of vagrancy could sign a "voluntary" labor contract with their former employer or some other white man who agreed to post bond. Workers who had no surety often wound up on chain gangs and were forced to labor through the convict-lease system.[26]

The planters favored a labor-repressive system of agricultural production. They had little incentive to use education and technology to increase efficiency and productivity or to use schooling as a means to train and discipline a more efficient work force. The postwar planters held to the beliefs and behavior of over two centuries of slavery; they did not trust the system of "free labor." Force, rather than rational free choice, was the basis of the South's political economy. Hence the region's slow development in education was in substantial part the result of the planters' stubborn adherence to a set of values inconsistent with democracy, modernization, rapid industrialization, and free schooling. To be sure, other factors militated against rapid educational change. Fundamentally, however, the South's slow rate of educational development and the planters' particular opposition to black education sprang from their clear economic and ideological interests in preserving the racially qualified system of coercive agricultural labor. Both race and class conflict existed between white planters and their black agricultural laborers.

Even though the long-term gains in public education for ex-slaves proved to be small and slow, their organized efforts and ideological imperatives laid the foundation for universal education in the South. Between 1860 and 1880 no organized challenge to the planters' interests came from the region's white middle or lower classes. Both groups were not only economically dependent on the planters, as were the ex-slaves, but also subservient to the planters' interests. Freedmen's Bureau officials were particularly alarmed by lower-class whites' general apathy toward public education. Bureau officials recognized that some planters were hostile to the idea of public education for poor whites. Louisiana's superintendent in 1869 observed planters' opposition to "the education of freedmen and poor whites." "In the parish of Franklin," he reported, "public sentiment, as to the education of freedmen and poor whites, is very decidedly against it." Unlike the ex-slaves, however, "the whites take little or no interest in educational matters, even for their own race." Throughout the bureau's history, its officials contrasted ex-slave and lower-class white attitudes toward public education. In 1866 Alvord noted: "We make no invidious comparisons of the ignorant freedman, and the ignorant Anglo-Saxon of the South. We only say the former has most creditably won his present position; and he has done it by good conduct, and rapid improvement under that instruction we are now reporting." In 1869 a bureau state school superintendent observed: "As a class they [ex-slaves] are eager to learn, while the poor whites are indifferent." Poor whites were not so much indifferent as they were bound to the planters' regime. Before the war poor children were unable to afford private schooling and only rarely had the opportunity to attend charity institutions. In the immediate postwar years the region's poor whites, in general, were still too closely tied to the planters' interests and ideology to pursue a different conception of education and society. White laborers and small farmers when organized in the Farmers' Alliance and Populist party challenged the planters' opposition to universal schooling only in the late 1880s. Ex-slaves, or black native southerners, had struggled for universal schooling over two decades before the Populist campaigns of the late 1880s and 1890s. The ex-slaves' campaign also predated the organized movement for free schooling by southern middle-class progressives. The South's white middle classes, unorganized and subservient to planter interests throughout the nineteenth century, did not begin their campaign for universal education until the dawn of the twentieth century. Hence, surrounded by planters who were hostile to public education, middle-class professionals who allied themselves with planter interests, and lower-class whites who were largely alienated from mass education, ex-slaves were the only native group to forge ahead to commit the South to a system of universal schooling in the immediate postwar years.[27]

Clearly, the freedmen's educational movement had an impact that reached far beyond their own communities. Their initiative forced whites of all classes to confront the question of universal schooling. From the Freedmen's Bureau superintendent came testimony that "the white population of the South feels the power of the [freedmen's] schools." "The poor whites are provoked by hearing Negroes read, while they are ignorant; and it is my belief that they will now receive schools, if furnished them, as never before," wrote Alvord in 1866. Further, "The educated class are not slow to perceive that their schools must be reopened, or fall behind humiliated, and that new schools must now be organized on a more popular plan than heretofore." Mass education was necessary for white children, insisted Robert Mills Lusher, white school superintendent of Louisiana, so that they would be "properly prepared to maintain the supremacy of the white race." The ex-slaves' initiative in establishing and supporting a system of secular and Sabbath schools and in demanding universal public education for all children presented a new challenge to the dominant-class whites—the possibility of an emerging literate black working class in the midst of a largely illiterate poor white class. This constituted a frontal assault on the racist myth of black inferiority, which was critical to the maintenance of the South's racial caste system. The planters, unable to wipe out the educational gains made by ex-slaves between 1860 and 1870, had to take a more liberal posture regarding universal education among whites of all classes. Moreover, poor whites became less indifferent toward the idea of public education. Thus the Populist demands for free schooling in the late 1880s and 1890s, as well as the middle-class educational reforms of the early twentieth century, were indebted to the ex-slaves' educational movement of the 1860s and 1870s.[28]

In the late 1870s and early 1880s, one could already detect a slight shift in southern white attitudes regarding universal schooling in general and particularly for black children. Southern whites began realizing the improbability of reversing the gains made by freedmen during the Civil War and Reconstruction years. Hence a growing, although small, minority of prominent southern whites began speaking in favor of universal schooling for the region's laboring classes, including Afro-Americans. Foremost among these whites were those promoting limited or rapid southern industrialization. Although traditional planters continued to favor a repressive system of agricultural labor and to discourage working-class literacy, proponents of southern industrialization increasingly viewed mass schooling as a means to produce efficient and contented labor and as a socialization process to instill in black and white children an acceptance of the southern racial hierarchy. In 1877 Thomas Muldrop Logan, former Confederate general and industrialist in Richmond, Virginia, spoke before the American Social Science Association on the question of education in the southern states. Logan, who became one of the South's most prominent railroad magnates, articulated a rationale for supporting working-class and Afro-American schooling that came to characterize the thinking of many dominant-class whites in the late nineteenth and early twentieth centuries. "Wherever public schools have been established," argued Logan, "the industrial classes, becoming more intelligent, have proved more skillful and efficient; and all competing countries must likewise establish public schools, or be supplanted in the markets of the world." Logan was well aware of the planters' argument against black schooling, "that when the freedman regards himself qualified to earn a support by mental work, he is unwilling to accept manual labor." Logan believed, however, that maintenance of caste distinctions and division of labor were possible if blacks were offered industrial education such as was practiced at the Hampton Normal and Agricultural Institute of Virginia. By training blacks "to perform, efficiently, their part in the social economy, this caste allotment of social duties might prove advantageous to southern society, as a whole, on the principle of a division of labor applied to races." These views were echoed by famous and little-known southern industrialists as they testified before a subcommittee of the United States Senate Committee on Education and Labor in 1883.[29]

But the prevailing philosophies of black education and the subjects taught in black schools were not geared to reproduce the caste distinctions or the racially segmented labor force desired by Logan and many other postbellum white industrialists. The black teachers, school officials, and secular and religious leaders who formed the vanguard of the postwar common school movement insisted that the ex-slaves must educate themselves, gather experience, and acquire a responsible awareness of the duties incumbent upon them as citizens and as male voters in the new social order. Their thinking on these questions indicated virtually no illusions about the power of schooling to ameliorate fundamental economic inequalities. Rather, it reflected their belief that education could help raise the freed people to an appreciation of their historic responsibility to develop a better society and that any significant reorganization of the southern political economy was indissolubly linked to their education in the principles, duties, and obligations appropriate to a democratic social order. Ex-slave communities pursued their educational objectives by developing various strata, but the one they stressed the most was leadership training. They believed that the masses could not achieve political and economic independence or self-determination without first becoming organized, and organization was impossible without well-trained intellectuals—teachers, ministers, politicians, managers, administrators, and businessmen.

Toward this end the black leaders and educators adopted the New England classical liberal curriculum, so the subjects taught in post—Civil War black elementary, normal, and collegiate schools did not differ appreciably from those taught in northern white schools. Students in elementary schools received instruction in reading, spelling, writing, grammar, diction, history, geography, arithmetic, and music. Normal school students took this standard English curriculum with additional courses in orthography, map drawing, physiology, algebra, and geometry, as well as the theory and practice of teaching. The college curriculum varied slightly among institutions, but the classical course leading to the BA usually required Latin, Greek, mathematics, science, philosophy, and, in a few cases, one modern language. Black leaders did not view their adoption of the classical liberal curriculum or its philosophical foundations as mere imitation of white schooling. Indeed, they knew many whites who had no education at all. Rather, they saw this curriculum as providing access to the best intellectual traditions of their era and the best means to understanding their own historical development and sociological uniqueness. To be sure, a study of the classical liberal curriculum was not a study of the historical and cultural forces that enabled Afro-Americans to survive the most dehumanized aspects of enslavement. Yet that curriculum did not necessarily convince black students that they were inferior to white people.[30]

For example, Richard Wright, one of the brightest and most influential educators of the post-Reconstruction era, found in his study of the classics solid evidence to counter claims of black inferiority. Wright was a student in an American Missionary Association school in Atlanta in 1868 when a group of visitors from the North, including General Oliver o. Howard, asked the black pupils what they should tell their friends in New England about the Georgia freedmen. Replied the young Wright, "Tell them we are rising." Wright graduated from Atlanta University in 1876 and in 1880, at age twenty-seven, he was principal of the Augusta, Georgia, "Colored High School" (later named E. A. Ware High School), the only public high school for blacks in the state. In 1883 principal Wright was sworn and examined by the U.S. Senate Committee on Education and Labor regarding conditions for education and work among blacks in Georgia. Senator Henry W. Blair of New Hampshire, the committee's chairman, queried Wright about the comparative inferiority and superiority of races. Drawing upon his understanding of the classics, Wright replied:

> It is generally admitted that religion has been a great means of human de-
> velopment and progress, and I think that about all the great religions which
> have blest this world have come from the colored races—all.... I believe too,
> that our methods of alphabetic writing all came from the colored race, and I
> think the majority of the sciences in their origin have come from the colored
> races.... Now I take the testimony of those people who know, and who, I
> feel are capable of instructing me on this point, and I find them saying that
> the Egyptians were actually woolly-haired negroes. In Humboldt's Cos-
> mos (Vol. z, p. 531) you will find that testimony, and Humboldt, I presume,
> is pretty good authority. The same thing is stated in Herodotus, and in a
> number of other authors with whom you gentlemen are doubtless familiar.
> Now, if that is true, the idea that this negro race is inherently inferior, seems
> to me to be at least a little limping.

Wright's study of the classical liberal tradition led him to conclude that "these differences of race, so called, are a mere matter of color and not of brain." For such educators as Wright, the classical course was not so much the imposition of an alien white culture that would make blacks feel inferior as it was a means to understanding the development of the Western world and blacks' inherent rights to equality within that world. Thus, with few exceptions, both the schools founded and sustained by black churches and secular organizations as well as those founded by northern missionary societies taught a basic English education supplemented with the classical courses at the normal school and collegiate levels.[31]

During the immediate postwar years the more conservative missionary societies made some attempts to superimpose upon the common school curriculum a set of readers designed specifically and exclusively for ex-slave children. The American Tract Society of the American Missionary Association published the largest collection of these materials. Such readers as *The Freedmen's Primer, The Freedmen's Spelling Book, The Lincoln Primer,* and the *First, Second* and *Third Freedmen's Readers* contained social values designed to inculcate in the ex-slaves an acceptance of economic and racial subordination. These books portrayed blacks in subservient roles and frequently assumed that blacks were morally and mentally inferior. Their use of such books to propagate ideas of racial subordination betray the conservative missionaries' perception that the appropriate regressive social values were not already contained in the New England common school course. Whether these special books had any widespread and long-range impact is extremely doubtful. First, even in the most conservative missionary schools the basic pattern of freedmen's education followed that of northern public schools. Second, the missionary-sponsored common school structure was much too weak and fragmented to affect the instruction of large numbers of ex-slaves. In 1870 the American Missionary Association, for instance, sustained 157 common schools. That number had declined to 70 in 1871 and to 13 in 1874. By the mid-1870s, the northern societies had already reduced their involvement in black southern education, particularly in the area of common schools. After this period, they concentrated their efforts and financial aid primarily on normal and higher education. Their normal schools and colleges offered the traditional classical liberal curriculum. This emphasis was important in determining curricular trends in black common schools because missionary colleges trained the bulk of black teachers until well into the twentieth century.[32]

The short-range purpose of black schooling was to provide the masses of ex-slaves with basic literacy skills plus the rudiments of citizenship training for participation in a democratic society. The long-range purpose was the intellectual and moral development of a responsible leadership class that would organize the masses and lead them to freedom and equality. Being educated and literate had an important cultural significance to Afro-Americans, and they pursued these goals in opposition to the economic and ideological interest of the planter-dominated South. Despite what seemed like overwhelming opposition to their educational campaigns, the masses of Afro-Americans persisted in becoming literate. Their 95 percent illiteracy rate in 1860 had dropped to 70 percent in 1880 and would drop to 30 percent by 1910. The former slaves were becoming literate; the process could be slowed but it could not be stopped or reversed.[33]

By 1880, many white southerners saw that any attempt to reverse the thrust of the ex-slaves' school campaigns would invite greater black resistance and possibly northern intervention. They began to make an uneasy peace with the Reconstruction-era educational reforms. Most did not agree with the idea of universal education for both races any more than they agreed with the Fifteenth Amendment and universal franchise for all men. They could agree, however, that it was politically unwise to attempt to repeal the legal basis of either. A particular class of southern whites began thinking more about controlling and restricting the expansion of public schooling in the black South and the possibility of adapting it to the region's traditional social structure and racial mores. Their interest in the schooling of Afro-American children differed in social origin and purpose from the ex-slaves' educational movement and even from the interests of the most conservative missionary societies. They called for the special instruction of the former slaves in a manner that could not be adapted from the curriculum and teaching materials of the classical liberal tradition. A full curriculum of special instruction for black students was being developed at that time by Samuel Armstrong at the Hampton Normal and Agricultural Institute in Hampton, Virginia. This new curriculum offered the possibility of adapting black education to the particular needs and interests of the South's dominant-class whites. Hence those southern and northern whites who thought it wiser to redirect the social purpose of freedmen's education rather than attempt to destroy it rallied to this new model of special instruction. This aspect of the ex-slaves' struggle for universal education—the development of a special form of industrial education for Afro-Americans—provoked more controversy than any other issue in black education during the late nineteenth and early twentieth centuries. As the period 1860 to 1880 was characterized by efforts to establish the legal, institutional, and moral foundation of universal schooling for ex-slaves, the quarter century following was characterized by movements to transform the content and purpose of instruction in black education.[34]

Abbreviations

GEB Papers	General Education Board Papers, Rockefeller Archive Center
HIA	Hampton Institute Archives
Home Mission Monthly	*American Baptist Home Mission Monthly*
JRFP-FU	Julius Rosenwald Fund Papers, Fisk University Library

Endnotes

1   Webber, *Deep Like the Rivers*, pp. 136-37; Stowe, "Education of the Freedmen," p. 128; Nordhoff quoted in Blassingame, *Black New Orleans*, p. 108; Washington quoted in DuBois, *Black Reconstruction in America*, pp. 641-42; Blassingame, "Union Army as an Educational Institution"; Butchart, "Educating for Freedom"; Sweat, "Some Notes on the Role of Negroes"; Hornsby, "Freedmen's Bureau Schools in Texas," pp. 397-417; Duncan, *Freedom's Shore*, pp. 23-25; Berlin, Reidy, and Rowland, editors, Freedom, pp. 28, 32, 420, 615-30.

2   Franklin, *Black Self-Determination*, pp. 168-69; Gutman, "Observations on Selected Trends in American Working-Class Historiography"; DuBois, *Black Reconstruction in America*, pp. 641-49.

3   Alvord, *Inspector's Report*, pp. 9-10.

4   Bullock, *History of Negro Education in the South*, p. 26; Butchart, "Educating for Freedom," pp. 2, 25; *New Orleans Union*, 12 July 1864; Gutman, "Observations on Selected Trends in American Working-Class Historiography"; Alvord, *Fifth Semi-Annual Report on Schools for the Freedmen*, p. 29.

5   Gutman, "Observations on Selected Trends in American Working-Class Historiography."

6   *New Orleans Union*, 12 July 1864; Blassingame, "Union Army as an Educational Institution," p. 154; Blassingame, *Black New Orleans*, pp. 108-9; White, *Freedmen's Bureau in Louisiana*, pp. 167, 172, 175; *New Orleans Tribune*, 22 Sept., 23 July 1864; Alvord, *Inspector's Report*, pp. 14-15; Howard, *Black Liberation in Kentucky*, pp. 160-61.

7   White, *Freedmen's Bureau in Louisiana*, pp. 172-75; Alvord, *Inspector's Report*, pp. 9-10, 14-15.

8   *New Orleans Tribune*, 5 Sept., 31 Oct., 6 Nov. 1866; White, *Freedmen's Bureau in Louisiana*, pp. 177-79; Blassingame, *Black New Orleans*, pp. 111-12.

9   Wright, "Development of Education for Blacks in Georgia," pp. 71-72; *Loyal Georgian*, 3 Feb. 1866; Alvord, *Fifth Semi-Annual Report*, p. 28; Alvord, *Third Semi-Annual Report*, p. 12; Jones, *Soldiers of Light and Love*, pp. 61, 73-74; Drago, *Black Politicians and Reconstruction in Georgia*, p. 27.

10 *Loyal Georgian*, 19, 16 May 1867, 3 Feb., 10 Mar. 1866; Jones, *Soldiers of Light and Love*, p. 84; Butchart, "Educating for Freedom," pp. 418-23; Duncan, *Freedom's Shore*, p. 45.

11 Horst, "Education for Manhood," p. 18; Alvord, *Inspector's Report*, pp. 9, 12; Blassingame, *Black New Orleans*, p. 113; Alvord, *Fifth Semi-Annual Report*, p. 5; Alvord, *Third Semi-Annual Report*, p. 30.

12 Alvord, *Ninth Semi-Annual Report*, p. 49; Alvord, *Eighth Semi-Annual Report*, p. 82; Butchart, "Educating for Freedom," p. 430; McPherson, *Struggle for Equality*, p. 406; Weinberg, *A Chance to Learn*, p. 43; Alvord, *Sixth Semi-Annual Report*, p. 74; Bass and Roberts, eds., *Proceedings of the 46 Indiana Annual Conference of the African Methodist Episcopal Church*, pp. 22, 31; Washington quoted in DuBois, *Black Reconstruction*, p. 642; Williams, "A.M.E. Christian Recorder"; Montgomery, "Negro Churches in the South."

13 DuBois, *Black Reconstruction*, pp. 649-56; Sweat, "Some Notes on the Role of Negroes"; Alvord, *Inspector's Report*, pp. 10, 20.

14 Blassingame, editor, *Slave Testimony*, pp. 173, 234, 267, 336, 382, 417, 544, 565, 620, 622, 643, 689, 710-12, 740-42; Heard, *From Slavery to the Bishopric in the A.M.E. Church*, p. 31; Jones, *The Experience of Thomas H. Jones*, pp. 14-21; Rawick, editor, *American Slave*, p. iii; Yetman, *Life under the "Peculiar Institution,"* pp. 257, 299; Feldstein, *Once a Slave*, pp. 62-63; Webber, *Deep Like the Rivers*, pp. 131-38; Cornelius, "'We Slipped and Learned to Read.'"

15 Gutman, *The Black Family in Slavery and Freedom*, p. 431; Butchart, "Educating for Freedom," p. 429; Alvord, *Fourth Semi-Annual Report*; Alvord, *Inspector's Report*, p. 15; Cohen, "Negro Involuntary Servitude in the South," p. 47; Litwack, *Been in the Storm So Long*, p. 489; Jones, *Soldiers of Light and Love*, p. 59.

16 *New Orleans Black Republican,* 29 Apr. 1865; *Loyal Georgian,* 19, 16 May 1867; Butchart, "Educating for Freedom," pp. 430-31; Alvord, *Fifth Semi-Annual Report,* p. 47; Blassingame, *Black New Orleans,* pp. 39, 72, 129, 157-58.

17 Bullock, *History of Negro Education in the South,* p. 29; Alvord, *Inspector's Report,* pp. 2, 13; Butchart, "Educating for Freedom," p. 418; Butchart, *Northern Schools, Southern Blacks, and Reconstruction,* pp. 13-21; DuBois, *Black Reconstruction,* pp. 649-56; Sweat, "Some Notes on the Role of Negroes"; Brown, *Education and Economic Development of the Negro in Virginia,* pp. 46-48; Weinberg, *A Chance to Learn,* p. 46.

18 Tyack and Lowe, "Constitutional Moment."

19 Ransom and Sutch, *One Kind of Freedom;* Mandie, *Roots of Black Poverty;* Wiener, *Social Origins of the New South;* Billings, *Planters and the Making of a "New South";* Woodman, "Sequel to Slavery."

20 Wiener, "Planter Persistence and Social Change," p. 257; Katz, "Origins of Public Education," p. 392; Alvord, *Inspector's Report,* p. 12; Southern writer and Schurz quoted in Butchart, "Educating for Freedom," pp. 458, 460.

21 Ransom and Sutch, *One Kind of Freedom,* pp. 44-47, 57, 67; Mandle, *Roots of Black Poverty,* p. 17; Billings, *Planters and the Making of a "New South,"* pp. 35-39.

22 Alvord, *Inspector's Report,* p. 13; Alvord, *Fourth Semi-Annual Report,* pp. 83-84; Chase quoted in ibid., p. 49.

23 White, *Freedmen's Bureau in Louisiana,* p. 186; Butchart, "Educating for Freedom," p. 474; Alvord, *Third Semi-Annual Report,* pp. 30-31; *New Orleans Tribune,* 23 July 1864; Bullock, *History of Negro Education in the South,* p. 43; Alvord, *Ninth Semi-Annual Report,* p. 42; Ransom and Sutch, *One Kind of Freedom,* p. 26.

24 Alvord, *Ninth Semi-Annual Report,* p. 33; Weinberg, *A Chance to Learn,* p. 52; Eaton quoted in Pinchbeck, *Virginia Negro Artisan and Tradesman,* p. 71.

25 Ransom and Sutch, *One Kind of Freedom,* p. 67; Butchart, "Educating for Freedom," pp. 455-57; Weinberg, *A Chance to Learn,* pp. 46-47; Bullock, *History of Negro Education in the South,* pp. 44-52; Billington, *American South,* pp. 189-96; Bond, *Education of the Negro in the American Social Order,* p. 115.

26 Cohen, "Negro Involuntary Servitude in the South"; Daniel, *Shadow of Slavery;* Wiener, "Planter-Merchant Conflict in Reconstruction Alabama," pp. 87-89.

27 Billings, *Planters and the Making of a "New South,"* pp. 37, 206-8; Louisiana superintendent quoted in Alvord, *Seventh Semi-Annual Report,* pp. 33-35; Alvord, *Inspector's Report,* p. 21; Harlan, *Separate and Unequal,* p. 37; Jones, *Soldiers of Light and Love,* p. 81.

28 DuBois, *Black Reconstruction,* p. 641; Alvord, *Inspector's Report,* p. 12; Lusher quoted in Blassingame, *Black New Orleans,* p. 113; Butchart, "Educating for Freedom," p. 461.

29 Logan, "Opposition in the South to the Free-School System"; for a discussion of southern white industrialists' views of black education, see chapter 2 of Anderson, "Education for Servitude," pp. 41-80; Anderson, "Education as a Vehicle for the Manipulation of Black Workers," pp. 21-26; for industrialists' original testimony, see U.S. Senate Committee on Education and Labor, *Report upon the Relations between Labor and Capital;* for an analysis of the South's middle-class educational campaign, see Harlan, *Separate and Unequal.*

30 Jones, *Soldiers of Light and Love*, p. 109; Morris, *Reading, 'Riting, and Reconstruction*, p. 211; Butchart, *Northern Schools, Southern Blacks, and Reconstruction*, p. 135; McPherson, *Abolitionist Legacy*, pp. 203-5; Richardson, *Christian Reconstruction*, p. 125; Sherer, *Subordination or Liberation*, p. 65.

31 Jones, *Soldiers of Light and Love*, p. 127; Patton, "Major Richard Robert Wright, Sr.," pp. 139-46; U.S. Senate, *Report upon Relations between Labor and Capital*, pp. 813-14.

32 Butchart, *Northern Schools, Southern Blacks, and Reconstruction*, pp. 131-68; Richardson, *Christian Reconstruction*, p. 113.

33 Webber, *Deep Like the Rivers*, pp. 131-38; Franklin, *Black Self-Determination*, p. 175.

34 For a discussion of the southern and northern whites who favored a redirection of the social purpose of black education, see Anderson, "Education for Servitude," chaps. 1-3.

Spreading the Word:
The Cultural Work of The Black Press

By Elizabeth McHenry

To FULLY UNDERSTAND the development of a readership and literary culture among free blacks in the antebellum United States, we must look not only at the contexts and situations in which reading and other literary activities took place but also at the avenues of production and distribution that gave free black Americans in the urban North access to printed texts. As the well-known example of Frederick Douglass illustrates, it was necessary for slaves to acquire reading and writing skills surreptitiously: Douglass records in his 1845 autobiography how, as a slave, he contrived ways to "steal" literacy from his white associates in a Baltimore shipyard.[1] Less well-known are stories of the efforts of free blacks in the urban North to acquire and use their literacy, or of the channels through which they gained access to and distributed printed texts at a time when bound books were, for the most part, prohibitively expensive and hard to come by. How did free black Americans come to value reading and how did they come to understand the uses to which printed texts could be put? How was reading presented as a compelling attraction for free blacks as they made choices about what to do with relative financial stability and increasing leisure time? And what were they reading, both within and outside of their literary societies?

It is no coincidence that the rise of the African American press paralleled the development of literary societies and literary culture in northern antebellum black communities: a primary goal of these texts was to foster the development of what one early contributor to the black press called "a literary character."[2] As Henry Louis Gates Jr., and others have persuasively argued, since the Enlightenment, "the index of any race's 'humanity' was its possession of reason, which was to be known through its representation in writing." Particularly admired was writing "in its more exalted or 'literary' forms," but all association with literature, as readers and writers, was seen by free black Americans living in the urban North as a means to becoming exemplary citizens who could fully participate in the civic life of their community. Evidence of literary skill and demonstrations of literary character would refute the claims of racists and proponents of slavery that the African was innately inferior and therefore, "by nature," fit for nothing but slavery. [3] The pursuit of literary culture in black communities that culminated, in the final years of the 1820s, in the formation of African American literary societies and the institution of an African American press must be seen as part of a constant and ongoing campaign launched by black Americans to prove the sublimity of the black mind by demonstrating literary abilities and a propensity for developing "literary character." Literary character offered black Americans a way to refute widespread claims of their miserable, degraded position; examples of it, made visible at meetings of African American literary societies or through the pages of an African American newspaper, would counter assumptions of African inferiority with displays of black genius.

Beginning in 1827 with the inaugural issue of *Freedom's Journal* newspapers published by and for the African American community were able to advance and advertise the existence of literary character in the black community. They provided black readers with common reading material that was relatively easily obtained and could be shared among multiple readers who possessed a range of literacy levels.

Equally important was the key role played by newspapers in shaping a black readership by disseminating a sense of the importance of reading and literary activity to the future of the black community. The antebellum black press both responded to and stimulated interest in literary interaction among antebellum free blacks, providing a context through which its readers could see how literary texts and the activities fostered by literary societies could be a source of empowerment for African Americans. It offered them a means to express themselves and instructed them in the ways that literature, both oral and written, could publicly mediate the radical disjuncture between "African" and "American." In doing so, it assisted free blacks in asserting agency in the construction and representation of themselves as new subjectivities and allowed them to position race within the context of an American identity.

In this chapter I explore the ways in which and the extent to which the antebellum African American press promoted the development of literary character and extended the formation of literary community among free blacks in the urban North. I argue that central to the mission of two of the earliest African American newspapers, **Freedom's Journal** and **The Colored American,** was the development of a black readership; they worked to illustrate the existence of a vibrant tradition of black literary arts while also encouraging black Americans to consider themselves integral to the future viability of that tradition. These publications launched a campaign to promote reading and literary activity as a component of citizenship and the responsibility of all free blacks living in the

North. These newspapers advocated through their content and style as well as through the very fact of their existence that reading and a commitment to literature were an essential means of assuming an intellectual identity and introducing oneself to the public conversations of civic life. They were a means of assuming a quality of respectability that, for African Americans who were presumed in the white imagination to be in every way inferior and incapable of rational thought, must be seen as both polite and political gesture. Rather than an alternative to political action, the pursuit of literary character became, in the decades that preceded the Civil War, a strategy that leaders in the free black community believed would open the doors of American society to black people. The antebellum black press was a chief agent in the emphatic delivery of this message. The extent to which it penetrated the black community is manifest in the extensive literary record that survived within its pages and in the sheer number of literary institutions that developed throughout the urban North in the decades that preceded the Civil War. I close this chapter by illustrating how vibrant the "literary character" of a significant portion of the free black community was and how determined they were to claim what they considered their literary rights as the Civil War began, even as the threat of imminent emancipation intensified debates about the character and the nature of "the Negro" and augmented hostility toward all African Americans, free and slave. In this turbulent time literary publications by and for the black community thrived, and the publishing division of the A.M.E. Church, the Book Concern, was able to claim that it was "really in a prosperous condition."[4]

The texts I consider here, first *Freedom's Journal* the *Colored American,* and *Frederick Douglass' Paper,* and later the *Repository of Religion and Literature, and of Science and Art,* the *Weekly Anglo-African* and the *Anglo-African Magazine,* and the *Christian Recorder,* were crucial to the formation of an ideal of community that affirmed reading and other literary activities as acts of public good on which the intellectual life and civic character of its members could be grounded. The sense of community created by these texts approximated the sort of "nationalism" Benedict Anderson defined as "an imagined political community-and imagined as both inherently limited and sovereign."[5] In the case of the black readership of the newspapers I address here, the "imagined community" was racially bounded and its sovereignty was perceived as free from the control of whites. In urban areas throughout the North, black men and women personally unknown to one another sought to realize a common destiny despite white attempts to derail this project. Their community was also imagined, since tensions and conflicts within the black community, between emigrationists and those who believed that their future lay in achieving full citizenship rights in the United States, for instance, coexisted alongside assumptions of a "deep horizontal comradeship."[6] Anderson points specifically to the role of print in the formation of nationalism. He cites the newspaper as an institution that connects its "assemblage of fellow-readers" by articulating a sameness of purpose and by defining specific cultural, social, and intellectual activities as common means of executing designs; in this way, newspapers help to create and sustain "imagined community."[7]

"We Wish To Plead Our Own Cause"

Generalizations about black illiteracy in the first half of the nineteenth century, coupled with the scholarly attention given to the slave narrative as the primary form of literary expression by black Americans between 1830 and 1865, have contributed to misrepresentations of the black press in the early nineteenth century. Traditionally, antebellum black newspapers have been examined as abolitionist publications whose primary focus was to expose the evils of slavery in order to free the slaves and put an end to the institution of slavery in the United States.[8] In keeping with that perspective, scholars have assumed that the newspapers: primary audience was located in the white population. But, as historian Frederick Cooper notes of the first African American newspaper, *Freedom's Journal* "in the two-year lifetime of [the paper], slavery was mentioned with some frequency, but rarely was it the subject of the featured article or the editorial."[9] Although the newspapers demonstrate that the free black population was sympathetic to the plight of the southern slaves and that they recognized the institution of slavery as "cruel in its practice and unlimited in duration, they *also* suggest that free blacks believed the prejudice to which they were victim was, to quote an anonymous contributor to the *Colored American,* "more wicked and fatal than even slavery itself."[10] In the inaugural issue of *Freedom's Journal* the editors lamented that "no publication, as yet, [had] been devoted to their improvement.[11] To focus exclusively on the antebellum black press as an antislavery concern is to misrepresent the newspapers' actual content and artificially limit the complex role they played in antebellum American society.

Given the extent to which literacy was broadly defined and widely practiced by free blacks well before the Civil War, a reconsideration of *Freedom's Journal* and other antebellum African American newspapers as a source of literature by and reading material for African Americans is especially pertinent. Systematic analysis of the content of the newspaper supports the editors' statement that their journalistic effort was specifically "designed for the reading of their coloured brethren."[12] *Freedoms Journal's* coeditors Samuel Cornish and John Russwurm estimated that "FIVE HUNDRED THOUSAND free persons of color [were among the total population of the United States], one half of whom might peruse, and the whole be benefitted by the publication of the Journal."[13] A network of agents located throughout the urban North and informal systems of distribution that enabled the publication to reach black readers as far away as Canada, the Caribbean, and England ensured that *Freedom's journal* would transcend its local New York City area to become a national newspaper. Even if verifiable circulation figures were available they would also be unreliable as indicators of the number of *Freedom's journal's* readers, as placement in reading rooms and the sharing of copies among whole congregations and associations as well as between friends and neighbors distinguishes the newspaper's actual readership from its list of subscribers. Systems of combined oral and written literacy, where those who could read to those who could not, further confounds assumptions that the African American "readership" of the early black press was insignificant.

The newspaper was at the heart of a new political strategy for the free black community: because of its ability to communicate a common message to a wide audience and thus facilitate organization, the editors believed it to be a "most economical and convenient method" of ensuring the "moral, religious, civic and literary improvement of the injured race" that was "daily slandered."[14] Indeed, whites' resentment of free blacks intensified throughout the antebellum period, paralleling the rising visibility of African Americans in urban spaces. In the 1820s and 1830s this was captured by the white popular press with increasing frequency in print and caricature.[15] Scholars have blamed increasing racial antipathy in the rapidly growing urban centers of Philadelphia, New York, and Boston after the War of 1812 on growing competition for jobs, housing, and political voice among the lower classes. Changing theories about race and racial difference, and a proliferation of arguments refuting the idea of human equality, encouraged middle- and upper-class white Americans to reconsider previous sympathies and voice concerns about the dangers of intermixing white "superior" blood with black "inferior" blood, both sexually and in terms of shared public space. Deteriorating race relations were exacerbated by the growing numbers of free blacks and their increasing social and, to some extent, economic stability. The rising aspirations of free black Americans—especially in terms of their rejection of subservient roles and claims of full citizenship rights—threatened to upset the established social order.[16] In this hostile climate, the white community was more and more willing to adopt the perspective advanced by the American Colonization Society, which argued in 1825 in the pages of its journal, the *African Repository,* that free blacks were "notoriously ignorant, degraded, and miserable, mentally diseased, broken spirited, acted upon by no motive to honourable exertions, [and] scarcely reached in their debasement by the heavenly light."[17] "Bond or free," proclaimed one writer for the *African Repository* in a June 1828 issue, black Americans were "the subjects of a degradation inevitable and incurable. The African in this country belongs by birth to the lowest station in society; and from that station he can never rise, be his talent, his enterprise, his virtues what they may."[18]

In response to such pronouncements, and with forms of political power like the ballot largely unavailable to them, free blacks developed alternative strategies to assert themselves and act on their determination to achieve equality in the United States.[19] The daily behavior and activities of black Americans, they believed, would sway public opinion and dispel negative attitudes toward free blacks. The newspaper was designed as a medium of socialization that would disseminate to the black community the standards of behavior that would make this strategy effective. Blacks must be encouraged to adopt and exercise visibly those habits that would help them to become and to be seen as useful in society: these included personal morality, temperance, industriousness, and, most importantly, an intellectual identity that was the result of the active pursuit of a literary education. Were white Americans to see blacks engaged in these activities, the editors idealistically believed, they would recognize them as worthy of democratic treatment regardless of their skin color. "When our too long neglected race shall have become proportionally intelligent and informed with the white community, prejudice will and must sink into insignificance and give place to liberty and impartiality," declared one writer in an early column promoting the need for perseverance in education.[20] The editors placed great faith in an ideal of American democracy that could embrace the black community, and they used their paper to outline for their readers what they must do to propel themselves to the point where they would be judged by their merit and morality and not by their skin color. Placing their belief in the ideal that the "world has grown too enlightened, to estimate any man's character by his personal appearance," they imagined a national community that transcended race and that could be achieved through, among other things, the presentation of a broad intellectual persona within the black community.[21]

To some extent, Samuel Cornish and John Russwurm identified discrimination against the free black population as a problem of misleading representation. The majority press's erroneous and incomplete reports on free blacks led to inaccuracies about black people becoming lodged in the white imagination. "From the press and the pulpit we have suffered much by being incorrectly represented," they announced. "Men, who we equally love and admire have not hesitated to represent us disadvantageously, without becoming personally acquainted with the true state of things, nor discerning between the virtue and vice among us." The editors acknowledged that there were many examples of corruption among African Americans, but they signaled that these were largely attributable to the lack of educational and economic opportunities in black communities. They asserted that without their own representation the black community was portrayed unfairly and inaccurately: while "our vices and our degradation are ever arrayed against us," they lamented, "our virtues are passed by unnoticed." Literary activities would mark black Americans as public and refined figures, giving them the positive reputation that they lacked. It would also help them to find and use their own voices. "We wish to plead our own cause," wrote Cornish and Russwurm in their inaugural editorial. "Too long have others spoken for us. Too long has the publick been deceived by misrepresentations, in things which concern us dearly." Coupled with strict adherence to "acceptable" forms of behavior, this simple act of self-representation, the editors believed, would "arrest the progress of prejudice, and . . . shield [the free black community] against the consequent evils."[22]

To this end, much of the content of *Freedom's Journal* was loyal to the editors' commitment to represent more fully the plight and achievements of black people and to document the white community's sympathetic response to unprejudiced representation of them. The newspaper balanced accounts of black delinquency alongside stories of black accomplishments, highlighting the fact that both existed in the community. Reports of social outcasts such as murderers, counterfeiters, and those who fell victim to the evils of alcohol were included not only to document the very real failures of the black community but also to provide a context through which to consider examples of the disciplined, orderly lives that enabled others to make contributions to the advancement of the race. A biographical article on Paul Cuffe, a successful black shipowner, was reprinted serially from the pages of England's *Liverpool Mercury* in the first five issues of *Freedom's Journal's* two-year run. By detailing Cuffe's life, the text emphasized how he came to be a recognized man by overcoming the difficulties and discrimination associated with his race.[23] To emphasize that such balanced representation of blacks elicited positive responses from the white community, *Freedom's Journal* also reprinted from other newspapers letters and occasional pieces written by sympathetic whites that dramatized their awakening to the cruelty inflicted on black people in the United States, free and slave, and to the depth and danger of American racism. A letter signed "Omega" and printed in the first issue of *Freedom's Journal* is representative. Writing of an unspecified injustice recently witnessed, she explained her horror at what she had seen: "It took hold of my feelings in a very particular manner, and excited within my bosom a greater detestation of slave dealings as well as of those who engage in this nefarious practice, than I ever realized before. "[24]

While stories establishing fair representation of the black community and the white community)s appropriate response to it served one of *Freedom's Journal's* purposes, the miscellaneous articles that filled the pages of each issue served another. They were lessons in literacy for both the young and the adult student. In subject matter at least, much of the miscellaneous material was unrelated to the immediate lives of its readers. The content of the paper's "Varieties" column exemplified this. In one early issue it included instructions for the proper burial of corpses alongside a table outlining the consumption of wheat and other grains in the United Kingdom. Other "newsworthy" items printed in the same column were titled "A Polish Joke," "Rare Instances of Self-Devotion," and "Curious Love Letter." The "Domestic News" column generally carried accounts of tragic but spectacular accidents in which victims suffered greatly before dramatically "expiring." "Foreign News" published in *Freedom's journal* consisted of equally diverse items. The paper's first edition carried articles on the egg trade in Ireland as well as on Chinese fashions. Later accounts of parliamentary activities and the installation of royalty in England were only slightly more pertinent to the immediate lives of free blacks in the United States.[25]

However random, these stories provided the free black community with narratives and reports that were educational tools. They supplied their readers with a steady stream of interesting and diverse reading material consumable by a readership of various ages and literacy levels. The vignettes included in the newspaper were interesting and compelling, if often sensational. Brief enough to be consumed in short periods of time, they were also convenient to read. Stories included in *Freedom's Journal* were written for sharing, in a format that lent itself to their being read aloud. In addition to their informational value, these features made the *Journal* an important resource for newly and semi-literate readers.[26] Furthermore, unlike bound books, *Freedom's Journal* was readily available; it could be read in the home and was also a primary text in the libraries of local reading rooms and literary societies. At least one of New York's African Free Schools received the newspaper, where it was used as a makeshift textbook. When Charles C. Andrews, a teacher at the African Free School on Mulberry Street, wrote to the editors to thank them for "furnishing gratuitously, the regular weekly numbers of the 'Freedom's Journal,' for the benefit of the Library in the School," he assured them that the newspaper was being put to use: "much good," he reported, "may be calculated to result from such a journal being perused by such readers, as will have access to its pages."[27]

As a means of facilitating the continual practice of literacy and encouraging the development of literary sophistication, *Freedom's Journal* was a timely addition to the free black community. As its editors pointed out, one paradoxical effect of the acquisition of the most basic literacy skills by many free blacks in the urban North was to mask the need for more profound literacy and the continued pursuit of education. "The day has been," they wrote, "when if any one of us could read it was considered a 'passing strange;' and we believe that this has been unfavorable to our improvement. This wonderment and praise from our fairer brethren, instead of exciting, has been the cause of many halting in their career of acquiring knowledge." The journal advanced the notion that the astonishment expressed by the white community over black Americans with even the most basic literacy skills served only to maintain educational and intellectual disparity between blacks and whites. For the "youthful mind, unsupported by the sage counsels of age and wisdom," the flattery that ostensibly praised blacks who possessed only basic skills was crippling; it was even more "dangerous to the middle-aged and intelligent." Rather than be content to "read and write a little," or "cypher and transact the common affairs of life, almost as well as other men," *Freedoms Journal* submitted that blacks needed to be more demanding of themselves and of their educational institutions.[28]

The newspaper itself responded to this imperative in two ways: it became a forum for the announcement of schools and other educational opportunities as well as the site of educational programs in themselves. Its pages were filled with advertisements for "Coloured schools" and other small, local institutions where children might be taught the rudiments of" reading, writing, arithmetic, English grammar, geography with the use of maps and globes, and history."[29] Along with advertisements for other commodities desperately needed by the black community-primarily cheap clothes and boardinghouses where they would be welcome-announcements of the opening of schools were among the most prominent features of *Freedom's Journal*. Most of these listed the name of a single individual, usually a man, who served as the school's primary instructor. Jeremiah Gloucester's notice of his Philadelphia school is typical of efforts that ran weekly to attract students to such institutions: "The subscriber wishes to return thanks to his friends, for the liberal encouragement of patronizing his school; and would be permitted to say, he still continues to teach in the same place, and hopes by increasing exertions, to merit a share of public encouragement." At Gloucester's school, "the branches attended to" were "Reading, Writing, Cyphering, Geography, English Grammar, and Natural Philosophy"; female students were taught "Needle Work."[30]

Increased opportunities for and improvements in the education of black children such as those offered by informal academies like Jeremiah Gloucester's and the network of Free African Schools in New York and Boston allowed leaders in free black communities to focus more of their energy on the educational needs of older African Americans. *Freedom's Journal* communicated to its readers that adults had to rely on diverse and independent means of educating themselves. Reading was depicted as a panacea for the sort of adult instruction needed in the free black community, and *Freedom's Journal* presented itself as a proper and practical source of that reading. In the first issue of the newspaper, Cornish and Russwurm promised that a central function of their publication would be to assist their readers in selecting "such authors as will not only enlarge their stock of useful knowledge, but such as will also serve to stimulate them to higher attainments in science." This service would help readers avoid "time ... lost, and wrong principles instilled, by the perusal of works of trivial importance."[31] Evident in this promise is the extent to which *Freedom's Journal* sought to influence its readers, not only in terms of what they read but in how they used their time generally. Articles included in *Freedom's Journal* were exemplary of the ways a written text might serve as a manual to self-improvement and the standards of good character and "respectable" behavior. Titles such as "Formation of Character," "Duty of Wives," "Duties of Children," "Accurate Judgement," and "Economy" suggest the way readers were provided with guidelines to "proper" behavior and the attitudes that would strengthen the moral condition of the individual, the race, and the nation.[32]

As educational reading, lessons that emphasized the parameters of respectable behavior and inspired discipline, especially in the disposal of excess time and money, were particularly popular. Early in its two-year run *Freedom's Journal* published the story of "Dick the Gentleman," whose fine clothing and dapper lifestyle suggested the superficial trappings of success but who was ultimately devoid of the qualities most needed in the black community. His story warned readers of the dangers of excess and alerted them as to how not to behave:

> DICK THE GENTLEMAN–Dicky Dash was born in the midst of a fine, flat, fertile county of the west, where there were plenty of potatoes, cabbage, and corn-but no gentlemen. Dicky had small hands, thin face, an idle disposition, and a bushy head. Dicky said he was a gentleman. The squire looked from top to toe of Dicky, and said he was a gentleman. The lawyer cross-examined him and said "Dicky's a gentleman," This being ascertained beyond a doubt, Dicky immediately kicked the potatoes from him, tossed away the cabbages and gave the plough over to satan. Dicky put a new shirt into his pocket, jumped on board the steamship, and hallowed out to the captain to start away his nine inches of steam for the city.

After setting himself up as a merchant, Dicky neglected to cultivate the qualities most important to the success of the black Americans, both individually and as a group. He supported his extravagant lifestyle with credit, "got a horse and a saddle and went to the races," and became a regular at the theater, the opera, and at concerts, where girls smiled at him and women "praised him." According to the story, he eventually became so debt-ridden that he had to leave the city and return to the country "as he came from it, with a shirt in his pocket and a flea in his ear."[33]

This satire reinforces the extent to which readers of *Freedom's Journal* were encouraged to see the disposition of free time and relative wealth as a novel dilemma: what should be done with them? Neither idleness nor superficial displays of culture and class had a place in the lives of even the most well-to-do African Americans in the antebellum urban North. Fine clothing, attendance at the races or the theatre—these activities would only provide opportunities for blacks to reinforce negative stereotypes of themselves as aimless and undisciplined, confirming white assumptions that black people were nuisances to society. In contrast, reading and other forms of literary study were depicted as ideal activities, providing the means not only of "edification, but merely to employ an idle hour."[34] The frequency with which the term "useful knowledge" is associated with literary study in *Freedom's Journal* suggests the extent to which a commitment to reading and other forms of literary activity had moral and, for blacks striving to be seen as Americans, political implications. *Freedom's Journal* worked to develop in the minds of its readers a binary opposition between what was "useful" and morally "good" and the many forms of "evil" that threatened to destroy black people, individually and as a group, by perpetuating racial stereotypes. Reading was presented as a vehicle of instruction, a positive elective for an African American population who had to negotiate on a daily basis a dense landscape of tempting hazards that included intemperance and lack of economy, the central targets of the moral reform movement that was sweeping the nation as a whole. As a habit, reading was a responsible way to engage the mind and give shape to what would otherwise be time lost. An alternative to the various forms of moral decay that threatened to bring down the individual and, ultimately, the race and nation, reading would convert "the many moments now spent in idleness" into hours "employed storing [free African Americans'] minds with all kinds of useful knowledge, and preparing themselves for future usefulness."[35]

The campaign launched by *Freedom's Journal* to promote literary study as an alternative to idleness and moral decay manifested itself institutionally in the development of African American literary societies, which were advertised in the pages of *Freedom's Journal* as definitive elixirs for societal "evils." Letters to the editor, original contributions, and other notices on the topic of literary associations in the first volume of *Freedom's Journal* record the escalation of literary activity in the free black community in 1827 and underscore the extent to which organized literary coalitions reinforced the political purposes that the newspaper advanced. "That man must be blind indeed," observed one correspondent in a letter to the editors of *Freedom's Journal* "who does not discover that the people of color, in these parts are rapidly improving in knowledge and virtue, notwithstanding all the great disadvantages to which they are subjected by prejudice." "Much of this improvement," the writer contended, "has arisen from the societies formed among themselves, and on these more than ever, must their future advancement depend." Believing that the intellectual achievements that resulted from participation in literary coalitions would promote the equal treatment of African Americans, the writer posed the rhetorical question: "Wha[t] man can attend an orderly ... literary, or charitable institution of coloured persons, and not feel the injustice of ranking t[h]em as inferior beings, while there are multitudes of white men, who never associate for any virtuous, or honourable purpose whatever?" Equally important to the writer's sense of the value of these institutions, however, was his contention that literary societies were "highly beneficial," not only "to their members," but to "society at large."[36]

From its earliest issues, *Freedom's Journal* devoted pages of print to supplying its readers with a sense of the rich history of black literary arts. It regularly published literary criticism, which appeared mainly in the form of biographical summaries of eighteenth-century black poets followed by brief extracts from their works. In the paper's first year of existence, Ignatius Sancho, Olaudah Equiano, Ottobah Cuagono, and "Cesar" were all reviewed. Hailed by the editors of *Freedom's Journal* alternatively as "our poetess" and as the "African genius," Phillis Wheatley was frequently evaluated and presented as a model of literary achievement. Her story and her literary work were important not only as examples of black achievement but also because they had had such a tremendous impact on those who believed the African to be inferior. Acknowledging that from the "want of education had also arisen the idea of *'African inferiority'* among many, who will not take the trouble to inquire into the cause," one correspondent for the *Freedom's Journal* submitted to the editors an account of Wheatley in November 1827, in which she was identified as a hero of the race:

> Boston is the place where that sweet poetess of nature, *Phillis Wheatley,* first tuned her lyre under the inspiration of the Muses, putting to shame the illiberal expressions of the advocates of slavery in all parts of the globe. So incredible were the public concerning the genuineness of poems, that they are ushered into the world with the signature of the Governor, the Lieutenant-Governor, and other distinguished men of Massachusetts affixed to *them.* O Liberality, thou art not certainly a being of this lower sphere! for why should the natural powers of man be rated by the fairness of his complexion?[37]

In an effort to create another, contemporary literary hero, the editors of *Freedom's Journal* launched a campaign in 1828 to free the slave-poet George Moses Horton. Described in a front-page story printed in an August 1828 issue of the paper as "an extraordinary young slave ... who has astonished all who have witnessed his poetic talent," Horton soon became a primary focus of *Freedom's Journal's* articles and correspondence. "It is with much pleasure that we inform our readers that measures are about to be taken to effect the emancipation of this interesting young man," the editors of *Freedoms Journal* wrote later that month. The importance of literary figures and their value to members of the free black community in the urban North is evident in the speed with which the campaign to free Horton became a principal concern. Horton quickly came to represent the belief of free blacks in the urban North that association with literature would lead to freedom. Their hopes for the elevating power of association with literature are reflected in the urgency they felt about the emancipation of this representative of black literary arts. *"Something must be done—George M. Horton must be liberated from a state of bondage,"* the editors wrote in a September 1828 issue of *Freedom's Journal* "Were each person of colour in [the city of New York] to give but one penny, there would be no danger about obtaining his liberty."[38] Although a significant amount of money was raised to secure Horton's freedom, his master would not permit his sale. Horton's publication in 1829 of the twenty two-page volume of his poetry, "The Hope of Liberty," reveals the extent to which antebellum blacks believed that in their literacy lay the key to liberation. Horton's hope that, with the proceeds of his volume of poetry, he might be permitted to purchase his freedom was in keeping with the perspective advanced by free blacks in the urban North, who connected their literary activities with the eventual literal freedom of all blacks in the United States and the immediate elevation of free blacks in the eyes of whites, many of whom doubted their very humanity.

Literary activity, engaged in through the pages of *Freedom's Journal* and in the context of the literary society, was presented as a prime means by which African Americans could contribute to their own self-improvement and, in turn, the making of "good society." It was considered a necessity for the community's young men, who were otherwise in danger of being lured into unproductive patterns of behavior. Disappointment that too many black men of promise were neglecting substantive activities in favor of more superficial forms of entertainment was the sentiment behind one writer's letter to the editor, printed in a July 1827 issue of *Freedom's Journal* "Many of our young men, whose situation in life afforded them the means to improve their minds, and whose prospects were so fair that they needed nothing except their assiduous attention to direct their course through life, after having obtained their rudiments of a liberal education, have degenerated into such insignificance, that their very existence has been a matter of no great concern," wrote "Muta." "This, I am sorry to say, has too long existed among us, and it is partly from the want of literary institutions."[39] Because, in this writer's assessment, they further not only intellectual development but also conversation and exchange, literary societies were the essential arena to ensure the lasting value of one's educational efforts. Much of the benefit of literary associations was the connection they established between sociability and the acquisition of knowledge. Literary societies, the author argued, "create a spirit of emulations, and, of course, a disposition for reading, which would tend to mature the judgement and expand the mind, causing it to germinate in all its native beauty, to contemplate on objects which ignorance had before veiled in obscurity . . . They will remove the very illiberal views which may have been taken of people of color."[40]

Certainly one effect of adopting positive habits such as reading and the associated activities of discussion and debate was to illustrate a readiness to learn. Through these activities, the negative stereotypes associated with blacks would be replaced with images of industry economy, and intellectual competence. But another outcome of literary activity was the development of literary character, an attribute that, when acquired and properly maintained, would serve not only to divert African Americans from the many "evils" that threatened to corrupt society but also endow them with the personality needed to participate in the civic debates that would sustain a healthy democracy. Literary activities and the character cultivated through them provided a means of equipping oneself with lasting benefits that would ensure the success of the individual and, in turn, the community. Developing literary character, the components of which included morality, self-discipline, intellectual curiosity, civic responsibility, and eloquence, was cast as both a private virtue and a civic duty: it benefited the individual, but it was essential for the common good as well. For Americans of African descent, the implications of the correlation between personal responsibility and civic duty were potentially far-reaching. In developing literary talents, they contributed not only to their own improvement but to the improvement of their race. In the words of Samuel Cornish, the acquisition of these skills would lead to the "good principles [that] will soon break down the barriers between [the black] and the white population."[41]

In this context, it is interesting to note that the editors of *Freedom's Journal* did not question the need for distinctions in their society: "We have never contended," they wrote, "that there should be no distinctions in society: but we have, and are still determined to maintain that distinctions should not exist merely on account of a man's complexion.[42] Rather than skin color or economic criteria, the quality of one's literary character should define one's standing in society. It also dictated one's usefulness in the struggle to obtain civil rights. Eloquence, for instance, one component of literary character, was considered a powerful attribute that would be instrumental in dismantling both institutionalized racism in the North and the institution of slavery in the South. Inspired to write to the paper on the "importance of forming a Debating Society, among our brethren of [New York City], one writer, who signed his name "A Young Man," asserted that "no one at the present day, will presume to dispute the extensive influence, which Eloquence exerts upon mankind." In the context of this writers comments, "Eloquence" gained from reading, writing, and debating in the company of others became a vital weapon. "What caused the Abolition of the Slave Trade," he argued, "but the glowing language and vivid colouring given to its abominations? I do not expect a Debating Society will make us all Sheridans, but it will enlarge our powers of reasoning by teaching us to express our thoughts as brief as possible, and to the best advantage. It will also enable us to detect at a glance whatever sophistry is contained in the arguments of an opponent."[43]

Such rehearsals of eloquence were essential to preparing black Americans to fully participate in the democratic culture advocated and exemplified by *Freedom's Journal*. As a forum for literary exchange, *Freedom's Journal* encouraged its readers to consider themselves and assume the responsibilities of citizens; giving voice to their opinions and perspectives through the pages of the newspaper was one way of doing this. Responses to the editors' appeals to "the pens of many of our respected friends" to contribute "practical pieces, having for their bases, the improvement of our brethren" filled the publication with Original Communications." These took the form of letters to the editors, testimonials, contributions to the "marriage and death" column, and poetry and occasional pieces.[44] Distinguished by the heading "For the Freedom's Journal," original contributions to the newspaper included a "short and imperfect account" of the eighteenth-century black poet Phillis Wheatley and a biographical sketch of Toussaint L'Ouverture. Poetry by the "masters" of European literature was published alongside the verses of "Amelia" and "Emma." Black readers' appetite for this material, and the extent of their desire to themselves become a part of the literary exchange, is recorded in the pages of the newspaper itself. A brief column called "To our Correspondents" encouraged readers to become contributors and informed them of the status of their submissions. In one 1827 issue of the paper the editors used this column to report that "'ACROSTIC' is under consideration" and to inform the author of "CLARKSON, No. 3" that it "has been received and will appear next week." They encouraged "ROSA, of our sister city," to "write frequently," but related that "Poetical lines by 'AMELIA, ' of N. York, we cannot insert, being too personal."[45]

Through the contributions of these and other writers, *Freedom's Journal* quickly became a forum for discussion and debate in the black community. Cornish and Russwurm were true to their promise that their "columns would ever be open to a temperate discussion of interesting subjects." In providing this "public channel" through which to communicate, they created for the black community a social and cultural space in which to articulate their opposition to white oppression while also providing an invaluable lesson in literary interaction and the power of print. The object of a literary education, they relayed through the pages of their newspaper, was not merely to learn how to read; black Americans needed to understand the public uses to which literature could be put. In the pages of *Freedom's Journal* reading was not presented as a passive or solitary activity; rather, it was an invitation to participate, a means of orienting the individual toward social and communal models of exchange, be they written or oral, that would enhance civic life and facilitate involvement in the public sphere. Readers were encouraged to respond to what they read as the basis for further exchange. In this sense, the ability to read was not an end in itself; it was a part of a larger process of training individuals to claim the authority of language and effectively use it to participate in reasoned and civil public debate.

"There Is A People Here . . ."

From 1827 until it folded in 1829, *Freedom's Journal* urged free African Americans to educate themselves by becoming readers and involving themselves in both the life of the newspaper and in literary societies and other associations through which they might exercise their intellects and make their voices heard. Blacks were encouraged to become active participants in the goals of a national society by taking part in literary activities and public discussions in hopes that by doing this, they would be considered a part of that society. Despite the sense of discouragement and disillusionment that dominated the final issues of *Freedom's Journal* evidence that an appetite for "literary character" had taken hold in the black community filled the pages of the newspaper from its inception. Even before the first issue of *Freedom's Journal* was released, free blacks in the urban North indicated their desire for a newspaper and their readiness to foster its success in their individual communities. The inaugural issue of the paper was released on March 16th, 1827, but almost four weeks earlier a group of black Bostonians had gathered in the home of David Walker to discuss the prospectus of the new venture and consider "giving aid and support to the Freedom's Journal." Those present agreed that "the enterprise is one of a laudable nature, reflecting great credit upon the projectors, and well worthy of our countenance and support." Their decision was not merely to give *Freedom's Journal* their "aid and support" as subscribers to and readers of it; in their determination "to use [their] utmost exertions to increase its patronage," they expressed their deep commitment to the life of the paper, from which they believed that "great good will result to the People of Colour."[46] This democratic assessment of the newspaper and the commitment of members of black communities throughout the urban North to work cooperatively toward its success indicate the extent to which *Freedom's Journal* was truly a communal effort and not merely the creation of its New York City editors. David Walker, whose own literary work and belief in the importance of spreading literacy throughout the black community was in keeping with the mission of *Freedom's Journal* himself became a distributing agent for the newspaper. When the Boston supporters of *Freedom's Journal* met a year later, in April 1828, "for the purpose of enquiring whether the Freedom's Journal had been conducted in a manner satisfactory to the subscribers and the Coloured community at large," Walker argued that indeed it had. In his comments in support of the newspaper he pointed specifically to the "disadvantages the people of Colour labour under, by the neglect of literature." He identified *Freedom's Journal* as a medium that was taking important steps to remedy that situation. The "very derision, violence, and oppression, with which we as a part of the community are treated by a benevolent and Christian people," he remarked, "ought to stimulate us to the greatest exertion for the acquirement of . . . literature."[47] *Freedom's Journal* was instrumental in facilitating that goal.

This appetite "for the acquirement of literature" filled the pages of the *Colored American* from its beginning in 1837. While the form and content of *Freedom's Journal* had promoted basic literacy, the *Colored American* assumed it and instead encouraged its readers to use their literary skills to acquire cultural literacy. Whereas *Freedom's Journal* had primarily encouraged black communities to form literary societies and avail themselves of their benefits, the *Colored American* acted as a coworker of these societies, operating in conjunction with them to further their shared mission. Like *Freedom's Journal* the *Colored American* was deeply sensitive to promoting reading as an activity that expanded opportunities and encouraged moral conduct." He that would be an intelligent person must be a reading person," announced one of the many articles published in the newspaper that underlined the role of reading in the productive use of leisure hours. "By reading you may visit all countries, converse with the wise, good, and great, who have lived in any age or country, imbibe their very feelings and sentiments and view every thing elegant in architecture, sculpture, and painting. By reading you may ascend to those remote regions where other spheres encircle other sums, where other stars illuminate a new expanse of skies, and enkindle the most sublime emotions that can animate the human soul." The extraordinary power of literature to expose readers to this expansive world is starkly contrasted to the dreary existence of nonreaders in the single sentence that composes the item's next paragraph. "Without being a reading person, your information must be limited, and of a local nature."[48] In addition to articles giving general counsel on reading, the *Colored American* reprinted articles from European American newspapers like the *New York Observer* that instructed the middle class how to choose the "right" books and chronicled the decline of "solid" reading and the rise of genres of literature, such as the novel, which were considered "fanciful and imaginative."[49]

One of the things communicated in this juxtaposition is the perceived difference between a program of "solid" reading and the informal, relaxed reading implied by the very nature of fiction and other "fanciful and imaginative" texts. Articles printed in the *Colored American* on the subject of reading reinforced the belief that to derive full benefit from one's reading required discipline, diligence, and direction; imaginative texts suggested a certain casual freedom, a release from the very moral and civic responsibility and sense of engagement with others that was at the heart of literary study. This distinction serves to underscore the extent to which reading was deemed a suitable activity only in terms of its association with notions of the appropriate use of leisure time. Like *Freedom's Journal,* the *Colored American* communicated to its readers that reading was not, in fact, to be thought of as a "pastime" in the casual sense of the word. The consumption of entertaining, imaginative literature was considered a passive, frivolous activity, one that threatened to falsely release readers from both civic responsibility and social interaction. "Proper" reading was associated with study or work rather than with amusement, and it required vigorous attention and active mental application for full benefit and appreciation.

This understanding of literary activity dictated that the *Colored American* would also share with *Freedom's Journal* a particular interest in promoting organized literary study as a positive alternative to the host of negative and "immoral" distractions that faced the free black community daily. Particular concern was expressed again and again for what one anonymous contributor to the *Colored American* described as "the rising generation," by which was meant those "young men whose evenings are unemployed, and who now spend their leisure hours in the theatre or porter house, (which leads to the brothel and gaming tables)." In an article titled "Literary Societies" this writer called these institutions "of more importance than any others in the present age of Societies and Associations." With more of them in the black community, susceptible young men "might be induced to make the reading room their place of resort, and thus instead of injuring their health, wasting their money, and acquring immoral habits, they might be storing their minds with useful knowledge, and erecting a reputation which would be far superior to the ephemeral renown which pleasure confers on their votaries, and they might also establish for themselves a character which time itself could not destroy."[30]

Announcements of new opportunities for literary study and interaction appeared regularly in the *Colored American* and expressed similar concern for the many obstacles to the development of literary character in the black community. Like the one placed by David Ruggles in the 16 June 1838 issue, most made reference both to the distractions of urban life and to the difficulties of finding access to literary texts or appropriate environments for their appreciation. Observing that "intelligence can only be acquired by observation, reading and reflection," Ruggles condemned the exclusion of African Americans "from Reading Rooms, popular lectures, and all places of literary attractions and general improvement" by those he termed "our fairer and more favored citizens." Ruggles expressed the commonly held fear that "without some centre of literary attraction for all young men whose mental appetites thirst for food, many are in danger of being led into idle and licentious habits by the allurements of vice which surround them on every side." He tried to remedy this situation by opening a READING ROOM, where those who wish to avail themselves of the opportunity, can have access to the principal daily and leading anti-slavery papers, and other popular periodicals of the day."

He concluded with an invitation and an exhortation: "We hope that the friends of literary improvement, among all classes of our citizens in this part of the city, will encourage our enterprise."[31] Inherent in this and similar announcements that appeared in the *Colored American* is the insistence that literary texts and the institutions that would provide access to them were vital to the "present and future prosperity of young men in this community."[32] Without them, black Americans could not cultivate public voices capable of withstanding the demands of any situation or subject.

Despite these similarities, however, the *Colored American* assumed a different kind of readership than had *Freedom's Journal*, with a different set of expertise and expectations. It was itself a testimony to the improved literacy skills and changing needs of black readers. As a "channel of communication for the interchange of thought," the newspaper provided a forum for energetic discussions that revolved around a variety of subjects.[33] Sophisticated debates-including the debate over the racial name by which blacks in the United States would be known- were waged in its pages, largely replacing the sensational domestic tragedies and international trivia that had padded the columns of *Freedom's Journal* Indeed, one reason for this debate and another significant way that the *Colored American* differed from *Freedom's Journal* had to do with the question of emigration, which the earlier *Freedom's Journal* had contemplated but which the *Colored American* thoroughly repudiated. When it dealt with the political issues of colonization and racial names, the *Colored American* did so with a combination of sharp political assertiveness and distinguished literary prose. "Many would gladly rob us of the endeared name, AMERICANS, a distinction more emphatically belonging to us, than five-sixths of this nation, and one which we will never yield," wrote Samuel Cornish, in his role as the *Colored American's* editor. The newspaper's first numbers were issued under the name the *Weekly Advocate;* by renaming the paper the *Colored American,* Cornish effectively stymied "enemies, who would rob [blacks] of [their] nationality and reproach [them] as exoticks" by moving beyond their terms of discussion.[54]

Although themes from *Freedom's Journal,* such as self-improvement and economy, formed a familiar foundation for the new publication, the *Colored American* presented itself from its beginning as a paper with a different attitude toward and different assumptions about the black community. According to the editorial address published in the first issue of the *Weekly Advocate* and titled "Our Undertaking," the new paper would be "devoted to the moral improvement and amelioration of [the] race"; no shift in objective took place when the name of the paper was changed to the *Colored American.*[55] Contributors to the *Colored American* expressed themselves largely without cushioning or disguising the authority they claimed through the very act of writing for publication. The words of one writer, who identified himself only as a "Free Man of Colour," exemplify the boldness and literary confidence largely absent in the contributions to *Freedom's Journal.*[56] Calling the term "free man of color" an "empty name" and "a mockery," his editorial asserted that "no man of color, be his talents, be his respectability, be his worth, or be his wealth what they may, enjoys, in any sense, the rights of a freeman."[57] This statement, with its directness and lack of artifice and the firmness and intensity that give it resonance, was exactly the sort of expression called for by Samuel Cornish in his first editorial for the *Colored American,* titled "Why we should have a paper." Because of the great distances that separated free people of color from one another, Cornish declared they must use the press, "that mighty vehicle for the transmission and transfusion of thought," to "speak out in THUNDER TONES, until the nation repents and renders to every man that which is his just and equal." The *Colored American* was to convey the grievances of black people expressly in order "to rouse them up" and "call their energies into action."[58]

Armed with the nickname "The American" and the place it asserted for free blacks in the United States, the newspaper proceeded to publish pointed political statements that disseminated the message that equal rights and citizenship were due "all men." The *Colored American* promised to be the organ through which free blacks would obtain these rights and sustain themselves.[59] It would be the "Advocate and Friend" of the free black population by making public specific incidents of injustice and inequality, as well as the efforts of black leaders and organizations to effect change in black communities.[60] This promise stimulated reports that reflected the subscribers' hopes for the new publication: "all we ask is light on [a] subject," wrote one reader, "full, free, and unbiased discussion, for the sake of arriving at truth and correct principles."[61] Without exception, the *Colored American* was "to be looked on as their own, and devoted to their interests." It was to serve as a vehicle through which free blacks could "communicate with each other and their friends," and "make known their views to the public."[62]

In exchange for the rights of citizenship, the *Colored American* suggested that claiming an American identity brought with it its own set of responsibilities; with the acquisition of basic literacy assumed to be one of these, the *Colored American* pushed its readers toward greater attention to intellectual exercise. "Our people must be supplied with mental resources," insisted the writer of an introductory editorial printed in the newspaper's inaugural issue.[63] The *Colored American* offered itself to the free black population as a means of access to these needed resources. "The paper is adapted in form, in matter, and in price to nearly the whole of our friends," this writer claimed; it would be instrumental in "persuad[ing] unthinking men (and women) to leave the haunts of vice and wretchedness" and join "the enviable ranks of virtuous, intelligent, and useful men."[64] One form of needed knowledge among the *Colored American's* target population was perceived to be a certain level of cultural literacy, not only about their own expanding and prosperous democracy but also about the distant regions increasingly within the national consciousness. The first three issues of the paper included a series of articles written for the *New York Weekly Advocate* on various historical and organizational aspects of the United States. After recounting the general history of the country from its "discovery," these articles outlined the origins of and relevant statistics on each state. Included in the knowledge communicated in this series as "useful for present and future reference" was the structure of local and Federal government, anticipated population figures for the various states in 1837 based on the population in 1830, and a listing of the "Vessels of War, in the United States Navy, 1836."[65] Subsequent issues of the *Colored American* featured an extensive article titled "Principal Features of the Various Nations of the Earth," compiled specifically for the newspaper, as well as a biographical sketch of Benjamin Franklin.[66] By offering its readers a kind of advanced course of study on national history, state statistics, and eminent American lives, the *Colored American* was implicitly demonstrating the kind of cultural literacy its editors believed necessary for creating an informed African American citizenry.

The acquisition of cultural literacy was also something that would be fostered in the literary societies that the publication supported. Like *Freedom's Journal* only to an even greater degree, the *Colored American* announced the meetings of African American literary societies, generally supporting their efforts and forming an alliance with them that advanced the mutual work of both institutions. By advertising and covering the activities and the events, such as public lectures and debates, that were sponsored by African American literary societies and were increasingly open to the public, the *Colored American* contributed to the societies' visibility and facilitated the spread of their influence. An early edition of the newspaper carried a review of "Our Literary Societies" that boasted of the status of literary societies in New York City's black community. "It is certainly gratifying to know that there is in existence, in this city, a number of associations, male and female, devoted to the mental and literary improvement of our people," the writer observed. "They will do us good." He suggested that the impact of literary societies was to be felt not from their numbers but from their activities. "These societies," he claimed, "will be productive of the happiest, and most beneficial results" and will "prove a readiness in us to avail ourselves of every means of improvement which lies within our reach." Literary societies would be responsible for the development of a new generation of black leaders, preparing them to be "useful and honorable members of society."[67]

In the pages of the *Colored American,* such general commentary on the benefits of organized literary study was combined with articles that systematically enumerated African American literary societies in the northeast and reprinted their founding documents. An article titled "Highly Important" and printed in the second issue of the *Weekly Advocate* issued a call to the black community for "a concise account" of the various literary societies. It was announced that a listing of these would "occupy a prominent place" in the paper's "forthcoming numbers."[68] Appearing periodically throughout the publication history of the paper, this list of literary societies across the nation suggests just how extensive the network of reading associations was and how diverse they were in their activities. Even more than cataloguing the names of various literary societies, the *Colored American* also published pertinent information on their organization and sometimes reprinted their founding documents. For instance, in the 24 June 1837 issue of the paper, the editors printed the constitution of the Philadelphia Society for the Moral and Mental Improvement of the People of Color; on 2 September 1837, the constitution and bylaws of Pittsburgh's Young Men's Literary and Moral Reform Society were featured. "Feeling the necessity and demand of literary talent among us," the society was established by and for "young [men] of known moral habits and respectability" between the ages of eighteen and thirty-five.

In a brief note written on behalf of the society, a member elaborated on its nature: "We have as it were only begun to exist," wrote the correspondent, as if to explain their membership of "only sixteen." He reported that "Our society has regular meetings which are spent for the improvement of our minds." He closed his communication by praising the *Colored American* and expressing the society's appreciation "that we have a press of our own, and a paper edited by a colored man." His description of the importance of the newspaper is noteworthy: through its pages, "the world might know there is a people here and [that] they have life. "[69]

Indeed, the *Colored American* used its pages to publish not only the constitutions but also the statements of purpose, bylaws, and schedules of upcoming topics to be discussed or debated in the meetings of local literary societies. On a practical level, this public information on the operation of reading groups served as a guideline for the formation of new literary societies. It also promoted the expansion of this alternative system of improvement by reiterating the imperative relationship that was believed to exist between the "moral and intellectual improvement" of people of color and their "civil and political elevation."[70] That the newspaper was a crucial institution through which the literary skills developed in the context of the literary society might be employed to reach a larger public was not lost on the organizers of African American literary societies, which often incorporated a commitment to support African American and abolitionist newspapers into their founding documents. Included in the constitution of the Phoenixonian Literary Society, for instance, was a resolution to "ascertain those persons who are able to subscribe for a newspaper that advocates the cause of immediate abolition of slavery and the elevation of the colored population to equal rights with whites."[71] Other literary organizations, such as New York's Ladies Literary Society, regularly held fairs and festivals "for the benefit of the Colored American." Engaged in the same project, the newspaper and the literary societies also shared the same economic troubles and were comfortable enough in their relationship to ask for mutual aid. As it struggled to succeed in November 1837, the *Colored American's* general agent, Charles Ray, felt at liberty to issue a general call to the members of literary societies to "send us of the funds they may have on hand, not wanted for present use, to aid us at this crisis, in sustaining our paper."[72]

As a coworker in the drive to "give our people a literary character," the *Colored American* documented the proceedings of African American literary societies in such a way as to approximate the experience of being present.[73] Associating its readers with the tangible social space of the lecture hall and the intellectual community implied by the activities practiced there was one reason for doing this. By revealing how literary characteristics were valued in the context of a specific literary society meeting, the reports also offered incentive to those who were not present to consider, critique, and correct their own literary performance. In addition, they reinforced the rigor and demands of literary study, a perspective easily lost when reading in solitude. These multiple purposes are perhaps best illustrated through the report of a meeting of the Phoenixonian Society that was included in the 18 February 1837 issue of the newspaper. In all, eight presentations had been made at the meeting of this "rising and deservedly popular institution"; due to time constraints, one presenter "read only extracts from his address." Although the correspondent, whose article was signed with only the initial "W," described the evening as "an affair which the members of the 'Phoenixonian Society' have every reason to be proud of," he also felt it his duty "to make some passing remarks on the general character" of the "original compositions which were delivered on the evening in question."[74]

What "W" chooses to focus on and report in the pages of the *Colored American* suggests the ways in which readers of the newspaper were trained and encouraged in literary pursuits even as they were informed of actual events at which they may or may not have been present. His comments also illustrate the extent to which speaking in public in nineteenth-century African American literary societies elicited a spectrum of critical discernment potentially as sophisticated as that which, within the modern rhetoric of literary study, would be applied to written texts. "W"'s "reading" of the orally presented texts includes not only summaries of the arguments made and examples given; a complex inventory of stylistic gestures, physical presence, and vocal quality suggests the virtual lack of distinction between the oral and written features of texts. While an essay titled

"The Influence of the Press" was praised for its evidence of "profound thought and extensive enquiry," for instance, "W" noted with equal emphasis that the document was "not
read with that spirit and energy which usually characterizes the author." Mr. G. Downing,
whose address was called "The Possibility of Great Changes," was advised to "exert himself
more"; "this young man has power," remarked his reviewer, "but he is not conscious of it."
Only Mr. Thomas Sidney received unqualified praise from "W" for his address on "The
Influence of Intellectual Ability." "It is not our province to flatter . . . ," remarked "W," "but
we must say candidly, this gentleman has abundant reason to congratulate himself on
being endowed with so large a share of that which was the subject of his discourse . . . . He
show(ed] an imagination, and depth of research, truly astonishing for his years."[75]

"W"'s criteria for a successful lecture imply the limited authority of written text on
its own. They point toward a social model of knowledge oriented toward the importance
of communication. Carefully chosen words, whether written or oral, were meaningless
unless compellingly conveyed to the audience. Well-spoken, effectively communicated
words, on the other hand, asserted the authority, prestige, and power of the speaker and
indicated his readiness to contribute to civic debate; they also inspired his audience to
respond and stimulated the conversations that were essential to the workings of community. By reporting on literary performances as if the reader were a participant, the
Colored American embraced this social model of knowledge and attempted to dupli-
cate it through its own content and structure. As a teacher of and model for an ideal of
democratic culture, literary societies offered the free black community an extraordinary
environment in which to read, exchange ideas, and study uses of language in relation
to their ability to inform their membership and inspire them to find and use their own
voices. By attempting to replicate the structure of a literary society and reproducing the
experience of being present at a meeting in its pages, by reprinting the constitutions
of literary societies and applauding their activities at every turn, the *Colored American*
embraced the values assumed by the term "society": only in the company of others and
through conversations with others could the ideal of democratic culture be realized and
a comprehensive literary character develop.

Like the libraries and reading rooms of literary societies, the *Colored American* as-
pired to supply its readers with access to lasting texts that would be central to their
acquisition of "useful knowledge" while also providing a basis for engagement with others in productive conversation. Singlehandedly, it fulfilled the role of a reading room by
distributing texts on a diverse range of subjects to an audience that could then come
together to discuss and debate what they had read. In this, the *Colored American* considered itself a valuable resource that should be preserved for future rereading and later
reference. Beginning with the first issue of the paper, the editors regularly published
this reminder to "File Your Papers": "As the advocate will not only be devoted to the
passing events of the day, but also in a great measure to useful and entertaining general
matter, which may be perused at any future time with as much interest as at the present,
we would suggest to our readers the importance of preserving a file of the journal. By

doing this, they will, at the end of a year, have a neat little volume, and also have at hand the means of amusing and improving their minds during leisure hours."[76] This advice is telling, especially when contrasted with the anxiety expressed over the modest size of the publication by the paper's editor in its first issue: "Our paper, though somewhat small in size, will be found valuable in contents."[77] Taken together, a year's worth of individual issues of the newspaper would form a "neat little volume"—practically a book. In the same way that the *Colored American* presented reading as an imperative activity, it presented books as items to be treasured: they were promoted as the agents and, increasingly, the emblems of an appropriately cultivated intellect. Later issues carried advertisements for "whole libraries" containing the "most valuable Standard Religious and Scientific Works," which were available for purchase for "only twelve dollars."[78] A library was advertised as something "every family ought to have," and the *Colored American* printed at least one list of guidelines to help its readers establish their own.[79] Those with the financial security to do *so* were to consider themselves "blessed."[80] For the unblessed majority, however, access to and the ownership of books was not impossible. The *Colored American* presented itself as an affordable substitute. For the sum of $1.50 per year, it provided free blacks with both an encyclopedia of "useful information" and a source of appropriate entertainment. Although its issues would remain unbound, possession of a full year's run of the *Colored American* was something of which to be proud. Like a library of bound books, the collection would testify to the social, civic, and moral standing of its owner.

"We Must Do Just What White Men Do"

I have shown so far that the connection between literary societies and *Freedom's Journal* and the *Colored American* is explicit, and the newspapers' deliberate involvement in the project of spreading literacy and literary culture throughout the communities of free blacks in the urban North is directly visible. Both newspapers included in their pages instructions on what and how to read; they also made readers aware of the development and rising popularity of literary societies in northern, urban free black communities. Literary societies were promoted in these newspapers as alternatives to society's evils, including idleness, financial irresponsibility, intemperance, and moral decay. The mere frequency with which meetings of literary societies were announced and their activities positively reviewed gives some indication of the partnership that developed between these early African American newspapers and African American literary organizations. Both *Freedoms Journal* and, to a greater extent, the *Colored American* carried detailed accounts of discussions surrounding literature that took place at meetings of literary societies, approximating for their readers the experience of being present at these meetings. In essence, these articles scripted for their readers-whether themselves members of literary societies or not-how literature might be discussed, debated, and put to use.

In contrast, all three of Frederick Douglass's newspapers, the *North Star, Frederick Douglass' Paper,* and *Douglass' Monthly* (the last of which I will not discuss here), took or granted that the black community understood the contexts in which literature would be enjoyed and the uses to which literature could be put. Unlike the earlier papers, the *North Star* and *Frederick Douglass' Paper* did not include didactic articles instructing readers on the importance of reading and the benefits of literary conversation, nor did it explicitly encourage black readers to consider literature within the context of organized literary activities. Instead, these newspapers served as libraries for what they assumed to be skilled and sophisticated readers, including in their pages all of the material, literary and political, that was the subject of literary discussions, both within the context of literary societies and in the larger community. In this, their connection to the organized literary activities of free blacks in the urban North that proliferated in the decades before the Civil War was no less definitive. That their relationship with black readers generally and with antebellum African American literary societies specifically is implicit rather than explicit points to a significant evolution in black literary culture and underscores the observation that the antebellum black press accommodated literature and served black readers in a variety of different ways.

It should be noted that Douglass's newspapers were complicated entities that served many purposes; but I am interested in uncovering some of the literary objectives in the *North Star* and *Frederick Douglass' Paper.* Because Douglass was able to assume that his readers understood the importance of reading—were themselves readers, whether literate or not—he was able to focus on more complex literary goals than were the editors of *Freedom's Journal* and the *Colored American.* First, Douglass hoped to make the pages of the *North Star* and *Frederick Douglass' Paper* a forum for black writers, whose work he actively solicited and reviewed and who eventually came to see his newspapers as a primary site for the publication of their work. Second, Douglass sought to capture the nuances of an emerging American literature that included the poetry and prose of European American authors like Ralph Waldo Emerson, Nathaniel Hawthorne, and John Greenleaf Whittier as well as the slave narratives and other writing composed by black authors. From Douglass's perspective, one important aspect of the emerging American literature was its dual positioning as both political and imaginative. In the work of white writers this duality was taken for granted; but one of Douglass's literary goals in his newspapers was to claim artistic license for black literary arts and the work of black authors, whose writing, with the rising popularity of the slave narrative in the 1830s and 1840s, had come to be valued only for its veracity and political force. Finally but perhaps most significantly, Douglass sought to advance the unprecedented idea of the creative parity between black and white writers. Although discussions that took place in the pages of Douglass's papers underscored the extent to which material equality between blacks and whites did not exist Douglass's placement of the work of the most celebrated white European and European American writers next to that of black writers insisted on the equality of their literary, cultural, and artistic pursuits.

Douglass's motivation in establishing the *North Star* in 1847 was in keeping with these aims. His objective was to create a "colored newspaper" that would "attack SLAVERY in all its forms and aspects, advocate UNIVERSAL EMANCIPATION; exalt the standard of PUBLIC MORALITY; promote the moral and intellectual improvement of the colored people; and hasten the day of FREEDOM to the THREE MILLION of our ENSLAVED FELLOW COUNTRYMEN."[81] Colored newspapers, he realized, were sometimes "objected to, on the ground that they serve to keep up an odious and wicked distinction between white and colored persons," but this distinction, while odious, was also very real. "Facts are facts," he wrote in an editorial that appeared early in the life of the *North Star*, "white is not black, and black is not white. There is neither good sense, nor common honesty, in trying to forget this distinction." "The distinction which degrades *us*," he continued,

> *is* not that which exists between a *white* MAN and a black MAN. They are
> equal men: the one is white, the other is black; but both are men, and equal
> men. The white man *is* only superior to the black man, when he outstrips
> him in the race of improvement; and the black man *is* only inferior, when he
> proves himself incapable of doing just what is done by his white brother. In
> order to remove this odious distinction, we must do just what white men do.
> It must no longer be white lawyer and black woodsawyer [sic], white editor,
> and black street cleaner: it must be no longer white, intelligent, and black,
> ignorant; but we must take our stand side by side with our white fellow
> countrymen, in all the trades, arts, profession[s] and callings of the day.[82]

That Douglass was relatively successful in helping black Americans "take their stand" in the arts was readily apparent by September 1854, when *Frederick Douglass' Paper* printed a review of Frances Ellen Watkins [Harper]'s *Poems on Miscellaneous Subjects.* Calling Watkins's collection "a credible production and . . . one tending, both on account of the excellence of its sentiments, and the source from which they emanate to interest and improve the hearts of those who may peruse it, " the reviewer hailed *Poems on Miscellaneous Subjects* as "one of the increasing number of evidences of the gradual and certain advancements of our long enthralled and deeply injured people." "We observe, in the papers, that Miss Watkins has recently taken the field as a lecturer, and that the impression made by her addresses is highly beneficial to the cause of Freedom, and the elevation of our people, the reviewer noted. His closing remarks seem equally directed to her literary accomplishments and her political presence: "It must have required no slight stretch of conviction, and no small amount of moral courage to bring one, identified as Miss W. is with a despised race, publicly before the oppressors, to plead the cause of her, people." "Let her be encouraged and cheered on in her good works, this reviewer wrote, shifting the focus of his comments directly to black readers who needed to be conscientious in their support of black authors and public figures. "Colored people, especially, should be forward in sustaining Miss

Watkins, and affording her the means of prosecuting her literary and oral labors in behalf of the slave."[83]

There are many noteworthy aspects of this review, and we will return to it later for the emphasis that the reviewer places on the coexistence in Watkins's writing of literary excellence and political power. For the time being, however, I want to focus on the way that Watkins's collection came to the attention of Douglass and his staff: It was sent to *Frederick Douglass' Paper* "by the author." That Watkins herself sent a copy of her volume of poetry to Douglass underscores the extent to which she considered *Frederick Douglass' Paper* an appropriate venue not only for the publication of her literary work but also for its critical analysis and its promotion. By 1854 the literary arts of African American authors filled the pages of *Frederick Douglass' Paper,* often accompanied by sophisticated literary criticism that analyzed both its content and its impact. As this review indicates, black readers still needed a bit of prodding to remind them of the importance of supporting authors of their own race. But Watkins's voluntary submission of *Poems on Miscellaneous Subjects* to Douglass in 1854 stands in striking contrast to Douglass's earlier struggle to solicit the work of black writers for the *North Star* and gives some indication of Douglass's challenge and his success in his bid to make his newspapers a literary forum for the work of black authors. Initially, the *North Star* struggled to be seen by authors and their promoters as a place where literary news would appear, and Douglass was more apt to stumble on the work of a promising African American author than to receive his or her work directly. Douglass's readers were first informed of the existence of Henry Bibb's *Narrative of the Life of Henry Bibb,* for instance, by Gerrit Smith, a white abolitionist and longtime supporter of the *North Star* and *Frederick Douglass' Paper.* In an early August issue of the *North Star,* Douglass printed a letter from Smith to Bibb written in July 1849. Smith's letter commends Bibb on his "deeply interesting Narrative" and expresses his wish that "every reader in the nation and in the world might read it." In his role as the *North Star's* editor, Douglass appended a note to the bottom of Smith's letter. "Why have we not seen this Narrative?" he asked rhetorically. "We should be glad to see it. Will the author favor us with a copy[?]"[84]

Whether Bibb did indeed forward a copy of his *Narrative* to Douglass, or whether Douglass gained access to the *Narrative* from another source, is unclear. A review of it, however, appeared in the *North Star* two weeks later. "Although we dislike the principle just acted on," Douglass wrote in reference to his belief that Bibb had overlooked him as the black editor of a black newspaper, "we are disposed to do justice to his book." Calling it "one of the most interesting and thrilling narratives of slavery ever laid before the American people," Douglass deem[ed] the work a most valuable acquisition to the anti-slavery cause. Douglass's positive assessment of Bibb's narrative and his understanding of its potential impact seems straightforward; to understand its subtlety, however, we must return momentarily to Gerrit Smith's letter to Bibb reprinted by Douglass in the *North Star.* The primary function of Smith's letter was to anticipate challenges to Bibb's credibility and assure potential readers of the character of the author and the authenticity of his story. "What a horrible thing slavery is in the light of your Narrative!" Smith wrote. "And your Narrative is true," he concluded, "for I know you to be a man of integrity. In his own review of Bibb's *Narrative,* Douglass also praised Bibb for the "exposure which the author makes of the horrors of slavery." He noted, however, that while Bibb's "narrations of the cruelty of slaveholders" was "natural," it was probably "not in every essential particular true."[85]

At first glance, it is easy to consider this comment as intended to be critical, prompted perhaps by Douglass's frustration and even anger or bitterness that Bibb did not immediately present his *Narrative* to Douglass for consideration by the *North Star.* In the antebellum political climate, Douglass's comments, which question the veracity of Bibb's *Narrative,* might well have threatened to undermine and devalue the *Narrative* by raising suspicions that it was untrue. As Gerrit Smith's letter affirming the quality of Bibb's character and the authenticity of his *Narrative* suggests, the issue of truth-telling that Douglass raises here was particularly relevant. "True" or verifiable slave narratives such as that written by Douglass himself were becoming more and more important to the abolitionist movement and to antislavery discourse; in fact, the political force that was believed to result from relaying the "truth" about slavery was the sole criterion by which the quality of black writing and black writers was assessed. As illustrated by the earlier case of James Williams, a black ex-slave who in 1838 dictated the story of his life in bondage and escape from slavery to the abolitionist poet John Greenleaf Whittier, the truth of which was later challenged by the southern press, slave narratives that were determined to be "false," no matter how compelling or effective they were in convey-ing the abolitionist message, were ultimately considered detrimental to the antislavery cause. Williams's narrative had been widely circulated both in book form and as a serial in the *Anti-Slavery Examiner.* But in the wake of the brouhaha surrounding its determi-nation as "wholly false," the publisher was ordered to discontinue sale of the work. In 1838 there was no place, it seemed, for works of literature that were, in the words of one commentator, "purely of the Negro imagination."[86]

Douglass's own experience as an antislavery lecturer and the author of a slave narra-tive would have made him familiar with the potentially fatal consequences of implying that Bibb's *Narrative* was "not in every essential particular true." But he was also aware of the extent to which the exclusive demand for "truthfulness" in the slave narrative threatened to effectively silence black writers whose perceived value lay in the political effectiveness of their stories while their creative, artistic abilities and literary style went unrecognized. Located in Douglass's apparent criticism of Bibbs work is an affirmation of the creative abilities of black writers and a desire to reclaim imagination as a feature of their literature. At the core of Douglass's dual assertion in his review of Bibb's *Narra-tive*-that Bibb's *Narrative* was probably not entirely true coupled with his assessment of it as "one of the most interesting and thrilling narratives of slavery ever laid before the American people" and "a most valuable acquisition to the anti-slavery cause is a powerful argument: literature by black Americans, Douglass contends, can be both political and imaginative. By positioning the imagination as a valuable and viable feature of black literary arts, Douglass refutes those who would judge it exclusively in the context of racial politics and for its political effectiveness. As the transcribers of slave narratives that provided firsthand accounts of slavery, black Americans had received wide recognition; yet the heavily mediated genre of the slave narrative threatened to become, for many black writers, a form of verbal bondage. These verbal bonds Douglass knew well. Readily embraced by William Lloyd Garrison, a principal sponsor of his 1845 *Narrative,* and others in the New England antislavery group as an effective spokesperson, Douglass never felt that he was recognized by them as an independent thinker, a creative writer, or a dynamic leader in his own right. This was one of the factors leading him to split with that group. His desire to break the verbal bonds that he came to feel had dominated his 1845 *Narrative* and infected his participation in Garrison's antislavery movement and to exercise authorial control over both the narrative he told and the way in which that narrative was told manifests itself in Douglass's pursuit of bolder and more independent literary efforts, of which his venture into journalism is but one example. In this light, Douglass's review of Henry Bibb's *Narrative,* with its potentially inflammatory suggestion that Bibb's work could be both artistically imaginative and politically powerful, is a bold and contentious statement. The dual criteria for the assessment of African American literature he outlines in it, still resonant in African American critical discourse today, would come to guide much of the literary criticism and assessments of literary value in the *North Star* and *Frederick Douglass' Paper.* Recall, for instance, the 1854 evaluation of Frances Ellen Watkins's *Poems on Miscellaneous Subjects,* which was praised simultaneously for the "excellence of its sentiments" and because Watkins's work would "interest and improve the hearts of those who may peruse it."

Douglass's critical voice would take on still greater and more deliberate force as he worked through the pages of the *North Star* and, later, *Frederick Douglass' Paper* to assert the place of black literature. In the fall of 1849, Douglass included in the *North Star* an extensive review of the *Narrative of Henry Box Brown.* Like those of other slave narrators, Brown's story offered an eyewitness account of the horrors of slavery, and Douglass's straightforward recommendation to his readers to "Get the book" reflects his assessment of the narrative's success as both a powerful indictment of slavery and the compelling story of one man's heroic pursuit of freedom.[87] Douglass's review of Henry Box Brown's *Narrative* was the occasion for a brief but resonant critical meditation on the emergence of American slave narratives as a literary genre. "America has the melancholy honor of being the sole producer of books such as this," Douglass wrote in his review. "She is so busy talking about the doctrine of human rights, that she has not time to put it in practice. Boasting forever of her republican institutions, where shall we find a nation that has less reason to boast? Shouting continually about freedom, and human equality; but in practice denying the existence of either."[88] Douglass points here to the ironic dichotomy between the romantic but ultimately insincere rhetoric of American revolutionary ideals and its genuine expression in the narratives of fugitive slaves. He believed that the hunger for freedom and human justice that had given shape to the American republic was exemplified in stories of the pursuit of freedom in the narratives of former slaves. This hunger for freedom and its passionate expression had given rise to what Douglass identified in his review of Henry Box Brown's *Narrative* as a uniquely American literary form. In advancing this perspective, Douglass echoed that of Boston Unitarian minister and abolitionist Ephraim Peabody, whose review-essay "Narratives of Fugitive Slaves" Douglass had excerpted in an earlier issue of the *North Star*. In his review of three prominent slave narratives, *Narrative of the Life of Frederick Douglass, an American Slave* (1845), *Narrative of William W Brown, a Fugitive Slave* (1847), and *The Life of Josiah Henson, Formerly a Slave, Now an Inhabitant of Canada* (1849), Peabody called slave narratives a "new department" in the "literature of civilization" whose appearance it was America's "mournful honor" to claim. Peabody went so far as to argue that this literature was superior to much of the fiction being produced: the "ordinary characters" of literature, he wrote, seem "dull and tame" when compared with those slave narrators "who have sufficient force of mind and heart to enable them to struggle up from hopeless bondage."[89] This perspective would also be advanced by transcendentalist and activist Theodore Parker, who argued in 1849 that "all of the original romance of Americans is in [slave narratives], not in the white man's novel."[90]

These comments indicate the extent to which, in the 1830s, 1840s, and into the 1850s, the narratives of fugitive slaves increasingly gained literary as well as political significance. Abolitionists hoped that slave narratives, by exposing the courage and perseverance of slaves in contrast to the cruelty of slavery, could potentially serve as powerful weapons in the fight against slavery because of their power to change prevailing skeptical attitudes lodged in the public imagination toward blacks in the United States. But Douglass, Peabody, Parker, and others asserted that in the narratives of fugitive slaves lay the basis of a distinct and distinctly American literature, one inseparable from the nation in which it was created and one which epitomized its national experience and its character. Slave narratives were in keeping with Ralph Waldo Emerson's 1837 assertion that a "cultural revolution, a democratization of literature, was underway." Emerson insisted that, "instead of the sublime and beautiful," American literature must instead explore "the near, the common." The best of the slave narratives, notes literary historian William Andrews, fulfilled this objective by "restor[ing] political and literary discourse on the subject of slavery to first considerations--the tangible experience and direct perceptions of the individual." It was the slave narrative's "absence of conventional art," Andrews continues, "its rejection of elegance and classic form, its apparent spontaneous rhythms of consciousness, and its dependence on plain speech and empirical facts" that contributed to its being recognized by a handful of black and white intellectuals of the day as a model for American literature's potential to combine spiritual self-examination, romantic self-consciousness, and democratic individualism in a format that was rhetorically eloquent yet resounded with language that was unpretentious, vibrant, true.[91]

That the *North Star* and *Frederick Douglass' Paper* were focused in part on capturing this emerging American literature in all its complexity and variety is apparent in the

literary selections and critical discussions about literature that took place in the newspapers. Slave narratives and other writing by black Americans were a vital component of
this emerging American literature; Douglass included literature by a variety of American
writers of European descent that he considered notable as well. A partial catalogue of
these authors reveals the names of some of the most significant literary figures of the
nineteenth century. References to and the writing of Henry Wadsworth Longfellow,
James Fenimore Cooper, Henry Beecher Ward, and Lydia Maria Child appeared frequently in the pages of the newspapers. Ralph Waldo Emerson was regularly discussed,
his lectures announced and reviewed, and his work excerpted. Nathaniel Hawthorne's
short story "The Pine Tree Shilling" was included in the 14 December 1849 issue of the
North Star; a selection from Herman Melville's *Typee,* titled "Tatooing," appeared in
the 2 June 1848 issue.[92] John Greenleaf Whittier was heralded as a major poet worthy of
extended study by readers of the newspaper. His verses were frequently included in the
"Poetry" column and often matched with biographical data and critical discussions of
the author's work. The terms for his praise and that of other European American writers
typically recalled the new standards for American literature that were embodied in the
narratives of fugitive slaves. Whittier, one writer asserted, "has made more than verses.
He has not only written, but done something .... He has perhaps, fulfilled the truest
vocation of the poet in this transition age by being in some sort the voice of one crying
in the wilderness."[93]

By situating the work of these emergent European American writers next to that of
black writers, by implying that these authors, black and white, were responsible for negotiating the terms of an emerging and distinct American literature, Douglass effectively
advanced the unprecedented idea of their creative parity. While much of the content of
the *North Star* and *Frederick Douglass' Paper* attested to the dramatic differences in the
material condition of the nation's black and white populations, the juxtaposition of the
creative literary work of black and white American writers in the pages of the newspapers was a testimony to their shared cultural pursuits. Like W.E.B. Du Bois's strategy of
pairing Negro spirituals with European verse as the epigraphs of each of his chapters of
The Souls of Black Folk (1903), Douglass is able to emphasize both the creative symmetry
and the complementarity of these forms of expression, all of which he considered as
indigenous, American literature.

To say the least, Douglass's assertion of the creative parity of black and white writers
was subversive to the cultural hierarchy of the time; many Americans questioned the
very humanity of black people, and even among sympathetic abolitionists their ability
to create literary art was viewed skeptically. By printing the work of the most celebrated
European authors alongside that of black and white American writers Douglass posed a
further challenge to early nineteenth-century assumptions about literary value, which
held that works of European literature were far superior to those of American literature.
The writing of Sir Walter Scott, Samuel Coleridge, and Felicia Hemans appeared regularly in the *North Star* and *Frederick Douglass' Paper.* Douglass's efforts to highlight the

work of one of the most popular English writers, Charles Dickens, is particularly notable. The editorial decision to serialize Dickens's latest novel, *Bleak House,* in the spring of 1852 is another sign of Douglass's determination to expose black readers to a variety of literature, including that which was more immediately associated with white readers. *Harper's Monthly,* a publication with increasing prestige as a literary journal, had secured an agreement with Dickens for the right to publish *Bleak House;* without securing such an agreement, Douglass seems to have taken the liberty of simultaneously publishing the novel, the installments in *Frederick Douglass' Paper* running slightly behind those in *Harpers Monthly.*

There is no shortage of questions to be asked and observations to be made about both Douglass's decision to print *Bleak House* and his readers' response to it. For the purposes of this discussion, it must suffice to leap straight to one of the most significant observations. Douglass promoted the publication of *Bleak House* as a significant event, supplying his readers with the supplemental texts, including biographical sketches of Dickens and notices informing readers of the record-breaking sales of his work abroad, that were traditionally employed by newspaper editors to stimulate and maintain their readers' interest in serialized fiction. Nevertheless, during the eighteen-month serialization of *Bleak House* in *Frederick Douglass' Paper,* the main literary attraction of the newspaper was not Dickens's novel but, rather, critical discussion of Harriet Beecher Stowe's *Uncle Tom's Cabin.* The serialization of *Bleak House,* which ran weekly with one exception from 15 April 1852 until 16 December 1853, coincided directly with extensive debates on the literary and political merit of *Uncle Tom's Cabin.* Black readers of *Frederick Douglass' Paper* were more focused on Stowe's novel, which was reviewed in the "Literary Notices" column of the newspaper on the same day that the commencement of *Bleak House* was announced. The one exception to the weekly inclusion of *Bleak House* in *Frederick Douglass' Paper* points to the literary and political priorities of Douglass's readers: on 1 October 1852 an editorial decision to reprint the text of Charles Sumner's speech addressing his motion to repeal the Fugitive Slave Act left no room for the weekly installment of the novel. Slavery and the future of black Americans in the United States were issues directly addressed by Stowe's novel. Initially serialized in the *National Era, Uncle Tom's Cabin* was, in the spring of 1852, released as a single volume. Frederick Douglass's review of that volume, issued before he had in fact seen it and based almost entirely on Stowe's reputation and on his knowledge that the book took up the question of slavery, posited his belief in its ability to work political wonders. "The touching portraiture [Stowe] has given of 'poor Uncle Tom' will, of itself, enlist the kind sympathies, of numbers, in behalf of the oppressed African race, and will raise up a host of enemies against the fearful system of slavery," concluded an early review of the novel.[94]

That Stowe's subject matter and the potential political impact of her novel were of more interest and personal concern to Douglass's readers than was Dickens's *Bleak House* is unsurprising, and editorial notices indicate that Douglass was certainly aware that some readers were critical of his decision even to include *Bleak House* in *Frederick*

Douglass' Paper. More to the point, the timing of the publication of the two novels seemed to have put them in direct competition with one another, an impression that the newspaper's editors seemed aware of and worked to dispel. As early as the end of April 1852, a note to readers in the newspaper's "Literary Notices" column highlighted this tension: "We make no apology to our readers for devoting our fourth page to Bleak House,'" it began. "To those among them who have read 'UNCLE TOM'S CABIN,' (and who has not read it ere this?) we commend this attractive story of the most popular of English writers."[95] In this implied contest, *Uncle Tom's Cabin* was the definitive victor; while *Bleak House* inspired little critical commentary, letters to the newspaper concerning the literary and political merits of Stowe's novel abounded.

It bears emphasizing that Douglass might have suspended the serialization of *Bleak House* at any time, either in order to make more room for the publication of critical perspectives on *Uncle Toms Cabin* or because he sensed his readers' waning interest in the novel. That he did not serves to underscore Douglass's literary priorities and commitments. As I have already argued, Douglass was intent on laying the work of European, American, and African American writers side by side in *Frederick Douglass' Paper*. His purpose in doing so was to prove by association that this writing was equal and to insist, at the same time, that literary talent was transracial. In the juxtaposition of all of this literature—fiction about legal injustice in *Bleak House,* fiction about racial injustice in *Uncle Tom's Cabin,* and nonfiction about slave experience in the slave narratives—the newspaper's readers were able to see them as connected by theme (injustice) and in political intent (to reform the Justice system, abolish slavery).

Douglass's editorial choice to serialize *Bleak House* alongside critical debates about *Uncle Tom's Cabin* demonstrates his commitment to producing both literature and literary criticism, both primary texts and the discussions that surrounded them, in the pages of *Frederick Douglass' Paper*. As I have argued, the ways in which Douglass's journalism supported efforts to foster the development of literary skills in the black community are not explicitly communicated in the pages of the newspapers. But a desire to enhance these talents and a keen sense of their importance was inherent in Douglass's literary decisions. His determination to provide his readers with both a variety of literature and an array of critical voices serves to illustrate the extent to which Douglass advocated an agenda for promoting black liberation and equality that was grounded in African American literary practice. The tangible focus of the critical debates waged in the pages of *Frederick Douglass' Paper,* the most visible and well-documented of which was that between Douglass and his former coeditor, Martin Delany, was Stowe's *Uncle Tom's Cabin;* but while the novel provided a concrete center for these conversations, it served as a point of departure for literary and political discussions that would shape and galvanize both black readers and the black community generally in myriad ways. Behind the various critical commentaries on the novel lurked a variety of questions crucial to the future of black Americans and the development of their literary and political voices. Did Stowe's novel, as Douglass initially believed, have the power to improve the condition of blacks in the United States? How was this impression of the novel compatible with its final chapter, in which Stowe promoted colonization? What were the limits of religious piety, and when was resistance not only justified but demanded? Could a white writer such as Stowe faithfully represent the black experience in slavery?[96]

Douglass's own response to these questions seems at once straightforward. Editorial pieces contributed to the newspaper in the years after the publication of *Uncle Tom's Cabin* attest to Douglass's belief in "Mrs. Stowe's power to do us good," and there is no doubt that he used the pages of *Frederick Douglass' Paper* to orchestrate a positive reading of *Uncle Tom's Cabin,* defending the novel valiantly against even its troubling advocacy of colonization. But at the height of his defense of the novel, Douglass included in the pages of *Frederick Douglass' Paper* a novella that he wrote which delivered a searching critique of Stowe's work. "The Heroic Slave," serialized in the paper early in 1853, tells the story of the slave Madison Washington who, in 1841, led a successful revolt against the slave ship *Creole.* Douglass's novella confirms in fictional form the belief he expressed in the context of his comments on *Uncle Tom's Cabin:* working in concert with black Americans, sympathetic whites could help to bring about the liberation and elevation of African Americans. At the same time, "The Heroic Slave" pointedly counters or revises some of the images put forth by Stowe's novel. Most notably, Washington is presented to the reader as a rebellious rather than a docile slave. He does share some of Uncle Tom's attributes: "A child might play in his arms, or dance on his shoulders," Douglass writes in a description of him. Yet unlike Stowe's Uncle Tom, Washington is also described as a man with the capacity to think for himself and act decisively: "He had the head to conceive, and the hand to execute. In a word, he was one to be sought as a friend, but to be dreaded as an enemy."[97]

Douglass's novella is an early example of African American fiction based on the conventions of the slave narrative. Douglass's familiarity and frustration with the slave narrative needs no further documentation, and his experimentation with fiction writing in "The Heroic Slave" is a tangible demonstration of his desire to assume control over both narrative strategy and creative voice. Taken in concert, Douglass's fictional response to *Uncle Tom's Cabin* and his critical assessments of the novel, laid side by side in the pages of *Frederick Douglass's Paper,* make visible a less straightforward, more complex response to it than allowed by either source alone. On the one hand, he embraced it because he believed it had the potential to mobilize Americans in support of the interests of both free and enslaved blacks. On the other hand, he used "The Heroic Slave" to posit a critical revision of some aspects of it. That Douglass relied on two different kinds of literary texts, imaginative and critical, to communicate the nuances of his thinking on Stowe's novel points to the important work Douglass relied on literary texts to do in 1853 and suggests the extent to which, in the 1850s and on the eve of the Civil War, he trusted literary texts to provide free blacks with a means of discussing questions to which definitive answers were scarce. One need only look as far as the rift between Douglass and Delany that found expression in the pages of *Frederick Douglass'*

Paper as a debate over the value of *Uncle Tom's Cabin* to see the complicated and often divisive nature of these discussions. The immorality of slavery and racist practices in the North, the validity of the Fugitive Slave Law, the complexity of issues of colonization and emigration, the intricacies inherent in the pursuit of freedom and citizenship, the desirability of religious otherworldliness, the advocacy of various strategies for effective leadership and representation and their political consequences--sorting through these issues presented great challenges to black Americans as they struggled to maintain. their focus on effecting communal change while remaining true to differences in perspectives on race and nation, political vision and public stance. Douglass's journalism reinforced for its black readers the extent to which literary texts could provide the basis for fruitful discussions; it is in these productive literary conversations that Douglass and other free blacks continued to struggle for their rights as well as to suggest how that struggle might best be waged.

"An Intimate Companion of All Classes"

Literary historians have noted with surprise that the first African American newspapers focused decisively on literature and the first African American literary magazines produced in and for the black community were launched in the politically turbulent 1850s, when legislation like the passage of the Fugitive Slave Act and court decisions like the *Dred Scott* case made fugitive slaves and free blacks more vulnerable than ever. Although the law and the Supreme Court decision exacerbated the situation of blacks enslaved in the South, they proved particularly problematic for the free black population who were now threatened with kidnapping and had their hopes for citizenship dashed by Judge Taney's firm assertion that all blacks constituted, a "subordinate and inferior class of beings" who essentially had no rights or privileges but such as those who held the power and the government might choose to grant them."[98] But against this desolate background, newspapers focused more decisively on literature like *Frederick Douglass' Paper* and the first black literary magazines were published; in this political situation, these publications counseled new strategies for literacy and literary work.

In the midst of deteriorating conditions, attention to literary pursuits generally and specifically to the development of journalism more literary in nature was one way to "uphold and encourage the now depressed hopes of thinking black men, in the United States. In the words of Thomas Hamilton, publisher of the *Anglo-African Magazine,* this population had, "for twenty years and more . . . been active in conventions, in public meetings, in societies, in the pulpit, and through the press, cheering on and laboring on to promote emancipation affranchisement *[sic]* and education." The "apparent result of their work and their sacrifices," however, was "only Fugitive Slave laws and Compromise bills, and the denial of citizenship on the part of the Federal and State Governments."[99] Despite their sense of discouragement, these individuals remained committed to achieving social and racial Justice in the United States; once literary character spread throughout the black community, they believed, prejudice and discrimination would disappear and the promise of democracy would be fulfilled. "If ever there was a time when our people should read," wrote one contributor to the *Christian Recorder* in 1854, "it is now, in order to improve their understanding, and cultivate their minds. We should read and study every book and paper, any thing and every thing that tends to religion, morality, science, and literature." Exposure to such literary learning, this writer advocated, would allow black Americans to "cultivate and improve ourselves, that we may be able to stand in juxtaposition with our friends, who think themselves the favoured of God."[100]

I close this chapter by looking summarily at two newspapers, the *Christian Recorder,* established in 1852, and the *Weekly Anglo-African,* begun in 1859, and two literary magazines, the *Repository of Religion and Literature, and of Science and Art* and the *Anglo-African Magazine,* begun in 1858 and 1859, respectively. All of these publications supported the concerns expressed by *Freedom's Journal,* the *Colored American,* and the *North Star* and *Frederick Douglass' Paper:* they regarded the need for self-representation as central to the future of black Americans in the United States and saw their columns as places where black voices would find a receptive audience. "We know that there are many well-educated, strong and powerful minds among us, that have need only to be discovered . . . in order to become the wonder and admiration of the world," wrote the editor of the *Christian Recorder* in an early issue of the newspaper. "Come friends, one and all, who are interested for [sic] the spread of useful knowledge . . . let us hear what you have to say upon these great questions."[101] Five years later, Thomas Hamilton used his introductory remarks in the *Anglo-African Magazine* to reiterate the imperative of creating a platform from which to counter what he recognized as a concerted "endeavor to write down the negro [sic] as something less than a man." "'The twelve millions of blacks in the United States and its environs,'" he wrote, "must speak for themselves; no outside tongue, however gifted with eloquence, can tell their story; no outside eye, however penetrating, can see their wants; no outside organization, however benevolently intended, nor however cunningly contrived, can develope [sic] the energies and aspirations that make up their mission."[102] Hamilton promised that "all articles in the Magazine, not otherwise designated, will be the products of the pens of colored men and women."[103] He told his readers of his intent, "if the requisite editorial matter can be furnished, to make this magazine one of the institutions of the country'."[104]

Hamilton's desire to create a publication composed exclusively of literature by black authors reflects an approach to fostering the development of "literary character" in the black community that differed significantly from that of Frederick Douglass. Their goals, however, were not dissimilar. In addition to providing a place in which literary production by African Americans would find a readership, the *Anglo-African Magazine* also furnished a forum in which black writers used sophisticated works of literature to engage in debates about the nature and function of black art and its role in racial uplift. Writers of such different political persuasions and artistic sensibilities as Frances E. W.

Harper and Martin R. Delany published significant pieces in the first volume of the *Anglo-African Magazine.* Published serially throughout 1859, Delany's *Blake: or the Huts of America* is the story of Henry Holland, a free black who attempts to organize a revolt among the slaves not only in the United States but throughout the western hemisphere. Harper's short story "The Two Offers," which also appeared serially, presents a radically different literary representation of black life. She contrasts the lives of two cousins to argue against complacency and to assert that marriage is but one option for women of intelligence and social conscience. While one cousin lives an unhappy life after marrying someone she does not love, the other does not marry; she becomes a writer and dedicates her life to "mak[ing] the world better by her example [and] gladder by her presence." Like Harper herself, her fictional character "had a higher and better object in all her writings than the mere acquisition of gold, or acquirement of fame . . . she had a high and holy mission on the battlefield of existence."[105] Harper and Delany represent two extremes in their aesthetic beliefs and social politics; like other authors who published in the *Anglo-African Magazine,* the *Weekly Anglo-African,* the *Repository,* and the *Christian Recorder,* both found an audience for their diverse agendas.[106]

   In their quest to become monuments to the intellectual abilities and the cultural achievements of black Americans, these publications shared with the earlier newspapers a commitment to working cooperatively with other institutions of literary activity. The *Christian Recorder,* for instance, was a product of the African Methodist Episcopal (A.M.E.) Church's Book Concern, a committee formed in 1817 to ensure the distribution of moral and religious texts to the black community. The newspaper was central to fulfilling the Book Concern's mission of extending literacy throughout the black community and seeing that black Americans were well represented in print. Founders of the *Christian Recorder* considered the publication a principal means of presenting the black community in its best light and "pledged to make It a paper—in print, in size, in type and in general appearance—that shall give respectability and credit to us."[107] The literary content of each issue of the newspaper supported this commitment, as well as the Book Concern's dedication to the distribution of texts and of literary knowledge generally. In addition to the original contributions written by both well-known and amateur black writers, the *Christian Recorder* published bibliographic essays and discussions about literary theory and reviewed and recommended recently published books by both African American and European American authors. Early in 1864, a column called "Books For Our Times" recommended Louisa May Alcott's Hospital Sketches and a collection of speeches and lectures by Wendell Phillips as well as William Wells Brown's recently published *The Black Man* and a biography of Toussaint L'Ouverture.[108] Some books received special acknowledgment. Under the heading Book Notices, a slave narrative by Rev. J. W. Loguen of Syracuse, New York, was called "a wonderful book" that "narrates the life of Bro. Loguen with startling power."[109] This and all other books mentioned in the *Christian Recorder* were available for purchase through what was advertised as "Our Very Own Bookstore." A full catalogue of "Books for Sale at the Book Depository of the

A. M. E. Church," located on Pine Street in Philadelphia, was regularly included in the *Christian Recorder*. In addition to "Sabbath School Books" and "Public School Books," the Book Depository also had available a vast array of titles aimed at a general audience.[110]

The *Repository of Religion and Literature, and of Science and Art* was formed in conjunction with not one but many literary institutions. It was first published by select "Literary Societies of the African Methodist Episcopal Church." By January 1862 the *Repository's* sponsorship shifted to all the Literary Societies that will contribute the annual sum of $24 for its support." Many of the features that were included in the *Repository* were lectures that had been given before or were prepared in the context of men's and women's literary societies, and the editors appealed regularly to members of the literary societies that sponsored the magazine to employ "their rich thought and polished pen" toward the production of "contributions of great value."[111] The *Repository* included "Literature" and "Poetry" sections as well as a "Young Ladies' Lecture Room." Stories for children were found in a section called the "Children's Room" and short reviews of books, pamphlets, and magazines appeared in the "Monthly Book-Table" section, or under the heading "Literary Notices."

So oriented toward literature was the *Weekly Anglo-African* that it inspired the formation of both informal literary coalitions and a formal reading room. Writing to the editors of the *Weekly Anglo-African* in October 1859, one of its readers, the Reverend Amos Gerry, made the following observation: "Long winter evenings are before us-- many hours are to be disposed of," he wrote. "How shall they be occupied?" "Now is the time to form Social Improvement Circles, Gerry suggested, "where the few, if no more are willing to Join, may meet at least *one* evening in each week, and read such selections as may be agreed upon, or recite from the great poets such portions as will expand the mind, strengthen the understanding, and improve the taste." He recalled one such "little company of five or six individuals," who gathered "to hear one of their number read through David Walker's Appeal to the Colored People of America." Gerry commended this activity, not only because of the importance of Walker's text specifically ("Would that that book could be read by every person within these United States," he wrote of it. "Its pages thunder, its paragraphs blaze"), but also because such reading circles were one way to expose African Americans to black authors and, in so doing, preserve black literary arts. It was an opportune time to think about the formation of such circles, Gerry believed, for several reasons. Surely free blacks such as those who had access to the *Weekly Anglo-African* were in need of improving their literary skills, and the approach of shorter days and colder weather made a renewed commitment to indoor activities like reading and extended literary discussion appropriate. It was the existence of the *Weekly Anglo-African*, however, and the unprecedented access to literary texts that it facilitated, that made it a Particularly auspicious time for free blacks to form literary circles. The "opportunities for gaining useful knowledge now presented, especially by the 'Anglo-African'" were tremendous, Gerry argued. He considered the newspaper an invaluable source of reading material as well as a forum through which the thinking and writing of black people could be appreciated and preserved. This was, in fact one of

Gerry's principal concerns. "An effort should be made to preserve the writings of colored persons, and we know of no better way than to form such 'improvement circles,' and to gather up all the books and writing so far as may be which refer to us as a people. If this is faithfully done," he concluded, "there will be many a library formed of no small value—of inestimable value—and of increasing interest."[112]

Indeed, the contents of the *Weekly Anglo-African* did form a library of no small value, each issue containing abundant material to support the activities of a reading circle. In addition to letters, essays, and extended book reviews, a regular feature of the newspaper was a "Poems, Anecdotes and Sketches" column. The content of this column was entirely explained in its title. In one issue, Frances Ellen Watkins's poem "Be Active" was followed by an anonymously authored poem called "He's None The Worse For That" and two works of short fiction, "The Negro of Brazil" by "An Old Tar" and "The Lost Diamond" by Mrs. F. D. Gage.[113] Short, moralistic vignettes appeared alongside excerpts from recently published novels. The close relationship between the *Weekly Anglo-African* and the *Anglo-African Magazine* ensured that a steady stream of texts would appear in both journals. James McCune Smith's "Chess," originally published in the September 1859 issue of the *Anglo-African Magazine,* was also included on the front page of the issue of the *Weekly Anglo-African* published on 10 September 1859, and Frances E. Watkins's contribution to the August 1859 issue of the *Anglo-African Magazine,* "The Dying Fugitive," also appeared in the *Weekly Anglo-African* on 20 August 1859. Even the extended book reviews that were included in the *Weekly Anglo-African* offered readers significant literary texts that enhanced their critical perspective as they suggested further reading. Reviews and advertisements for Douglass's *My Bondage and My Freedom,* a biography of the Reverend Jermain W. Loguen, and William C. Nell's *The Colored Patriots of the American Revolution* shared space with recommendations for Lydia Maria Child's "The Right Way, The Safe Way."[114] The number as well as the diversity of texts supplied on a weekly basis by the *Weekly Anglo-African* was appreciated by readers, who recognized the advantages that would accompany such literary exposure. In the words of one of the newspaper's patrons, through active interaction with the literary texts included in the *Weekly Anglo-African,* "readers are taught to think for themselves, and are stimulated to express their thoughts in appropriate language." By this means, this reader recognized, "they will make rapid advances in literature."[115] Evidently, the newspaper's audience's eagerness to consume its literary offerings sometimes came at the expense of their reading of another text commonly associated with African American readers: the Bible. A small item included in a February 1860 issue of the newspaper and titled "Popularity of the Anglo-African" reported that one New York City preacher had complained to his congregation that "he knew Christians who could be found sitting up late at night reading the 'African Paper,' while their Bibles were totally neglected."[116]

Capitalizing on the interest in literature and literary texts in part created by the *Weekly Anglo-African,* its editors moved to open their own reading room in November 1859. Located in 178 Prince Street in New York City, the Anglo-African Reading Room opened with much fanfare. To publicize the existence of the reading room and ensure its immediate popularity, the committee responsible for organizing the Anglo-African Reading Room instigated "a course of popular lectures" to be held periodically at the reading room. Although they chose to promote the lectures, rather than the reading room itself, in their initial announcement, the text of it makes clear that "the object of the course [of lectures]" was to "aid in the establishment of a reading room." By providing ready access to literary material and promoting attention to literary character in the black community, the reading room this group recognized, would constitute an essential and lasting addition to the black community. Organizers hoped that the reading room would be inviting to "the masses," a space "where the barriers of complexion, sect, or party shall have no existence whatever-a place where young and old may resort to inform themselves upon the current events of the age, and enjoy the various and piquant pleasures produced by the learned review or the well stored magazine." Intergenerational as well as interracial, the Anglo-African Reading Room was envisioned as a "place . . . not for the *colored man,* and not for the *white man,* but for the PEOPLE."[117]

To this end, the "list of lecturers" was to "comprehend the representatives of color and those who are not." Speakers were to encompass a wide range of subject matters and perspectives, representing "the pulpit, the bar, the bench, the editorial chair—the Presbyterian, the Congregationalist, the Methodist, the Baptist, the Universalist—learning, eloquence, and enthusiasm."[118] Meetings were often sponsored by independent literary societies, including those whose membership was female. Reports of lectures and meetings held in the Anglo-African Reading Room suggest that these events, serious or playful, were dominated by a spirit of interaction rather than opposition. Speakers assembled could be contentious, their addresses challenging, but they were thought-provoking as well. Exposure to this sort of environment and the intellectually challenging climate it encouraged seems to have been precisely the type of exercise the reading room hoped to provide. Surely gatherings advertised as "A little literature and lemonade—a few declamations and doughnuts!" were playful and entertaining; but they were serious and academic, too. As had traditionally been the case with African American literary coalitions, the success of the reading room was in its combination of intellectual exercise and society. "To sit alone and gorge one's self with venison and wine, is not our taste, " wrote one correspondent for the *Weekly Anglo-African* in praise of the reading room's activities. "An association of kindred spirits can sometimes find profitable conversation over a cup of coffee, refreshing our minds as well as bodies, and sharpening the ideas by social interchange of sentiment."[119] This understanding was shared by readers of the *Weekly Anglo-African* who did not live near the Anglo-African Reading Room. Writing from Hartford, Connecticut "Sigma" used these words to express her belief in the advantages of the social aspect of literary study afforded by reading rooms, for both men and women: "We feel glad to know that a reading room has been started in your city, and although we cannot enjoy its benefits yet we console ourselves with the idea that it will be productive of good, especially if the ladies patronize it and enter into discussions upon the merits of the different periodicals on the files. Nothing calls into action and better strengthens one's judgement as this habit of conversing on what we read."[120]

Despite the emphasis of all of these publications on nurturing black readers and writers and preserving a record of their accomplishments, most have until recently been overlooked by literary historians as sources of early African American literature. An exception to this is the *Anglo-African Magazine,* widely considered the first literary magazine produced by and for the black community. Contemporary definitions of journalism have prevented us from dissociating our understanding of the newspaper's coverage of "news" from the actual literary contexts of early nineteenth-century African American newspapers. Furthermore, contemporary distinctions between church and state, between "high" and "popular" literary productions, have limited our ability to see either the *Repository* or the *Christian Recorder* as anything other than religious publications. But, as Frances Smith Foster has recently reminded us, "the Afro-Protestant press rarely if ever confined itself to what we might understand as 'religious' subjects. To the publishers and contributors, as to their intended readers, the sacred and the secular were not discrete elements of their lives and their experiences."[121] Foster's own recovery of three novels by Frances E. W. Harper that were published serially in the *Christian Recorder* between1868 and 1888 reinforces her argument that the Afro-Protestant press must be reconsidered as a major source of literature by and for African Americans. By ignoring or dismissing such sources, scholars of African American literary history will necessarily perpetuate what Foster calls "ahistorical and overdisciplined ways of thinking" about the literary habits of and literary production by African Americans in the mid-nineteenth century.[122] The diverse literary content of publications like the *Repository of Religion and Literature, and of Science and Art* and the *Christian Recorder* serves as an important reminder that many non-religious documents were included in church-based sources, and that the black church encouraged African American readers to acquaint themselves with literature that was not limited to the Bible.

Scholarly neglect of these critical sources has had tremendous repercussions, not only in terms of our knowledge of early African American literature but also in terms of our understanding of the habits of African Americans as readers as they faced the definitional crises that marked the 1850s. During this time, for instance, the *Repository,* the *Anglo-African Magazine,* and the *Christian Recorder* all shared what in the *Colored American* had been a fledgling concern with the creation of an enduring record of African American accomplishments and cultural production. The editors considered the durability of their publications a prime aspect of their appeal; in promoting them, they distanced the publications from the ephemeral qualities of a newspaper by representing them as booklike. This was true even of the *Christian Recorder,* which was published more frequently and printed on sheets larger than the new literary magazines. The founders of the *Christian Recorder* emphasized in the prospectus that it would be "in a form so as to be folded as a book or pamphlet, that families and individuals may have books made of it and preserved for future references."[123] A statement regularly included in issues of the *Repository* cited the magazine's durability as a principal appeal when it enumerated the reasons it should be patronized. "Because being in bookform," this announcement stated, "it is better adapted to preserve the current literature of our Church, and of sister denominations for the use of posterity—for where you will find one copy of our newspapers fifty years hence, you will doubtless find fifty copies of the Repository." Although the *Repository* would remain unbound, it was as good as having a book: "People seldom preserve newspapers, but almost always preserve their books. Indeed, books preserve themselves." The creation of durable sources of literature was considered critical to the support of black authors and the development of an African American literary tradition. The *Repository* claimed that "because of [its] conservative power it is better adapted to develope [*sic*] the talents of our young people, and to furnish data for future comparison."[124] This and similar assertions offer further insight into the literary aesthetics of early African American readers, who were reminded in multiple ways that literature was, above all, functional. It could not serve to educate or inspire the people if it did not survive to reach multiple generations of black readers.

What finally distinguishes the literary journalism of the period just before the Civil War is that, in addition to attempting to recreate the shared space of literary societies, as *Freedoms Journal* and the *Colored American* had, it also encouraged independent reading and fostered the development of individual reading habits. A distinctive feature of the new literary magazines was their portability; individual issues of the *Repository*, for instance, were but twenty-two pages, bound by a single thread, and small enough to fit conveniently in a pocket. The *Repository* highlighted its portability as a primary appeal to subscribers in a statement repeated monthly on the back cover of the publication. "If you bind newspapers into book form it then becomes too large to be portable, too unhandy for use," explained the editors, "but the Repository *will always be portable, always easily used.*"[125] This portable source of literature was designed to convey the experience and the benefits of organized literary activity to individual readers and to each solitary reading experience. The implication here is that, because of its portability, the magazine insisted on being read; it was, according to the *Repository's* editors, "an intimate companion of all classes," capable of providing the individual reader with opportunities to engage in a communal model of literary activity even when away from the company of peers at the literary society meeting or in the lecture hall.[126] Literary magazines would provide constant company for black readers, ensuring that they were kept in regular contact with appropriate literature. As if they were at a meeting of a literary society, readers of the new literary magazines would be tutored in the civic responsibilities and democratic process that formed the basis of all literary engagement as they read. In this way, the editors of the *Repository* suggested, the solitary reading experience would be another means of exposing black Americans to the literary environments that would contribute to their becoming "fit for society, [and] better neighbors in any community."[127]

The design of these publications to expand the literary habits of black readers to include more attention to individual, solitary reading is representative of notable changes taking place in the black community on the eve of the Civil War. Despite significant restrictions on their freedom, free blacks responded to the legislative assaults of the 1850s through different and more decisively political organizational channels than they had in earlier decades. In response to the political setbacks of the 1850s, some black Americans revisited the idea of emigration, not only to Africa but also to Canada and Haiti. Others became involved in greater numbers in antislavery societies and the activities that directly supported the abolitionist effort. African Americans in New York and Ohio renewed their dedication to organizing annual conventions, and throughout the North blacks held meetings to consider how to respond to the infuriating disregard for their rights and their freedom. In this increasingly polarized, increasingly hostile pre-Civil War environment, black Americans had less energy to dedicate to organized literary efforts, and the number of organizations specifically focused around reading and literature declined. Literary study, however, remained no less important, and the literary publications of the 1850s and early 1860s addressed this continued need for attention to literature by cultivating the development of more solitary and individual reading habits. Although they appreciated the institutions that continued to support organized literary activities, the idea of literacy communicated by these publications was not tied to the specific context of the literary society or reading room. It is not that the communal context associated with literary societies became any less important in the decade preceding the Civil War. In fact, never had there been greater need for free blacks to assert in strong, public voices their commitment to liberty and equality. The terms of literary practice shaped and communicated by the literary journalism of the 1850s and early 1860s insisted that individual readers must remain oriented toward uses of literacy and language that allowed them to forcefully enter into public debates about the future of black Americans in the United States and to raise the voice of conscience in a society seemingly deaf to its own ideals.

Endnotes

1   See Frederick Douglass, *Narrative of the Life of Frederick Douglass, an American Slave*, 81-87. Few stories of the impact of the acquisition of public voice are more powerful than that of Frederick Douglass. While still a slave, Douglass acquired a copy of Caleb Bingham's *Columbian Orator*; among other examples of powerful rhetoric he found in it was the story of a slave who, in the course of a series of conversations, persuaded his master that slavery was wrong. "The reading of these speeches," he wrote in *My Bondage and My Freedom*, "added much to my limited stock of language, and enabled me to give tongue to many interesting thoughts, which had recently flashed through my soul, and died away for want of utterance." What Douglass describes is how his reading literally transformed him, giving him the voice that would eventually allow him to enter the public sphere. See Douglass, *My Bondage and My Freedom* (1855; reprint, Urbana: University of Illinois Press, 1987), 99-101. The quotation is from page 100. Douglass speaks of the impact of what he read in the *Columbian Orator* in similar terms in *Narrative of the Life*, 83-84.

2 "Examiner," "Characteristics of the People of Color-No. 3: Literary Character," *Colored American*, 16 May 1840, unpaginated. Readers should note that the pagination of ante-bellum black newspapers is inconsistent (and often inaccurate); for instance, the *Colored American* was paginated consistently only in 1838 and from March to December 1841. Whenever possible I have included page numbers in my citations; in all cases the citations given are indicative of the most complete information available.

3 Henry Louis Gates Jr., "From Wheatley to Douglass: The Politics of Displacement," in *Frederick Douglass: New Literary and Historical Essays,* edited by Eric Sundquist (New York: Cambridge University Press, 1990), 52.

4 *Christian Recorder,* 27 December 1862, 206.

5 Benedict Anderson, *Imagined Communities: Reflections on the Origins and Spread of Nationalism,* rev. ed. (London: Verso, 1991), 6.

6 Ibid., 7.

7 For discussion of the role of print in the formation of nationalism and "imagined community," see ibid., 62–63, 7 4–75. The quotation is from page 62.

8 African American historian Garland Penn's groundbreaking history of black journalism, *The Afro-American Press and Its Editors* (1891; reprint, New York: Arno Press, 1969), laid the groundwork for future historians to consider the early black press primarily in the context of abolitionist efforts when he observed that *Freedom's Journal* "contended for our freedom from bondage, or our deliverance from a human curse which then seemed riveted about us with a most tenacious grip" (27). Later studies that consider *Freedom's Journal* and other antebellum black newspapers as abolitionist publications include Frederick G. Detweiler, *The Negro Press in the United States* (College Park, Md.: McGrath, 1968), 35–37; Carter R. Bryan, "Negro Journalism in America Before Emancipation," *Journalism Monographs* 12 (September 1969): 8–10; Roland E. Wolseley, *The Black Press, U.S.A.* (Ames: Iowa State University Press, 1971), 17–18. Edwin Emery, *The Press and America* (Englewood Cliffs, N.J.: Prentice-Hall, 1972), 219, stresses the abolitionist focus of *Freedom's Journal* but mentions that the paper had other content as well.

9 Frederick Cooper, "Elevating the Race: The Social Thought of Black Leaders, 1829- 1850," *American Quarterly* 24 (December 1972): 606. Cooper adds, "articles on slavery were often reprints from other journals, while the editors themselves wrote about other subjects" (606). The editors shared this perspective: "We would not be unmindful of our brethren who are still in the iron fetters of bondage. They are our kindred by all the ties of nature; and though but little can be effected by us, still let our sympathies be poured forth, and our prayers in their behalf, ascend to Him who is able to sucour them." See "To Our Patrons," *Freedom's Journal,* 16 March 1827, 1.

10 "Why we should have a Paper," *Colored American,* 4 March 1837, unpaginated.

11 "To Our Patrons," *Freedom's Journal,* 16 March, 1827, 1. As Frankie Hutton notes in her study of the antebellum black press, *The Early Black Press in America, 1827- 1860* (Westport, Conn.: Greenwood Press, 1993), "many of the newspaper's editors were active abolitionists outside of their editorships whereas their newspapers were pragmatically focused on upbeat news and activities from free black communities" (4). Hutton's analysis of the early black press provides the most complete recent assessment of it; especially useful is the first part of her study in which she concentrates on the editors of the earliest black

newspapers and their beliefs. Further details on the lives of the editors of the early black press are available elsewhere. I have not focused on them here as I am interested in *Freedom's Journal* and the other publications I address in this chapter as institutions rather than as reflections of their editors' own desires and beliefs.

12   Reverend Samuel Cox, "Recommendations," *Freedom's Journal,* 23 March 1827, 4. Along with the editors' own perspective on their primary audience, this comment calls into question earlier assumptions that, because of the illiteracy rate in the black population, the majority of the readers of *Freedom's Journal* were white. In the northern states, my research suggests a higher literacy rate than has traditionally been assumed. By 1850, the census reports that 86 percent of black Bostonians were literate; by 1860, that number had risen to 92 percent. The reliability of census figures, especially concerning people of color, and the very definition of literacy they assume are problematic. Furthermore, literacy rates in New England and along the Atlantic seaboard in the nineteenth century were not typical of the entire United States. But these figures do suggest the extent to which literacy was both known and manifest by African Americans long before the Civil War.

13   "To Our Patrons," *Freedom's Journal,* 16 March 1827, 1.

14   "Proposals for Publishing the Freedom's Journal: Prospectus," *Freedom's Journal,* 25 April 1828, 37. The same column was reprinted in the 16 May and 30 May 1828 issues of the newspaper.

15   Evidence of the mixture of hostility and resentment that brewed in northern, urban spaces filled the pages of the white press at the end of the 1820s. It is perhaps best captured in the series of cartoons produced by caricaturist Edward Clay titled "Life in Philadelphia." Clay's cartoons, popular in both the United States and England, ridicule the strivings and aspirations of urban, upwardly mobile African Americans. As broadsides, they were published by William Simpson and C. S. Hart in Philadelphia and by Tregear and several other publishing houses in London. Nancy Reynolds Davison offers a cogent analysis of Clay's caricatures in her study "E. W Clay: American Political Caricaturist of the Jacksonian Era" (Ph.D. diss., University of Michigan, 1980).

16   For a fuller analysis of the development and growth of urban spaces in the antebellum free North and the lives of free blacks within these spaces, see Gary B. Nash, *Forging Freedom,* esp. chap. 7; Emma Lapsansky, "'Since They Got Those Separate Churches'"; James Oliver Horton, *Free People of Color;* James Oliver Horton and Lois E. Horton, *In Hope of Liberty.*

17   *African Repository* I (1825): 68.

18   *African Repository* 4 (1828): 118. As Peter P. Hinks asserts, *Freedom's Journal* was "probably begun in part as a response to the publication two years earlier of the ACS [American Colonization Society] organ *African Repository.*" The creation of the *African Repository* in 1825 had fueled the rapid growth of the American Colonization Society in part because it contributed dramatically to the Society's ability to communicate its message to a wide audience and facilitated the organization of its supporters. See Hinks, *To Awaken My Afflicted Brethren,* 101.

19   As James Oliver Horton and Lois E. Horton note in their study of free blacks in the antebellum United States, "the expansion of the franchise for white men [in the first decades of the nineteenth century] was often accompanied by the restriction or elimination of the franchise for black men." The Hortons discuss black voting rights in *In Hope of Liberty,*

167- 70; the quotation is from page 168. The extent to which free blacks were excluded from traditional means of political expression and participation can be seen in the fact that in New York City, out of a black population of 12,575, only 16 voted in 1825. See Philip S. Foner, *History of Black Americans* (Westport, Conn.: Greenwood Press, 1975), 517–20; statistics on page 520.

20   "Education, No. 1," *Freedom's Journal*, 30 March 1827, 10.

21   "To Our Patrons," *Freedom's Journal*, 16 March 1827, 1.

22   "To Our Patrons," *Freedom's Journal*, 16 March 1827, I. All quotations in this paragraph are from this source.

23   As was customary of all antebellum newspapers, much of the material that appeared in *Freedom's journal* was reprinted from other publications in the United States and England.

24   "Effects of Slavery," *Freedom's Journal*, 16 March 1827, 4. The letter appeared originally in New York's *Christian Advocate* and was reprinted in *Freedom's Journal*.

25   "Foreign News," *Freedom's Journal*, 27 May 1827, 43.

26   As Kenneth D. Nordin notes, "since *Freedom's Journal's* target audience was essentially semi-literate, the strategy of making the paper entertaining was a sound one." See Nordin, "In Search of Black Unity: An Interpretation of the Content and Function of *Freedom's Journal*," in *Journalism History* 4 (winter 1977-78): 126.

27   Charles C. Andrews, "New York African Free School," *Freedom's Journal*, 9 November 1827, 138. In his letter, Andrews called it "a pleasing fact" that *Freedom's Journal* joined "three hundred well selected volumes" in the school's library. His pride in the collection is evident in the anecdote he relayed to readers of the newspaper: "One of our little scholars, aged about ten years, was questioned on some astronomical and other scientific subjects a few months ago, by a celebrated and learned doctor of this city; the boy answered so readily and so accurately to the queries, [and] was at last asked, how it was that he was so well acquainted with such subjects. His reply was, that he remembered to have read of them in the books in the School Library."

28   "African Free Schools in the United States," *Freedom's Journal*, 18 May 1827, 38.

29   Advertisement: "B. F. Hughes School, for Coloured Children of both Sexes," *Freedom's Journal*, 16 March 1827, 4. Similar advertisements and announcements appear throughout the paper.

30   "School Notice," *Freedom's Journal*, 2 November 1827, 136.

31   "To Our Patrons," *Freedom's Journal*, 16 March 1827, 1.

32   See *Freedom's Journal*, 14, 21, 28 February 1828 and 21 March 1828.

33   "Dick the Gentleman," *Freedom's Journal*, 27 April 1827, 26.

34   "To the Senior Editor," *Freedom's Journal*, 31 August 1827, 99.

35   "Libraries," *Freedom's Journal*, 5 October 1827, 119. For a valuable history of the nineteenth-century middle-class culture of self-control, see Mary Ryan, *The Cradle of the Middle Class: The Family in Oneida County, New York, 1790- 1865* (Cambridge: Cambridge University Press, 1981), esp. chaps. 2 and 4.

36   "R," "For the Freedom's Journal," *Freedom's Journal*, 1 June 1827, 46.

37   "Letter, No. V. To Rev. Samuel E. Cornish," *Freedom's Journal*, 2 November 1827, 135.

38   "George M. Horton," *Freedom's Journal*, 8 August 1828, 153; "GEORGE M. HORTON,"
     Freedom's Journal, 29 August 1828, 179; "GEORGE M. HORTON," *Freedom's Journal*, 12
     September 1828, 194–95, emphasis in original. Horton's case is discussed and these pas-
     sages are quoted in Gates, "From Wheatley to Douglass," 54–56.

39   "Muta," "Original Communications," *Freedom's Journal*, 27 July 1827, 78.

40   Ibid.

41   Samuel E. Cornish, "Original Communications," *Freedom's Journal*, 13 July 1827, 70. As
     Kenneth Cmiel argues in his study of linguistic usage in the United States, the "nine-
     teenth-century debate over language was a fight over what kind of personality was needed
     to sustain a healthy democracy" (14). In this context, the possession of literary character
     "implied far more than the ability to handle words deftly; it invoked larger concerns about
     audience, personality, and social order" (24). Literary character was always a reflection of
     the individual, but its focus was always civic as well. Early Americans looked to literary
     performances to distinguish individuals with the "cultivated sensibilities . . . needed to
     check their own self-interest and encourage a humane but unsentimental concern for
     the common good" (30). See Cmiel, *Democratic Eloquence: The Fight over Popular Speech
     in Nineteenth-Century America* (New York: William Morrow, 1990); he discusses the de-
     velopment of this understanding of rhetoric in the revolutionary era in the first chapter.

42   "Libraries," *Freedom's Journal*, 5 October 1827, 119.

43   "A Young Man," *Freedom's Journal*, 7 September 1827, 102.

44   "To Our Patrons," *Freedom's Journal*, 16 March 1827, 1.

45   "To Correspondents," *Freedom's Journal*, 2 November 1827, 136.

46   Untitled, *Freedom's Journal*, 16 March 1827, 2.

47   "FREEDOM'S JOURNAL," *Freedom's Journal*, 25 April 1828, 38.

48   "Miscellaneous: Reading," *Weekly Advocate*, 11 February 1837, unpaginated.

49   "Selection of Books," *Colored American*, 16 February 1839, unpaginated; "Solid Reading,"
     Colored American, 20 July 1839, unpaginated. In the 1830s it was still common for all news-
     papers to reprint articles from other newspapers. This was one of the ways that the literary
     values embraced by the European American population were communicated to the black
     community. As Thomas Augst documents in his research on New York's Mercantile Library
     Company, the distinction between the business of reading and reading for amusement was
     hotly contested in the 1830s and 1840s. This process of literary valuation is reflected and
     paralleled in the discussions of literature that appear in the columns of the *Colored Ameri-
     can*. See Augst, "The Business of Reading in Nineteenth-Century America: The New York
     Mercantile Library," *American Quarterly* 50 (June 1998): 267–305, esp. 292–99.

50   "Literary Societies," *Colored American*, 5 October 1839, unpaginated.

51   "Circular," *Colored American*, 16 June 1838, 69. Charges for the use of the facilities under-
     score Ruggles's commitment to making it accessible to all. "Strangers" were welcomed
     free of charge. All others were to pay according to how long they wished to use the library:
     yearly rates were $2.75; monthly the charge was $0.25, and the library could be used for a
     week for 6 ½ cents.

52   Ibid.

53   *Weekly Advocate,* 7 January 1837, unpaginated.

54   "Title of this Journal," *Colored American,* 4 March 1837, unpaginated. The *Colored American* began publication on 7 January 1837 as the *Weekly Advocate,* with Samuel Cornish, former editor of *Freedom's Journal* as its editor, Phillip Bell as proprietor, and Charles Ray as general agent. After two months, the publication was renamed the *Colored American* to signify the centrality of the black population's demand for full citizenship rights. It appeared under that name from the 4 March 1837 issue until it suspended publication with the 25 December 1841 issue. In 1838 Charles Ray became one of the paper's proprietors; the following year, after the withdrawal of Phillip Bell from the enterprise, Ray became the paper's sole publisher. It is significant to note that the National Negro Conventions met annually from 1830 until 1835, when the convention was held in Philadelphia. The next National Negro Convention did not take place until 1843, when it met in Buffalo, New York. The publication run of the *Colored American* (1837–41) coincides roughly with the interval during which no national conventions were held.

55   "Our Undertaking," *Weekly Advocate,* 7 January 1837, unpaginated.

56   Original contributions published in *Freedom's Journal* often began with disclaimers that asserted the inexperience of the writer or made reference to the "better pens" who might be more suited to address the topic at hand. To some extent, the anxiety expressed in these introductory clauses must be taken at face value: because *Freedom's Journal* was one of the first publication venues available to black writers in the United States, its contributors were often giving voice to their very real inexperience. The writers' increasing experience, especially in the newspaper's second year of publication, suggests that these disclaimers of authority were also at times unauthentic. Surely the acknowledgments of "better pens" was to some extent a humbling strategy used by many experienced American writers throughout the nineteenth century. But rather than signs of their humility or lack of experience, these introductory remarks and apologies emphasize that the conditions under which black people lived in the United States often required strategies of representation and framing devices that would disguise the control and authority implied by the very act of writing. As Frances Smith Foster argues, "such declarations are not accurate, nor were they meant to be"; she describes them rather as "masks" that "riff the readers away to new, different, and compelling interpretations" (165). Foster reviews the ways a handful of early African American authors, including Phillis Wheatley and Frederick Douglass, used this strategy in her groundbreaking book *Written by Herself Literary Production by African-American Women, 1746- 1892* (Bloomington: Indiana University Press, 1993). It should be noted that framing devices such as disclaimers were not entirely absent from contributions to the *Colored American.* Female writers were most apt to express apparent self-consciousness in their texts. In an article for the *Colored American* titled "Female Influence" (30 September 1837), a writer who signed her name "Ellen" included this paragraph: "There is a delicacy in a young and unknown female writing for the public press, which naught but my anxiety for the elevation of my people, and the improvement of my sex, together with the importance of the subject, could induce me to overcome. But with these objects in view, and with the consciousness of right, I feel impelled by an irresistible impulse, to incite the mind of community to the deep responsibility which rests upon them, in consequence of their neglect of a subject of such vital interest."

57   "Free Man of Colour," *Weekly Advocate,* 14 January 1837, unpaginated.

58 "Why we should have a Paper," *Colored American*, 4 March 1837, unpaginated.

59 Periodically, the *Colored American* ran a column titled "The Importance of Our Paper." In the beginning of the paper's second year, this column asked the question: "Without a paper- an organ of communication through which we may keep up an interchange of views, and maintain a unity of feeling and effort, how could we possibly sustain our-selves?" *Colored American*, 3 February 1838, 15.

60 "To Our Friends and Subscribers," *Colored American*, 7 January 1837, unpaginated; the editors introduced the *Colored American* as its readers' "ADVOCATE and FRIEND."

61 William Whipper, "To the Editor of the 'Colored American,'" *Colored American*, 3 February 1838, 15. Whipper, who in 1828 was one of the organizers of Philadelphia's Colored Reading Society, wrote to criticize the editor of the *Colored American* for not printing a letter expressing his opinion on the "principles and measures of the American Moral Reform Society," the organization with which he had been associated since its founding in August 1837.

62 *Colored American*, 1 April 1837, unpaginated.

63 "To Our Friends and Subscribers," *Weekly Advocate*, 7 January 1837, unpaginated.

64 "Original Communication," *Weekly Advocate*, 7 January 1837, unpaginated.

65 Table: "Vessels of War, in the U.S. Navy, 1836," *Weekly Advocate*, 7 January 1837, unpaginated. For subsequent installments of the same series, "A Brief Description of the United States," see the 14 and 21 January 1837 issues.

66 "Principal Features of the Various Nations of the Earth" and "Useful Knowledge: Life of Ben Franklin," *Weekly Advocate*, 28 January 1837, unpaginated.

67 "AMICUS," *Colored American*, 11 March 1837, unpaginated.

68 "Highly Important," *Colored American*, 14 January 1837. This announcement is repeated periodically, sometimes under the heading "Societies among the People of Color." See, for instance, the 21 January, 18 February, and 22 July 1837 issues of the paper. The overall objective of the newspaper in gathering this information was to create "a concise account of our various Benevolent and Literary Institutions to be carefully prepared from the most official sources" (7 July 1837). Societies were asked to send "a copy of their constitutions, or extracts therefrom: [and] also, answers to the following questions": "1. Male or Female; 2. How long since they were formed; 3. Who were the founders; 4. How many members; 5. Whether incorporated; 6. Names of present officers; 7. Whether Benevolent, Literary or Moral; 8. If Benevolent, how much is expended annually [for beneficial purposes]; 9. If Literary, what advancement made; 10. Whether they have a Library; 11. How many Volumes." Perhaps as an incentive to the societies to participate in the survey, the *Colored American* promised "To any society, or Secretary of a Society, who may send us answers to the above questions, or any other information relative to their respective institutions, (post paid) we will send several copies of the number containing the account of their Society" (29 July 1837). Despite these efforts, no such directory seems to have ever been created. Had the project been completed or, if completed, had the resulting directory of African American literary, moral, and benevolent associations survived, it would have offered a remarkable record of these institutions.

69 "Constitution and By-Laws of the Philadelphia Association for the Moral and Mental improvement of the People of Color," *Colored American,* 24 June 1837, unpaginated; John N. Templeton, "We, the young men of color of the city of Pittsburgh . . . ," *The Colored American,* 2 September 1837, unpaginated. The most prominent member of the Young Men's Literary and Moral Reform Society was Martin R. Delany. According to Delany's biographer Victor Ullman, the Young Men's Literary and Moral Reform Society was a new name for the Theban Literary Society, a coalition formed by Delany and a classmate, Molliston Clark, in 1832. Delany and Clark's use of this name reflects their knowledge of the rich history of the Egyptian city of Thebes and their appreciation for the vibrant intellectual traditions associated with this African civilization. According to Ullman, members of the Theban Literary Society "were occupied [during their meetings] with reading and criticism of each other's literary efforts and intellectual wanderings" (25). Ullman implies that the Theban Literary Society provided its members with a somewhat shallow experience when he comments that the atmosphere of the club was "quite divorced from the immediate problems of the day." The lifelong literary and political pursuits of both Delany and Clark, however, suggest that, while this early literary association may have been pretentious, it was neither devoid of substance nor did it remove its members from sincere engagement with the issues facing African Americans in the midnineteenth century. Significantly, both Clark and Delany went on to prominent and fulfilling literary careers, aligning themselves with publications whose commitment to the welfare of the black community was unwavering. Clark became a significant figure in the A.M.E. Church and served as the editor of its organ, the *Christian Recorder.* Delany began his own newspaper, the *Mystery,* in 1843; he became a coeditor with Frederick Douglass of the *North Star* (which would later become *Frederick Douglass's Paper*) in 1847. Delany's *Blake: or the Huts of America, A Tale of the Mississippi Valley, the Southern United States, and Cuba,* published serially in the *Anglo-African Magazine* between January and July 1859, and in the *Weekly Anglo-African* in 1861 and 1862, is one of the first novels to be written by an African American. Ullman's biography of Delany, *Martin R. Delany: The Beginnings of Black Nationalism* (Boston: Beacon, 1971), is a marvelous source of information on his life. Its usefulness to researchers, however, is limited, as his sources are largely undocumented. Similarly another source of information on Martin Delany, Dorothy Sterling's *The Making of an Afro-American* (New York: Doubleday, 1971), also suffers from its lack of specific documentation. Sterling discusses Delany's involvement in the Theban Literary Society and the Young Men's Literary and Moral Reform Society on pages 45–46.

70 "A Good Example," *Colored American,* 1 April 1837, unpaginated. These comments are made about the Female Benevolence Society of Troy, New York. A report on the fourth anniversary of this society appears on the first page of this issue.

71 "Constitution of the New-York 'Phoenix Society,'" *Liberator,* 29 June 1833, 104.

72 Sarah Melvin and Eliza Richards, "A Fair," *Colored American,* 23 December 1837, unpaginated; Charles B. Ray, "New Agencies," *Colored American,* II November 1837, unpaginated. In the 20 January 1838 issue, *Colored American* printed the note from the Ladies Literary Society that had accompanied the proceeds from the fair. "The expenses of the fair having been much greater than they anticipated," the society sent less than they had originally hoped; nevertheless, they wrote, "while they regret the smallness of the sum, [they] are buoyed up with the hope that it may be of some benefit to the Paper."

73   "Examiner," "Characteristics of the People of Color- No. 3: Literary Character," *Colored American,"* 16 May 1840, unpaginated.

74   "W.," "We take this opportunity . . . ," *Weekly Advocate,* 18 February 1837, unpaginated.

75   Ibid.

76   "File Your Papers," *Weekly Advocate,* 7 January 1837, unpaginated.

77   "Our Undertaking," *Weekly Advocate,* 7 January 18 3 7, unpaginated.

78   "The Cheapest Publications in the World!: Whole Library for Twelve Dollars," *Colored American,* 9 June 1838, 64. "The Christian Library" is advertised as "handsomely bound in sheep, fine paper, and in separate volumes, consisting of 64 of the most valuable Standard religious and Scientific Works, elegantly printed, without any alteration."

79   See "Household Libraries," *Colored American,* 7 July 1838, 80. This list of seven guidelines emphasizes the importance of a physical space for study, respect for books, and general economy as much as it does the acquisition of the texts themselves: "1. Select a room, or at least a corner of some room, where the Bible a11d other books, together with inkstand and paper, shall be kept. [. . .] 2. Obtain a good, convenient book case, and writing table, or desk, or both. Let the dust be brushed off, daily used, and kept constantly neat and clean. 3. Whenever a book has been taken into another room for use, let it always be returned to the library for safekeeping. 4. Avoid subscribing for books, unless you feel that the book cannot be published without a subscription . . . . 5. Lay out your money carefully. Buy no books but good ones. Select the best. Seek to make, from month to month, some increase to the library. Learn your children, servants, and friends to use the books with care. 6. Admit no novels. 7. Select, in addition to religious works, books of reference, school books, scientific works, and philosophical, a few of the best productions of the best poets. In all departments get works of established and solid reputation." A library was cast as something that even those of the most modest economic stature could possess: "By pursuing this course a few years, every farmer and mechanic can have a library which will be of great value to his children, when he is gone, as well as to himself while living."

80   "The Blessing of Books," *Colored American,* 17 February 1838, 24.

81   "The Object of the NORTH STAR," *North Star,* 3 December 1847, 1.

82   "COLORED NEWSPAPERS," *North Star,* 7 January 1848, 2.

83   Review of *Poems on Miscellaneous Subjects, Frederick Douglass' Paper,* 15 September 1854, 2. In an effort to continue the promotion of her work, *Frederick Douglass' Paper* included in the next issue, published on 22 September 1854, one of Frances Ellen Watkins's poems, "The Slave Auction."

84   *North Star,* 3 August 1849, 3.

85   Frederick Douglass, review of *Narrative of the Life of Henry Bibb, North Star,* 17 August 1849, 2.

86   Quoted in Gates, "From Wheatley to Douglass," 58, 59. The New York branch of the American Anti-Slavery Society, led by James G. Birney and Lewis Tappan, took the lead in declaring Williams's narrative "wholly false"; they retracted their support for it and requested that publishers discontinue its sale in a statement printed in the *Liberator* on 2 November 1838. In fact, as Marion Wilson Starling has noted, attacks on the narrative's credibility had "not attacked the *substance* of the narrative to any considerable extent, but rather the *names* Williams had given his characters." Although the conditions of slavery Williams depicted were

uncontested, his strategy of disguising the name of the place in which he was enslaved and the people with whom he had contact (a strategy Frederick Douglass would also adopt in the 1845 telling of his escape from slavery) destroyed the credibility of his narrative. For more detailed analyses of this case, see Starling, *The Slave Narrative: Its Place in American History* (Washington, D.C.: Howard University Press, 1988), 228-31 (the above quote is from page 230), and William L. Andrews, *To Tell a Free Story: The First Century of Afro-American Autobiography, 1790-1865* (Urbana: University of Illinois Press, 1986), 87–90.

87   "Narrative of Henry Box Brown," *North Star*, 28 September 1849, 2. The *Narrative of Henry Box Brown, Who Escaped from Slavery Enclosed in a Box 3 Feet Long and 2 Wide* (Boston: Brown and Stearns, 1849) was ghostwritten by Charles Stearns, who claimed to have received the facts of the story from Henry Brown. Stearns also wrote an introduction to the *Narrative*. As Douglass emphasized in his review, however, Brown's experience as a slave may first appear to readers as atypical. His narrative included "stories of partial kindness on the part of his master" and "he never, during thirty years of bondage, received a whipping." These facts about the circumstances of Brown's enslavement are important, Douglass implies: although they fail to expose the institution of slavery as physically violent, they point in distinctive ways to the untold emotional and psychological brutality that drove Brown to risk his life to escape from bondage.

88   Ibid.

89   The 3 August 1849 issue of the *North Star* includes a note to readers informing them that "EXTRACTS from Mr. Peabody's review of Narratives of Fugitive Slaves, are crowded out this week. They will appear in [the] next number." It was included on the front page of the 10 August 1848 issue of the *North Star*. Ephraim Peabody's review mentions but does not extensively review two other slave narratives: the *Narrative of Henry Watson, a Fugitive Slave* (1848) and *Narrative of the Sufferings of Lewis and Milton Clarke* (1846). I have quoted here from the version of "Narratives of Fugitive Slaves" printed in the *Christian Examiner*, July 1849, 61, 62; the text runs from 61- 93.

90   Theodore Parker, "The American Scholar," in George Willis Cooke, editor, *The American Scholar*, vol. 8 of *Centenary Edition of Theodore Parker's Writings* (Boston: American Unitarian Association, 1907), 37. "The American Scholar" was first delivered as a commencement speech at Colby College, 8 August 1849.

91   Andrews, *To Tell a Free Story*, 101 - 02.

92   Nathaniel Hawthorne, "The Pine Tree Shilling," *North Star*, 14 December 1849, 4; Herman Melville, "Tatooing," *North Star*, 2 June 1848, 4.

93   "Barton and Whittier," *North Star*, 26 January 1849, 4.

94   It should be noted that the entries in the "Literary Notices" column of the paper during this time may have been written by Douglass but are more likely the work of Julia Griffiths, Douglass's English comrade, financial supporter, and literary editor. While many of the earliest reviews in the *North Star* are signed with the initials "F. D.," indicating Frederick Douglass's authorship of them, assessment of the literary choices made in the *North Star* and *Frederick Douglass' Paper* is complicated by the fact that the newspapers reveal few clues about the editorial processes by which literary selections or assessments were made. During the height of *Frederick Douglass' Paper's* popularity, Douglass announced that Griffiths would take over as editor of the newspaper's literary column, describing her as "a lady well qualified, by her talents, tastes, industry, and acquirements, to discharge the duties

of this department." It is likely that hers was the principal voice in making many of the decisions about the selection of authors to be included in the newspaper between 1850 and 1855. But, as Benjamin Quarles has noted and as the name of the newspaper during this time unambiguously asserts, *Frederick Douglass' Paper* was "to an unusual degree the product of one man's thinking." For Douglass's announcement of Griffiths's role as literary editor, see "Prospectus of the Eighth Volume of 'Frederick Douglass' Paper,'" *Frederick Douglass' Paper,* 8 December 1854, 2. Quarles's comments about *Frederick Douglass' Paper* are included in his *Frederick Douglass* [Washington, D.C.: Associated Publishers, 1948), 83. For a detailed discussion of the relationship between Douglass and Griffiths, see William S. McFeely's *Frederick Douglass* (New York: Simon and Schuster, 1991), 163- 82.

95   J. G. [Julia Griffiths], "Literary Notices," *Frederick Douglass' Paper,* 29 April 1852, 2.

96   In *Martin Delany, Frederick Douglass, and the Politics of Representative Identity* (Chapel Hill: University of North Carolina Press, 1997), Robert S. Levine skillfully traces the public debate between Douglass and his former coeditor, Martin R. Delany, waged in the pages of *Frederick Douglass' Paper,* on the subject of *Uncle Tom's Cabin.* As Levine points out, the disagreement between these two well-respected men was not motivated by the publication of Stowe's novel alone, and although the text itself became the tangible focus of their debate, they were also, to some extent, struggling over the right to be the "main voice" in the black community (60). The novel's publication coincided with the April 1852 publication of Delany's *The Condition, Elevation, Emigration, and Destiny of the Colored People of the United States* (reprint: New York: Arno Press, 1968), in which he expressed his mounting doubts about the effectiveness of white abolitionists and his disillusionment with the possibility that blacks could elevate themselves in the United States. Delany sent a copy of *Condition* to Douglass in May 1852. But whereas *Frederick Douglass' Paper* quickly heralded Stowe's novel as a literary sensation bound to have a tremendous impact on the status of African Americans in the United States, the newspaper entirely neglected the publication of Delany's *Condition,* failing to review it or even announce its appearance. That Douglass ignored this work, choosing instead to focus the attention of his readers on the thinking and perspective of a white woman whose text promoted both religious otherworldliness and colonization, was to Delany astonishing and infuriating. Surely it contributed to the overwhelming sense of disillusionment he expressed in a letter to William Lloyd Garrison, who had directly criticized his emigrationist treatise while openly praising Stowe's colonizationist novel. "I have no hopes in this country," he wrote. "[I have] no confidence in the American people" (quoted in Levine, 70). Specifically, Delany found *Uncle Tom's Cabin* to be racist and paternalist. Despite his own suggestion expressed in *Condition* that emigration might be best for African Americans, he was also troubled by Stowe's apparent advocacy of Liberian colonization. But as Levine points out, behind Delany's various criticisms of *Uncle Tom's Cabin* lurked a broader but equally pressing question: "Can a white writer such as Stowe faithfully represent the black experience in slavery?" (75). Delany had reflected on this question in *Condition,* arguing that "Our elevation must be the result of *self-efforts,* and the work of our *own hands*" (45). In this light, Delany felt that Douglass was misguided in championing *Uncle Tom's Cabin* as a text with the potential to improve the condition of blacks in the United States. He believed that Douglass relied too heavily on the words and ideas of whites at the expense of talented black leaders and their perception of the black community's particular needs and interests. "We have always fallen into great errors in efforts of this kind, giving to others [more] than the *intelligent* and *experienced* among *ourselves,*" Delany wrote in April 1853 on the subject

of Douglass's promotion of Stowe as a representative voice for black Americans. "In all respect and difference [sic] to Mrs. Stowe, I beg leave to say that she knows nothing about us, 'the Free Colored people of the United States,' neither does any other white person, and consequently, can contrive no successful scheme for our elevation; it must be done for ourselves." See Martin L. Delany to Frederick Douglass, letter of 20 March 1853, *Frederick Douglass' Paper*, 1 April 1853, 2. Levine's chapter on the Douglass-Delany debate (58- 98) was instrumental in my understanding of Douglass's literary objectives in his newspaper.

97   Frederick Douglass, "The Heroic Slave," reprinted in *The Life and Writings of Frederick Douglass, Volume 5*, edited by Philip S. Foner *(New York: International Publishers, 1975), 476. My reading here follows that of Levine; see Martin Delany, Frederick Douglass, and the Politics of Representative Identity, 83-85.*

98   *Dred Scott v. John EA. Sandford*, 19 Howard 393 (1857), 404- 05.

99   Thomas Hamilton, "Apology (Introductory)," *Anglo-African Magazine* I (January 1859): 3.

100 Jer. V. R. Thomas, "The Success of Our Paper," *Christian Recorder*, 16 September 1854, 79.

101 "Editor," "Our Expectation," *Christian Recorder*, 13 July 1854, 62.

102 Hamilton, "Apology (Introductory)," *Anglo-African Magazine* I (January 1859): 1. About Thomas Hamilton we know very little. In his "Apology" he described himself as "'brought up' among Newspapers, Magazines." Boasting of his experience in the publishing industry, he summarized his lifelong aspirations and accomplishments in this way: "To become a Publisher, was the dream of his youth . . . and the aim of his manhood." In 1843, "while yet a boy," Hamilton established the *People's Press*, "a not unnoticed weekly paper," that denounced slavery and urged free blacks to refrain from participating in the nation's wars until their services were recognized and their freedom and equality guaranteed. The *People's Press* survived until 1847; it is unclear what Hamilton did in the twenty years between his publishing ventures.

103 Ibid., 4.

104 Ibid., 1.

105 Frances E. Watkins [Harper], "The Two Offers," *Anglo-African Magazine* 1 (September and October 1859): 288-91, 311-13; the quotations are both from p. 313.

106 Evidence suggests that most writers for these publications were unpaid, either by design or because the financial situation of the publication would not allow it. For instance, Thomas Hamilton insisted in his introductory comments to the first issue of the *Anglo-African Magazine* that literary contributions to the magazine, "when used, will be paid for, according to the means of the Publisher"; he had to admit at the end of the first year of his venture, however, that the "contributors to this Magazine have performed a labor of love- the publisher has not yet been able to pay them." See Hamilton, "Apology (Introduction)," *Anglo-African Magazine* 1 (January 1859): 4; and Hamilton, "The Anglo-African Magazine for 1860," *Anglo-African Magazine* (December 1859): 400.

107 M. M. Clark, "Prospectus of the Christian Recorder of the African Methodist Episcopal Church," in Daniel Payne, *History of the African Methodist Episcopal Church* (Nashville, Tenn.: Publishing House of the A.M.E. Sunday-School Union, 1891), 278–79.

108 "Books For Our Times," *Christian Recorder*, 23 January 1864, 15. This column appears regularly in the newspaper, sometimes under the heading "Books For The Times."

109 "Book Notices," *Christian Recorder,* 9 July 1864, 110.

110 Advertisements for "Our Own Book-Store" or "Our Very Own Book-Store" appear regularly in the newspaper. See, for instance, the *Christian Recorder,* 21 November 1863, 187.

111 "Editor's Repository: Our Duty to Aid Ourselves and Support Our Literature," *Repository of Religion and Literature, and of Science and Art* 5 (January 1863): 21.

112 Amos Gerry Beman, letter from Rev. Amos Gerry Beman, *Weekly Anglo-African,* 29 October 1859, 1.

113 "Poems, Anecdotes and Sketches," *Weekly Anglo-African,* 30 July 1859, l.

114 "A New and Exciting Book [review of *Life of Rev. J W Longuen*]," *Weekly Anglo-African,* 1 October 1859, I; a review of William C. Nell's *Colored Patriots of the American Revolution* was published in the 30 July 1859 issue of the *Weekly Anglo-African* (3); Child's work was reviewed in "New Books," *Weekly Anglo-African,* 2 June 1860, 2.

115 "Should the 'Anglo-African' Be Sustained?" *Weekly Anglo-African,* 9 June 1860, 2. This correspondent, whose name is not attached to the letter, refers here to the importance of "both the weekly and the magazine. "

116 "Popularity of the 'Anglo-African,'" *Weekly Anglo-African,* 4 February 1860, 3.

117 "Anglo-African Lectures," *Weekly Anglo-African,* 15 October 1859, 2.

118 Ibid.

119 "Amusements," *Weekly Anglo-African,* 31 March 1860, 3.

120 Sigma, "Letter from Hartford," *Weekly Anglo-African,* 3 December 1859, I.

121 Frances Smith Foster, introduction to *Minnie's Sacrifice; Sowing and Reaping; Trial and Triumph: Three Rediscovered Novels,* by Frances E.W. Harper, xxvi. Foster's essay provides an invaluable overview of the literary legacy of African Americans.

122 Ibid., XXXV.

123 M. M. Clark, "Prospectus of the Christian Recorder of the African Methodist Episcopal Church," in Daniel Payne, *History of the African Methodist Episcopal Church,* 278- 79. In 1855 the Book Concern entertained a proposal to change the newspaper into a monthly magazine: "Having duly considered all the circumstances in the case, and finding themselves without funds, and furthermore, without a reasonable prospect of obtaining sufficient means to sustain the semi-monthly publication of our paper, in its present form, the Book Committee have [sic] concluded that it be greatly to the advantage of the Book Concern, and the whole connexion, to change the present form of our little sheet from a semi-monthly newspaper to a monthly magazine." Apparently, there was little support for this proposition and the newspaper retained its status but continued to be published inconsistently. See "Proposed Change in The Christian Recorder," *Christian Recorder,* 18 August 1855, 130.

124 "Reasons why the Repository should be Continued and Patronized, *"Repository of Religion and of Literature, and of Science and Art.* This announcement is reprinted on the inside back cover of virtually every issue of the *Repository;* see, for instance, January 1862.

125 Ibid.

126 J[ohn] M. B[rown], "Salutatory," *Repository of Religion and Literature, and of Science and Art I* (April 1859): 1. See also: "Prospectus" (February 1862), unpaginated; John M. Brown, "A Word to Our Subscribers and Friends" (April 1861), 51.

127 E[lisha] W[eaver], "To Our Subscribers," *Repository of Religion and Literature, and of Science and Art* 4 (October 1859): 192.

Bibliography

ARCHIVAL SOURCES AND PERIODICALS

Readers interested in learning more about the publications listed here should consult *African-American Newspapers and Periodicals: A National Bibliography,* edited by James P. Danky (Cambridge: Harvard University Press, 1998). This two-volume bibliography, arranged alphabetically by title, accounts for over six thousand newspapers and periodicals by or about African Americans in the United States, Canada, and the Caribbean. Entries list the frequency of publication, subscription rates, publisher, and variations in title and place or frequency of publication. The bibliography also informs researchers where issues of the publications can be found, either on microfilm or hard copy. Readers should also note that increasingly, access to nineteenth-century African American newspapers and periodicals is available through web-accessible archives.

> *African Repository*
> *Anglo-African Magazine*
> *Christian Advocate* (New York)
> *Christian Recorder* (Philadelphia, PA.)
> *Freedom's Journal* (New York)
> *Liberator* (Boston, Mass.)
> *Mystery* (Pittsburgh, PA.)
> *North Star* (Rochester, N.Y.)
> *Weekly Advocate* (New York)
> *Weekly Anglo-African* (New York)

ARTICLES AND BOOKS

Anderson, Benedict. *Imagined Communities: Reflections on the Origins and Spread of Nationalism.* London: Verso, 1991.

Andrews, William L. *To Tell a Free Story: The First Century of Afro-American Autobiography, 1790-1865.* Urbana: University of Illinois Press, 1986.

Augst, Thomas. "The Business of Reading in Nineteenth-Century America: The New York Mercantile Library." *American Quarterly* 50 (June 1998): 267–305.

Bryan, Carter R. "Negro Journalism in America Before Emancipation." *Journalism Monographs* 12 (September 1969): 8–10.

Clark, M. M. "Prospectus of the Christian Recorder of the African Methodist Episcopal Church." In *History of the African Methodist Episcopal Church*, by Daniel Payne, 278–79. Nashville, Tenn.: Publishing House of the A.M.E. Sunday School Union, 1891.

Cmiel, Kenneth. *Democratic Eloquence: The Fight over Popular Speech in Nineteenth-Century America.* New York: William Morrow, 1990.

Cooper, Frederick. "Elevating the Race: The Social Thought of Black Leaders, 1829-1850." *American Quarterly* 24 (December 1972): 604–25.

Davison, Nancy Reynolds. "E. W. Clay: American Political Caricaturist of the Jacksonian Era." Ph.D. diss., University of Michigan, 1980.

Delany, Martin R. *The Condition, Elevation, Emigration, and Destiny of the Colored People of the United States.* 1852. Reprint, New York: Arno Press, 1968.

Detweiler, Frederick G. *The Negro Press in the United States.* College Park, Md.: McGrath, 1968.

Douglass, Frederick. "The Heroic Slave." In *The Life and Writings of Frederick Douglass.* Vol. 5, edited by Philip S. Foner, 473–505. New York: International Publishers, 1975.

- -. *My Bondage and My Freedom.* 1855. Reprint, Urbana: University of Illinois Press, 1987.

- -. *Narrative of the Life of Frederick Douglass, an American Slave.* 1845. Reprint, New York: Penguin, 1983.

Du Bois, W. E. B. *Black Reconstruction in America.* 1935. Reprint, New York: Atheneum, 1992.

- - . *The Souls of Black Folk.* 1903. Reprint, New York: Penguin, 1989.

Emery, Edwin. *The Press and America.* Englewood Cliffs, N.J.: Prentice Hall, 1972.

Foner, Philip S. *History of Black Americans.* Westport, Conn.: Greenwood Press, 1975.

Foster, Frances Smith. Introduction to *Minnie's Sacrifice; Sowing and Reaping; Trial and Triumph: Three Rediscovered Novels,* by Frances E. W. Harper. Boston: Beacon, 1994.

- - . *Written by Herself Literary Production of African-American Women, 1746-1892.* Bloomington: Indiana University Press, 1993.

Gates, Henry Louis, Jr. "From Wheatley to Douglass: The Politics of Displacement." In *Frederick Douglass: New Literary and Historical Essays,* edited by Eric Sundquist, 47–65. New York: Cambridge University Press, 1990.

Hutton, Frankie. *The Early Black Press in America, 1827- 1860.* Westport, Conn.: Greenwood Press, 1993.

Lapsansky, Emma. "'Since They Got Those Separate Churches': Afro-Americans and Racism in Jacksonian Philadelphia." *American Quarterly* 32 (1980): 54-78.

Levine, Robert S. "Circulating the Nation: The Missouri Compromise, David Walker's *Appeal,* and the Rise of the Black Press." In *The Black Press: Literary and Historical Essays on the "Other" Front Page,* edited by Todd Vogel. New Brunswick: Rutgers University Press, 2001.

--. *Martin Delany, Frederick Douglass, and the Politics of Representative Identity.* Chapel Hill: University of North Carolina Press, 1997.

McFeely, William S. *Frederick Douglass.* New York: Simon and Schuster, 1991.

Nash, Gary. "Black Americans in a White Republic." *Race and Revolution.* Madison: University of Wisconsin Press, 1990.

- - . *Forging Freedom: The Formation of Philadelphia's Black Community, 1720-1840.* Cambridge: Harvard University Press, 1988.

Nordin, Kenneth D. "In Search of Black Unity: An Interpretation of the Content and Function of *Freedom's Journal*" *Journalism History* 4 (winter 1977-78): 123–28.

Parker, Theodore. "The American Scholar." In *The American Scholar,* edited by George Willis Cooke, 1–53. Vol. 8 of *Centenary Edition of Theodore Parker's Writings.* Boston: American Unitarian Association, 1907.

Penn, Garland. *The Afro-American Press and Its Editors*. 1891. Reprint, New York: Arno Press, 1969.

Quarles, Benjamin. *Frederick Douglass*. Washington, D.C.: Associated Publishers, 1948.

Ryan, Mary. *The Cradle of the Middle Class: The Family in Oneida County, New York, 1790–1865*. Cambridge: Cambridge University Press, 1981.

Starling, Marion Wilson. *The Slave Narrative: Its Place in American History*. Washington, D.C.: Howard University Press, 1988.

Sterling, Dorothy. *The Making of an Afro-American*. New York: Doubleday, 1971.

Ullman, Victor. *Martin R. Delany: The Beginnings of Black Nationalism*. Boston: Beacon, 1971.

Walker, David. *Appeal in Four Articles; Together with a Preamble, to the Colored Citizens of the World, but in Particular, and Very Expressly to Those of the United States of America*. 1829. Edited by Sean Wilentz. Reprint, New York: Hill and Wang, 1965.

Wolseley, Roland E. *The Black Press, U.S.A.* Ames: Iowa State University Press, 1971.

SELECTION 4

The Spread of Northern School Segregation, 1890-1940

By D.M. Douglas

> *Some of us went to some of the influential Negroes and told them, conditions being as they were, we thought it would be better to establish some separate schools for the colored people in the lower grades. That would give some of the colored people positions as teachers in the colored schools. They agreed to this and they were established.*
> — A WHITE SCHOOL OFFICIAL IN CHESTER, PENNSYLVANIA, 1922[1]

THE POLITICAL INFLUENCE that African Americans enjoyed in most northern states following the end of the Civil War that resulted in anti-segregation legislation had begun to fade by the end of the nineteenth century. White insistence on racial separation in northern schools increased in response to the northern migration of southern blacks that began during the last decade of the nineteenth century and exploded during and after World War I. This influx of southern blacks exacerbated racial tensions, and many white school officials who had tolerated school integration when the number of African Americans was relatively small began to insist on racial separation. By the late 1930s, northern school segregation was considerably more extensive than it had been at the turn of the century. Although much of this racial separation was due to residential segregation, in many communities school officials engaged in explicit racial assignments. For much of the North, the antisegregation legislation of the nineteenth century was long forgotten.

Growing White Hostility in Response to Migration of Southern Blacks

Northern commitments to racial equality deteriorated during the late nineteenth and early twentieth centuries, contemporaneous with increasing white hostility to blacks in southern states. During the last decade of the nineteenth century and the first decade of the twentieth century, many northern whites began to insist on racial separation in various aspects of public life, including education. In 1890, the *New York Times,* which had previously championed black school desegregation efforts, criticized—in extraordinary fashion—a black parent in southern Illinois for seeking the admission of his children to a white school: "Some of the negroes insist that their children shall . . . be taught in the same schools [as white children.] The Constitution [of Illinois] seems to uphold this pretension, but the negroes are none the less foolish and ill advised to make it . . . . Whoever insists upon forcing himself where he is not wanted is a public nuisance, and his offensiveness is not in the least mitigated by the circumstance that he is black." In 1906, the *New York Commercial* commented on the growing trend toward segregation across the country: "Northern sentiment on the race question is not at bottom a million miles away from Southern sentiment." In 1916, Seth Low, a former mayor of New York City and president of Columbia University, wrote to Robert Moton, Booker T. Washington's successor as president of Tuskegee Institute: "race purity is as strong an instinct at the North as it is at the South." Racist southern educator Thomas Bailey, in his 1914 study *Race Orthodoxy in the South,* noted, in a self-serving manner, the decline in northern opposition to southern racism: "Is not the South being *encouraged* to treat the negroes *as aliens* by the growing discrimination against the negro in the North, a discrimination that is social as well as economic? Does not the South perceive that all the fire has gone out of the Northern philanthropic fight for the rights of man? *The North has surrendered!*"[2]

The migration of tens of thousands of southern blacks to northern cities during the late nineteenth and early twentieth centuries exacerbated white hostility toward African Americans. Migration northward began in significant numbers during the 1890s. Whereas only 88,000 blacks left the South during the 1880s, 185,000 departed during the 1880s and 194,000 during the first decade of the twentieth century. Between 1890 and 1910, about 2.5 percent of the South's black population moved north. Of the five northern states with the largest black populations in 1910—Pennsylvania (191,000), New York (120,000), Ohio (110,000), Illinois (109,000), and New Jersey (88,000)—each experienced an increase in black population between 1900 and 1910 of over 25 percent. Urban population increases were even more dramatic. During the decade of the 1890s, the black populations of Chicago, Cleveland, and Pittsburgh doubled, while the populations of Detroit, New York, and Philadelphia also sharply increased. In 1903, W. E. B. Du Bois noted that "the most significant economic change among Negroes in the last ten or twenty years has been their influx into northern cities." This trend would continue. Between 1900 and 1910, the number of African Americans living in Chicago and New York increased by about 50 percent.[3]

Given the correlation between the enfranchisement of northern blacks and the increase in political influence that African Americans enjoyed in much of the North during the 1870s and 1880s, one might have expected this increase in black population during the 1890s and the first decade of the twentieth century to have positively affected the status of northern blacks. With a few exceptions, however, the status of northern blacks declined with the onset of the migration of southern blacks into northern cities. The special conditions of the 1870s and 1880s—Radical Republican commitments to removing legal disabilities imposed on African Americans, closely contested elections, and the paucity of black residents in much of the North—had faded by the early twentieth century. The growth of the northern city, populated by northern-born whites and blacks alongside growing numbers of European immigrants and southern blacks, produced an array of tensions that led to the diminishment of the status of African Americans. As historian Judy Mohraz has noted: "the rising percentage of Negroes in northern cities in the last decades of the nineteenth century altered the previous obscurity of the black residents and triggered varying degrees of racial hostility and tension. Heightened friction followed the greater visibility of Negroes in the early twentieth century city—on the streets, in residential areas, on the job, and in the schools."[4]

The migration of southern blacks during the late nineteenth and early twentieth centuries accompanied a rise in racist ideology across the country grounded in white supremacy. In the South, this racist ideology manifested itself in segregation laws and disfranchisement. In the North, many whites also began to embrace white supremacist views that dismissed blacks as inferior and unfit for full participation in white civilization. Leading scholars during the 1890s and the first decade of the twentieth century, particularly in the field of anthropology, offered scientific justifications for racial separation, rejecting notions that the poorer social outcomes of many blacks were due to environmental influences. University of Chicago anthropologist Frederick Starr, in an 1897 essay "The Degeneracy of the American Negro," emphasized inherent racial differences between blacks and whites: "[I]t is certain that race differences are real and persistent . . . . Study of criminality in the two races gives astonishing results. Of the total prisoners in the United States in 1890, nearly 30 percent were colored; the negro, however forms but 11 percent of the population . . . . Conditions of life and bad social opportunities cannot be urged in excuse . . . . The difference is *racial*." Starr held little optimism that education would improve the situation for African Americans: "What can be done? Not much. But faith in school-book education as a means of grace must die . . . . Recognition of difference between white men and black men is fundamental. The desire and effort to turn bright black boys into inefficient white men should cease. . . . We may expect the race here to die and disappear; the sooner perhaps the better." Economist Frederick Hoffman, writing in 1896, agreed: "In marked contrast with the frequent assertions . . . that race is not important and that environment or conditions of life are the most important factors in the final result of the struggle for life, . . . we have here abundant evidence that we find in race and heredity the determining factors in the upward or downward course of mankind . . . . [T] he colored race is shown to be on the downward grade, tending toward a condition in which matters will be worse than they are now . . . . Neither religion nor education nor a higher degree of economic well-being have been able to raise the race from a low and anti-social condition . . ."⁵

At the same time, many white Americans applied Darwinian notions of "survival of the fittest" to social relations, arguing that weaker groups, such as blacks, would fail while others would prosper. The burgeoning new "science" of eugenics lent support to notions of racial superiority. Two leading educational theorists of the early twentieth century, G. Stanley Hall and G. E. Partridge, articulated a "genetic philosophy of education" pursuant to which "[e]ach race must be educated and governed according to the stage of culture and development to which it belongs": "The greatest mistakes have been made in trying to cope with the negro question, in not understanding the nature of the negro, who is so different from the white man, both in body and mind, that the two races should not be treated alike in any particular . . . . [The negro] must be trained according to his own nature . . . . His whole training must centre in industry rather than in mental development disconnected from motor expression . . . . Given the proper conditions, the negro will make progress naturally toward a higher stage of civilisation, but he cannot be hurried by imitating the white man's nature."⁶

As the northern black population grew, so did opportunities for interracial conflict, as many whites began to fear competition for jobs, housing, and political influence. The immigration of millions of southern and eastern Europeans to northern cities during the 1880s had already triggered fears of job loss among native whites and anxieties about dilution of the "Anglo Saxon racial stock." The northward migration of southern blacks beginning during the 1890s provoked additional resentment among many white workers and exacerbated racial hostility. The Supreme Court's 1896 *Plessy v. Ferguson* decision, which legitimated "separate but equal," gave voice to what was already becoming the dominant mood throughout the country. Not surprisingly, the *Plessy* decision provoked minimal coverage in the nation's leading newspapers.⁷

This growing racial antagonism manifested itself in a variety of ways. Lynchings sharply increased in some midwestern states during the 1890s. The governor of Georgia, one of the nation's leaders in lynchings, attempted to condone his state's record by citing the large number of lynchings in Indiana. During the first decade of the twentieth century, a number of northern communities such as New York City, Philadelphia, Akron and Springfield (Ohio), Belville and Springfield (Illinois), and Evansville and Greensburg (Indiana) were torn by race riots. In several of these riots, white mobs destroyed homes and drove blacks out of the community. The Evansville riot, for example, triggered in part by white working-class apprehensions about economic competition from African Americans, left many dead or wounded, inflicted substantial damage on black homes and businesses, and caused the evacuation of many blacks from the city. The Springfield, Illinois, riot of 1908 captured nationwide attention for its brutal attacks on black lives and property. William English Walling, a distinguished white writer who would later help found the NAACP, commented about the Springfield riot: "Either the spirit of the abolitionists, of Lincoln and of [Elijah] Lovejoy, must be revived . . . or [James K] Vardaman and [Ben] Tillman will soon have transferred the race war to the North." Mississippi Governor Vardaman, for his part, commented that the Springfield riot would "cause the people of the North to look with more toleration upon the methods employed by the Southern people."[8]

Discrimination in public accommodations significantly increased during the late nineteenth and early twentieth centuries. Indeed, as early as the 1890s, many communities in the racially liberal Western Reserve of Ohio began, for the first time, to experience racial discrimination in public accommodations. By the onset of World War I, many hotels and restaurants in Cleveland that had once freely served black customers had implemented a color line. At the same time, many northern state legislatures considered or enacted legislation banning interracial marriage during the first decade of the new century, as did Congress during the second decade of the century.[9]

Blacks who migrated north during the late nineteenth and early twentieth centuries were confronted with increasing residential segregation. Indeed, many scholars have labeled the late nineteenth and early twentieth centuries as "the formative years of the black ghetto" in northern cities. For example, in Cleveland, which enjoyed considerable residential integration for most of the nineteenth century, an influx of blacks during the late nineteenth century and the first decade of the twentieth century brought residential segregation, as restrictive real estate practices forced blacks into the Central Avenue area of the city. [10]

Chicago also experienced an increase in segregationist pressure during the early twentieth century. White property owners urged real estate agents and property owners in white neighborhoods to sell or rent only to whites. The Hyde Park Improvement Protective Club in Chicago was especially aggressive in its efforts to keep blacks out, threatening to blacklist real estate firms that sold or rented housing to blacks and to boycott white merchants who did business with blacks. The Hyde Park club also attempted to buy property or leases from blacks who had purchased or rented property in white neighborhoods. Black families that resisted experienced vandalism. These efforts were successful: most of Hyde Park remained white until the middle of the twentieth century.[11]

A few northern communities did more than insist on residential segregation. Some communities, such as Syracuse, Ohio, Lawrenceburg, Salem, and Ellwood, Indiana, simply forbade blacks to settle within their limits. One writer described the Syracuse practice in 1913: "When a colored man is seen in the town during the day he is generally told of these traditions and is warned to leave before sun-down. If he fails to take heed, he is surrounded at about the time that darkness begins, and is addressed by the leaders of the gang in about this language: 'No nigger is allowed to stay in this town overnight. . . . Get out of here now, and get out quick.' . . . The command is always effective, for it is backed by stones in the ready hands of boys none too friendly.[12]

Employment discrimination also increased throughout the North during the early twentieth century as blacks in many northern cities were pushed out of skilled labor positions. Between 1870 and 1910, the percentage of blacks in Cleveland working in skilled trades declined from 32 percent to 11 percent. In Gary, Indiana, the community's white leaders sponsored a "clean out the Negro" campaign in 1909 aimed at removing those black workers that U.S. Steel had brought to the city to build new factories. In 1911, the *Gary Evening Post* reported that "any Negro in Gary who hasn't got a job had better lose no time in getting one" and reported that fifty blacks had been run out of the city in the prior two days. Many industrial employers simply excluded blacks from employment, while union apprenticeship programs—essential for learning necessary job skills—were typically closed to blacks, as labor unions were frequently hostile to black workers.[13]

As a result, domestic work emerged as the most promising line of work for many northern blacks during the late nineteenth and early twentieth centuries. A survey in Philadelphia during the late 1890s found about 60 percent of all black working men and about 90 percent of black working women employed as low-paid domestics; these figures would hold constant for the next forty years. By comparison, fewer than 30 percent of white immigrants and about 10 percent of native-born white workers in Philadelphia were employed as domestics during this time period.[14]

Strikebreaking provided the best opportunity for blacks to secure higher-paid jobs during the early twentieth century. Such work was short term, however, as white workers generally reclaimed these jobs with the resolution of the strike. Moreover, the strikebreaking activities of African Americans provoked bitter antagonism from white workers. The hiring of black strikebreakers during the 1904 stockyards strike and the 1905 teamsters strike in Chicago, for example, triggered "the most serious racial conflicts" in that city's history.[15]

A dramatic example of this increasing racist sentiment in the North took place at Oberlin College in Ohio. Founded by abolitionists, Oberlin had been one of the first colleges in America to admit students without regard to race during the 1830s. Moreover, the town of Oberlin was one of the few northern communities during the 1830s and 1840s to admit black children to the public schools on a nonsegregated basis. Both the town and college were important antislavery outposts, serving as a stop on the Underground Railroad and as a training ground for teachers in the Freedmen's schools after the Civil War.[16]

By the end of the nineteenth century, however, the racial idealism at Oberlin had faded. As early as 1882, white Oberlin students began to protest having to eat at the same dining hall tables with black students. Although the college president forbade racial segregation, pressure from white students for racial separation continued. In 1905, literary societies, a critical element in the Oberlin education, formally excluded black male students from membership, and in 1909 the college established separate housing for black female students. One white Oberlin student justified the exclusion of blacks from the literary societies in 1910 by citing larger patterns of societal discrimination: "[E]ven if he had been taken in and made one of us in every way, many of you older men know full well how small a degree of any such treatment he could receive outside Oberlin walls. Would you tantalize a human soul with the vision of a promised land from which an impassable gulf will soon shut him off?" The *Cleveland Plain Dealer,* no friend of Oberlin, reported the white students' position, noting that "the feeling against the African is shifting from the south to the north more and more, and the ultimatum of Oberlin's students is but added proof of that." Oberlin's president agreed: "I think the attitude of the students towards the colored question as a whole is merely a representative of the attitude of the whole north toward the question." Oberlin's president announced in 1914 that "I do not . . . see how we can avoid having some separate colored boarding houses for colored students." Mary Church Terrell, one of the school's most distinguished alumnae, replied: "I try to be optimistic in this wicked and cruel country . . . [but] nothing has come so near forcing me to give up hope, and resigning myself to the cruel fate which many people are certain awaits us, than the heartbreaking backsliding of Oberlin College."[17]

The Great Migration

During the First World War, hundreds of thousands of southern blacks moved north, launching what would become over the course of the next four decades the most significant internal migration in American history. This increase in the number of African Americans living in the North would further intensify antiblack sentiment among many whites.

Between 1915 and 1920, about 500,000 blacks left the South, moving to northern cities. Another 800,000 to 1 million southern blacks migrated north during the 1920s. All told, about 10 percent of blacks living in the South moved to the North between 1915 and 1930. Whereas in 1910 90 percent of the country's black population lived in the South, those demographics would dramatically shift over the course of the next half century. By 1960, half of the nation's black population lived outside the South.[18]

Those states receiving the largest number of black migrants during World War I were, in descending order, Pennsylvania, Illinois, Ohio, New York, and Michigan. Most black migrants settled in cities. Indeed, by 1920, almost 40 percent of northern blacks resided in just eight cities—New York, Philadelphia, Chicago, Detroit, Pittsburgh, Cleveland, Cincinnati, and Columbus—each of which experienced a dramatic increase in its black population as a result of the migration. For example, between 1910 and 1930, New York City's black population increased from 91,700 to 327,700; Chicago's from 44,100 to 233,900; Philadelphia's from 84,500 to 219,600; Detroit's from 5,700 to 120,100; and Cleveland's from 8,400 to 71,900. Smaller cities experienced sharp increases in their black population as well. The black population of Buffalo, for example, more than doubled between 1910 and 1920 and then doubled again between 1920 and 1925.[19]

Several factors contributed to the Great Migration of southern blacks to northern cities during and after World War I. Economic concerns were highly significant. First of all, sharp declines in southern agriculture due to the devastations of the boll weevil—that "ashy-colored rascal"—the reduction in cotton prices in 1913 and 1914, and the floods of 1915 and 1916 forced southern blacks to look elsewhere for work. These economic problems were coupled with the lure of employment opportunities in the North created by sharp declines in foreign immigration, the labor needs of wartime industry, and the loss of American workers to the battlefields of Europe. Immigration declines were particularly dramatic. Whereas 1,200,000 foreign immigrants entered the United States in 1914, only 110,000 arrived in 1918.[20]

Desperate for labor, many northern industries during World War I sent labor agents to the South to recruit black workers. These recruitment efforts were aided by numerous northern black newspapers and journals that relentlessly promoted job opportunities in northern cities and devoted considerable time and space to the lives and wages of northern blacks compared to their southern counterparts. The most vigorous promoter of northern work opportunities was the *Chicago Defender,* which had become the most widely read and influential black newspaper in the nation. In response, many southern communities banned the sale of the *Chicago Defender* and tightened labor agent restrictions. Moreover, many migrants wrote or returned home for visits and encouraged their friends and families to come North, spreading tales of abundant work and good wages. Following the conclusion of World War I, the northern migration continued, fueled by the postwar industrial boom and restrictions on foreign immigration.[21]

Yet economic factors were not the only ones that accounted for the Great Migration. Many African Americans left the South to escape the region's racial oppression. In letters to the *Chicago Defender,* migrants cited hope for better treatment as a reason for departing as well as the lure of higher wages. As one black Alabamian wrote the *Chicago Defender* during World War I: "I am in the darkness of the south . . . . [P]lease help me to get of this low down country [where] I am counted as no more than a dog." Lynching also increased during World War I in parts of the South, almost doubling between 1917 and 1918 alone.[22]

Some migrants were drawn northward by the promise of better educational opportunities, as southern black schools were grossly underfunded. Both migrants and northern black newspapers cited better schools as a major draw for migration. One Georgia migrant commented: "My children I wished to be educated in a different community than here. Where the school facilities are better and less prejudice [is] shown and in fact where advantages are better for our people in all respect." Studies of the Great Migration show that a very high percentage of migrant children quickly found their way into the public schools. The *Chicago Defender,* with some exaggeration, trumpeted "the splendid unrestricted system of learning in the northern cities," in comparison with southern schools, "where Jim-Crowism is to be the first lesson taught.[23]

Racial integration, however, was not foremost on the minds of southern black migrants. As historian James Grossman has written of the migration to Chicago: "There is little evidence that black southerners coming to Chicago were especially interested in integration per se; most were more concerned about legal protection, political rights, and access to the paths of security or mobility . . . In some aspects of everyday life, many newcomers looked forward to freedom from whites; they evinced little desire to attend integrated churches or spend leisure time with white people."[24]

Impact of the Great Migration on White Hostility toward Blacks

The black migration during World War I and the postwar era dramatically increased racial tensions in the North and accelerated the racial separation that had already begun during the early twentieth century. "It is a gentle conceit of northern people that race prejudice is a vice peculiar to the south," Detroit minister Reinhold Niebuhr observed in 1927. "The tremendous migration of southern Negroes into the industrial centers of the north is rapidly dispelling this illusion." The arrival of southern blacks provoked profound anxiety in many northern whites. Cleveland City Manager W. R. Hopkins announced in 1925 that "I don't know of any problem confronting the city that contains more potential menace than the fact that 40,000 southern Negroes have been dumped into Cleveland within the last few years." White demands for segregation in public accommodations, housing, and education sharply increased during the 1920s. As Harvard Sitkoff has written of the Great Migration: "Some who followed the North Star looking for the Promised Land found hell instead: educational and residential segregation, dilapidated housing milked by white slumlords, discrimination by labor unions and employers, brutality by white policemen, and liquor and narcotics the only means of escape."[25]

Public accommodations discrimination sharply increased in the wake of the Great Migration, as many restaurants, hotels, stores, and theaters employed a variety of tactics to discourage black patronage. As W. E. B. Du Bois noted in 1934, in the early twentieth century "not a single hotel in Boston dared to refuse colored guests," but after the Great Migration, there remained "few Boston hotels where colored people are received." This reversal was not confined to Boston. Du Bois also noted that "[i]n 1910, colored men could be entertained in the best hotels in Cleveland, Detroit and Chicago. Today [in 1934], there is not a single Northern city, except New York, where a Negro can be a guest at a first-class hotel." Black leader George Schuyler made a similar observation in 1937: "Literally thousands of hotels, theaters, tourist camps, restaurants, amusement parks, swimming pools, soda fountains and even some stores either completely bar or jim crow Negroes in hundreds of cities and towns in the 'free' North." Confronted with white hostility, many northern blacks simply gave up. The leading black newspaper in Indianapolis, the *Freeman*, commented: "We have learned to forego some rights that are common, and because we know the price . . . . We have not insisted that hotels should entertain our race, or the theaters, rights that are clearly ours." In fact, blacks would be excluded from most theaters, public hospitals, and public parks in Indianapolis, except on a segregated basis, until after World War II.[26]

Although most northern states had enacted laws during the 1880s prohibiting racial discrimination in public accommodations, those laws were frequently disregarded

Figure 4.1.

Sign in restaurant window, Lancaster, Ohio, 1930s. Reprinted from the Library of Congress, Prints & Photographs Division, FSA/OWI Collection, LC-USF33-6392-M4

during the 1920s and 1930s. Some states, like New Jersey, weakened their nineteenth-century public accommodations statutes in the wake of the migration of southern blacks. Moreover, prosecutors were reluctant to enforce the criminal aspects of public accommodations legislation, as juries frequently refused to convict despite clear violations. Private plaintiffs were dissuaded from filing suit by restrictive court decisions and the fact that successful litigation typically resulted in nominal damages, often not enough to cover court costs.[27]

One of the most striking effects of the Great Migration was a significant increase in northern urban residential segregation. As southern blacks settled in northern cities, they were segregated into certain neighborhoods through a series of private and public tactics. With the exception of Indianapolis, northern cities did not promulgate local ordinances requiring residential segregation, a tactic the Supreme Court declared unconstitutional in 1917, but did so with equal efficacy through racially restrictive covenants and discriminatory real estate practices, zoning regulations, and neighborhood associations. Throughout the North, local real estate agents steered black families away from white neighborhoods. In Cincinnati, for example, the local real estate board during the 1920s instructed its employees that "no agent shall rent or sell property to colored people in an established white section or neighborhood and this inhibition shall be particularly applicable to the hill tops and suburban property." White realtors in Indianapolis refused to show blacks homes in white neighborhoods and used a two-tier pricing structure: "a realistic market price to whites and a ridiculously inflated price to Negroes." Indianapolis newspaper want ads would continue to describe certain property "for colored" until the mid-1960s. In Chicago, the local real estate board took action in 1917 to restrict black migrants to certain blocks in the city, resolving that "each block [in black neighborhoods] be filled solidly and that further expansion ... be confined to contiguous blocks," and that "owners' societies ... [be created] ... in every white block for the purpose of mutual defense." Other cities, like Pittsburgh, followed suit. From 1924 until 1950, realtors throughout the nation subscribed to a national code that provided that "a realtor should never be instrumental in introducing into a neighborhood ... members of any race or nationality, or any individual whose presence will clearly be detrimental to property values in the neighborhood".[28]

In many parts of the North, vigilante violence accompanied black attempts to move into white neighborhoods or their refusal to vacate homes in white neighborhoods. One such incident provoked murder charges against Ossian Sweet, a black doctor in Detroit who confronted a white mob seeking to drive him from his home. Legal scholar John Frank has persuasively argued that the explosion of violence in racially mixed neighborhoods during the 1910s and early 1920s helped persuade courts to uphold racially restrictive covenants.[29]

Some governmental officials also played a role in the preservation of residential segregation. For example, in 1923, the mayor of Johnstown, Pennsylvania, ordered all black southern migrants to leave his town. Moreover, with the onset of federal loan programs in the 1930s, racial discrimination in housing continued. A 1933 report of the Federal Home Owners Loan Corporation stated that the presence of "Russian Jews of lower class, South Italians, Negroes, and Mexicans" caused declining property values and that in these neighborhoods no mortgages should be financed. Federal loans, available under the National Housing Act of 1934, encouraged residential segregation, as the Federal Housing Administration (FHA) rated the presence of blacks in a neighborhood a risk that factored into the availability of mortgages.[30]

The effect of these various public and private acts of discrimination was dramatic. In 1910, only 30 percent of Chicago's African Americans lived in predominantly black neighborhoods; by 1920, a majority did so. In Cleveland, the number of census tracts with no black residents more than doubled between 1910 and 1920, from seventeen to thirty-eight. Racially restrictive covenants in San Francisco caused one black newspaper in that city to announce in 1927: "Residential Segregation is as real in California as in Mississippi. A mob is unnecessary. All that's needed is a neighbor [hood] meeting and agreement in writing not to rent, lease, or sell to blacks, and the Courts will do the rest." Even in Minnesota, neighborhoods embraced racially restrictive covenants during the 1920s despite having a paucity of African Americans.[31]

The Great Migration also triggered increasing violence toward blacks, particularly during and after World War I. Race riots erupted in several northern cities—including East St. Louis, Chicago, Philadelphia, and Syracuse, New York—sparked in part by white—black competition for jobs and housing. In East St. Louis, the hiring of black workers triggered mass destruction in the black community in 1917 by a white mob that left 125 blacks dead and hundreds of others maimed. Some of the worst violence took place in Chicago. Between 1917 and 1921, fifty-eight racially inspired bombings took place there, most directed at the homes of black families in racially mixed neighborhoods. The most significant outbreak in Chicago was the July 1919 riot that took 38 lives and injured more than 500; blacks bore the brunt of the violence. Historian John Hope Franklin has called the last six months of 1919 "the greatest period of interracial strife the nation had ever witnessed." As a result of the violence, white demands for segregation increased. As the *Chicago Tribune* editorialized: "Despite the possible justice of Negro demands, the fact is that the races are not living in harmony.... How long will it be before segregation will be the only means of preventing murders?" [32]

Employer and labor union discrimination against black workers increased in the wake of the Great Migration, particularly in skilled labor positions. White workers opposed hiring black workers, and employers readily acceded to this opposition. A survey by the Cincinnati Chamber of Commerce between 1925 and 1930 found that the most frequent reason employers gave for their failure to hire black workers was that they were "unable or unwilling to mix white and Negro workers." White employers in Minneapolis refused to hire black workers except for certain jobs; as a result, 80 percent of the black men in Minneapolis in 1926 worked as porters, janitors, and night watchmen. White workers in an integrated munitions factory in Chicago during World War I placed a sign in the factory lavatory: "Niggers not allowed to use this toilet." Although the number of blacks employed in skilled and semiskilled work had dramatically increased during World War I, racial discrimination among both northern employers and northern unions sharply curtailed these advances after the conclusion of the war. [33]

Increase in Northern School Segregation in Response to the Migration of Southern Blacks

One important manifestation of this growing racial antagonism was a sharp increase in white insistence on school segregation. Despite state antisegregation laws, school segregation increased in much of the North during the two decades prior to World War I, and then increased even more dramatically following the onset of the Great Migration.

A number of local school boards introduced school segregation between 1897 and 1910 — even in states that expressly prohibited such segregation — including Alton, Illinois (1897), Brooklyn, Illinois (1901), Sheffield, Massachusetts (1904), East Orange, New Jersey (1905), and Oxford, Pennsylvania (1909). Other northern school boards with a tradition of integrated schools fought to preserve racial mixing in the face of intense segregationist pressure. For example, Chicago schools had been desegregated since 1865, but white insistence on school segregation dramatically increased during the early twentieth century in response to the arrival of thousands of African Americans. One black Chicago attorney noted in 1910 of the growth of the city's black population since 1890: "Colored children have appeared in numbers in many schools ... [T]hese things have a tendency to cause whites to resort to jim crow tactics." Chicago whites sought both school board action and a city charter amendment to reverse a half-century history of integrated schools. A leader of the antiblack Hyde Park Improvement Protective Club announced in 1909 that "[i]t is only a question of time when there will be separate schools for Negroes throughout Illinois." Many white students joined the struggle for racial separation. In 1905, a group of white students in Chicago rioted when they were transferred to a predominantly black school, and in 1908 over 150 white students staged a boycott when they were transferred to an integrated school. Moreover, in 1909, when two black children were transferred to a white school, they were beaten by their new classmates. Although black resistance prevented explicit segregation during the first decade of the twentieth century, the Chicago school board did allow white children to transfer out of mixed schools and racially gerrymandered school attendance zones to increase racial cohesion.[34]

During the first decade of the twentieth century, a few state legislatures altered their laws to permit segregation. In 1900, the Kansas state legislature, in response to the murder of a white boy by an African American, enacted legislation permitting school segregation in the high schools of Kansas City. Thereafter, pressure for school segregation in other parts of Kansas increased. In 1906, the superintendent of the public schools of Kansas wrote his counterpart in North Carolina requesting information about North Carolina's school segregation statute: "There is a movement in Kansas looking toward the segregation of the races in the public schools, where the per cent of colored population will warrant the separation . . . . Have you any laws on the subject?" In 1909, the Kansas state legislature, in response to overwhelming demand, enacted special legislation allowing Wichita to segregate its schools, reversing a decision of the Kansas Supreme Court that had declared school segregation in Wichita unlawful. Arizona also enacted legislation in 1909 *permitting school* segregation throughout the state; in 1912, the Arizona legislature *mandated* segregation in all elementary schools and permitted local school officials to decide whether to segregate high schools. Specifically, if an Arizona high school had at least twenty-five black students, the local school board was obliged to hold a referendum on segregated schools if 15 percent of the electorate called for such an election. New Mexico enacted legislation permitting school segregation in 1923. In 1911, the Ohio legislature considered but ultimately declined to enact legislation that would have again permitted school segregation in the Buckeye state, while segregationists in New York sought similar legislation the same year.[35]

In the wake of the Great Migration, school segregation sharply increased throughout the North, even in communities that had long enjoyed a tradition of racially mixed schools. As Kelly Miller of Howard University noted in 1929: "The issue of separate schooling is moving Northward with the rising tide of Negro migration. The color line in public education is vigorously asserting itself across the continent." Much of this increase in segregation took place in the southern portions of those states bordering the South. As a 1922 study of northern race relations aptly noted: "There is . . . along the Southern border of Pennsylvania, Ohio, Indiana, Illinois, and Kansas a semi-legal segregation in the schools in force. At least, it amounts to a tacit understanding, in some of the towns, that the colored children must go to the colored schools, and that they will not be admitted to the schools attended by white children. In fact, in any Northern town where they are proportionately numerous, there is just the same tendency and desire to have them separated from the whites that there is in the South."[36]

Northern school segregation during the post—World War I era took many forms. Although some racial separation was due to the burgeoning residential segregation of northern cities, much of it resulted from specific actions taken by local school officials to preserve racial separation. The most explicit form of school segregation was the establishment of separate schools for black and white children, with pupil assignments conducted on a racial basis. School segregation in New Jersey, for example, already widespread in the state's southern counties by the end of the nineteenth century, substantially increased during the first four decades of the twentieth century as school officials in many communities formally established dual school systems—sometimes by local ordinance—in which school assignments were explicitly based on race rather than geography. A 1925 report found: "[F]rom the university town of Princeton, including the capital city of Trenton, southward to Cape May, every city or town with a considerable Negro population supports the dual educational system, with a building for its white and a building for its Negro pupils of the grammar grades." A few southern counties in New Jersey segregated black students not only at the elementary school level but also at the high school level. A study published in the early 1950s noted striking similarities between segregation in southern New Jersey and the South throughout the first half of the twentieth century: "While most of New Jersey is geographically above the Mason-Dixon line, the history of its public school education, especially at the elementary and junior high school levels, has had more in common with states below than above the line. In the [state's] southern counties both basic policies and prevailing practices have been essentially similar to those of the Southern states."[37]

But this increase in school segregation in New Jersey was not confined to the state's southern counties. During the two decades following World War I, a few northern New Jersey communities, most of which had integrated their schools during the 1870s, reintroduced racially separate schools in response to the increase in black population. A 1939 report to the state legislature found that "in recent years . . . many communities in northern New Jersey have either instituted or plan to institute experiments of their own in separate school facilities." Across the state, the number of separate schools for African-American children increased by 35 percent between 1919 and 1935, and by 1940 there were more segregated schools in New Jersey than at any time since the enactment of the 1881 antisegregation legislation. This increase in school segregation clearly violated New Jersey law. As one lawyer noted, New Jersey engaged in the "theoretical admission of colored children to white schools by terms of legislation and simultaneously actual exclusion by method of administration."[38]

School boards in other northern states also engaged in explicit racial assignments, rejecting the practice of assigning children to school based on geography. Many small towns in eastern Pennsylvania established racially separate schools during the 1910s and 1920s. Chester, for example, which had segregated its elementary schools in 1912, established a separate black junior high school in 1929 and a separate black senior high school in 1934. The Chester school board assigned all of the town's black children to Frederick Douglass High School and all of the white children to Chester High School. School authorities in Lower Oxford maintained a black and a white school across the street from each other, justifying such segregation on the grounds that black children are "not as bright as whites." Some Pennsylvania and New Jersey school districts retained geographic assignments, but nevertheless assigned white children who lived in "black" school districts to the closest white school and black children living in "white" school districts to the closest black school. Philadelphia engaged in this practice after the city experienced a fourfold increase in black population during and after World War I. The Philadelphia school superintendent explained in 1926 that "whenever the colored element was in predominance [at a given school] it was deemed wise to transfer all of the white students and faculty members and install a colored faculty." As a result, by the mid-1920s, almost one-third of Philadelphia's black students attended single-race schools, due in significant measure to the race-conscious assignment policies of the school board.[39]

In some communities, school officials placed black children in a separate building on the grounds of a white school or in separate classrooms in an otherwise racially mixed school. For example, in Gary, Indiana, school officials established racially segregated elementary schools—East Pulaski and West Pulaski—on the same parcel of land, with separate teachers, classrooms, and American flags. The two schools operated on slightly different schedules to reduce racial interaction. In many counties in southern New Jersey, school buildings were divided into white and black sections, with white teachers for white children and black teachers for black children. Some Pennsylvania and New Jersey school districts established racially separate classrooms, with "Union Rooms" for black children of all ages and graded classrooms for whites. Although the Pennsylvania state legislature enacted legislation in 1925 prohibiting racially separate classrooms, the new legislation was frequently ignored.[40]

Several Ohio cities, including Cincinnati, Cleveland, Columbus, and Dayton, also established racially separate classrooms in the wake of the Great Migration. Dayton, for example, established separate classrooms for black children in racially mixed schools in 1912, a practice it had previously used prior to the 1887 antisegregation legislation in Ohio. During World War I, a number of southern black families migrated to Dayton, many of whom settled in the attendance area of the Garfield elementary school, a white school. In 1917, the Dayton school board assigned these newly arrived black students to a poorly heated and maintained frame building behind the Garfield School to keep them separate from the white children educated inside the main building. These black students were crowded into classrooms with more than twice as many pupils as the classrooms in the main building that housed the white children. Even black children at Dayton's racially mixed orphanage were assigned across town to black classes at Garfield, whereas white orphans went to a nearby school, a practice that continued until after the 1954 *Brown* decision.[41]

Cleveland reversed its long-standing commitment to racially integrated schools during the 1920s by assigning black children to racially separate classrooms, prompting a local black newspaper, the *Call and Post,* to comment in 1928: "Daily it becomes more apparent that the virus of southern race prejudice is bearing its malignant fruit in this cosmopolitan city of Cleveland. With amazing rapidity it is spreading through the very arteries of this city—once famous for its liberality to minority groups." The trend towards segregation increased during the 1930s as the Cleveland school board began to assign most of the city's black high school students to Central High School, even those who lived closer to other high schools, and to permit white students who lived near Central High School to transfer to other schools.[42]

Where there were too few black children to justify a racially separate classroom, some teachers insisted on racial separation within the classroom. Prior to the establishment of a separate black senior high school in Chester, Pennsylvania, for example, some teachers required segregated seating. A white teacher in Dayton in the 1920s told a black student that "even though I was a good student I was not to sit in the front of the class because most of the colored children sat in the back." One Arizona school teacher went to an even greater extreme, placing a screen around the desk of a black student to shield him from his white classmates.[43]

In some racially mixed schools, black and white children were segregated during recreational activities. For example, some New Jersey schools, as in Asbury Park, fenced their playgrounds to keep black and white children apart. A Wichita school also designated a specific part of the school playground for black children. Several school districts throughout the North, including districts in New Jersey, New York, Ohio, Illinois, Indiana, and Kansas, excluded black students from high school swimming pools or else forced them to swim on Friday afternoons, after which the pools would be drained. Many northern school districts with racially mixed schools excluded black children from a variety of extracurricular activities such as athletics, the school band, and ROTC, forcing the black community to organize private extracurricular activities for their children. For example, during the early twentieth century, blacks in Portland, Oregon, used churches to stage plays and oratorical contests to provide black children with opportunities denied them in the public schools. Students at high school graduation ceremonies in Montclair, New Jersey, marched in a racially segregated fashion until the NAACP petitioned for an end to the practice in 1925.[44]

Some local school authorities preserved racial separation through racially gerrymandered school district lines accompanied by discriminatory transfer policies that permitted only white students to transfer to a school in another district. The experience in New Rochelle, New York, illustrates this practice. In 1889, school authorities closed New Rochelle's one black school, which dated from the antebellum era, and assigned the town's black children to white schools. Thereafter, black children in New Rochelle attended racially mixed schools. But in 1930, faced with a growing black population, the New Rochelle school board opened a new school, the Webster School, and racially gerrymandered its attendance zone lines so that it would be a predominantly white school, while the nearby Lincoln School would be a predominantly black school. The New Rochelle school board permitted all white children who lived in the Lincoln school district to transfer to the Webster School but denied black children living in the Lincoln district the same right. The effect of these actions was dramatic. Between 1930 and 1933, black enrollment at Lincoln increased from 25 to 75 percent, and by 1949 Lincoln was an all-black school. Finally, in 1949, confronted with the inequities of its transfer policy, the school board ceased to allow transfers, although it did not redraw its racially gerrymandered district lines.[45]

Other school districts also used racial gerrymandering to preserve racial separation. The Columbus Board of Education—which had desegregated its schools and used racially mixed faculties during the 1880s—resegregated many of its schools during the early twentieth century through racially gerrymandered school district lines and the assignment of teachers on a racial basis. In 1909, the Columbus school board established a new elementary school in the middle of a black neighborhood and gerrymandered the school's attendance zone to preserve its character as a black school. As a result, the new school—Champion Elementary—was more than 80 percent black, whereas two other elementary schools, each about three blocks away, were less than 4 percent black. Many African Americans, fearing that the Champion School's placement would lead to school segregation, had petitioned the school board—unsuccessfully—to build the school elsewhere, claiming that "the boundary lines of certain school districts in this city [had already] been drawn as to segregate colored children." During the 1920s, the Columbus school board grew bolder in its segregation efforts, expanding its use of gerrymandered school districts and racially explicit teacher assignments to preserve the racial integrity of the city's schools. In addition, in 1925, the school board established a "portable school" to house black students living in a predominantly white neighborhood in the northern section of the city, rather than assign these children to a nearby white elementary school. A 1931 report from the Ohio director of education to the governor found that 1,269 black children in Columbus attended "special schools for colored children." A 1937 report on the Columbus schools concluded that the problem of black education "seems to be met satisfactorily with separate schools wherever possible." School district lines would remain racially gerrymandered in Columbus until after the 1954 *Brown* decision.[46]

Chicago racially gerrymandered its school district lines as well. Prior to the Great Migration, Chicago school officials had largely resisted school segregation in the face of white pressure. But as the number of blacks living in Chicago sharply increased during and after World War I, pressure for school segregation mounted, as many whites argued that "white children should not be compelled to sit with colored children." In response, school authorities racially gerrymandered school district lines and liberally granted white children transfers from predominantly black schools to which they had been assigned based on residence. Black children were denied such transfer rights. The effect of these practices was dramatic. Whereas in 1916, only one Chicago school—Keith Elementary—was 90 percent black and it enrolled only about eight percent of the city's 4,500 black students, by 1930, 26 of the city's schools were at least 90 percent black and they enrolled about 82 percent of the city's 34,000 black students. These shifting patterns were due in significant measure to residential segregation caused by an array of practices by realtors, mortgage lenders, and local politicians in response to the Great Migration that led to the creation of a rigid, permanent black ghetto in Chicago, but racially gerrymandered district lines also played a role. In 1945, the president of the Chicago NAACP would declare with some exaggeration: "We have segregated schools outright . . . . They are as much segregated as the schools in Savannah, Georgia, or Vicksburg, Mississippi.[47]

Figure 4.2.
Students at Keith Elementary School, Chicago, 1936. National Archives photo, no. 69-N-5442-C (Works Progress Administration photo).

Where racial gerrymandering could not preserve school segregation, some local school boards established "undistricted" attendance zones; white children living in these zones were permitted to attend certain designated white schools, but black children were required to attend a black school. Gary, Indiana, followed this strategy. Other northern school districts deployed undistricted attendance zones but only encouraged, not required, black children in those areas to attend separate black schools. Cincinnati, for example, had eliminated most of its separate black schools after the enactment of antisegregation legislation in 1887, but the school board reestablished several black schools during the first three decades of the twentieth century. In residentially integrated areas of the city, the school board did not utilize geographic attendance zones; rather, the board maintained both white and colored schools. In theory, black children could choose the school they wished to attend, but frequent mistreatment in the white schools caused most to choose one of the colored schools. The Cincinnati school board would continue to exclude several black elementary schools, designated "Separate Schools," from the city's general geographic assignment plan until the early 1950s. By the same token, in the 1920s, the Cincinnati school board introduced a disciplinary policy pursuant to which black children in racially mixed schools who misbehaved were transferred to one of the separate colored schools.[48]

Patterns of racial segregation varied between elementary schools and high schools. In many northern cities, such as Atlantic City, Camden, Trenton, Cincinnati, and Philadelphia, elementary schools were segregated, while high schools were integrated. However, some communities, such as Dayton, Ohio, and Chester, Pennsylvania, maintained segregated elementary schools and high schools. Some northern school districts provided elementary schools for black children but no high schools. Several school districts in southern Illinois, for example, excluded black children from all local high schools, requiring them to travel to segregated high schools in neighboring counties or, more typically, to go without.[49]

In a few instances, black children were excluded from public schools altogether. For example, during the 1920s, as southern blacks moved to Oregon to work in the lumber industry, their children were denied entry into public schools in some communities. In the town of Maxville in eastern Oregon, the public schools barred black children, instead hiring a black woman to teach them in her home during the evenings. Some black children in Maxville traveled to other towns to attend school.[50]

Figure 4.3.
New York City school, 1937. National Archives photo, no. 69-N-9609 (Work Progress Administration photo).

To be sure, in some parts of the North, school segregation was minimal in the wake of the Great Migration. New England experienced the smallest increase in school segregation due in significant measure to the fact that relatively few southern blacks migrated to New England during and after World War I. New Haven, Connecticut, for example, experienced minimal school segregation during the first three decades of the twentieth century; during those years, black students comprised less than 3.5 percent of the New Haven student population. Both Boston and Providence, each of which also received relatively few black migrants during the Great Migration, also retained racially mixed schools. In fact, the black population in Rhode Island increased only slightly during the 1910s and actually *declined* during the 1920s.[51]

Figure 4.4.
New York City school, 1930s. National Archives photo, no. 69-N9597 (Works Progress Administration photo).

Patterns of segregation were also less rigid in New York City even though many blacks did migrate there during and after World War I. In fact, New York City is somewhat unique among northern cities, as it experienced a large black influx but generally declined to engage in deliberate efforts to segregate its schools during the 1910s and 1920s. A 1913 study of black education in New York City revealed that assignment patterns in the city's elementary schools were generally consistent with residential patterns. Another 1913 study found black students present in every school in the city. After World War I, black students in New York City were increasingly concentrated in certain schools due to residential segregation, but the NAACP made few claims of intentional segregation during the 1920s and 1930s and offered the New York City elementary schools as a model for other cities to emulate. Similarly, the biracial Mayor's Commission on

Conditions in Harlem, appointed in 1935, made no mention of school segregation even though by 1934, Harlem had thirteen virtually all-black schools due to residential segregation. Alain Locke, upon reviewing the Mayor's Commission report, commented that "the comparative absence of racial discrimination in the school system is one of the bright features of the report." A 1939 report of the New York State Temporary Commission on the Condition of the Colored Urban Population, created by the state legislature, also found no intentional segregation in New York City's elementary schools, although it did find that high school district lines had been gerrymandered in and around Harlem to preserve racial segregation.[52]

In Indiana, the one northern state that expressly permitted school segregation by local option until the middle of the twentieth century, the number of racially separate schools sharply increased during the 1920s due to a variety of segregationist tactics. Indeed, by the 1930s, most of Indiana's larger cities had partial or complete school segregation, as did several smaller towns and cities, particularly in the southern counties of the state. Moreover, in 1935, the Indiana General Assembly took action in further support of school segregation. In 1907, the state legislature had provided for the closure of any public school with a daily average attendance of fewer than 12 students—a provision that led to integration in a few rural communities. In 1935, however, the legislature provided that that closure provision did not apply to separate black schools and ordered all school districts that had previously closed black schools pursuant to the 1907 statute to reopen them. As a federal judge later characterized the 1935 statute, the state legislature ordered local school authorities "to furnish a separate school building and teacher for the instruction of . . . one Negro child attending primary school rather than permit that child to attend a white school." Despite the gross inefficiency of school segregation in certain areas, many Indiana school authorities retained their separate black schools. During the 1948-9 school year, for example, nine counties in Indiana averaged five or fewer students per grade in their separate black schools.[53]

Indianapolis, though most of its black elementary schoolchildren had always attended racially separate schools, had never segregated its public high schools. In 1922, however, several white groups, including the Indianapolis Chamber of Commerce, petitioned the school board for the establishment of a separate black high school; thereafter, the board agreed to build such a school. The *Indianapolis Recorder*, a black newspaper, bemoaned the board's decision: "The Colored High School is to be a reality. Jim-Crowism is rapidly encroaching the colored citizens of Indianapolis. Color-phobia is rampant. First came segregation in the theatres, department stores, and other public places. Next our own city park. Now . . . the Negroes' only weapon of defense has failed, the ballot. Politicians no longer fear the wrath of the Negro vote."[54]

As racial separation in northern public schools increased in response to the Great Migration, ignorance of the illegality of school segregation under state law remained widespread. One of the leading education texts of the period, Stanford Professor Ellwood Cubberley's *State and County Educational Reorganization*, published in 1914, noted that "[a]ny county or city school-district may also establish separate schools for children of the negro race, when there are enough to make such separate instruction advantageous," advice that ran directly contrary to the antisegregation legislation in most northern states. The same year, Cubberley wrote "an ideal state school code" that noted, again contrary to the law of most northern states, that school officials may set up separate schools for "defective, delinquent, or . . . negro" children. Finally, Cubberley erroneously advised local school districts that they could either provide separate secondary schools for their black students or else contract with a neighboring school district to educate them. Even the United States Bureau of Education displayed ignorance of the nineteenth-century antisegregation legislation. In a 1917 report, the Bureau made the preposterous claim that Pennsylvania and Illinois had "no law governing separation of the races in the public schools"—ignoring the fact that both of those states clearly prohibited school segregation by statute.[55]

Reasons for the Increase in Northern School Segregation

This impetus toward increased school segregation in the early twentieth century had many causes. Central to white insistence on segregation was the influx of southern black children into northern school districts. Indeed, white insistence on school segregation was generally strongest in those cities that received the largest number of southern migrants and generally increased in proportion to the number of black children in the school district. A 1932 study of New Jersey schools, for example, found that when the black population in a given community reached 10 percent, pressure to segregate black children substantially increased.[56]

Many white principals, teachers, and school boards justified school segregation on the grounds that the newly arrived southern migrant children were not equipped to engage in studies alongside white children because of their poor educational backgrounds. In the South, black children had typically attended school for only a few months a year, and the quality of southern black education was vastly inferior to that available in most northern schools. The Chicago Commission on Race Relations concluded in 1922 that "the great majority of the retarded Negro children were from southern states" and that their retardation was due in significant measure to their poor educational backgrounds. A 1926 survey of the Detroit Bureau of Governmental Research also found that most black children who had fallen behind their grade level were migrant children with inferior educational backgrounds.[57]

As a result of their educational deficiencies, many black children were placed in classrooms in which they were considerably older than their peers. These age gaps, coupled with cultural differences, produced socialization problems that adversely affected the attitudes of white school administrators toward the migrant children. Black sociologist Charles Johnson reported in 1932 that when southern black children "come into northern schools . . . the usual problems of overage children develop. Truancy, delinquency and incorrigibility are expressions of this and require special and concerted efforts to correct."[58]

Under the best of circumstances, the assimilation of poorly educated southern black children into northern schools would have required patience and care from teachers, most of whom were white. But many white teachers were neither prepared nor willing to assist these students in making the necessary adjustment to their new school. Instead, the limited academic preparation of the southern migrant children gave way to racist stereotypes about the deficiencies of African Americans. Many white administrators openly urged school segregation, notwithstanding state laws that prohibited such action.

For example, a survey of educational attitudes among New Jersey school superintendents found widespread support for segregation. The superintendent of Trenton schools explained his support in 1927: "The problem of retardation is more serious among colored children than among any other racial group. I am inclined to believe that the further extension of segregation . . . is the only real practical solution." Philadelphia's school superintendent also urged separate schools in the early twentieth century: "[Segregation] has given to the colored child better opportunity to move at its [sic] own rate of progress through the materials of the curriculum, which rate of progress is in some respects different from the rate of progress of other children. "[59]

At the same time, many northern white teachers preferred school segregation. In a 1921 survey in Columbus, Ohio, 115 out of 130 school teachers reported that they favored school segregation. A majority of these teachers stated that black children were "backward" and impeded the progress of white children. Many of these teachers also believed that black children were inherently inferior to white children. When asked about the wisdom of racial mixing, one Columbus high school teacher remarked that "their capacities are not the same, thus one retards the possible progress of the other." Another Columbus school teacher commented that "[t]he very make-up of the races are different, and one race is repulsive to the other. Thus the teacher if she be of the white race cannot and will not give the attention to the negro that he should have."[60]

Other northern educators shared these views. The assistant principal of a predominantly black school in Buffalo commented that "other children should not be mixed-up with the colored as their standard of morals is so much lower." In Gary, Indiana, most of the white teachers in a racially integrated school (but with segregated classrooms) petitioned their principal in 1918 to remove the black children from their school: "The promiscuous association of the white and colored pupils is a terrible thing. It should not be allowed, particularly in a school with a large number of foreign pupils. They will soon lose sight of the color line." The Gary teachers also complained that black children posed discipline problems due to their poor educational backgrounds and the age disparity between many black and white children.[61]

Many white education scholars argued that black children would fare better in separate schools under the tutelage of black teachers.[62] Louis A. Pechstein, dean of the University of Cincinnati School of Education and a prominent northern white educator, wrote in 1929:

"While all would prefer to have democracy in education, this goal has not been reached and is not likely to be reached in the northern cities studied, since the separation of the races in all walks of life is operating and seems likely to continue.... [T]he ideal separate public school for negroes in northern cities will, under a staff of well-trained negro teachers, function in providing a closer parent-pupil-teacher relation as well as a clearer insight into the treatment of mental deficiency, social maladjustments, special disabilities, and irregularities in behavior."[63]

Many northern school officials were blatantly racist in their resistance to pupil integration, arguing that black children were inherently inferior and not fit to associate with white children. A white principal in Atlantic City, New Jersey, explained his support for school segregation: "I believe in segregation.... [Black children] are like little animals. There is no civilization in their homes. They shouldn't hold up white children who have had these things for centuries. They are not as clean. They are careless about their bodies. Why should we contaminate our race?" Another white school principal in Toms River, New Jersey, dismissed an objection by black parents to the midyear removal of thirty black students from their racially mixed school to a poorly equipped church: "I've just returned from a trip to Texas, and, believe me, they know how to treat colored people down there.... Why, if these people had done in Texas what they've done here, or had done it in any of the Southern states, they'd have been lynched. They would have gone to whatever school the whites told them to and be mighty glad to have the chance." The president of the Westhampton Township, New Jersey, Board of Education announced in 1939 that "[o]ur plan is to have a separate school for colored children from the first grade through high school. The reason is because the colored children are objectionable." Not surprisingly, many black leaders called New Jersey the "Mississippi of the north."[64]

Such racist attitudes were prevalent among school administrators in other parts of the North as well. In Madison, Indiana, one student recalled the white school superintendent visiting his black school: "[He talked] to us like we were just something that came in from darkest Africa or somewhere. He told us that we were worthless, dumb, that we couldn't learn anything, that we would never learn. I will never forget it." Upon hearing a white student comment that "if Negroes should ever try to enroll in our school, we'll get machine guns and see that they leave as quick as they came," a white principal in Gary replied: "I wouldn't blame them either, might even help them."[65]

Many white parents also opposed school integration. When a teacher in Flushing, New York, in 1911 required a white girl to dance with a black boy, provoking taunts from her white classmates that she was a "nigger's partner," white parents demanded a return to separate schools. A 1921 study in Columbus, Ohio, found that a majority of white parents surveyed objected to racially mixed schools on the grounds that black children were backward and that their presence in the classroom retarded white children in their school work. Such parental attitudes were widespread. One white man in Gary urged school segregation: "After all, they came from Africa quite recently, and as slaves at that.

They have no tradition of civilization and education as we have . . . . They are still dirty, lazy, loud and not too pleasant to have living nearby. "[66]

Many white students also expressed strong opposition to the presence of black children in their classrooms. White high school students in Cincinnati engaged in an unsuccessful strike to exclude their black classmates in 1916. In 1919, white students in Gallipolis, Ohio, conducted a boycott to protest a court decision that black children could not be excluded from their school. White high school students in Darby, Pennsylvania, unsuccessfully protested the announcement of a black student as their valedictorian in 1924 and threatened to hold separate commencement exercises. White students in Gary engaged in a massive walkout in 1927 when a few black students were assigned to their school; eventually, school authorities did reassign most of the black students to another school. To be sure, some northern white students did oppose racial segregation, particularly when the numbers of black children were quite small. In 1929, more than 400 white students in Dorchester, Massachusetts, refused to hold their high school prom at a hotel that announced that it would exclude the school's sole black student.[67]

Figure 4.5.

Ku Klux Klan cross burning, Indianapolis, 1920s. Reprinted with permission of the Indiana Historical Society, Indianapolis Recorder Collection, PO 303, Box 81, Folder 14.

Moreover, the Ku Klux Klan experienced a striking resurgence throughout much of the North and West during the 1920s and 1930s that led to increased pressure for school segregation. In many northern communities, newly energized Klan groups pressured school officials to establish or maintain segregated schools. The Grand Dragon of the Indiana Klan urged support in 1924 for a variety of positions including "White American supremacy and the segregating of Negroes, especially in schools." Klan support contributed to the establishment of the first segregated high school in Indianapolis. In

Ohio, the Klan waged a public campaign for both school segregation and a ban on inter-racial marriage throughout the 1920s and early 1930s. George McCord, superintendent of the Springfield, Ohio, schools during that city's reestablishment of segregated schools during the early 1920s, along with two members of the local school board, were Klan members. The Columbus, New Jersey, school superintendent during the 1920s was also a local Klan leader. In 1922, the rare hiring of a black teacher to teach white children in Hackensack, New Jersey, prompted a Ku Klux Klan parade in opposition and a barrage of threats. Similarly, in 1936, the Klan threatened to intervene in a school segregation dispute in East Orange, New Jersey. The Oregon Klan used death threats to drive the only black resident out of Oregon City and threatened blacks who moved into white neighborhoods in Portland.[68]

At the same time, many educational theorists of the 1920s urged a "scientific basis for educational policy" that included ability groupings, intelligence tests, and a differentiated curriculum for slower learners. White educators used intelligence testing, which became increasingly popular during the 1910s, to support their notions of the intellectual inferi-ority of blacks and to justify school segregation. Indeed, African Americans migrated north in large numbers at a time when prevailing social science described blacks as a "social problem" and many educational researchers made scientific claims of black intel-lectual inferiority. For example, Lewis Terman, a prominent professor of psychology at Stanford and an important figure in the eugenics movement, concluded in an influential 1916 book, *The Measurement of Intelligence,* that low levels of intelligence were "very, very common among Spanish—Indian and Mexican families of the Southwest and also in-herent negroes" and that these deficiencies were "racial, or at least inherent in the family stocks from which they come." Terman also believed that intelligence tests could be used to forecast a child's later station in life, which would "be of great value . . . in planning the differentiated curriculum here recommended."[69]

The wartime intelligence tests given to Army recruits provided further fodder for those who believed in the intellectual inferiority of black children, as the scores of white soldiers were, on average, higher than the scores of black soldiers. Many white psychol-ogists concluded that the lower test scores of certain racial and ethnic group members were due to their inherent inferiority. For example, University of Oregon psychologist Kimball Young, a protege of Lewis Terman, concluded that the poorer test results of Latin American and southern European children were due to a "considerable negroid strain" in their population and that "amalgamation of inferior with average and superior" groups must be avoided. Schools were encouraged to separate children accordingly.[70]

Black scholars attacked this reliance on intelligence testing to justify school segrega-tion. *Opportunity,* the journal of the National Urban League, emerged as a leading voice of black scholars during the 1920s, including Horace Mann Bond, E. Franklin Frazier, How-ard H. Long, Ira de A. Reid, Alain Locke, Joseph St. Clair Price, and Charles Johnson, the last of whom served as the publication's editor from 1925 until 1928. *Opportunity* published a number of articles attacking the use of intelligence testing to suggest that black children were intellectually inferior. Johnson published a major critique of the Army intelligence testing in 1923, arguing that the tests did not support a theory of inherent black inferiority, but rather demonstrated that blacks had had poorer educational opportunities. Johnson noted that black recruits from northern states, on average, scored significantly higher than did white recruits from southern states due to better educational opportunities in northern schools. In another article in *Opportunity,* Long concluded that "extreme advocates of race superiority who are also devotees of mental tests" would "be put to their wit's end" in trying to harmonize their point of view with "the state of affairs revealed by the army tests."[71]

In fact, in some northern states, such as Ohio, black recruits scored on average higher than white recruits from almost every southern state. As one contemporary noted sarcastically: "A [white] southerner can still boast of being above a 'n—r,' as long as he is certain that the latter is not a New York or Ohio Negro." Black educator Horace Mann Bond conducted a study of the Army intelligence tests, correlating the test results with various educational data such as teachers' salaries, state funding, length of the school term, and school attendance. Bond concluded: "the indisputable truth [is] that Alpha [the Army test] measures environment, and not native and inherent capacity. Instead of furnishing the material for racial propagandists and agitators, it should show the sad deficiency of opportunity which is the lot of every child, white or black, whose misfortune it is to be born and reared in a community backward and reactionary in cultural and educational avenues of expression."[72]

Other contemporary data supported the view that educational success was influenced significantly by educational opportunity. A study of Chicago schoolchildren in 1920 found "relatively little difference between the reading accomplishments of . . . [Chicago-born] colored pupils and white pupils who have had the advantages of the same method of instruction and environment." This same report, however, found that the reading scores of southern black migrant children were considerably lower than those of both whites and blacks born in Chicago. Subsequent tests would also show the effect of cultural factors such as educational opportunities and parents' vocation on pupils' achievement test scores.[73]

Some white psychologists rejected the notion that differing educational opportunities accounted for the differences between northern and southern black intelligence scores. When confronted with the sharp variations in test results between southern and northern blacks, Princeton's Carl Brigham in his 1922 analysis of the World War I Army intelligence test data, *A Study of American Intelligence,* claimed, with no apparent support, that the higher scores of northern blacks were due in part to their "admixture of white blood" and that "the more intelligent negro" had migrated north. Brigham dismissed the notion that the dramatic differences in educational opportunities between North and South could fully explain the test score differences.[74]

But many other psychologists during the 1920s and 1930s challenged this notion of black inferiority. In fact, during this period, social scientists increasingly argued that culture and environment were largely responsible for observable differences between social groups. Sociologists Franz Boas, E. Franklin Frazier, Robert Park, and Edward Reuter would be particularly influential in their assault on widely held assumptions that the poor social outcomes of many blacks were due to innate inferiority. For example, in 1927, Reuter, a University of Iowa sociologist, published a book, *The American Race Problem,* in which he concluded that the intelligence test score gap was due not to "any innate intellectual difference" between whites and blacks but to "a difference in education and in educational opportunity."[75]

Moreover, during the 1930s, Columbia University psychologist Otto Klineberg found that blacks who migrated north were no more intelligent than those who remained behind, but that their length of residence in the North did positively influence their test scores—confirming the positive impact of superior northern education. Klineberg's *Race Differences,* published in 1935, found no compelling evidence of inherent race differences and concluded that social and cultural environment accounted for test scores differences. In particular, Klineberg, who administered intelligence test scores to more than 3,000 Harlem blacks, found that the longer southern-born black children remained in the North, the higher their intelligence scores were. Klineberg would later offer testimony in one of the cases that comprised *Brown v. Board of Education* that blacks had the same learning abilities as whites. Other studies supported Klineberg's conclusions. For example, studies of children in Los Angeles during the early 1930s found that black students had slightly higher IQs than white students; contemporaneous studies in New York City found the test scores of the two racial groups to be roughly equivalent.[76]

At the same time that many northern white educators insisted on separate schooling for African Americans, assimilation of white immigrant children remained a central imperative of contemporary educational theory. Though many white immigrant children came from poor backgrounds, experienced dismal living conditions, and spoke no English, white administrators and teachers were generally confident in the ability of the public school to assimilate them. They deplored the isolation of white ethnic groups in their own neighborhoods and communities and urged assimilation into the American mainstream. As one New York educator noted: "In a commonwealth such as the United States social inequalities are largely the result of difference in up-bringing, and to this extent the problem of assimilation is one of *education* in the broadest sense of the word. In all progressive communities the school is recognized as the chief instrument of socialization and civilization." Although this assimilationist perspective played a central role in urban educational theory in the early twentieth century, in many northern communities it did not include the black southern migrant.[77]

Curricular Variations for White and Black Children

In addition to school segregation, many northern white school authorities during the first four decades of the twentieth century urged separate "tracks" for black (and, in some instances, certain immigrant) children with different curricula on the grounds that they were intellectually ill-equipped to engage in rigorous academic study. Proponents of separate tracks also argued that the reality of employment discrimination rendered certain educational pursuits superfluous for black children. This sorting out of students into separate tracks, an early twentieth-century educational innovation, frequently placed black students in the lowest curricular levels. In many school districts, such as that of Buffalo, psychological and intelligence tests were used during and after World War I for the purpose of placing certain students—typically black children who had recently migrated from the South—in dead-end special classes or schools that emphasized low-skill training, such as broom- and rug-making. Black girls in Buffalo were frequently placed in the Domestic Arts Curriculum, which the director described in 1926: "The girls, most of them Negro and many of them strangers to our gates, are divided into small working groups . . . . The actual sewing is but a medium for putting over much necessary instruction in hygiene of person and clothing and worthy home membership." Another school administrator described these special programs as designed to teach children "habits of industry, accuracy, promptness, loyalty to superiors, obedience, courtesy, patience, respect for the rights of others and care of equipment." Preparing black children to assume a particular social and economic role in society emerged as an important educational goal in many northern school districts during the 1920s. Many immigrant children from southern and eastern Europe also landed in these separate tracks.[78]

Many of these vocational schools tended to be in dismal condition. Buffalo's vocational school for black children was housed in a building that had been closed in 1918 due to "intolerable conditions." A 1931 United States Office of Education survey of the Buffalo schools found in the city's "development" school "loose and broken boards on landings, dark corners with no means of lighting and an old, inefficient boiler system. Loose plaster threatened the safety of children and the lavatory arrangements were totally unsanitary and unworthy of any modern school system."[79]

Other northern cities followed similar patterns. In Cleveland, school administrators reduced elective courses such as foreign languages in black schools during the 1920s and increased vocational courses such as cooking, sewing, and manual shop work. A 1933 study found that in the predominantly black Central High School in Cleveland, the majority of students studied no math, and home economics courses placed primary emphasis on laundry procedures. In Providence, Rhode Island, the percentage of black students at the city's Technical High School, which provided basic vocational training, sharply increased between 1915 and 1925. As historian Joel Perlmann has noted, "by 1925, when the Tech program had become clearly identified as the less academically elite and less socially elite program, and the more likely to prepare students for manual work, black males were concentrated there." Black girls were also concentrated in the Tech program, where they were taught cooking and sewing rather than typing and stenography.[80]

By the same token, black children were frequently excluded from those technical schools that provided training for skilled labor positions. Such exclusions were justified in part on the grounds that skilled labor jobs would not be available to black workers. Buffalo was one such city. Members of the Buffalo Board of Education concluded that

vocational education in skilled trades made no sense for black students because no employer would hire them. Accordingly, the Buffalo Technical High School, which offered
training in skilled trades and which was located across the street from a black school, had
only 10 black students out of 1,400 in 1923. During the 1930s, black students in Buffalo
were not allowed to attend classes in aircraft construction because the Curtiss-Wright
and Bell Aircraft Corporations publicly announced that they did not employ black
workers. The Buffalo Urban League, noting the discrimination among Buffalo's labor
unions, reported in 1939: "The complete absence of Negroes in the vocational schools
was striking. Vocational instruction, undoubtedly, holds the greatest opportunity for
the minority race in the community to improve their social position." In Cleveland, the
school board operated a trade school to train the city's youth for skilled labor positions.
Local unions, however, controlled admission to the program, which led to the exclusion
of most black children from the school. This racial discrimination continued until at least
the mid-1950s; in 1956, the local school board finally adopted a policy of nondiscrimina-
tion for the trade school.[81]

Blacks confronted barriers to vocational training for skilled labor positions in New
York City as well. The Mayor's Commission on conditions in Harlem found in its 1936
report extensive channeling of black students into low-skill vocational courses, such as
domestic science, while discouraging enrollment in academic courses of high skill vocational courses. The Mayor's commission explained: "These [school] advisers, often
reflecting the traditional belief concerning the capacity of the Negro for purely academic
pursuits, direct these girls from taking the commercial courses on the ground that opportunities are not open to Negro girls in the commercial field." In 1933, a counselor at the
Girls' High School in Brooklyn discouraged a black girl from taking courses that would
prepare her to study medicine, stating erroneously that "they weren't allowing Negroes
to study medicine." The Mayor's Commission found that school authorities placed many
black girls in the "dumping ground" of the Harlem annex to the Straubmuller Textile
High School, where there were no facilities for training in meaningful work, and excluded
black boys from "real vocational training" at the Manhattan Trade School for Boys. The
Commission blamed this exclusion in part "on the principals who make the selection and
partly on the American Federation of Labor's policies in regard to the Negro in certain
trades" The 1939 report of the New York State Temporary Commission on the Condition
of the Colored Urban Population concluded that school officials, encouraged by trade
union discrimination, shunted black students into courses with limited vocational opportunities. As on city official conceded: "Let's not mince words; let's be practical about
this matter; the Negro is not employed in certain trades, so why permit him to waste his
time taking such courses" The Mayor's Commission indicted the policy as "narrow in
outlook and vicious in consequence. It is the completion of a vicious cycle in that Negroes
cannot find jobs without training and they are refused training because they might not
be able to find the jobs."[82]

Blacks understood the effects of these exclusions. An investigator in New York reported that the exclusion of black children from skilled vocational training programs "was sapping the ambition of colored boys and girls, and that they were not making the effort put out by their parents and grandparents to secure an education." A 1940 study of black high school graduates found that the more education black persons received, the more job dissatisfaction they experienced because so many higher-level jobs were foreclosed to blacks.[83]

African Americans had made substantial strides toward full inclusion in the public education systems of the North during the late nineteenth century, but the migration of hundreds of thousands of southern blacks into northern cities during the early twentieth century provoked renewed white insistence on racial separation in much of the North. Stung by this growing web of racial separation, the northern black community divided on the appropriate response. The 1920s and 1930s would bring the greatest turmoil around the issue of northern school segregation since Reconstruction.

Endnotes

1   Quoted in Duncan, *The Changing Race Relationship*, pp. 38–9.

2   For the *New York Times* quote, see "Race in Education," *New York Times*, Jan. 16, 1890, p. 4; for the *New York Commercial* quote, see "Jim Crow School in New Jersey," *Raleigh Daily News and Observer*, Feb. 18, 1906, p. 4; for the Low quote, see Fairclough, *Teaching Equality*, p. 21; for the Bailey quote, see Woodward, *The Strange Career of Jim Crow*, p. 113.

3   For population data, see U.S. Bureau of Census, 1890, 1900, 1910; Diner, *A Very Different Age*, p. 131; Department of Interior, Bureau of Education, *Negro Education*, pp. 677–89. For the Du Bois quote, see Meier and Rudwick, *From Plantation to Ghetto*, p. 215

4   Mohraz, *The Separate Problem*, pp. 3–4.

5   For the rise of racist ideology, see Spear, *Black Chicago*, p. 8; Hatfield, "The Impact of the New Deal," p. 20; Woodward, *The Strange Career of Jim Crow*, p. 70; Fishel, "The North and the Negro," p. 370; Baker, *From Savage to Negro*, p. 3. For the Starr quotes, see Starr, "The Degeneracy of the American Negro," pp. 17–18. For the Hoffman quote, see Hoffman, *Race Traits and Tendencies*, pp. 310, 312.

6   Partridge, *Genetic Philosophy of Education*, pp. 378, 379–80.

7   For immigration fears, see Klarman, *From Crow to Civil Rights*, p. 12. For dilution of Anglo-Saxon stock, see Walker, "Restriction of Immigration," pp. 828–9 (arguing in the *Atlantic Monthly* that these new European immigrants, "degraded below our utmost conceptions" and "representing the worst failures in the struggle for existence," posed "great danger to the health and life of the nation"). For the reaction to *Plessy*, see Lofgren, *The Plessy Case*, pp. 196–7.

8   For lynchings, see, for example, "An Illinois Lynching," *Cleveland Gazette*, June 13, 1903, p. 1; for the Georgia governor, see Thornbrough, *The Negro in Indiana*, pp. 179-80. For race riots, see Franklin, *From Slavery to Freedom*, pp. 443-4; Woodward, *Origins of the New South*,

p. 351; Bigham, *Towns and Villages,* pp. 234-5. For the Walling and Vardaman quotes, see Walling, "The Race War in the North," p. 534.

9   For Cleveland segregation, see Washington, "The Black Struggle for Desegregated Quality Education," p. 79; Moore, "The Limits of Black Power," p. 13; "Euclid Ave. Store Tries Out Segregation," *Cleveland Advocate,* Sept. 25, 1920, p. 4; for interracial marriage bans, see Taylor, *In Search of the Racial Frontier,* p. 212; Moore, *Leading the Race,* p. 206.

10 For the black ghetto quote, see Kusmer, *A Ghetto Takes Shape,* p. 35; for Cleveland segregation, see Moore, "The Limits of Black Power," p. 12; Mosey, "Testing, Tracking, and Curriculum," pp. 17-18.

11 Spear, *Black Chicago,* pp. 21-3.

12 For exclusion of blacks from certain communities, see Thornbrough, "Segregation in Indiana," p. 596; Franklin, *From Slavery to Freedom,* p. 443; for the quote, see Quillin, *The Color Line in Ohio,* p. 160.

13 For Cleveland, see Moore, "The Limits of Black Power," p. 13; for Gary, see Betten and Mohl, "The Evolution of Racism," p. 53 (quote, p. 54).

14 Licht, *Getting Work,* p. 48.

15 Trotter, *Black Milwaukee,* pp. 13–14; Spear, *Black Chicago,* p. 36 (quote).

16 Waite, "Permission to Remain among Us," pp. 3–4, 38–9.

17 For a discussion of the increasing segregationist sentiment at Oberlin, see Waite, "Permission to Remain among Us," pp. 86-98, 117-18, 132-5. For quotes, see ibid., pp. 121, 126, 128, 139, 142. See also letter from William Pickens to Frances J. Hosford, May 1, 1919, NAACP Papers, Box I-C-271 (efforts to exclude black students from Oberlin dormitories).

18 For demographic changes, see Trotter, *River Jordan,* p. 95; Hardy, "Race and Opportunity," p. v; Anyon, *Ghetto Schooling,* p. 61; Meier and Rudwick, *From Plantation to Ghetto,* p. 213. Between 1910 and 1940, approximately 1.8 million blacks left the South for the North in pursuit of better jobs. McAdam, *Political Process and the Development of Black Insurgency,* p. 80

19 U.S. Bureau of Census, 1910, 1920, 1930; Spear, *Black Chicago,* p. 139; Mosey, "Testing, Tracking, and Curriculum," p. 13; Hine, "Black Migration to the Urban Midwest, p. 242; Robisch, "Educational Segregation," p. 24.

20 Phillips, *AlabamaNorth,* p. 43 (quote); Waller, "Holding Back the Dawn," p. 127; Spear, *Black Chicago,* p. 131.

21 Buni, *Robert L. Vann,* p. 72; Barnett, "The Role of the Press," p. 479; Phillips, *AlabamaNorth,* p. 46; Spear, *Black Chicago,* pp. 184–5; Grossman, "Blowing the Trumpet," pp. 90-6; Diner, *A Very Different Age,* p. 153; Miller, "The Black Migration to Philadelphia," p. 316

22 For the letter to the *Chicago Defender,* see Fultz, "'Agitate Then, Brother,'" p. 24; for the increase in lynchings, see Phillips, *AlabamaNorth,* pp. 44-5.

23 For the importance of schools to migrants, see Waller, "Holding Back the Dawn," pp. 137, 145; Miller, "The Black Migration to Philadelphia," p. 346. For the quote from a Georgia migrant, see Marks, *Farewell—We're Good and Gone,* p. 77; for the quote from the *Chicago Defender,* see Homel, "The Politics of Public Education," p. 179.

24 Grossman, *Land of Hope,* p. 161.

25 For the Niebuhr quote, see Niebuhr, "Race Prejudice in the North," p. 583; for the Hopkins quote, see "Hopkins, Schrembs and Jones," *Cleveland Gazette*, Jan. 31, 1925, p. 2; for the Sitkoff quote, see Sitkoff, *The Struggle for Black Equality*, p. 8.

26 For the first Du Bois quote, see Du Bois, "William Monroe Trotter," *The Crisis* (May 1934), p. 134; for the second quote, see Du Bois, "Postscript," *The Crisis* (Apr. 1934), pp. 115–17; for the Schuyler quote, see Schuyler, "Do We Really Want Equality?" p. 103; for the quote from the *Freeman*, see Thornbrough, "Segregation in Indiana," p. 597. For exclusion of Indianapolis blacks, see *United States v. Board of Commissioners*, 332 F. Supp. 655, 661 (S.D. Ind. 1971).

27 For New Jersey, see Price, *Freedom Not Far Distant*, p. 142; for other limitations of these statutes, see Spear, *Black Chicago*, pp. 41–3, 207; Russell H. Davis, "Civil Rights in Cleveland 1912 through 1961," p. 15 (1973), Russell Howard Davis Papers, Container 9; for restrictive court decisions, see, for example, *Chocos v. Burden*, 74 Ind. App. 242 (1920), and *Harvey v. Sissle*, 53 Ohio App. 405 (1936).

28 For the Supreme Court decision, see *Buchanan v. Warley*, 245 U.S. 60 (1917); for other residential segregation tactics, see Trotter, *Black Milwaukee*, p. 233. For the Cincinnati quote, see Trotter, *River Jordan*, p. 106; for the Indianapolis discussion, see *United States v. Board of Commissioners*, 332 F. Supp. 655, 662–3 (S.D. Ind. 1971); for the Chicago discussion, see Mosey, "Testing, Tracking, and Curriculum," p. 16; *The Chicago Real Estate Board Bulletin*, Apr. 25, 1917, pp. 315–17; for Pittsburgh, see Buni, *Robert L. Vann*, p. 62; for the realtor code quote, see Lipsitz, *The Possessive Investment in Whiteness*, pp. 25–6.

29 For vigilante violence, see "In Henry Sweet Trial," *Cleveland Gazette*, May 15, 1926, p. 1; "Three Telling Victories," *Cleveland Gazette*, June 13, 1925, p. 1; *Cleveland Gazette*, Feb. 20, 1926, p. 2; Meyer, *As Long as They Don't Move Next Door*, pp. 38–45. See also Frank, "Can the Courts Erase the Color Line?" p. 309 ("the cases of the 1920's appearing to condone restrictive covenants were a direct retreat because of the racial violence which shortly preceded them").

30 For Johnstown, see *Cleveland Gazette*, Sept. 29, 1923, p. 2; for the 1933 report, see Anyon, *Ghetto Schooling*, pp. 62-3.

31 For Chicago, see Spear, *Black Chicago*, p. 17; for Cleveland, see Reid, "Race, Class, Gender and the Teaching Profession," p. 39; for the 1927 quote, see Taylor, *In Search of the Racial Frontier*, p. 236; for Minnesota, see Delton, "Forging of a Northern Strategy," p. 118.

32 For East St. Louis, see Baker, *From Savage to Negro*, p. 138; for Chicago, see Spear, *Black Chicago*, pp. 211-16; for the Franklin quote, see Franklin, *From Slavery to Freedom*, p. 480; for the *Chicago Tribune* quote, see Spear, *Black Chicago*, p. 217.

33 For the Cincinnati quote, see Trotter, *River Jordan*, pp. 101-2; for Minneapolis, see Delton, "Forging of a Northern Strategy," pp. 120-2; for the Chicago quote, see 'Judge John Richardson Gives Jim Crow' Decision," *Ohio State Monitor*, Sept. 14, 1918, p. 4; for union discrimination, see Trotter, *Black Milwaukee*, pp. 46-7.

34 For the increase in school segregation, see Meier and Rudwick, "Early Boycotts of Segregated Schools: The Alton, Illinois, Case"; Meier and Rudwick, "Early Boycotts of Segregated Schools: The East Orange, New Jersey, Experience"; Cha-Jua, *America's First Black Town*, p. 135; "Arson Follows Race War," *New York Times*, Jan. 1, 1904, p. 7; "Bay State Jim Crow' School," *New York Times*, Jan 6, 1904, p. 1; "Negroes Win School Fight," *New York Times*,

Feb. 12, 1906, p. 2. For the Chicago attorney quote, see Spear, *Black Chicago*, p. 48; for the Hyde Park quote, see Mohraz, *The Separate Problem*, p. 100; for school riots in Chicago, see Spear, *Black Chicago*, pp. 44-5; for Chicago school board policies, see Mohraz, *The Separate Problem*, pp. 98-100; Spear, *Black Chicago*, pp. 204-5.

35 For Kansas legislation, see Duncan, "The Changing Race Relationship," p. 37; for the quote, see "Segregation of Races: Kansas Superintendent of Schools Wants Information," *Raleigh Daily News and Observer*, Aug. 24, 1906, p. 5; for 1909 legislation reversing *Rowles v. Board of Education*, 76 Kan. 361 (1907), see Van Meeter, "Black Resistance to Segregation," pp. 73-4, 77; for Arizona and New Mexico statutes, see Murray, *States' Laws on Race and Color*, pp. 35-6, 290. For proposed Ohio legislation, see Montgomery, "Racial History of the Cincinnati and Suburban Schools," p. 95 (1983), Cincinnati Historical Society; for New York, see "To Demand Separate Schools for Negroes," *New York Times*, Jan. 18, 1911, p. 3.

36 For the Miller quote, see Miller, "Is the Color Line Crumbling?," p. 284; for the 1922 study, see Duncan, "Changing Race Relationship," p. 37.

37 For the 1925 study, see Granger, "Race Relations and the School System," p. 327. For other sources on the increase of segregation in New Jersey, see Crocco, Munro, and Weiler, *Pedagogies of Resistance*, p. 67; Payne, "Negroes in the Public Elementary Schools," p. 227; Weinberg, *A Chance to Learn*, p. 75; Mumford, "Double V in New Jersey," p. 25. For the 1950s study, see Williams and Ryan, *Schools in Transition*, p. 121.

38 For the increase in New Jersey segregation, see Wright, *The Education of Negroes*, pp. 185, 194; Oak and Oak, "The Development of Separate Education in New Jersey, p. 110; Wright, "Racial Integration in the Public Schools," p. 282. For the 1939 report, see *Report of the New Jersey State Temporary Commission*, p. 41. For the lawyer quote, see Satterthwait, "The Color-Line in New Jersey," p. 395.

39 For segregation in eastern Pennsylvania, including Carlisle, Chester, Coatesville, Frankford, Germantown, Lansdown, Lower Oxford, Sharon Hill, Swarthmore, West Chester, and York, see "World War II Brought Change in Jim Crow School Pattern," *York Gazette and Daily*, July 1,1954, NAACP Papers, Box II-A-228; Letter from S. B. Randolph to National Office of the NAACP, July 1944, NAACP Papers, Box II-B-146; Duncan, "The Changing Race Relationship," pp. 39–40; Hatfield, "The Impact of the New Deal," pp. 205–6; Kennedy, *The Negro Peasant Turns Cityward*, p. 194. For Chester, see "Chester Creates First Jim Crow High School in State," *Philadelphia Tribune*, Feb. 22, 1934, p. 1; Mohraz, *The Separate Problem*, p. 92; *Murray v. School District of the City of Chester*, Bill of Complaint, May 29, 1934, Arthur Spingarn Papers, Box 33. For Lower Oxford, see "Say Negroes 'Not Bright,'" *Houston Informer*, July 31, 1948, NAACP Papers, Box II-B-146; for assignment policies, see Kennedy, *The Negro Peasant Turns Cityward*, p. 194; Pennsylvania Department of Public Welfare, "Negro Survey of Pennsylvania," p. 58; Henri, *Black Migration*, p. 181; Mosey, "Testing, Tracking, and Curriculum," pp. 13–14; " Annual Report of the Urban Colored Population Commission, State of New Jersey" (1945), Lett Papers. For the school superintendent quote, sec Franklin, *The Education of Black Philadelphia*, p. 82. For Philadelphia patterns, see Franklin, *The Education of Black Philadelphia*, p. 66; Licht, *Getting Work*, p. 84; Daniels, "Schools," pp. 178–82; "How Separate Schools Menace!" *Cleveland Gazette*, July 21, 1928, p. 1.

40 For separate buildings and classrooms, see New Jersey Conference of Social Work, *The Negro in New Jersey*, p. 37; Granger, "Race Relations and the School System," p. 329; Devore, "The Education of Blacks in New Jersey," pp. 101–2, 144–5; Johnson, *The Negro in American Civilization*, pp. 268-9; *Report of the New Jersey State Temporary Commission*, P. 40; Henri,

Black Migration, p. 181; Tyack, *The One Best System,* p. 124; Pennsylvania Department of Public Welfare, "Negro Survey of Pennsylvania," pp. 58-9; Kennedy, *The Negro Peasant Turns Cityward,* pp. 193–5. For Gary schools, see Tipton, *Community in Crisis,* p. 21; Millender, *Yesterday in Gary,* p. 57; for fenced playgrounds, see Payne, "Negroes in the Public Elementary Schools of the North," p. 227; for failed legislation banning separate classrooms, see Letter from Theodore O. Spaulding to Roy Wilkins, Mar. 25, 1940; Letter from W. M. Gilmore to Constance Baker Motley, Feb. 22, 1950, NAACP Papers, Box II-B-146; Untitled and undated article on Segregation in Northern Schools, NAACP Papers, Box II-B-137.

41   For racially separate classrooms in Ohio, see "'Jim Crow' School Rooms," *Cleveland Gazette,* May 22, 1937, p. 1; "Is the Ohio Supreme Court K.K.K.?" *Cleveland Gazette,* Apr. 4, 1925, p. 1; Porter, "The Problem of Negro Education," p. 124. For Dayton, see *Brinkman v. Gilligan,* 583 F.2d 243, 249, n.19 (6th Cir. 1978); *Board of Education v. State ex rel. Reese, 114* Ohio St. 188 (1926); Watras, *Politics, Race, and Schools,* p. 85; Appendix to Brief in Opposition to Petition for Writ of Certiorari, pp. 3a, n.3, 5a, n.6, *Brinkmann v. Gilligan,* United States Supreme Court, 1979.

42   For integrated schools in Cleveland, see "Cleveland's Schools," *Cleveland Advocate,* Sept. 18, 1915, p. 4; Kusmer, *A Ghetto Takes Shape,* pp. 182–4, 187 (quote, p. 187).

43   For racially separate seating, see "Girl Fought 'Jim-Crow,'" *Cleveland Gazette,* Apr. 4, 1931, p. 1 (Chester); Appendix to Brief in Opposition to Petition for Writ of Certiorari, p. 4a, n. 4, *Brinkmann v. Gilligan,* United States Supreme Court, 1979 (Dayton – quote); Taylor, *In Search of the Racial Frontier,* p. 217 (Arizona).

44   For separate playgrounds, see Granger, "Race Relations and the School System," p.329 (New Jersey); Payne, "Negroes in the Public Elementary Schools of the North," p. 227 (New Jersey); Taylor, *In Search of the Racial Frontier,* p. 218 (Wichita). For separate swimming pools, see *Patterson v. Board of Education of Trenton,* 11 N.J. Misc. 179 (1933), *aff'd,* 112 N.J.L. 99 (1934) (Trenton); "Court Upholds Ban on Race Segregation," *New York Times,* Jan. 6, 1934, p. 17 (Trenton); Thomas, "Schooling as a Political Instrument," p. 587 (Buffalo); "Our Student Strike!" *Cleveland Gazette,* Sept. 27, 1930, p. 1 (Sandusky, Ohio); "Atlantic's 'Jim Crowists,'" *Cleveland Gazette,* June 7, 1924, p. 1 (Atlantic City); Tipton, *Community in Crisis,* pp. 25-6 (Gary); "Along the N.A.A.C.P. Battlefront," *The Crisis* 43 (June 1936), p. 182 (Kankakee, Illinois); "Victory against School Segregation," *Cleveland Gazette,* Apr. 26, 1924, p. 1 (Wichita). Other districts required black and white children to swim at separate times. Interview with Robert Carter, Aug. 7, 2003 (East Orange, New Jersey); Robisch, "Educational Segregation and Desegregation," p. 71 (Dayton, Ohio). For example, in Gary, school authorities during the early 1940s finally permitted black boys to swim in the school pool, but only on Fridays, and then required that the pool be thoroughly cleaned over the weekend before white children used it again. Tipton, *Community in Crisis,* pp. 25–6. For exclusion of blacks from school activities, see Homel, "Two Worlds of Race?" pp. 241–2 (Chicago); Betten and Mohl, "The Evolution of Racism," pp. 54–5 (Gary); Wallis, *All We Had Was Each Other,* p. 6 (Madison County, Indiana); McElderry, "The Problem of the Color Line," p. 67 (Portland). For Montclair graduation ceremonies, see "Alter Graduation March," *New York Times,* June 13, 1925, p. 6.

45   "Protest to Governor on 'Jim Crow' Schools," *New York Times,* Sept. 10, 1930, p. 22; *Taylor v. Board of Education of New Rochelle,* 191 F. Supp. 181, 184-6 (S.D.N.Y. 1961); United States Commission on Civil Rights, *Civil Rights U.S.A.: Public Schools Cities in the North and West,* pp. 46, 48, 68; Ment, "Racial Segregation in the Public Schools," pp. 264–73.

46 For the discussion of Columbus, see "Would Draw a 'Color Line' in the Public Schools,"
    Cleveland Gazette, Sept. 26, 1903, p. 1; Columbus Board of Education Minutes, Sept. 30,
    1907, May 1 1, 1908, June 8, 1908, cited in Testimony of W. A. Montgomery, Appendix, pp.
    368–71, *Columbus Board of Education v. Penick,* 443 U.S. 449 (1979); Gerber, *Black Ohio and
    the Color Line,* pp. 266–7; Minor, "The Negro in Columbus," pp. 147-53. For the black pe-
    tition quote, see Brief for Respondents, p. 14, n. 12, *Columbus Board of Education v. Penick,*
    443 U.S. 449 (1979); for the 1931 report, see *Penick v. Columbus Board of Education,* 519 F.
    Supp. 925, 929 (S.D. Ohio 1981); for the 1937 quote, see Robisch, "Educational Segregation
    and Desegregation," p. 69.

47 For the discussion of Chicago, see Homel, "Two Worlds of Race?" pp. 241–2; Spear, *Black
    Chicago,* pp. 201–2, 204; Homel, *Down from Equality,* pp. 27–8. For the quote concerning
    whites sitting with blacks, see Spear, *Black Chicago,* p. 205; for the quote from the NAACP
    president, see Homel, "Two Worlds of Race?" p. 242.

48 For Gary, see Tipton, *Community in Crisis,* p. 22 ; for Cincinnati, see Washington, "The Black
    Struggle for Desegregated Quality Education," pp. 83, 101, 103; Montgomery, "Racial His-
    tory of the Cincinnati and Suburban Public Schools," pp. 125–6 (1983), Cincinnati Historical
    Society.

49 For variations in segregation, see Homel, "Two Worlds of Race?" p. 242; for exclusion of
    blacks from high school, see Valien, "Racial Desegregation," p. 304 (Illinois) "Gallipolis
    School Situation," *Ohio State Monitor,* Oct. 19, 1918, p. 8 (Ohio); Letter from William Hastie
    to Walter White, Oct. 2, 1933, Hastie Papers, Box 102-2 (New Jersey).

50 McLagan, *A Peculiar Paradise,* pp. 111, 115, 123, 131, 135, 141, 165; see also letter from "Non de
    plume" to W. E. B. Du Bois, Apr. 9, 1914, NAACP Papers, Box II-L-14 (exclusion of blacks
    from public schools in Nogales, Arizona).

51 For New Haven, see Homel, "Two Worlds of Race?" p. 241; Warner, *New Haven Negroes,* pp.
    275-8; Ment, "Racial Segregation in the Public Schools," pp. 275–6; for Boston, see Daniels,
    In Freedom's Birthplace, p. 188; for Providence, see Perlmann, *Ethnic Differences,* pp. 182–3;
    for the Rhode Island black population, see U.S. Bureau of Census, 1910, 1920, 1930.

52 For the first 1913 study, see Blascoer, *Colored School Children in New York;* for the second 1913
    study, see Henri, *Black Migration,* p. 181; for New York schools after World War I, see Stern,
    Jim Crow Goes to School in New York," pp. 201–2; Ment, "Racial Segregation in the Public
    Schools," pp. 228–9, 235–51; Thompson, "The Negro Separate School," p. 242; Homel, "Two
    Worlds of Race?" p. 241. For the Locke quote, see Ment, "Racial Segregation in the Public
    Schools," p. 245, n. 1.

53 For the discussion of Indiana, see *United States v. Board of Commissioners,* 332 F. Supp. 655
    (S.D. Ind. 1971) (quote, pp. 664-5); Reynolds, "The Challenge of Racial Equality" p. 177.

54 For Indianapolis segregation, see Thornbrough, "Segregation in Indiana," pp. 601–4; Wil-
    liams and Ryan, *Schools in Transition,* p. 50. For the quote, see "Jim-Crow High School
    Reality, To Build in April," *Indianapolis Recorder,* Nov. 29, 1924, in NAACP Papers, Box
    I-D-58.

55 For the first quote, see Cubberley, *State and County Educational Reorganization,* pp. 83–4;
    for the second quote, see ibid., p. 4; for erroneous advice, see ibid., pp. 83–4. For the final
    quote, see Department of the Interior, Bureau of Education, *Negro Education,* pp. 677, 683,
    688.

56 For white insistence on segregation, see Henri, *Black Migration*, p. 182; Kennedy, *The Negro Peasant Turns Cityward*, p. 193; for the New Jersey study, see Wright, *The Education of Negroes*, p. 192.

57 For justifications of segregation, see Spear, *Black Chicago*, p. 204; Woofter, *Negro Problems in Cities* pp. 175–6; "The Segregation of Negro Children at Toms River, N.J.," 25 *School and Society* 365 (Mar. 26, 1927); Meier and Rudwick, "Early Boycotts of Segregated Schools: The East Orange, New Jersey, Experience," pp. 23–4; Johnson, *The Negro in American Civilization*, p. 270; Kennedy, *The Negro Peasant Turns Cityward*, pp. 196–8; Chicago Commission on Race Relations, *The Negro in Chicago*, pp. 239, 256 (quote, p. 260). For Detroit survey, see Kennedy, *The Negro Peasant Turns Cityward*, p. 199.

58 For socialization problems, see Mosey, "Testing, Tracking, and Curriculum," p. 64; for the Johnson quote, see C. S. Johnson, "The Need of Social Work in Cities—in the North," January 30, 1932, p. 4, Johnson Papers, Box 166, Folder 16.

59 For racial stereotypes, see Frazier, *The Negro in the United States*, pp. 440–1; for the New Jersey survey, see *Report of the New Jersey State Temporary Commission*, pp. 38–42. For the Trenton superintendent quote, see Payne, "Negroes in the Public Elementary Schools," p. 230; for the Philadelphia superintendent quote, see Tyack, *The One Best System*, p. 227.

60 Harshman, "Race Contact in Columbus," pp. 19–20.

61 For the Buffalo quote, see Mosey, "Testing, Tracking, and Curriculum," p. 63; for the Gary discussion and quote, see Cohen, *Children of the Mill*, p. 69.

62 Frazier, *The Negro in the United States*, p. 441.

63 Pechstein, "The Problem of Negro Education," pp. 197–8.

64 For the Atlantic City quote, see Johnson, *Background to Patterns of Negro Segregation*, p. 198; for the Toms River quote, see Wilson, "Citizens Protest to Governor," *Pittsburgh Courier*, Apr. 2, 1927, p. 1; for the Westhampton quote, see *Report of the New Jersey State Temporary Commission*, p. 41; for the Mississippi quote, see Morse, "New Jersey, New Laboratory in Race Relations," p. 156. The *New Jersey Herald News* reported in 1941 that white teachers in Trenton "have a reputation for gross prejudice against colored children." "Little Hitlers in School System," *New Jersey Herald News*, Feb. 22, 1941, p. 8.

65 For the Madison quote, see Wallis, *All We Had Was Each Other*, p. 65; for the Gary quote, see Tipton, *Community in Crisis*, p. 99.

66 For Flushing, see "To Demand Separate Schools for Negroes," *New York Times*, Jan. 18, 1911, p. 3; for the Columbus study, see Harshman, "Race Contact in Columbus, pp. 16–18; for the Gary quote, see Tipton, *Community in Crisis*, p. 16.

67 For the Cincinnati strike, see "No Racial Lines for Cincinnati Schools," *New York Age*, Feb. 3, 1916, p. 1; for the Gallipolis boycott, see "Court Refuses to Stand for Segregation in Public Schools," *Colorado Statesman*, Jan. 25, 1919, in NAACP Papers, Box I-C-405; for the Darby protest, see *Cleveland Gazette*, July 26, 1924, p. 2; for the Gary walkout, see Betten and Mohl, "The Evolution of Racism," p. 55; for the Dorchester prom, see "400 White Hi Grads Loyal," *Cleveland Gazette*, July 27, 1929, p. 2.

68 For resurgence of the Klan, see Trotter, *River Jordan*, p. 105; for the Indiana quote, see Proclamation of Grand Dragon of Ku Klux Klan, Realm of Indiana, Nov. 1924, NAACP Papers, Box I-G-63; for the Klan in Indianapolis, see Press Release, "N.A.A.C.P. Contributes $200

to Fight Indianapolis School Segregation," Mar. 20, 1925, NAACP Papers, Box I-D-58; for the Klan in Ohio, see "Kluxers Out in the Open," *Cleveland Gazette*, Oct. 3, 1931, p. 1; *Cleveland Gazette*, Feb. 21, 1925, p. 2; "The Dayton School Fight," *Cleveland Gazette*, June 20, 1925, p. 2; "Ku Klux Klan Victory!" *Cleveland Gazette*, June 13, 1925, p. 2; for the Klan in New Jersey, see Moore, "Full Citizenship in New Jersey," p. 272; Morrow, *Way Down South Up North*, pp. 94–5; "Black Legion Shows Hand in New Jersey School Teacher Campaign," *Norfolk Journal and Guide*, Aug. 22, 1936, p. 10; for the Klan in Oregon, see McLagan, *A Peculiar Paradise*, pp. 138–40.

69 For the use of intelligence tests, see Priest, "A Historical Study of the Royal Elementary School," p. 39; Du Bois, "Literacy Tests in the Army," p. 86; for claims of black inferiority, see Tyack, *The One Best System*, p. 217. For the first Terman quote, see Terman, *The Measurement of Intelligence*, p. 91; for the second quote, see Terman, et al., *Intelligence Tests and School Reorganization*, p. 28.

70 For psychologist views, see Thomas, "Black Intellectuals," p. 477; for Young's views, see Hendrick, *The Education of Non-Whites*, p. 88; Mosey, "Testing, Tracking, and Curriculum," p. 23.

71 For *Opportunity*, see Fultz, "'Agitate Then, Brother,'" pp. 213–14; for Johnson's views, see Johnson, "Mental Measurements of Negro Groups," pp. 21–5; for the Long quote, see Long, "Race and Mental Tests," p. 28.

72 For black recruit scores, see C. S. Johnson, "Mr. Waring and the Lonely Crowd," Jan. 10, 1954, p. 6, Johnson Papers, Box 166, Folder 10; for the "boast" quote, see "Boasted Bunk" *Cleveland Gazette*, Dec. 8, 1923, p. 1 (reprint of an article in *Pearson's Magazine* by Herbert Alexander); for the Bond quote, see Bond, "What the Army 'Intelligence' Tests Measured," p. 201.

73 For the Chicago study, see Daniel, "A History of Discrimination Against Black Students," p. 151. The 1922 Chicago Commission on Race Relations, charged with investigating the 1919 riot, found that "Negro children born in the North had, as a rule, no higher rate of retardation" than white children. Chicago Commission on Race Relations, *The Negro in Chicago*, p. 261. For other tests, see Thomas, "Black Intellectuals," pp. 482–5,

74 Brigham, *A Study of American Intelligence*, p. 192.

75 For social scientists, see Scott, *Contempt and Pity*, pp. 19–70; for the Reuter quote, see Reuter, *The American Race Problem*, p. 89.

76 For Klineberg, see Klineberg, "The Question of Negro Intelligence," pp. 361–7; Klineberg, *Race Differences*, pp. 184–9; Pettigrew, *Negro American Intelligence*, p. 18; Kluger, *Simple Justice*, p. 439. For other studies see Klineberg, *Race Differences*, pp. 183, 185–9; Hendrick, *The Education of Non-Whites*, p. 89.

77 For the quote, see Tyack, *The One Best System*, p. 233.

78 For the discussion of tracks, see Tyack, *The One Best System*, p. 221; for the discussion of Buffalo vocational education, see Thomas, "Urban Schooling for Black Migrant Youth," p. 282. For the first quote, see Mosey, "Testing, Tracking, and Curriculum," pp. 65, 68–71, 76–7; for the second quote, see ibid., p. 72 (quoting Principal James Farrell).

79 For Buffalo vocational education, see Mosey, "Testing, Tracking, and Curriculum," p. 66; for the Survey quote, see ibid., pp. 91–2.

80 For Cleveland, see Homel, "Two Worlds of Race?" p. 252; Kusmer, *A Ghetto Takes Shape*, pp. 182–4; Lieberson, *A Piece of the Pie*, pp. 236–7; Mosey, "Testing, Tracking, and Curriculum," pp. 28–9. For the Perlmann quote, see Perlmann, *Ethnic Differences*, p. 183.

81 For Buffalo, see Thomas, "Urban Schooling for Black Migrant Youth," pp. 276–81 (quote, p. 281); Mosey, "Testing, Tracking, and Curriculum," pp. 106-8; for Cleveland, see Moore, "The Limits of Black Power," pp. 61–3.

82 For vocational schools in New York City, see Stern, "Jim Crow Goes to School in New York," p. 202; Ment, "Racial Segregation in the Public Schools," pp. 251–2 (first quote, ibid., p. 252; second quote, ibid., p. 250; third quote, ibid., p. 253; fourth and fifth quotes, ibid., p.254.

83 Quote in Blascoer, *Colored School Children in New York*, pp. 18–19; 1940 study Tyack, *The One Best System*, p. 222.

Organized Resistance and Black Educators' Quest for School Equality, 1878–1938

Vanessa Siddle Walker, Emory University

Historical accounts of advocacy for equality in educational facilities and resources for Blacks during de jure segregation in the South have generally minimized, or ignored, the role of Black educators. This article challenges the omission of Black educators in the historical portrait by providing a historical analysis of four periods of teacher activism in Georgia prior to Brown. Results indicate that, through their organizational structure, Black educators consistently advocated for improved facilities, bus transportation, longer school terms, high schools, and better salaries. Although the success of their activities was mediated by the Southern political context of the era in which they advocated, the Black teachers' organization was the most organized agent for change throughout this period.

HISTORICAL ACCOUNTS OF advocacy for equality in educational facilities and resources for Blacks during *de jure* segregation in the South have generally minimized, or ignored, the role of Black educators. Black educators are characterized as being dependent upon school boards, as being reticent to become involved in civil rights issues, and as being frightened of desegregation because of the likely loss of employment.[1] Although these characterizations are accurate representations of the reality of the era, the descriptions have been popularly and historically generalized to create the widely held conclusion that Black educators were sidelined in efforts to achieve equality, and that their primary concern was to protect their own self-centered individual interests. Richard Kluger's citation of the editor of a Black newspaper in Columbia, South Carolina, captures the beliefs emanating from this perspective. Describing Black teachers as shiftless and un-grateful for the work that had been accomplished on their behalf, the editorial concludes that "most [Black teachers] are as worthless to aiding fights for the race as the most worthless of citizens."[2]

Instead of considering the role that may have been played by Black educators, achieve-ment of equality in Black educational opportunity has been attributed most consistently to the National Association for the Advancement of Colored People (NAACP). The re-sulting portrait is one of legal victories, and of courageous parents and ministers who participated to accomplish these legal victories. Local NAACP chapters are described as being sufficiently strong that other organizations did not intrude on their efforts to broker change; indeed, some portraits suggest that the NAACP was the only organization pushing for change.[3] Except for some few exceptional teachers and consultants in higher education, the dominant portrait of NAACP activity generally omits references to Black educators as having any agency in seeking equality of opportunities for Black children. This characterization is widely found in general historical accounts of the era, NAACP histories, state histories, and histories of Blacks in America.[4]

Even in research that purports to focus specifically on education, the story has re-mained largely one of legal success. In Michael John Schultz's history of *The National Educational Association and the Black Teacher*, for example, the NAACP is described as beginning a "vigorous assault upon the segregated practice of education," with no refer-ence to the role of Black educators.[5] Donohue, Heckman, and Todd review 17 states to explore variables influencing Black educational uplift in the South. They conclude that private philanthropy and the NAACP explain most gains in the South.[6] In other analy-ses, some scant attention to Black educational efforts is captured in reports of financial contributions of teacher organizations to the legal effort and the hint that teachers may have been more than inactive bystanders.[7] Yet, none explores the ways in which financial contributions were representative of an ongoing comprehensive strategy of resistance on the part of Black educators.

The role of Black educators as organized advocates is likewise not captured in the recent revisionist accounts of Black segregated schools. Focusing on the resilience of Black school communities in the midst of oppressive circumstances, this literature has demonstrated the interplay between Black parents and educators, the professional roles and training of teachers and principals, and the interpersonal and institutional caring that characterized the environments of many of the schools.[8] However, despite its lens that captures more intimately the environments of segregated schools, the research has failed to incorporate the paucity of sources that suggest that many of the reported activi-ties, such as fighting for buses, may have been part of a larger rubric of Black educational activity. This omission has occurred despite earlier historical research by Linda Perkins on Black teachers that should have created the foundation for an expanded interpreta-tion of some of the examples found in this research. Perkins describes the emergence of Black teacher organizations throughout the South by 1900, arguing that the Alabama

State Teachers Association was interested in improving teacher salaries and having longer school terms as early as 1910. Her article also demonstrates that by the 1930s Black educators were campaigning vigorously for equality of educational opportunity in individual states and through their national organization, the American Teachers Association (ATA).[9] Though not as well developed, some other historical accounts, such as the history of the ATA and Black teachers in the NEA, along with more recent research on Black teachers by Michael Fultz, also support these findings.[10] In large measure, however, the implication of these references for a broader research agenda on Black educational agency has been overlooked, and the most commonly accepted portrait has remained one of Black educators who may have been caring facilitators in individual communities, but who were disinterested spectators in the broader struggle for equality.

This article challenges the dominant portrayal of Black educators and explores specifically the organized advocacy of Black educators for decades before, and subsequently in cooperation with, the well-documented legal campaigns. It does not lessen the importance of the NAACP activity, or organizations and individuals who supported the court cases, including Black educators themselves (whose role during the era of litigation is discussed in a forthcoming work). Indeed, equality of educational opportunity for Blacks has consistently been determined by the degree to which federal court opinions upheld beliefs about U.S. constitutional claims of equality, and individuals sufficiently skilled and courageous challenged contradictions in constitutional intent and implementation. However, the current analysis does extend the one-dimensional portrait of progress that has been consistently accepted. By investigating the organized historical role played by Black educators in achieving equality and analyzing the systematic ways in which these educators resisted inequalities, a more textured, contextualized, and historically accurate pre-Brown portrait emerges. In its intent, this article is the first stage in a rejoinder to the question asked by a Black educator during a session of ATA with Thurgood Marshall in 1950. The attendee wished to know whether the time had come for the ATA and NAACP to "give more publicity to the contributions being made annually by the ATA to the cause of the judicial effort."[11] Although Marshall's response is unrecorded, as the record shows, the speaker's goal of a more comprehensive account has yet to be realized.

This paper focuses upon the early decades of organized teacher resistance, before the period when many Black educational organizations formed more formal collaborations with the NAACP. It extends the historical literature on the influence and active stance of Black educators during *de jure* segregation in the South by extraditing and illuminating the agency, voice, and advocacy evident in the organization of Black teachers between 1879 and 1938. Using historical methodology to describe and put in context their activities as represented in newspaper accounts, teacher association records, state archival documents, NAACP records, interviews, primary source books, and secondary literature for the period covered, the paper explores the resistance of educators in the Georgia Teachers and Education Association (GTEA) during four time frames. These periods, which emerged from the research, have been identified as: 1) association building and interracial collaboration, 2) intellectual activity and national collaboration, 3) petitions and shielded collaboration, and 4) direct appeal. In each period, the paper explores the issues that formed the foundation and context for resistance, the mechanisms Black educators used to advocate for Black education, and the external factors that facilitated or impeded their success. Although the primary source document analysis is limited to Georgia, the evidence in the secondary source literature of other states suggests strongly that the basic tenants of the story were replicated across the South.[12]

Results indicate that the resistance of Black educators during these periods was intentionally vested in their professional organizations, rather than in the easily recognized behaviors of individual Black teachers. Through their organization, Black educators spoke continuously and emphatically on the inequality in facilities, length of school term, buses, teacher salaries, and vocational educational opportunities evident in the educational system. Between 1878 and 1938, their activities may be characterized by efforts to advocate for equality by working primarily *within* the Southern educational system, seeking to effect change by reasoning with the White leadership through letters, petitions, and meetings.

Viewed by contemporary standards, and compared with the well-documented examples of personal risk and death that permeate the civil rights portraits of the 1950s and beyond, the resistance of the teachers during these early periods may be assumed to be mild, tentative, and overly placating. Yet, characterized by the standards of their own era, where teachers could be beaten or killed for educating children, where freedom of speech for Blacks was routinely denied, where even White university professors could be forced from their jobs as a result of speaking forthrightly about inequality, and where lynching ruled as the dominant White response to Blacks who no longer understood their place in the social order, the behavior of the teachers assumes a different characterization. Sterling Stuckey's portrait of slave culture provides a useful interpretive frame for understanding their response. Stuckey argues that any effort by oppressed people to affirm their humanity can be characterized as an act of resistance. Guided by this definition, the organized response of Black teachers to inequalities and the careful way in which they shield individual members from reprisal constitute an act of rebellion within their time period no less difficult and risky than that of their successors who would later openly march for civil rights. Historian James Anderson argues that without understanding this context of oppression, the meaning of their agency and resistance can not be appropriately understood.[13] Yet, when their actions are contextually measured, they exist as the primary, most consistent, and best organized mechanism advocating for change for the segregated schools in the Georgia during this period.

Early Resistance, 1878–1894: Association Building And Interracial Collaboration

The Black teachers' association in Georgia, eventually to be known as the Georgia Teachers and Education Association (GTEA), dates its organizational history to 1878. According to *Rising in the Sun*, the official history of the GTEA written in 1966 with historian Horace Mann Bond as part of the editorial team, the formation of a continuous Black teachers' group in Georgia was "unquestionably" the brainchild of Richard R. Wright, Sr. Wright, who has been described by James Anderson as "one of the brightest and most influential educators of the post-Reconstruction era," convened 300 Black educators who were the "leaders and representative men of the state" in 1787 in Atlanta to plan for Black education.[14] At the time of the convention, Wright had been principal of the only high school for Blacks in Georgia for seven years, and had already appeared before a U.S. Senate Committee on Education and Labor to report on conditions in Georgia. With his broad classical training—Wright graduated from Atlanta University in 1878—and a forthrightness that had characterized him since childhood, he ostensibly laid before the group the critical needs confronting the race. At the conclusion of the convention, the attendees named themselves the Georgia Teachers Association and elected Wright as their president.[15]

This convention marks the beginning of a Black teachers' association in Georgia that would continue until it was dismantled in the wake of desegregation mergers in 1970. However, this particular convention does not mark the beginning of educational activity in Georgia. As captured vividly by James Anderson, Jacqueline Jones, and Ronald Butchart, educational activities for Blacks in Georgia dated to the Civil War.[16] Indeed, Wright himself, a former slave and student of the American Missionary Association (AMA) teachers, recounts in his 1894 book, *A Brief Historical Sketch of Negro Education in Georgia*, an 1864 meeting led by Black ministers as the beginning of collaborations in the interest of Black children. By 1865, Jones notes that ministers in Savannah had formed the Savannah Education Association (SEA). According to Jones, the SEA had raised $800 by January 1, 1865, to support the education of 500 Black children, tuition-free.

Other educational activity also spanned the state during Reconstruction, though historians disagree on the exact dates. The Georgia Equal Rights Association, later renamed the Georgia Education Association, was one of the earliest organizations and was formed as a way to supervise the growing number of Black schools.[17] Georgia historians describe the Equal Rights Association as an almost entirely Black organization that devoted itself to building schools and educational opportunities.[18] By 1870, at least 200 schools controlled by native Black men and women existed in 70 counties in Georgia.[19] Numan V. Bartley notes that the Equal Rights Association held its first convention in 1866 and spawned the creation of local education units among Blacks throughout the state. Given the proximity in time of its formation to the 1867 Constitutional Convention, and the overlap of some of the members, one might also infer that it provided the intellectual catalyst for the 37 Black delegates who helped write the Georgia constitution that first created a system of public schooling in the state.[20] In other activity, Wright also describes the era as one in which former slaves and sympathetic White Republicans worked collaboratively to certify teachers and to discuss educational ideas.[21]

Wright's call for a convention in 1878 reflects neither a new focus for the Black community nor a new strategy. However, the call does signal the attribution of agency in the written record to educators rather than ministers, and its timing coincides with a shift in political climate.[22] By 1876, in part because of the poll tax that disabled Black voter participation, the Republican Party was a diminished political force, and by the time of Wright's call, the spirit of White supremacy had emerged as a dominant political force.[23] Wright's convention, for example, occurred two years after a new state constitution, written in 1877, restricted the public education commitment of the earlier constitution to public education only at the elementary levels and changed the "equal" provisions for Black and White education to "equal so far as practicable."[24] Georgia's constitutional efforts to limit the potential of Negro attainment during this period is entirely consistent with the federal abandonment of the Negro in Georgia, as signaled in Hayes Compromise of 1876, and with the desire among Democratic Whites to regain dominance within the state. Indeed, the intent of one former Confederate officer in the rewriting of a new constitution, according to Georgia historian Donald Grant, was to create a document in which "the Negro shall never be heard from" again.[25]

When Wright convened his leading men of the state, Blacks were transferring their children from AMA schools to the newly forming public schools of Georgia, where White Southern officials were willing to hire Black teachers as a way of ridding the state of the Northern influence of AMA teachers. Blacks had always resisted the AMA paternalistic attitude, making the placement of Black teachers in the public schools an end upon which Southern Whites and Blacks could agree, despite the difference in rationale. Black school attendance was also rising by 1875 in the Georgia public schools, reportedly two-thirds the attendance of Whites even though the children faced harsh economic conditions. Thus, Wright's convention appears to be spawned by an understanding of the ominous political events that threatened to thwart the budding Black educational effort, and perhaps also by an effort to build coalitions with White Democrats, some of whose ends coincided with those of the Black community.

In planning a strategy to effect change, the organization continued the utilization of interracial interaction that was begun during Reconstruction. At its meetings between 1878 and 1898, Wright quotes Henry Walker as recording the presence of men of both races at the annual meetings of teachers. These White participants are described as "friendly to the Negro cause." As the Association convened its meetings in the major cities, such as Macon, Augusta, Savannah, Milledgeville, and Atlanta, Wright says that "the superintendents of the local systems have recognized and acknowledged the importance of this body and lent their presence."[26] Into 1893, a meeting acknowledged to be "the best in its history," this strategy of collaboration continues. The meeting records addresses from Governor Northern; Commissioner Bradwell, who is described as an untiring worker for the education of all children in the state; Superintendent Slaton; and others.[27]

Over the years, the Black Georgia Teachers Association grew in membership and influence. Walker is recorded by Wright as reporting that the organization continued to grow after its founding, "gathering momentum year by year until the present day [1894], when its influence can not well be calculated." Throughout these years, sympathetic White educators continued to support the Black group, and their display of support created a climate that was conducive to growth in the membership of the organization.[28] With superintendent support, Black teachers could exercise freedom in attending meetings and maintaining visibility in leadership in the state gatherings. The collaboration thus served the purpose of utilizing White voices as allies to create a climate that would allow for growth of the organization.

However, the presence of influential Whites at the meetings of Black educators cannot be misinterpreted as a signal that Whites shared the aims of education that were consistent with the members of the Black association. White participation during these years reveals deeply held differences about attainment that model the contradictions between Northern philanthropists and Blacks themselves. Gustavus Orr provides an example of this contradiction. Orr became the second state school commissioner in 1872, after the ouster of Governor Rufus Bullock, the Reconstruction governor who had the audacity to denounce slavery and White supremacy.[29] Orr's almost 16-year term, which overlapped with the growth of the teachers' organization, was one that supported Negro education. He argued that Negro children had a legal right to free education as well as the White children. Blacks consulted with Orr and, ostensibly, sought to work with him to achieve equality of opportunity.[30] However, in a twist that represents the difficulty of attaining comparable education for Blacks during the era, Orr also represented the return of White rule, disfavored funding Atlanta University because of the intermingling of the races and generally sought to appease White educational interests.[31] In these beliefs, he exemplifies the contradiction of Whites who simultaneously sought to help the Negro, but who limited his rise to the place the White South appointed.[32] Local Whites such as Orr placed Black educators in the ongoing dilemma of needing to seek whatever good a White leader could offer while, as Georgia historian Donald Grant has supposed, holding onto the hope that the next person/administration would do better.[33]

The interracial meetings also masked differing beliefs between Whites and Blacks about the financing and structuring of Black education. While Whites largely supported the development of public education that increasingly granted fewer opportunities to Blacks, Black educators soon began to denounce openly such inequalities. After Orr's death in 1887, and in the face of decreasing expenditures and inequalities as they related to Black education, Wright began "strongly urging that the colored people be given a larger share in the appropriation made for the school support."[34] Although Black schools were growing in number, as were Black teachers and attendance, and the length of the school term had increased, Wright believed these "encouraging gains" were undermined by a Southern environment that was growing increasingly hostile.

In addition to interracial collaborations, the program list of the Black teachers' association during these early years also indicates the beginning of interstate collaborations among Black educators. Although collaborations with educators in other states would not fully emerge until the forthcoming period, the era did provide the groundwork for later exchanges of information across Black educational groups. For example, Booker T. Washington was present at the 1893 Georgia Teachers Association meeting, as well as some subsequent meetings. Although he had not yet delivered the Atlanta Compromise speech for which he would become famous, he was by 1893 an accomplished speaker. In 1884, he had spoken before the National Education Association (NEA); moreover, in 1882 he had helped found the Black Alabama State Teachers Association, speaking to those educators with classical references akin to those used by Wright during his 1883 congressional appearances. While the nature of Washington's talk to the Georgia association in 1893 is undocumented, his presence affirms the beginning of informed activity across states.[35]

In sum, this first identifiable period of the association was born of a political climate that threatened to jeopardize the gains Blacks had made during Reconstruction. It relied primarily upon organization building, interracial cooperation, and emergent inter-state information networks as mechanisms to affect change. Although it differed in purpose from that of Whites who functioned as part of association meetings, the period was one that netted increasing schools, attendance, and length of school term.

As the climate became increasingly restricted, however, Blacks would have to identify new avenues to support Black education. In his 1894 book Wright hints at the shifts in attitude among Georgia Whites that would reconfigure the interracial collaborations. Although his 1894 writing was at the height of the Populist movement, Wright notes that the Negro "is becoming more sensitive with regard to discourtesies and insults," attributing his "restiveness" to the "natural result of his increased intelligence and love for his country."[36] Although not named, Wright must surely be referring to the election violence that threatened to undermine Black political influence and the increasing peonage and sharecropping that threatened to dismantle Black gains during this period.[37] He likely also was referencing school funding, since Blacks contributed a total of $288,500 to the school fund through various taxes, while only $167,857 was spent on Black education.[38] Wright predicted that if the "outrages" continue, Black "defiance will increase in proportion as the lawless outrages increase." Amidst a text that generally applauds the efforts of all agencies in uplift and appears particularly kind to White efforts, these predictive remarks loom as a blatant reminder of the ways in which the era of even the appearance of interracial collaboration was in the midst of change. When Wright published his history in 1894, he still maintained the hope that there would be "no possibility of trouble between the intelligent and upright colored people and the intelligent and upright white people."[39] Unfortunately, Wright was wrong. While the organization itself would continue, the period of Black and White cooperation on school issues, fueled by the hope among Black educators that they could spur equal educational opportunities for Black children, was reaching an end.

Responding to shifting attitudes, 1894–1916: intellectual activity and national collaborations

With the turn of the century, Black educational organized activity on the state level decreased as hardening White attitudes manifested themselves in social and political legislation that separated the races. Indeed, *Plessy v. Ferguson* in 1896 gave Whites permission to recreate a world where White supremacy ruled. By the turn of the century, restrictions had been placed in the mingling of the races in Georgia and throughout the South, including segregation laws on trains, in restaurants, and in other public facilities. In Georgia, the 1906 gubernatorial campaign and its aftermath exemplified the new era. Supported, ironically, by former Populist leader Tom Watson who was angered by Black votes that dismantled his Populist campaign, candidate Hoke Smith stomped the state, inciting racial divisions.[40] The heightened tension erupted into the Atlanta Race Riot of 1906, a bloody confrontation that included Whites invading Black neighborhoods and Blacks (including Walter White, who would later head the Atlanta NAACP and subsequently the national NAACP) having to defend themselves with weapons. Blacks were also accused of bartering votes in the 1906 election. This action would lend further support to efforts to maintain White solidarity and eliminate Black political strength. Despite Black protest, formal disfranchisement soon followed in 1908.[41]

Additionally, the year 1906 saw the end of effective Black protest against unjust laws. While boycotts by Black citizens had been useful in stalling segregation laws in the late 1890s, these measures ceased to be effective in the new climate.[42] For example, an 18-month boycott in Savannah, organized by ministers and supported by the Black press, failed when Whites refused to weaken as they had in earlier times.[43] Moreover, despite protests by W. E. B. Du Bois and other Black leaders, by 1915, *Birth of a Nation* premiered across the South, romanticizing an imagined "old South" with such vigor that it would inspire the rebirth of the Georgia Klan at the foot of Stone Mountain, Georgia.

Given these events, unsurprisingly the educational climate for Blacks also became more oppressive. Three years after Wright's hopeful evaluation of the school situation in 1894, the strong academic high school of which he was principal, and the only one of four in the Southern states, was closed by the local school board. As Anderson describes this event, the closing occurred in 1897 despite protests by the Black community, and despite its obvious violation of *Plessy v. Ferguson* decision, which required separate, but equal accommodations. Upheld by the Supreme Court in 1899, this judicial action signaled Whites that they could sacrifice high school education for Blacks while providing it for Whites.[44]

The years that followed reaped the ramifications of this judicial opinion and the national climate touting industrial education for Blacks. Despite a subsidy of $140,000 that Blacks paid for White education in 1908, Whites continued to resist equitable resources for Black education.[45] The gap between Black teachers' and White teachers' salary, which was minimal in 1896 with only $6.56 separating the highest Black teacher salary from the highest White teacher salary, plummeted to a gap in which the Black teacher's salary was less than half the salary of the White teacher by 1915.[46] Adhering to the 1870 school law that allowed "equal [facilities] so far as *practicable* [italics mine]," Whites demonstrated the impracticability of equality.[47] In addition to differences in salary and expenditure per child, differences during this time were evident in inequitable distribution of funds for agriculture in public schools, inequitable distribution of funds for higher education, inaccessibility to high school education, and limited access to elementary grades offered in some Black schools. As this era unfolded, Whites blatantly ignored the "equal" clause of *Plessy* and sought to orchestrate a "new South" still "firmly anchored in White supremacy."[48] Their activities caused Du Bois to note in 1911 that the Negro common schools for Blacks were worse off than it had been 20 years previously.

In this new climate also, the teachers' organization that had grown and received accolades in the mid to late 1800s, began to diminish in membership. The history of GTEA reports that the teachers seemed to have lost some interest in the Georgia Teachers Association; in 1894, compared with previous years, the meeting was the smallest gathering. By 1906, ironically the same year that Blacks ceased to be effective in protesting unjust laws, the history reports teacher participation down to about 300 teachers, causing the *Atlanta Independent* to lament that Georgia teachers had "absolutely no interest in their profession."[49] Although the meetings continued, the president of the organization spurred teachers in 1913 by pleading for "every Negro teacher in Georgia [to] join us in an effort to bring once more to life and activity our state teachers' association." He encouraged every teacher to "rise up and lend his aid in making [the] association [be] what it ought to be."[50]

Several contextual forces help explain the decline in teacher attendance at the annual meetings. According to *Rising in the Sun*, the decline in participation was directly associated with the rise of White supremacy and the disenfranchisement of the Negro vote.[51] Moreover, the climate in Georgia was becoming increasingly hostile to those who supported Black education. For example, in 1899, the homes of Black teachers were gunfire targets in Twiggs County, while promoters of Black education were whipped along with their children.[52]

However, several other factors may explain the decline as well. The *Atlanta Independent* hints that infighting between Atlanta University students and other colleges helped to destroy the public display of support that existed in its early days.[53] Although this firsthand account likely has some basis for explaining the difficulties of the era, its support is not immediately evident in the documentation. In contrast, Du Bois' claim that systemic efforts were at the root of the decline in Black professionalism may have important explanatory power. Du Bois' 1901 report during the Negro Common School Conference suggests that Black teachers during this era were being systematically invited to a status of inferiority, different from that they held in the previous era. He contrasted Black teachers to White teachers, who had received state incentives such as scholarships and increased salaries to entice them to complete normal and collegiate training, arguing that White teachers showed "marked improvement." Noting that "20 years ago [White] teachers were not as good as the Negro teachers," he bemoaned that during this same period Negro teachers were being discouraged by "starvation wages and the idea that any training will do for a teacher."[34] These behaviors stand in contradiction to the support of superintendents during the previous era that allowed teachers to attend professional conventions, and reveal intentional structures to promote inferior Black education. The environment of the era was thus one with severe restrictions upon Black educational activity, and the decline in professional participation is consistent with its tenets.

During these years, Black educational leaders attempted to maintain the organization, now crippled by an overtly repressive climate that made it difficult for teachers to attend. Ostensibly as a way to meet the needs of their constituency, they organized the association into a departmental plan that included an emphasis on the common school, the high school, the college, and the industrial education. Moreover, in 1913, they established 12 congressional districts, each headed by a vice-president, apparently as a means of creating a statewide organizational structure.[55]

In addition to restructuring the organization, its leaders also sought other collaborations that would forward the interests of Black education. For example, Black educators, led by Wright and joined by others who have been described as the "ultimate of the talented tenth," formed in Georgia the American Negro Academy in 1897. Likely not coincidentally, this event occurred immediately after the *Plessy* decision and the demise of Wright's school. The academy was designed by the intellectual leaders of the race into the state to provide a program that would "furnish data and discussion along the most important lines of education."[56] Between 1898 and 1904, W. E. B. Du Bois served as its president. Before its demise in 1929, the academy published 22 scholarly papers.[57] Concurrent with the famed Atlanta University Conferences that were likewise designed to provide accurate academic information about the state of the Negro, individuals who were leaders of the existing state teachers' group sought scholarly means to disseminate information about the Negro. Presumably these efforts were motivated by the belief that if Whites simply understood the plight of Blacks, they would loosen some of the structures that were constricting Black attainment.

During this period, Black leaders of the teachers' group also became part of national collaborations that might be able to effect change. One of these groups was the National Association of Teachers in Colored Schools (NATCS), later renamed the American Teachers Association (ATA). This group held its first "full-fledged" meeting of Black representatives across the Southern states in 1907. From 1909–1910, Georgia's

R. R. Wright served as its president. According to Thelma Perry, historian for the ATA, Wright believed that unions between and among educators would add strength to the educational cause. Through NATCS, Black educators were able to develop a systematic agenda for challenging educational inequality that would later be seen echoed throughout the Southern states.[58] Consistent with their concerns on the state level, Perry notes that every president of this association was interested in educational equality.

Wright's association with the national group was replayed in the associations of other Georgia educational leaders such as John Hope, president of the school that would later become Morehouse College, and Lucy Laney. Both would become leaders in NATCS. However, their associations were not merely ones with other educators. Indeed, Wright and Hope were also both invited to the Niagara Conference in 1909 that would prompt the beginning of the NAACP. Although Wright was unable to attend, Hope was present. The presence of these men at the beginning of the national movement suggests that the NAACP, like the NATCS, was embraced as another national forum through which individual educators may have believed that could advocate for the issues of the Black education. Unlike the NATCS, however, the NAACP would also represent a way to agitate against the larger structural issues that kept the Black man's status expendable in the South.[59]

The influence of these intellectual and national pursuits revealed itself in Georgia in the efforts to revive the fervor of state organization among teachers who had more to fear in openly supporting the organization be- cause of the oppressive environments in which they worked. Using information that could only be available through the national networks, President W. W. Reddick compared the Georgia state association with that of other states in 1913 and lamented that Georgia is the most "backward state in the whole south with respect to teachers' organizations."[60] Meetings also continued during this era at places like Georgia State College in 1914 (the industrial school of which Wright had now become president).

But, despite the maintenance, and even expansion, of the organizational structure during this oppressive climate, the history characterizes the dominant portrayal of the era is one where the leaders of the association participated in creating broader organizational networks that crossed states and individuals. The silence of Black newspaper accounts, such as the *Savannah Tribune*, on educational activity of the association during this era, as compared with their earlier and later reports, confirms the impotence of the association during the era.[61]

The period of 1894 to 1916 nets little visible change for Black education. Although the NATCS had the structure to facilitate disseminating information and the vision to eradicate inequality, it did not have the resources or power to influence individual states. Likewise, the scholarship emerging from the American Negro Academy and the Atlanta University Conferences did little to mitigate the influence of the scholarship of White academics who employed biology, theology, sociology, and history to justify the Negro's innate inferiority.[62] Finally, the NAACP was not then sufficiently networked throughout the South to effect local change, even though it included education among its concerns. Indeed, as the lynching numbers of the period reveal, the mass of Black educators themselves existed in a world that was overtly threatening both physically and politically. Although educational leaders sought strategies to address the needs of their era, the success, or lack thereof, of the organization's efforts was directly linked to the oppressive external circumstances. The year was 1917 before a pivotal moment occurred that had the potential to bring about organized change.

New Beginnings, 1917–1921: Shields and Direct Petition

Historical and newspaper accounts concur that a shift in the national and local climate in 1917 prompted a new educational effort among Black educational leaders. Several events converged to create this climate. Notably, the great migration of Blacks from the South had been underway since 1914, with Georgians part of the exodus that claimed 100,000 Southern Blacks a year for a 15-year period.[63] The departure of Black farmers from Georgia began at time when the Georgia cotton crop had tripled, and White Georgia farmers were experiencing greater prosperity than they had since the 1850s.[64] Yet, as reprinted from the *Houston Post* in the *Savannah Times* in 1917, the Negro was not satisfied with the compensation he was receiving. "He wants more money for his work, he wants more money with greater regularity, and he wants to feel that he always receives the worth of his money," wrote the editorialist.[65] As Georgia's economic interests began to be threatened, its White citizens became more amenable to listening to Black complaints, among them the continued discontent about the quality of schooling. The new governor, Hugh Dorsey, understood that the prosperity of Georgia was being jeopardized because of the economic pressure of Black departure. In 1917, he inferred that he would improve Negro education as a way of checking the migration of Blacks to Northern cities.[66]

The federal government and Black newspapers also spurred a more conducive climate for local corporation. As the United States entered World War I with its talk of protecting democracy, Black newspapers consistently and widely denounced U.S. failure to attend to democracy at home. Unrelentingly, and sometimes at financial risk, they pounded the irony of a country using the citizens against whom it discriminated at home to fight a war to protect democracy abroad. With increasing White interest, they created the image of a "New Negro" who demanded citizenship and was willing to agitate for equality.[67] The claim was believable. Two years earlier, in 1915 the NAACP had some legal success in striking the grandfather clause that kept many Southern blacks from voting.[68] Blacks, therefore, had the potential to wield political power in ways they were denied in the previous era. Concurrent with these national changes, Georgia was also provided an incentive by the federal government on February 23, 1917, when Congress passed the Smith-Hughes Act. This bill provided for the first time $42,000 in federal aid to Georgia high schools for industrial, agricultural and home-economics education.[69]

The conflation of these events ostensibly seeded the possibility of change. One month after the passage of the Smith-Hughes Act, a group of Black attendees at the March 1917 Workers Conference at Fort Valley High and Industrial School, with principal H. A. Hunt as the leader in that gathering, put forth the need for an educational body designed to take advantage of the new climate. The older Georgia Teachers Association still existed, but the older body was composed primarily of teachers who still existed in local racial climates that were hostile to Negro education. Thus, teachers, as single agitators, were viewed as unable to advocate in a visible capacity for the needs of the Black youth. In this climate, the power to act, as the fiery Black minister and organizational leader Henry M. Turner had warned during Reconstruction, would come through organizational power, and organizational power came through unity.[70]

Jesse O. Thomas, a contemporary of the 1917 events, was interviewed on November 17, 1961. His first-person account reflects the tension of the period in the need to create organizational, rather than individual, agency. Recalling Hunt's reasons for organizing the association, Thomas notes:

> Negroes at that time could not participate in the democratic primary; therefore, they could not engage in the selection of candidates for public office. The Teachers then represented a voteless element of the population. Since they were employed by the City, County and State, they were easily identifiable in the zone of reprisal It was Mr. Hunt's idea that since the Negro Teachers were voteless and also employees of the City, County or State, they were helpless to make any contribution toward significant changes in the educational pattern. He therefore organized the Georgia Education Association which took into its membership non-teaching citizens such as physicians, head of fraternal organizations, representatives of Insurance Companies and other self-employed persons.[71]

According to Thomas, the intended strategy was to use a professional organization, openly publicized as including other professionals, to create shields for the teachers, whose jobs were perceived to be in jeopardy if they advocated directly. The local Black newspaper, *The Savannah Tribune*, echoes Thomas' memory of the importance of this strategy in the creation of a new association. Writing in 1919, the newspaper noted: "Formerly, efforts have been made by a handful of Negro schools teachers in their associations to do something, but it has become evident that no handful of teachers, however earnest, can bring about the change we all wish." Lamenting that the school teachers' hands were tied to their jobs, the editorial vested agency in an educational organization that would encompass all members of the community as a way to effect change.[72] At its inception, then, the organization both acknowledged the previous efforts led by teachers and created as its foundation the belief that teachers in this climate should be shielded by having a strong group inclusive of members who, though still susceptible to White retaliation, were not as directly accountable to the White class for financial support.

Two months after a new organization had been discussed at the Workers Conference, the new group was organized in Macon, Georgia, on May 4, 1917. All accounts give educator H. A. Hunt the credit for beginning this new association. In these activities, Hunt's actions appear to be an enigma. His reputation with the Northern philanthropists was one of accommodation, and he appeared to maintain a program as principal of Fort Valley that was consistent with their limited and menial objectives for Black education. Yet, as leader of the new association, Hunt embraced both vision and determination to use this season in U.S. history to advocate for the educational rights of Blacks. His advocacy of industrial education was certainly consistent with the beliefs of other Black Georgia educators at the time, including Wright and Du Bois. But other Black educators did not embrace industrial education to the exclusion of a classical curriculum in the ways Hunt has previously been characterized. While Hunt's actual beliefs are unknown, his actions here and in subsequent political efforts suggest, as James Anderson has subsequently argued, that Hunt learned well how to play the game of pretending to accommodate Northern philanthropists, while quietly seeking ways to agitate for change. In these behaviors, his were not unlike those of another complicated and subversive educator, Booker T. Washington.[73] The timing of the meeting was no accident. In the call for the meeting of a new educational association, the planners noted: "This seems a particularly opportune time for such a gathering and there is good reason to believe that the state school authorities will take some action to better the educational interests of Negroes if the matter is properly presented."[74] In their behaviors, the group reflected the surge of activity throughout Georgia that reflected beliefs in the possibility for change.[75] Their activities also mirrored those of NATACS, which spurred educators to believe that World War I presented opportunities for racial progress in education.[76]

The new association met at the same time as the White Georgia Educational Association (GEA) so that members could take advantage of reduced rates on all the railroads that had been made available for White teachers. They advertised their gathering six days before its occurrence with the newspaper headline "Great Meeting in the Interest of Education." The text invited "everyone interested in the educational advancement of Negroes who can possibly do so" to "attend this meeting and lend a hand."[77] At the conclusion of the gathering, the new association had formulated clear advocacy objectives for its program. It wanted: "1) better salaries for teachers, 2) better schoolhouses and equipment, 3) the establishment of a normal training school for colored with adequate funds for maintenance, 4) District agricultural school to better prepare farmers, 5) securing appropriation for summer schools."[78] According to the *Savannah Tribune* in a later article, the group believed in the need for an "educational awakening" among the Negroes of Georgia. "There was also general agreement," they reported, "on the need of bringing to bear upon the public authorities of the state all the influences we possibly can to the end that more liberal appropriations be made and better facilities provided for the education of Negro youth."[79]

Immediately, the group began to implement its agenda by petitioning state leaders for equality. By August 2, 1919, the group claimed to have already "memoralized" the State Board of Education. The *Savannah Tribune* noted that "in this memorial the needs of Negro education were set forth and these bodies were asked to see to it that better pay for teachers and better facilities be given for teaching." The White Atlanta newspaper, the *Atlanta Journal and Constitution*, reported that 100 Negroes appeared before the State Board. The enumerated items listed requested are consistent with the ones articulated by the association. In addition, they also advocated for a more equitable share of the monies Georgia was receiving from the federal government.[80] Of the response they received, the *Savannah Tribune* recorded that "the officers of the executive committee had a very respectful hearing and were responded to through a written statement by a special committee on education." However, Joiner reports that their requests had a "definite influence" in the passage of the Elders-Carswell Bill, which provided a comprehensive series of measures designed to increase school opportunities in Georgia education. Moreover, other historical sources report some gains in Black education by 1919 under the Dorsey administration.[81] The evidence suggests that these gains may be linked to the activity of the new educational association.

For a five-year period, the new association promoted itself widely in the Black press for its ability to draw a diverse group of supporters among the Black citizens, and for the next five years membership and influence grew. In May 1919, 500 people reportedly attended their meeting. Attendance was expected to be 1,000 in 1920.[82] However, despite the public portrayal of an organization led by the people, the participants in this group were reportedly the same people who were participants in the older Georgia Teachers Association. Thus, the conceptual leadership appears to have remained among educators, while other members functioned as shields for their activities.

The new education association was not alone in its advocacy of equality of educational opportunity during this era. The period of 1917 is also one that saw critical and focused educational activity on the part of the Atlanta chapter of the NAACP. The December before, the young Walter White, a recent graduate of Atlanta University and associate of Du Bois, indicated a desire to begin a NAACP chapter in Atlanta. By February 3, 1917, the new group had met and decided to fight for education, an event that occurred three days before they would formally request a charter. Within 17 days of the charter request, the group reported to the national office its victory in saving the second grade in Atlanta public schools.[83] It had used reasoned petition and presentation, the same activities utilized by the teachers' association, along with a skilled analysis of the educational situation in Atlanta to make its pleas. As aptly described by Edgar Tappin and verified in NAACP records, the Atlanta NAACP continued to focus on educational issues throughout September of 1917, with careful detail on the nature of the school sessions as they influenced Black children. But by December of that year, the branch had become inactive. With only rare spurts, the lethargy continued into the 1920s, with very little activity of any type inspiring membership. Only one other local NAACP branch, in Savannah, also pushed educational issues, using unsuccessfully the same strategies of petition that had been successful in Atlanta. The other branches throughout the state assume charters during this period or shortly thereafter and quickly die.[84]

A direct correlation can not be proven between the activities of the educational group under Hunt, which focused on statewide activity, and the NAACP, which focused its activity in Atlanta. However, reasons exist to believe that the NAACP was an avenue through which educators and other education-minded individuals in Atlanta accomplished their agenda. While they operated under different organizational names, as one 1970s NAACP state president explained, "we were (after all) the same people." The "same people" argument may be applicable in the 1917 period as well. As noted previously, John Hope was part of the original teachers' organization, serving as a member of the executive committee in 1913 and is listed as working with President M. W. Reddick to reinvigorate the program of the association. He was also actively associated with the NATCS, which was advocating for educational equality on a national level through the interconnection of states. He attended all meetings and is reported to have actively supported the NATCS program, and to have advocated for Black educational equality in other venues. But Hope, who attended the Niagara Conference in 1909, was also one of the signers of the NAACP petition in 1917.[85] In this capacity, his signature clearly represents his membership in the NAACP. Yet, Hope necessarily brought to bear in this organization the education interests that he had long held. Evidence of the possibility of other individuals being members of both organizations is also evident in Charles Harper, the young principal on the membership list in 1917, but later clearly identified with the educational association. In general, the weight of evidence suggests strongly that similar ideas and some overlap in people fueled both initiatives in 1917. Such an interpretation explains the detailed evidence about the educational needs in the city that the NAACP was able to compile so quickly to make its case.[86]

This era, in sum, was one of focused direct activity using a variety of shielded mechanisms. Both the NAACP and the teachers' association used petitions to protest, and both organizations capitalized upon the climate of the era that made Whites more willing to listen to Black demands. In these activities, they met with some limited success, as specifically evident in the passage of the Elders-Carswell Bill. As becomes evident, however, the efforts to pressure local agencies for educational ends would soon be placed in the hands of the state education association, and educators, under the name of the teachers' association, would continue the battle for the next 20 years.

Educational Leadership, 1921–1938: Direct Appeal

Shortly after the its invigorating success in Atlanta to save elementary education, the Atlanta NAACP began a downward trend. To the chagrin of the national office, the branch rarely spoke on educational issues for the next two decades. Likewise, NAACP

local chapters initiated by Atlanta University graduate James Weldon Johnson under
the auspices of the national office also quickly sputtered and died.[87] Their lack of sus-
tainability is reasonably linked to the hostile climate in Georgia during the era which
was less conducive to local NAACP activity, particularly in the smaller cities and rural
areas where members suffered immediate reprisal for membership. How- ever, since this
explanation does not capture the inactivity of the Atlanta branch, another explanation
may be that for unarticulated reasons the community chose to support educators and to
continue the utilization of the teachers' organization as the primary way to effect change.

By 1921 the Georgia Association of Educators, formed in 1917 under H. A. Hunt, and
the Georgia Teachers Association, formed in 1878 under R. R. Wright, appointed a committee to begin the process of merging to form one organization. Since the Georgia Teachers
Association never regained its effectiveness in drawing large numbers of teachers and
membership across the two associations, members of both groups accepted the belief that
a combined effort would create the best strategy. After meeting together for several years,
they formed a new association, the Georgia Teachers and Education Association (GTEA),
which throughout its history would continue the advocacy effort to achieve equality for
Black children that had been present in both parent organizations. Although the association also maintained an active program of professional development, this more visible,
easily recognized aspect does not represent the full range of its activities. To the contrary,
GTEA developed a coordinated mechanism through which it maintained continual pressure in a variety of ways upon Southern educational leaders to provide Negro children a
fair and equitable share of state resources.[88]

In many ways, the advocacy of this era was one of more direct confrontation and
explicit naming of requests on the part of the organization than is evident in earlier
periods. Yet, despite the shifting climate as the United States embraced New Deal policies and began its move toward World War II, the period was nonetheless one in which
Southern law and reprisal would not allow the teachers to take liberties in their approach
with Whites. Many forms of repression still existed, and Black teachers necessarily maintained a stance of placating Whites even as they pressured for change. This stance is
particularly evident in public records and personal communications where they were
careful not to offend the sensibilities of those who financially controlled the schooling of
Black children. However, notwithstanding the challenges, the teachers organizationally
maintained an active resistance to inequality in facilities, resources, terms, and salary.

The consistency of GTEA to pressure for educational equality during this era is
evident in a variety of published and unpublished documents. At the 1925 conference,
for example, GTEA called for "better schoolhouses, better teachers, better school appropriations, and a better correlation of all the forces looking forward to an equal division
of educational funds."[89] This sentiment is echoed in the minutes of the opening session
of the GTEA held in 1926. The secretary noted that the president brought before the
audience the objectives of the association. They were: "Better teachers, schoolhouses,
salaries, terms, larger appropriations to Negro schools and better attendance by Negro

children." Throughout the years, this advocacy theme reappeared with little variation in the addresses and/or reports of its presidents or other officers. According to *Rising in the Sun,* the 1928 presidential address included the statement that "better teachers and better school houses with better pay for those who teach shall be our motto. . . ." The report noted that this theme was reiterated in "numerous speeches delivered by guest speakers and other association members."[90] When H. A. Hunt was re-elected president in 1930, the objectives remained unchanged from his focus in 1917. Likewise, President B. F. Hubert's address in 1938 continued the trend, with a specific emphasis upon the need to equalize Black teacher salaries.[91]

In addition to the visible exhortation at GTEA meetings, the message that the goal was to advocate for the needs of Negro children was also reinforced in the materials distributed to members and in the private discussions evident in the executive committee minutes. For example, in 1930 on the last page of the official publication of GTEA, *The Herald,* teachers were reminded of the goals: "Let us work and ask for better teachers, salaries, school houses and longer school terms."[92] Likewise, in 1936, the in-house document that outlines the vision of the administration of the new president, M. Agnes Jones, appropriates national sentiment by calling the theme of her administration "A New Deal for the Negro School Child." Among her goals are the increase in the salary of qualified teachers, the improvement of facilities for Negro children, the consolidation of single-room schools, the achievement of adequate expenditures for transportation, the implementation of a minimum seven-month school term (though she desired a nine-month term), and the expansion of the number of high schools.[93] In multiple published and unpublished sources, the evidence of GTEA's consistency in focus through this period is evident.

To accomplish the GTEA advocacy agenda, the organization relied primarily upon three strategies. The first, most central strategy was the development of a numerically strong professional association. As captured in the president's message in 1928: "[E]ffective organization was necessary to advance the cause of the race; individuals standing alone could not be effective."[94] Minutes of the Executive Committee, the nine-member team of leaders elected by the membership to represent the needs of all segments of the state, indicate that their "greatest objective was to build up an effective organization for the advancement of education among [the] people of Georgia."[95] The superintendent of education for Negroes in Georgia also made a plea in 1932, pointing out the role teachers must play in the educational uplift of the race. "If there is to be any leadership in educational activities in Georgia today it must come from the ranks of the professionally minded teachers," he proclaimed.[96] Throughout its years, GTEA continued to believe that it had to be a strong body comprised of most of the Black teachers of the state to have maximum influence and to protect its individual members since the group was viewed as the means through which "individual members [of the group] could express themselves."[97] To this end, teachers were expected to join and those districts with 100% representation were widely and publicly recognized.

Membership during this post World War I period never attained 100% participation, but the teachers did enroll in increasing numbers throughout the 1920s. In 1925, for example, GTEA boasted 982 members; by 1929, this number had risen to 2,500, which was approximately half the number of Black teachers employed. Membership in the early 1930s averaged from 1,800 to 2,000 members.[98] Some information about the perspective of teachers regarding GTEA is captured in reports of district and state meetings that were reportedly largely attended, and in information that describes their interest in the work of the organization. Reported the executive director in 1933: "I have just returned from Savannah where the interest is very good and the teachers are all anxious to do more because of the adverse conditions." In another county, despite the lack of support of the superintendent, GTEA received $32 in dues ($1.00 per teacher) in 1933, even though the minimum salary in the county for Black teachers was only $18 per month. Although these reports are incomplete accounts, the existing evidence does indicate sacrifice on the part of many teachers to maintain membership in the organization through the 1930s.[99] Given the hard economic times that descended upon Georgia during the Depression, and the reports of Black teachers not being paid at all, or not being paid their pittance salaries on time, their continued enthusiasm for the work of GTEA may be as indicative of their support as their membership.

Petitions, letters, and personal contacts were the primary means through which advocacy was addressed during this period. In 1930, when H. A. Hunt has been re-elected president of the organization, he notes that he and other members of the executive committee have petitioned the state superintendent of schools requesting better salaries, teachers, equipment, schools, and so forth.[100] Another president in 1938 noted that a committee "has conferences with the Division of Negro Education, the State Department of Education, and the Governor of Georgia on the issue of teacher salaries, and promises that they will keep this matter constantly before the people who are responsible for the apportionment of public funds in the Public School System of Georgia." He also noted that during the year he had traveled over 7,000 miles and written 318 letters to superintendents in the state of Georgia. This type of activity is consistent throughout the period.

In addition to letters to Southern White educators sent by the president of the association, the executive committee was also vested with power to meet with groups and represent the interests of GTEA. In 1929 the executive committee was provided a list of seven "duties," all of which expected that they would "effect improvement" in numbers of teachers, facilities, transportation, consolidation, salaries, and other items on the advocacy agenda (no professional activities are listed as objectives).[101] This 1929 executive committee included a "legislative committee" that suggested, among other things, that in the name of the association, the message of publicity concerning legislation be sent through all newspaper editors.[102] Minutes of the April 1930 meeting in Macon show that a "committee" appeared before the "Superintendents of State." Among other items, their petition asked that the superintendents give more attention to salaries, better teachers, better equipment, longer terms, larger buildings, better location of buildings, consolidation of one-teacher schools, and appropriations for teachers to attend summer schools.[103]

The delivery of their petitions and letters was the outgrown of a finely-tuned communication flow. Generally very well educated and part of the network of Black academic thought, those members who served on the executive committee or as president held the responsibility for direct advocacy with superintendents and those on the state level who could effect change.[104] For example, in the 1929 executive committee minutes, one speaker argued that the committee should "build up a fine, strong sentiment in behalf of that which [they] most desire. Use key-men to exert this influence. Make a plea for justice to our schools and to our teachers' salaries."[105] Unlike previous eras when education was visibly championed by other professionals who would not suffer direct reprisals from Whites if they functioned as shields, the "key people" during this era who were to advocate through petitions, letters, and meetings were primarily GTEA elected leaders. As part of the communication flow, the elected leaders obtained the critical documentation on inequalities from individual teachers who were closest to the local situations across the state; in turn, these leaders utilized the information to maintain political pressure. In this structured manner, individual teachers were protected from the fear of local reprisal that might occur if White employers knew that their employees were part of any agitation for change. GTEA understood the vulnerability of its members, and even in its public programs that superintendents might read, focused more on professional matters than on the advocacy agenda clearly evident in its private documents.[106]

President Hunt's activities in 1932 provide some insight on the implementation of the communication and advocacy pattern. In *The Herald*, Hunt explicitly encouraged teachers to refrain from speaking directly to local superintendents, yet simultaneously provided them with a copy of the letter that has gone out to superintendents in their behalf. Similar sentiment was also expressed in the instructions given teachers after the executive committee meeting in 1936. The teachers were asked to "stay informed" on situations and then "write to [their Black] district president and the state president [of GTEA], calling on them for assistance."[107] This carefully crafted communication flow of petition and protection was the second way in which advocacy worked during this period.

The final GTEA strategy was the utilization of philanthropic aid as a way of implementing its agenda. At the 1925 conference, GTEA noted that its major objective was to match a Rosenwald Foundation grant in order to hire a state worker in the field who could provide the information necessary for spurring activities that would lead to educational equality.[108] This goal was eventually accomplished, and the fieldworker, also called the executive secretary and the Rosenwald Foundation agent, became an integral part of the GTEA activities. While a full discussion of the relationship between the state director of Negro Education, and the Rosenwald agent/executive director of the association for this complete period is outside the scope of this article, the years 1930–1933 are instructive in providing an overview of this working relationship and how it was used to forward the interests of GTEA.

Vincent H. Harris was employed as executive director of GTEA and Rosenwald field agent in December 1930, following several other GTEA members who had been employed in the 1920s. Harris' appointment coincided with the appointment of J. C. Dixon as the White supervisor of Negro education in 1930. Harris received his salary from GTEA and, in an equal amount, a travel allowance from the Department of Education through Dixon's office. Throughout the years, in these dual roles Harris worked with local school Boards and trustees, traveled extensively throughout the state, met regularly with the executive committee and the president of GTEA, wrote petitions and letters, provided formal communications to members, published the *Herald*, and handled the details of GTEA meetings. Ostensibly, he was expected to report on his activities to Dixon, who was to implement the Rosenwald plan for industrial education in the South.[109]

In the early communication disseminated from his office, evidence for Dixon as a representative of the industrial goals of the General Education Board is evident. For example, he traveled with representatives of the Rosenwald Foundation to inspect new schools that were being built with the help of the foundation, and he appeared to be committed to the vocational education that Northern industrialists espoused. His misunderstanding of the ways in which Black educators advocated is also revealed in his naïve suggestion that Black teachers speak to the House and Senate members of the Legislature—an advocacy plan that would make teachers vulnerable and that is never discernable in GTEA materials. However, over the course of Dixon's relationship with Harris, his communications suggest a shift in commitment to the cause of GTEA. He meets with the GTEA executive committee, receiving their suggestions about the content and timing of his letters to White superintendents requesting support for Black teachers. He seeks the advice of Harris to help construct the wording of his letters and, utilizing his access to the networks of White superintendents, gives Harris advice on when the timing may be right for him to make an appearance in a local district or contact the state superintendent. By 1932, he indicated his reluctance for himself or his White assistant to be part of the program at a state meeting, noting that he didn't want to be perceived as "dictating" the activities of GTEA. To be sure, Dixon never wanted to alienate White support and he cajoled Whites as necessary; yet, his actions appear to indicate an evolution of his role. Over time, and presumably through his association with Harris and other Black educators, Dixon appeared to become more an agent of GTEA even though he was employed the General Education Board.[110]

The addition of this level of advocacy reveals the final layer of a carefully concealed information flow that began with local teachers and extended through the leadership and into the office of the Division of Negro Education. However, the flow of information did not merely provide information from teachers to GTEA officials; it also received information from GTEA officials and utilized teachers to communicate critical needs back to the community. The building of the Rosenwald schools in Georgia provides an illustration of this reversed communication pattern. In a 1932 editorial in the *Herald*, Harris told teachers that they should organize an educational committee within their communities, especially in rural communities. Using his extensive knowledge of the state and aided by Dixon's information on the monetary developments in funding, Harris explained that the local Black trustees have no program, that teachers are to make a program, and that they are to call the trustees together themselves, and "tell them what [they] expect them to do for the school. Tell them that it is their duty to go before the Local Board when it meets on the first Tuesday in the court house and to ask for things that are fair and just and in keeping with the needs of your school."[111] Coupled with a call to teachers in the 1932 *Herald* to "[h]elp us build Rosenwald Schools, shops, and teachers' homes in every county in Georgia," the evidence suggests that the teachers were the conduits through which GTEA information was disseminated from leaders to Black parents so that parents could approach boards and request Rosenwald schools. Of course, the teachers were not the only recipients of this information. Though outside of the purview of this article, GTEA also simultaneously encouraged members of the Black state Parent Teachers Association, who met at the same time as teachers and were considered a functioning part of GTEA, to organize and to cooperate with the teachers and principals. Yet, that teachers could have been part of the mechanism that explains that the attainment of 262 Rosenwald schools in Georgia by 1937 is not a correlation that has been explicitly made in the scholarly literature.[112]

These activities of GTEA stand in stark contrast to those of the White teacher association in Georgia, the Georgia Education Association (GEA). Even though both organizations shared the same organizational structure, they held different values in the education of Black children. GEA occasionally reported on Negro education, possibly as a result of Dixon's urgings; but the general thrust does not reflect a disposition on the part of the organization that suggested that it desired to advocate to eradicate the in- equalities in Black education.[113] Attention to the needs of Black education is also not evident in its resolutions. Indeed, to the contrary, some actions of GEA supported overtly hurt Black educators.[114] Moreover, their journal is congratulatory toward Governor Eugene Talmadge for getting school debts paid, while ignoring the overtly denigrating and racist behavior he exhibited as governor during this period toward Blacks.[115] With a membership of the superintendents and state school leaders who resisted change in Black education and a model in the National Education Association (NEA) of lack attention to salary differentials between Black and White teachers, the GEA consistently chose a course that maintained the status quo. Because of their silence, the Black organization was left to its own devices as the single voice to agitate for improved Black education.

By the end of 1938, though some gains, such as a longer school term and textbooks, had been accomplished, many of the items for which GTEA had advocated had remained unfilled.[116] Some of their difficulties may be at- tributed to the real economic difficulties in Georgia during the Depression; some reflect the continuation of the prevailing Southern belief in limited educational opportunities for Blacks. In the years to come, GTEA would cease to attempt to reason with Whites in the manner that some Black national leaders argued was necessary during the 1930s. Instead, they would embrace the ideology of other Black leaders who, referring to the pervasiveness of racism, argued that "appeals to [a] sense of fairness among Whites [was] likely to be useless."[117]. The NAACP victory in the *Gaines* decision in 1938 helped prompt this move, as did the adoption of the Virginia Teachers Association use of legal means in 1938 to address the complaints the Virginia teachers had long held. As chronicled in forthcoming work, the new era of Black educational advocacy would mark one of direct confrontation as GTEA employed local attorneys, requested assistance from the NAACP Legal Defense fund for its efforts, provided plaintiffs, and formed formal relationships with the NAACP and other groups to accomplish its agenda.

Conclusion

The four periods described—association building and interracial collaboration, intellectual activity and national collaboration, petitions and shielded collaboration, and direct appeal—provide evidence of the resistance of Black educators to inequality from 1878 to 1938. Their organization was born as a result of overt structures designed to thwart Black educational opportunities, and it sustained and recreated itself for over 50 years in response to various forms of White neglect or hostility. Yet, despite continual delays, generally without the support of the White teachers' association, and through clever strategies of concealment, Black educators assumed the lead in advocating for Black educational opportunity in a way that is unparalleled within the state. In these behaviors, they were arguably, as Horace Tate, the former executive director of GTEA has captured them, the "engine behind the civil rights movement."

This portrait of Black educators in their various iterations of activity does not discount earlier historical interpretations of Black teachers as afraid of losing their jobs during desegregation. Indeed, the data indicate that fear of economic reprisal for teachers was an accurate concern during this period of restrictive and oppressive race relations. However, earlier interpretations have failed to explore the ways in which Black teachers used their organizational structure as a means of resistance. Indeed, GTEA represented a concerted effort to preserve agency and voice, while minimizing individual reprisal. The very fear that has been used to discount Black educators in striving for equality, in reality, became the basis upon which the organizers developed political and united voice. To focus only on individual agency and not the organizational agency, as most previous research has done, does not reveal this structure.

The educators' efforts during this period yield little structural change since their capacity for effectiveness appears inextricably linked to the federal and state climate in which they lived. Yet, their efforts provide important context for the legal movement that follows. Indeed, the data demonstrate that the legal battle was not the first, but the fifth in the series of movements by Black educators to accomplish equality for Black children. The historical context thus centers Black educators as agents in the advocacy of equality in ways they have been heretofore generally ignored. In this year in which the legal victory ultimately accomplished in the *Brown v. Board of Education* decision is being rightly celebrated, unmasking the roles of Black teachers in educational advocacy is critically important for historical accuracy.

Endnotes

1   Numerous historical accounts depict Black teachers for their concern about employment loss and/or render them invisible in the struggle equality. See David Cecelski, *Along Freedom Road: Hyde County, North Carolina and the Fate of Black Schools in the South* (Chapel Hill, University of North Carolina Press, 1994); Richard Kluger, *Simple Justice* (New York: Vintage Books, 1977); Liva Baker, *The Second Battle of New Orleans* (New York: HarperCollins, 1996); Matthew D. Lassiter and Andrew B. Lewis, editors, *The Moderates' Dilemma: Massive Resistance to School Desegregation in Virginia* (Charlottesville: University Press of Virginia, 1998); Robert A. Pratt, *The Color of Their Skin: Education and Race in Richmond, Virginia, 1954–89* (Charlottesville: University Press of Virginia, 1992); David R. Goldfield, *Black, White, and SOUTHERN: Race Relations and Southern Culture* (Baton Rouge: Louisiana State University Press, 1990), 12–16; Charles Payne, "Debating the Civil Rights Movement: The View from the Trenches," in Steven F. Lawson and Charles Payne, *Debating the Civil Rights Movement, 1945–1968* (Lanham: Rowman and Littlefield, 1998), 124.

2   Kluger, *Simple Justice*, 339.

3   Aldon D. Morris, *The Origins of the Civil Rights Movement: Black Communities Organizing for Change* (New York: The Free Press, 1984); Karen Ferguson, *Black Politics in New Deal Atlanta* (Chapel Hill: University of North Carolina Press, 2002).

4   Donald Grant, *The Way It Was in the South: The Black Experience in Georgia* (Athens: University of Georgia Press, 1993); Stephen N. Tuck, *Beyond Atlanta: The Struggle for Racial Equality in Georgia, 1940–1980* (Athens: University of Georgia Press, 2001); Kenneth Coleman, editor, *A History of Georgia* (Athens: University of Georgia Press, 1977); Oscar H. Joiner, *A History of Public Education in Georgia, 1734–1976* (Columbia, SC: R. L. Bryan Company, 1979). For more general civil rights accounts that neglect teachers, see also Taylor Branch, *Parting the Waters: America in the King Years, 1954–63* (New York: Touchstone, 1988); Aldon D. Morris, *The Origins of the Civil Rights Movement: Black Communities Organizing for Change* (New York: The Free Press, 1984); Philip A. Klinkneer with Rogers M. Smith, *The Unsteady March: The Rise and Decline of Racial Equality in America* (Chicago: University of Chicago Press, 1999) and Harvard Sitkoff, *The Struggle for Black Equality, 1954–1992* (New York: Hill and Wang, 1981); Robert Margo, *Race and Schooling in the South*. Chicago: University of Chicago Press, 53, 63.

5   *The National Educational Association and the Black Teacher*, 55.

6   John J. Donohue, III, J. J. Heckman, and P.E. Todd, "The Schooling of Southern Blacks: The Roles of Legal Activism and Private Philanthropy, 1910–1950," *The Quarterly Journal of Economics* (February 2002).

7   See Adam Fairclough, *Teaching Equality: Black Schools in the Age of Jim Crow* (Athens: University of Georgia Press, 2001), and Mark Tushnet, *The NAACP's Legal Strategy Against Segregated Education, 1925–1950* (Chapel Hill: University of North Carolina Press, 1987).

8   The first set of studies on Black segregated schools included Alvis V. Adair, *Desegregation: The Illusion of Black Progress* (Lanham, Maryland: University of America, 1984); M. G. Hundley, *The Dunbar Story (1870–1955)* (New York: Vantage Press, 1965); Russell Irvine and Jackie Irvine, "The Impact of the Desegregation Process on the Education of Black Students: Key Variables," Journal of Negro Education 52 (1983), 410–422; Faustine Jones, *A Traditional Model of Educational Excellence: Dunbar High School of Little Rock, Arkansas* (Washington: Howard University Press, 1981); F. Rodgers, *The Black High School and Its Community* (Lexington, MA: Lexington Books, 1967); Thomas Sowell, "Black Excellence: The Case of Dunbar High School," Public Interest, 35 (1974), 1–21; Thomas Sowell, "Patterns of Black Excellence," Public Interest, 43 (1976), 26–58. More recent scholarship emerged in the 1990s. Generally, it has been more widely disseminated and discussed than the earlier studies. See Tamara Beauboeuf-Lafontant, "A Movement Against and Beyond Boundaries: 'Politically Relevant Teaching' Among African American Teachers," *Teachers College Record,* 100 (1999), 702–723; Cecelski, *Along Freedom Road*; Michele Foster, "Constancy, Connectedness, and Constraints in the Lives of African American Teachers," *NWSA Journal,* 3 (1990), 233–61; Michele Foster, "The Politics of Race: Through the Eyes of African American Teachers," *Journal of Education,* 172 (1990), 123–41; Michele Foster, *Black Teachers on Teaching* (New York: The New Press); Rhonda Jeffries, "The Trickster Figure in African American Teaching: Pre- and Post-Desegregation," *The Urban Review,* 26 (1994), 289–304; Alicia McCullough-Garrett, "Reclaiming the African American Vision for Teaching: Toward and Educational Conversation," Journal of Negro Education, 62 (1993), 433–440; Vivian Morris and Curtis Morris, *Creating Caring and Nurturing Educational Environments for African American Children* (Westport, CT: Bergin and Garvey, 2000); George Noblit and Van Dempsey, *The Social Construction of Virtue: The Moral Life of Schools* (Albany, NY: State University of New York Press, 1996); Vanessa Siddle Walker, *Their Highest Potential: An African American School Community in the Segregated South* (Chapel Hill: University of North Carolina Press, 1996); Vanessa Siddle Walker, "Caswell County Training School, 1933–1969: Relationships Between Community and School," Harvard Educational Review, 63 (1993), 161–182; Vanessa Siddle Walker, "Valued Segregated Schools for African American Children in the South, 1935–1969: A Review of Common Themes and Characteristics," *Review of Educational Research,* 70 (Fall 2000), 253–285; Vanessa Siddle Walker, "African American Teachers in Segregated Schools in the South, 1940–1969," *American Educational Research Journal, 38* (2001). These scholarly descriptions are accompanied by a number of locally published histories that span both time periods. See Lenwood Davis, *A History of Queen Street High School: 1928–1968* (Kingston, NY: Tri State Services, 1996); W. C. Edwards, Preston Royster, and Lazurus Bates, *The Education of Black Citizens in Halifax County: 1866–1969* (Springfield, VA: Banister Press, 1979); T. Tilford-Weathers, *A History of Louisville Central High School, 1882–1982* (Louisville: Central High School Alumni Association, 1996).

9   Linda Perkins, "The History of Blacks in Teaching," in Donald Warren, *American Teachers: Histories of a Profession at Work* (New York: Macmillan, 1989), 351–357.

10 Thelma Perry, *History of the American Teachers Association* (Washington, DC: NEA, 1975); Michael John Schultz, Jr., *The National Education Association and the Black Teacher* (Michael Fultz, "African-American teachers in the South, 1890–1940: Growth, Feminization, and

Salary Discrimination," *Teachers College Record* 96 (Spring 1995) 40–64; Thomas O'Brien, *The Politics of Race and Schooling: Public Education in Georgia, 1900–1961* (Lanham: Lexington Books,1999).

11 *The Bulletin*, Jan–March, 1950, 26 (1), 14. Horace Tate Private Collection.

12 Rupert Picott, *History of the Virginia Teachers Association* (Washington, DC: NEA, 1975); Thomas Patterson, *History of the Arkansas Teachers Association* (Washington, DC: NEA, 1981); Ancella Bickley, *History of the West Virginia State Teachers' Association* (Washington, DC: NEA, 1975); Gilbert Porter and Leedell Neyland, *History of the Florida State Teachers Association* (Washington, DC: NEA, 1977); John Potts, Sr., *A History of the Palmetto Education Association* (Washington, DC: NEA, 1978); Percy Murray, *History of the North Carolina Teachers Association* (Washington, DC: NEA n.d.).

13 Sterling Stuckey, *Slave Culture: Nationalist theory and the foundations of Black America* (New York: Oxford University Press, 1987).

14 *Rising in the Sun*, 23.

15 For descriptions of Wright, see Leon F. Litwack, *Trouble in Mind* (New York: Vintage Books, 1999), 75–76; James D. Anderson, *The Education of Blacks in the South, 1860–1935* (Chapel Hill: University of North Carolina Press, 1988), 29–30.

16 Anderson, *The Education of Blacks in the South*; Jacqueline Jones, *Soldiers of Light and Love: Northern Teachers and Georgia Blacks, 1865–1873* (Chapel Hill: University of North Carolina Press, 1980).

17 Anderson, *The Education of Blacks:* 11, records the founding as 1865; Jones, *Soldiers of Light and Love*, 54: records the founding as 1866.

18 Numan V. Bartley, *The Creation of Modern Georgia* (Athens: University of Georgia Press, 1983), 51.

19 For early educational activities in Georgia, see Jones, *Soldiers of Light and Love*, 541–563.

20 Bartley, *The Creation of Modern Georgia*, 51–55; Jones, *Soldiers of Light and Love*, 72. Oscar H. Joiner et al., *History of Public Education in Georgia* (Columbia, SC: R. L.Bryan Company, 1979) do not mention the Black association. Joiner et al. chronicles instead 25 white educators from schools and colleges who met in Atlanta and formed the Georgia Teachers Association four months before the convention. Reportedly, they consulted with the George Peabody Fund in 1867 and received money to study needs and to develop a system of public schools, 70.

21 Richard R. Wright, *A Brief Historical Sketch of Negro Education in Georgia* (Savannah, GA: Robinson Printing House, 1894), 18.

22 The earlier leaders, described as ministers, also were likely educators. Thus, this shift may be one of name only rather than actuality. See Wright, *A Brief Historical Sketch*, 7.

23 See Jones, *Soldiers of Light and Love*, 195–201; Bartley, *The Creation of Modern Georgia*, 69; Grant, *The Way It Was in the South*, 126–128.

24 See Joiner et al., *History of Public Education in Georgia*, 89; Bartley, *The Creation of Modern Georgia*, 80.

25 Grant, *The Way it was in the South*, 130.

26 Wright, *A Brief Historical Sketch*, 47.

27 *Rising in the Sun,* 24.

28 Wright, *A Brief Historical Sketch,* 47.

29 Joiner et al., *History of Public Education in Georgia,* 87–88; Bartley, *The Creation of Modern Georgia,* 61.

30 Wright, *A Brief Historical Sketch,* 47.

31 Hines Lafayette Hill, *Negro Education in Rural Georgia* (A thesis submitted to Emory University, August 1939), 12.

32 Anderson, *The Education of Blacks in the South,* provides the most comprehensive description of the variety of ways Whites educated Blacks for their roles in the South.

33 Grant, *The Way It Was in the South,* 127.

34 *Rising in the Sun,* 23.

35 Louis R. Harlan, *Booker T. Washington: The Making of a Black Leader, 1856–1901* (New York: Oxford University Press, 1972), 154.

36 For a discussion of the populist movement in Georgia, see Bartley, *The Creation of Modern Georgia,* 91–94. For commentary on inequality, see Wright, *A Brief Historical Sketch,* 52.

37 Grant, *The It Was in the South,* 127–128.

38 Ibid, 232.

39 Wright, *A Brief Historical Sketch, 33,* 52.

40 Kevin K. Gaines, *Uplifting the Race: Black Leadership, Politics and Culture in the 20th Century* (Chapel Hill: University of North Carolina Press, 1996).

41 For comprehensive accounts of the rise of Southern racism, see C. Vann Woodard, *The Strange Career of Jim Crow* (New York: Oxford University Press, 1974); Kluger, *Simple Justice.* For information specific to Georgia, see Bartley, *The Creation of Modern Georgia*; Grant, *The Way It Was in the South,* 209.

42 In 1892, Atlanta Blacks boycotted streetcars, which resulted in non-enforcement of the segregation requirement. See Grant, *The Way It Was in the South,* 217; Coleman, *A History of Georgia,* 277. In other activism, in 1891 officers of the Colored Farmer's Alliance addressed the General Assembly and urged that Jim Crow laws not be passed and the laws were not passed. See Coleman, *A History of Georgia,* 277.

43 Grant, *The Way It Was in the South,* 216.

44 Anderson, *The Education of Blacks in the South,* 188, 192–193.

45 Grant, *The Way It Was in the South,* 232.

46 *Rising in the Sun,* 16. Grant reports that before disenfranchisement, Black teachers averaged 58% of the White teacher scale; three years after disfranchisement, Black teachers received only 38% of the scale. The average salary of Black teachers declined $5 a year, whereas white teachers' salaries increased by more than $100. Grant, *The Way It Was in the South,* 235.

47 Coleman, *A History of Georgia,* 239.

48 Bartley, *The Creation of Modern Georgia,* 85.

49 *Rising in the Sun,* 25.

50 "Special Notice to Colored Teachers," *Savannah Tribune* 28 (August 16, 1913), 4.

51 Ibid.

52 Grant, *The Way It Was in the South*, 228.

53 Reported in *Rising in the Sun*, 25.

54 W. E. Burghardt Du Bois, "The Negro Common School," in *The Atlanta University Publi-cations* (New York: Arno Press and The New York Times, 1969), 117.

55 *Rising in the Sun*, 24–25.

56 "National Association of Teachers in Colored Schools to Meet," *Savannah Tribune* 32 (July 7, 1917), 1.

57 Grant, *The Way it was in the South*, 244.

58 Perry, *History of the American Teachers Association*, 47–48; Donald H. Parkerson and Jo Ann Parkerson, *Transitions in American Education: A Social History of Teaching* (New York: Routledge Farmer, 2001), 87

59 For leadership of Wright, Laner, and Hope in NATCS, see Perry, *History of American Teach-ers Association*, 103, 104, 107. Wright was unable to attend the 1909 meeting; however, Hope attended. See Ridgely Torrence, *The Story of John Hope* (New York: Macmillan Company, 1948), 161.

60 "Special Notice to Colored Teachers," *Savannah Tribune* 28 (August 16, 1913), 4.

61 For references to newspaper accounts of Black educational activity in the 1880s, see *Rising in the Sun*, 22–24. Except for the 1913 reference, reported activity in the *Savannah Tribune* does not resume until 1917. For example, see "Georgia Association for Negro Education Holds Successful Meeting in Atlanta," *Savannah Tribune* 36 (May 14, 1921), 1; "Educational Associ-ation Planning Big Meeting," *Savannah Tribune* (April 13, 1918), 2; "Many Attend Educational Mass Meeting," *Savannah Tribune* 31 (May 10, 1919). Others are cited in references below.

62 Kluger, *Simple Justice*, 85–86.

63 Grant, *The Way It Was in the South*, 293; Kluger, *Simple Justice*, 100.

64 Coleman, *A History of Georgia*, 261.

65 "The Negro 'Exodus' in Texas," *Savannah Times* 32 (July 17, 1979), 1.

66 Grant, *The Way It Was in the South*, 293–294.

67 William G. Jordan, *Black Newspapers & America's War for Democracy, 1914–1920* (Chapel Hill: University of North Carolina Press, 2001), 145.

68 Kluger, *Simple Justice*, 100–104.

69 Joiner et al., *History of Public Education in Georgia*, 200.

70 Jones, *Soldiers of Light and Mercy*, 72.

71 "Jesse O. Thomas Interview" (1961). Tate Papers.

72 "Big Educational Meeting Next Month," *Savannah Tribune* 34 (April 19, 1919), 1.

73 Hunt may have been mirroring the behavior of Booker T. Washington. For a description of Washington's actions politically behind the scenes and Tuskegee students studying national philosophy, ancient history, and civil government in 1897, see Harlan, *Booker*

T. Washington; David Levering Lewis, *W. E. B. Du Bois: Biography of a Race* (New York: Henry Holt and Company, 1993), 197–198. On Hunt's liberal arts curriculum in 1915, see also Lewis, 545. On the evolution of Hunt, James Anderson argues that Hunt may have learned from his predecessor what happens to Blacks who fail to play the game of vocational education correctly. This understanding, coupled with his familial associations with Tuskegee faculty, allow him to publicly pretend to eschew his Atlanta University training, while quietly finding ways to generate resistance. James Anderson, personal communication.

74 "Great Meeting in the Interest of Education," *Savannah Tribune* (April 28, 1917), 1.

75 Grant, *The Way It Was in Georgia,* 294.

76 "National Teachers at Harper's Ferry," *Savannah Tribune* (July 27, 1918), 1.

77 "Great Meeting in the Interest of Education," *Savannah Tribune* (April 28, 1917), 1.

78 *Rising in the Sun,* 26. Interestingly, these points are the same points argued by Waycross leaders during that same year. Though no explicit link has been identified, the leaders of that group quite likely are part of the new educational group. For a description of the Waycross activity, see Grant, *The Way It Was in the South,* 294.

79 "Need Felt for Educational Awakening," *Savannah Tribune* (March 2, 1918), 1.

80 Joiner et al., *History of Public Education in Georgia,* 212.

81 Thomas O'Brien, *The Politics of Race and Schooling,* 15.

82 "Many Attend Educational Mass Meeting," *Savannah Tribune* (May 10, 1919); "Educational Ass'n to Meet in Macon," *Savannah Tribune* (April 24, 1920), 1.

83 Walter W. White to Roy Nash, New York, 16 December 1916; Walter White to Roy Nash, New York, 3 February 1917; Walter W. White to Roy Nash, New York, 3 February 1917; Walter W. White to James W. Johnson, Florida, 22 February 1917. NAACP Branch Files, Atlanta, Georgia, 1913–1917. NAACP Records, Library of Congress.

84 Edgar Tappin, "Walter White and the Atlanta NAACP's Fight for Equal Schools, 1916–1917," *History of Education Quarterly* 7 (Spring 1967), 3–17. For Atlanta branch activity, see also Walter White to James W. Johnson, New York, 27 March 1917; Walter White to Roy Nash, New York, 19 March 1917; Walter White to Roy Nash, New York, 3 February 1917; Walter W. White to Roy Nash, New York, 3 March 1917; Walter W. White to James W. Johnson, New York, 27 September 1917. For lessened activity in the Branch, see Acting Secretary to Harry H. Pace, Atlanta, 12 December 1917; Acting Secretary to Walter White, Atlanta, 12 December 1917; Walter W. White to James W. Johnson, New York, 5 December 1917; Director of Branches to Austin T. Walden 27 January 1925; Director of Branches to E. Franklin Frazier, Atlanta, 21 January 1925; Director of Branches to E. Franklin Frazier, Atlanta, 24 February 1925; 2–27–27; 6–19–19. For charter requests and demise of other Georgia branches, as evidenced by lack of communication , see examples of correspondence in Branch Files for Albany, GA, 1919–1933; Americus, GA, 1919, 1922–1924; Athens, GA, 1917–1918; Brunswick, GA, 1918–1938; Columbus, GA; Cordele, GA; For branch activity in the 1930s, see branch files for Augusta, GA, Jan.- Nov. 1933; Bainbridge, GA; Albany, GA 1934; Baxley, GA, Apr-Nov. 1936; Cartersville, GA; Cedartown, GA; Collins, GA; Cuthbert, GA, 1934–1939. Savannah activity can be documented in the Savannah Branch Files. NAACP Records, Library of Congress.

85 "Special Notice to Colored Teachers," *Savannah Tribune* 18 (August 16, 1913), 4; Perry, *History of American Teachers Association*, 105; Lewis, *W. E. B. DuBois*, 550; Walter White to James W. Johnson, New York, 22 February 1917.

86 Tour guides at the King center currently describe the King home as the place where educators met with A. D. Williams, NAACP president, to plan advocacy. Public Parks, Atlanta, GA.

87 Grant, *The Way It Was in the South*, 311. As noted in footnote 83, Georgia branches formed circa 1917–19. The branch files reveal little activity in the 1920s. For branch activity in the 1930s, see, for example, branch files for Augusta, GA, Jan.-Nov. 1933; Bainbridge, GA; Albany, GA, 1934; Baxley, GA, Apr.-Nov. 1936; Cartersville, GA; Cedartown, GA; Collins, GA; Cuthbert, GA, 1934–1939.

88 The association continued to evolve until 1926. *Rising in the Sun*, 41, notes that several other previous associations, such as the Georgia Business and Professional League and the Organization of Private Colleges and Schools, also became part of GTEA. During the 1920s, this association is known as the Georgia State Teachers and Educational Association. For clarity, I refer to the organization throughout as the Georgia Teachers and Education Association (GTEA).

89 *Rising in the Sun*, 29.

90 Ibid 50–51.

91 "Annual Address of President B. F. Hubert," *The Herald* 4 (June 1938), 4–5.

92 *The Herald* 2, (April 1930), 15. Horace Tate Collection, Atlanta, GA.

93 "A New Deal for the Negro School Child," 1–2. Horace Tate Collection, Atlanta, GA. In these and other excerpts, I omit other concerns of the Association that relate to curricular matters, increasing teacher qualifications, and so forth. Although the teachers were equally interested in these areas, this topic is not the focus of the present paper.

94 *Rising in the Sun*, 51.

95 GTEA Executive Meeting minutes, June 28, 1929. Horace Tate Collection, Atlanta, GA. This statement is also recorded in *Rising in the Sun*, 51

96 J. C. Dixon, "Everyone to the Annual Convention in Macon," *The Herald* 2 (April 1932), 7.

97 J. C. Dixon to Jeanes teachers, Georgia, 6 December 1933. Vincent H. Harris File, Georgia State Archives.

98 *Rising in the Sun*, 54; Vincent Harris, "Editorial," *The Herald* 2 (April 1932), 7.

99 Descriptions of teacher response are most evident in the Vincent Harris file, Georgia State Archives. See Vincent Harris to Dorothy Millsap, Atlanta, 31 January 1931; H. A. Hunt to Vincent H. Harris, Atlanta, 25 January 1932; Vincent Harris to Dorothy Millsap, Atlanta, 28 March 1932; Vincent Harris to Mayme R. Brown, Cuthbert, GA, 16 February 1933; Mayme R. Brown to J. C. Dixon, Atlanta, 31 January 1933. For their response during the Depression, see Vincent Harris to W. P. Stephens, Calhoun, GA, 4 October 1931; Walter Stephens to J. C. Dixon, Atlanta, 18 October 1932, 10–18–32; J. C. Dixon to Mason Williams, Morven, GA, 20 February 1933; Dixon to J. Mason Williams, Morven, GA, 7 March 1933.

100 *Rising in the Sun*, 56.

101 *Rising in the Sun*, 56.

102 Ibid.

103 "Minutes of annual Meeting," April 17, 1930, 20. Horace Tate Collection, Atlanta, GA.

104 W. E. B. Du Bois served on the advisory board for GTEA for 1936 and 1937 and lectured
     at one of the GTEA meetings in 1937. At least two copies of the Herald carry articles/
     speeches by him during his affiliation with GTEA. See "Dr. W. E. B. Du Bois speaks at
     Georgia State College," *The Herald* 5 (February 1939), 10–11 and "Curriculum Revision,"
     The Herald 3 (March 1937), 13.

105 Executive Meeting Minutes, June 28, 1929. Horace Tate Collection, Atlanta, GA.

106 In public materials, the advocacy is often concealed under such categories as "presidential
     recommendations," or, in later years, "teacher improvement." The contrast between the
     minutes of the executive committee and the annual meeting suggest a concealment or
     minimization of the advocacy in public discourse. Minutes of Annual Meeting, Savan-
     nah, GA, April 17, 1929. Horace Tate Collection, Atlanta, GA.

107 Vincent Harris, "Editorial," *The Herald* 2 (April 1932), 7; H. A. Hunt, Letter to Fellow
     Teachers, *The Herald* 2 (April 1932), 14; Agnes Jones, "A New Deal for the Negro School
     Child," 4. Horace Tate; Collection, Atlanta, GA.

108 *Rising in the Sun*, 29.

109 Vincent Harris to J. C. Dixon, Atlanta, 21 March 1932; J. C. Dixon to Vincent Harris,
     Atlanta, 11 April 1932; Vincent Harris to Dixon, Atlanta, 4 October 1932.

110 For Dixon's evolution, see J. C. Dixon to Vincent Harris, Atlanta, 12 January 1931; Vincent
     Harris to J. C. Dixon, Atlanta, 9 March 1931; Vincent Harris to J. C. Dixon, Atlanta, 8 April
     1931; J. C. Dixon to Vincent Harris, Atlanta, 24 July 1931; Vincent Harris to J. C. Dixon, At-
     lanta, 6 January 1932; Vincent Harris to J. c. Dixon, Atlanta 8 December 1933; J. C. Dixon
     to Vincent Harris, Atlanta, 6 April 1933; Vincent Harris to J. C. Dixon, Atlanta, 1 March
     1933. The evolution of Dixon may shed meaning on the statement of his contemporary,
     captured in James Anderson, *The Education of Blacks in the South*. Anderson records that
     Newbold notes, "If only these walls could talk." Newbold may, in fact, be suggesting a
     relationship occurring within those walls that was not publicly unveiled.

111 "Vincent H. Harris, Editorial," *The Herald* 2 (April 1932), 7. The relationship between
     Dixon and vocational education is as yet unclear. GTEA members themselves advocated
     for vocational education, and had since the Smith-Hughes Act. They seemed to see no
     contra- diction between this advocacy and classical education, indeed allowing both of
     them to exist side by side in local school settings.

112 "The Julius Rosenwald Fund," *The Herald* 3 (March 1937), 4. Horace Tate Collection,
     Atlanta, GA; *Rising in the Sun*, 51.

113 See "Negro School Conditions," *Georgia Education Journal*, 27 (January 1935), 33, for an
     example of one of the few reports on Negro education.

114 See, for example, "Editorial," *Georgia Education Journal* 28 (February 1936), 20. "Editorial,"
     Georgia Education Journal 28 (November 1935), 20.

115 "Editorial," *Georgia Education Journal* 28 (January 1936), 20.

116 For various reports on teacher certification, building program enrollment gains, see *The
     Herald* 3 (March 1937), 12. However, it must be noted that it is difficult to disaggregate

this activity from the GEA influence, since GEA also advocated for general issues such as school term.

117 Tushnet, *The NAACP's Legal Strategy*, 12.

SELECTION 6

Patterns of Black Excellence

Thomas Sowell

THE HISTORY OF the advancement of black Americans is almost a laboratory study of human achievement, for it extends back to slavery and was accomplished in the face of the strongest opposition confronting any American racial or ethnic group. Yet this mass advancement is little discussed and seldom researched, except for lionizing some individuals or compiling a record of *political* milestones. But the story of how millions of people developed from the depths of slavery—acquired work skills, personal discipline, human ideals, and the whole complex of knowledge and values required for achievement in a modern society—is a largely untold story. A glance at the mass of human misery around the world shows that such development is by no means an automatic process. Yet how it was accomplished remains a matter of little concern—in contrast to the unflagging interest in social pathology.

One small, but important, part of the advancement of black Americans has been educational achievement. Here, as in other areas, the pathology is well known and extensively documented, while the healthy or outstanding functioning is almost totally unknown and unstudied. Yet educational excellence has been achieved by black Americans.[1] Current speculative discussions of the "prerequisites" for the quality education of black children proceed as if educational excellence were only a remote possibility, to be reached by futuristic experimental methods—indeed, as if black children were a special breed who could be "reached" only on special wave lengths. When quality education for black youngsters is seen, instead, as something that has *already* been achieved—that happened decades ago—then an attempt to understand the ingredients of such education can be made on the basis of that experience, rather than as a search for exotic revelations. The problem is to assess the nature of black excellence, its sources, and its wider implications for contemporary education and for social policy in general.

There are a number of successful black schools in various cities that exemplify this educational excellence—for the purposes of this study, six high schools and two elementary schools were selected. The high schools were chosen from a list, compiled by the late Horace Mann Bond, which shows those black high schools whose alumni included the most doctorates during the period from 1957 through 1962. The two elementary schools were added because of their outstanding performance by other indices. Some of the schools were once outstanding but are no longer, while others are currently academically successful. The schools were researched not only in terms of such "hard" data as test scores but also in terms of such intangibles as atmosphere and school/community relations, as these could be either observed or reconstructed from documents and from interviews with alumni, former teachers, and others. On the basis of this research, several questions were raised:

1. Is black "success" largely an individual phenomenon—simply "cream rising to the top"—or are the successes produced in such isolated concentrations as to suggest powerful forces at work in special social or institutional settings? Strong and clear patterns would indicate that there are things that can be done through social policy to create or enhance the prospect of individual development.

2. Does the environment for successful black education have to be a special "black" environment—either culturally, or in terms of the race of the principals and teachers, or in terms of the particular teaching methods used? Are such conventional indices as test scores more or less relevant to black students? For example, do these top black schools have average I.Q. scores higher than the average (around 85) for black youngsters in the country as a whole? Are their I.Q. scores as high as white schools of comparable performance by other criteria?

3. How much of the academic success of these schools can be explained as a product of the "middle-class" origins of its students? Have most of the children taught in these schools been the sons and daughters of doctors and lawyers, or have they represented a cross section of the black community?

4. How important was the surrounding community as an influence on the quality of education in these schools? Did this influence come through involvement in school decision-making or through moral support in other ways?

5. How many of the assumed "prerequisites" of quality education actually existed in these outstanding schools? Did they have good facilities, an adequate budget, innovative programs, internal harmony, etc.?

6. What kind of individual was shaped by these institutions? More bluntly, was the black excellence of the past an accommodationist or "Uncle Tom" success molded by meek or cautious educators, or the product of bold individuals with high personal and racial pride?

Although these questions will be treated in the course of this article, the first question is perhaps the easiest to answer immediately. Black successes—whether measured by academic degrees or by career achievement—have not occurred randomly among the millions of black people scattered across the United States, as might be expected if individual natural ability were the major factor. On the contrary, a very few institutions in a few urban centers with a special history have produced a disproportionate share of black pioneers and high achievers. In Horace Mann Bond's study, five percent of the high schools produced 21 percent of the later PhDs.[2] Four of the six high schools studied here—McDonough 35 High School, in New Orleans; Frederick Douglass High School, in Baltimore; Dunbar High School, in Washington, D.C.; and Booker T. Washington High School, in Atlanta—produced a long list of black breakthroughs, including the first black state superintendent of schools (Wilson Riles, from McDonough 35), the first black Supreme Court Justice (Thurgood Marshall, from Frederick Douglass), the first black general (Benjamin O. Davis, Sr., from Dunbar), the first black Cabinet member (Robert C. Weaver, from Dunbar), the discoverer of blood plasma (Charles R. Drew, from Dunbar), a Nobel Prize winner (Martin Luther King, Jr., from Booker T. Washington), and the only black Senator in this century (Edward W. Brooke, from Dunbar). From the same four schools, this list can be extended down to many regional and local "firsts," as well as such national "firsts" as the first black federal judge (William H. Hastie, from Dunbar), the first black professor at a major university (Allison Davis, from Dunbar, at the University of Chicago), and others. All of this from just four schools suggests some systematic social process at work, rather than anything as geographically random as outstanding individual ability—though these particular individuals had to be personally outstanding, besides being the products of special conditions.

The locations of these four schools are suggestive: Washington, D.C., Baltimore, New Orleans, and Atlanta. Baltimore, New Orleans, and Washington were the three largest communities of "free persons of color" in the Southern or border states in 1850.[3] None of these schools goes back to 1850, and some of them are relatively new; but the communities in which they developed had long traditions among the old families, and historical head starts apparently have enduring consequences. New Orleans had the most prosperous and culturally advanced community of "free persons of color" and the largest number of high schools on H. M. Bond's list—all three of which are still outstanding high schools today.

Atlanta: Booker T. Washington High School

When Booker T. Washington High School was founded in 1924, it was the first public high school for Negroes in Atlanta and in the state of Georgia, and one of the first in the nation. However, the black community of Atlanta had had both primary and secondary education for its children long before that. In 1869, the American Missionary Society—which greatly influenced quality education for Southern blacks—established in Atlanta several "colleges" and "universities," whose initial enrollments were actually concentrated in elementary and secondary study, with only a few real college students.[4] The first principal of Booker T. Washington High School was, in fact, a man who had been in charge of the high school program at Morris Brown College.

Professor Charles Lincoln Harper was principal of Booker T. Washington for its first 19 years, and a major influence on the shaping of the institution. By all accounts, he was a man of great courage, ability, and capacity for hard work. Far from being middle-class in origin, he came from a black farm family living on a white-owned plantation. As a child, he attended the only available school, which was 10 miles away and which held classes only three months of the year. Somehow Harper managed to educate himself and go on to college, and later to graduate work at the University of Chicago and Columbia. In addition to becoming a principal, Harper was a civil rights activist at a time when economic retaliation, lynchings, and Ku Klux Klan violence were an ever-present threat. The times were such that many blacks gave money to the NAACP *anonymously* through Harper, who bore the onus of converting it into checks to mail to the NAACP headquarters in New York. Thurgood Marshall said that Harper "stood out head and shoulders above many others because of his complete lack of fear of physical or economic repercussions."[5]

As principal, it was common for Harper to work Saturdays, and to spend part of his summer vacation taking promising students to various colleges and universities, trying to gain admission or scholarships for them. A contemporary described him as a man of "utter sincerity" who "lives on the job." Though he was a man who drove himself, with teachers he was "affable" and "easy to approach," and he showed "vast stores of patience" with students. A man of modest means—he owned only one suit—he nevertheless gave small sums of money to poor children in his school when they needed it. Yet for all his dedication to black people, he was not uncritical of black institutions. As late as 1950, he said, "There is not a single first-class, accredited college in the state for the education of Negro students."[6] To say that must have required considerable courage in Atlanta, home of Morehouse, Spelman, and Morris Brown colleges, and of many proud alumni.

The cohesion of the Atlanta black community and the political sophistication of its leaders were directly responsible for the building of Booker T. Washington High School. A public high school for Negroes was unprecedented in the state of Georgia, and some members of the all-white school board considered it an outrageous demand. Black voters enforced their demand by turning out in sufficient numbers—in the heyday of the Ku Klux Klan—repeatedly to defeat school bond issues until it was agreed that the high school would be built. But the board of education did not go one step beyond its grudging agreement: The school building alone was built on bare land. Harper conducted a fundraising campaign in the community to provide landscaping and to build a statue of the school's namesake in front of the entrance. The board of education's tightfistedness continued to be a problem for the school for decades. Classes were large in the early years: 45 to 50 pupils per class was not unusual. The students received hand-me-down textbooks discarded after years of use in white schools.

Extra efforts by Harper, the staff, and the community overcame these obstacles. The community contributed money for the building of an athletic stadium and helped support school athletics out of their own pockets. The board of education provided no money at all for athletic uniforms, or for athletes to travel. However, the coach obtained uniforms from a local sports store and drove the teams in his own car, with gas supplied free by a gas station in the community. The team ate hot dogs donated by a black drugstore. On their own time, teachers drove students to cultural events during the spring vacation. The teachers of this era also maintained closets full of second-hand clothing and shoes for needy pupils—all brought to school in paper bags, so that no one would ever know whose old clothes he was wearing.

The atmosphere in the school during this era was a blend of support, encouragement, and rigid standards. One alumnus described it as a "happy school" with "hard taskmasters." Of one teacher it was said: "She did not tolerate sloppy work any more than a Marine sergeant tolerates a coward on a battlefield." Another teacher "threw homework at you like you were in college instead of the sixth grade." Those who did not learn on the first try in school stayed after school for as many days as it took to learn. Yet the students found the teachers inspiring rather than oppressive. A sense of individual worth and pride of achievement were constantly sought. "You couldn't go wrong," an alumnus said: "The teachers wouldn't let you."

Racial and political awareness were part of the early curriculum but traditional subjects—including Latin—dominated. Racial pride was developed by example as well as by words. Many teachers refused the indignity of riding in the back of segregated buses, which meant that some of them had to walk during years when cars were rare.

In the 50 years of its existence, Booker T. Washington has had only five principals: C. L. Harper for 17 years (1924-1941), C. N. Cornell for 20 years (1941-1961), J. Y. Moreland for eight years (1961-1969), before being promoted to area superintendent, and A. A. Dawson for four years (1969-1973), also before being promoted to area superintendent. The present principal, Robert L. Collins, Jr., assumed the post in 1973. He is a graduate of the school, and his daughter is the third generation of his family to attend.

The school has undergone some metamorphoses in the half-century of its existence. It is no longer the only black high school in the city, and the neighborhood in which it is located is run down—both factors tending to lower academic performance—while there are such offsetting tendencies as better financial support and better physical equipment. The available records do not go back far enough to permit comparison with the performance of the early years, but the current academic performance of Booker T. Washington is far from that of an elite school. On a variety of tests, its students scored significantly below the national average, and below the average of other Atlanta high schools. The demeanor of its students also seems much more in keeping with that of a typical urban ghetto school than a school with a distinguished past. Black Atlantans seemed defensive about discussing these changes, though one characterized the school as "a little thuggish" today. It is not unusual for a school which loses its monopoly of black high school students and is located in a declining neighborhood to have difficulties maintaining standards. Other schools in this study have suffered similar fates. But the justifiable pride of Atlantans in the school's past makes it difficult to trace the process by which the present uninspiring situation came about. Certainly it is clear that the present financial resources and political clout—a black superintendent of schools and a black mayor of the city—are no substitute for the human resources that enabled earlier generations to overcome heavy handicaps.

Interestingly enough, the current principal is not as defensive as other Atlantans inside or outside the school system. While he will not openly concede a decline in academic performance, he freely acknowledges a number of factors which make it a harder job to get good performance from students of a given level of ability. Chief among these is less parental support and cooperation: Parents may be more "involved" in school decisions today, but they are less cooperative than in earlier decades. In particular, parents are less willing to take the side of the school teacher or principal who wants an able student to take more demanding courses instead of following the path of least resistance. Even when the parents understand the long-run educational need, they are often not willing to risk immediate problems in relations with their children. Discipline problems are also more numerous and more difficult, and there are fewer methods available for dealing with them. Corporal punishment was still permissible in the mid-1940s, when Collins was a student, but it is no longer an option. Moreover, whatever discipline is imposed is less likely to have parental support or reinforcement, and more likely to provoke parental indignation. Still, Collins works at it—12 hours or more a day. It is too early to tell if he can turn the situation around, especially since the general problem extends well beyond Atlanta, is not limited to black schools, and has had a varying impact on schools across the country.

Atlanta: St. Paul of the Cross

A very different school in many ways is St. Paul of the Cross. Its openness was the first of many contrasts. Records just received from a testing organization were taken straight from the envelope and spread out on the table for inspection. This confidence was based on years of solid performance. A sample of I.Q. scores for this Catholic elementary school shows them consistently at or above the national norm of 100—which is to say, significantly above the national average of about 85 for other black children. This school came to our attention as a result of an earlier research project surveying I.Q. scores. The mean I.Q. of the St. Paul student body for the years surveyed (1960-1972) ranged from 99 to 107.

St. Paul is located in a middle-class black suburban area of Atlanta, but its students are drawn from various parts of the city. Of all the schools in this study for which we were able to obtain the data, St. Paul has the highest proportion of white-collar and professional occupations among its students' parents. For the period 1960-1972, 40 per cent of the parents were either white-collar or professional. Our breakdown shows 33 per cent white-collar and seven per cent professional, but that is based on counting school teachers in the white-collar category, and the two categories are presented together simply to avoid needless (and endless) debate over where the line should be drawn. For the other schools in this study, this internal breakdown is of little significance, since the two categories together usually add up to no more than 10 per cent. But although St. Paul has a substantial proportion of white-collar and professional parents for a black school, it is still not predominantly middle-class, in the usual sense of having children whose parents are doctors, engineers, or professors, or are in similar occupations.

Quiet, calm, and orderliness prevail in St. Paul's modem building, even during the changing of class. Yet the students do not seem either repressed or apprehensive. There was talking during the change of classes, but no yelling or fighting. Corporal punishment is one of the disciplinary options, but it is seldom used. Discipline is usually maintained through individual discussions between the teachers—half nuns and half laity—and the children. For example, a little boy who had spilled his soda in the hall without cleaning it up was told that the cleaning woman works hard to keep the school nice, and it was suggested that he apologize to her for making her job harder—but all this was done very gently without burdening him with guilt. This calm, low-key approach is made possible by small classes (about 30), small student body (about 200), and an automatically self-selective admissions process, since hard-core troublemakers are unlikely to apply for admission to a private school.

Instruction is highly individualized. Instead of the classic picture of the teacher standing in front of the class lecturing, the more usual scene in the classroom at St. Paul was a teacher very much engaged with an individual student or a small group, while the other members of the class worked intently on their respective assignments. This individualized approach extended even to allowing students to go to the library on their own. The child's self-confidence is built up in subtle ways. However, there was no single teaching method or formula imposed from above. The usual bureaucratic paperwork was absent at St. Paul. Records were well kept and complete, but not cluttered with trivia. Administrators had time to circulate through the school and get to know the students, rather than being stuck at their desks behind piles of paper. Morale is high enough to attract lay teachers at lower salaries than they receive elsewhere.

St. Paul has had only four principals in its 21-year history. Three of these were nuns of the Sisters of St. Joseph, and the other was a black layman appointed in the 1960s at the height of the emphasis on "blackness." However, the initiative for a black lay principal came from whites in the religious order, rather than from either the black community or black parents. The current principal is a white nun.

The children are encouraged to take pride in their black heritage, but the curriculum is heavily oriented toward the basics of education—especially reading. There is also religious instruction, but the student body is about 70 percent non-Catholic, though it was initially predominantly Catholic. Black non-Catholic students in Catholic schools are common in cities around the country, as black parents seek the education, the discipline, and the sheer physical safety which the public schools often cannot offer. The tuition is modest—about $450 per year for non-Catholics and $360 for Catholics—and the school runs a deficit, which is made up from general church funds.

Though quite different from Booker T. Washington High School in many ways, St. Paul has one problem in common with it: Some parents think that the school is *too* intellectually challenging for their children. Interestingly, this view is more common among those parents who are public school teachers.

Baltimore: Frederick Douglass High School

As of 1850, the 25,000 "free persons of color" in Baltimore were the largest number in any city in the United States, so it is not surprising that Baltimore's high school for black children was among the earliest founded, in 1892. Like many other black schools throughout the United States, Frederick Douglass High School survived for decades with inadequate financial support, was located in a succession of hand-me-down buildings that whites had discarded, and was stocked with old textbooks used for years before by white students, refinished desks from white schools, second-hand sports equipment, and so on. Douglass was for many years the only black high school in Baltimore. The school contained academic, vocational, commercial, and "general" programs. Because the surrounding communities had no high schools for Negro children, black students from outside Baltimore also came to Douglass—some legitimately, through stiff tests given to outsiders, and many others by the simple expedient of giving false addresses in Baltimore, often the addresses of relatives or friends.

Although pupils from Baltimore faced no tests for admission, there was a self-selection factor at work. Those without sufficient interest or skills would have dropped out before high school, in an era when students left school at earlier ages and when substandard students repeated grades, instead of today's automatic promotion. In short, while Frederick Douglass in its early decades was formally an all-inclusive black high school serving Baltimore and vicinity, in practice there were automatic selection factors which screened out the wholly uninterested or negative student. These were not high academic admission standards, such as elite private schools imposed, but even this wholly informal screening was sufficient to keep the school free of "discipline problems."

The teachers included men and women trained at the leading colleges and universities in the country. An alumnus of the 1930's recalls that his principal, Mason Hawkins, had a PhD from the University of Pennsylvania and his teachers included individuals with degrees from Harvard, Brown, Smith, and Cornell. They were trained in content rather than educational "methods"—and their teaching styles approximated those of rigorous colleges: discussions rather than lectures, reading lists rather than day-by-day assignments, papers rather than exclusive reliance on "objective" tests. But there was no single teaching method imposed from above. The teachers often put in extra time, without pay, especially to work with promising students from low socioeconomic backgrounds.

Students were given pride in their achievements as individuals, but no mystique of "blackness." Negro history week was observed, and there was an elective course in black history, but it was not a prominent element in the curriculum. Although formal guidance counselling was minimal, the individual teachers actively counselled students on their own. But the teachers' concern for the students took the form of getting them to meet standards, not of bringing the standards down to their level of preparation. In reminiscing about her 40 years as teacher and administrator at Douglass High School, former principal Mrs. Edna Campbell said of her students, "Even though you are pushing for them, and dying inside for them, you have to let them know that they have to produce."

The interest of the teachers in the students was reciprocated by the interest of the parents in supporting the teachers and the school. "The school could do no wrong" in the eyes of parents, according to alumni. Parental involvement was of this supportive nature rather than an actual involvement in school decision-making. "Parent power" or "community control" were unheard-of concepts then.

Most of the whites in Baltimore were relatively unaware of Frederick Douglass High School—they did not know or care whether it was good or bad—and this indifference extended to the board of education as well. Under the dual school system in the era of racial segregation, the lack of interest in black schools by the all-white board of education allowed wide latitude to black subordinates to run the black part of the system, so long as no problems became visible. "Benign neglect" is perhaps the most charitable characterization of this policy. In short, Douglass High School's achievements were not a result of white input, at either the administrative or the teaching levels.

Color differences within the black community were significant in the school as well. Light-skinned alumni tended to minimize this factor, but darker-skinned alumni sometimes still carry bitter memories. One man, now an official of the Baltimore school system, recalls being maneuvered out of the honor of being class valedictorian at Douglass, in favor of a lighter-skinned student from a socially prominent family.

Like several of the schools studied, Douglass' days of glory are past. A decline began with the building of other black high schools in Baltimore and became precipitous in the wake of the Supreme Court's desegregation decision in 1954. While the mean I.Q. in the academic program at Douglass ranged from 93 to 105 for the 20 years before the 1954 decision, it fell immediately below 90 in 1955 and remained in the 80s from February 1955 through February 1958. This reflected the exodus of more capable students to white high schools. A concerted effort was made to reverse this trend in the 1960s, especially from 1965 to 1973, when Mrs. Edna Campbell was the principal. Our sampling of test scores for this period indicates some success. I.Q. scores went back into the 90s from 1965 through 1971, the last year for which we have a sample of 20 or more scores.

Today, in its decline, Frederick Douglass High School has better physical facilities, some integration of the faculty, and more parental input into the decision-making process, as well as a Baltimore school system dominated by black officials. There is little evidence that this compensates for what it has lost. Indeed, some knowledgeable people in Baltimore believe that it is precisely the growth of "student rights" and "parent power" that is responsible for declining discipline in schools. There certainly was evidence of such discipline problems at Douglass. A researcher collecting data for this study had her purse snatched in the school building itself, and some weeks earlier there had been a shooting there. This was a far cry from the school that had once been second in the nation in black PhDs among its alumni, and the only black school to produce a Supreme Court justice.

New Orleans: McDonough 35 High School

New Orleans has had a unique role in the history of American race relations, and so it is not surprising that the city has had not one, but three outstanding black high schools on Horace Mann Bond's list—and all three are *still* outstanding. Long before the Civil War, the free Negro community in New Orleans had rights, privileges, and economic success well in advance of its counterpart in any other American city. By 1850, "free persons of color" owned *$15 million* worth of taxable property in New Orleans—one fifth of the total taxable property in the city.

The pattern of race relations in New Orleans had been established before the city became a part of the United States as a result of the Louisiana Purchase in 1812, and it was—and largely remained—the pattern common to Latin America, rather than the pattern of Anglo-Saxon slave societies in the Western Hemisphere. For example, the "free colored" population of Latin America had a far wider range of occupations open to them than did American Negroes, and they often dominated the skilled artisan trades in Latin countries—simply because there were just not enough whites. The French, Spanish, and Portuguese who colonized the Western Hemisphere did not bring women, families, or a working class with them to the extent that the Anglo-Saxons did, and so were both economically and sexually more dependent upon the indigenous populations and those of African descent. This dependency led to a greater relaxation of racism in practice, even though the Latins subscribed in principle to the same "white supremacy" doctrines as the Anglo-Saxons.

New Orleans, as a former French (and Spanish) colony, reflected the Latin pattern in the skills of "free persons of color," few of whom were laborers, many of whom were small businessmen, some of whom were wealthy, and a few of whom were even commercial slave owners. New Orleans also reflected the multicolored caste system characteristic of Latin American countries, in contrast to the stark black/white dichotomy of Anglo-Saxon nations. The celebrated "quadroon balls" of antebellum New Orleans were but one aspect of this system.

Segments of the "free colored" population of New Orleans had been giving their children quality education (sometimes including college abroad) for more than a century before the first black public high school was founded in 1916. This school—McDonough 35 High School—was for many years the only public high school for New Orleans Negroes, but it was preceded by, and accompanied by, private black secondary schools, including Catholic schools—again, reflecting the Latin influence. Two Catholic high schools—St. Augustine and Xavier Preparatory—and McDonough 35 make up today's three outstanding black high schools in New Orleans.

So many schools in New Orleans are named for philanthropist John McDonough that numbers are added to distinguish them. McDonough 35 High School is outstanding among these. It has had only four principals in its nearly 50-year history. The first principal, John W. Hoffman, was a well-traveled man with a cosmopolitan outlook. The second principal, Lucien V. Alexis, was a graduate of Phillips Exeter Academy ('14) and Harvard ('18), and was an "iron-fisted" ex-Army officer. The third principal, Mack J. Spears, was a more diplomatic man with considerable political savvy—which proved to be decisive in saving the school from the physical or educational extinction which came upon other outstanding black high schools during the time when "integration" was regarded as an educational panacea. The current principal, Clifford J. Francis, is a quiet, thoughtful man who accepts overtime work as a normal part of his job. He runs a smoothly operating, high-quality school which, for the first time, has a good physical plant and a good racially-integrated staff.

When McDonough 35 was opened in 1917, it was housed in a building built in the 1880's. As late as 1954, this building was heated by potbellied stoves, with the students keeping the fires going by carrying coal. When a hurricane passed through New Orleans in 1965, the ancient building simply collapsed. At this point, the all-white board of education decided to disband the school and assign its pupils to other schools in New Orleans. But, unlike other outstanding black schools which were destroyed by white officials who were unaware of their quality, McDonough 35 fought back. Principal Mack Spears organized community support to save the school, lobbied Congressmen, and ultimately obtained the use of an abandoned federal court house to house the institution until a new school building could be constructed.

The institution he saved was one which was an inspiration to its students, as well as a leading producer of later black PhDs. By chance, I happened to encounter Wilson Riles, the California State Superintendent of Schools, the day after my first visit to McDonough 35, and the very mention of the school's name caused his face to light up and provoked a flood of warm memories of his student days there. He credited the school with taking him and other black youngsters from an economically and culturally limited background, and giving them both the education and the self-confidence to advance in later life. Mack Spears, a student and later a principal at McDonough 35, told a very similar story. Spears was the son of a poor farmer, but he remembers vividly how his teachers promoted the idea of the worth of the individual—how they always called the boys "Mister" and the girls "Miss," emotionally important titles denied even adult Negroes throughout the South at that time.

Although the school had few counsellors in its earlier days, the teachers acted as counsellors, and as instructors and role models. But with all the psychological strengthening that was an integral part of the educational process, there was no parochial "blackness" in McDonough 35. Cultural expansion was the goal. Questions about "black English" in McDonough 35 brought a "hell no!" from Spears. The current principal more gently observed that this was a recent and minor matter, of interest to only a few young white teachers.

Like some other outstanding black high schools, McDonough 35 suffered a decline in quality as other black high schools were built in the same city and as neighborhood changes left it in a less desirable part of town. At one point in the 1950s, there was a controversy over the right of its teachers to carry guns for self-protection. The academic deterioration of this period matched the deterioration in social conditions and morale. The median I.Q. of the school population in the mid-1950s was in the low 80s; but under the new policies introduced when Spears became principal in 1954, I.Q.s began to rise, to a peak of 99 in the 1965-1966 school year; and they have remained in the mid-to-upper 90s since then. Unfortunately, there are no I.Q. data available for the earlier period of the school's academic excellence—the period during which the PhDs studied by H. M. Bond would have been high school students there. The present I.Q. scores—at about the national average, and therefore significantly above the average for black students—must be interpreted in the context of a city where private Catholic schools attract large numbers of both white and black students with higher educational aspirations and achievements. McDonough 35 median I.Q.s have consistently been above the city-wide average for public school students—white and black—for the past decade.

The policies introduced in the mid-1950s which reversed McDonough 35's decline included keeping neighborhood derelicts out of the school, ability-grouping, or "tracking," to deal with the variation in student capabilities and interests, and a widening of school boundaries beyond the immediate neighborhood. Spears, a former football player, was perfect for keeping the derelicts out of the school—for even though he spoke softly, the big stick was implicit in his very presence. Instead of explaining away low test scores by "cultural deprivation" or dismissing them as "irrelevant," Spears used those scores to demonstrate to parents and to the black community the full depth of the problem and to get support for educational change, including ability-grouping to deal with the wide range of scores and a self-selection admissions system to supersede neighborhood boundaries.

All was not harmony in McDonough 35, even in its heyday. The internal class differences within the black community—which revolved around color differences going back to the era of slavery—were more pronounced in New Orleans, just as intra-group color differences in Latin cultures generally exceeded those in Anglo-Saxon cultures. However, light-skinned Negroes were *not* noticeably overrepresented among students, faculty, or administrators. And darker Negroes, such as Riles and Spears, were nevertheless accepted by the school, even though the larger community was divided socially along internal color lines.

Whites were, at best, a negligible factor in the development of McDonough 35 High School. According to former principal Spears, the all-white board of education "did not give a damn—and we took *advantage* of that to build academic excellence."

New Orleans: St. Augustine High School

St. Augustine High School is a school for boys founded in 1951 by the Josephite Fathers. Its first principal was a young priest, Father Matthew O'Rourke, with neither experience nor training in education. Keenly aware of these gaps in his preparation, Father O'Rourke began a crash program, taking education courses at a local university—but found them "empty" and "a big zero." He and the other similarly inexperienced young priests and laymen on the faculty proceeded by trial and error—and dedication.

One of the first issues to arise came with the introduction of corporal punishment. In an era of growing racial sensitivities, some white priests outside the school were disturbed by the thought of white men (even in priestly garb) beating black youths. But Father O'Rourke and the other priests felt no guilt—the Josephite Order had been founded in the 19th century to serve blacks—and viewed the problem in purely pragmatic terms. Their options were to allow disruptive students to undo their work with others, to save the school by expelling such students, or to attempt to save both the students and the school by an occasional paddling. They elected to try the last. Despite the misgivings of some outside priests, the black parents backed the teachers completely, and the system worked. It has remained a feature of St. Augustine to the present—strongly believed in, but infrequently used. The student/teacher relations in St. Augustine are more relaxed and warm than in most public schools, where corporal punishment is usually forbidden by law.

The school was neither wedded to tradition nor seeking to be in the vanguard of "innovation." It did whatever worked educationally, and abandoned what did not. The wide range of student preparation led to ability-grouping, and to the jettisoning of the traditional English courses for the least prepared students in favor of an emphasis on reading, at virtually any cost. *Time* magazine was found to be an effective vocabulary tool for many students, and hundreds of St. Augustine students subscribed, at the urging of their teachers. A special summer course featured speed reading, with assignments of a novel per week, including reports.

The teachers' inexperience and lack of familiarity with educational fashions paid off handsomely. The first Southern Negro student to win a National Merit Scholarship came from St. Augustine. So did the first Presidential Scholar of any race from the state of Louisiana in 1964, and 10 years later, St. Augustine had produced 20 per cent of all the Presidential Scholars in the history of the state. In the National Achievement Scholarship program for black students, St. Augustine has produced more finalists and semi-finalists than any other school in the nation. In *1964—before* the big college drive to enroll black students—St. Augustine's students won more than $100,000 in college scholarship money. This is all the more remarkable since the total enrollment is less than 700.

The pattern of I.Q. scores over time at St. Augustine shows a generally upward movement, beginning at a level very similar to the average for black students and reaching a level at or above that for the United States population as a whole. In its early years, St. Augustine had mean I.Q.s as low as 86; but during the period from 1964 through 1972, I.Q.s were just over 100 for every year except one.

The reasons for the rising I.Q.s at St. Augustine cannot be easily determined. Father O'Rourke is reluctant to claim credit for the school itself. But in recalling his years as principal, he cited a number of instances where students with potential, but without cultural development, had improved after extra attention—improved not only on achievement tests, but also on I.Q. tests, "though that's not supposed to happen." Test scores were never used as a rigid admissions cutoff at St. Augustine. Our sample includes individual I.Q.s in the 60s, as well as many others more than twice as high.

Father O'Rourke was succeeded as principal in 1960 by Father Robert H. Grant, one of the other young priests teaching at St. Augustine. Where Father O'Rourke had been universally liked, Father Grant tended to have both enthusiasts and detractors. Under Father Grant's administration, a heavy emphasis on academic achievement and tighter discipline brought Merit and Presidential scholars, school-wide I.Q.s averaging over 100—and murmurs of discontent in the community. The discontented usually were *not* parents of students at St. Augustine. The rise of racial militancy raised questions about a white principal of a black school and brought demands for a "black" orientation of the curriculum. In retrospect, Father Grant describes his administration as "benignly autocratic" and himself as "blunt." "We didn't spend much time hassling, debating, or dialoguing." The teachers and principal had their meetings, but once an agreement had been reached, they did not "waste time" with "parent power" or "student rights," but relied instead on parental trust and on student achievement as a vindication of that trust. He met the demands for "black studies" by establishing an elective course on the subject—meeting at a time that was otherwise available as a study period. Only six students enrolled, out of more than 600 students in the school.

Although Father Grant fought a legal battle to integrate Louisiana's high school athletics, and was sympathetic to the civil rights movement in general, he was also opposed to the introduction of "extraneous elements, issues, and concerns" into the school itself. Keenly aware of both the students' cultural disadvantages and the need to overcome them, he felt that "we absolutely could not do the two things well," though both were important. It was a matter of time and priorities: "Don't consume my time with extraneous issues and then expect me to have enough time left over to dedicate myself to a strong academic program where I will turn out strong, intelligent, competent kids."

In 1969, Father Grant accepted a post in Switzerland and was replaced by a black lay principal—just what the doctor ordered politically, but apparently not administratively or educationally. He was replaced after a few years. The current principal, Leo A. Johnson, is also a black layman and, in addition, the first alumnus of St. Augustine to head the school. His term began in 1974, and it is too early to assess his impact on the school.

Teaching methods at St. Augustine are traditional, and both its academic and behavioral standards are strict. Students must wear "a dress shirt with a collar," and the shirttail "must be worn inside the trousers at all times." The general atmosphere at St. Augustine is relaxed, but serious. Its halls are quiet and its students are attentive and engrossed in what they are doing, as are the teachers. Yet it is not a wholly bookish place. Its athletic teams have won many local championships in football, basketball, and baseball. At lunch time, the students were as noisy as any other high school students, and the boys in the lunch room were visibly appreciative of a shapely young woman who was part of our research team. One of the real accomplishments of St. Augustine has been to give education a masculine image so that black youths need not consider intellectual activity "sissy."

The achievements of St. Augustine cannot be explained by the usual phrase of dismissal, "middle-class." Although it is a private school, its modest tuition ($645 per year) does not require affluence, and about 15 per cent of the students pay no tuition at all, while others pay reduced tuition because of their parents' low income. The school runs a chronic deficit, despite the low pay scale for those teachers who are clergy. Despite the color/caste history of New Orleans, the students at St. Augustine are physically indistinguishable from the students at any other black high school. Their demeanor and their work are very different, but their skin color is the same. Our statistical tabulation of parents' occupations covers only the years from 1951 through 1957, but in each year during that span more than half of the known parental occupations were in the "unskilled and semi-skilled" category, and the parents with professional or white-collar jobs added up to less than one tenth as many. While the students are seldom from the lowest poverty level, there is only occasionally the son of a doctor. Many come from families where the father is a bricklayer, carpenter, or other artisan, and has only a modest educational background. They are not middle-class in income, career security, culture, or lifestyle. Many are ambitious for their children and send them to school with attitudes that allow the education to "take." But such attitudes are not a monopoly of the middle class, despite sociological stereotyping. If such attitudes were in fact a monopoly of the middle class, neither blacks nor other ethnic minorities could ever have risen.

New Orleans: Xavier Prep

Xavier Prep is an all-girl Catholic school run by the Sisters of the Blessed Sacrament. It was founded in 1915, and was coeducational until 1970. It had 18 graduating seniors in 1918, and the enrollment increased to about 500 in 1940. It has about 350 students today, after the male students were phased out in the 1960s. Even when it was coeducational, it had more female than male students. One of the reasons for the difficulty of maintaining a masculine image for education among black youths is that, throughout the country and down through the years, Negro girls have outperformed Negro boys by a wide margin on grades, tests, and virtually every measure of intellectual ability. Studies of high I.Q. black students have consistently found the girls outnumbering the boys, by from two-to-one to more than five-to-one.

Over 90% of the graduates of Xavier Prep go on to college. Until the 1960s, almost all went to Xavier University in New Orleans, run by the same order of nuns. Today about 60% of the graduates go to either Xavier University, Loyola, or Tulane —all in New Orleans—even though their academic preparation would make them eligible for many other colleges and universities in other parts of the country.

I.Q. scores and other test scores vary considerably among Xavier students, but the average score of the school as a whole has fluctuated around the national norm—which is to say, higher than for Southerners of either race, higher than for black students nationally, and considerably higher than for black Southern children from the modest socioeconomic backgrounds of Xavier students. The mean I.Q. of the school as a whole ranged from 96 to 108 during the 1960s, and has been at or above 100 for each year surveyed during the 1970s.

In the earliest years of Xavier Prep, many of the students were from Creole back-grounds. But today the colors and conditions of the students represent a cross section of black America. Over the years, about 40-50 percent of the students have come from low-income families, many entering with serious educational deficiencies, requiring re-medial work. More than 60 percent of its students are eligible for the free lunch program. While Xavier is a private school, its tuition is only $35 a month. Our statistical tabulation of parental occupation shows that from one half to four fifths of the parents' occupations have been in the "unskilled or semi-skilled" category, in the period from 1949 to 1972 for which we have data. Parents in professional or white-collar occupations put together added up to only seven per cent of the total during that same span. The principal, Sister Anne Louise Bechtold, recalls "one dentist" this year and "one lawyer last year" among the parents, but no engineers or college professors, and a small percentage of public school teachers—and otherwise parents of very modest socioeconomic backgrounds, with some of the mothers being domestics or store clerks and the fathers in similar occupations.

Unlike middle-class parents, the parents of Xavier students tend to be very cautious about their input into the school—even when invited and encouraged to participate. They seek discipline and an emphasis on basic education, and seem particularly pleased when their children's teachers are nuns. The caution of the parents is also a factor in the narrow range of colleges which most Xavier graduates attend. Ivy League and other Northern colleges attempt to recruit Xavier graduates, but the parents are reluctant to have their daughters exposed to strange influences in faraway colleges. In some cases, the teachers or counsellors fight a losing battle to get a promising student to accept an offer from a top-level college or university. This is not all the result of the limited cultural horizons of the parents. Economic pressures make it difficult for many of the parents to finance the travel involved, much less the living expenses, even if the student has a full scholarship.

Classes at Xavier Prep in the past tended to be large (35-40 students), but since boys were phased out in the mid-1960s, classes have been reduced to about 25 to 30 students. These students are "tracked" by academic ability. The less prepared students are given intensive and imaginative remedial work. Unlike St. Augustine, Xavier Prep has neither corporal punishment nor an emphasis on athletics. But the general atmosphere—described by one nun as "reserved but informal"—is very similar. Nuns and lay teachers are about equally represented on its faculty, and its principal is a nun. It is a quiet, low-key place where the changing of classes produces swarms of black teenagers in the halls, but little noise. The classes in session have students and teachers absorbed in mutual endeavor, but with a certain relaxed geniality. Discussions with Xavier teachers indicate that they put much thought and work, on their own time, into the preparation of their classes. Although subject to the guidance of superiors both inside and outside the school, the teachers seem to have more scope for personal initiative than do public school teachers. Among alumni of the school, their teachers' personal interest in them is a factor often cited as having given them the inspiration and self-confidence that came before the educational achievements themselves.

Brooklyn: P. S. 91

Perhaps the most remarkable of all the schools in this study is P.S. 91, an elementary school in a rundown neighborhood of Brooklyn. Here, where over half the students are eligible for the free lunch program and a significant proportion are on welfare, *every grade approximates or (usually) exceeds the national norms* in reading comprehension. A tour of the ancient school building is even more surprising than these statistics. Here, in class after class, the students—overwhelmingly ghetto youngsters—work quietly, intently, and pleasantly under the direction of obviously intelligent and interested teachers and teacher aides who represent a wide range of ages, races, and personal styles. The sheer silence of the school was eerie to one who had attended elementary school in central Harlem and had recently researched similar schools elsewhere.

In class after class, discussion periods brought lively exchanges between teachers and pupils—the children speaking in complete sentences, grammatically and directly to the point, and returning to the subject if the teacher's response was not clear or satisfactory to them. To see this happening with children identical in appearance and dress to those who are dull, withdrawn, or hostile in untold other ghetto schools can only be described as an emotional experience. After leaving one classroom where a lively discussion was still in progress, the principal said matter-of-factly, "That was our slow learners' class. They are doing all right, but I think there is need for improvement."

That was the remarkable attitude of a remarkable man. Martin Shor, the principal, is white and was principal of the school when the school was white. As the Crown Heights section of Brooklyn changed its racial composition and the socioeconomic level fell, the school population reflected these changes. Now there are only a few white or oriental children in P.S. 91. But unlike other schools whose academic standards have fallen along with the socioeconomic level of their neighborhoods, P.S. 91 has had a *rising* proportion of its students scoring above the national norms in reading. In 1971, just over 49 percent of its students exceeded the national norms, in 1972 it was 51 percent, in 1973 it was 54 percent, and in 1974 it was 57 percent. To put these numbers in perspective, *none* of the 12 other schools in its district had even 40 percent of their students above the national norms, even though some of these other schools are in higher-socioeconomic-status neighborhoods. The highest percentage in the whole borough of Brooklyn—with more than 600 elementary schools—is 60% above the national norms.

The handicaps under which P.S. 91 operates include a very high turnover rate, characteristic of ghetto schools. There was a 34 percent turnover in just three months. This means that the school loses many of the good students it has prepared in the early grades and receives from other ghetto schools badly prepared youngsters whom it must reeducate in later grades. This is apparently a factor in the pattern of scores whereby the lower grades at P.S. 91 exceed the national norms by wider margins than the higher grades (see Table 6.1.). However, it should be noted that other black schools in other cities also tend to score relatively higher in their earlier grades—sometimes even exceeding the national norms in the early grades, in schools far below the national norms overall. How much of the later disastrous decline in scores in ghetto schools is the result of high turnover and how much is the result of the negative effects of the school itself, or the development of negative attitudes by the students toward the school (or life), is a subject which has scarcely been explored. Indeed, the phenomenon itself has hardly been recognized. It is well known that black children tend to fall progressively further behind as they go through school systems, but just how well they do in the first or second grades—even in school systems with dreadful overall results, such as in Chicago or Philadelphia—is a largely unrecognized phenomena.

Martin Shor puts heavy emphasis on teaching the P.S. 91 pupils to read well in the first grade. Indeed, half of the P.S. 91 children can read when they have finished kindergarten. While the school bears the imprint of his own special methods and approach, Shor argues that none of these methods would work unless the students first knew how to read. A disproportionate amount of the school's money and teaching talent goes into preparing the first-graders to read, write, and express themselves orally.

Table 6.1. *Reading Scores, P.S. 91, Brooklyn*

GRADE	NATIONAL NORMS	P.S. 91 MEDIAN
2	2.7	3.5
3	3.7	4.1
4	4.7	4.5
5	5.7	6.3
6	6.7	6.7

Source: *Compilation from District 17, Brooklyn.*

The higher grades use a variety of self-teaching materials, including programmed books, teaching machines, and tape recorders. Many of these materials are *a year or more ahead* of the "age" or "grade" level of the students using them. Students are separated into small groups by ability within each class as well as between classes, and each group has its own assignment. "This may look like an 'open' classroom," Shor said. "But it's not. Every group is working on its own *assigned* task." When asked if this "tracking" system did not originally lead to certain racial imbalances in classes within the school, Shor pointed out that initially disadvantaged students advanced enough to produce more racial balance eventually.

"But if other schools followed your system," I asked, "wouldn't that mean that, in the interim, a multi-racial school would have the appearance of internal segregation, which would lead to a lot of political flack?" "Then you just take the flack," he said. He had taken flack during the period of racial transition at P.S. 91, but the educational results silenced critics and gained parental support. How many other white principals in a ghetto neighborhood have that kind of courage is another question. A study of unusually successful ghetto schools by the Office of Educational Personnel Review in New York concluded that "the quality and attitude of the administrator seemed to be the only real difference" between these schools and less successful ones. A few hours with Martin Shor reinforce that conclusion. He is a quietly confident, forceful man, with an incisive mind, much experience and resourcefulness, and the implicit faith that the job *can* be done. His talk is free of the educational clichés and public relations smoothness normally associated with school administrators. He comes to the ghetto to do a job, does it well, and then goes home elsewhere—contrary to the emotional cries about the need for indigenous community leadership in the school.

P.S. 91 does not teach "black English" or black studies, though its many books and other materials do include a few items of special interest to black children. The school tries to *expand* the students' cultural horizons: Several hundred of these elementary school pupils study foreign languages. P.S. 91 students also read excerpts from translations of the classics of world literature, such as Cervantes or Aesop. They are constantly exposed to material that allows their minds to see beyond the drab school building, the decaying tenements, and the area that caused a friend to tell me, "You sure are brave to park a car in *that* neighborhood." The usual "middle-class" label used to dismiss black educational achievements is only a bad joke when applied to P.S. 91.

Washington, D.C.: Dunbar High School

The oldest and most illustrious of the black elite schools was Dunbar High School in Washington, D.C., during the period from 1870 to 1955. Over that 85-year span, most of its graduates went to college—rare for whites or blacks, then—and many went on to outstanding academic achievements and distinguished careers. Back at the turn of the century, Dunbar was sending students to Harvard, and in the period 1918-1923, Dunbar graduates earned 15 degrees from Ivy League colleges, and 10 degrees from Amherst, Williams, and Wesleyan. During World War II, Dunbar alumni in the Army included "nearly a score of Majors, nine Colonels and Lieutenant Colonels, and a Brigadier General" —a substantial percentage of all high-ranking black officers at that time.

Dunbar was the first black public high school in the United States. Its unique position allowed it to select some of the best of the educated blacks in the country for its teachers and principals. Of its first nine principals, seven had degrees from either Harvard, Oberlin, Dartmouth, or Amherst. Of the remaining two, one was educated in Glasgow and London, and the other was a Phi Beta Kappa from Western Reserve. The principals included the first black woman in the United States to receive a college degree (from Oberlin, 1862) and the first black man to graduate from Harvard (in 1870). Clearly they were remarkable people even to attempt what they did, when they did.

So too was the man who spearheaded the drive that led to the founding of the school which ultimately became Dunbar High School (after several changes of name and location). William Syphax was a "free person of color," born in 1826 and active in civic affairs and civil rights issues, "fearing no man regardless of position or color." As a trustee of the Negro schools in Washington, Syphax preferred to hire black teachers, but only when their qualifications were equal to those of white teachers—for the trustees "deem it a violation of our official oath to employ inferior teachers when superior teachers can be had for the same money." He addressed demands not only to whites in power, but also to his own people, exhorting them to send their children to school with discipline, respect, and a willingness to work hard. These became hallmarks of Dunbar High School, as did the academic success that flowed from them. As early as 1899, Dunbar scored higher in city-wide tests than any of the white high schools in the District of Columbia. Down through the years its attendance records were generally better than those of the white high schools, and its rate of tardiness was lower. Dunbar meant business.

The teachers at Dunbar usually held degrees in liberal arts from top institutions, not education degrees from teachers colleges. The scarcity of alternative occupations for educated Negroes allowed Dunbar to pick the cream of the crop. As late as the 1920's, its staff included individuals with Ph.D.'s from leading universities, including the distinguished historian Carter G. Woodson. The teachers were as dedicated and demanding as they were qualified. Extracurricular tutoring, securing scholarships for graduating seniors, getting parents of promising students to keep them in school despite desperate family finances—all these were part of the voluntary work load of Dunbar teachers and principals. In a city that remained racially segregated into the 1950s, there were also constant efforts to bring cultural attractions to the school that were unavailable to black youngsters in theaters, concert halls, or other cultural and entertainment centers. While individual pride and racial awareness were part of the atmosphere at Dunbar High School, cultural expansion was the educational goal. Latin was taught throughout the period from 1870 to 1955, and in the early decades, Greek was taught as well. In the 1940s, Dunbar fought a losing battle with the superintendent of schools to have calculus added.

Throughout the 85-year period of its academic ascendancy, Dunbar never had adequate financial support. At its founding it was allowed to draw only on taxes collected in the black community. While this arrangement eventually gave way to drawing on the general taxes of the city, so too did the separate administration of Negro schools by black trustees give way to city-wide administration by an all-white board of education, which never provided equal support. Large classes were the norm from the 1870s, when there were more than 40 students per teacher, to the 1950s, when Dunbar's student/teacher ratio exceeded that of any white high school in Washington. The school was in operation more than 40 years before it had a lunch room, which then was so small that many children had to eat lunch out on the street. Blackboards were "cracked with confusing lines resembling a map." It was 1950 before the school had a public address system.

The social origins of Dunbar students were diverse. For three decades, Dunbar was the only black high school in Washington, D.C., and for three more decades it was the only black academic high school in the city, so it drew on a broad cross section of students. As late as 1948, one third of all black high school students in Washington were enrolled in Dunbar. Nevertheless, the "middle-class" label has been stuck on Dunbar, and no amount of facts dispels it. According to a *Washington Post* reporter, the one word "Dunbar" will divide any room of middle-aged black Washingtonians into "outraged warring factions." Some are fiercely loyal to Dunbar as a monumental educational achievement, while others see it as snobbish elitism for middle-class mulattoes who either excluded poor blacks from the school or ostracized them if they attended. A look through old yearbook photographs will disprove the myth of mulatto predominance, and our statistical tabulation of parental occupations from 1938 through 1955 shows 38% of known parental occupations to have been "unskilled and semiskilled" (including many maids), while "white-collar" and "professional" occupations together added up to only 17 percent.

Unquestionably, almost all middle-class Negroes in Washington sent their children to Dunbar during the period from 1870 to 1955, and for historical reasons, middle-class Negroes tended to be lighter in color—but that is very different from saying that most Dunbar students were either middle class or mulattoes. Former Dunbar Principal

Charles Lofton calls it all "an old wives' tale." "If we took only the children of doctors and lawyers," he asked, "how could we have had 1400 black students at one time?" Yet the persistence and power of the myth suggests something of the depth of the hurt felt by those who either did not go to Dunbar because of fear of social rejection or did go and did not feel accepted. To this day, one Dunbar alumna has a policy at social gatherings in Washington of never mentioning where she went to high school.

Dunbar alumni claim that the school was at its academic peak in the 1920's or earlier—in particular that the "M Street School," which was the name prior to 1917, was superior to "Dunbar," which was the name attached to the building constructed that year. There is some inconclusive evidence—graduation years of distinguished alumni, numbers of graduates attending top colleges, etc.—supporting this view, but no standard tests were given in both eras that would permit a direct comparison. The earliest I.Q. records available are for 1938, so that our data cover only its supposedly declining years. Nonetheless, for this 18-year period, the average I.Q. in the school was below 100 for only one year (when it was 99) and was as high as 111 (in 1939).

There is general agreement that Dunbar declined precipitously and catastrophically after the school reorganization of 1955 made it a neighborhood school for the first time in its history. Its neighborhood was one of the worst in the city, and as its new students entered, advanced elective courses gave way to remedial math and English, and its quiet building now became the scene of "discipline problems." The past excellence of the school had caused many teachers to stay on past the retirement age, and now many of them began to retire at once. By the 1960s a newspaper story on the school was titled "Black Elite Institution Now Typical Slum Facility." It remains a typical slum school today—its past recalled only in the heat of a bitter controversy over the tearing down of the old building standing alongside a modern school bearing the same name. One of several city councilmen who favored demolition said that Dunbar "represents a symbol of elitism among blacks that should never appear again." But a Dunbar alumnus wondered if the real problem was that the new school fears the "silent competition" of the old building and the achievement it represents.

Educational "Law and Order"

Contrary to current fashions, it has not been necessary (or usual) to have a special method of teaching to "reach" black children in order to have high-quality education. Teaching methods used in the schools studied here have varied enormously from school to school, and even in particular schools the variation from teacher to teacher has been so great as to defy general characterization. Everything from religious principles to corporal punishment has been used to maintain order. The buildings have ranged from the most dilapidated wrecks to a sparkling plate-glass palace. The teachers and principals have been black and white, religious and secular, authoritarian and gentle, community leaders and visitors from another social world. Some have had a warm "human touch" and others would have failed Public Relations I. Their only common denominators have been dedication to education, commitment to the children, and faith in what it was possible to achieve. The institutional common denominators of these schools are a larger and more complex question.

In general, test scores have been significantly higher at these schools than at black schools in general, and have been highest at the most elite and oldest—Dunbar High School in Washington, in its academic heyday. Yet their I.Q. scores have not been as high as those at white high schools of comparable achievement, and all of the schools studied have included students well below national test score norms. In short, test scores are not "irrelevant" for black achievement, but neither are they the be-all and end-all. One of the tragedies in the wake of the Jensen controversy is that many schools and school systems avoid giving I.Q. tests for fear of political repercussions, when in fact much useful information can be obtained from this imperfect instrument, once its limitations are understood. Even where I.Q. tests are used, the results are often handled in a politicized way. For example, the Austin (Texas) public school system refused to release data on a school being considered for inclusion in this study because of "legal" reasons—but only after a lengthy cross-examination on my personal beliefs about various issues involved in the I.Q. controversy. Sometimes the data are suppressed for more directly institutional political reasons—as in the case of a large metropolitan black school on the West Coast whose outstanding performance is kept quiet for fear of citizen demands to know why the other black schools in the same city cannot produce similar results.

Perhaps the most basic characteristic of all these schools could be called "law and order," if these had not become politically dirty words. Each of these schools currently maintaining high standards was a very quiet and orderly school, whether located in a middle-class suburb of Atlanta or in the heart of a deteriorating ghetto in Brooklyn. Schools formerly of high quality were repeatedly described by alumni, teachers, and others as places where "discipline problems" were virtually unheard-of. "Respect" was the word most used by those interviewed to describe the attitudes of students and parents toward these schools. "The teacher was *always* right" was a phrase that was used again and again to describe the attitude of the black parents of a generation or more ago. Most Negro students of that era would not have dreamed of complaining to their parents after being punished by a teacher, for that would have been likely to bring on a second—and worse—punishment at home. Even today, in those few instances where schools have the confidence of black parents, a wise student maintains a discreet silence at home about his difficulties with teachers, and hopes that the teachers do the same. The black culture is not a permissive culture. But in more and more cases, "student rights" activists among adults—particularly adults with an eye to political exposure—create a more contentious environment in which it is the teacher or the principal who maintains a discreet silence for fear of legal or physical retaliation. The sheer exhaustion of going through "due process" for every disruptive student who needs to be suspended is enough to discourage decisive action by many school officials.

The destruction of high-quality black schools has been associated with a breakdown in the basic framework of law and order. Nor did it require mass violence to destroy these or other black schools. Again and again those interviewed who were working in the field of education pointed out that only a fraction—perhaps no more than one tenth of the students—need to be hard-core troublemakers in order for good education to become impossible. Another way of looking at this is that only a small amount of initial selectivity (including student self-selection) or subsequent ability to suspend or expel is necessary to free a school of a major obstacle to education. At one time this small amount of selectivity was provided automatically for black (and other) high schools, because most uninterested students did not go on to high school. Those whose educational performances were substandard in the lower grades were left back often enough to reach the age to leave school before reaching high school. Moreover, that legal age was lower then; and, in addition, those utterly uninterested in school were unlikely to be zealously pursued by attendance officers in the era before the "dropout" problem became an emotionally important political issue.

Formal selectivity, in terms of entrance examination cutoff scores, was the exception rather than the rule for the schools studied here. Most of these were public schools serving all students in a given area; and for some period of their history, that area has included all black children in the city, in the cases of Dunbar, Douglass, and Booker T. Washington High Schools. The private schools—St. Augustine, Xavier, and St. Paul—have entrance examinations, but these do not automatically admit or exclude, and the wide range of student test scores in these schools indicates that such scores are far from decisive in admissions. In short, no stringent "elitism" is necessary to achieve high-quality education. It is only necessary to select, or have students self-select, in such a way as to exclude the tiny fraction who are troublemakers.

At one time, it was a relatively simple matter to suspend, expel, or transfer a disruptive student to some "special" class or "dumping ground" vocational school, allowing the rest of the educational system to proceed undisturbed. Now this has become more difficult with the growth of "student rights" and "parent power"— and, more generally, with an agonizing preoccupation with the question of what can be done for the disruptive student to "solve" his "problem." This mass projection of the academic paradigm of problem-solving to the whole society is part of the general spirit of the times, but it overlooks the vital question whether there is, in fact, a solution—whether we have it within our grasp today, and whether we shall allow the "problem" to take its fullest destructive toll before such indefinite time as we have it "solved." Recent campaigns to "get the drunk driver off the road" suggest that there are cases where the primary concern is to protect society, and where whatever remedies can be offered the individual are secondary. The enormous toll of a few destructive students on black education is one of the tragic untold stories of our time—perhaps because there is no political gain to be made by telling it, and much political capital to reap from championing "student rights."

Recovering the Past

While order and respect have been universal characteristics of the schools studied here, other ingredients have also been necessary to create academic excellence. Chief among these have been the character and ability of the principals, Some of these principals have been of heroic dimensions—fighters for civil rights at a time when that was a dangerous role—and others have been simply dedicated educators. The number of these principals who have trained at top colleges and universities in the country suggests that investments made in promising Negro youths more than half a century ago have paid off large and continuing dividends.

Ability grouping has been a prominent feature of most of these schools during their periods of academic excellence—contrary to the "democratic" trends in contemporary education. For many reasons going back into history, there are very wide ranges of educational preparation and orientation among black children, and accommodating them all in one standard curriculum may often be impractical. Among Dunbar students in the period from 1938 to 1955, it was not uncommon to find individuals with I.Q.s in the 80s and individuals with I.Q.s in the 140s in the same grade. In P.S. 91 today, the ability-grouping principle includes not only several different classes in the same grade but also several different ability groupings within each class—all told, perhaps two dozen ability levels in a single grade. This may not sound plausible as an educational policy, but it works—and it works in an unpromising social setting where many more popular ideas fail to show any results.

Perhaps the most disturbing aspect of contemporary education is the extent to which the very process of testing ideas and procedures by their actual *results* has been superseded by a process of testing them by their consonance with existing *preconceptions* about education and society. Father Grant, even after his remarkable successes as principal of St. Augustine, found no receptivity at the Ford Foundation either to his appeals for money for the school or to his ideas about education. He was out of step with the rhetoric of his time and did not use the "innovative" methods that were preconceived to be necessary or beneficial to black students. Xavier Prep, even after more than half a century of demonstrable results, is still looking for a modest sum of money to improve its library, but libraries are not "exciting" or "imaginative"—as "black English" or "black studies" are.

The social settings of the schools studied here are also significant. Every one of them was an urban school. This is remarkable because during the academic heyday of most of these schools most American Negroes lived in rural and small-town settings. This suggests that the rise of such prominent blacks as those who came from these schools—which is to say, most of the top black pioneers in the history of this country—seems a matter less of innate ability and more of special social settings in which individual ability could develop and that the settings from which such black leadership arose were quite different from the social settings in which the mass of the black population lived. The second point needs emphasis only because of the recent mystique surrounding "grass roots" origins and/or the faithful reflection of "grass roots" attitudes by leaders. Much of this is nothing more than brazen presumption and reckless semantics: No one ever applies labels like "middle-class" to Angela Davis or LeRoi Jones (or others of their persuasion), though that is in fact their origin, while those with a more moderate philosophy are often condemned as "middle-class"—no matter that they may actually have come from desperate poverty, and no matter how many polls show that their opinions are shared by the masses of blacks.

The particular cities in which the high-quality black schools arose were distinctive as centers of concentration for the "free persons of color" in the antebellum era. Except in the case of Dunbar High School in Washington, there was no unbroken historical line traceable back to the free Negroes of the early 19th century, but it seems more than coincidence that these schools took root in places where there had been schools for black children (usually private schools) 50 or 100 years earlier. That is, an old black community with a demand for good education existed even before good schools became an institutional reality. It is not that the bulk of the Negroes in these cities necessarily wanted quality education, but that there was an important nucleus that understood what was needed, and that the others recognized and respected good education when it appeared.

Apparently the great bulk of black children who benefited from these schools were *not* descendants of "free persons of color" or of middle-class Negroes in general. But the knowledge, experience, and values of the more fortunate segment of the race became their heritage. While the black educated classes were not angels—they could be as snobbish and insufferable as any other privileged group—they were a vital source of knowledge, discipline, and competence. They opened a window on a wider world of human history and culture. They did not glorify provincialism or tribalism, in the manner of some of today's black middle-class radicals who attempt to expiate their own past by being "blacker-than-thou." Those white officials who have successfully run high-quality black schools have, without exception, been men and women who were neither impressed nor intimidated by the militant vogues of the 1960s.

Whatever is the objective importance of social history in any final assessment of black education, that history must be dealt with—if only to counter the *fictitious* history that has become part of current stereotypes. Messianic movements of whatever place or time tend to denigrate the past as a means of making themselves unique and their vision glorious. Recent black messianic movements, and white messianic movements speaking in the name of blacks, have been no exception. The picture that emerges from these visions is of an inert, fearful, and unconcerned black leadership in the past—leaders only recently superseded by bold men of vision, like themselves. This is a libel on the men and women who faced up to far more serious dangers than our generation will ever confront, who took the children of slaves and made them educated men and women, and who put in the long hours of hard work required to turn a despised mass into a cohesive community. In many ways, those communities had far more cohesion, stability, mutual respect, and plain humanity than the ghettos of today.

Endnotes

1   Thomas Sowell, "Black Excellence: The Case of Dunbar High School," *The Public Interest*, No. 35 (Spring 1974), pp. 1-21.

2   Horace Mann Bond, "The Negro Scholar and Professional in America," *The American Negro Reference Book* (Englewood Cliffs, Prentice-Hall, 1970), p. 562.

3   E. Franklin Frazier, *The Negro in the United States* (New York, Macmillan, 1971), p. 74.

4   Henry Reid Hunter, *The Development of the Public Secondary Schools of Atlanta, Georgia: 1845-1937* (Office of the School System Historian, Atlanta Public Schools, 1974), pp. 49-52.

5   "They Knew Charles L. Harper," *The Herald* (October 1955), p. 19. Quoted in V. W. Hodges, "Georgians Join Atlantans in Tribute to Mr. Harper," in *The Atlanta World* (June 14, 1950).

The Price of Desegregation

By Trudier Harris

EVERY YEAR A pattern is set into motion in January that continues into February. That is the time of year, as Langston Hughes would say, when "the Negro is in vogue." Or, to use the more contemporary phrase, when African Americans have lots of attention focused on them because of Dr. Martin Luther King, Jr.'s birthday and because of Black History Month. Although many of us keep standing up and asserting that we are black all year-round, it never seems to affect the programming in our communities, schools, colleges, and universities. So during January we dredge up all our memories and readings of Dr. King and blow our trumpets about civil rights and progress since Dr. King's sojourn here. But every now and then, I want to say, Saint Peter, would you please pass me through to Dr. King? I want to bring him up to date on a little American and African American history. I would start off by telling him an anecdote about Zora Neale Hurston—just in case he hadn't gotten around to talking with her—and I would tell him about so-called progress in my hometown, what kind of impact the civil rights movement has had on it. And I would tell him about what a treasure trove of abuse has been heaped on him.

When the U.S. Supreme Court's decision on desegregation was passed down in 1954, Zora Neale Hurston, novelist, playwright, folklore collector, and general preserver of African American culture, was one of the few national voices opposed to that decision. Desegregating schools, Hurston maintained, was really a slap in the face of those black teachers who had done a superb job of taking care of the minds and the development of

African American children. Such a decision cast aspersion on their abilities to do well what they had long been in the habit of doing. Obviously, most people thought Hurston was crazy. They asked, How could any sane, right-thinking black person in these United States of America really believe that segregation was best for black people?

As early as the mid-1960s, careful observers began to see some of the negative effects of desegregation, and if they had ever heard of Zora Neale Hurston, they probably would have discovered that they shared a lot in common with her. Those institutions that many black people held dear—the schools that three and four generations of their families had grown up in, the churches where their great-grandparents had been baptized—were gradually being destroyed or relocated. Many of these blacks discovered, therefore, that they were equal enough to be singled out as losers.

Consider my hometown of Tuscaloosa, Alabama. In Tuscaloosa, which is commonly called the Druid City, Druid High School had evolved from Industrial High School, which had been founded in 1944. Its principal, McDonald Hughes, had guided its growth into a well-respected institution. Many of the teachers under Mr. Hughes's leadership and example-setting had earned their master's degrees, and several of them were on their way to earning doctoral degrees. They studied at schools such as Columbia, Indiana University, and Northwestern. They were practiced in the art of education as well as in the art of discipline (no small feat in a school of 1600 students).

Then along came the civil rights movement and desegregation. In 1971 the school was desegregated, which meant that a certain number of black students and teachers were transferred to the formerly all-white high school across town and an equal number of white students and teachers were to come to Druid. A fascinating dynamic was set in motion. Teachers from Druid with twenty and thirty years of experience and near doctoral degrees were sent to the formerly all-white school. Druid in turn got wives of white law students at the University of Alabama who needed something to do while their husbands finished their degrees and who had little, if any, classroom experience. Picture, then, a petite blond woman coming into a classroom of primarily black students, many of them athletes towering over her. When she says, "Please take your seats," they respond, rather gruffly, "Who you talking to?" and she wilts into silence. From that moment forward, she has no control over the classroom, and no learning occurs.

The so-called exchange was a fiasco. The former white school became solidly integrated; the former black school ended up with a few white teachers and a few white students. Most of the white parents responded by sending their children to recently established "Christian" and other private schools in order to avoid sending them to Druid (a common story in countless cities during this period). Consequently, a move was started in the late 1970s to turn Druid into the lower division of the senior high school. All tenth graders throughout the city would go there; it would now be called Central West. All eleventh and twelfth graders would go to the former white high school, which would become Central East. Central East would have the basketball and football teams, the cheerleaders and the symphony orchestra, and all the other things that make high school extracurricular activities interesting. Druid would simply be the holding pen for those students waiting to go to Central East.

Needless to say, those of us who graduated from Druid High School between 1944 and 1970 were not thrilled with these developments, but we lost in our fights with the Board of Education as well as with the city. Today we still have our two schools, and the Dragons, the former mascots of Druid High School, are in hibernation. We are still curious to see if we will get museum space for our mementos. We still wear our red and blue and refer to the upper-division school in our community as Druid High School. All of the black kids who have graduated from that school in the past 30 years similarly refer to it as Druid High School. It's sort of like the situation in Toni Morrison's novel *Song of Solomon*. Although the white folks change the name of the major street in the black neighborhood from "Doctor Street," because the town's only black doctor lives there, to "Mains Avenue," the black folks retort by calling it "Not Doctor Street." Black reality prevails.

I moved away from Tuscaloosa in 1969, but I return three, four, and sometimes as many as five times a year. It is not only home for me; it provides a fascinating study in the consequences of so-called integration, of the impact that the civil rights movement has had on black culture, on the people and the institutions instrumental in the shaping of values within and among black children. I valued the time when teachers were surrogate parents, when neighbors felt a responsibility in the shaping of a child's growth. Now the schools have changed, and the old neighborhoods have given way to shopping centers and freeways. I valued the time when Mrs. Sawyer, the fifth-grade teacher at Thirty-second Avenue Elementary School, came to see my mother because my brother had been naughty in school (she lived only two blocks away). I valued the time when my aunt—though I never could figure out exactly how she was related to me—would admonish me to sit or otherwise behave like a young lady. I valued the time when you could work for your teacher if she was having a club meeting and make a few extra dollars, or when a teacher would come to your house if you were ill to see how you were doing, or bring a bolt of cloth for your mother to make new dresses for you if you could not afford to buy new ones. I do not wax romantic. I merely paint a picture of the way things used to be before we decided that so-called integration was better, before our teachers moved out of our neighborhoods, and before disciplining a child became a criminal offense instead of neighborly intervention.

There is a price for change, and black people throughout this country have paid the price of desegregation. Don't misunderstand me; I am not suggesting that it was the wrong step to have taken at the time. And please do not class me with whites who advocate maintaining the purity of ethnic neighborhoods. What I am suggesting is that few, if any, African American individuals ever stopped to think through some of the potentially destructive consequences of desegregation. They never stopped, for example, to think what desegregation would do to black schools and colleges. The general feeling was that the meeting of black and white would be glorious; we would all join hands and traipse off into the sunset together, in a vision that would have been the envy of the Communist party of the 1930s. But something else happened. There was a great gap between what was taken away and what was put in its place. The schools and colleges that had given the world the likes of Booker T. Washington, George Washington Carver, James Weldon Johnson, and Dr. Martin Luther King, Jr., were now looked on with suspicion. "Go to a black college?" some of our misguided young minds would question, "Why, only the folks who can't get into white colleges go to those things."

One of the negative consequences of the civil rights movement, therefore, was that it taught some black people—and I emphasize *some*—to disparage their own roots. I maintain that we have lost a couple of generations of young black people who are insensitive to their history and to their ancestors. I keep coming across junior high school students who have gone to their integrated schools and who don't know any of the names I just mentioned. I keep coming across black college students who never heard of Brer Rabbit and the Tar Baby, or of John and Old Massa, or of John Henry. And indeed, many of the junior and senior high school students sometimes cannot relate a single piece of factual information about Dr. Martin Luther King, Jr. Although I am sometimes surprised and always saddened by these revelations, I am more often angered. I am angry with the teachers who would prefer babysitting to teaching. I am angry—even as I understand— that many black parents are afraid to meet with white teachers about their children's performances in classrooms. I am angry with all the circumstances that none of us, individually, can control, but for which all of us, collectively, are responsible.

Although I obviously cannot advocate returning to those days before 1954, I can certainly understand Zora Neale Hurston's point of view. She had the foresight to see some of the things that others are only now becoming aware of. It is a fact that we have achieved a lot of vertical integration; we eat in the same dining halls, sit in the same classrooms, and sometimes chitchat about things of no specific consequence to either blacks or whites. Our relationships are still too fragile to be tested in the fire of amicable but serious disagreement. So we operate at a surface level that is a mere tranquil covering for the boiling depths beneath. And I ask myself, Is this what Dr. King wanted? I imagine myself talking to him sometimes. Black folks, after all, have a long history of dealing with Saint Peter. He is a constant character in our folk narratives about Heaven. So he lets me through.

"Excuse me, Dr. King," I say, "but it's January again, and you're being whipped again. For the past two weeks I have heard more boring speeches and platitudes in your name than the law allows. And they are usually so solemn and *un*-eloquent, not at all like anything you would ever say or anything that would ever appeal to you. The speechifiers paint you as serious, serious, serious, without even a hint of the sense of humor that I know you had. They believe that you were an activist twenty-four hours a day, walking five feet above the soil on which the rest of us tread heavily. They lament what they call the tragedy of your life, your early death, without ever considering the fact that your view of the situation might have been entirely different. People take out their handkerchiefs, shed a few tears, and convince themselves that they are somehow in touch with you. Sometimes it gets to be disgusting, but it's sort of un-American for anyone to say that out loud.

"In every city worth its name in the United States, you are being taken out of musty drawers and called into action again. Doesn't it just make you mad? Every petty city official from Maine to California and from Michigan to Florida thinks he can increase his black vote by mentioning your name. It would be great if half of them meant it. But they drag out your name as if you were some magical potion, then they chant a few syllables and put you away until the next year.

"And black folks are no better. Every year, the society ladies and their clubs sell tickets to some fancy dinner where all the people who think they are somebody come to show off their finery. I went to one of those recently, but not because I had any finery to show off. I paid one of my fraternity brothers fifty dollars for two tickets because I was his soror and he needed my support. The dinner was supposed to start at 7:00 p.m. At first, we were delayed because some of the *stars* hadn't shown up; then, when they got there, we were delayed another twenty minutes or so because all the folks scheduled to sit at the head table had to be properly lined up—according to somebody's sense of their self-worth. Then the mistress of ceremonies had to introduce the twenty-some folks at the head table, after which they started speechifying. By the time somebody realized that this was a banquet, and that we were supposed to be eating, it was 8:15. Then dinner was spoiled throughout by people getting up and mouthing off platitudes. I don't know, Dr. King, but it seemed to me that you would have preferred to be remembered in some other way. "And have you noticed how city administrators use you as a pacifier? Have you looked at any maps recently and seen how many streets in this country are Martin Luther King, Jr., Roads, or Boulevards, or Avenues? Or elementary schools or cultural centers? And have you noticed where those streets, schools, and institutions usually are? One thing's for sure; they're seldom—if ever—in those sections of town where the lawns are perfectly manicured and eighty-thousand-dollar cars grace the driveways. Practically every street they ever named after you, Dr. King, is in a predominantly black, segregated neighborhood. That's not what you stood for, Dr. King. Does that bother you?

"And what about all those housing projects and schools? Have you observed how many of them have your name? I have never seen a King Heights, a King Club, or a King Estates. It's always a visible project with your name on the street that runs through it. And any time the black folks are screaming for more of whatever, they get a black school named after you. These schools are all over the South. Again and again, county commissioners and members of Boards of Education suggest that you were—and are—relevant only for black folks.

"Only when it's convenient do organizers of celebrations in your honor suggest that you have greater meaning. After that banquet I attended, everybody got up and sang 'We Shall Overcome.' It was dead and dry and perfunctory, but they tried, and at least the context was historically connected to you. Now gays, lesbians, and feminists have adopted the song as a rallying point. You've become such a handy catchall for so many things, causes, and groups that people tend to forget what you really stood for: the complete political, moral, and social transformation of America, especially in terms of racial understanding. You were not a mere token. I wonder if you're up there shaking your head in disbelief at all this confusion, or if you just turn away and refuse to look in this direction.

"Did you ever have any idea that schools in the South would end up the way they have? Do you ever have second thoughts about the tactics you used? Do you and Gandhi discuss these things? Do you ever want to be reincarnated and try to set the record straight? One thing's for sure, Dr. King; folks who profess to honor you have worn you to a frazzle. I think black folks and white folks—and everybody else who has become interested in you—ought to come up with some new names to toss around. After all, why must all the black folks' heroes be dead and martyred? Why can't we come up with somebody else who could articulate the concerns of the times? Would you like your name to take a rest, Dr. King? It's hard for people to give up their heroes, and I'm not suggesting that we forget you. But I do think that we should be clear in conveying to others that your dream of racial harmony and understanding almost forty years ago cannot forever sustain more than thirty million people. And if we're *not* going to give you a rest—and that seems likely—we ought to try at least to recapture your ideals in a meaningful way: work to make laws apply equally across racial lines, get more black kids adopted, and improve educational access for poor black kids."

Yes, I talk to Dr. King. I like to think that he listens. I like to think that every now and again he wants to say something back to me. But I think Saint Peter insists that the communication be one way. That way, he doesn't have to mediate between disgruntled saints trying to come back to earth to straighten out the confusion that ensued after their deaths and supplicants on earth who would like that to happen. Not me. I don't want Dr. King to come back and have to go through this madness again. But I do think he should encourage the archangel Gabriel to hurl a lightning bolt in this direction every now and then—just enough to set a little fire under someone who will realize that saints are saints and that this world needs some flesh and blood bodies to carry on whatever battles must be fought in this realm.

If the consequences of the civil rights movement—those anticipated and those not—are ever to be balanced in some way, Dr. King cannot do it. The spirit of his work cannot do it. But perhaps, just perhaps, some of the people who keep standing on his shoulders and claiming kinship to him will find philosophies and practical ways to make "We Shall Overcome" an obsolete tune.

Part II
A (Black) Nation at Risk

A (Black) Nation at Risk?

BY THE 1980s, a national educational crisis compelled the U.S. government to reclaim dominance on the world stage at the expense of equality and multiculturalism. At the local, state, and federal levels, educational authorities claimed that American schools were struggling to remain competitive at home and abroad. The national focus, then, needed to be on excellence, not segregation (Urban, 2015). Whether this rhetoric was a manufactured crisis or not, the National Commission on Excellence in Education's (1983) publication of *A Nation at Risk* declared resolutely: "The educational foundations of our society are presently being eroded by a rising tide of mediocrity that threatens our very future as a Nation and a people" (p. 9). Black students became the quintessential "at-risk" population in classrooms, schools, and some communities—30 years after the *Brown* decision. One scholar, for instance, used animalistic tropes to describe Black boys' academic performance and deemed them an "endangered species" (Gibbs, 1988). Scholars of Black education tend to agree that the 1980s ushered in a state-sponsored attack on the lives of Black youth that reneged on the promise of *Brown*.

Part II explores Black students and the afterlife of school segregation from 1980 to the present. We contend that this historical moment is marked by "too much schooling, too little education," to borrow the words of Black education scholar Mwalimu Shujaa

(1994). It is marked by Black students and parents demanding true integration in the form of equality, access, opportunities, equity, and inclusion. It is marked by a reductionist move away from "Black liberation" to "Black Lives Matter." Here we highlight scholars of Black education who are thinking about Black students' lives and fashioning pedagogies, curricula, and relationships that can benefit *all* students. The refusal of the "at-risk" trope permeates each and every selected reading.

We begin with pioneering work from scholars who have sought to explain Black underachievement and a widening racial achievement gap between Blacks and Whites. In "Black Students' School Success: Coping with the Burden of 'Acting White,'" Signithia Fordham and John Ogbu (1986) introduce the "burden of 'acting White'" thesis to explain the underachievement of Black students in public schools. Drawing on ethnographic methods in schools, Fordham and Ogbu argue: "One major reason Black students do poorly in school is that they experience inordinate ambivalence and affective dissonance in regard to academic effort and success" (p. 177). Rejecting this line of thinking, many scholars have reacted negatively to the "burden of 'acting White'" thesis by refusing the seductive nature of the argument in the late 1980s. Many of them returned to classrooms, as well as school cafeterias and hallways, to investigate whether a "burden of 'acting White'" exists (Akom, 2003; Carter, 2003, 2005; Horvat & Lewis, 2003; Horvat & O'Connor, 2006; O'Connor et al., 2006; Tyson, 2011). For a witty and informative response to her critics, read Fordham (2008), who offers fascinating background on what she calls "the strange career of the 'burden of "acting White."'"

In one of many possible examples of a counterargument to Fordham and Ogbu, we selected Antwi A. Akom's (2003) "Reexamining Resistance as Oppositional Behavior: The Nation of Islam and the Creation of a Black Achievement Ideology" to highlight a plausible response to the "burden of 'acting White'" thesis. Drawing on ethnographic methods as well, he persuasively challenges Fordham and Ogbu's (1986) groundbreaking scholarship

> by demonstrating that through the religious tenets and practices of the Nation of Islam (NOI), young female members develop a black achievement ideology, resulting in the adoption of the kind of studious orientation to school that is usually demonstrated by voluntary immigrant groups . . . demonstrating the ways in which black people differentially make sense of and enact what it means to be black that challenge previous binary or dichotomized accounts of black oppositional social identity. (Akom, 2003, p. 305)

Akom is one of many scholars who see resistance as transformative rather than oppositional. To date, there has been no final word on the "burden of 'acting White.'"

In "The Canary in the Mine: The Achievement Gap Between Black and White Students," physicist Mano Singham (1998) addresses the Black–White achievement gap in the context of larger political realities, arguing that we have to look at the educational system as a whole and understand Black students as "canaries in the mine." Singham's work can explain the ubiquitous presence of the achievement gap, even in middle- and upper middle-class integrated communities where middle-class and upper middle-class Black students should thrive. His commentary disrupts the widely accepted belief that only low-income Black students are marginalized within urban, public schools.

A cadre of Black education scholars have focused on pedagogy, or the art of teaching, as a way to address the significance of Black teachers' lives and work in thinking about teaching African American students successfully during the 1980s and 1990s (Beauboeuf-Lafontant, 2002; Foster, 1990, 1993, 1997; hooks, 1994; Jeffries, 1994; Ladson-Billings, 1995, 2000, 2009; Lynn & Jennings, 2009). Gloria Ladson-Billings and bell hooks have demonstrated that culturally relevant pedagogy and transgressive teaching practices are necessary and essential for the education of Black children in a White-dominant world. While each author has argued that high-quality instruction should be the prerogative of *all* teachers who are committed to equitable educational possibilities for all students, they are mainly concerned with the education of Black children. Their thinking, research, and writing challenge the notion that Black students are "at-risk" underachievers who do not value education. While we understand that there are many more brilliant scholars that we could have included in this volume, we have selected readings that touched our lives personally and continue to shape how we think about educating Black children.

In "Toward a Theory of Culturally Relevant Pedagogy," Gloria Ladson-Billings (1995) introduces a groundbreaking construct. Drawing on the lives and work of Black teachers, she builds a theoretical intervention around the idea that teachers should possess Black cultural knowledge about the students they teach to support academic achievement, cultural competence, and a sociopolitical consciousness. Unwavering in her stance that successful teachers of Black children must incorporate a culturally relevant pedagogy into their pedagogical repertoire, Ladson-Billings (1995) implicates all teachers in contributing to student underachievement when they do not affirm students' cultural identities and when they are unable to help students "develop critical perspectives that challenge inequities in schools" (p. 469). Contrary to Fordham and Ogbu (1986), Ladson-Billings thinks that an oppositional consciousness is critical for Black teachers and their students in an oppressive world where teaching and learning are power-laden situations.

With a focus on personal and pedagogical transformation, the late bell hooks (1994) embraced the adage "it takes a village" to raise a child and reflects on how Black communities fostered Black excellence and achievement in the past. Having been inspired by her Black women teachers in grade school, hooks wrote about their commitment to nurturing Black intellect in spite of state-sponsored prejudice and discrimination. In *Teaching to Transgress: Education as the Practice of Freedom*, hooks (1994) reflected, "We learned early that our devotion to learning, to a life of the mind, was a counter-hegemonic act, a fundamental way to resist every strategy of white racist colonization" (p. 2). Overall, her work represents the best of critical pedagogy that pushes teachers and schools to eliminate their reliance on rote memorization and banking education—simply depositing information into the minds of students (see also Freire, 2007).

One of the biggest challenges to cultural explanations of Black underachievement, from "at risk" to "the burden of 'acting White,'" has been critical race scholarship from the Derrick Bell tradition (Delgado & Stefancic, 2005). Critical race theory (CRT) grew out of a critical legal studies movement in the 1970s and 1980s and sought to examine the relationship between race, racism, and power in the law (Delgado & Stefancic, 2001; Dixson & Rousseau, 2006; Ladson-Billings & Tate, 1995). In the field of education, Black education scholars Gloria Ladson-Billings and William Tate (1995) published "Toward a Critical Race Theory in Education" to think through the implications of CRT in education and to demonstrate the use of "race" as an analytical tool for understanding school inequity. They offer a groundbreaking critique of multiculturalism in school, which dominated the field throughout the 1980s and 1990s. Ladson-Billings and Tate explain:

> We make this observation of the limits of the current multicultural paradigm not to disparage the scholarly efforts and sacrifices of many of its proponents, but to underscore the difficulty (indeed, impossibility) of maintaining the spirit and intent of justice for the oppressed while simultaneously permitting the hegemonic rule of the oppressor. (p. 62)

Beyond "diversity" and "multiculturalism," Ladson-Billings and Tate introduced new key words from the tenets of critical race theory, such as *racial realism, Whiteness as property*, and *intersectionality*. In addition, they borrowed from older traditions within critical Black studies, such as oppression, hegemony, and liberation.

Given a national focus on gendered experiences in U.S. schooling, some Black scholars in education have pointed out that there are a set of underlying experiences impacting Black boys and girls differently. For example, in "Early Schooling and Academic Achievement of African American Males," James Earl Davis (2003) explains the important factors needed to understand the achievement gap for African American males in early education. According to Davis, who is a leading scholar on Black males in education, "the current plight of young African American males in schools demands much more focus, both theoretically and methodologically" (p. 517). He considers multiple explanations for Black boys' early disengagement with schooling and questions the role of the school in shaping their educational trajectories.

In "Those Loud Black Girls," Signithia Fordham (1993) documents and analyzes the everyday schooling experiences of Black girls at Capital High School. Academic achievement for Black girls is defined by their adoption of "gender passing" or a scholarly posture that imitates White American males and females (p. 3). She describes the ways that schools homogenize students in the absence of gender diversity in academic settings. Fordham's discussion of gender and Blackness complements Davis's scholarship on Black boys in schools. Both should make us question the promise of *Brown* and the afterlife of school segregation for the growth and development of a large number of Black youth in desegregated and resegregated schools.

Hip-hop has become a new area of focus for some scholars of Black education (Alim, 2004; Alridge, 2005; Baszile, 2009; Bridges, 2011; Hill, 2009; Ibrahim, 2004; Ladson-Billings, 2014; Love, 2015; Stovall, 2006). But as Emery Petchauer (2009) demonstrates in "Framing and Reviewing Hip-Hop Educational Research," the world of hip-hop has become relevant to the field of education, in general, and Black education, in particular. Petchauer outlines three key areas:

> (a) hip-hop-based education—studies that use hip-hop, especially rap songs and lyrics, as curricular and pedagogical resources; (b) hip-hop, meaning(s), and identities—studies that focus on how students mobilize these texts and how they intersect with identities; and (c) hip-hop aesthetic forms—studies that conceptualize the ways of doing or habits of mind produced by hip-hop practices. (p. 952)

Faced with the dilemma of having so many great authors whose work could represent this new area of research, we selected Petchauer's review because it is interdisciplinary and comprehensive. His work best demonstrates what a cadre of scholars of Black education think hip-hop pedagogy and curriculum can do to critically educate Black students today.

We conclude Part II with a provocative selection making the case for critical Black theory, or BlackCrit, in educational studies. BlackCrit is one of the latest emergent areas of research centering anti-Blackness and borrowing from Black studies and Black educational theory foundations across centuries. In "'Be Real Black for Me': Imagining BlackCrit in Education," Michael J. Dumas and kihana miraya ross (2016) offer a careful, studied, and frank critique of critical race theory (CRT) in education, which became a dominant approach to thinking about Black education at the end of the 20th century (see Ladson-Billings & Tate, in this volume). Dumas and ross proclaim resolutely: "CRT in education functions much more as a critique of white supremacy and the limits of the hegemonic liberal multiculturalism, which guides policy, practices, and research in the field" (p. 416). Such observations about the limits of a particular way of viewing Black education are admittedly part of the impetus for this interdisciplinary reader. We have been concerned about "thinking about Black education" and the fact that some of the most liberating thoughts, histories, and stories have been overlooked, lost, or forgotten. The emergent research focused on "anti-Blackness in education," or Black critical theory, or BlackCrit, or Afropessimism is connected to a long history of Black struggle, aspiration, resilience, quiet, and resistance. BlackCrit scholars, as Dumas and ross demonstrate, neither center Whiteness nor subscribe to it as they seek to understand, explain, and write about Blackness and anti-Blackness. The final reading in the volume is important because it promises a new way of thinking and talking about Black education.

References

Akom, A. A. (2003). Reexamining resistance as oppositional behavior: The Nation of Islam and the creation of a Black achievement ideology. *Sociology of Education, 76,* 305–325.

Alim, H. S. (2004). Hip-hop nation language. In C. A. Ferguson, E. Finegan, S. B. Heath, & J. R. Rickford (Eds.), *Language in the USA: Themes for the twenty-first century* (pp. 387–406). Cambridge University Press.

Alridge, D. P. (2005). From civil rights to hip hop: Toward a nexus of ideas. *Journal of African American History, 90*(3), 226–252.

Baszile, D. T. (2009). Deal with it we must: Education, social justice, and the curriculum of hip-hop culture. *Equity & Excellence in Education, 42*(1), 6–19.

Beauboeuf-Lafontant, T. (2002). A womanist experience of caring: Understanding the pedagogy of exemplary Black women teachers. *The Urban Review, 34*(1), 71–86.

Bridges, T. (2011). Towards a pedagogy of hip hop in urban teacher education. *The Journal of Negro Education, 80*(3), 325–338, 435.

Carter, P. (2003). Black cultural capital, status positioning and schooling conflicts for low-income African American youth. *Social Problems, 50*(1), 136–155.

Carter, P. (2005). *Keepin' it real: School success beyond Black and White.* Oxford University Press.

Davis, J. E. (2003). Early schooling and academic achievement of African American males. *Urban Education, 38*(5), 515–537.

Delgado, R., & Stefancic, J. (2001) *Critical race theory: An introduction.* New York University Press.

Delgado, R., & Stefancic, J. (2005). *The Derrick Bell reader.* New York University Press.

Dixson, A., & Rousseau, C. (2006). *Critical race theory in education: All God's children got a song.* Routledge Press.

Dumas, M. J., & ross, k. m. (2016). "Be real Black for me": Imagining BlackCrit in education. *Urban Education, 51*(4), 415–442.

Fordham, S. (1993). Those loud Black girls: (Black) Women, silence, and gender "passing" in the academy. *Anthropology & Education Quarterly, 24*(1), 3–32.

Fordham, S. (2008). Beyond Capital High: On dual citizenship and the strange career of "acting White." *Anthropology & Education Quarterly, 39*(3), 227–246.

Fordham, S., & Ogbu, J. (1986). Black students' school success: Coping with the burden of "acting White." *Urban Review, 18,* 176–206.

Foster, M. (1990). The politics of race: Through the eyes of African-American teachers. *Journal of Education, 172*(3), 123–141.

Foster, M. (1993). Educating for competence in community and culture: Exploring the views of exemplary African-American teachers. *Urban Education, 27*(4), 370–394.

Foster, M. (1997). *Black teachers on teaching.* New Press.

Freire, P. (2007). *Pedagogy of the oppressed.* Continuum.

Gibbs, J. (1988). Young Black males in America: Endangered, embittered, and embattled. In J. Gibbs, A. Brunswick, M. Connor, R. Dembo, T. Larson, R. Reed, & B. Solomon (Eds.), *Young, Black and male in America: An endangered species* (pp. 1–36). Auburn House.

Hill, M. (2009). *Beats, rhymes, and classroom life: Hip hop pedagogy and the politics of identity.* Teachers College Press.

hooks, b. (1994). *Teaching to transgress: Education as the practice of freedom.* Routledge.

Horvat, E. M., & Lewis, K. (2003). Reassessing the "burden of acting white": The importance of peer groups in managing academic success. *Sociology of Education, 76,* 265–280.

Horvat, E., & O'Connor, C. (2006). *Beyond acting White: Reassessments and new directions in research on Black students and school success.* Rowman and Littlefield.

Ibrahim, A. (2004). Operation under erasure: Hip-hop and the pedagogy of affective. *Journal of Curriculum Theorizing, 20*(1), 113–133.

Jeffries, R. (1994). The trickster figure in African-American teaching: Pre- and post-desegregation. *The Urban Review, 26*(4), 289–304.

Ladson-Billings, G. (1995). Toward a theory of culturally relevant pedagogy. *American Educational Research Journal, 32,* 465–491.

Ladson-Billings, G. (2000). Fighting for our lives: Preparing teachers to teach African American students. *Journal of Teacher Education, 51*(3), 206–214.

Ladson-Billings, G. (2006). From the achievement gap to the education debt: Understanding achievement in U.S. schools. *Educational Researcher, 35*(7), 3–12.

Ladson-Billings, G. (2009). *The dreamkeepers: Successful teachers of African American children* (2nd ed.). Jossey-Bass.

Ladson-Billings, G. (2014). *Culturally relevant pedagogy 2.0: A. K. A. the remix. Harvard Educational Review, 84*(1), 74–84.

Ladson-Billings, G., & Tate, W. (1995). Toward a critical race theory of education. *Teachers College Record, 97*(1), 47–68.

Love, B. (2015). What is hip-hop-based education doing in nice fields such as early childhood and elementary education? *Urban Education, 50*(1), 106–131.

Lynn, M., & Jennings, M. (2009). Power, politics and critical race pedagogy: A critical race analysis of Black male teachers' pedagogy. *Race Ethnicity and Education, 12*(2), 173–196.

The National Commission on Excellence in Education. (1983). *A nation at risk: The imperative for educational reform.* U.S. Department of Education.

O'Connor, C., Horvat, E., & Lewis, A. E. (2006). Framing the field: Past and future research on the historic underachievement of Black students. In E. Horvat & C. O'Connor (Eds.), *Beyond acting White: Reassessments and new directions in research on Black students and school success* (pp. 1–24). Rowman and Littlefield.

Petchauer, E. (2009). Framing and reviewing hip-hop educational research. *Review of Educational Research, 79*(2), 946–978.

Shujaa, M. J. (Ed.). (1994). *Too much schooling, too little education: A paradox of Black life in White societies.* Africa World Press, Inc.

Singham, M. (1998). The canary in the mine: The achievement gap between Black and White students. *Phi Delta Kappan, 80*(1), 8–15.

Stovall, D. (2006). We can relate: Hip-hop culture, critical pedagogy, and the secondary classroom. *Urban Education, 41*(6), 585–602.

Tyson, K. (2011). *Integration interrupted: Tracking, Black students, and acting White after Brown.* Oxford University Press.

Urban, W. J., & Jennings, W. L., Jr. (2013). *American education: A history* (5th ed.). Routledge.

Black Students' School Success:
Coping with the "Burden of 'Acting White'"[1]

Signithia Fordham and John U. Ogbu

THE AUTHORS REVIEW their previous explanation of black students' underachievement. They now suggest the importance of considering black people's expressive responses to their historical status and experience in America. "Fictive kinship" is proposed as a framework for understanding how a sense of collective identity enters into the process of schooling and affects academic achievement The authors support their argument with ethnographic data from a high school in Washington, D.C., showing how the fear of being accused of "acting white" causes a social and psychological situation which diminishes black students' academic effort and thus leads to underachievement. Policy and programmatic implications are discussed.

The following vignettes point to the central problem addressed in this paper. The first is from Dorothy Gilliam's column in the *Washington Post* of February 15, 1982, entitled "Success":

> My friend was talking to her son, who is 20, when he blurted out a secret half as old as he. It was the explanation for his ambivalence toward success. It began, he said, in his early school years, when a fifth-grade teacher questioned whether he had really written the outstanding essay he'd turned in about the life of squirrels. It ended when the teacher gave him a grade that clearly showed that she did not believe the boy's outraged denial of plagiarism.

Because the young man is black and the teacher is white, and because such incidents had happened before, he arrived at a youthful solution: "I never tried again," he recently told his mother, who had suffered misery as her son's grades had plummeted and his interest in school had waned. He had sold himself short because he was humiliated.

Today he reads the classics but has only a high school diploma; today he can finally articulate his feelings. Today he feels he was manipulated by society not to achieve, and feels he has been tricked into lowering his performance. He is furious that he blocked his own talents.

As my distraught friend recounted this disturbing episode, we looked at each other and grimaced. Each of us know people of her son's generation, and of our own, who are ambivalent about success (p. B1).

Gilliam goes on to recount how the existing ecological conditions have led black parents unwittingly to teach their children a double message: "You must be twice as good to go half as far," and "Don't get the big head, don't blow your own horn." Generations of black children have learned this lesson so well that what appears to have emerged in some segments of the black community is a kind of cultural orientation which defines academic learning in school as "acting white," and academic success as the prerogative of white Americans. This orientation embodies both social pressures against striving for academic success and fear of striving for academic success. The following passage from Abdul-Jabbar's autobiography illustrates a part of this *evolved cultural orientation toward schooling*:

> I got there [Holy Providence School in Cornwall Heights, right outside of Philadelphia] and immediately found I could read better than anyone in the school. My father's example and my mother's training had made that come easy; I could pick up a book, read it out loud, pronounce the words with proper inflections and actually know what they meant. When the nuns found this out they paid me a lot of attention, once even asking me, a fourth grader, to read to the seventh grade. When the kids found this out I became a target.
>
> It was my first time away from home, my first experience in an all-black situation, and I found myself being punished for doing everything I'd ever been taught was right. I got all A's and was hated for it; I spoke correctly and was called a punk. I had to learn a new language simply to be able to deal with the threats. I had good manners and was a good little boy and paid for it with my hide. (Abdul-Jabbar, 1983, p. 16)

Our main point in this paper is that *one major reason* black students do poorly in school is that they experience inordinate ambivalence and affective dissonance in regard to academic effort and success. This problem arose partly because white Americans traditionally refused to acknowledge that black Americans are capable of intellectual achievement, and partly because black Americans subsequently began to doubt their own intellectual ability, began to define academic success as white people's prerogative, and began to discourage their peers, perhaps unconsciously, from emulating white people in academic striving, i.e., from "acting white." Because of the ambivalence, affective dissonance, and social pressures, many black students who are academically able do not put forth the necessary effort and perseverance in their schoolwork and, consequently, do poorly in school. Even black students who do not fail generally perform well below their potential for the same reasons. We will illustrate this phenomenon with data from a recent ethnographic study of both successful and unsuccessful students in a predominantly black high school in Washington, D.C.

We will begin with a conceptual background and framework. This will be followed by a presentation of the case study from Washington, D.C. In the third section we will show that the phenomenon exists in other parts of the United States and probably can be found among other, similar minority groups in the U.S. and other societies. We will discuss the implications of our paper for policy and programs designed to increase minority school performance in the last, concluding section of the paper.

BACKGROUND AND CONCEPTUAL FRAMEWORK

Cultural-Ecological Influences on Schooling

It is well known that some minority groups are academically successful in school, while other minority groups are not (Coleman et al., 1966). The differences in the school performance of the various minority groups exist even when the minority groups face similar language, cultural, and educational barriers in school as well as barriers in the opportunity structure (e.g., job discrimination) in adult life (see Ogbu, 1984, in press; Ogbu and MatuteBianchi, 1986). In order to account for this variability, we have suggested that minority groups should be classified into three types: *autonomous minorities,* who are minorities primarily in a numerical sense; *immigrant minorities,* who came to America more or less *voluntarily* with the expectation of improving their economic, political, and social status; and *subordinate* or *castelike minorities,* who were *involuntarily and permanently* incorporated into American society through slavery or conquest. Black Americans are an example par excellence of castelike minorities because they were brought to America as slaves and after emancipation were relegated to menial status through legal and extralegal devices (Berreman, 1960; Myrdal, 1944). American Indians, Mexican Americans, and Native Hawaiians share, to some extent, features of castelike minorities. American Indians, the original owners of the land, were conquered and sent to live on reservations (Spicer, 1962). Mexican Americans in the Southwest were also conquered and displaced from power; and Mexicans who later immigrated from Mexico were given the status of the conquered group and treated in the same manner (Aeuna, 1972; Ogbu, 1978; Schmidt, 1970).

We initially explained the disproportionate and persistent high rates of school failure of subordinate minorities from a cultural-ecological perspective because this perspective allowed us to examine the school performance of the minorities in the context of historical, structural, and cultural forces which affect the schooling of such groups (Ogbu, 1978, 1981). In the case of black Americans we suggested that the disproportionately high rate of low school performance is a kind of adaptation to their limited social and economic opportunities in adult life. That is, the low school performance is an adaptive response to the requirements of cultural imperatives within their ecological structure.

Within their ecological structure black Americans traditionally have been provided with substandard schooling, based on white Americans' perceptions of the educational needs of black Americans; and white Americans have controlled black Americans' education. Another feature of their ecological structure is that black Americans have faced a job ceiling, so that even when they achieved in school in the past, i.e., had good educational credentials, they were not necessarily given access to jobs, wages, and other benefits commensurate with their academic accomplishments. The third component of the ecological structure is that in response to substandard schooling and barriers in the adult opportunity structure, black Americans developed several "survival strategies" and other coping mechanisms.

We suggested how these ecological factors might enter into the schooling of black children and adversely affect their academic performance. The job ceiling, for example, tends to give rise to disillusionment about the real value of schooling, especially among older children, and thereby discourages them from working hard in school (Hunter, 1980; Ogbu, 1974) Frustrations over the job ceiling and substandard schooling create conflicts and distrust between black Americans and the public schools, making it more difficult for black Americans than for white Americans to believe what the schools say and to behave according to school norms. Survival strategies, such as collective struggle, uncle tomming, and hustling, may encourage black Americans to develop attitudes, perceptions, behaviors, and competencies that are not necessarily congruent with those required to do well in school. The job ceiling and other discriminatory treatment engender among black Americans a feeling of impotence and a lack of self-confidence that they can compete successfully with whites *in matters considered traditionally as white people's domain,* such as good jobs and academic tasks. Finally, the experience of slavery with its attendant "compulsory ignorance" has meant that black Americans have had a limited development of academic tradition.

Under these circumstances, attitudes and behaviors of black students, though different from those of white students, are not deviant or pathological but should be considered as a mode of adaptation necessitated by the ecological structure or effective environment of the black community. That is, the attitudes and behaviors which black children learn in this community as they grow up and which they bring to school are those required by and appropriate for the niche black Americans have traditionally occupied in the American corporate economy and racial stratification system. In sum, the low school performance of black children stems from the following factors: first, white people provide them with inferior schooling and treat them differently in school; second, by imposing a job ceiling, white people fail to reward them adequately for their educational accomplishments in adult life; and third, black Americans develop coping devices which, in turn, further limit their striving for academic success.

A concept which allows one to comprehend more fully the academic attitudes and behaviors of black Americans under this circumstance is that of *status mobility system* (LeVine, 1967; Ogbu, 1978). A status mobility system is the socially or culturally approved strategy for getting ahead within a given population or a given society. It is the people's *folk theory of making it* or getting ahead, however the particular population defines getting ahead. A central premise of the concept is that a given status mobility system generates its own ideal personality types, distinguished by those orientations, qualities, and competencies which one needs to get ahead in the particular population. Furthermore, the way members of a population, including a subordinate population, prepare their children for adulthood, through child rearing as well as formal schooling, is influenced by their ideal images and characteristics of successful members of the population, living or dead; these images are incorporated into the value systems of parents and others responsible for the upbringing of children. As the children get older and begin to understand the status mobility system of their group, they themselves tend to play an active role in learning how to get ahead in the manner prescribed by their culture.

In a given population the orientations, qualities, competencies, and behaviors fostered by the system of status mobility will reflect the social and economic realities of its members. Thus, people's way of bringing up children, through which they inculcate those orientations, qualities, competencies, and behaviors they consider essential for competence in adulthood, is not divorced from their social and economic realities. In the case of subordinate minorities like black Americans, the schooling offered to them by the dominant group usually reflects the dominant group members' perceptions of the place of the minorities in the opportunity structure; equally important, however, are the responses of the minorities, which reflect their perceptions of their social and economic realities, their strategies for getting ahead.

The cultural-ecological explanation has undergone modifications because the original formulation did not explain differences in school success among black students. Why, for example, are some black children academically successful even though as a group black Americans face a limited adult opportunity structure and are given substandard education? The original formulation has also been criticized for focusing on black school failure while ignoring possible explanations for black school success (Fordham, 1981). But in fairness to the theory, it should be pointed out that it was initially proposed as a response to earlier theories that attributed disproportionately high rates of black school failure to genetic factors (Jensen, 1969) or to cultural deprivation (Bloom, Davis, and Hess, 1965).

Collective Identity, Cultural Frame, and Schooling

Since 1980 (Ogbu, 1980, 1982) the recognition of the above weakness, as well as the need to explain better the academic success of some other minority groups, has led the authors to modify the cultural-ecological explanation. The modification has involved going beyond factors of instrumental exploitation (limitations in opportunity structure, such as "job ceilings") and instrumental responses, to examine the expressive dimension of the relationship between the dominant group and the minorities. Specifically, in studying the expressive dimension of minority-majority group relations, we have isolated two additional factors we believe make the relationship between blacks and whites in America qualitatively different from the relationship between white Americans and other types of minorities, especially the immigrants. These additional factors also shed some light on the intragroup differences or individual differences within the black population. The two factors are an *oppositional collective* or *social identity* and an *oppositional cultural frame of reference* (Fordham, 1981, 1982a; Ogbu, 1980, 1981, 1984).

Our clue to the twin phenomena comes from reviewing cross-cultural studies of minorities. We have found the work of Spicer (1966, 1971), DeVos (1967, 1984). Castile and Kushner (1981), Green (1981), and others particularly helpful in this regard. These scholars have analyzed conflicts and oppositional processes between minority groups and dominant groups in both traditional societies and contemporary urban industrial societies, and they have concluded that the conflicts and opposition often cause the minorities to form oppositional social identities and oppositional cultural frames of reference (Ogbu, 1986a). A close analysis of the relationship between subordinate minorities and the dominant white Americans reveals these same kinds of conflicts and oppositional processes.

Subordinate minorities like black Americans develop a sense of collective identity or sense of peoplehood in opposition to the social identity of white Americans because of the way white Americans treat them in economic, political, social, and psychological domains, including white exclusion of these groups from true assimilation. The oppositional identity of the minority evolves also because they perceive and experience the treatment by whites as collective and enduring oppression. They realize and believe that, regardless of their individual ability and training or education, and regardless of their place of origin (e.g., in Africa) or residence in America, regardless of their individual economic status or physical appearance, they cannot expect to be treated like white Americans, their "fellow citizens"; nor can they easily escape from their more or less birth-ascribed membership in a subordinate and disparaged group by "passing" or by returning to "a homeland" (Green, 1981).

Along with the formation of an oppositional social identity, subordinate minorities also develop an oppositional cultural frame of reference which includes devices for protecting their identity and for maintaining boundaries between them and white Americans. Thus subordinate minorities regard certain forms of behavior and certain activities or events, symbols, and meanings as *not appropriate* for them because those behaviors, events, symbols, and meanings are characteristic of white Americans. At the same time they emphasize other forms of behavior and other events, symbols, and meanings as more appropriate for them because these are *not* a part of white Americans' way of life. To behave in the manner defined as falling within a white cultural frame of reference is to "act white" and is negatively sanctioned.

The cultural frame of reference of subordinate minorities is emotionally charged because it is closely tied to their sense of collective identity and security. Therefore individuals who try to behave like white Americans or try to cross cultural boundaries or to "act white" *in forbidden domains* face opposition from their peers and probably from other members of the minority community. Their peers often construe such behaviors as trying to join the enemy (DeVos, 1967). Individuals trying to cross cultural boundaries or pass culturally may also experience internal stress, what DeVos (1967) calls "affective dissonance." The reason for the affective dissonance is that such individuals share their minority-group's sense of collective oppositional identity, a belief which may cause them to feel that they are, indeed, betraying their group and its cause. The individuals may also experience psychological stress because they are uncertain that white Americans will accept them if they succeed in learning to "act white" (Fordham, 1985; Ogbu, 1986b). Indeed, DeVos (1984) argues that in a situation involving an oppositional process, subordinate-group members may automatically or unconsciously perceive learning some aspects of the culture of their "oppressors" as harmful to their identity. That is, learning itself may arouse a sense of "impending conflict over one's future identity." Of course, not every member of the minority group feels this way. Some do not identify with the oppositional identity and oppositional cultural frame of reference of their group. Some identify only marginally; and some even repudiate their group's social identity and cultural frame of reference (Fordham, 1985).

An oppositional cultural frame of reference is applied by the minorities selectively. The target areas appear to be those traditionally defined as prerogatives of white Americans, both by white people themselves and by the minorities. These are areas in which it was long believed that only whites could perform well and in which few minorities traditionally were given the opportunity to try or were rewarded if they tried and succeeded. They are areas where criteria of performance have been established by whites and competence in performance is judged by whites or their representatives, and where rewards for performance are determined by white people according to white criteria. Academic tasks represent one such area, as was noted in our comment in the vignettes presented earlier.

How do the oppositional identity and oppositional cultural frame of reference enter into the process of subordinate minorities' schooling? The oppositional identity and oppositional cultural frame of reference enter into the process of minority schooling through the minorities' perceptions and interpretations of schooling as learning the white American cultural frame of reference which they have come to assume to have adverse effects on their own cultural and identity integrity. Learning school curriculum and learning to follow the standard academic practices of the school are often equated by the minorities with learning to "act white" or as actually "acting white" while simultaneously giving up acting like a minority person. School learning is therefore consciously or unconsciously perceived as a *subtractive process:* a minority person who learns successfully in school or who follows the standard practices of the school is perceived as becoming acculturated into the white American cultural frame of reference at the expense of the minorities' cultural frame of reference and collective welfare. *It is important to point out that, even though the perceptions and behavioral responses are manifested by students, as peer groups and individuals, the perceptions and interpretations are a part of a cultural orientation toward schooling which exists within the minority community and which evolved during many generations when white Americans insisted that minorities were incapable of academic success, denied them the opportunity to succeed academically, and did not reward them adequately when they succeeded.*

The perception of schooling as a subtractive process causes subordinate minorities to "oppose" or "resist" academic striving, both socially and psychologically. At the social level, peer groups discourage their members from putting forth the time and effort required to do well in school and from adopting the attitudes and standard practices that enhance academic success. They oppose adopting appropriate academic attitudes and behaviors because they are considered "white." Peer group pressures against academic striving take many forms, including labeling (e.g., "brainiac" for students who receive good grades in their courses), exclusion from peer activities or ostracism, and physical assault. Individuals "resist" striving to do well academically partly out of fear of peer responses and partly to avoid affective dissonance. Because they also share their group's sense of collective identity and cultural frame of reference, individuals may not want to behave in a manner they themselves define as "acting white."

Fictive Kinship and Schooling

In our study of the twin phenomena of oppositional social identity and oppositional cultural frame of reference among black Americans, we have found the concept of fictive kinship (see Fordham 1981, 1985) an appropriate one to convey their meanings. In anthropology, fictive kinship refers to a kinship like relationship between persons not related by blood or marriage in a society, but who have some reciprocal social or economic relationship. There is usually a native term for it, or a number of native terms expressing or indicating its presence (Brain, 1971; Freed, 1973; Norbeck and Befu, 1958; Pitt-Rivers, 1968). Fictive kinship in the anthropological sense also exists among black Americans. Sometimes black people refer to persons in that kind of relationship as "play-kin" (Shimkin, Shimkin, and Frate, 1978).

But there is a much wider meaning of fictive kinship among black Americans. In this latter sense the term conveys the idea of "brotherhood" and "sisterhood" of all black Americans. This sense of peoplehood or collective social identity is evident in numerous kinship and pseudo kinship terms that black Americans use to refer to one another. The following are examples of the kinship and pseudo kinship terms most commonly used by adolescents and adults: "brother," "sister," "soul brother," "soul sister," "blood," "bleed," "folk," "members," "the people," "my people" (see Folb, 1980; Liebow, 1967; Sargent, 1985; Stack, 1974). In this paper we are using the term fictive kinship in the second, wider sense; that is, fictive kinship is used to denote a cultural symbol of collective identity of black Americans.

More specifically, fictive kinship is used to describe the particular mind set, i.e., the specific world view of those persons who are appropriately labeled "black." Since "blackness" is more than a skin color, fictive kinship is the concept used to denote the moral judgment the group makes on its members (see Brain, 1972). Essentially, the concept suggests that the mere possession of African features and/ or being of African descent does not automatically make one a black person, nor does it suggest that one is a member in good standing of the group. One can be black in color, but choose not to seek membership in the fictive kinship system, and/ or be denied membership by the group because one's behavior, activities, and lack of manifest loyalty are at variance with those thought to be appropriate and group-specific.

The black American fictive kinship system probably developed from their responses to two types of treatment they received from white Americans. One is the economic and other instrumental exploitation by whites both during and after slavery (Anderson, 1975; Bullock, 1970; Drake and cayton, 1970; Myrdal, 1944; Spivey, 1978). The other kind of treatment is the tendency of white Americans historically to treat blacks as an undifferentiated mass of people, ascribing to them indiscriminately certain inherent strengths and weaknesses. It appears that blacks have sometimes responded by inverting the negative stereotypes and assumptions of whites into positive and functional attributes (Fordham, 1982a; Holt, 1972; Ogbu, 1983). Thus, blacks may have transformed white assumptions of black homogeneity into a collective identity system and a coping strategy.

An example of collective treatment by white Americans which may have promoted the formation of black people's sense of collective identity *in opposition* to white identity *and* expressed the oppositional identity in the idiom of fictive kinship occurred following Nat Turner's "insurrection" in Southampton, Virginia, in 1831. After that incident whites restricted the movement of blacks as well as black contact amongst themselves, regardless of their place of residence or personal involvement in the insurrection (Haley, 1976; Styron, 1966). Even black children in Washington, D.C., were forbidden by whites from attending Sunday school with white children after the incident, although local whites knew that black children in Washington, D.C., had no part in the insurrection. What was well understood by blacks in Southampton, Virginia, in Washington, D.C., and elsewhere in the country was that the *onus* for Turner's behavior was extended to all black Americans solely on the basis of their being black. Numerous arbitrary treatments of this kind, coupled with a knowledge that they were denied true assimilation into the mainstream of American life, encouraged blacks to develop what DeVos (1967) calls "ethnic consolidation," a sense of peoplehood (Green, 1981) expressed in fictive kinship feelings and language.

Because fictive kinship symbolizes a black American sense of peoplehood in opposition to white American social identity, we suggest that it is closely tied to their various boundary-maintaining behaviors and attitudes towards whites. An example is the tendency for black Americans to emphasize *group loyalty* in situations involving conflict or competition with whites. Furthermore, black people have a tendency to negatively sanction behaviors and attitudes they consider to be at variance with their group identity symbols and criteria of membership. We also note that, since only black Americans are involved in the evaluation of group members' eligibility for membership in the fictive kinship system, they control the criteria used to judge one's worthiness for membership, and the criteria are totally group-specific. That is, the determination and control of the criteria for membership in the fictive kinship system are in contrast to the determination and control of the criteria for earning grades in school or promotion in the mainstream workplace by white people. Fictive kinship means a lot to black people because they regard it as the ideal by which members of the group are judged; it is also the medium through which blacks distinguish "real" from "spurious" members (M. Williams, 1981).

Black children learn the meaning of fictive kinship from their parents and peers while they are growing up. And it appears that the children learn it early and well enough so that they more or less unconsciously but strongly tend to associate their life chances and "success" potential with those of their peers and members of their community. Group membership is important in black peer relationships; as a result, when it comes to dealing with whites and white institutions, the unexpressed assumption guiding behavior seems to be that "my brother is my brother regardless of what he does or has done" (Haskins, 1976; Sargent, 1985). In the next section we will illustrate how the fictive kinship phenomenon enters into and affects the schooling of black children in one local community, Washington, D.C.

"ACTING WHITE" AT CAPITAL HIGH

The setting of the study, Capital High School and its surrounding community, has been described in detail elsewhere (Fordham, 1982b, 1984, 1985). Suffice it here to say that Capital High is a predominantly black high school (some 99% black 1,868 out of 1,886 students at the start of the research effort in 1982). It is located in a historically black section of Washington, D.C., in a relatively low-income area.

The influence of fictive kinship is extensive among the students at Capital High. It shows up not only in conflicts between blacks and whites and between black students and black teachers, who are often perceived to be "functionaries" of the dominant society, but also in the students' constant need to reassure one another of black loyalty and identity. They appear to achieve this group loyalty by defining certain attitudes and behaviors as "white" and therefore unacceptable, and then employing numerous devices to discourage one another from engaging in those behaviors and attitudes, i.e., from "acting white."

Among the attitudes and behaviors that black students at Capital High identify as "acting white" and therefore unacceptable are: (1) speaking standard English; (2) listening to white music and white radio stations; (3) going to the opera or ballet; (4) spending a lot of time in the library studying; (5) working hard to get good grades in school; (6) getting good grades in school (those who get good grades are labeled "brainiacs"); (7) going to the Smithsonian; (8) going to a Rolling Stones concert at the Capital Center; (9) doing volunteer work; (10) going camping, hiking, or mountain climbing; (11) having cocktails or a cocktail party; (12) going to a symphony orchestra concert; (13) having a party with no music; (14) listening to classical music; (15) being on time; (16) reading and writing poetry; and (17) putting on "airs," and so forth. This list is not exhaustive, but indicates kinds of attitudes and behaviors likely to be negatively sanctioned and therefore avoided by a large number of students.

As operationally defined in this paper, the idea of "coping with the burden of 'acting white'" suggests the various strategies that black students at Capital High use to resolve, successfully or unsuccessfully, the tension between students desiring to do well academically and meet the expectations of school authorities on the one hand and the demands of peers for conformity to group-sanctioned attitudes and behaviors that validate black identity and cultural frame on the other. Black students at Capital High who choose to pursue academic success are perceived by their peers as "being kind of white" (Weis, 1985, p. 101) and therefore not truly black. This gives rise to the tension between those who want to succeed (i.e., who in the eyes of their peers want to "act white") and others insisting on highlighting group-sanctioned attitudes and behaviors. Under the circumstance, students who want to do well in school must find some strategy to resolve the tension. This tension, along with the extra responsibility it places on students who choose to pursue academic success in spite of it, and its effects on the performance of those who resolve the tension successfully and those who do not, constitute "the burden of 'acting white.'" The few high-achieving students, as we will show, have learned how to cope successfully with the burden of acting white; the many underachieving students have not succeeded in a manner that enhances academic success. It is this tension and its effects on black students' academic efforts and outcomes that are explored in the case study of Capital High students.

Ethnographic data in the study were collected over a period of more than one year. During the study some 33 students in the eleventh grade were studied intensively, and our examples are drawn from this sample. Below we describe 8 cases, 4 males and 4 females. Two of the males and 2 of the females are underachievers, while 2 of the males and 2 of the females are high achievers.

Underachieving black students in the sample appear to have the ability to do well in school, at least better than their present records show. But they have apparently decided, consciously or unconsciously, to avoid "acting white." That is, they choose to avoid adopting attitudes and putting in enough time and effort in their schoolwork because their peers (and they themselves) would interpret their behaviors as "white." Their main strategy for coping with the burden of acting white tends, therefore, to be *avoidance*.

Our first example of an underachieving male is *Sidney*. Like most students in the sample, Sidney took the Preliminary Scholastic Aptitude Test (PSAT) and did fairly well, scoring at the 67th percentile on the math section of the test and at the 54th percentile on the verbal section. His scores on the Comprehensive Test of Basic Skills (CTBS) in the ninth grade indicate that he was performing well above grade level: His composite score in reading was 12.2; he scored at the college level on the language component (13.6); on the math component he scored just above eleventh grade (11.3), making his total battery on these three components 11.8. He scored above college level in the reference skills, science, and social studies sections. On the whole, his performance on standardized tests is far higher than that of many high-achieving males in our sample.

In spite of this relatively good performance on standardized tests, his grade point average is only C. Sidney is surprised and disgusted with his inability to earn grades comparable to those he earned in elementary and junior high school. While he takes most of the courses available to eleventh graders from the Advanced Placement sequence, he is not making the A's and B's at Capital High that he consistently made during his earlier schooling.

Sidney is an outstanding football player who appears to be encapsulated in the very forces which he maintains are largely responsible for the lack of upward mobility in the local black community. He is very much aware of the need to earn good grades in school in order to take advantage of the few opportunities he thinks are available to black Americans. However, he appears unable to control his life and act in opposition to the forces he identifies as detrimental to his academic progress.

His friends are primarily football players and other athletes. He is able to mix and mingle easily with them despite the fact that, unlike most of them, he takes advanced courses; he claims that this is because of his status as an athlete. His friends are aware of his decision to take these advanced courses, and they jokingly refer to him as "Mr. Advanced Placement."

Sidney readily admits that he could do a lot better in school, but says that he, like many of his friends, does not value what he is asked to learn in school. He also reluctantly admits that the fear of being called a "brainiac" prevents him from putting more time and effort into his schoolwork. According to him, the term "brainiac" is used in a disparaging manner at Capital High for students who do well in their courses:

Anthropologist:	Have you heard the word "brainiac" used here?
Sidney:	Yes. [When referring to students who take the Advanced Placement courses here.] That's a term for the smartest person in class. Brainiac—jerk—you know, those terms. If you're smart, you're a jerk, you're a brainiac.
Anthro:	Are all those words synonyms?
Sidney:	Yes.
Anthro:	So it's not a positive [term]?
Sidney:	No, it's a negative [term], as far as brilliant academic students are concerned.
Anthro:	Why is that?
Sidney:	That's just the way the school population is.

Although Sidney takes the Advanced Placement Courses, he is not making much effort to get good grades; instead, he spends his time and effort developing a persona that will nullify any claims that he is a brainiac, as can be seen in the following interview excerpt:

Anthropologist:	Has anyone ever called you a [brainiac]?
Sidney:	Brainiac? No.
Anthro:	Why not?
Sidney:	Well, I haven't given them a reason to. And, too, well, I don't excel in all my classes like I *should* be—that's another reason. . . . I couldn't blame it on the environment. I have come to blame it on myself—for partaking *in* the environment. But I *can* tell you that—going back to what we *were* talking about—another reason why they don't call me a "brainiac," because I'm an athlete.
Anthro:	So … if a kid is smart, for example, one of the ways to limit the negative reaction to him or her, and his or her is . . . .
Sidney:	Yeah, do something extracurricular in the school . . . [like] being an athlete, cheerleader squad, in the band—like that. . . . Yeah, *something that's important* [emphasis added], that has something to do with—that represents your school.

Sidney admits that the fear of being known as a brainiac has negatively affected his academic effort a great deal. The fear of being discovered as an "imposter" among his friends, leads him to choose carefully those persons with whom he will interact within the classroom; all of the males with whom he interacts who also take Advanced Placement courses are, like him, primarily concerned with "mak[ing] it over the hump."

He also attributes his lack of greater effort in school to his lack of will power and time on task. And he thinks that his low performance is due to his greater emphasis on athletic achievement and his emerging manhood, and less emphasis on the core curriculum. He does not study. He spends very little time completing his homework assignments, usually fifteen minutes before breakfast. On the whole, Sidney is not proud of his academic record. But he does not feel that he can change the direction of his school career because he does not want to be known as a brainiac.

The second example of an underachieving male student is *Max*. Max scored higher than many high-achieving males on the PSAT, scoring at the 58th percentile on the verbal and at the 52nd percentile on the math component. But his course grades, at all levels, have been mostly C's with a few B's and an occasional A. Since coming to Capital High, his grades have fallen even further from their earlier low in junior high. For example, during his first year at Capital High he earned two F's, two D's, one C, and one A.

Max, like Sidney, is a football player who "puts brakes," i.e., limitations, on his academic effort. He also takes most of his courses from the Advanced Placement courses for eleventh graders. However, unlike Sidney, who chose to come to Capital High because of the advanced courses, Max takes these courses only because his parents insist that he take them.

Listening to this student's responses to questions, or hearing him talk about his life experiences, one is struck by the tenacity of his desire to remain encapsulated in peer-group relations and norms. This is quite contrary to his mother's constant effort to "liberate" him from that encapsulation. Max is different from his friends because of his middle-class background. He knows that he is different, but values their friendship very much:

> We don't think the same, me and my friends. That's why I used to think that I wasn't—I used to think that I wasn't—I used to always put myself down, I wasn't good enough. Because I could—the things they'd want to do, I didn't want to do because I knew it was wrong, and that I wouldn't get anything out of it. And, really, a cheap thrill isn't really all that much to me—really it isn't. It's just not worth it, you know. Why go through the trouble? So— that's just the way I think. I used to try and change it, but it didn't work . . . not for me, it didn't, anyways.

Because his friends are critically important to him and his sense of identity, Max not only holds on to them at the expense of his academic progress, but he also resorts to necessary role playing to ensure that he retains the integrity of his social identity. For him, role playing means underestimating his level of intelligence and insight. In fact, he argues that the role he has played over the years has become so much a part of him that he is forced at different junctures to say to himself that he must snap out of the socially constructed persona. This role—limiting his academic effort and performance—is so much a part of who he is seen to be, that Max claims it is "something like a split personality, kind of, but it isn't."

What is the effect of these factors on Max's school career? He feels sad when he reflects on his school career thus far:

> You know, I just sacrificed a whole lot out of myself, what I could do, just to make my friends happy, you know. And it never—it just didn't work. They—you know, all of them didn't take advantage of me. They really didn't bother—it bothered me, but it wasn't that they were all trying just to take advantage of me, it was just that, you know, sometimes when I got my mind—you know, I just got—I'd get myself psyched out, worrying about what other people thought of me. But it really doesn't matter all that much, anymore. Not as much as it did then. I guess that's just growing up.

Shelvy is our first example of the underachieving female students. Her performance on standardized tests supports her teachers' evaluation of her academic ability. On her eleventh grade CTBS, her composite score in the three major areas—reading, language, and mathematics—was the highest overall grade equivalent (OGE) possible, 13.6. Because she assumes that she will not be able to go to college (her parents are very poor), she did not see any value in trying to convince her parents to give her the five dollars needed to pay for the PSAT, and so she opted not to take it.

In the elementary school her grades were "mostly VG's, A's, B's and stuff like that." Despite the resistance to academic success by students in the two elementary and two junior high schools (all in the Capital community) she attended prior to coming to Capital High, she continued to obtain good grades. In fact, in the second junior high school she was placed in the only honors section of the ninth grade class. This made it much easier for her because everybody there had been identified as a potentially good student. As she puts it:

> I went to Garden [Junior High School]. That was *fairly* well, but in the eighth grade I had the problem of the same thing—everybody saying, "Well, she thinks she's smart," and all this. I had the same problem in the eighth grade. But in the ninth grade, they placed me in an all-academic section and, you know, everyone in there was smart, so it wasn't recognized—they recognized everybody as being a smart section, instead of an individual.

She made the Honor Roll during both her eighth and ninth grade years, and this pattern of academic success continued during her first year at Capital High when she earned two B's, two A's, and two C's.

At the time of this study, however, things had changed for Shelvy. She is no longer enthusiastic about school and is not making any concerted effort to improve the level of her performance. The reason for this development is unclear. However, from her account of students' attitudes and behaviors in the schools she attended and at Capital, we speculate that she finally submitted to peer pressures not to "act white." Therefore she has not resorted to the coping strategies that worked for her in earlier school years.

Speaking of her earlier school experiences, Shelvy says that her first contact with the notion of success as a risky task began in the elementary school, and probably came to full fruition during the sixth grade when, for the first time in her life, she heard the word "brainiac" used to refer to her. She says that ideally everybody wants to be a brainiac, but one is paralyzed with fear that if he or she performs well in school he or she will be discovered, and that would bring some added responsibilities and problems.

Perhaps more than any other underachieving female, Shelvy's academic performance reflects the pain and frustrations associated with trying to camouflage one's abilities from peers. Having been a "good student" in elementary school, she knows firsthand how difficult it is to avoid encapsulation in antiacademic peer groups:

> In the sixth grade, it was me and these two girls, we used to hang together all the time. They used to say we was brainiacs, and no one really liked us... It's not something—well, *it's something that you want to be, but you don't want your friends to know* [emphasis added]... Because once they find out you're a brainiac, then the first thing they'll say is, "Well, she thinks she's cute, and she thinks she's smart, she thinks she's better than anyone else." So what most brainiacs do, they sit back and they know an answer, and they won't answer it.... 'Cause, see, first thing everybody say, "Well, they're trying to show off." So they really don't—they might answer once in a while, but.... Because if you let... all your friends know how smart you are, then when you take a test or something, then they're going to know you know the answer and they're going to want the answers. And if you don't give them to them, then they're going to get upset with you.

When asked how their being upset would be manifested, Shelvy replied, "Well, they might start rumors about you, might give you a bad name or something like that."

Shelvy's analysis of the dilemma of the brainiac clearly suggests that the academically successful black student's life is fraught with conflicts and ambivalence. The fear of being differentiated and labeled as a brainiac often leads to social isolation and a social self which is hurt by negative perceptions. Essentially Shelvy claims that a student who is identified as a brainiac is more vulnerable to "social death" than one who is not.

Shelvy is more aware than many of her peers concerning why she is not performing as well academically as she could and perhaps should. As she explains it, she is keenly aware of her peers' concurrent "embracement and rejection" of school norms and behaviors. In that sense she realizes that seeking school success at Capital High is immersed in boundary-maintaining devices. It is the boundary-maintaining tendencies of her peers, which negatively sanction behaviors associated with the label "brainiac," that are negatively affecting her school performance. Her fear of being labeled a "brainiac" and burdened with all the expectations attendant thereto, as well as her negative perception of the opportunity structure, has led her to resort to lowering her effort in school. Her fear of academic excellence is readily apparent when observed in the classroom context. When she is called upon by teachers, she responds quickly and correctly; however, having learned from negative experiences associated with academic success in the elementary and junior high schools, she "puts brakes" on her academic effort to minimize bringing attention to herself.

Kaela is our second example of an underachieving female student. Kaela did not take the PSAT in the eleventh grade, so it is not one of the available measures of her academic ability. Nor did she take the CTBS. She did, however, take the Life Skills Examination, a standardized test required of all eleventh graders by the D.C. Public School System. In fact, she had a perfect score on that exam.

Kaela's teachers say that she not only has the ability to do the work required in their courses, but she is also more capable than most other students taking their courses. Yet, Kaela failed nearly all her major courses during her first semester at Capital High. The primary reason for her failure is her unwillingness to come to school regularly, i.e., her repeated absence from her assigned classes. For example, her English teacher was pleased with her performance, but could not give her a passing grade because of poor attendance. Her history teacher was "forced" to give her a failing grade because of excessive absenteeism, although she scored 88% on the semester examination.

Kaela attended Catholic elementary and junior high schools in the Washington, D.C., area, and her academic records from those schools show that she was a good student and a high achiever. For example, during her ninth grade year, she earned high honors and received a full scholarship. She apparently attended school regularly before coming to Capital High. When questioned directly about her repeated absence at Capital High, Kaela says that she does not know why she and other students are absent:

> I don't really know why. I don't even know why I don't come, when I know I should come. It's just that we [black students] don't have that much support. We don't get—I know we know that we should do things, but it's—you know, you know something pushing you. And when you don't have that, sometimes you feel like nobody cares, so why should *you* care? It gets like that sometimes. But then other times, I don't know why. Sometimes I don't want to come if I haven't done my homework. And then—I don't understand. I don't know why. I think we're scared to take responsibility and stuff. And that's because the people we keep company with, you know. And it's just—I don't know—people—when we see people, you know, and they're like role models. But they don't necessarily have to be *good* role models. And then we just settle for that. And we—I know that! don't *want* to settle for that, but it's just something *in* me that won't let me do more. So I settle. I know I could make the Honor Roll here.

An examination of Kaela's schooling history shows that her problem probably began to develop back in Catholic schools when she started to develop a sense of collective identity. She says that she began to lose interest in her schoolwork after she found that the parochial school administrators were treating her differently from the way they treated other black students, as if she were special. Since she, too, is a black person, she began to seriously limit her school effort and could not be persuaded by her teachers or parents to believe that she was unlike the other black students. Thus, while her teachers insist on treating her as an individual, Kaela sees herself first and foremost as a black person, and it is her growing sense of identity as a black person which has negatively affected her school performance. She appears convinced that opportunities for black Americans are small and her personal future very limited because (a) she is black, (b) her family is very poor and cannot pay for her college education, and (c) the competition for highly valued positions in school and the workplace is too keen for her. Therefore she decided to "put brakes" on her academic effort in order to reduce the frustration from being overqualified for the low-status jobs she thinks she will get eventually.

Kaela attributes the behaviors and low academic achievement of other black Americans at Capital High to the same factors as those operating in her situation. She says that students perceive an opportunity structure in which they are judged primarily on the basis of their race. This discourages students from persevering in their schoolwork and from academic success. As Kaela was being interviewed at a time when students were selecting their classes for the next year, she used the event to point out the effect of students' perceptions of dismal futures on their course selections:

> [The students at Capital High would try harder to make good grades in school if they thought they had a real chance.] I *know* that. Because I've heard a lot of people say, "Well, I don't know why I'm taking all these hard classes. I ain't never going to see this stuff again in my life! Why am I going to sit up here and make my record look bad, trying to take all these hard classes and get bad grades? I ain't going to need this stuff. I'm just going to take what I need to get my diploma. Forget all that other stuff." And, you know, *I thought like that for a while too* [emphasis added]. But it's not the right way. I mean, we should try to better ourselves in any possible way. But a lot of people don't think that way.

Kaela's views of black Americans' opportunity structure as being racially biased have contributed to her diminishing interest and effort in school. Her refusal to put forth the necessary effort to do well in school also stems from her growing identification with the problems and concerns of black people. Her growing racial awareness is thus inversely related to her school effort and achievement. It seems that Kaela's absence from school is one way she tries to cope with the "burden of 'acting white.'"

High-Achieving Students

Students at Capital High who are relatively successful academically also face the problem of coping with the "burden of 'acting white.'" But they have usually adopted strategies that enable them to succeed. These students decide more or less consciously (a) to pursue academic success and (b) to use specific strategies to cope with the burden of acting white.

Martin is our first example of a high-achieving male student. His scores on the standardized tests, PSAT and CTBS, are unfortunately not available to help us assess his ability. But he has a relatively good academic record. He graduated tenth in his junior high school class; and in the tenth grade at Capital High, he earned three B's, one A-, and a D. He is a member of the school's chapter of the National Honor Society. Although Martin is still uncertain about his overall academic ability because of absence of reliable scores on standardized tests, he gets good grades in class, attends school regularly, has a positive attitude about school, and receives good evaluations from teachers.

Martin is fully aware of peer pressures to discourage male students at Capital High from striving toward academic success. The most discouraging factor, in his view, is the fear of being labeled a "brainiac" or, worse, a "pervert brainiac." To be known as a brainiac is bad enough, but to be known as a pervert brainiac is tantamount to receiving a kiss of death. For a male student to be known as a brainiac, according to Martin, is to question his manhood; to be known as a pervert brainiac leaves little doubt. He claims that there are persistent rumors that some male students taking all or a large number of the Advanced Placement courses are homosexuals; this is far less the case for male students who do not take the advanced courses. Also it is believed at Capital High that males who do *not* make good grades are less likely to be gay.

Martin says that the best strategy for a male student making good grades or wanting to succeed academically and yet escape the label of brainiac is for him to handle his school persona carefully and to cloak it in other activities that minimize hostility against academically successful students. One such "cloaking activity" is "lunching": that is, to avoid being called a brainiac and thereby bringing one's manhood into question, a male student who desires good grades will often resort to behaviors suggesting that he is a clown, comedian, or does not work very hard to earn the grades he receives.

Martin:	Okay. Lunching is like when you be acting crazy, you know, having fun with women, you know. Okay, you still be going to class, but you—like me, okay, they call *me* crazy, 'cause I'll be having fun.
Anthropologist:	Do they say you're "lunching"?
Martin:	Yeah. Go ask [my girlfriend]. She be saying I'm lunching. 'cause I be— 'cause I be doin' my homework, and I be playin' at the same time, and I get it done. I don't know how I do that.
Anthro:	So It's important to be a clown, too—I mean, to be a comedian?

Martin: Yeah. Yeah, a comedian, because you—yeah.

Anthro: A comedian is a male? There's no doubt that a comedian is a male?

Martin: A male, uh-huh! 'Cause if you be all about [concerned only about] your schoolwork, right? And you know a lot of your *friends* not about it, if you don't act like a clown, your friends gonna start calling you a brainiac.

Anthro: And it's not good to be called a brainiac?

Martin: Yeah, it's—I don't want nobody to be calling *me* one, 'cause I know I ain't no brainiac. But if they call you one, you might seem odd to them. 'Cause they'll always be joning on you. See? When I was at Kaplan [Junior High school], that's what they called me—"brainiac," 'cause I made straight A's and B's, that's all in the First Advisory. So that's why . . . .

The interview with Martin left us with the impression that he does not put forth as much effort and time as he might have were he not shackled with the burden of worrying about his peers' perceptions of him as a brainiac. Therefore, although he comes to school every day (he missed only one day during the tenth grade) and completes most of his homework, he does not do more than the officially required academic tasks.

Norris is another high-achieving male student who has developed specific strategies for coping with the burden of acting white. His performance on the verbal and math sections of the PSAT was at the 85th and 96th percentile, respectively. His scores on the CTBS are similarly impressive. His overall grade equivalent in every section—reading, language, math, reference skills, science, and social studies, as well as in every subsection—is at the college level (13.6 OGE—overall grade equivalent).

He has maintained an outstanding academic record since elementary school, where he was recommended to skip the fifth grade. He graduated from Garden Junior High as the Valedictorian of his class. He also received several ancillary awards, including "the most improved student," "the most likely to succeed," etc. He earned all A's in his first semester at Capital High, taking Advanced Placement courses. His cumulative grade average is A.

How does Norris do so well in school and still cope with the burden of acting white? Norris says that he has faced the problem of coping with the burden of acting white since his elementary school days, when he discovered that he was academically ahead of other students, and that they did not like anyone doing well academically like himself. He says that what has been critically important in his acceptance by his peers, even though he is a good student, is his appearance of not putting forth much academic effort. At the elementary and junior high schools, where his peers thought that he got good grades without studying, they attributed his academic success to his "natural talent" or special gift. Therefore they did not view him as a pervert brainiac.

The public elementary school he attended was "filled with hoodlums, thugs, and the dregs of society," in his words. Fighting was a frequent pastime among the students. Under this circumstance Norris's strategy was to choose friends who would protect him in exchange for his helping them with homework assignments, tests, etc. He explains the strategy as follows:

> I didn't want to—you know, be with anybody that was like me, 'cause I didn't want to get beat up. The school I went to, Berkeley, was really rough, see? It was really tough, you know. Lived in the projects and everything, and known tough and everything. So I used to hang with them. If anybody ever came in my face and wanted to pick on me, they'd always be there to help me. So I always made sure I had at least two or three bullies to be my friends. Even though if it does mean I had to give up answers in class.... I was willing to give up a little to get a lot. So I did that for elementary school. Then, by the time I got to junior high school, I said, "Forget it. If people don't tend to accept me the way I am, that's too bad. I don't need any friends, I have myself."

His alliance with "bullies" and "hoodlums" worked at the elementary school. At the junior high level, he had a second factor in his favor, namely, his growing athletic prowess. This helped to lessen the image of him as a pervert brainiac. But he also deliberately employed another strategy, this time acting as a clown or comedian. He explains it this way:

> [In junior high school] I had to act crazy then . . . you know, nutty, kind of loony, they say . . . [the students would then say], "He's crazy"—not a *class* clown, to get on the teachers' nerves, I never did that to the—around *them*. I'd be crazy. As soon as I hit that class, it was serious business.... Only the people who knew me knew my crazy side, when they found out I was smart, they wouldn't believe it. And the people that knew that I was smart, wouldn't believe it if they were told that I was crazy. So I went through that. I'm still like that *now*, though.

Norris continues his comedian strategy at Capital High. He says that it is important for him to employ this strategy because he wants to do well in order to go to college on scholarships.

High-achieving females use certain gender-specific strategies to cope with the burden of acting white. But, like the males, they camouflage to avoid being perceived as brainiacs. More than the males, the female high achievers work to maintain low profiles in school. Katrina and Rita will serve as examples.

Katrina's performance on the math component of the PSAT was at the 95th percentile. Only one other student, Norris, scored higher and another student had a comparable score. Katrina's score on the verbal component was not as high, being at the 75th percentile. But her overall score far surpassed those of most other students. Her performance on the CTBS was equally impressive, with an overall grade equivalent of 13.6, or college level, in every section—math, reading, and language, and in every subsection, as well as in the ancillary sections, namely, reference skills, social studies, and science. She also performed well on the Life Skills examination which measures students' ability to process information in nine different areas. Katrina scored 100% in each of the nine areas.

In the classroom her performance has been equally outstanding. She had A in all subjects except handwriting in the elementary school, Her final grades in the ninth grade (i.e., junior high school) were all A's; and in the tenth grade, her first year at Capital High, her final grades were all A's.

Katrina has heard of the term "brainiac" not only at Capital High, but as far back as at the elementary and junior high school levels. And she is very much aware of the nuances associated with the term. She explains:

> When they [other students] call someone a "brainiac," they mean he's always in the books. But he probably isn't always in the books. Straight A, maybe—you know, or A's and B's. A Goody-Two-Shoes with the teacher, maybe—you know, the teacher always calling on them, and they're always the leaders in the class or something.

She acknowledges that she is often referred to as a brainiac, but that she always denies it because she does not want her peers to see her that way. To treat her as a brainiac "blows her cover" and exposes her to the very forces she has sought so hard to avoid: alienation, ridicule, physical harm, and the inability to live up to the name.

How does Katrina avoid being called a brainiac and treated with hostility while at the same time managing to keep up her outstanding academic performance? Katrina admits that she has had to "put brakes" on her academic performance in order to minimize the stress she experiences. She says that she is much better at handling subject matter than at handling her peers. To solve the peer problem, she tries not to be conspicuous. As she puts it:

> Junior high, I didn't have much problem. I mean, I didn't have—there were always a lot of people in the classroom who did the work, so I wasn't like, the only one who did this assignment. So—I mean, I might do better at it, but I wasn't the only one. And so a lot of times, I'd let other kids answer—I mean, not *let* them, but. . . . All right, I *let* them answer questions [laughter], and I'd hold back. So I never really got into any arguments, you know, about school and my grades or anything.

She is extremely fearful of peer reactions if she were identified as acting white. Since she wants to continue doing well in school, she chooses to "go underground," that is, not to bring attention to herself. Her reluctance to participate in Capital High's "It's Academic" Club, a TV competition program, illustrates her desire to maintain a low profile. "It's Academic" is perhaps the most "intellectual" extracurricular activity at the school. To participate in the three-person team, a student must take a test prepared by the faculty sponsoring it. The three top scorers are eligible to represent the school in the TV competition. Katrina reluctantly took the test at the suggestion of her physics teacher, the club sponsor. However, she had a prior agreement that she would not be selected to participate on the team *even if she had the top score.* She was one of the three top scorers, but because of the prior agreement was made only an alternate member of the team.

Rita, our second high-achieving female, had one of the best performances on the standardized tests given at Capital High. She had the highest score on the verbal component of the PSAT, at the 96th percentile. Her math score was not as high, being at the 62nd percentile. As a result of her high performance on the PSAT, Rita was one of only five students from Capital High nominated for the National Merit Scholarship for Outstanding Negro Students. Her performance on the CTBS was equally outstanding: she scored at the OGE of 13.6 on all except the spelling subsection where she scored almost at grade level, 11.8. On the Life Skills Examination, she scored higher on each of the nine areas than the minimum required.

Rita makes fairly good grades in school, although her effort and her performance are not consistent. She switches from being a good student to an average or near-average student. For example, during her first year at Capital High, she received four C's, two D's, and one B. But in the second year she got three A's, three B's, and one C.

The inconsistency in Rita's performance appears to be due to one of the strategies she claims to have adopted to cope with the burden of acting white, namely, irregular class attendance as a way of maintaining a low profile. She readily admits that she strategically cuts classes and makes deliberate plans for achieving her goal of getting the most in return for as little effort as possible in all her classes.

Rita's current main strategy is, however, comedic. She is seen as a clown and is often described by friends, peers and classmates as "that crazy Rita." This is true even though they know that her academic performance is among the best at the school. But her main impression on people is that she is "crazy," because of the way she interacts with peers, classmates, and even with her teachers. Rita believes that this comedic behavior enables her to cope with pressures of schoolwork and pressure from peers. The comedic strategy is unusual among the female students at Capital High; but it works for Rita just as it works for Norris: it thwarts latent hostility of peers, while allowing her to do well on some measures of school success.

To summarize, all the high-achieving students wrestle with the conflict inherent in the unique relationship of black people with the dominant institution: the struggle to achieve success while retaining group support and approval. In school, the immediate issue is how to obtain good grades and meet the expectations of school authorities without being rejected by peers for acting white. Our examples show that successful students at Capital High generally adopt specific strategies to solve this problem.

THE BURDEN OF ACTING WHITE
IN COMPARATIVE PERSPECTIVE

The burden of acting white, how black adolescents cope with it, and its effects on their academic careers have not been generally recognized, let alone systematically studied. Nevertheless, there are references here and there suggesting that similar problems are faced by black students in other schools and in other parts of the United States. One example from Philadelphia, that of Abdul-Jabbar, has already been cited. Another is that of E. Sargent, a journalist with the *Washington Post*, who attended public schools in Washington, D.C.

Sargent describes, in a column in the *Washington Post*, (Feb. 10, 1985) how he used his emerging sense of black identity to minimize the conflicts associated with academic success among black students. He attributes his ability to deal with the burden of acting white to his broader sense of black American history which he acquired *outside* the public schools. As he puts it:

> While I had always been a good student, I became a better one as a result of my sense of black history. I began to notice that my public-school teachers very rarely mentioned black contributions to the sciences, math, and other areas of study. They never talked about ways blacks could collectively use their education to solve the great economic and social problems facing the race.
>
> My mind was undergoing a metamorphosis that made the world change its texture. Everything became relevant because I knew blacks had made an impact on all facets of life. *I felt a part of things that most blacks thought only white people had a claim to* [our emphasis]. Knowing that there is a serious speculation that Beethoven was black—a mullato [sic]—made me enjoy classical music. "Man, why do you listen to that junk? That's white music," my friends would say. "Wrong. Beethoven was a brother." I was now bicultural, a distinction most Americans could not claim. I could switch from boogie to rock, from funk to jazz and from rhythm-and-blues to Beethoven and Bach... I moved from thinking of myself as disadvantaged to realizing that I was actually "super-advantaged." (pp. DI, D4)

Black students in desegregated and integrated schools also face the burden of acting white. A study by Petroni and Hirsch (1970) shows how the phenomenon operates in a Midwestern city. They present several examples of academically successful students at Plains High School and the problems confronting them, as well as the strategies they adopt to cope with the burden of acting white. Take the case of Pat, an academically successful black female whose dilemma they describe. Pat appears to be different from other black students in the school, and she seems to be subjected to different kinds of pressures from black and white students. However, she indicates that the more difficult pressures come from black students:

> I [feel] the greatest pressure from members of my own race. I'm an all A student; I'm always on the Honor Roll; I'm in Madrigals, and so on. Because of these small accomplishments, there's a tendency for the [blacks] to think that I'm better than they are. They think I'm boasting. Take Nancy—Nancy ran for office, and I've heard other [black students] say, "She thinks she's so good." I don't think of it this way. These small accomplishments that I've achieved aren't just for me, but they're to help the black cause. I do things for my race, not just for myself. Most of the time, though, I don't pay too much attention to these kids. It's just a small percentage of [blacks] anyway, who're the troublemakers, and they resent the fact that I'm doing something, and they aren't. (Petroni and Hirsch, 1970, p. 20)

The burden of acting white becomes heavier when academically able black students face both pressures from blacks peers to conform, and doubts from whites about their ability, as the following cases show. The former is described in a series of articles on adolescents' school behavior in a predominantly white suburban school system near Washington, D.C., by Elsa Walsh (1984). Her account highlights the problems of high-achieving black students in integrated schools, especially the paralyzing effects of coping with the burden of acting white.

Our first case is that of "K," who Walsh identifies as a 13-year-old, academically gifted, female black student. Walsh describes K's feeling of loneliness and isolation in the predominantly white honors courses to which she was assigned. She also points out that black students at the school reject K and often accuse her of being "stuck up" and thinking she is "too good for them." At the same time, K's white classmates doubt that she actually has the ability to do the work in the honors courses. All of these factors erode K's confidence.

An example of a similar dilemma is Gray's (1985) description of the futility of her efforts to minimize her "blackness" through academic excellence in a predominantly white school and community:

> No matter how refined my speech, or how well educated or assimiliated [sic] I become, I fear I will always be an outsider. I'm almost like a naturalized alien—in this place but not of it. During my pompous period, I dealt with my insecurities by wearing a veil of superiority. Except around my family and neighbors, I played the role—the un-black.
>
> To whites I tried to appear perfect—I earned good grades and spoke impeccable English, was well-mannered and well-groomed. Poor whites, however, made me nervous. They seldom concealed their contempt for blacks, especially

"uppity" ones like myself . . . To blacks, I was all of the above and extremely stuck up. I pretended not to see them on the street, spoke to them only when spoken to and cringed in the presence of blacks being loud in front of whites. The more integrated my Catholic grammar school became, the more uncomfortable I was there. I had heard white parents on TV, grumbling about blacks ruining their schools; I didn't want anyone to think that I, too, might bring down Sacred Heart Academy. So I behaved, hoping that no one would associated [sic] me with "them". (Gray, 1985, pp. E1, E5)

In summary, black students elsewhere, like those at Capital High, in predominantly black schools as well as in integrated schools, appear to face the burden of acting white. Under this circumstance students who are clever enough to use certain deliberate strategies succeed in "making it." In predominantly black schools, they succeed in protecting themselves from the antagonisms of black peers who define their academic striving negatively as acting white. In integrated schools, their problem is further complicated by the negative and often implicit assumptions of whites about the intellectual ability of black people. In such schools, white Americans' doubts may erode the academic confidence of black students who are taking "white courses."

Other Minority Groups

Other subordinate minorities in the United States and elsewhere also appear to face a similar problem. There are indications, for instance, that American Indians and Mexican Americans perceive the public schools as an agent of assimilation into the white American or Anglo cultural frame of reference; and that these minorities consider such assimilation or linear acculturation to be detrimental to the integrity of their cultures, languages, and identities (Virgil, 1980; Ogbu and Matute-Bianchi, 1986). Some Mexican-American students have been reported to say that school learning is "doing the anglo thing" and to appear to resist learning what is taught in the school context (Ogbu and Matute-Bianchi 1986; Matute-Bianchi, 1986).

The problem of coping with the burden of acting white has also been reported for some American Indian students. Studies by Erickson and Mohan (1982) among Odawa Indian students, and by Philips (1983) among Warm Springs Reservation Indian students suggest that older elementary school students are already affected by it. These children come to the classroom "resisting" school rules and standard practices. That is, they enter the classroom with a sort of cultural convention which dictates that they should not adopt the rules of behavior and standard practices expected of children in the public schools taught by the white teachers. This indicates that for them perhaps the rules and practices are considered white.

Outside the United States, there are also subordinate minorities who perceive the learning of the formal school curriculum as *a subtractive process*, i.e., as one-way acculturation into the cultural frame of reference of the dominant group members of their society. Among these subordinate minorities are Australian Aborigines (Bourke, 1983), the Buraku Outcastes in Japan (DeVos & Wagatsuma, 1967), some Indians of South America (Varese, 1985), and the Maoris of New Zealand (Smith, 1983). Good ethnographic studies of actual school and classroom attitudes and behaviors of these minorities are needed to determine the strategies of the students for coping with the burden of acting like the dominant group.

SUMMARY AND IMPLICATIONS

We have suggested in this paper that black students' academic efforts are hampered by both external factors and within-group factors. We have tried to show that black students who are academically successful in the face of these factors have usually adopted specific strategies to avoid them. Although we recognize and have described elsewhere in detail the external, including school, factors which adversely affect black adolescents' school performance (Fordham, 1982a, 1985; Ogbu, 1974, 1978), our focus in this paper is on the within-group factors, especially on how black students respond to other black students who are trying to "make it" academically.

We began by noting that the instrumental factors postulated in our earlier cultural-ecological explanation of minority school performance, namely, inferior schooling, limited opportunity structure, and such peoples' own perceptions of and responses to schooling, are important, but that there are additional factors involved. We identified the additional factors as an oppositional collective or social identity and an oppositional cultural frame of reference, both symbolized, in the case of black Americans, by a fictive kinship system.

Fictive kinship is, then, not only a symbol of social identity for black Americans, it is also a medium of boundary maintenance vis-à-vis white Americans. The school experience of black children is implicated because, under the circumstance, schooling is perceived by blacks, especially by black adolescents, as learning to act white, as acting white, or as trying to cross cultural boundaries. And, importantly, school learning is viewed as a subtractive process. In our view, then, the academic learning and performance problems of black children arise not only from a limited opportunity structure and black people's responses to it, but also from the way black people attempt to cope with the "burden of 'acting white.'" The sources of their school difficulties—perceptions of and responses to the limited opportunity structure and the burden of acting white—are particularly important during the adolescent period in the children's school careers.

We chose to focus our analysis on the burden of acting white and its effects on the academic effort and performance of black children because it seems to us to be a very important but as yet widely unrecognized dilemma of black students, particularly black adolescents. In other words, while we fully recognize the role of external forces—societal and school forces—in creating academic problems for the students, *we also argue that how black students respond to other black students who are trying to make it is also important in determining the outcome of their education.*

In the case study of Capital High School in Washington, D.C., we showed that coping with the burden of acting white affects the academic performance of both underachieving and high-achieving students. Black students who are encapsulated in the fictive kinship system or oppositional process experience greater difficulty in crossing cultural boundaries; i.e., in accepting standard academic attitudes and practices of the school and in investing sufficient time and effort in pursuing their educational goals. Some of the high-achieving students do not identify with the fictive kinship system; others more or less deliberately adopt sex-specific strategies to camouflage their academic pursuits and achievements.

The strategies of the academically successful students include engaging in activities which mute perceptions of their being preoccupied with academic excellence leading eventually to individual success outside the group, i.e., eventual upward mobility. Among them are athletic activities (which are regarded as "black activities") and other "team"-oriented activities, for male students. Other high-achieving students camouflage their academic effort by clowning. Still others do well in school by acquiring the protection of "bullies" and "hoodlums" in return for assisting the latter in their schoolwork and homework. In general, academically successful black students at Capital High (and probably elsewhere) are careful not to brag about their achievements or otherwise bring too much attention to themselves. We conclude, however, from this study of high-achieving students at Capital High, that they would do much better if they did not have to divert time and effort into strategies designed to camouflage their academic pursuit.

There are several implications of our analysis, and the implications are at different levels. As this analysis clearly demonstrates, the first and critically important change must occur in the existing opportunity structure, through an elimination of the job ceiling and related barriers. Changes in the opportunity structure are a prerequisite to changes in the behaviors and expectations of black adolescents for two salient reasons: (1) to change the students' perceptions of what is available to them as adult workers in the labor force and (2) to minimize the exacerbation of the extant achievement problem of black adolescents who are expected to master the technical skills taught and condoned in the school context but who are, nonetheless, unable to find employment in areas where they demonstrate exemplary expertise. Barring changes in the opportunity structure, the perceptions, behaviors, and academic effort of black adolescents are unlikely to change to the extent necessary to have a significant effect on the existing boundary-maintaining mechanisms in the community. Therefore, until the perceptions of the nature and configuration of the opportunity structure change (see J. Williams, 1985), the response of black students in the school context is likely to continue to be one which suggests that school achievement is a kind of risk which necessitates strategies enabling them to cope with the "burden of acting white." Second, educational barriers, both the gross and subtle mechanisms by which schools differentiate the academic careers of black and white children, should be eliminated.

Third, and particularly important in terms of our analysis, *the unique academic learning and performance problems created by the burden of acting white should be recognized and made a target of educational policies and remediation effort.* Both the schools and the black community have important roles to play in this regard. School personnel should try to understand the influence of the fictive kinship system in the students' perceptions of learning and the standard academic attitudes and practices or behaviors expected. The schools should then develop programs, including appropriate counseling, to help the students learn to divorce academic pursuit from the idea of acting white. The schools should also reinforce black identity in a manner compatible with academic pursuit, as in the case of Sargent (1985).

The black community has an important part to play in changing the situation. The community should develop programs to teach black children that academic pursuit is not synonymous with one-way acculturation into a white cultural frame of reference or acting white. To do this effectively, however, the black community must reexamine its own perceptions and interpretations of school learning. Apparently, black children's general perception that academic pursuit is "acting white" is learned in the black community. The ideology of the community in regard to the cultural meaning of schooling is, therefore, implicated and needs to be reexamined. Another thing the black community can do is to provide visible and concrete evidence for black youths that the community appreciates and encourages academic effort and success. Cultural or public recognition of those who are academically successful should be made a frequent event, as is generally done in the case of those who succeed in the fields of sports and entertainment.

Acknowledgments

This paper is based on Fordham's two-year ethnographic study as part of doctoral dissertation requirements. The research and preparation of the paper were made possible by grants from the National Institute of Education (N1E-G82 0037) and the Spencer Foundation, by a Dissertation Research Grant from The American University, Washington, D.C., and by the Faculty Research Fund, University of California, Berkeley. We wish to thank the District of Columbia Public School System and the faculty, staff, and students at Capital High (a pseudonym), without whose cooperation and assistance this study would not have been possible. We are grateful to Dr. John L. Johnson of the University of the District of Columbia for his characterization of the research effort as one which centers around how black adolescents struggle with the "burden of 'acting white."' An earlier version of the paper was presented by Fordham at the 84th Annual Meeting of the American Anthropological Association, Washington, D.C., December 5, 1985.

Endnotes

1   Capital High and all other proper names are pseudonyms.

References

Abdul-Jabbar, K., and Knobles, P. (1983). *Giant Steps: The Autobiography of Kareem Abdul-Jabbar.* New York: Bantam Books.

Acuna, R. (1972). *Occupied America: The Chicano's Struggle Toward Liberation.* San Francisco: Canfield Press.

Anderson, J. D. (1975). Education and the manipulation of black workers. In W. Feinberg and H. Rosemont, Jr. (Eds.), *Work, technology, and education: Dissenting essays in the intellectual foundations of American education.* Chicago: University of Illinois Press.

Berreman, G. D. (1960), Caste in India and the United States. *The American Journal of Sociology* LXVI: 120-127.

Bloom, B. S., Davis, A., and Hess, R. (1965). *Compensatory education for cultural deprivation.* New York: Holt.

Bourke, C. J. (1983). Reactions to these concepts from aboriginal Australia. In OECD, *The education of minority groups: An enquiry into problems and practices of fifteen countries,* pp. 317-335. Paris: OECD, Center for Educational Research and Innovation. Brain, J. J. (1972). Kinship terms, *Man* 7(1): 137-138.

Bullock, H. A. (1970). *A history of Negro education in the South: From 1619 to the present.* New York: Praeger.

Castile, G. P., and Kushner, G., Eds. (1981). *Persistent peoples: Cultural enclaves in perspective.* Tucson: University of Arizona Press.

Coleman, J. S., et al. (1966). *Equality of educational opportunity.* Washington, D.C.: U.S. Government Printing Office.

DeVos, G. A. (1984). *Ethnic persistence and role degradation: An illustration from Japan [unpublished manuscript].* Prepared for the American-Soviet Symposium on Contemporary Ethnic Processes in the USA and the USSR, New Orleans, April 14-16.

DeVos, G. A. (1967). Essential elements of caste: psychological determinants in structural theory. In G. A. DeVos and H. Wagatsuma (eds.), *Japan's invisible race: Caste in culture and personality,* pp. 332-384. Berkeley: University of California Press.

DeVos, G. A., and Wagatsuma, H., eds. (1967). *Japan's invisible race: Caste in culture and personality.* Berkeley: University of California Press.

Drake, S. C., and Cayton, H. (1970). *Black Metropolis.* New York: Harcourt, Brace. Erickson, F., and Mohatt, J. (1982). Cultural organization of participant structure in two classrooms of Indian students. In G. D. Spindler (Ed.), *Doing the ethnography of schooling: Educational anthropology in action,* pp. 132-175. New York: Holt.

Folb, E. A. (1980). *Runnin' down some lines: The language and culture of black teenagers.* Cambridge, Mass.: Harvard University Press.

Fordham, S. (1985). Black student school success as related to fictive kinship. Final Report. The National Institute of Education, Washington, D.C.

Fordham, S. (1984). Ethnography in a black high school: learning not to be a native. A paper presented at the 83rd Annual Meeting, American Anthropological Association, Denver, Nov. 14-18.

Fordham, S. (1982a). Black student school success as related to fictive kinship: an ethnographic study in the Washington, D.C., public school system. A research proposal submitted to the National Institute of Education.

Fordham, S. (1982b). Cultural inversion and black children's school performance. Paper presented at the 81st Annual Meeting, American Anthropological Association, Washington, D.C., Dec. 3-7.

Fordham, S. (1981). Black student school success as related to fictive kinship: a study in the Washington, D.C. public school system. A dissertation proposal submitted to the Department of Anthropology, The American University.

Freed, S. A. (1973). Fictive kinship in a Northern Indian village. *Ethnology 11(1)*: 86-103.

Gray, J. (1985). A black American princess: new game, new rules. The Washington Post, March 17, pp. El, E5.

Green, V. (1981). Blacks in the United States: the creation of an enduring people? In G. P. Castile and G. Kushner (Eds.), *Persistent peoples: Cultural eEnclaves in perspective*, pp. 69-77. Tucscon: University of Arizona Press.

Haley, A. (1976). *Roots: The saga of an American family*. Garden City, N.Y.: Doubleday.

Haskins, K. (1976). You have no right to put a kid out of school. *The Urban Review 8(4)*: 273-287.

Holt, G. S. (1972). "Inversion" in black communication. In T. Kachman (Ed.), *Rappin' and stylin' out: Communication in urban black America*. Chicago: University of Illinois Press.

Hunter, D. (1980). Ducks vs. hard rocks. *Newsweek*, Aug. 18, pp. 14-15.

Jensen, A. R. (1969). How much can we boost IQ and scholastic achievement? *Harvard Educational Review 39*: 1-123.

LeVine, R. A. (1967). *Dreams and deeds: Achievement motivation in Nigeria*. Chicago: University of Chicago Press.

Liebow, E. (1967). *Tally's corner*. Boston: Little, Brown.

Matute-Bianchi, M. D. (1986). Variations in patterns of school performance among Mexican, Chicano and Japanese Youth [unpublished manuscript]. Santa Cruz, Calif.: Merrill College, University of California.

Myrdal, G. (1944). *An American dilemma: The Negro problem and modern democracy*. New York: Harper.

Norbeck, E., and Befu, H. (1958). Informal fictive kinship in Japan. *American Anthropologist 60*: 102-117.

Ogbu, J. U. (in press). Variability in minority responses to schooling: non-immigrants vs. immigrants. In G. D. Spindler (Ed.), *Education and cultural process*.

Ogbu, J. U. (1986a). Class stratification, racial stratification and schooling. In L. Weis, (Ed.), *Race, class and schooling: Special Studies in Comparative Education*, #17, pp. 6-35. Comparative Education Center, State University of New York at Buffalo.

Ogbu, J. U. (1986b). Cross-cultural study of minority education: contributions from Stockton research. 23rd Annual J. William Harris Lecture, School of Education, University of the Pacific, Stockton, Calif.

Ogbu, J. U. (1984). Understanding community forces affecting minority students' academic effort. Paper prepared for the Achievement Council, Oakland, Calif.

Ogbu, J. U. (1983). Minority status and schooling in plural societies. *Comparative Education Review 27(2)*: 168-190.

Ogbu, J. U. (1982). Cultural discontinuities and schooling. *Anthropology and Education Quarterly 13(4)*: 290-307.

Ogbu, J. U. (1981). Schooling in the ghetto: an ecological perspective on community and home influences. Prepared for NIE Conference on Follow Through, Philadelphia, Feb. 10-11.

Ogbu, J. U. (1980). Cultural differences vs. alternative cultures: a critique of 'cultural discontinuity' hypothesis in classroom ethnographies. A paper presented at the 79th Annual Meeting, American Anthropological Association, Washington, D.C.

Ogbu, J. U. (1978). *Minority education and caste: The American system in cross-cultural perspective.* New York: Academic Press.

Ogbu, J. U. (1974). *The next generation: An ethnography of education in an urban neighborhood.* New York: Academic Press.

Ogbu, J. U., and Matute-Bianchi, M. E. (1986). Understanding sociocultural factors in education: knowledge, identity, and adjustment. In *Beyond language: Sociocultural factors in schooling, language, and minority students. California State Department of Education. Los Angeles:* Education Dissemination and Assessment center, California State University, Los Angeles, pp. 71-143.

Petroni, F. A., and Hirsch, E. A. (1970). *Two, four, six, eight, When you gonna integrate?* New York: Behavioral Publications.

Philips, S. U. (1983). *The invisible culture: Communication in classroom and community on the warm springs Indian reservation.* New York: Longman.

Pitt-Rivers, J. (1968). Pseudo-kinship. In D. L. Sills (Ed.), *The international encyclopedia of social science.* New York: Macmillan.

Sargent, E. (1985). Freeing myself: discoveries that unshackle *the* mind. *The Washington Post,* Feb. 10.

Schmidt, F. H. (1970). *Spanish surname American Employment in the Southwest.* Washington, D.C.: U.S. Government Printing Office.

Shimkin, D. B., Shimkin, E. M., and Frate, D. A. (Eds.) (1978). *The extended family in black societies.* The Hague: Mouton.

Smith, A. F. (1983). A response for the Maori population of New Zealand. In *The education of minority groups: An enquiry into problems and practices of fifteen countries,* pp. 293-315. Paris: OECD, Center for Educational Research and Innovation.

Spicer, E. H. (1971). Persistent cultural systems: a comparative study of identity systems that can adapt to contrasting environments. *Science* 174: 795-800.

Spicer, E. H. (1966). The process of cultural enslavement in Middle America. Proceedings, *35th Congreso Internacional de Americanistas,* Vol. 3, pp. 267-279. Seville.

Spicer, E. H., (1962). *Cycles of conquest: The impact of Spain, Mexico and the United States on the Indians of the Southwest, 1533-1960.* Tucson: University of Arizona Press.

Spivey, D. (1978). *Schooling for the new slavery: Black industrial education, 1868-1915.* Westport, Conn.: Greenwood Press.

Stack, C. (1974). *All our kin: Strategies for survival in a black community.* New York: Harper & Row.

Styron, W. (1966). *The confessions of Nat Turner.* New York: Random House.

Varese, S. (1985). Cultural development in ethnic groups: anthropological explorations in education. *International Social Science Journal* 37(2): 201-216.

Virgil, J. D. (1980). *From Indians to Chicanos: A sociocultural history.* St. Louis: C. V. Mosby.

Walsh, E. (1984). Trouble at thirteen: being black poses special problems. *The Washington Post,* April 24, pp. A1, A6.

Weis, L. (1985). *Between two worlds: Black students in an urban community college.* Boston: Routledge & Kegan Paul.

Williams, J. (1985). The vast gap between black and white visions of reality. *The Washington Post,* March 31, pp. K1, K4.

Williams, M. D. (1981). *On the street where I lived.* New York: Holt, Rinehart & Winston.

Reexamining Resistance as Oppositional Behavior:
The Nation of Islam and the Creation of a Black Achievement Ideology

By A.A. Akom

THE OPPOSITIONAL-CULTURE EXPLANATION for racial disparities in educational achievement, introduced by Ogbu (1978, 1991), suggests that individuals from historically oppressed groups (involuntary minorities) display their antagonism toward the dominant group by resisting educational goals. According to this line of argument, castelike minorities (including native-born blacks, Puerto Ricans, Mexicans, and American Indians) withdraw from academic pursuits because they believe that racial discrimination and prejudice limit their access to high-paying jobs. Ironically however, in their unwillingness to play the "credentializing" game, they reproduce existing class relations and remain mired in subordinate economic positions (Solomon 1992; Willis 1977).

In contrast, individuals from the dominant group and groups who migrated to the United States on their own accord (voluntary-immigrant minorities) maintain optimistic views of their chances for educational and occupational success. A key component in this explanation is the difference between the migratory trajectories of involuntary and voluntary minorities and their children.

Voluntary minorities, on the one hand, tend to develop positive attitudes regarding their chances for success and remain optimistic in their outlook on educational advancement. On the other hand, involuntary minorities, in response to unfavorable conditions, tend to behave in four ways: First, they equate schooling with assimilation into the dominant group. Second, they do not try to achieve academically. Third, they pay a unique psychological wage, which Fordham and Ogbu (1986) referred to as the "burden of acting white," if they do try to achieve academically. And, finally, they engage in actions of resistance against the school and societal norms.

In the case of the Nation of Islam (NOI), a religious organization composed primarily of black Americans, I did not find patterns of oppositional behavior in the way this construct has been traditionally documented and defined. Although an oppositional-culture frame of reference was evident among the young women whom I studied and observed, it was distinct in character from that offered by Ogbu and his associates and did not produce the academic outcomes that are commonly associated with this model (Ogbu & Simons 1998). Instead, I observed an involuntary minority culture of mobility whereby involuntary-minority students in the NOI resisted schooling and societal practices that they viewed as being at odds with their religious tenets and practices, yet drew on the moral, spiritual, and material resources facilitated by their tightly knit community to achieve social mobility and academic success.

Previous research that assigned involuntary minorities an oppositional orientation to educational and social mobility neglected the class and cultural heterogeneity inherent within all minority communities. Even poor minority neighborhoods are culturally diverse and include people who hold to conventional norms of behavior, those who choose a street-oriented or oppositional lifestyle, and those who vacillate between the two (Anderson 1999; Patillo-McCoy 1999). Other theories of black educational underachievement are underdeveloped as well, first, because of their tendency to reduce the relationship between cultural identity and academic engagement to a zero-sum game for involuntary minorities and second, because of their inability to capture the ways in which blacks (or other racial-ethnic groups) maintain their own cultural identities and strategies for collective mobility in the context of discrimination and group disadvantage (Flores-Gonzalez 1999; Foley 1990; Hemmings 1996).

This article seeks to complicate and extend previous accounts of a unidimensional oppositional social identity that have frequently been ascribed to involuntary-minority individuals and communities by focusing on the experiences of seven young women in the NOI. More specifically, I demonstrate that involuntary minorities do not have to choose between performing well in school and maintaining their racial-ethnic identities. Instead, I show that it is possible simultaneously to be an "involuntary"; an "oppositional"; and, to a certain degree, a "model" student (Hemmings 1996).

To illustrate the ways in which a group of low-income black students associated school success neither with acting white nor with a middle-class trait, I invoke the concept of organizational habitus (McDonough 1997; see also Downey and Ainsworth-Darnell 1998). *Organizational habitus* refers to a set of dispositions, perceptions, and appreciations transmitted to individuals through a common organizational culture (McDonough 1997). Although Bourdieu (1986) conceptualized and wrote about habitus as a function of social class, less attention has been paid to incorporating race into structures that shape habitus, as well as the ways in which organizations, such as the NOI, act to shape structures that influence individuals in everyday life.

I use the notion of organizational habitus to gain a better understanding of the ways in which the NOI as a religious organization transmits racial and religious ideologies to individual actors, which work, in the school context, to enhance educational outcomes. Race and religious orientation not only influence individual members in the NOI, but play an important role in shaping how the school acts and reacts to NOI members. The interaction of race and religion influences how NOI young women construct their academic and social identities, as well as the strategies they choose to succeed in school.

This article is divided into four sections. The first section explains the historical origins of the NOI's black achievement ideology—a central component of the NOI's organizational habitus—and its relation to the formation of an oppositional social identity. The second section describes the research setting and methods. The third section presents the research data and suggests that it is how members of an involuntary-minority group construct their racial-ethnic identities, internalize and display an achievement ideology, and are guided by forces in the community that affect their performance in school. The final section illustrates the ways in which black people differentially make sense of and enact what it means to be black that challenge previous binary or dichotomized accounts of black oppositional social identity.

ORIGINS OF THE NOI'S BLACK ACHIEVEMENT IDEOLOGY

In the United States, although all Muslims may be called Muslim or refer to their religion as Islam, the experience of black American Muslims is different from that of Muslims who were born and raised in Muslim countries or in an immigrant Muslim cultural milieu. The earliest black American Muslim communities were established in reaction to racist practices, evasive actions, and exploitative relationships fostered by segregation during the Jim Crow era (Gardell 1996). The black social and cultural institutions and ideologies that emerged out of this social context constructed what Lipsitz (1988) referred to as a "culture of opposition." According to Lipsitz, these cultures of opposition constituted a partial refuge from the humiliation of racism, class pretensions, and low-wage work for blacks and allowed them to nurture collectivist values that were markedly different from the prevailing individualistic ideology of the white ruling class. Ironically, then, segregation facilitated the creation and development of the NOI.

The expressed goals of the NOI are as follows: (1) to gain self-determination in North America—not in Africa as preceding movements, such as Garveyism or the Moorish Science temple, had proposed; (2) to reconstitute the black nation by embracing blackness as an ideal (according to the NOI, the black man is the original man, and all black people are members of the NOI, whether they are conscious of it or not);

and (3), to achieve collective economic independence through individual achievement (Lincoln 1973). These goals, in conjunction with the belief that a black man variously named W. D. Fard or W. F. Muhammad was God in the flesh and that the Honorable Elijah Muhammad was his prophet, are some of the essential elements that constitute the NOI's black achievement ideology (see Table 1).

This dialectical understanding of white power and black resistance suggests that the NOI's black achievement ideology offers a set of cultural tools that provides strategies for educational and economic mobility in the context of historical discrimination and group disadvantage. The NOI's black achievement ideology is not a whole culture but, rather, a set of cultural elements that are relevant to the problems of educational and economic mobility in the face of instrumental discrimination (e.g., in employment and wages), relational discrimination (e.g., social and residential segregation), and symbolic discrimination (e.g., denigration of the minority culture and language) (Massey and Denton 1993).

Within the NOI, the black achievement ideology often coexists with an oppositional social identity. Members of the NOI are often familiar with each ideology, and the relative influence of both is dependent on the social context, as well as individual factors, such as personality or school or work trajectories. Thus, even though oppositional social identity may seem antithetical to the NOI's black achievement ideology, historically the two emerged in tandem, as dual responses to conditions of racism and group discrimination.

In short, rigid morals, self-determination, nontraditional Islam, and black nationalism are the key elements that constitute what I refer to as the NOI's black achievement ideology. The black achievement ideology is a theory about the world—how and why it was created and how human beings relate to and should act in the world (Gardell 1996). Since the black achievement ideology in this context is essentially a religious construct, it provides adherents with a frame of reference that governs their interpretation and experiences in the world *(see Table 9.1 on next page).*

RESEARCH METHODOLOGY

Despite the fact that Islam is well on its way to surpassing Judaism as the second-largest religion in the United States—dwarfing Protestant denominations, such as the Episcopal church—there has been little qualitative research on it (Essien-Udom 1962; Gardell 1996; see also Halasa 1990; M. Lee 1996; Lincoln 1973). Studies on the NOI, with some notable exceptions, have been based mainly on secondary sources, partly because of the NOI's unwillingness to be the object of inquiry.

The study presented here, which was based on participant observation, field notes, and recorded interviews, began in September 1996 and ended in August 1998. During that time, I—a young black, non-Muslim, man—conducted an ethnographic study of Eastern High (a pseudonym), an urban high school located in a predominantly black

Table 9.1.

Differences and Similarities Between Achievement Ideologies

Nation of Islam's Black Achievement Ideology	Mainstream Achievement Ideology
Differences	
Absolute ethnic difference and racial Consciousness	Pluralism and color blindness
Institutional Discrimination is a pervasive factor that can impede mobility	Institutional discrimination does not exist or is minimal
Visibility: Loud or overt cultural nationalism	Invisibility: Quiet or cryptonationalism
Resistance to cultural assimilation via cultural preservation	Cultural assimilation
Collectivist values and community goals, informed by Islamic law and a work ethic	Individual achievement, individual goals informed by the Protestant work ethic [b]
Nontraditional Islam: The belief that a black man, variously name W. D. Fard or W. F. Muhammad, was God in the flesh and that the Honorable Elijah Muhammad was his prophet	Modernity: The belief in Judeo-Christian or secular values
Similarities	
Self-reliance, hard work, sobriety, Individual effort and sacrifice	

These principles are collectively termed the "achievement ideology" because of the widely shared belief that adherence to such values brings monetary rewards, economic advancement, and educational mobility

[a] Admittedly the terms *black achievement ideology and mainstream achievement ideology* are unsatisfactory ways of naming the process of cultural mutation, yet as processes of inclusion and exclusion, as well as mobility processes, they are integral to identity formation and defining community boundaries.

[b] Weber (1958) argued that "the Protestant ethic," "the inner-wordly asceticism" rationally expressed in work as a calling, resulted in the creation of "the spirit of capitalism." A similar process can be discerned in the NOI's version of the Protestant work ethic, which because of its ban on wastefulness and demands for hard work, has resulted in the formation of an economic empire with assets that have been estimated to be as much as $80 million (Mamiya 1983:245).

neighborhood in West Philadelphia. The social fabric of Eastern High, including demographics (98 percent black), attendance, suspension rates, dropout rates, poverty levels, and test scores—parallels other comprehensive high schools that suffer from deindustrialization, resegregation, and the transition to a postindustrial economy. For example, in 1995-96, the average daily attendance at Eastern High (total population 1,700) was 76 percent, 40 percent of the student body was suspended at least once, and roughly 40 percent to 50 percent of the ninth graders who entered in fall 1990-91 failed to graduate four years later. As an indication of students' economic status, 86 percent of the student population at Eastern High were from low-income families or families who were then receiving Aid to Families with Dependent Children (now Temporary Assistance to Needy Families).

When I began collecting data, the goal was to examine the relationship among black students' self-perceptions, aspirations, and low academic achievement. However, after two years of fieldwork, extensive participant observation, and intensive interviews with 50 students, 10 teachers, 2 administrators, and 6 members of the community, what emerged was not a group of low-achieving black students. Instead, the interviews, together with participant observation, directed my attention to a group of high-achieving black students with a history of disciplinary problems and resisting school authority. By high-achieving students, I mean those who were in good academic standing with at least a B grade point average (GPA), were on schedule to graduate in four years, were college eligible, and were not in danger of dropping out. These students, according to interviews with the students and staff, had developed an interesting set of strategies for maintaining their academic, racial, and cultural identities at school while resisting schooling and societal practices that they viewed as being at odds with their religious tenets and practices.

Clusters of interviews with these students, all American-born young black women who had converted to the NOI, became the basis for my use of the extended case method, which ascertains a social phenomenon by looking at what is "interesting" and "surprising" in a particular social situation (Burawoy, Camson, and Burton, 1991). Consequently, from an initial group of three 11th-grade female students, snowball sampling, which was based on mutual associations, produced three more 11th-grade and one 10th-grade female students.

All seven primary participants came from low-income families in which no parent had an advanced degree (*see Table 9.2*), and all self-identified as black.

To test whether the general cultural norm of peer sanctioning for high achievement was prevalent among female students in the NOI, I conducted intensive in-depth life-history interviews and focus groups with these students. I ended up with an average of three or four interviews per week that became the basis for detailed case studies in which every attempt was made to understand the young women's entire networks of social relations and socioeconomic circumstances that may have influenced their orientation to school and achievement.

As my field notes and interviews began to accumulate, analyses of issues and themes across individuals and groups became increasingly possible. It also became possible to analyze the school as an institution and, finally, to analyze the importance of the relationship between external community forces and academic achievement for the seven primary participants.

The advantage of focusing on a small number of participants lies in the detail and richness of the data gathered. Although the small sample may limit generalization of the results, my findings are consistent with those of recent related research on school success and ethnic identity cited earlier. Most interviews took place at school. However, informal discussions and conversations took place in lunchrooms or hallways or outside the temple.

Most interviews were audiotaped. School records, school reports, and other school documents complemented the observations, interviews, and focus groups.

Table 9.2.

Summary of Interview Data

Name	Grade	Highest Parental/Guardian Level of Education	Mother's or Grandmother's Occupation	Family Structure
Aisha	11th	High school dropout	Dishwasher	Single parent; resides with mother; has no siblings
Erikka	11th	High school diploma	Provider of care to the elderly	Parents separated; resides with mother and three siblings, one older
Kesha	11th	High School diploma	Disabled	Resides with grandmother; has one younger sibling
Latasha	11th	High School dropout	Unemployed; living on welfare	Single parent; resides with mother; has two siblings, one older
Rochelle	10th	High School dropout	Employed at local fast-food restaurant	Single parent; Resdies with mother; has two older siblings
Safiya	11th	High School diploma	Unemployed; living on welfare	Parents separated; Resides with mother; has one younger sibling
Tiffany	11th	High School dropout	Unemployed; living on social security	Resides with grandmother; has no siblings

Although the research described here focused on the experiences of seven young black women, gender was not a major focus of the analysis. To be sure, gender has been shown to influence students' school experience and social identities (Collins 1990). However, in this article, gender is addressed only to the extent that the primary participants were all young women. As a result, my findings may not reflect similar individual and organizational interactions experienced by young men in similar settings.

The Setting and Establishing Rapport

I attended Eastern High three to five days a week to assess how school culture and climate influenced the participants' everyday lives. Given my frequent presence and constant interaction, I established good rapport with the participants. However, like many other qualitative-oriented researchers, I view the research act as one that is far from value free (Denzin and Lincoln, 1994). Part of the research endeavor is the process of making meaning—not just observing, but shaping, interpreting, and framing the research process. Consequently, rather than ignore my own subjectivity, I engaged in formal systematic monitoring of myself throughout the course of the data collection, which enabled me to monitor my personal and professional growth and evolution in the research process. Toward this end, I wrote self-reflective memoranda, shared the manuscripts of analyzed data with the participants, and discussed emerging themes with colleagues who were familiar with the project.

Moreover, I believe that my background shaped my role as a researcher. First, I am a black man in my late 20s who grew up in Pennsylvania, about two hours from the area in which the research was conducted. Second, I grew up in a single-parent female-headed household, as did all the primary participants. Third, my adolescent schooling experiences were entirely within public institutions.

Given my background as a young black non-Muslim man, I am often asked how I was able to establish rapport with the young women in this study and how I was certain that I could adequately appreciate the standpoint from and context within which they lived. My ability to establish rapport was greatly enhanced by my being of the same race as the primary participants (individuals who share the same race as NOI members are often viewed as potential members). In other words, even though there were gender differences—and, to a lesser extent, class differences, given my mother's advanced education—to overcome in establishing a connection with each student, race was always the same. Consequently, our commonness as "blacks" who were committed to community development and nation building provided the bridge that we needed to connect with one another, while other shared experiences (parents' divorce, the universal traits of adolescence, or shared hobbies) served as additional reference points.

Rapport was evidenced by displays of affection from the primary participants (friendly greetings), the sharing of personal confidences, and the open expression of trust (many participants called me to asked about preparing for college). Moreover, I was able to interact informally with the primary participants while I observed them at the school. Often these informal interactions served as icebreakers before the interviews.

However, my findings must not be viewed as some objective representation of the "truth" about the social world of the NOI or of Eastern High. Rather, my findings are my most accurate representation of the perspectives that were gathered during this study.

RESULTS

Becoming a Member of the NW

The NOI is an extremely hierarchical organization. To transform raw recruits into NOI members, young Muslim brothers visit jails and penitentiaries, pool halls and barber-shops, college campuses and street corners. The goal of this proselytizing is to "restore black people in America to their original industrial and commercial greatness so that African Americans can become self-sufficient in the production of food, clothing, shelter, health care, education, and employment" (Gardell 1996:319).

The NOI's recruitment efforts have been particularly successful with respect to incarcerated criminals and drug addicts. Its members' record of rehabilitating former convicts and addicts has been acknowledged by social workers and documented by scholars and journalists alike (Lincoln 1973:84).

In addition, true to its ideology of "do for self," the NOI rejects the American welfare system. Although he did not condemn Americans who live on welfare, the present leader of the NOI, Minister Louis Farrakhan Muhammad (1991), warned of the system's consequences: "Welfare if you turn it around means farewell. It means bye to the spirit of self-determination. It means so long to the spirit that God gives to every human being to do something for self. It makes you a slave. Welfare, farewell."

Discussions with the primary participants about their life experiences before they joined the NOI showed how conversion not only introduces new sets of beliefs but, more fundamentally, entails the displacement of one universe or discourse by another (Snow and Machalek 1984). The following interviews with Latasha and Erikka demonstrate the ways in which acculturation into the NOI positively influenced their racial identity, educational aspirations, and desire to uplift the black community:

> Latsha: Once I joined the NOI, I started getting a real education—a black education—an education that made me see the truth about me and my history . . . and that made me see who I really was—a black queen. . . . Now I love my black skin—not that I didn't before—but I don't think I was aware before like I am now of what it means to be black . . . . We have a great history—that's way different than the white lies that white people tell—and now I feel more responsible and proud to be what I am, and I work harder

in school because I know I have to put Islam and submission to the Will of
Allah first in everything I do.... And that gives me power—lots of power—I
feel powerful like nothin' can hold me back from gettin' my goal of goin' to
college and raisin' a family.

These students also stated that both their mindsets and their behavior changed after
they joined the NOI.

> Erikka: Before joining the NOI. I didn't do well in school. . . . I wasn't fo-
> cused; . . . I was unsure of myself, . . . but the Messenger teaches us that you
> have to take responsibility for your own success. . . . He teaches us that no
> individual in the Nation stands alone because we are one Nation—the last
> independent nation on earth.... I mean a real nation within a nation—with
> our own flag, laws, rules, and stuff.... And with all these strong black people
> behind me, . . . I feel like I can do whatever it is that needs to get done.
>
> AA: But what is it that you're trying to accomplish? What are your personal
> goals?
>
> Erikka: Well, I know for sure I want to graduate from high school, . . . go to
> college, . . . and get a good job.
>
> AA: And has the Nation helped you accomplish these goals?
>
> Erikka: Yea. Like I just said, . . . before I joined the Nation, I wasn't doing
> that well in school. . . . Studying was hard for me . . . 'cause no matter how
> hard I studied, I still got bad grades.... And then when I joined the Nation,
> this sister took me by the hand and taught me how to study.
>
> AA: What do you mean how to study?
>
> Erikka: You see, now when I sit down to read something, I got a system. .
> . . I get my notebook out . . . I get my dictionary . . . and sit and really read .
> . . you know, . . . not just memorize the words, but really try to understand
> what their trying to say to me. . . . And then I write out questions ... just so
> I can really figure out if what there saying is true . . . and if it really makes
> sense. . . . What I'm saying is . . . not only did sister Muhammad (the sister
> who pulled her aside) teach me how to study, . . . but she made me believe
> that I was smart. . . . I went from studying once or twice a week to five or
> six hours a day.

By marking their members as part of a special group and providing them with a black
achievement ideology, as well as a visible means of support, the NOI fosters the development of new social and academic identities. An important component of the conversion
process is the development of a dual frame of reference. Women in the NOI, although not

voluntary immigrants, acquire a dual frame of reference that works in a similar manner as it does for immigrants. That is, instead of associating being black with underachievement or with the social pathologies that are often ascribed to black youths and those of other minorities, young women in the NOI use previous economic and political oppression, as well as religious socialization, as catalysts to make present sacrifices more tolerable. Safiya's description of her preconversion attitudes and behaviors illustrates this point:

> Before I joined the NOI, I was all wrong—I smoked weed a lot, . . . I hung out with the wrong people, . . . didn't do well in school. . . . Basically, I was like a lot of these other [black] students who don't even like themselves or their own people, . . . and with me, you could tell I was all wrong because I would fight for mines . . . or talk about other people. . . . I've even watched fools get killed. . . . It's like slaves of the past gonna be slaves of the future unless you make a change, . . . but we're taught [by the NOI] the other way around. . . . It's foolish not to love yo' self and yo' people, especially if you want to get anywhere, . . . you have to love yo' self and work hard.

Aisha, who before she joined the NOI, "was about relaxin" reported:

> Before I joined two years ago, I used to kick it all the time and watch music videos. . . . Now I organize meetings, go to study group. . . . I don't even watch TV. . . . I do fund-raisin,' bake sales, and stuff. . . I speak Arabic. . . I eat right . . . I read more . . . I am more focused. I think . . . I think about the world in a different way. . . . I feel more awake ...more conscious . . . like I'm tryin' to liberate myself and my people. . . . I wasn't about that before.

A teacher who knew Aisha before she joined the NOI commented:

> Teacher: When I first met her, I didn't think she was going to make it at this school . . . knowing where she grew up and the type of neighborhood she comes from and who her friends were, . . . but she is a totally different person now, . . . and I suppose a lot of students change at this age, . . . but you rarely see kids change from bad behavior to good behavior so dramatically—not the way that Aisha did.
>
> M: And what do you think accounted for the change?
>
> Teacher: What jumps out at me are her religious beliefs. . . . I think they had a lot to do with it. . . . It's like she took on a different culture, . . . so now she's a different person—she dresses different, acts totally different, hangs out with different people—so in my opinion, her conversion to Islam had a lot

to do with her improvement in school—not just educationally, but socially and emotionally.

To seal the conversion or personal rebirth, converts to the NOI first have to cast off their old selves and take on new identities, which involves changing their name, religion, language, style of dress, moral and cultural values, and very purpose in living. To commemorate their rebirth, converts drop their last name and become known simply by their first name and the last name of Muhammad (referring to W. D. Muhammad, the founder of the NOI).

For the young women in the NOI, changing their name was important because it signaled a change in social networks, conversion of their identities, and collective ownership and formal membership in the organization. Conversion also had a strong effect on the young women's educational aspirations and performance in school.

From the Burden of Acting White to the Honor of Being Black

Young women in the NOI present a special challenge to the thesis of the burden of acting white proposed by Fordham and Ogbu (1986). More specifically, the organizational habitus of the NOI has inverted the cultural construct of acting white, so that instead of associating it with positive educational outcomes (i.e., academic achievement) and potentially negative cultural outcomes (disassociation from black cultural forms), the NOI associates it with negative attitudes and behaviors that do not conform to the notion of uplifting black individuals or the black community. Conversely, the NOI associates being black with positive educational and cultural outcomes. Thus, by changing a community's interpretation of both itself and its history and redefining morality and acceptable social behavior, the NOI has been able systematically to create an organizational habitus that encourages achievement for its members, resulting in the transformation of the burden of acting white into the honor of being black. The following comments from the interviews illustrate this point:

> AA: What does acting white mean to you?
>
> Erikka: To me, actin' white means gettin' by the easy way—like takin' things that don't belong to you . . . or cheatin'. . . . or not workin' hard, . . . but actin' like you somethin' you're not . . . like actin' like you don't want to be black. . . . That's what actin' white means to me—actin' fake.

Safiya expressed a similar view:

> I would say lookin' down on poor people. . . . or you know . . . people who ain't doin' too good—that's what actin' white means to me . . . And I see lots of kids in this school actin' a fool—like white people got a hold of their

minds—and those are the kids who I try to talk to, . . . so I can shake em' up. 'Cause they're ain't nothin' wrong with being poor.

One member, Rochelle, spoke of elements of hip-hop music as acting white:

I think a lot of hip-hop music is actin' white. I know that sounds funny, but I think it is. . . . A lot of these so-called artists be fillin' our heads with garbage and filth . . . and to me, that's just another way to keep the white man on top—just another form of white supremacy . . . another way white people got black people miseducatin' each other.

When I asked Rochelle to describe for me what she thinks of when she thinks of black culture, she responded:

When I think of black culture, I think about how great we are, how we are really the chosen people—black gods in a lost world, the creators of all science, wisdom, and history.. That's what we learn at the temple, and that's what I think about. . . . I think about how just cause you see black people perpetuatin' ignorance . . . don't mean you have to act ignorant, . . and just cause you see ignorance, that ain't black culture.

The notion of black greatness and entitlement is central to understanding the organizational habitus of the NOI. The following field note from my observations at a local temple the young women regularly attended illustrates how the NOI combines black and religious nationalism in a way that makes the imagined community of the NOI a priority over other racial and ethnic communities.

Minister: Black people, you have been brainwashed into thinking that this country doesn't owe you anything. . . . But I ask you, have we put our blood, sweat, and tears into this country?

Congregation: Yes, Sir!

Minister: Have our women broken their backs for the white man? Cooked his meals, . . . raised his children, . . . and taken out his trash?

Congregation: Yes, Sir!

Minister (voice strong and proud): White people don't think we deserve what we deserve. . . . And after all we've done for this country, . . . they still don't want to treat us right. . . . But I say, don't let em' brainwash you . . . don't let em' trick you into not getting' what you deserve. If you're going to college and there is only a handful of scholarships for us black folks, . . . you are entitled to those scholarships. . . . If you are going for a job and there are only a handful of jobs for us black folks, you are entitled to those jobs. . . . But don't stop there . . . 'cause [you are] black kings and queens—divine creators of the universe—and you don't have to beg the white man for anything. . . . You have to learn to do for yourself.

Congregation (with vigor): Yes, Sir!

Minister: How else are we going to build a better future for our nation and our children? How else are we gonna build a nation unless we have a strong black family? . . . We need to have our own economic institutions. . . . . We already have our own companies, . . . we've built our own industries. . . . We own this building—this land that I am standing on. . . . We own ourselves. . . . And that's why we don't need the white man . . . because we are independent . . . Isn't that right?

Congregation: Yes, Sir!

In group interviews, all seven young women spoke of how these aspects of the NOI's creed are drilled into them. Kesha explained that once she joined, she could no longer "flirt with boys anymore or go out dancin' and actin all crazy." Tiffany and Latasha discussed how they have been told countless times that "black people are supreme" and that "black people are the original people" or "How important it is to avoid drugs and alcohol to keep the mind and the body clean." Latasha added: "Once I really believed this, I knew nothin' could stop me from achievin' my goals." The goal of this form of indoctrination is to get converts to adopt a new frame of reference that restructures their perceptions and "sense of ultimate grounding" (Heirich 1977:673).

My field notes and transcripts of interviews illustrate the ways in which the organizational habitus of the NOI has inverted the racial code that equates acting white with school success and instead equates the notion with historical, psychological, institutional, and subjective levels of oppression. In this manner, NOI women not only demonstrate the heterogeneity of the black experience, but illustrate the ways in which black people differentially make sense of and enact what it means to be black that challenge dichotomized or binary accounts of how black cultural identity is implicated in the underperformance of black youths.

Non-NOI Attitudes Toward NOI Students

Although the seven young women had strong opinions about acting white, no one in the school expressed animosity toward them for doing well in school. They were not singled out or harassed because of their academic accomplishments. They were not labeled, ostracized, or physically assaulted for doing well in school, as Fordham and Ogbu (1986) reported happened to the black high achievers they studied. Yet, the high achievers in the NOI were not simply seen as another group among the few high achievers at the school. Rather, interviews with students and teachers revealed that although these young women enjoyed high social and academic standing, they also had a reputation for being disruptive and argumentative.

NOI Women as Strong Academic Performers

The NOI young women were seen as high academic achievers. The following excerpts, taken from group and individual interviews with non-NOI students, demonstrate the extent to which the NOI members were viewed as strong academic performers *by* their peers and as offering help to others:

> Them Islamic heads are serious people. . . I always see them studyin.'

> They work hard. . . . That's why I think people respect them 'cause they're serious about their business—they're the hardest-working students at this school.

> They help me out. . . . I ask them for help because they really know what their doin'. . . . They help me get better grades because they take studyin' seriously, and they're just down for black people. . . . They ain't afraid to say the truth. . . . That's what I like about them, they'll tell anybody to their face what time it is.

The teachers had similar responses to the NOI students. They reported that when they saw NOI students coming to class on time, taking notes in class, and turning assignments in on time, it indicated to them that these students had a strong desire to excel in school. In interviews with the 10 teachers, 7 specifically identified the NOI young women as strong academic performers:

> Teacher: Sometimes they dominate class discussion, but that's because they want to be the best they can be—and I admire that. . . . I also think that other kids can learn from it. . . . Look at the example they're setting—[they] come to class on time, study hard, [are] prepared, and get good grades. . . . They're almost perfect students, . . . but I'm not saying I agree with everything they do or stand for. . . There are some things about them that I don't respect.

> AA: For instance?

> Teacher: Their religion.

Another teacher added:

> I think they get more attention than the other kids because of the way they dress—both good and bad. . . . But overall, they complete all their assignments on time and bring a critical perspective into the classroom. . . . In fact, they're frequently the ones who challenge students on topics we're

discussing in class or their personal beliefs.... Sometimes that can become a disruption, though 'cause they don't know when enough is enough.... And they kind of have an arrogance about them—like a gang mentality. Maybe it comes from them studying together or just hanging out, ... but if you mess with one, you're messing with them all.... For the most part, though, they're good kids—not angels—but good kids.

Studying Together

The NOI young women were not solitary learners. Instead, they formed academic communities that were composed of other NOI young women who shared a common purpose. The following interview with a teacher illustrates this point:

> Teacher: I offer my classroom for anybody to come [after school, and often ... it is only the NOI girls who come into the study hall.... They study hard; ... they ask each other questions and help each other with their homework. ... They're definitely good at working together, ... and I think that's why they—at least the students who attend my study hall—do well in school.
>
> M: How do you know they do well in school?
>
> Teacher: I saw a couple of their names on the honor roll.

The NOI young women participated in formal and informal study groups in which they would ask each other questions, critique each other's work, and help each other with homework problems. Their collaboration was guided by the NOI's formal study-group sessions, which emphasize a merger, rather than a separation, of academic and social identities (Treisman 1985). The following field note illustrates how the NOI's formal study-group sessions systematically taught the NOI students to form academic communities in which their social and academic identities could begin to merge:

> One evening, around 7 o'clock, I went to an NOI study group held at a local temple. As I joined the group, Brother Muhammad (the study-group instructor) briefly explained to me general tips for note taking.... He stressed compiling main ideas and generating dissenting views to help potential members, such as myself, ascertain "the truth." He also gave general instructions about how to sit and behave.... Here, he emphasized sitting upright and erect... respecting one another, ... and helping each other's moral and spiritual development.... Last, ... he expressed the importance of keeping this notebook and the accompanying strategies that he just shared at all times. ... He said "being consciously reflective would help me grow and develop as a man." At the end of the study group, the students broke up into two

small groups. . . . One group practiced vocabulary words and analogies—"the kinds of problems that individuals may encounter in rhetorical debate," said Brother Muhammad, and another group practiced math. . . . In this group, one of the members explained that he could teach us better "math tricks than the white students use in their schools" and emphasized that "it was important for us to study together so that we can have each other's backs in a world full of white duplicitousness and deceit.

I attended many other study groups, and each time a number of supplementary educational activities were emphasized: writing, inquiry, collaboration, role modeling-mentoring, and exploring careers. By encouraging the use of academic techniques in their religious indoctrination, the NOI gives explicit instruction in the invisible culture of schools. Bourdieu (1986) labeled the invisible culture that the NOI teaches "cultural capital." The organizational habitus of the NOI gives low-income individuals some of the cultural capital in the temple that is similar to the cultural capital that more economically advantaged parents give to their children at home. (Bourdieu, 1986)

NOI Women in a Dysfunctional School

At Eastern High, the NOI young women were strong achievers in the midst of a dysfunctional school. As evidence, I observed teachers not only allowing, but encouraging the students to watch the Jerry Springer show on a daily basis. The following field notes highlight the students' low level of expectations and the teachers' meager instruction and support, as well as the ways in which the NOI young women responded to this dysfunctional educational environment:

> One morning in October, I went to observe a Spanish class. . . . Two students in the NOI were the first people to arrive—the teacher arrived 15 minutes late. . . . The 2 students in the NOI were among 7 students who actually stayed . . . and about 10 more students actually showed up but left. . . . When the regular teacher finally arrived, the teacher promptly put in a Jerry Springer tape in English—not as an educational exercise, but as a way to "kill time and make sure students' behaved." The 2 students in the NOI were the only students to ask the teacher for a homework assignment and to sit in the back of the class and complete their work. All the other students either listened to Walkmen, played cards, or left. . . . This teacher practices this sort of instructional neglect and blatant disregard for the teaching standards two to three times a week.

In other classrooms, I observed similar instances of institutional and instructional neglect:

On a midmorning in November, I was observing a health class. Two NOI young women were in the class (different students from those in the Spanish class). Again, the teacher, as well as the instructional assistants, arrived late.... Besides handing out some below grade-level handouts, ... the main instructional activity was to turn on a "boom box," place it in front of the classroom, and abandon the students to "educate" themselves for the entire period. The teachers in this school practice this sort of instructional neglect and blatant disregard for the teaching standards daily. The young women in the NOI initially responded by complaining directly to the teacher about the lack of "real education" offered at the school.... However, by the end of the month, they had resorted to skipping the class altogether.... Instead of going to class, they began to go to the library or into the hallway to do their homework and study for other classes.

The young women in the NOI not only voiced the power of their own agency, but their statements about Advanced Placement courses also displayed a critical awareness of structural inequality, as this comment by Tiffany illustrates:

> We don't even have any Advanced courses at this school.... And we have been the ones askin' for them—like almost beggin.' How do you expect us to go to college if we don't have the same chance to learn?

Although many students at Eastern High "acquired ritual competency," as Goffman (1959) termed it, by putting their heads down, listening to Walkmen, sleeping in class, reading magazines, engaging in practical jokes, and becoming part of the "dropout rate"—which Fine (1991) more accurately called the "push-out" rate—the NOI students did not. Instead, I encountered a set of institutional arrangements in which the NOI young women developed a different ideology and adopted a different course of action than has been described by previous research. More specifically, the NOI provided highly valuable forms of academic and social support by connecting these seven young women (and other members of the NOI) to an organizational collectivity that was committed to helping them achieve.

Resistance as Oppositional Behavior

The NOI young women expressed a belief in their own efficacy to improve their lives and to uplift the black community. They translated this belief into action by actively participating in classroom discussions and resisting school practices that they viewed as being at odds with their religious tenets and practices. The following field note illustrates one of the ways in which cultural differences between the NOI students and school authorities became politically charged and created conflict:

On a Tuesday morning in mid-March, around 10 o'clock, I went to observe an American History class. . . . In the midst of distributing a written quiz, . . . the teacher made the following statements: "You know I don't trust any of you. . . . All students will cheat if they get a chance, and I'm paranoid . . . because I don't trust any of you in this classroom.

Immediately three female students in the NOI (Tiffany, Safiya, and Latasha) protested. . . . Tiffany led off by saying that she was "very insulted, and unless she received an apology, she wouldn't take the quiz." Safiya said that "her religion doesn't permit her to cheat—cheating is for white people." And Latasha followed by stating succinctly: "You ain't no teacher to me . . . 'cause you act like a white lady [the teacher was black). . . . You don't teach us nothin' that's gonna make us smart. . . . You just give us the same book to read over and over again, . . . and then you be actin' all paranoid and everthin' . . . We don't even need to cheat . . . and white people ain't shit."

The teacher responded in a voice full of authority: "I am the teacher, . . . and you are not allowed to talk to me like that in this classroom. . . . Do you understand me, young lady? I don't care if you think that you are holier than thou . . . wearin' that stuff on your head. . . . I don't give a damn. . . . You can't talk to me like that." Safiya responded, "But this is a democracy, ain't it? Don't we have freedom of speech—don't we? The teacher said: "Well your right and wrong, young lady, 'cause you see, I teach about democracy, but that doesn't mean I run my class that way. Tiffany chimed in, "But who is runnin' this class—cause you sure as hell aren't."

As the quiz continued, three students were caught cheating. . . . However, none was a member of the NOI. . . . The overt resistance by the NOI students was acknowledged by the teacher: "I respect those girls—everybody does—but what I don't like is they think they know everything . . . when really they're the ones who are always causing problems. . . . I mean, they think that 'cause they dress funny, they can accuse people of not being black enough. . . . Who do they think they are? They don't know what I've been through. . . . That's like the pot callin' the kettle black."

Many educational researchers have found that black students often protect their pride as black students by adopting anti-school behaviors (see, e.g., Erickson, 1987).

However, the NOI students did not respond in this manner. Their actions and statements of belief were not conformist, assimilationist, or regressive. Rather, to handle the complexities that they encountered, they adopted an instrumental view of education (as the means to an end), yet were highly critical of their school, teachers, and peers. In other words, unlike Willis's (1977) "lads," who were blind to the connection between schooling and mobility; MacLeod's (1987) "Hallway Hangers"; or Foley's (1990) "vatos," who withdrew from academic pursuits, acted up in class, ignored homework assignments, and cut classes, and unlike Ogbu and Simon's (1998) involuntary minorities, who tended to equate schooling with assimilation into the dominant group and thus did not try to achieve academically, members of the NOI resisted the cultural and linguistic patterns of the majority culture, yet embraced educational achievement.

As a result, the NOI young women's response to schooling may be considered transformative, rather than merely reproductive, because the agency the students displayed came from a unique form of religious socialization that produces a social consciousness whereby students are encouraged to politicize their cultural resistance and develop counterideologies, while they assess the costs and benefits of not playing the game. By using a black achievement ideology, the NOI students avoided what Ogbu (1991) referred to as the victims contributing to their own victimization by transforming, rather than reproducing, educational outcomes that are commonly associated with oppositional identity and resistance for blacks.

Another cultural incongruity between the NOI young women and the school was the lack of opportunity to practice their faith in accordance with Islamic principles. Generally, Black Muslims are required to pray five times a day, an obligation that does not cease on school days. Prayer times vary in accordance with sunrise and sunset, and early and late prayers usually do not conflict with the school day. However, the midday and midafternoon prayers did present problems for the seven students who were interviewed, as did rituals of absolution that are required before each prayer. The following interviews with Safiya and Kesha highlight the ways in which these NOI young women resisted schooling practices that they viewed as being at odds with their religious tenets yet maintained a strong orientation to academic achievement.

> AA: Is it difficult to find prayer time at school?
>
> Safiya: Yes, whenever I have to pray, I either ask to go to the bathroom or just skip out of class all together.
>
> M: So does that mean that you skip school everyday?
>
> Safiya: Yeah, but I make up for it in the study group that we have at the temple every week.
>
> Kesha added:
>
> This school don't respect our beliefs. . . . So sometimes we have no choice but to break the rules, . . . but I ain't gonna let that stop me from getting to college . . . or from doin' what I'm supposed to be doin' in school. . . . I'll do whatever it takes to keep up. . . . I don't mind workin' hard, . . . but I'm a Black Muslim first—before I'm anything else.

Members of the NOI withdrew from classes not only to pray, but to avoid unacceptable or offensive curricula. Tiffany stated this point succinctly:

> All I know is [that] in history class, all they teach about is white people.... We don't learn nothin' about black history or black achievements, ... and even when we do, it is like a little tiny bit of class time.... But when we learn about white people, it goes on and on and on—for weeks.... That's why other kids listen to me... 'cause they know that I know about black history.

Tiffany added:

> People don't respect our religion around here.... They don't care if we pray or where we pray, they don't care what we eat, and they don't honor how we dress or our need to fast.... But I guarantee you if it's a white holiday, their gonna celebrate it.... Why do you think that is? It's 'cause we don't believe in a white God, that's why.... That's why they treat us bad even though we're good honest people.

These interviews and field notes illustrate that at Eastern High, a simple dichotomy between resistance and conformity overlooks the complexity of students' behaviors and responses. More specifically, the young women in the NOI demonstrated that accommodation is not the only path to success in school and that opposition does not necessarily lead to failure. Rather, they resisted what they perceived as acts of oppression within the school and, at the same time, pursued strategies that enabled them to be academically successful. By combining strategies that have been attributed to recent immigrants to the United States with a black achievement ideology, these young women displayed a unique mobility strategy that is, according to the social science literature, usually not expressed by low-income black American youths or other involuntary minority groups, although historical records suggest otherwise (Gibson, 1998; Perry, Steele, and Hilliard, 2003). Adding these complexities to notions of resistance suggests that we need to reexamine the link between resistance and failure and accommodation and success (S. Lee, 1996) because the young women in the NOI both qualities were exhibited.

FROM ANALYSIS TO RECONSTRUCTION OF THEORY

This article has charted a theory of black educational achievement. It did so by challenging the work of Ogbu and Simon (1998) and others by examining which claims have held up, need to be complicated, or need to be reconstructed. I began by illustrating how a group's original terms of incorporation, although significant, are one of a number of different variables that shape the school-adaptation patterns for an involuntary minority group. Academic engagement depends not only on the historical, political, and economic realities that students face, but on the students' day-to-day experiences in school, in the community, and in what Jackson (2001) referred to as the "performative dimension" of race—that is, how specific cultural practices are used to constitute racial identity. In the case of the NOI, its black achievement ideology is intentionally organized in opposition to the ideology of white supremacy and, as such, counters folk theories of black intellectual inferiority and hence contributes to a culture of academic achievement.

The NOI's ability to create a black achievement ideology suggests that we need to re-construct Ogbu's typology that categorizes separate and distinct ideologies for voluntary and involuntary immigrant groups (see Figure 9.1). The young women in the NOI did not fit this typology. Although they described a system that is not sympathetic toward blacks, in general, or Islamic women, in particular, they maintained that it is possible to better themselves, their subcultural community, and the society at large by being disciplined, avoiding drugs and other vices, practicing ethical integrity, and working hard.

The NOI's black achievement ideology, which is simultaneously culturally and ac-ademically affirming, further complicates the traditional relationship among academic achievement, socioeconomic status, and educational success. The young women in the NOI understood the importance of developing culturally appropriate social behavior and academic skills and achieving academically. At the same time, because they prac-ticed Islam in a non-Islamic setting, they also represented a challenge to commonsense notions of what are (or are not) culturally appropriate norms, attitudes, and behaviors.

The NOI's black achievement ideology also challenges the burden-of-acting-white thesis because the NOI young women transformed the burden of acting white into the honor of being black. In this manner, they demonstrated the heterogeneity of the black American experience.

Previous research assumed a binary or dichotomous pattern of cultural orientation for low-income students, such as those in the NOI—one in which individuals are either accommodating or resisting, succeeding or failing, involuntary or voluntary. However, my research documented how innovation occurs precisely because these NOI young women simultaneously engaged in structural assimilation (promoting traditional val-ues, such as hard work), separation (affirming their own racial and cultural identities), and resistance (challenging key tenets of the achievement ideology by not conforming or assimilating to school rules or social etiquette) and, at the same time, understood the importance of academic achievement.

Figure 9.1.

Akom's Extension of Ogbu's Cultural-Ecological Model of Racial-Ethnic School Performance

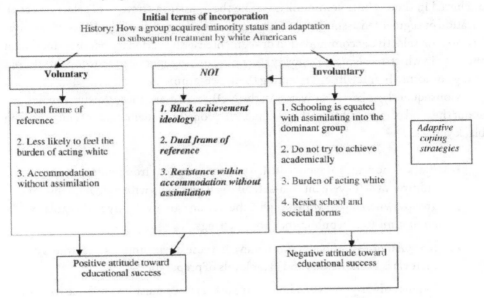

As a result, NOI young women provide fertile ground for reinterpreting popular notions of resistance that suggest that working-class students get working-class jobs because they refuse to develop skills, attitudes, manners, and speech that are necessary for achievement in a capitalist society. My research contradicted key aspects of resistance theory by documenting how resistance for young women in the NOI is transformative, rather than merely reproductive of existing patterns of social relations. The NOI students' response to schooling may be considered transformative because these young women used a black achievement ideology and a dual frame of reference to produce positive educational and social outcomes and to achieve working-class mobility. Willis (1977), in particular, and resistance theory, in general, have tended to understate the role of race, immigrant status, community forces, and power relations in the production of educational achievement and, as a result, have not adequately accounted for nuances in variations of achievement among involuntary minority groups.

However, focusing on the NOI does not mean that I place the onus of educational success squarely within the minority communities themselves and exempt the educational system from responsibility. Rather, by extending Bourdieu's (1986) theoretical framework, I have attempted to reveal how individual actors' lives are influenced by an organizational habitus that is rooted in racial and religious distinctions and how the concept of oppositionality often originates in and is nurtured by schools themselves.

In sum, this research has suggested that *guided* cultural and social resources within an ethnic community, regardless of voluntary or involuntary status, increase the chance for educational success and increase the likelihood that youths will not deviate from paths of mobility. In other words, the best course for many youths is to remain securely anchored in their ethnic communities while they pursue a strategy of selective acculturation or segmented assimilation. However, my findings differ from those of previous research on selective accommodation or segmented assimilation in that they document the ways in which *involuntary* minority students can be academically successful without being conformists and without rejecting their race-ethnicity.

Consequently, if I extend the case of the NOI, I can make the following predictions about the kind of environments that are likely to promote academic achievement among black youths:

- Black American students will achieve in school environments that create cultures of achievement that extend to all members with a strong sense of group ownership in which high expectations are explicitly and regularly communicated in public and group settings.

- Black American students can achieve in these environments, regardless of their class backgrounds and prior levels of preparation.

- Regular and rigorous academic support services must be available to ensure that all students are able to achieve.

- Deliberate socialization is important so that all students develop practices, beliefs, behaviors, and values that support cultures of achievement (Perry et al., 2003).

Obviously, further research is needed to uncover the extent to which the case of the NOI is generalizable, as well as to determine the extent to which school racial composition, gender, grade level, and other socioeconomic factors affect school-related behavior and attitudes among black students, in general, and NOI students, in particular. I hope that this work will stimulate other researchers to address similar questions. I expect that, with time, some of what is presented here will be superseded by knowledge generated by better research. I theorize that there are other achievement ideologies that exist and that society, social science, and the media will benefit from the illumination of their complexity.

Endnotes

1   The oppositional-culture explanation has three main components. The first component is the way in which minorities are treated or mistreated in education in terms of educational policies, pedagogy, and returns for their investment or school credentials. Ogbu and Simons (1998) referred to this as the *system*. The second component is the way in which minorities perceive or respond to schooling as a consequence of their mistreatment. The third component is how and why a group became a minority in the United States in the first

place. All these factors, including explaining minority disadvantage in education as a result of a culture that discourages academic effort by branding it as acting white, constitute the oppositional cultural explanation.

2   Authors, ranging from Ogbu (1987) to Portes and Stepick (1993), have written about the ways in which voluntary immigrants who want to be identified as "American," not foreign, acculturate into an oppositional subculture developed by involuntary youths (i.e., black Americans). Portes and Stepick cited the example of Haitian children in Miami who feel pressured to choose between remaining "Haitian" and being looked down on by their black American peers or adopting a black American identity, which generally carries with it counter school attitudes and behaviors. Although these studies have added much to our understanding of the relationship between "community forces" and immigrants' positive school performance, few have taken sufficient account of the role of involuntary-minority cultures of mobility in shaping students' identity, school experience, and academic performance.

3   According to Hemmings (1996), black high achievers in different school contexts have different definitions of "blackness." In comparing black high achievers in two high schools, Hemmings found that they differed in the way in which they reconciled being model students and being black. Black high achievers in a predominantly middle-class high school experienced pressure to act middle class and made no distinction between white and black middle-class behavior, whereas those in a working-class high school experienced pressure to conform to peers' images of blackness, which involved a rejection of whiteness. Hemmings's findings point to the significance of school context and social class in shaping involuntary perceptions of model student, resistant student, and approaches to academic success.

4   For this study, I found the concept of organizational habitus to be more useful than the similar concept of organizational culture because of the former's emphasis on structure (Horvat and Antonio, 1999). While organizational culture concentrates on the meaning conferred by the set of practices, beliefs, and rules of an organization, organizational habitus is concerned more with how the same set of (in this case) religious-based practices, beliefs, and rules not only provide meaning but structure social interaction.

5   According to the *New World Dictionary*, second edition, ideology refers to (1) the body of ideas reflecting the social needs and aspirations of an individual, a group, a class, or a culture or (2) a set of doctrines or beliefs that form the basis of a political, economic, or other systems.

6   In the United States, Islam is also a mosaic of many different ethnic, racial, and national groups. The majority are first- or second-generation immigrants or black American converts (Haddad and Esposito 2000).

7   None of the studies mentioned in the text dealt with the relationship between the NOI's religious socialization and enhanced educational aspirations and performance. Previous research that did address religious socialization and its impact on educational outcomes suggested that many of the socialization experiences that emanate from religion are conducive to a number of positive outcomes, including educational achievement (Hopson & Hopson, 1990). However most of these studies focused on Protestantism, the black church, or Catholicism and failed to illustrate the ways in which processes of religious socialization influence educational achievement for non-conventional faiths (such as Black Muslims).

8   Within the research literature, aspirations is often defined as the life outcomes that are preferred or desired by individuals (MacLeod, 1987).

9   Data on improvements in grades were taken mainly from three sources: self-reports, school records provided by the students, and teachers' records regarding course examinations. At Eastern High, students are divided into what are known as small learning communities (SLCs), which range from 165 to 330 students. Seven teachers generally provide basic instruction in various subjects—mathematics, English, science, and social studies (the two largest SLCs, out of nine, have 28 teachers between them). Many of the young women I interviewed were in different SLCs, but all spoke of a noticeable increase in educational and occupational aspirations, study habits, and skills since they had joined the NOI. Five out of seven indicated that their GPAs had increased .3 percent to .9 percent per year since they had joined the NOI. And the other two indicated one-year increases of 1.1 percent to 1.3 percent. All had joined the NOI in the 9th or 10th grade.

10 In the population of 1,700 students, it was impossible to measure the exact number of Black Muslim students because this information was not included in the school records. However, the Black Muslim population "appeared" to be significant.

11 Information on the fathers' occupations was omitted because none of the participants had significant economic or social ties with their fathers. All the participants were the first in their immediate families to join the NOI.

12 Ogbu (1987) and Ogbu and Simons (1998) hypothesized "that the study of community forces would shed light on why immigrant minorities do well in school while non-immigrants do less well" (Ogbu and Simons 1998:157). However, to my knowledge neither of these studies analyzed or provided empirical data on the role of community forces in the academic achievement of involuntary minorities.

13 I also disagree with the notion that unless individuals have shared a specific experience or background, they will be unable to understand and appreciate one another. Indeed, as Collins (1990:225) noted, black feminist thought challenges the notion of additive oppression and replaces it with a conceptual framework in which "all groups possess varying amounts of penalty and privilege in one historically created system"; one need not win the oppression sweepstakes to understand and appreciate the pain of exclusion and domination (Horvat and Antonio, 1999).

14 This point is important because it rules out the possibility that the associations between NOI membership and strong academic habits and aspirations are due to selection into the NOI, rather than to the effects of NOI membership.

15 Similar to Advancement via Individual Determination (Mehan, Hubbard, and Villanueva, 1994) the NOI's formal study groups emphasized writing, inquiry, and collaboration, as well as role modeling-mentoring and exploring careers. For the NOI, writing is seen as a learning tool. The students are encouraged to take notes and develop questions that are based on their notes. In addition, they are encouraged to work through curricular readers on topics of import to the organization. Inquiry for the NOI is viewed as a rhetorical strategy that is used to help combat discrimination and prejudice, as well as a tool to facilitate self-empowerment. To develop inquiry as a rhetorical strategy, NOI ministers often use a Socratic method of questioning in their "speeches" that inevitably guides members to a logical conclusion foreseen by the ministers (see the earlier dialogue between a minister and his congregation). The Socratic method is also practiced in study groups by encouraging

the students to clarify their thoughts through provocative questioning, not giving them answers. Collaboration is another formal instructional strategy used by the NOI to encourage members to work together for educational or entrepreneurial goals. Specifically, collaborative groups allow members to work together as sources of information and to establish boundaries to differentiate between who belongs to the NOI and who does not.

16 In 2002, the dysfunctional nature of the schools—low expectations and the loss of "state social capital"—came to fruition when Philadelphia became the first city in the country to turn over 42 of its public schools to private and nonprofit organizations.

17 Mac an Ghaill (1988) termed this strategy "resistance within accommodation." However, the young women in the NOI complicated this terminology on two counts. First, a central tenet of their religious indoctrination advocates for accommodation leading to separation, and second, unlike Mac an Ghaill's "black sisters" or Gibson's (1988) voluntary minorities, these young women felt that they had to (and did) speak out when the school was operating in discriminatory ways. Consequently, the accommodation that they displayed is not consistent with the accommodation hypothesis offered by Gibson or Mac an Ghaill.

References

Anderson, Elijah. 1990. *Street wise.* Chicago: University of Chicago Press.

Bourdieu, Pierre. 1986. "The Forms of Capital." In *Handbook of theory and research for the sociology of education.* Pp. 241-58. Edited by John G. Richardson. New York: Greenwood Press.

Burawoy, Michael, Joshua Camson, and Alice Burton. 1991. *Ethnography unbound: Power and resistance in the modern metropolis.* Berkeley: University of California Press.

Collins, Patricia Hill. 1990. *Black feminist thought, knowledge, consciousness, and the politics of empowerment.* New York: Routledge.

Denzin, Norman K., and Yvonna S. Lincoln. 1994. "Entering the Field of Qualitative Research." Pp. 1-17 in *Handbook of Qualitative Research,* edited by Norman K. Denzin and Yvonna S. Lincoln. Newbury Park, CA: Sage.

Downey, Douglas B., & James W. Ainsworth-Darnell. 1998. "Assessing the Oppositional Culture Explanation for Racial/Ethnic Differences in School Performance." *American Sociological Review* 63:536-53.

Erickson, Fred. 1987. "Transforming School Success: The Politics and Culture of Educational Achievement." *Anthropology and Education Quarterly* 18:335-56.

Essien-Udom, E. U. 1962. *Black Nationalism.* Chicago: University of Chicago Press.

Farrakhan. Louis. 1991, April 22. "Who Is God? Part Three? *Final call.*

Fine, Michelle. 1991. *Framing dropouts.* Albany: State University of New York Press.

Flores-Gonzalez, Nilda. 1999. Puerto Rican High Achievers. *Anthropology and Education Quarterly* 30:343-62.

Foley, Douglas E. 1990. *Learning capitalist culture: Deep in the heart of Tejas.* Philadelphia: University of Pennsylvania Press.

Fordham, Signithia, and John U. Ogbu. 1986. "Black Students' School Success: Coping with the 'Burden of Acting White.'" *Urban Review* 18:176-206.

Gardell, Mattias. 1996. *In the name of Elijah Muhammad: Louis Farrakhan and the nation of Islam.* Durham, NC: Duke University Press.

Gibson, Margaret 1988. *Accommodation without assimilation: Sikh immigrants in an American high school.* Ithaca, NY: Cornell University Press.

---, ed. 1998. "Ethnicity and School Performance: Complicating the Immigrant/Involuntary Minority Typology" [Special issue]. *Anthropology and Education Quarterly* 28(3).

Goffman, Erving. 1959. *The presentation of self in everyday life.* Garden City, NY: Doubleday.

Haddad, Yvonne Yasbeck, and John Esposito, editors 2000. *Muslims in the Americanization path.* New York: Oxford University Press.

Halasa, Malu. 1990. *Elijah Muhammad.* New York: Chelsea House.

Heirich, Max. 1977. "Change of Heart: A Test of Some Widely Held Theories about Religious Conversion." *American Journal of Sociology* 83:653-80.

Hemmings, Annette. 1996. "Conflicting Images? Being Black and a Model High School Student." *Anthropology and Education Quarterly* 27:20-50.

Hopson, Darlene Powell, and Derek S. Hopson. 1990. *Different and wonderful: Raising black children in a race-conscious society.* Englewood Cliffs, NJ: Prentice-Hall.

Horvat, Erin McNamara, and Anthony Lising Antonio. 1999. "Hey, Those Shoes Are Out of Uniform: African American Girls in an Elite High School and the Importance of Habitus." *Anthropology and Education Quarterly* 30:317-42.

Jackson, John L. 2001. *Harlem world: Doing race and class in contemporary black America.* Chicago: University of Chicago Press.

Lee, Martha F. 1996. *The nation of Islam: An American millenarian movement.* Syracuse, NY: Syracuse University Press.

Lee, Stacey. 1996. *Unraveling the "Moral Minority" stereotype: Listening to Asian American youth.* New York: Teachers College Press.

Lincoln, C. Eric. 1973. *The black muslims in America.* Boston: Beacon Press.

Lipsitz, George. 1988. *A life in the struggle: Ivory Perry and the culture of opposition.* Philadelphia: Temple University Press.

Mac An Ghail, Mairtin. 1988. *Young, gifted, and black.* Milton Keynes, England: Open University Press.

MacLeod, Jay. 1987. *Ain't no makin' it: Leveled aspirations in a low-income neighborhood.* Boulder, CO: Westview Press.

Mamiya, Lawrence. 1982. "From Black Muslim to Bilalian: the Evolution of a Movement." *Journal for the scientific study of religion,* 21:138-52.

Massey, Douglas S., and Nancy A. Denton. 1993. *American apartheid: Segregation and the making of the underclass.* Cambridge, MA: Harvard University Press.

McDonough, Patricia M. 1997. *Choosing colleges: How social class and schools structure opportunity.* Albany: State University of New York Press.

Mehan, Hugh, Lea Hubbard, and Irene Villanueva. 1994. "Forming Academic Identities: Accomodation Without Assimilation Among Involuntary Minorities." *Anthropology and Education Quarterly* 25:91-117.

Ogbu, John U. 1978. *Minority education and caste: The American system in cross-cultural perspective.* New York: Academic Press.

---. 1987. "Variability in Minority School Performance: A Problem in Search of an Explanation." *Anthropology and Education Quarterly* 18:312-34.

---. 1991. "Immigrant and Involuntary Minorities in Comparative Perspective." Pp. 3-37 in *Minority status and schooling,* edited by Margaret Gibson and John U. Ogbu. New York: Garland.

Ogbu, John, and Simons, Herbert D. 1998. "Voluntary and Involuntary Minorities: A Cultural-Ecological Theory of School Performance with Some Implications for Education." *Anthropology and Education Quarterly* 29:155-88.

Pattillo-McCoy, Mary. 1999. *Black picket fences: Privilege and peril among the black middle class.* Chicago: University of Chicago Press.

Perry, Theresa, Claude Steele, and Asa G. Hilliard, III. 2003. *Young, gifted, and black: Promoting high achievement among African-American students.* Boston: Beacon Press.

Portes, Alejandro, and Alex Stepik. 1993. *City on the edge: The transformation of Miami.* Berkeley: University of California Press.

Snow, David, and Richard Machalek. 1984. "Sociology of Conversion." *Annual Review of Sociology* 10:167-90.

Solomon, R. Patrick. 1992. *Black resistance in school: Forging a separatist culture.* Albany: State University of New York Press.

Treisman, Urie. 1985. *A study of the mathematics performance of black students at the University of California at Berkeley.* University of California at Berkeley, PhD dissertation.

Weber, Max. 1958. *The protestant ethic and the spirit of capitalism.* New York: Charles Scribner's Sons.

Willis. Paul. 1977. *Learning to labor: How working class kids get working class jobs.* New York: Columbia University Press.

A. A. Akom is a Ph.D. candidate, University of Pennsylvania, and a Research Fellow, Institute for the Study of Social Change, University of California—Berkeley. His fields of interest are urban inequality, race-ethnicity, and social stratification. He is currently conducting research on urban inequality, social stratification, and public policy at the Institute for the Study of Social Change.

This research was part of a comparative urban ethnography project, directed by Elijah Anderson and Pedro Noguera and funded by the American Educational Research Association. Additional writing support was provided by the Institute for the Study of Social Change in Urban Inequality, Urban Education, and Public Policy at the University of California at Berkeley. I thank Pedro Noguera, Elijah Anderson, Michelle Fine, Howard Winant, Doug Massey, Michael Omi, Patricia Fernandez-Kelly, Randall Collins, Michael Hout, Martin Sanchez-Jankowski, Kathy Neckerman, Fred Erickson, Erick Klineberg, Jeannine Villasenor, David Minkus, Brett Cook, and Lemlem Milo for their assistance at various stages of this project. Any errors of fact or interpretation in this article are my responsibility. Direct correspondence to A. A. Akom, Institute for the Study of Social Change, University of California-Berkeley, 2420 Bowditch Street, Berkeley, CA 94720; e-mail: akom@udink4.berkeley.edu.

The Canary In the Mine
The Achievement Gap Between Black and White Students

By Mano Singham

The Achievement Gap

The educational achievement gap is real and has serious social, economic, and political consequences, Mr. Singham points out. But the situation is by no means hopeless, if we start looking at the problem in new ways and avoid simplistic one-shot solutions.

SHAKER HEIGHTS IS not your typical community. It is a small inner-ring bedroom suburb of Cleveland, covering an area of about five square miles and having a population of 30,000. It is a carefully planned city with tree-lined streets winding past well-maintained homes and manicured lawns, lakes, parks, and red-brick schools nestled in campus-like grounds. The city is about one-third African American and two-thirds white, with a sprinkling of other minorities. Although income levels in the city range from the poor (about 10% below the poverty level) to millionaires, the image of Shaker Heights is that of a primarily middle- and upper-middle-class community (median family income of $66,000) that is home to many of the academics, professionals, and corporate executives of all ethnic groups who work in the Cleveland area. It is also a highly educated community, with more than 60% of all residents over the age of 25 holding at least a bachelor's degree—a figure three times the national average.

FAVORED EXPLANATIONS FOR THE ACHIEVEMENT GAP SEEM TO DEPEND ON WHERE ONE STANDS ON THE IDEOLOGICAL SPECTRUM.

Shaker Heights prides itself on the excellence of its school system, taxing itself voluntarily with one of the highest rates in the state of Ohio in order to maintain the wide range of academic and extracurricular programs that provide the students who take advantage of them with an education that would be the envy of any child in the nation.

Hence the city tends to attract as residents relatively well-off people who seek both an integrated community and a high-quality education for their children. Every year, the school district sends off about 85% of its graduating seniors to four-year colleges, many of them prestigious, and boasts a remarkably high number of the National Merit Scholarship semifinalists, way out of proportion to the small size of its student enrollment (about 5,500).

But all is not well, and the problem is immediately apparent when you walk into classrooms. Although the school population has equal numbers of black students and white ones, in the highest-achievement tracks (the Advanced Placement sections) you find only a handful of blacks (about 10%), while the lowest-achievement tracks (called "general education") are populated almost exclusively by blacks (about 95%). When educational statistics are disaggregated by ethnicity. It is found that black Shaker Heights students on average do better than black students elsewhere, just as white Shaker Heights students do better than their counterparts in other school systems. The real puzzle has been why, although both communities have equal access to all the school district's educational opportunities, the academic performance of black Shaker Heights students lags significantly behind that of their white peers. For example, the average black SAT score in 1996 was 956 (compared to a national black average of 856), while the average for white students was 1198 (compared to a national white average of 1049).

This ethnic educational achievement gap is hardly news. It is a well-studied and well-established fact that, using almost any measure (the famous 15-point average I.Q. gap between blacks and whites sensationalized by The Bell Curve, SAT scores, college and high school grade-point averages, graduation and dropout rates), black students nationwide do not perform as well as whites.[1] While the phenomenon itself is indisputable, there is no clear consensus on the causes, and favored explanations seem to depend on where one stands on the ideological spectrum.

The so-called liberal interpretation is that this gap is the result of economic disparities between the two ethnic communities that can be traced back to the legacy of slavery and other forms of oppression that blacks have suffered. Support for this view (which I will call the socioeconomic model) comes from the fact that educational achievement correlates more strongly (although not perfectly) with economic status than with any other single variable. Proponents of this model argue that, since the black community lags badly behind the white in both income and wealth, the educational disparities are caused by the socioeconomic disparities. Once economic disparities disappear, proponents of this model say, educational (and other social) disparities will vanish along with them.

Those at the so-called conservative end of the ideological spectrum are not convinced that economic factors are the primary cause of black educational underachievement. As evidence, they point to the fact that other minority groups such as Asians, some of whom are economically worse off than blacks, excel in school. They believe that, while the legacy of slavery and segregation was indeed harsh, the civil rights legislation of the Fifties and Sixties has removed all legal roadblocks to black advancement and we have now achieved a color-blind society. This view leads them to conclude that various social pathologies within the black community (lumped under the euphemism "black culture") must be at fault. They point to unstable families; poor parenting skills; lack of drive and ambition; negative peer pressure and poor choice of role models; high levels of teenage pregnancies, drugs, and crime; and lack of parental involvement in their children's education as the causes of a lack of interest in education among black students.

Believers in this type of explanation (which I will call the sociopathological model) tend to lecture black communities constantly about the need for a wholesale spiritual awakening to traditional virtues and the work ethic. While they appreciate the hardships that blacks suffered in the past, their solution is to say, in effect, "Get over it. The real victims and perpetrators of that unjust system are dead. Stop looking to the past and claiming to be a victim. Pull yourself up by your bootstraps, and take advantage of what is now equally available to everyone." This group concedes that, while racial prejudice still exists, it is essentially a personal matter that should be dealt with on a personal level.

A third view (which I will call the genetic model) is best represented by Charles Murray and Richard Herrnstein, authors of The Bell Curve, who, after making the appropriate regretful noises to indicate their lack of racial prejudice, essentially conclude that the educational disparity is a fact of nature, the result of long term evolutionary selection that has resulted in blacks' simply not having the genetic smarts to compete equally with whites. Instead of engaging in well- meaning, heroic, but ultimately futile efforts to solve an inherently insoluble problem, the authors argue, the best thing to do would be to accept this situation and then determine how to minimize its adverse social consequences.

THE GOOD news is that there is little evidence for the belief that black students are somehow genetically inferior to whites and that this constitutes an insurmountable barrier to their ever achieving academic equality.[2] The further good news is that there are some very promising studies that indicate that the achievement gap in education can be narrowed dramatically and even eliminated. The bad news is that it is not going to be easy to achieve this goal. The problem needs to be addressed on many fronts—educationally, socially, and psychologically—and there is no single "magic bullet" that is going to take care of it.

The first thing to note is that there is one odd feature that characterizes the discussion of any social problem that is analyzed on the basis of how different ethnic groups compare. Statistics for whites are usually taken as a measure of the "natural" state of society, and black statistics are used as a measure of the problem. If the problem is viewed in this way, then the solution lies in getting black people to "act white," i.e., to adopt the values, behavior, attitudes, and mannerisms of white people, so that blacks will perform as well as whites. Much of the preaching of virtues to the black community about their social pathology (the sociopathological model) seems to have this belief as a basis.

There are many problems with this approach. One is that black people are not as impressed with the virtues of whites as whites are and see no need to emulate them. Given the behavior of whites during the time of slavery, to ask blacks to regard whites as role models for virtuousness seems presumptuous, to put it mildly. James Baldwin captured this difference in perception when he said in The Fire Next Time "White Americans find it as difficult as white people elsewhere do to divest themselves of the notion that they are in possession of some intrinsic value that black people need or want [T]here is certainly little enough in the white man's public or private life that one should desire to imitate."[3]

It would also be presumptuous to assume that rejecting the white behavior model is an act designed merely to give perverse satisfaction to blacks, even though it might hurt their chances of economic and educational success in life. Researcher Signithia Fordham, in her studies of black high school students in Washington, D.C., found that there was a marked difference in attitudes toward academic and career success between the generation of blacks that came of age during the civil rights struggle and their children.[4]

For black parents, the success of any one black person in any new field was perceived also as a vicarious victory for the whole black community because that individual was opening doors that had hitherto been closed to blacks. Other blacks could then emulate the example of the pioneer and follow in his or her footsteps. Thus eventually the community as a whole could pull itself out of the miserable conditions that were the legacy of slavery. So the black community rejoiced when Thurgood Marshall became a Supreme Court justice, when Ralph Bunche became an undersecretary-general of the United Nations and a winner of the Nobel Prize, when Arthur Ashe became Wimbledon and U.S. Open tennis champion, and when others became lawyers, doctors, nurses, college professors, and other kinds of professionals and administrators. It seemed to be only a matter of time before all members of the black community would obtain their share of the American dream that had long been denied them.

There was a price that was paid by these trailblazers, though. They recognized that all eyes were on them to see if they would measure up. Ever mindful of their responsibility not to jeopardize the chances of those who were to come after them, these black pioneers had to prove themselves "worthy" in white eyes, and this was done by "acting white" (at least in their work environment), by adopting the values and behavior of the white-dominated establishment they were trying to penetrate. In his autobiography, Malcolm X speaks sardonically of what he calls these "firsts," black people who were hailed as the first to occupy any position that had previously been denied to blacks. He said that very often it was these people, even more than whites, who would vociferously condemn other blacks like himself who did not buy into the notion of having to act white in order to advance themselves and their community. But by and large, such "white" behavior was tolerated and excused by blacks as a temporary strategy for the long-term benefit of their community.

But Fordham found that young black people now, following Malcolm X's lead, see things quite differently. What they have observed is that the success of the pioneers did not breed widespread success. A few more blacks made it into the professions but nowhere near the numbers necessary to lift up the whole community. Fordham reports that young black people see the strategy of using individual success to lead to community success as a fatally flawed one. They have replaced it with a largely unarticulated but nevertheless powerfully cohesive strategy that is based on the premise that the only way that the black community as a whole will advance is if all its members stick together and advance together. This way they can keep their ethnic identity intact (i.e., not have to "act white"). Hence the attempt by any individual black to achieve academic success is seen as a betrayal because it would involve eventually conforming to the norms of white behavior and attitudes.

This view causes immense problems for those black students who have higher academic aspirations. Many are torn between wanting to achieve academic success because of their parents' expectations and sacrifices on their behalf and the natural desire to stay in step with their peers and retain important adolescent friendships. Many of them adopt a middle road, keeping their grades just high enough to avoid trouble at home and preserve good relations with their teachers but no more. Fordham calls their strategy "racelessness"—behaving in what they see as a race neutral manner so as not to draw attention to themselves. They also tend to study alone and in secret so that they cannot be accused of breaking ranks with their peers. This pattern of isolated study leads to disastrous consequences when these same students confront the more challenging college environment.

By itself, Fordham's explanation of why black students underperform may not be sufficiently compelling. But Claude Steele of Stanford University (along with Joshua Aronson) has done research that indicates that other complementary factors contribute to poor academic performance by blacks.[5] Steele's research on college students at Stanford and the University of Michigan indicates that when students are placed in a situation in which a poor performance on a standardized test would support a stereotype of inferior abilities because of the student's ethnicity or gender, then the student's performance suffers when compared with those who do not labor under this preconception. For example, when black students and white ones were given tests that they were told measured their academic abilities, black students did worse than whites. But when a control group of black students and white ones were given the same test but were told that the test did not have any such significance but was merely a laboratory tool, the difference in performance disappeared. He calls this phenomenon "stereotype threat."

What is interesting about Steele's research results is that they do not apply only to black/white comparisons. The same phenomenon occurred with men and women. The women's performance deteriorated when they were told that the standardized mathematics test they were taking had shown gender differences, whereas the male/ female difference disappeared in the control group when the women were told that the identical test had not shown any gender differences. The white men, who were outperforming black and women students, were themselves not immune to the stereotype threat. When they were told that the same tests were being used to compare their abilities with Asians, their performance deteriorated.

Another interesting fact that Steele uncovered is that the "threat" of stereotyping that depresses performance does not have to be very obvious. Just being required to check off their gender or ethnicity on the answer sheet was sufficient to trigger the weaker performance by the students. Steele concludes that the fear that a poor performance on a test will confirm a stereotype in the mind of an examiner imposes an anxiety on the test-taker that is difficult to overcome. Given the widespread suspicion that blacks cannot cut it in the academic world or that women are not good in math, both these groups enter any test-taking situation with a disadvantage compared with those who do not have this fear. Steele suggests that it is this fear that causes these groups to disinvest in education, to assert that it is not important and that they are not going to expend any effort on mastering it. That way, a poor performance is only a measure of the individual's lack of interest in the subject and is not a sign of his or her inability to master it.

Anthropologist John Ogbu's and other researchers' studies of the effects of minority/ dominant relationships on academic performance are more complex.[6] They looked at studies of the performance of different ethnic minority groups in the same society (such as African Americans, Hispanics, Asians, and Native Americans in the U.S.) and of the same ethnic minority groups in different societies (such as Koreans in Japan and the U.S.). Their results indicate that the performance of any given minority depends on a complex interplay of factors, such as whether the minority is a voluntary one (such as Asians now and earlier generations of Jews, Irish, and Germans) or an involuntary one (such as blacks due to enslavement, Native Americans due to conquest, and Hispanics due to colonization), and the perceptions of the dominant community toward the minority. For example, Koreans and the Buraku (a tribe in Japan that is ethnically identical with other Japanese) do poorly in Japanese schools, where both groups are considered to be academically inferior. But members of the same groups excel when they come to the U.S., which tends to view any Koreans or Japanese (being Asian) as academic high fliers.

Ogbu points out the importance to academic performance of the perception of the relationship between effort and reward. People are more likely to work harder if they can see a benefit in return and have a realistic expectation of receiving that benefit. In the case of education, this link lies in the belief that educational effort leads to academic credentials, which in turn lead to gainful employment.

This effort/reward scenario lies at the basis of the white work ethic and forms an important component of the lectures delivered to blacks by those who adhere to the socio-pathological view of underachievement. Ogbu points out that the effort/reward relationship is not at all obvious to blacks. For years blacks were denied employment and education commensurate with their efforts. It did not matter how much they valued education or strove to master it; higher levels of education and employment were routinely denied them purely on the basis of their ethnicity. Hence it is unreasonable to expect them to see the work/credential/employment linkage as applying to them, as most whites do.

But it could be argued that this difference in perception is something that will disappear with time (or, as some might contend, should have disappeared by now if not for blacks' clinging to their "victim" status.) But Ogbu points out that there is a more pernicious effect still at work. He finds that the value of the "reward" lies very much in the eye of the beholder, because this perception is strongly affected by the group with which one compares oneself. Ogbu argues that members of voluntary minorities (i.e., the immigrant groups against whom blacks are routinely and adversely compared) judge their status and rewards against those of their peers whom they left behind in their native country. So even if they are working in lower-status jobs in the U.S. than those they left behind to come here, they tend to be earning more than their peers who stayed at home, and they also feel that their children (for whom they made the sacrifice to come to the U.S.) will have greater educational opportunities and chances for advancement than the children of their peers back home. Hence they have a strong sense of achievement that makes them strive even harder and instill these values in their children.

But blacks (an involuntary minority) have a different group as a basis for comparison. They have no reference points to groups outside the U.S. They compare their achievement with that of white people (usually suburban, middle-class whites), and they invariably suffer in the comparison. Ogbu says that in his interviews with "successful" blacks (however one measures that), it does not take long for the sentiment to be expressed that, of course, if they had been white, they would be even more successful, would have advanced more in their careers, or would have made more money. So for blacks, the perceived link between effort and reward is far weaker than it is for whites and voluntary minorities, and we should not be too surprised if the weakness of this link manifests itself in a lower commitment to academic effort.

The causes of black underachievement identified by Fordham, Steele, and Ogbu cannot simply be swept away by legislative or administrative action, by exhortations, or by identifying people with racial prejudice and weeding them out of public life. They lie in factors that are rooted deeply in history and that will not go away by themselves and may even worsen if not addressed. The good news is that there are specific educational strategies that provide hope for change.

One study originated around 1974 at the University of California, Berkeley, and was the result of an observation by a mathematics instructor named Uri Treisman.[7] He noticed (as had countless other college instructors) that black and Hispanic students were failing in the introductory mathematics course in far greater numbers than were members of any other ethnic group and were thus more likely to drop out of college. This occurred despite remedial courses, interventions, and other efforts aimed directly at this at-risk group.

Treisman inquired among his colleagues as to the possible reasons for this phenomenon and was given the usual list of suspect causes: black students tended to come from homes characterized by more poverty, less stability, and a lack of emphasis on education; they went to poorer high schools and were thus not as well prepared; they lacked motivation; and so forth. Rather than accept this boilerplate diagnosis, Treisman actually investigated to see if it was true. He found that the black students at Berkeley came from families that placed an intense emphasis on education. Their parents took great pride in and were highly supportive of their going to college. Many of these black students had gone to excellent high schools and were as well prepared as any other group. There was also a wide diversity among them—some came from integrated middle-class suburban neighborhoods; others, from inner-city segregated ones. Clearly the conventional wisdom did not hold, and the cause of their poor achievement lay elsewhere.

THE CHINESE STUDENTS, UNLIKE THE BLACKS, STUDIED TOGETHER, ROUTINELY ANALYZING LECTURES AND SHARING TIPS AND STRATEGIES.

What Treisman then did was to narrow his investigation to just two groups—blacks and the high-achieving ethnic Chinese minority. He studied all aspects of the two groups' lives to see what factors might be contributing to their hugely different performances, and what he found was interesting. He discovered that, while both blacks and Chinese socialized with other students in their group, the Chinese also studied together, routinely analyzing lectures and instructors, sharing tips and explanations and strategies for success. They had an enormously efficient information network for sharing what worked and what didn't. If someone made a mistake, others quickly learned of it and did not repeat it. In contrast, the black students partied together, just like the Chinese, but then went their separate ways for studying, perhaps as a result of the high school experience Fordham describes. This tendency resulted in a much slower pace of learning, as well as the suffering that comes with having to learn from mistakes. Black students typically had no idea where they stood with respect to the rest of the class, and they were usually surprised by the fact that they received poor grades despite doing exactly what they thought was expected of them, such as going to class, handing in all their assignments on time, and studying for as many hours as other students.

Treisman addressed this problem by creating a workshop for his mathematics students. In these workshops, students were formed into groups and worked on mathematics problems together. Discussion and sharing of information were actively encouraged and rewarded. By this means, Treisman sought to introduce to all his students (not just those who happened to chance upon this effective strategy) the value of group academic effort and sharing as methods of achieving academic success. One notable feature of this experiment was that the working groups were mixed ethnically and in terms of prior achievement. The second noteworthy feature was that the students were given very challenging problems to work on, much harder than the ones that they would normally have encountered in the regular courses.

It is interesting that both these features, although they preceded Claude Steele's research, avoided triggering the stereotype threat identified by him. The ethnically mixed nature of the groups avoided the perception that this was a remedial program aimed at blacks, while the explicitly challenging nature of the problems posed to the students meant that there was no stigma attached to failing to solve them. Failure was simply due to the difficulty of the problems, not to membership in an ethnic group that was assumed to be incapable of achieving academic success. In addition, when students did succeed in solving a problem, they experienced a sense of exhilaration and power at having achieved mastery of something difficult, which, as anyone who has experienced it will testify, is the only real and lasting incentive to high achievement. What Treisman found was that, as a result of his workshops, black students' performance improved by as much as one letter grade.

Much research supports the effectiveness of Treisman's strategy. Traditional "remedial" courses designed for underachieving students are largely based on the assumption that poor performance is due to lack of adequate preparation: that weaker students are handicapped by a lack of so-called basic skills. Hence these courses tend to have a strong emphasis on drilling students on the basics. But what such courses ignore is that students fall behind academically for a variety of reasons, not the least of which is that they have not mastered the higher-level reasoning and problem-solving skills that are the prerequisites for success in real life. So even if you drill students in the basics so that they reach the same hypothetical starting line as others, they start falling behind again as soon as they encounter new material because they do not know how to process the new information efficiently. Even worse, the drilling methods often used in remedial courses bore the students (turning them off to education even more) and tend to reinforce the low-level thinking skills that caused them to fall behind in the first place at the expense of the higher-level ones, thus compounding the problem instead of solving it. On the other hand, if students are given interesting and challenging problems to work on, things that pique their interest and are relevant to their lives, they are more likely to acquire the so-called basic skills as a means to solving the problems of interest.

THE ACADEMIC ACHIEVEMENT GAP MAY REALLY BE TELLING US THAT THERE ARE FUNDAMENTAL PROBLEMS WITH THE WAY EDUCATION IS DELIVERED TO ALL STUDENTS.

In his book *Color-Blind* Ellis Cose describes another success story of black education, this time at Xavier University, a historically black college in New Orleans.[8] This university took to heart the message of psychometrician Arthur Whimbey, who argued in *Intelligence Can Be Taught* that students can be taught to perform better academically by a suitably planned program that stresses the importance of higher-level thinking skills.[9] When the school adopted a Whimbey-inspired curriculum, incoming freshmen so improved their academic performance that Xavier is now the single biggest supplier of black graduates to medical schools, despite its relatively small enrollment. Once again it must be emphasized that what was stressed in this program was the challenging nature of the academic program, the drive for excellence as opposed to remediation.

I HAVE argued here that perceiving the academic performance of white students as the norm and that of blacks as a measure of the problem naturally leads to the proposing of solutions that have as their basis the attempt to persuade blacks to "act white" or at least to adopt white values. But the implicit notion that black behavior and values are somehow inferior to whites' makes these solutions offensive and unacceptable to many blacks.

There is an even more serious objection to this strategy of trying to get everyone to adopt the "white ethic" as a means of reducing the educational achievement gap. It is that it might be masking the true nature of the problem by assuming that there is no real problem in the educational delivery system as such but only in the way that it is received by different groups: that is, black students don't respond to education in the proper manner.

An alternative explanation is that the primary problem lies not in the way black children view education but in the way we teach all children, black, white, or other. The traditional model of education is one that largely requires children to work alone or to listen to an instructor. It is a passive model, based on the assumption that extrinsic rewards (such as credentials and jobs) are sufficient motivators for students to go to school and learn. Education is regarded as medicine; it is good for you but not necessarily pleasurable or worth doing for its own sake. Much emphasis is placed on teaching students "facts" that are unrelated to their interests or immediate experience but that they are told will be useful to them in the future. There is very little emphasis on exploiting the intrinsic curiosity that children have about the world around them or on using this as a springboard for challenging, self-motivated, and self-directed investigative studies.

Alternative, "active learning" methods of education (which have variants that come under the labels of "inquiry" or "discovery" learning) have as their primary motivator intrinsic rewards, the satisfaction that students experience when they, by their own efforts, solve some complex and challenging problem. Anyone who has struggled to understand a complex issue he or she cared deeply about and has succeeded knows the feeling of exhilaration and confidence in one's abilities that ensues. It is truly a high. Unfortunately, this happens far too rarely in education. Instead, most students (irrespective of gender or ethnicity) see the classroom as a place where they are made to learn material and jump through assessment hoops that have no meaning for them, with the carrot being rewarding employment far into the future.

Research indicates that active learning methods produce significant academic gains for students, with more on-task behavior in class. These methods also reduce the achievement gap -- but not, as it might be feared, by "dumbing down" the curriculum or depressing the performance of traditional high achievers. These students gain too, but the most dramatic gains tend to be for those who are not well served by the traditional passive model (i.e., involuntary minorities and women). This is because these students are the ones who lagged behind more in the traditional classroom and thus have more room to improve their performance.[10]

Such a deep-rooted criticism of the current education system is hard for many people to accept, especially those who are already highly credentialed academically. After all, they reasonably point out, the system worked for me, and I became a success. In addition, the U.S. has become an economic, scientific, and technological superpower. So how could its education system be so bad?

The issue is not whether any given education system is good or bad, and framing the question in this way is to go down a blind alley. The issue is what fraction of the student population you want to achieve excellence. The fact is that there never was a majority of students "just like us." What is true is that there has always been a relatively small fraction of students (possibly as high as 25%) from families that expect them to pursue a college education. For this fraction, the links between effort, credentials, and rewards are sufficiently realistic and compelling to act as an extrinsic motivator for academic effort. But even in these families, many students sense that school is not a very interesting or challenging place, and they simply go through the motions, hoping to escape with just enough success to avoid parental censure before they enter the real world and do something meaningful with their lives. Once they do get into real jobs and are confronted with challenging problems, some of them soon develop the higher-level thinking skills required for success.

But in those communities and families in which the perception of the link between effort and reward is weaker (as is the case with low-income families of all ethnicities and with involuntary minorities), these extrinsic rewards become even less compelling as motivators for academic effort and excellence, and the students' performance suffers. In fact, the effort/reward link may actually work against education since life on the streets may seem to provide a more realistic expectation of material reward. As long as society requires only a small fraction of educated people and does not care about gender or ethnic or socioeconomic equity issues, then the present system of education is quite adequate.

What the academic achievement gap may really be telling us is that, while the symptoms of the education system's ills are more clearly visible in the black community than in the white, there are fundamental problems with the way education is delivered to all students.

It used to be that coal miners took canaries into the mines as detectors of noxious gases. If the canary died, then the miners realized that they were in a region of danger and took the necessary precautions. The educational performance of the black community is like the canary, and the coal mine is the education system. The warning signals are apparent. But treating the problem by trying to make blacks "like whites" would be like replacing the canary in the coal mine with a bird that is more resistant to poisonous gases. It simply ignores the real problem.

While we cannot change history, we should not try to dismiss it as irrelevant either. We must come to terms with its very real and serious consequences for our lives now if we are to go beyond shallow analyses of important problems such as the achievement gap in education. Such shallow analyses, in the long run, do more harm than good because they force even well-meaning people to choose between two unsavory options: either to adopt a race-neutral socioeconomic explanation that clashes with everyday experience (and is hence secretly rejected though lip service is paid to it) or to look for pathologies in the character or culture of the involuntary minority communities. Neither option reflects the reality.

The educational achievement gap is not an artifact. It is real and has serious social, economic, and political consequences. Its roots lie in complex and historically rooted ethnic relationships and characteristics. But the situation is by no means hopeless. We can be encouraged by very promising experiments that have narrowed this gap. But we have to start looking at the problem in new and deep ways, and we must avoid the temptation to seek simplistic one-shot solutions if we are going to make any real headway.

Endnotes

1   Richard J. Herrnstein and Charles Murray, The Bell Curve (New York: Free Press, 1994).

2   Mano Singham, "Race and Intelligence: What Are the Issues?," Phi Delta Kappan, December 1995, pp. 271-78; Stephen Jay Gould, The Mismeasure of Man (New York: Norton, 1981); and R. C. Lewonton, Steven Rose, and Leon J. Kamin, Not in Our Genes (New York: Pantheon, 1984).

3   James Baldwin, The Fire Next Time (New York: Dial Press, 1963), p. 108.

4   Signithia Fordham, "Racelessness as a Factor in Black Students' School Success," Harvard Educational Review, February 1988, pp. 54-84.

5   Claude M. Steele, "Race and the Schooling of Black Americans," Atlantic, April 1992, pp. 68-78; Claude M. Steele and Joshua Aronson, "Stereotype Threat and the Intellectual Test Performance of African Americans," Journal of Personality and Social Psychology, vol. 69, 1995, pp. 797-811; and David J. Lewin, "Subtle Clues Elicit Stereotypes' Impact on Black Students," Journal of NIH Research, November 1995, pp. 24-26.

6 See, for example, John Ogbu, "Immigrant and Involuntary Minorities in Comparative Perspective"; Yongsook Lee, "Koreans in Japan and the United States"; and Nobuo K. Shimahara, "Social Mobility and Education: Burakumin in Japan," in John Ogbu and Margaret Gibson, eds., Minority Status and Schooling (New York: Garland. 1991).

7 P. Uri Treisman, "Studying Students Studying Calculus:' College Mathematics Journal, vol. 23, 1992, pp. 362-72.

8 Ellis Cose, Color-Blind: Seeing Beyond Race in a Race-Obsessed World (New York: HarperCollins, 1997).

9 Arthur Whimbey with Linda Shaw Whimbey, Intelligence Can Be Taught (New York: Dutton, 1975).

10 David W. Johnson, Roger T. Johnson, and Karl A. Smith, Active Learning: Cooperation in the College Classroom (Edina, Minn.: Interaction Book Co., 1991); Mark Keegan, "Psychological and Physiological Mechanisms by Which Discovery and Didactic Methods Work," School Science and Mathematics, vol. 95, 1995, pp. 3-10; Chet Meyers and Thomas B. Jones, Promoting Active Learning (San Francisco: Jossey-Bass, 1993); Jane Butler Kahle, "Systemic Reform: Challenges and Changes," Science Educator, Spring 1997, pp. 1-5; and Jane Butler Kahle and Arta Damnjanovic, "The Effect of Inquiry Activities on Elementary Students' Enjoyment, Ease, and Confidence in Doing Science: An Analysis by Sex and Race," Journal of Women and Minorities in Science and Engineering, vol. 1, 1994, pp. 17-28.

Toward a Theory of Culturally Relevant Pedagogy

Gloria Ladson-Billings

TEACHER EDUCATION PROGRAMS throughout the nation have coupled their efforts at reform with revised programs committed to social justice and equity. Thus, their focus has become the preparation of prospective teachers in ways that support equitable and just educational experiences for all students. Examples of such efforts include work in Alaska (Kleinfeld, 1992; Noordhoff, 1990; Noordhoff & Kleinfeld, 1991), California (King & Ladson-Billings, 1990), Illinois (Beyer, 1991), and Wisconsin (Murrell, 1990, 1991),

Currently, there are debates in the educational research Literature concerning both locating efforts at social reform in schools (Popkewitz, 1991) and the possibilities of "re-educating" typical teacher candidates for the variety of student populations in U. S. public schools (Grant, 1989; Haberman, 1991a, 1991b). Rather than looking at pro-grammatic reform, this article considers educational theorizing about teaching itself and proposes a theory of culturally focused pedagogy that might be considered in the reformation of teacher education.

Shulman's often cited article, "Knowledge and Teaching: Foundations of the New Reform" (1987), considers philosophical and psychological perspectives, underscored by case knowledge of novice and experienced practitioners. Although Shulman's work mentions the importance of both the knowledge of learners and their characteristics and knowledge of educational contexts, it generally minimizes the culturally based analyses of teaching that have preceded it. In this article, I attempt to build on the educational anthropological literature and suggest a new theoretical perspective to address the specific concerns of educating teachers for success with African-American students.

Teaching and Culture

For more than a decade, anthropologists have examined ways that teaching can better match the home and community cultures of students of color who have previously not had academic success in schools. Au and Jordan (1981, p. 139) termed "culturally appropriate" the pedagogy of teachers in a Hawaiian school who incorporated aspects of students' cultural backgrounds into their reading instruction. By permitting students to use *talk-story,* a language interaction style common among Native Hawaiian children, teachers were able to help students achieve at higher than predicted levels on, standardized reading tests.

Mohatt and Erickson (1981) conducted similar work with Native American students. As they observed teacher–student interactions and participation structures, they found teachers who used language interaction patterns that approximated the students' home cultural patterns were more successful in improving student academic performance. Improved student achievement also was evident among teachers who used what they termed, "mixed forms" (p. 117)—a combination of Native American and Anglo language interaction patterns. They termed this instruction, "culturally congruent" (p. 110).

Cazden and Leggett (1981) and Erickson and Mohan (1982) used the term "culturally responsive" (p. 167) to describe similar language interactions of teachers with linguistically diverse and Native American students, respectively. Later, Jordan (1985, p. 110) and Vogt, Jordan, and Tharp (1987, p. 281) began using the term "culturally compatible" to explain the success of classroom teachers with Hawaiian children. By observing the students in their home/community environment, teachers were able to include aspects of the students' cultural environment in the organization and instruction of the classroom. More specifically, Jordan (1985) discusses cultural compatibility in this way:

> Educational practices must match with the children's culture in ways which ensure the generation of academically important behaviors. It does not mean that all school practices need be completely congruent with natal cultural practices, in the sense of exactly or even closely matching or agreeing with them. The point of cultural compatibility is that the natal culture is used as a guide in the selection of educational program elements so that academically desired behaviors are produced and undesired behaviors are avoided. (p.110)

These studies have several common features. Each locates the source of student failure and subsequent achievement within the nexus of speech and language interaction patterns of the teacher and the students. Each suggests that student "success" is represented in achievement within the current social structures extant in schools, Thus, the goal of education becomes how to "fit" students constructed as "other" by virtue of their race/ethnicity, language, or social class into a hierarchical structure that is defined as a *meritocracy*. However, it is unclear how these conceptions do more than reproduce the current inequities. Singer (1988) suggests that "cultural congruence in an inherently moderate pedagogical strategy that accepts that the goal of educating minority students *is* to train individuals in those skills needed to succeed in mainstream society" (p. 1).

Three of the terms employed by studies on cultural mismatch between school and home—culturally appropriate, culturally congruent, and culturally compatible—seem to connote accommodation of student culture to mainstream culture. Only the term *culturally responsive* appears to refer to a more dynamic or synergistic relationship between home/community culture and school culture. Erickson and Mohatt (1982) suggest their notion of culturally responsive teaching can be seen as a beginning step for bridging the gap between home and school:

> It may well be that, by discovering the small differences in social relations which make a big difference in the interactional ways children engage the content of the school curriculum, anthropologists can make practical contributions to the improvement of minority children's school achievement and to the improvement of the everyday school life for such children and their teachers. Making small changes in everyday participation structures may be one of the means by which more culturally responsive pedagogy can be developed. (p. 170)

For the most part, studies of cultural appropriateness, congruence, or compatibility have been conducted within small-scale communities—for example, Native Hawaiian, Native Americans. However, an earlier generation of work considered the mismatch between the language patterns of African Americans and the school in larger, urban settings (Gay & Abrahamson, 1972; Labov, 1969; Piestrup, 1973).

Villegas (1988) challenged the microsocial explanations advanced by sociolinguists by suggesting that the source of cultural mismatch *is* located in larger social structures and that schools as institutions serve to reproduce social inequalities. She argued that

> As long as school performs this sorting function in society, it must necessarily produce winners and losers. Therefore, culturally sensitive remedies to educational problems of oppressed minority students that ignore the political aspect of schooling are doomed to failure. (pp. 262-263)

Although I would agree with Villegas's attention to the larger social structure, other scholars in the cultural ecological paradigm (Ogbu, 1981, 1983) are ahistorical and limited, particularly in their ability to explain African-American student success (Perry, 1993).[1]

The long history of African-American educational struggle and achievement is well documented (Anderson, 1988; Billingsley, 1992; Bond, 1969; Bullock, 1967; Clark, 1983; Harding, 1981; Harris, 1992; Johnson, 1936; Rury, 1983; Woodson, 1919; Weinberg, 1977). This historical record contradicts the glib pronouncements that, "Black people don't value education."

Second, more recent analyses of successful schooling for African-American students (King, 1991a; Ladson-Billings, 1992a, 1994; Siddle-Walker, 1993) challenge the explanatory power of the cultural ecologists' caste-like category and raise questions about what schools can and should be doing to promote academic success for African-American students.[2]

Despite their limitations, the microanalytic work of sociolinguists and the macrostructural analysis of cultural ecologists both are important in helping scholars think about their intersections and consider possible classroom/instructional adjustments. For scholars interested in the success of students of color in complex, urban environments, this work provides some important theoretical and conceptual groundwork.

Irvine (1990) developed the concept of *cultural synchronization* to describe the necessary interpersonal context that must exist between the teacher and African-American students to maximize learning. Rather than focus solely on speech and language interactions, Irvine's work describes the acceptance of students' communication patterns, along with a constellation of African-American cultural mores such as mutuality, reciprocity, spirituality, deference, and responsibility (King & Mitchell, 1990).

Irvine's work on African-American students and school failure considers both micro- and macro-analyses, including: teacher–student interpersonal contexts, teacher and student expectations, institutional contexts, and the societal context. This work is important for its break with the cultural deficit or cultural disadvantage explanations which led to compensatory educational interventions.[3] A next step for positing effective pedagogical practice is a theoretical model that not only addresses student achievement but also helps students to accept and affirm their cultural identity while developing critical perspectives that challenge inequities that schools (and other institutions) perpetuate term this pedagogy, *culturally relevant pedagogy*.

Several questions, some of which are beyond the scope of this discussion, drive this attempt to formulate a theoretical model of culturally relevant pedagogy. What constitutes student success? How can academic success and cultural success complement each other in settings where student alienation and hostility characterize the school experience? How can pedagogy promote the kind of student success that engages larger social structural issues in a critical way? How do researchers recognize that pedagogy in action? And, what are the implications for teacher preparation generated by this pedagogy?

The Illusion of Atheoretical Inquiry

Educational research is greeted with suspicion both within and outside of the academy. Among practitioners, it is regarded as *too theoretical* (Kaestle, 1993). For many academicians, it is regarded as *atheoretical* (Kamer, Cook, & Crouch, 1978). It is the latter notion that I address in this section of the article.

Clearly, much of educational research fails to make explicit its theoretical underpinnings (Argyris, 1980; Amundson, Serlin, & Lehrer, 1992). However, I want to suggest that even without explicating a theoretical framework, researchers do have explanations for why things "work the way they do," These theories may be partial, poorly articulated, conflated, or contradictory, but they exist. What is regarded as traditional educational theory—theories of reproduction (as described by Apple & Weis, 1983; Bowles, 1977; Weiler, 1988) or neoconservative traditional theory (as described in Young, 1990)—may actually be a *default* theory that researchers feel no need to make explicit. Thus, the theory's objectivity is unquestioned, and studies undergirded by these theories are regarded as truth or objective reality.

Citing the *ranking,* or privileging, of theoretical knowledge, Code (1991) observes:

> Even when empiricist *theories* of knowledge prevail, knowledgeable *practice* constructs positions of power and privilege that are by no means as impartially ordered as strict empiricism would require. Knowledge gained from practical (untheorized) experience is commonly regarded as inferior to theoretically derived or theory-confirming knowledge, and theory is elevated above practice. (p.243)

In education, work that recognizes the import of practical experience owes an intellectual debt to scholars such as Smith (1978), Atkin (1973), Glaser and Strauss (1967), and Lutz and Ramsey (1974) who explored notions of grounded theory as an important tool for educational research. Additionally, work by scholars in teacher education such as Stenhouse (1983), Elliott (1991), Carr and Kemmis (1986), Zeichner (1990), and Cochran-Smith and Lytle (1992) illuminates the action research tradition where teachers look reflexively at their practice to solve pedagogical problems and assist colleagues and researchers interested in teaching practice. Even some scholars in the logical positivist tradition acknowledged the value of a more experientially grounded research approach in education (Cronbach, 1975). More fundamental than arguing the merits of quantitative versus qualitative methodology (Gage, 1989) have been calls for broader understanding about the limits of any research methodology (Rist, 1990). In using selected citations from Kuhn, Patton, Becker, and Gouldner, Rist (1990) helps researchers understand the significance of research paradigms in education. For example:

Since no paradigm ever solves all of the problems it defines and since no two
paradigms leave all the same problems unsolved, paradigm debates always
involve the question: Which problems is it more significant to have solved?
(Kuhn, 1970, p. 46)

A paradigm is a world view, a general perspective, a way of breaking down
the complexity of the real world. As such, paradigms are deeply embedded
in the socialization of adherents and practitioners, telling them what is important, what is reasonable. (Patton, 1975, p. 9)

The issue is not research strategies, per se. Rather, the adherence to one
paradigm as opposed to another predisposes one to view the world and the
events within it in profoundly differing ways. (Rist, 1990, p. 83)

The power and pull of a paradigm is more than simply a methodological
orientation. It is a means by which to grasp reality and give it meaning and
predictability. (Rist, 1990, p. 83)

It is with this orientation toward the inherent subjectivity of educational research that I
have approached this work. In this next section, I discuss some of the specific perspectives that have informed my work.

The Participant-Observer Role for Researchers Who Are "Other"

Increasingly, researchers have a story to tell about themselves as well as their work (Carter, 1993; Peterson & Neumann, in press). I, too, share a concern for situating myself as
a researcher—who I am, what I believe, what experiences I have had all impact what,
how, and why I research. What may make these research revelations more problematic
for me is my own membership in a marginalized racial/cultural group.

One possible problem I face is the presumption of a "native" perspective (Banks,
1992; Narayan, 1993; Padilla, 1994; Rosaldo, 1989) as I study effective practice for African-
American students. To this end, the questions raised by Narayan seem relevant:

"Native" anthropologists, then, are perceived as insiders regardless of
their complex backgrounds. The differences between kinds of "native"
anthropologists are also obviously passed over. Can a person from an im-
poverished American minority background who, despite all prejudices,
manages to get an education and study her own community be equated
with a member of a Third World elite group who, backed by excellent
schooling and parental funds, studies anthropology abroad yet returns
home for fieldwork among the less privileged? Is it not insensitive to suppress the issue of location, acknowledging that a scholar who chooses an

institutional base in the Third World might have a different engagement with Western-based theories, books, political stances, and technologies of written production? Is a middle-class white professional researching aspects of her own society also a "native" anthropologist? (p. 677)

This location of myself as native can work against me (Banks, 1992; Padilla, 1994). My work may be perceived as biased or, at the least, skewed, because of my vested interests in the African-American community. Thus, I have attempted to search for theoretical grounding that acknowledges my standpoint and simultaneously forces me to problematize it. The work of Patricia Hill Collins (1991) on Black feminist thought has been most helpful.

Briefly, Collins's work is based on four propositions: (1) concrete experiences as a criterion of meaning, (2) the use of dialogue in assessing knowledge claims, (3) the ethic of caring, and (4) the ethic of personal accountability. Below, I briefly describe the context and methodology of my study and then attempt to link each of these propositions to a 3-year study I conducted with successful teachers of African-American students.

Issues of Context and Methodology

While it is not possible to fully explicate the context and method of this study in this article, it is necessary to provide readers with some sense of both for better continuity. I have provided more elaborate explanations of these aspects of the work in other writings (Ladson-Billings, 1990; 1992a, 1992b, 1994). Included here is a truncated explanation of the research context and method,

> In 1988, I began working as a lone investigator with a group of eight teachers in a small (less than 3,000 students) predominantly African-American, low-income elementary school district in Northern California. The teachers were identified through a process of *community nomination* (Foster, 1991), with African-American parents (in this case, all mothers) who attended local churches suggesting who they thought were outstanding teachers, The parents' criteria for teaching excellence included being accorded respect by the teacher, student enthusiasm toward school and academic tasks, and student attitudes toward themselves and others. The parents' selections were cross-checked by an independent list of excellent teachers generated by principals and some teaching colleagues. Principals' criteria for teaching excellence included excellent classroom management skills, student achievement (as measured by standardized test scores), and personal observations of teaching practice. Nine teachers' names appeared on both the parents' and principals' lists and were selected to be in the study. One teacher declined to participate because of the time commitment. The teachers were all females; five were African American and three were White.

The study was composed of four phases. During the first phase, each teacher participated in an ethnographic interview (Spradley, 1979) to discuss her background, philosophy of teaching, and ideas about curriculum, classroom management, and parent and community involvement. In the second phase of the study, teachers agreed to be observed by me. This agreement meant that the teachers gave me carte blanche to visit their classrooms. These visits were not scheduled beforehand. I visited the classrooms regularly for almost 2 years, an average of 3 days a week. During each visit, I took field notes, audio-taped the class, and talked with the teacher after the visit, either on-site or by telephone. The third phase of the study, which overlapped the second phase, involved videotaping the teachers. I made decisions about what to videotape as a result of my having become familiar with the teachers' styles and classroom routines.

The fourth and final phase of the study required that the teachers work together as a research collective or collaborative to view segments of one another's videotapes. In a series of ten 2-3-hour meetings, the teachers participated in analysis and interpretation of their own and one another's practice. It was during this phase of the study that formulations about culturally relevant pedagogy that had emerged in the initial interviews were confirmed by teaching practice.

My own interest in these *issues* of teaching excellence for African-American students came as a result of my desire to challenge deficit paradigms (Bloom, Davis, & Hess, 1965) that prevailed in the Literature on African-American learners. Partly as a result of my own experiences as a learner, a teacher, and a parent, I was convinced that, despite the literature, there were teachers who were capable of excellent teaching for African-American students. Thus, my work required a paradigmatic shift toward looking in the classrooms of excellent teachers, *through* the reality of those teachers. In this next section, I discuss how my understanding of my own theoretical grounding connected with the study.

Concrete Experiences as a Criterion of Meaning

According to Collins, "individuals who have lived through the experiences about which they claim to be experts are more believable and credible than those who have merely read and thought about such experience" (p. 209).

My work with successful teachers of African-American students began with a search for "expert" assessment of good teachers. The experts I chose were parents who had children attending the schools where I planned to conduct the research. The parents were willing to talk openly about who they thought were excellent teachers for their children, citing examples of teachers' respect for them as parents, their children's enthusiasm and changed attitudes toward learning, and improved academics in conjunction with support for the students' home culture. In most cases, the basis for their assessments were comparative, both from the standpoint of having had experiences with many teachers (for each individual child) and having had several school-age children. Thus, they could talk about how an individual child fared in different classrooms and how their children collectively performed at specific grade levels with specific teachers.

The second area where concrete experiences as a criterion of meaning was evident was with the teachers themselves, The eight teachers who participated in this study had from 12 to 40 years of teaching experience, most of it with African-American students. Their reflections on what was important in teaching African-American students were undergirded by their daily teaching experiences.

The Use of Dialogue in Assessing Knowledge Claims

This second criterion suggests that knowledge emerges in dialectical relationships. Rather than the voice of one authority, meaning is made as a product of dialogue between and among individuals. In the case of my study, dialogue was critical in assessing knowledge claims, Early in the study, each teacher participated in an ethnographic interview (Spradley, 1979). Although I had specific areas I wanted to broach with each teacher, the teachers' own life histories and interests determined how much time was spent on the various areas, In some cases, the interviews reflect a teacher's belief in the salience of his or her family background and education. In other instances, teachers talked more about their pedagogical, philosophical, and political perspectives. Even after I began collecting data via classroom observations, it was the teachers' explanations and clarifications that helped to construct the meaning of what transpired in the classrooms.

Additionally, after I collected data from classroom observations and classroom videotaping, the teachers convened as a research collaborative to examine both their own and one anothers' pedagogy.[4] In these meetings, meaning was constructed through reciprocal dialogue. Instead of merely accepting Berliner's (1988) notions that "experts" operate on a level of automaticity and intuition that does not allow for accurate individual critique and interpretation—that is, they cannot explain how they do what they do—together the teachers were able to make sense of their own and their colleagues' practices. The ongoing dialogue allowed them the opportunity to re-examine and re-think their practices.

The Ethic of Caring

Much has been discussed in feminist literature about women and caring (Gilligan, 1982; Noddings, 1984, 1991). Other feminists have been critical of any essentialized notion of women (Weiler, 1988) and suggest that no empirical evidence exists to support the notion that women care in ways different from men or that any such caring informs their scholarship and work. I argue that Collins's use of caring refers not merely to affective connections between and among people but to the articulation of a greater sense of commitment to what scholarship and/or pedagogy can mean in the lives of people.

For example, in this study, the teachers were not all demonstrative and affectionate toward the students. Instead, their common thread of caring was their concern for the implications their work had on their students' lives, the welfare of the community, and unjust social arrangements. Thus, rather than the idiosyncratic caring for individual students (for whom they did seem to care), the teachers spoke of the import of their work for preparing the students for confronting inequitable and undemocratic social structures.

The Ethic of Personal Accountability

In this final dimension, Collins addresses the notion that *who* makes knowledge claims is as important as *what* those knowledge claims are. Thus, the idea that individuals can ˉobjectively" argue a position whether they themselves agree with the position, as in public debating, is foreign. Individuals' commitments to ideological and/or value positions are important in understanding knowledge claims.

In this study, the teachers demonstrated this ethic of personal accountability in the kind of pedagogical stands they took. Several of the teachers spoke of defying administrative mandates in order to do what they believed was right for students. Others gave examples of proactive actions they took to engage in pedagogical practices more consistent with their beliefs and values. For example, one teacher was convinced that the school district's mandated reading program was inconsistent with what she was learning about literacy teaching/learning from a critical perspective. She decided to write a proposal to the school board asking for experimental status for a literacy approach she wanted to use in her classroom. Her proposal was buttressed by current research in literacy and would not cost the district any more than the proposed program. Ultimately, she was granted permission to conduct her experiment, and its success allowed other teachers to attempt it in subsequent years.

Although Collins's work provided me with a way to think about my work as a researcher, it did not provide me with a way to theorize about the teachers' practices. Ultimately, it was my responsibility to generate theory as I practiced theory. As previously mentioned, this work builds on earlier anthropological and sociolinguistic attempts at a cultural "fit" between students' home culture and school culture. However, by situating it in a more critical paradigm, a theory of culturally relevant pedagogy would necessarily propose to do three things—produce students who can achieve academically, produce students who demonstrate cultural competence, and develop students who can both understand and critique the existing social order. The next section discusses each of these elements of culturally relevant pedagogy.

Culturally Relevant Pedagogy and Student Achievement

Much has been written about the school failure of African-American students (see, e.g., African American Male Task Force, 1990; Clark, 1983; Corner, 1984; Irvine, 1990; Ogbu, 1981; Slaughter & Kuehne, 1988). However, explanations for this failure have varied widely. One often-cited explanation situates African-American students' failure in their "caste-like minority" (p.169) or "involuntary immigrant" status (Ogbu, 1983, p. 171). Other explanations posit *cultural difference* (Erickson, 1987, 1993; Piestrup, 1973) as the reason for this failure and, as previously mentioned, locate student failure in the cultural mismatch between students and the school.

Regardless of these failure explanations, little research has been done to examine academic success among African-American students. The *effective schools* literature (Brookover, 1985; Brookover, Beady, Flood, Schweitzer, & Wisenbaker, 1979; Edmonds, 1979) argued that a group of school-wide correlates were a reliable predictor of student success.[5] The basis for adjudging a school "effective" in this literature was how far above predicted levels students performed on standardized achievement tests. Whether or not scholars can agree on the significance of standardized tests, their meaning in the real world serves to rank and characterize both schools and individuals, Thus, teachers in urban schools are compelled to demonstrate that their students can achieve literacy and numeracy (Delpit, 1992). No matter how good a fit develops between home and school culture, students must achieve. No theory of pedagogy can escape this reality.

Students in the eight classrooms I observed did achieve. Despite the low ranking of the school district, the teachers were able to help students perform at higher levels than their district counterparts. In general, compared to students in middle-class communities, the students still lagged behind. But, more students in these classrooms were at or above grade level on standardized achievement tests.[6] Fortunately, academic achievement in these classrooms was not limited to standardized assessments. Classroom observations revealed a variety of demonstrated student achievements too numerous to list here. Briefly, students demonstrated an ability to read, write, speak, compute, pose and solve problems at sophisticated levels—that is, pose their own questions about the nature of teacher- or text-posed problems and engage in peer review of problem solutions. Each of the teachers felt that helping the students become academically successful was one of their primary responsibilities.

Culturally Relevant Teaching and Cultural Competence

Among the scholarship that has examined academically successful African-American students, a disturbing finding has emerged—the students' academic success came at the expense of their cultural and psychosocial well-being (Fine, 1986; Fordham 1988), Fordham and Ogbu (1986) identified a phenomenon entitled, "acting White" (p. 176) where African-American students who were academically successful were ostracized by their peers. Bacon (1981) found that, among African-American high school students identified as gifted in their elementary grades, only about half were continuing to do well at the high school level. A closer examination of the successful students' progress indicated that they were social isolates, with neither African-American nor White friends. The students believed that it was necessary for them to stand apart from other African-American students so that teachers would not attribute to them the negative characteristics they may have attributed to African-American students in general.

The dilemma for African-American students becomes one of negotiating the academic demands of school while demonstrating cultural competence. [7] Thus, culturally relevant pedagogy must provide a way for students to maintain their cultural integrity while succeeding academically. One of the teachers in the study used the lyrics of rap songs as a way to teach elements of poetry.[8] From the rap lyrics, she went on to more conventional poetry. Students who were more skilled at creating and improvising raps were encouraged and reinforced. Another teacher worked to channel the peer group leadership of her students into classroom and school-wide leadership. One of her African-American male students who had experienced multiple suspensions and other school problems before coming to her classroom demonstrated some obvious leadership abilities. He could be described as culturally competent in his language and interaction *styles* and demonstrated pride in himself and his cultural heritage. Rather than attempt to minimize his influence, the teacher encouraged him to run for sixth-grade president and mobilized the entire class to organize and help run his campaign. To the young man's surprise, he was elected. His position as president provided the teacher with many opportunities to respond to potential behavior problems. This same teacher made a point of encouraging the African-American males in her classroom to assume the role of academic leaders. Their academic leadership allowed their cultural values and styles to be appreciated and affirmed. Because these African-American male students were permitted, indeed encouraged, to be themselves in dress, language style, and interaction styles while achieving in school, the other students, who regarded them highly (because of their popularity), were able to see academic engagement as "cool."

Many of the self-described African-centered public schools have focused on *this* notion of cultural competence.[9] To date, little data has been reported on the academic success of students in these programs. However, the work of African-American scholars such as Ratteray (1994), Lee (1994), Hilliard (1992), Murrell (1993), Asante (1991), and others indicates that African-centered education does develop students who maintain cultural competence and demonstrate academic achievement.

Culturally Relevant Teaching and Cultural Critique

Not only must teachers encourage academic success and cultural competence, they must help students to recognize, understand, and critique current social inequities. This notion presumes that teachers themselves recognize social inequities and their causes. However, teacher educators (Grant, 1989; Haberman, 1991b; King, 1991b; King & Ladson-Billings, 1990; Zeichner, 1992) have demonstrated that many prospective teachers not only lack these understandings but reject information regarding social inequity. This suggests that more work on recruiting particular kinds of students into teaching must be done. Also, we are fortunate to have models for this kind of cultural critique emanating from the work of civil rights workers here in the U. S. (Aaronsohn, 1992; Morris, 1984; Clark, 1964; Clark, with Brown, 1990) and the international work of Freire (1973, 1974) that has been incorporated into the critical and feminist work currently being done by numerous scholars (see, e.g., Ellsworth, 1989; Giroux, 1983; Hooks, 1989; Lather, 1986; McLaren, 1989). Teachers who meet the cultural critique criteria must be engaged in a critical pedagogy which is:

> a deliberate attempt to influence how and what knowledge and identities are produced within and among particular sets of social relations. It can be understood as a practice through which people are incited to acquire a particular "moral character." As both a political and practical activity, it attempts to influence the occurrence and qualities of experiences. (Giroux & Simon., 1989, p, 239)

Thus, the teachers in this study were not reluctant to identify political underpinnings of the students' community and social world. One teacher worked with her students to identify poorly utilized space in the community, examine heretofore inaccessible archival records about the early history of the community, plan alternative uses for a vacant shopping mall, and write urban plans which they presented before the city council.

In a description of similar political activity, a *class* of African-American, middle-school students in Dallas identified the problem of their school's being surrounded by liquor stores (Robinson, 1993). Zoning regulations in the city made some areas dry while the students' school was in a wet area. The students identified the fact that schools serving White, upper middle-class students were located in dry areas, while schools in poor communities were in wet areas. The students, assisted by their teacher, planned a strategy for exposing this inequity. By using mathematics, literacy, social, and political skills, the students were able to prove their points with reports, editorials, charts, maps, and graphs. In both of these examples, teachers allowed students to use their community circumstances as official knowledge (Apple, 1993). Their pedagogy and the students' learning became a form of cultural critique.

Theoretical Underpinnings of Culturally Relevant Pedagogy

As I looked (and listened) to exemplary teachers of African-American students, I began to develop a grounded theory of culturally relevant pedagogy. The teachers in the study met the aforementioned criteria of helping their students to be academically successful, culturally competent, and sociopolitically critical. However, the ways in which they met these criteria seemed to differ markedly on the surface. Some teachers seemed more structured or rigid in their pedagogy. Others seemed to adopt more progressive teaching strategies. What theoretical perspective(s) held them together and allowed them to meet the criteria of culturally relevant teaching?

One of the places I began to look for these commonalties was in teachers' beliefs and ideologies. Lipman (1993) has suggested that, despite massive attempts at school reform and restructuring, teacher ideologies and *beliefs* often remain unchanged, particularly toward African-American children and their intellectual potential. Thus, in the analysis of the teacher interviews, classroom observations, and group analysis of videotaped segments of their teaching, I was able to deduce some broad propositions (or characteristics) that serve as theoretical underpinnings of culturally relevant pedagogy.

I approach the following propositions tentatively to avoid an essentialized and/or dichotomized notion of the pedagogy of excellent teachers. What I propose represents a range or continuum of teaching behaviors, not fixed or rigid behaviors that teachers must adhere to in order to merit the designation "culturally relevant." The need for these theoretical understandings may be more academic than pragmatic. The teachers themselves feel no need to name their practice culturally relevant. However, as a researcher and teacher educator, I am compelled to try to make this practice more accessible, particularly for those prospective teachers who do not share the cultural knowledge, experiences, and understandings of their students (Haberman, 1994).

The three broad propositions that have emerged from this research center around the following:[10]

- the conceptions of self and others held by culturally relevant teachers,

- the manner in which social relations are structured by culturally relevant teachers,

- the conceptions of knowledge held by culturally relevant teachers.

Conceptions of Self and Others

The sociology of teaching literature suggests that, despite the increasing professionalization of teaching (Strike, 1993), the status of teaching as a profession continues to decline. The feeling of low status is exacerbated when teachers work with what they perceive to be low-status students (Foster, 1986). However, as I acted as a participant-observer in the classrooms of exemplary teachers of African-American students, both what they said and did challenged this notion. In brief, the teachers:

- believed that all the students were capable of academic success,

- saw their pedagogy as art—unpredictable, always in the process of becoming,

- saw themselves as members of the community,
- saw teaching as a way to give back to the community,
- believed in a Freirean notion of "teaching as mining" (1974, p. 76) or pulling knowledge out.

The teachers demonstrated their commitment to these conceptions of self and others in a consistent and deliberate manner. Students were not permitted to choose failure in their classrooms. They cajoled, nagged, pestered, and bribed the students to work at high intellectual *levels.* Absent from their discourse about students was the 'language of lacking." Students were never referred to as being from a single-parent household, being on AFDC (welfare), or needing psychological evaluation. Instead, teachers talked about their own shortcomings and limitations and ways they needed to change to ensure student success.

As I observed them teach, I witnessed spontaneity and energy that came from experience and their willingness to be risk takers. In the midst of a lesson, one teacher, seemingly bewildered by her students' expressed belief that every princess had long blond hair, swiftly went to her book shelf, pulled down an African folk tale about a princess, and shared the story with the students to challenge their assertion. In our conference afterward, she commented,

> I didn't plan to insert that book, but I just couldn't let them go on thinking that only blond-haired, white women were eligible for royalty. I know where they get those ideas, but I have a responsibility to contradict some of that. The consequences of that kind of thinking are more devastating for *our* children. (sp-6, Field notes)[11]

The teachers made conscious decisions to be a part of the community from which their students come. Three of the eight teachers in this study live in the school community. The others made deliberate efforts to come to the community for goods, services, and leisure activities, demonstrating their belief in the community as an important and worthwhile *place* in both their lives and the lives of the students.

A final example I present here is an elaboration of a point made earlier. It reflects the teachers' attempt to support and instill community pride in the students. One teacher used the community as the basis of her curriculum. Her students searched the county historical archives, interviewed long-term residents, constructed and administered surveys and a questionnaire, and invited and listened to guest speakers to get a sense of *the* historical development of their community. Their ultimate goal was to develop a land use proposal for an abandoned shopping center that was a magnet for illegal drug use and other dangerous activities. The project ended with the students' making a presentation before the City Council and Urban Planning Commission. One of the students remarked to me, "This [community] is not such a bad place. There are a lot of good things that happened here, and some of that is still going on," The teacher told me that she was concerned that too many of the students believed that their only option for success involved moving out of the community, rather than participating in its reclamation.

Social Relations

Much has been written about classroom social interactions (see, e.g., Brophy & Good, 1970; Rist, 1970; Wilcox, 1982). Perhaps the strength of some of the research in this area is evidenced by its impact on classroom practices. For example, teachers throughout the nation have either heard of or implemented various forms of cooperative learning (Cohen & Benton, 1988; Slavin, 1987): cross-aged, multi-aged, and heterogeneous ability groupings. While these classroom arrangements may be designed to improve student achievement, culturally relevant teachers consciously create social interactions to help them meet the three previously mentioned criteria of academic success, cultural competence, and critical consciousness. Briefly, the teachers:

- maintain fluid student-teacher relationships,
- demonstrate a connectedness with all of the students,
- develop a community of learners,
- encourage students to learn collaboratively and be responsible for another.

In these teachers' classrooms, the teacher-student relationships are equitable and reciprocal. All of the teachers gave students opportunities to act as teachers. In one class, the teacher regularly sat at a student's desk, while the student stood at the front of the roam and explained a concept or some aspect of student culture, Another teacher highlighted the expertise of various students and required other students to consult those students before coming to her for help: "Did you ask Jamal how to do those math problems?" "Make sure you check with Latasha before you turn in your reading." Because she acknowledged a wide range of expertise, the individual students were not isolated from their peers as teacher's pets. Instead, all of the students were made aware that they were expected to excel at something and that the teacher would call on them to share that expertise with classmates.

The culturally relevant teachers encouraged a community of learners rather than competitive, individual achievement. By demanding a higher level of academic success for the entire class, individual success did not suffer. However, rather than lifting up individuals (and, perhaps, contributing to feelings of peer alienation), the teachers made it clear that they were working with smart classes. For many of the students, this identification with academic success was a new experience. "Calvin was a bad student last year," said one student. "And that was last year," replied the teacher, as she designated Calvin to lead a discussion group. Another example of this community of learners was exemplified by a teacher who, herself, was a graduate student. She made a conscious decision to share what she was learning with her sixth graders. Every Friday, after her Thursday evening class, the students queried her about what she had learned.

A demonstration of the students' understanding of what she was learning occurred during the principal's observation of her teaching. A few minutes into a discussion where students were required to come up with questions they wanted answered about the book they were reading, a young man seated at a table near the rear of the class remarked with seeming disgust, "We're never gonna learn anything if y'all don't stop asking all of these low level questions!" His comment was evidence of the fact that the teacher had shared Bloom's *Taxonomy of Educational Objectives* (1956) with the class. At another time, two African-American boys were arguing over a notebook. "What seems to be the problem?" asked the teacher. "He's got my meta-cognitive journal!" replied one of the boys. By using the language of the teacher's graduate class, the students demonstrated their ability to assimilate her language with their own experiences.

To solidify the social relationships in their classes, the teachers encouraged the students to learn collaboratively, teach each other, and be responsible for the academic success of others, These collaborative arrangements were not necessarily structured like those of cooperative learning. Instead, the teachers used a combination of formal and informal peer collaborations. One teacher used a buddy system, where each student was paired with another. The buddies checked each other's homework and class assignments. Buddies quizzed each other for tests, and, if one buddy was absent, it was the responsibility of the other to call to see why and to help with makeup work. The teachers used this ethos of reciprocity and mutuality to insist that one person's success was the success of all and one person's failure was the failure of all. These feelings were exemplified by the teacher who insisted, "We're a family. We have to care for one another as if our very survival depended on it . . . Actually, it does!"

Conceptions of Knowledge

The third proposition that emerged from this study was one that indicated how the teachers thought about knowledge—the curriculum or content they taught—and the assessment of that knowledge. Once again, I will summarize their conceptions or beliefs about knowledge:

- Knowledge is not static; it is shared, recycled, and constructed.

- Knowledge must be viewed critically.

- Teachers must be passionate about knowledge and learning.

- Teachers must *scaffold,* or build bridges, to facilitate learning.

- Assessment must be multifaceted, incorporating multiple forms of excellence.

For the teachers in this study, knowledge was about doing. The students listened and learned from one another as well as the teacher. Early in the school year, one teacher asked the students to identify one area in which they believed they had expertise. She then compiled a list of "classroom experts" for distribution to the class. Later, she developed a calendar and asked students to select a date that they would like to make a presentation in their area of expertise. When students made their presentations, their knowledge and expertise was a given. Their classmates were expected to be an attentive audience and to take seriously the knowledge that was being shared by taking notes and/ or asking relevant questions. The variety of topics the students offered included rap music, basketball, gospel singing, cooking, hair braiding, and baby-sitting. Other students listed more school-like areas of expertise such as reading, writing, and mathematics. However, all students were required to share their expertise.

Another example of the teachers' conceptions of knowledge was demonstrated in the critical stance the teachers took toward the school curriculum. Although cognizant of the need to teach certain things because of a districtwide testing policy, the teachers helped their students engage in a variety of forms of critical analyses. For one teacher, this meant critique of the social studies textbooks that were under consideration by a state evaluation panel. For two of the other teachers, critique came in the form of resistance to district-approved reading materials. Both of these teachers showed the students what it was they were supposed to be using along with what they were going to use and why. They both trusted the students with this information and enlisted them as allies against the school district's policies.

A final example in this category concerns the teachers' use of complex assessment strategies. Several of the teachers actively fought the students' *right-answer* approach to school tasks without putting the students' down. They provided them with problems and situations and helped the students to say aloud the kinds of questions they had in their minds but had been taught to suppress in most other classrooms. For one teacher, it was the simple requiring of students to always be prepared to ask, "Why?" Thus, when she posed a mathematical word problem, the first question usually went something like this: "Why are we interested in knowing this?" Or, someone would simply ask, "Why are we doing this problem?" The teacher's response was sometimes another question: "Who thinks they can respond to that question?" Other times, the teacher would offer an explanation and then ask, Are you satisfied with that answer?" If a student said "Yes," she might say, "You shouldn't be. Just because I'm the teacher doesn't mean I'm always right." The teacher was careful to help students to understand the difference between an intellectual challenge and a challenge to the authority of their parents. Thus, just as the students were affirmed in their ability to code-switch, or move with facility, in language between African-American language and a standard form of English, they were supported in the attempts at role-switching between school and home.

Another teacher helped her students to choose both the standards by which they were to be evaluated and the pieces of evidence they wanted to use as proof of their mastery of particular concepts and skills. None of the teachers or their students seemed to have test anxiety about the school district's standardized tests. Instead, they viewed the tests as necessary irritations, took them, scored better than their age-grade mates at their school, and quickly returned to the rhythm of learning in their classroom.

Conclusion

I began this article arguing for a theory of culturally relevant pedagogy. I also suggested that the tensions that surround my position as a native in the research field force me to face the theoretical and philosophical biases I bring to my work in overt and explicit ways. Thus, I situated my work in the context of Black feminist thought. I suggested that culturally relevant teaching must meet three criteria: an ability to develop students academically, a willingness to nurture and support cultural competence, and the development of a sociopolitical or critical consciousness. Next, I argued that culturally relevant teaching is distinguishable by three broad propositions or conceptions regarding self and other, social relations, and knowledge. With this theoretical perspective, I attempted to broaden notions of pedagogy beyond strictly psychological models. I also have argued that earlier sociolinguistic explanations have failed to include the larger social and cultural contexts of students and the cultural ecologists have failed to explain student success. I predicated the need for a culturally relevant theoretical perspective on the growing disparity between the racial, ethnic, and cultural characteristics of teachers and students along with the continued academic failure of African-American, Native American and Latino students.

Although I agree with Haberman's (1991b) assertion that teacher educators are unlikely to make much of a difference in the preparation of teachers to work with students in urban poverty unless they are able to recruit "better" teacher candidates, I still believe researchers are obligated to re-educate the candidates we currently attract toward a more expansive view of pedagogy (Bartolome, 1994). This can be accomplished partly by helping prospective teachers understand culture (their own and others) and the ways it functions in education. Rather than add on versions of multicultural education or human relations courses (Zeichner, 1992) that serve to exoticize diverse students as "other," a culturally relevant pedagogy is designed to problematize teaching and encourage teachers to ask about the nature of the student—teacher relationship, the curriculum, schooling, and society.

This study represents a beginning look at ways that teachers might systematically include student culture in the classroom as authorized or official knowledge. It also is a way to encourage praxis as an important aspect of research (Lather, 1986). This kind of research needs to continue in order to support new conceptions of collaboration between teachers and researchers (practitioners and theoreticians). We need research that proposes alternate models of pedagogy, coupled with exemplars of successful pedagogues. More importantly, we need to be willing to look for exemplary practice in those classrooms and communities that too many of us are ready to dismiss as incapable of producing excellence.

The implication of continuing this kind of work means that research grounded in the practice of exemplary teachers will form a significant part of the knowledge base on which we build teacher preparation. It means that the research community will have to *be* willing to listen to and heed the"wisdom of practice" (Shulman, 1987, p. 12) of these excellent practitioners. Additionally, we need to consider methodologies that present more robust portraits of teaching. Meaningful combinations of quantitative and qualitative inquiries must be employed to help us understand the deeply textured, multi-layered enterprise of teaching.

I presume that the work I have been doing raises more questions than it answers. A common question asked by practitioners is, "Isn't what you described just 'good teaching'?" And, while I do not deny that it is good teaching, I pose a counter question: why does so little of it seem to occur in classrooms populated by African-American students? Another question that arises is whether or not this pedagogy is so idiosyncratic that only "certain" teachers can engage in it. I would argue that the diversity of these teachers and the variety of teaching strategies they employed challenge that notion. The common feature they shared was a classroom practice grounded in what they believed about the educability of the students. Unfortunately, this raises troubling thoughts about those teachers who are not successful, but we cannot assume that they do not believe that some students are incapable (or unworthy) of being educated. The reasons for their lack of success are far too complex for this discussion.

Ultimately, my responsibility as a teacher educator who works primarily with young, middle-class, White women is to provide them with the examples of culturally relevant teaching in both theory and practice. My responsibility as a researcher is to continue to inquire in order to move toward a theory of culturally relevant pedagogy.

Notes

I am grateful to the National Academy of Education's Spencer postdoctoral fellowship program for providing me with the funding to conduct this research. However, the ideas expressed here are my own and do not necessarily reflect those of the National Academy of Education or the Spencer Foundation.

Endnotes

1 Although issues of culturally relevant teaching can and should be considered cross-culturally, this work looks specifically at the case of African-American students.

2   It is interesting to note that a number of trade books have emerged that detail the rage
and frustration **of** academically successful, professional, middle-class, African-American
adults, which suggests that, even with the proper educational credentials, their lives continue to be plagued by racism and a questioning of their competence Among the more
recent books are Jill Nelson's *Volunteer Slavery* (1993), Brent Staples's *Parallel Time* (1994),
and Ellis Cose's *The Rage of a Privileged Class* (1993).

3   It should be noted that the "cultural deficit" notion has been reinscribed under the rubric
of "at-risk" (Cuban, 1989). Initially, the U. S. Commission on Excellence in Education
defined the nation as at risk. Now, almost 10 years later, it appears that only some children
are at risk. Too often, in the case of African-American students, their racial/cultural group
membership defines them as at risk.

4   The research collaborative met to view portions of the classroom videotapes that I, as
researcher, selected for common viewing.

5   These correlates include: a clear and focused mission, instructional leadership, a safe and
orderly environment, regular monitoring of student progress, high expectations, and positive home—school relations.

6   Students in this district took the California Achievement Test (CAT) in October and
May of each school year. Growth scores in the classrooms *of* the teachers in the study were
significantly above those of others in the district.

7   *This is* not to suggest that cultural competence for African-American students means
being a failure. The problem that African-American students face is the constant devaluation of their culture both in school and in the larger society. Thus, the styles apparent in
African-American youth culture—e.g., dress, music, walk, language—are equated with
poor academic performance. The student who identifies with "hip-hop" culture may he
regarded as dangerous and/or a gang member for whom academic success is not expected.
He (and it usually is a male) is perceived as not having the *cultural* capital (Bourdieu, 1984)
necessary for academic success.

8   An examination of rap music reveals a wide variety of messages. Despite the high profile of
"gansta rap," which seems to glorify violence, particularly against the police and Whites,
and the misogynistic messages found in some of this music, there is a segment of rap music
that serves as cultural critique and urges African Americans to educate themselves because
schools fail to do so. Prominent rap artists in this tradition are Arrested Development,
Diggable Planets, KRS-1, and Queen Latifah.

9   I am indebted to Mwalimu Shuiaa for sharing his working paper, "Afrikan-Centered *Education* in Afrikan-Centered Schools: The Need far Consensus Building," which elaborates
the multiplicity of thinking on this issue extant in the African-centered movement.

10 Readers should note that [have listed these as separate and distinct categories for analytical purposes, In practice, they intersect and overlap, continuously.

11 These letters and numbers represent codes I employed to distinguish among the interview
data and field notes I collected during the study.

References

Aaronsohn, L. (1992). Learning to teach for empowerment. *Radical Teacher 40*, 44-46.

African American Male Task Force. (1990). *Educating African American males: A dream deferred* (Report). Washington, DC: Author.

Amundson, R., Serlin, R. C., & Lehrer, R. (1992). On the threats that do not face educational research. *Educational Researcher, 21(9)*, 19-24.

Anderson, J. (1988). *The education of Blacks in the South, 1860-1935.* Chapel Hill, NC: University of North Carolina Press.

Apple, M. (1993). *Official knowledge.* New York: Routledge.

Apple, M., & Weiss, L (1983). *Ideology and practice in schooling.* Philadelphia: Temple University Press.

Argyris, C. (1980). *Inner contradictions of rigorous research.* New York: Academic.

Asante, M. K. (1991). The Afrocentric idea in education. *The Journal of Negro Education, 60*, 170-180.

Atkin, J. M. (1973). Practice-oriented inquiry: A third approach to research in education. *Educational Researcher, 2(7)*, 3-4.

Au, K., & Jordan, C. (1981). Teaching reading to Hawaiian children: Finding a culturally appropriate solution. In H. Trueba, G. Guthrie, & K. Au (Eds.), *Culture and the bilingual classroom: Studies in classroom ethnography (pp. 139-152).* Rowley, MA: Newbury.

Bacon, M. (1981, May). *High potential children from Ravenswood Elementary School District* (Follow-up study). Redwood City, CA: Sequoia Union High School District.

Banks, J. A. (1992). African American scholarship and the evolution of multicultural education. *The Journal of Negro Education, 61*, 273-286.

Bartolome, L. (1994). Beyond the methods fetish: Toward a humanizing pedagogy. *Harvard Educational Review, 64*, 173-194.

Becker, H. S. (1967). Whose side are we on? *Social Problems, 14*, 239-247.

Berliner, D. (1988, October). *Implications of studies of expertise in pedagogy for teacher education and evaluation. New directions for teacher assessment.* Conference proceedings of the ETS Invitational Conference. Princeton, NJ: Educational Testing Service.

Beyer, L. E (1991). Teacher education, reflective inquiry, and moral action. In B. R. Tabachnick & K. M. Zeichner (Eds.), *Inquiry-oriented practice teacher education* (pp. 112-129). London: Falmer.

Billingsley, A. (1992). *Climbing Jacob's ladder The enduring legacy of African American families.* New York: Simon & Schuster.

Bloom, B. (1956). *Taxonomy of educational objectives* (1st ed.). New York: Longman, Green.

Bloom, B. S., Davis, A., & Hess, R. (1965). *Compensatory education for cultural deprivation.* New York: Holt.

Bond, H. M. (1969). *A Negro education: A study in cotton and steel.* NY: Octagon.

Bourdieu, P. (1984). *Distinctions: The social critique of the judgment of taste,* Cambridge, MA: Harvard University Press.

Bowles, S. (1977). Unequal education and the reproduction of the social division of labor. In J. Karabel & A. H. Halsey (Eds.), *Power and ideology in education* (pp. 137-153) New York: Oxford University Press.

Brookover, W. (1985). Can we make schools *effective* for minority students? *The Journal of Negro Education, 54*, 257-268.

Brookover, W., Beady, C., Flood, P., Schweitzer, J., & Wisenbaker, J. (1979). *School social systems and student achievement: Schools can make a difference.* New York: Praeger.

Brophy, J., & Good, T. (1970), Teachers' communication of differential expectations for children's classroom performance. *Journal of Educational Psychology, 61,* 365-374.

Bullock, H. A. (1967). *A history of Negro education in the South from 1614 to the present.* Cambridge, MA: Harvard University Press.

Carr, W., & Kemmis, S. (1986). *Becoming critical, education, knowledge and action research (Rev. ed.).* Victoria, Australia: Deakin University Press.

Carter, K. (1993), The place of story in the study of teaching and teacher education. *Educational Researcher 22(1),* 5-12, 18.

Cazden, C., & Leggett, E. (1981). Culturally responsive education: Recommendations for achieving Lau remedies II. In H. Tateba, G. Guthrie, & K. Au (Eds.), *Culture and the bilingual classroom: Studies in classroom ethnography* (pp. 69-86). Rowley, MA: Newbury.

Clark, R. (1983). *Family and school achievement: Why poor Black children succeed or fail.* Chicago: Chicago University Press.

Clark, S. (1964, First Quarter). Literacy and liberation. *Freedomways,* pp. 113-124.

Clark, S., with Brown, C. (1990). *Ready from within: A first person narrative.* Trenton, NJ: Africa World Press.

Cochran-Smith, M., & Lytle, S. (1992). *Inside/outside: Teachers, research, and knowledge.* NY: Teachers College Press,

Code, L. (1991). *What can she know? Feminist theory and the construction of knowledge.* Ithaca, NY: Cornell University Press.

Cohen, E., & Benton, J. (1988, Fall). Making groupwork work. *American Educator,* pp. 10-17, 45-46.

Collins, P. H. (1991). *Black feminist thought.* New York: Routledge.

Comer, J. (1984). Home school relationships as they affect the academic success of children, *Education and Urban Society, 16,* 323-337.

Cose, E. (1993). *The rage of a privileged class.* New York: HarperCollins.

Cronbach, L. J. (1975). Beyond the two disciplines of scientific psychology. *American Psychologist, 30,* 116-127.

Cuban, L. (1989). The "at-risk" label and the problem of urban school reform. *Phi Delta Kappan, 70,* 264-271.

Delpit, L. (1992). Acquisition of literate discourse: Bowing before the master? *Theory into Practice, 31,* 296-271.

Edmonds, R. (1979). Effective schools for the urban poor. *Educational Leadership, 37,* 15-24.

Elliot, J. (1991). *Action research for educational change.* Philadelphia Open University Press.

Ellsworth, E. (1989). Why doesn't this feel empowering? Working through the repressive myths of critical pedagogy. *Harvard Educational Review, 59,* 297-324.

Erickson, F. (1987). Transformation and school success: The politics and culture of educational achievement. *Anthropology and Education, 18,* 335-356.

Erickson, F. (1993). Transformation and school success: The politics and culture of educational achievement. In E. Jacob & C. Jordan (Eds.), *Minority education: Anthropological perspectives* (pp. 27-51). Norwood, NJ: Ablex.

Erickson, F., & Mohatt, G. (1982). Cultural organization and participation structures in two classrooms of Indian students. In G. Spindler (Ed.), *Doing the ethnography of schooling* (pp, 131-174). New York: Holt, Rinehart & Winston.

Fine, M. (1986). Why urban adolescents drop into and out of high school. *Teachers College Record, 87,* 393-109.

Fordham, S. (1988). Racelessness as a factor in Black student's school success: Pragmatic strategy or pyrrhic victory? *Harvard Educational Review, 58,* 54-84.

Fordham, S., & Ogbu, J. (1986). Black students' school success: Coping with the burden of "acting white." *The Urban Review, 18,* 176-206.

Foster, H. L. (1986). *Ribbirti, jivin' and playin' the dozens.* Cambridge, MA: Ballinger.

Foster, M. (1991). Constancy, connectedness, and constraints in the *lives* of African American teachers. *National Women's Studies Journal, 3,* 233-261.

Freire, P. (1973), *Education for critical consciousness.* New York: Seabury.

Freire, P. (1974), *Pedagogy of the oppressed.* New York: Seabury.

Gage, N. L. (1989). The paradigm wars and their aftermath. *Educational Researcher, 18* (7), 4-10.

Gay, G., & Abrahamson, R. D. (1972). Talking black in the classroom. In R. D. Abrahamson & R. Troike (Eds.), *Language and cultural diversity in education* (pp.200-208). Englewood Cliffs, NJ: Prentice-Hall.

Gilligan, C. (1982). *In a different voice.* Cambridge, MA: Harvard University Press.

Giroux, H. (1983). *Theory and resistance: A pedagogy for the opposition.* Hadley, MA: Bergin & Garvey.

Giroux, H., & Simon, R. (1989). Popular culture and critical pedagogy: Everyday life as a basis for curriculum knowledge. In H. Giroux & P. McLaren (Eds.), *Critical pedagogy, the state, and cultural struggle* (pp. 236-252). Albany, NY: State University of New York Press.

Glaser, B. G., & Strauss, A, L. (1967). *The discovery of grounded theory: Strategies for qualitative research.* Chicago: Aldine.

Gouldner, A. (1970). *The coming crisis in western sociology.* New York: Basic.

Grant, C. A. (1989). Urban teachers: Their new colleagues and curriculum, *Phi Delta Kappan, 70,* 764-770.

Haberman, M. (1991a). The rationale for training adults as teachers. In C. E. Sleeter (Ed.), *Empowerment through multicultural education* (pp. 275-286). Albany, NY: State University of New York Press.

Haberman, M. (1991b). Can cultural awareness be taught in teacher education programs? *Teaching Education, 4,* 25-32.

Harding, V. (1981). *There is a river: The Black struggle for freedom in America.* Harcourt Brace Jovanovich.

Harris, V. (1992). African American conceptions of literacy, A historical perspective. *Theory into Practice, 31,* 276-286.

Hilliard, A. (1992). Behavioral style, culture, and teaching and learning. *The Journal of Negro Education, 61,* 370-377.

Hooks, B. (1989). *Talking back: Thinking feminist, thinking black.* Boston: South End Press.

Irvine, J. (1990). *Black students and school failure.* Westport, CT. Greenwood.

Johnson, C. (1936). The education of the Negro child. *American Sociological Review, 1,* 264-272.

Jordan, C. (1985). Translating culture, From ethnographic information to educational program. *Anthropology and Education Quarterly, 16,* 105-123.

Kaestle, C. 0993). The awful reputation of educational research. *Educational Researcher, 22* (1), 23, 26-31

Katzer, J., Cook, K, & Crouch, W. (1978). *Evaluating information.* Menlo Park, CA: Addison-Wesley.

King, J. (1991a). Unfinished business, Black student alienation and Black teachers' emancipatory pedagogy. In M. Foster (Ed.), *Readings on equal education* (Vol. 11, pp. 245-271). New York AMS.

King, J. (1991b). Dysconscious racism: Ideology, identity, and the miseducation of teachers. *The Journal of Negro Education, 60,* 133-146.

King, J., & Ladson-Billings, G. (1990). The teacher education challenge in elite university settings: Developing critical perspectives for teaching in a democratic and multicultural society. *European Journal Intercultural Studies*, 1, 15-30.

King, J., & Mitchell, C. A (1990). *Black mothers to sons: Juxtaposing African American literature with social practice*. New York: Peter Lang

Kleinfeld, J. (1992). Learning to think like a teacher: The study of cases. In J. Shulman (Ed.), *Case methods in teacher education* (pp. 33-49). New York, Teachers College Press.

Kuhn, T. S. (1970). *The origins of scientific revolutions*. Chicago: University of Chicago Press.

Labov, W. (1969). The logic of non-standard Negro English. In J. E. Alatis (Ed.), *Linguistics and the teaching of standard English* (Monograph Series on Language and Linguistics, No. 22). Washington, DC: Georgetown University Press.

Ladson-Billings, G. (1990). Like lightning in a bottle: Attempting to capture the pedagogical excellence of successful teachers of Black students. *International Journal of Qualitative Studies in Education*, 3, 335-344.

Ladson-Billings, G. (1992a). Liberatory consequences of literacy: A case of culturally relevant instruction for African American students. *The Journal of Negro Education*, 61, 378-391.

Ladson-Billings, G. (1992b). Reading between the lines and beyond the pages, A culturally relevant approach to literacy teaching. *Theory into Practice*, 31, 312-320.

Ladson-Billings, G (1994). *The dreamkeepers: Successful teaching for African American students*. San Francisco: Jossey-Bass.

Lather, P. (1986). Research as praxis. *Harvard Educational Review*, 56, 257-277.

Lee, C. (1994). African-centered pedagogy: Complexities and possibilities. In M. J. Shujaa (Ed.), *Too much schooling, too little education* (pp. 295-318). Trenton, NJ: Africa World Press.

Lipman, P. (1993). *The influence of restructuring on teachers' beliefs about and practices with African American students*. Unpublished doctoral dissertation, University of Wisconsin, Madison.

Lutz, F., & Ramsey, M. (1974). The use of anthropological field methods in education. *Educational Researcher*, 3 (10), 5-9.

McLaren, P. (1989). *Life in schools*. White Plains, NY: Longman.

Mohatt, G., & Erickson, F. (1981). Cultural differences in teaching styles in an Odawa school: A sociolinguistic approach. In H. Trueba, G. Guthrie, & K. Au (Eds.), *Culture and the bilingual classroom: Studies in classroom ethnography* (pp. 105-119). Rowley, MA: Newbury.

Morris, A. (1984). *The origins of the civil rights movement*. New York: The Free Press.

Murrell, P. (1990, April). *Cultural politics in teacher education: What's missing in the preparation of African American teachers?* Paper presented at the Annual Meeting of the American Educational Research Association, Boston.

Murrell, P. (1991, April). *Deconstructing informal knowledge of exemplary teaching in diverse urban communities: Apprenticing preservice teachers as case study researchers in cultural sites*. Paper presented at the Annual Meeting of the American Educational Research Association, Chicago.

Murrell, P. (1993). Afrocentric immersion: Academic and personal development of African American males in public schools. In T. Perry & J. Fraser (Eds.), *Freedom's plow: Teaching in the multicultural classroom* (pp. 231-259). New York: Routledge.

Narayan, K. (1993). How native is a "native" anthropologist? *American Anthropologist*, 95, 671-686.

Nelson, J. (1993). *Volunteer slavery*. Chicago: Noble.

Noddings, N (1984). *Caring*. Berkeley: University of California Press.

Noddings, N. (1991). Stories in dialogue: Caring and interpersonal reasoning. In C. Witherell & N. Noddings (Eds.), *Stories lives tell: Narrative and dialogue in education* (pp. 157-170). New York: Teachers College Press.

Noordhoff, K. (1990). Shaping the rhetoric of reflection for multicultural settings. In R. T. Cliff, W. R. Houston, & M.C. Pugach (Eds.), *Encouraging reflective practice in education* (pp. 163-185). New York: Teachers College Press.

Noordhoff, K., & Kleinfeld, J. (1991, April). *Preparing teachers for multicultural classrooms: A case study in rural Alaska.* Paper presented at the Annual Meeting of the American Educational Research Association, Chicago.

Ogbu, J. (1981). Black education: A cultural-ecological perspective. In H.P. McAdoo (Ed.), *Black families* (pp. 139-154). Beverly Hills: Sage.

Ogbu, J. (1983). Minority status and schooling in plural societies. *Comparative Education Review, 27*, 168-190.

Padilla, A. (1994). Ethnic minority scholars, research, and mentoring: Current and future issues. *Educational Researcher, 23* (4), 24-27.

Patton, M. Q. (1975). *Alternative evaluation research paradigm.* Grand Forks, ND: University of North Dakota Press.

Perry, T. 0993). *Toward a theory of African American school achievement* (Report No. 16). Wheelock College, Boston, MA: Center on Families, Communities, Schools, and Children's Learning.

Peterson, P., & Neumann, A. (Eds.). (1995). *Research and everyday life: The personal sources of educational inquiry.* New York, Teachers College Press.

Piestrup, A. (1973), *Black dialect interference and accommodation of reading instruction in first grade* (Monograph No. 4). Berkeley, Language Behavior Research Laboratory.

Popkewitz, T. S. (1991). *A political sociology of educational reform.* New York: Teachers College Press.

Ratteray, J. D. (1994). The search for access and content in the education of African Americans. In M. J. Shujaa (Ed.), *Too much schooling, too little education* (pp. 123-142). Trenton, NJ: Africa World Press.

Rist, R. (1970). Student social class and teacher expectations: The self-fulfilling prophecy in ghetto schools. *Harvard Educational Review, 40*, 411-450.

Rist, R. (1990). On the relations among educational research paradigms: From disdain to dètentes. In K. Dougherty & F. Hammack (Eds), *Education and society: A reader* (pp. 81-95). New York: Harcourt Brace Javanovich.

Robinson, R. (1993, February 25). P. C. Anderson students try hand at problem solving. *Dallas Examiner,* pp. 1, 8.

Rosaldo, R. (1989). *Culture and truth: The remaking of social analysis.* Boston: Beacon.

Rury, J. (1983). The New York African Free School, 1827-1836: Conflict over community control of Black education. *Phylon, 44*, 187, 198.

Shulman, L (1987). Knowledge and teaching: Foundations of the new reform. *Harvard Educational Review, 63*, 161-182.

Siddle-Walker, V. (1993). Caswell County Training School, 1933-1969: Relationships between community and school. *Harvard Educational Review, 63*, 161-182.

Singer, E. (1988). *What is cultural congruence, and why are they saying such terrible things about it?* (Occasional Paper). East Lansing, MI: Institute for Research on Teaching.

Slaughter, D., & Kuehne, V. (1988). Improving Black education: Perspectives on parent involvement. *Urban League Review, 11*, 59-75.

Slavin, R. (1987). Cooperative learning and the cooperative school. *Educational Leadership, 45*, 7-13.

Smith, L M. (1978). An evolving logic of participant observation, education ethnography, and other case studies. In L. Shulman (Ed.), *Review of research in education* (pp. 316-377). Itasca, IL: Peacock/AERA.

Spradley, J. (1979). *The ethnographic interview.* New York: Holt, Rinehart & Winston.

Staples, B. (1994). *Parallel time: Growing up in black and white.* New York: Pantheon.

Stenhouse, L (1983). The relevance of practice to theory. *Theory into Practice, 22,* 211-215.

Strike, K. (1993). Professionalism, democracy, and discursive communities, Normative reflections on restructuring. *American Educational Research Journal, 30,* 255-275.

Villegas, A. (1988). School failure and cultural mismatch: Another view. *The Urban Review, 20,* 253-265.

Vogt, L, Jordan, C., & Tharp, R. (1987). Explaining school failure, producing school success: Two cases. *Anthropology and Education Quarterly, 18,* 276-286.

Weiler, K. (1988). *Women teaching for change.* New York: Bergin & Garvey.

Weinberg, M. (1977). *A chance to learn: A history of race and education in the United States.* Cambridge, MA: Cambridge University Press.

Wilcox, K. (1982). Differential socialization in the classroom: Implications for equal opportunity. In G. Spindler (Ed.), *Doing the ethnography of schooling* (pp. 268-309). Prospect Heights, IL: Waveland.

Woodson, C. G. (1919). *The education of the Negro prior to 1861.* Washington, DC: Associated Publishers.

Young R. (1990). *A critical theory of education.* New York, Teachers College Press.

Zeichner, K. (1990). Preparing teachers for democratic schools. *Action in Teacher Education, 11,* 5-10

Zeichner, K. (1992). *Educating teachers for cultural diversity* (Special Report). East Lansing, MI: National Center for Research on Teacher Learning.

Introduction: Teaching to Transgress (p. 341) *and* Feminist Scholarship: Black Scholars (p. 349)

By bell hooks

Introduction

IN THE WEEKS before the English Department at Oberlin College was about to decide whether or not I would be granted tenure, I was haunted by dreams of running away—of disappearing—yes, even of dying. These dreams were not a response to fear that I would not be granted tenure. They were a response to the reality that I would be granted tenure. I was afraid that I would be trapped in the academy forever.

Instead of feeling elated when I received tenure, I fell into a deep, life-threatening depression. Since everyone around me believed that I should be relieved, thrilled, proud, I felt "guilty" about my "real" feelings and could not share them with anyone. The lecture circuit took me to sunny California and the New Age world of my sister's house in Laguna Beach where I was able to chill out for a month. When I shared my feelings with my sister (she's a therapist), she reassured me that they were entirely appropriate because, she said, "You never wanted to be a teacher. Since we were little, all you ever wanted to do was write." She was right. It was always assumed by everyone else that I would become a teacher. In the apartheid South, black girls from working-class backgrounds had three career choices. We could marry. We could work as maids. We could become school teachers. And since, according to the sexist thinking of the time, men did not really desire "smart" women, it was assumed that signs of intelligence sealed one's fate. From grade school on, I was destined to become a teacher.

But the dream of becoming a writer was always present within me. From childhood, I believed that I would teach and write. Writing would be the serious work, teaching would be the not-so-serious-I-need-to-make-a-living "job." Writing, I believed then, was all about private longing and personal glory, but teaching was about service, giving back to one's community. For black folks teaching—educating—was fundamentally political because it was rooted in antiracist struggle. Indeed, my all black grade schools became the location where I experienced learning as revolution.

Almost all our teachers at Booker T. Washington were black women. They were committed to nurturing intellect so that we could become scholars, thinkers, and cultural workers—black folks who used our "minds." We learned early that our devotion to learning, to a life of the mind, was a counter-hegemonic act, a fundamental way to resist every strategy of white racist colonization. Though they did not define or articulate these practices in theoretical terms, my teachers were enacting a revolutionary pedagogy of resistance that was profoundly anticolonial. Within these segregated schools, black children who were deemed exceptional, gifted, were given special care. Teachers worked with and for us to ensure that we would fulfill our intellectual destiny and by so doing uplift the race. My teachers were on a mission.

To fulfill that mission, my teachers made sure they "knew" us. They knew our parents, our economic status, where we worshipped, what our homes were like, and how we were treated in the family. I went to school at a historical moment where I was being taught by the same teachers who had taught my mother, her sisters, and brothers. My effort and ability to learn was always contextualized within the framework of generational family experience. Certain behaviors, gestures, habits of being were traced back.

Attending school then was sheer joy. I loved being a student. I loved learning. School was the place of ecstasy—pleasure and danger. To be changed by ideas was pure pleasure. But to learn ideas that ran counter to values and beliefs learned at home was to place oneself at risk, to enter the danger zone. Home was the place where I was forced to conform to someone else's image of who and what I should be. School was the place where I could forget that self and, through ideas, reinvent myself.

School changed utterly with racial integration. Gone was the messianic zeal to transform our minds and beings that had characterized teachers and their pedagogical practices in our all-black schools. Knowledge was suddenly about information only. It had no relation to how one lived, behaved. It was no longer connected to antiracist struggle. Bussed to white schools, we soon learned that obedience, and not a zealous will to learn, was what was expected of us. Too much eagerness to learn could easily be seen as a threat to white authority.

When we entered racist, desegregated, white schools we left a world where teachers believed that to educate black children rightly would require a political commitment. Now, we were mainly taught by white teachers whose lessons reinforced racist stereotypes.

For black children, education was no longer about the practice of freedom. Realizing this, I lost my love of school. The classroom was no longer a place of pleasure or ecstasy. School was still a political place, since we were always having to counter white racist assumptions that we were genetically inferior, never as capable as white peers, even unable to learn. Yet, the politics were no longer counter-hegemonic. We were always and only responding and reacting to white folks.

That shift from beloved, all-black schools to white schools where black students were always seen as interlopers, as not really belonging, taught me the difference between education as the practice of freedom and education that merely strives to reinforce domination. The rare white teacher who dared to resist, who would not allow racist biases to determine how we were taught, sustained the belief that learning at its most powerful could indeed liberate. A few black teachers had joined us in the desegregation process. And, although it was more difficult, they continued to nurture black students even as their efforts were constrained by the suspicion they were favoring their own race.

Despite intensely negative experiences, I graduated from school still believing that education was enabling, that it enhanced our capacity to be free. When I began undergraduate work at Stanford University, I was enthralled with the process of becoming an insurgent black intellectual. It surprised and shocked me to sit in classes where professors were not excited about teaching, where they did not seem to have a clue that education was about the practice of freedom. During college, the primary lesson was reinforced: we were to learn obedience to authority.

In graduate school the classroom became a place I hated, yet a place where I struggled to claim and maintain the right to be an independent thinker. The university and the classroom began to feel more like a prison, a place of punishment and confinement rather than a place of promise and possibility. I wrote my first book during those undergraduate years, even though it was not published until years later. I was writing; but more importantly I was preparing to become a teacher.

Accepting the teaching profession as my destiny, I was tormented by the classroom reality I had known both as an undergraduate and a graduate student. The vast majority of our professors lacked basic communication skills, they were not self-actualized, and they often used the classroom to enact rituals of control that were about domination and the unjust exercise of power. In these settings I learned a lot about the kind of teacher I did not want to become.

In graduate school I found that I was often bored in classes. The banking system of education (based on the assumption that memorizing information and regurgitating it represented gaining knowledge that could be deposited, stored and used at a later date) did not interest me. I wanted to become a critical thinker. Yet that longing was often seen as a threat to authority. Individual white male students who were seen as "exceptional," were often allowed to chart their intellectual journeys, but the rest of us (and particularly those from marginal groups) were always expected to conform. Nonconformity on our part was viewed with suspicion, as empty gestures of defiance aimed at masking inferiority or substandard work. In those days, those of us from marginal groups who were allowed to enter prestigious, predominantly white colleges were made to feel that we were there not to learn but to prove that we were the equal of whites. We were there to prove this by showing how well we could become clones of our peers. As we constantly confronted biases, an undercurrent of stress diminished our learning experience.

My reaction to this stress and to the ever-present boredom and apathy that pervaded my classes was to imagine ways that teaching and the learning experience could be different. When I discovered the work of the Brazilian thinker Paulo Freire, my first introduction to critical pedagogy, I found a mentor and a guide, someone who understood that learning could be liberatory. With his teachings and my growing understanding of the ways in which the education I had received in all-black Southern schools had been empowering, I began to develop a blueprint for my own pedagogical practice. Already deeply engaged with feminist thinking, I had no difficulty bringing that critique to Freire's work. Significantly, I felt that this mentor and guide, whom I had never seen in the flesh, would encourage and support my challenge to his ideas if he was truly committed to education as the practice of freedom. At the same time, I used his pedagogical paradigms to critique the limitations of feminist classrooms.

During my undergraduate and graduate school years, only white women professors were involved in developing Women's Studies programs. And even though I taught my first class as a graduate student on black women writers from a feminist perspective, it was in the context of a Black Studies program. At that time, I found, white women professors were not eager to nurture any interest in feminist thinking and scholarship on the part of black female students if that interest included critical challenge. Yet their lack of interest did not discourage me from involvement with feminist ideas or participation in the feminist classroom. Those classrooms were the one space where pedagogical practices were interrogated, where it was assumed that the knowledge offered students would empower them to be better scholars, to live more fully in the world beyond academe. The feminist classroom was the one space where students could raise critical questions about pedagogical process. These critiques were not always encouraged or well received, but they were allowed. That small acceptance of critical interrogation was a crucial challenge inviting us as students to think seriously about pedagogy in relation to the practice of freedom.

When I entered my first undergraduate classroom to teach, I relied on the example of those inspired black women teachers in my grade school, on Freire's work, and on feminist thinking about radical pedagogy. I longed passionately to teach differently from the way I had been taught since high school. The first paradigm that shaped my pedagogy was the idea that the classroom should be an exciting place, never boring. And if boredom should prevail, then pedagogical strategies were needed that would intervene, alter, even disrupt the atmosphere. Neither Freire's work nor feminist pedagogy examined the notion of pleasure in the classroom. The idea that learning should be exciting, sometimes even "fun," was the subject of critical discussion by educators writing about pedagogical practices in grade schools, and sometimes even high schools. But there seemed to be no interest among either traditional or radical educators in discussing the role of excitement in higher education.

Excitement in higher education was viewed as potentially disruptive of the atmosphere of seriousness assumed to be essential to the learning process. To enter classroom settings in colleges and universities with the will to share the desire to encourage excitement, was to transgress. Not only did it require movement beyond accepted boundaries, but excitement could not be generated without a full recognition of the fact that there could never be an absolute set agenda governing teaching practices. Agendas had to be flexible, had to allow for spontaneous shifts in direction. Students had to be seen in their particularity as individuals (I drew on the strategies my grade-school teachers used to get to know us) and interacted with according to their needs (here Freire was useful). Critical reflection on my experience as a student in unexciting classrooms enabled me not only to imagine that the classroom could be exciting but that this excitement could co-exist with and even stimulate serious intellectual and/or academic engagement.

But excitement about ideas was not sufficient to create an exciting learning process. As a classroom community, our capacity to generate excitement is deeply affected by our interest in one another, in hearing one another's voices, in recognizing one another's presence. Since the vast majority of students learn through conservative, traditional educational practices and concern themselves only with the presence of the professor, any radical pedagogy must insist that everyone's presence is acknowledged. That insistence cannot be simply stated. It has to be demonstrated through pedagogical practices. To begin, the professor must genuinely *value* everyone's presence. There must be an ongoing recognition that everyone influences the classroom dynamic, that everyone contributes. These contributions are resources. Used constructively they enhance the capacity of any class to create an open learning community. Often before this process can begin there has to be some deconstruction of the traditional notion that only the professor is responsible for classroom dynamics. That responsibility is relative to status. Indeed, the professor will always be more responsible because the larger institutional structures will always ensure that accountability for what happens in the classroom rests with the teacher. It is rare that any professor, no matter how eloquent a lecturer, can generate through his or her actions enough excitement to create an exciting classroom. Excitement is generated through collective effort.

Seeing the classroom always as a communal place enhances the likelihood of collective effort in creating and sustaining a learning community. One semester, I had a very difficult class, one that completely failed on the communal level. Throughout the term, I thought that the major drawback inhibiting the development of a learning community was that the class was scheduled in the early morning, before nine. Almost always between a third and a half of the class was not fully awake. This, coupled with the tensions of "differences," was impossible to overcome. Every now and then we had an exciting session, but mostly it was a dull class. I came to hate this class so much that I had a tremendous fear that I would not awaken to attend it; the night before (despite alarm clocks, wake-up calls, and the experiential knowledge that I had never forgotten to attend class) I still could not sleep. Rather than making me arrive sleepy, I tended to arrive wired, full of an energy few students mirrored.

Time was just one of the factors that prevented this class from becoming a learning community. For reasons I cannot explain it was also full of "resisting" students who did not want to learn new pedagogical processes, who did not want to be in a classroom that differed in any way from the norm. To these students, transgressing boundaries was frightening. And though they were not the majority, their spirit of rigid resistance seemed always to be more powerful than any will to intellectual openness and pleasure in learning. More than any other class I had taught, this one compelled me to abandon the sense that the professor could, by sheer strength of will and desire, make the classroom an exciting, learning community.

Before this class, I considered that *Teaching to Transgress: Education as the Practice of Freedom* would be a book of essays mostly directed to teachers. After the class ended, I began writing with the understanding that I was speaking to and with both students and professors. The scholarly field of writing on critical pedagogy and/or feminist pedagogy continues to be primarily a discourse engaged by white women and men. Freire, too, in conversation with me, as in much of his written work, has always acknowledged that he occupies the location of white maleness, particularly in this country. But the work of various thinkers on radical pedagogy (I use this term to include critical and/or feminist perspectives) has in recent years truly included a recognition of differences—those determined by class, race, sexual practice, nationality, and so on. Yet this movement forward does not seem to coincide with any significant increase in black or other nonwhite voices joining discussions about radical pedagogical practices.

My pedagogical practices have emerged from the mutually illuminating interplay of anticolonial, critical, and feminist pedagogies. This complex and unique blending of multiple perspectives has been an engaging and powerful standpoint from which to work. Expanding beyond boundaries, it has made it possible for me to imagine and enact pedagogical practices that engage directly both the concern for interrogating biases in curricula that reinscribe systems of domination (such as racism and sexism) while simultaneously providing new ways to teach diverse groups of students.

In this book I want to share insights, strategies, and critical reflections on pedagogical practice. I intend these essays to be an intervention—countering the devaluation of teaching even as they address the urgent need for changes in teaching practices. They are meant to serve as constructive commentary. Hopeful and exuberant, they convey the pleasure and joy I experience teaching; these essays are celebratory! To emphasize that the pleasure of teaching is an act of resistance countering the overwhelming boredom, uninterest, and apathy that so often characterize the way professors and students feel about teaching and learning, about the classroom experience.

Each essay addresses common themes that surface again and again in discussions of pedagogy, offering ways to rethink teaching practices and constructive strategies to enhance learning. Written separately for a variety of contexts there is unavoidably some degree of overlap; ideas are repeated, key phrases used again and again. Even though I share strategies, these works do not offer blueprints for ways to make the classroom an exciting place for learning. To do so would undermine the insistence that engaged pedagogy recognize each classroom as different, that strategies must constantly be changed, invented, reconceptualized to address each new teaching experience

Teaching is a performative act. And it is that aspect of our work that offers the space for change, invention, spontaneous shifts, that can serve as a catalyst drawing out the unique elements in each classroom. To embrace the performative aspect of teaching we are compelled to engage "audiences," to consider issues of reciprocity. Teachers are not performers in the traditional sense of the word in that our work is not meant to be a spectacle. Yet it is meant to serve as a catalyst that calls everyone to become more and more engaged, to become active participants in learning.

Just as the way we perform changes, so should our sense of "voice." In our everyday lives we speak differently to diverse audiences. We communicate best by choosing that way of speaking that is inform ed by the particularity and uniqueness of whom we are speaking to and with. In keeping with this spirit, these essays do not all sound alike. They reflect my effort to use language in ways that speak to specific contexts, as well as my desire to communicate with a diverse audience. To teach in varied communities not only our paradigms must shift but also the way we think, write, speak. The engaged voice must never be fixed and absolute but always changing, always evolving in dialogue with a world beyond itself.

These essays reflect my experience of critical discussions with teachers, students, and individuals who have entered my classes to observe. Multilayered, then, these essays are meant to stand as testimony, bearing witness to education as the practice of freedom. Long before a public ever recognized me as a thinker or writer, I was recognized in the classroom by students—seen by them as a teacher who worked hard to create a dynamic learning experience for all of us. Nowadays, I am recognized more for insurgent intellectual practice. Indeed, the academic public that I encounter at my lectures always shows surprise when I speak intimately and deeply about the classroom. That public seemed particularly surprised when I said that I was working on a collection of essays about teaching. This surprise is a sad reminder of the way teaching is seen as a duller, less valuable aspect of the academic profession. This perspective on teaching is a common one. Yet it must be challenged if we are to meet the needs of our students, if we are to restore to education and the classroom excitement about ideas and the will to learn.

There is a serious crisis in education. Students often do not want to learn and teachers do not want to teach. More than ever before in the recent history of this nation, educators are compelled to confront the biases that have shaped teaching practices in our society and to create new ways of knowing, different strategies for the sharing of knowledge. We cannot address this crisis if progressive critical thinkers and social critics act as though teaching is not a subject worthy of our regard.

The classroom remains the most radical space of possibility in the academy. For years it has been a place where education has been undermined by teachers and students alike who seek to use it as a platform for opportunistic concerns rather than as a place to learn. With these essays, I add my voice to the collective call for renewal and rejuvenation in our teaching practices. Urging all of us to open our minds and hearts so that we can know beyond the boundaries of what is acceptable, so that we can think and rethink, so that we can create new visions, I celebrate teaching that enables transgressions—a movement against and beyond boundaries. It is that movement which makes education the practice of freedom.

Feminist Scholarship: Black Scholars

MORE THAN TWENTY years have passed since I wrote my first feminist book, *Ain't I a Woman: Black Women and Feminism*. Like many precocious girls growing up in a male-dominated household, I understood the significance of gender inequality at an early age. Our daily life was full of patriarchal drama—the use of coercion, violent punishment, verbal harassment, to maintain male domination. As small children we understood that our father was more important than our mother because he was a man. This knowledge was reinforced by the reality that any decision our mother made could be overruled by our dad's authority. Since we were raised during racial segregation, we lived in an all-black neighborhood, went to black schools, attended a black church. Black males held more power and authority than black females in all these institutions. It was only when I entered college that I learned that black males had supposedly been "emasculated," that the trauma of slavery was primarily that it had stripped black men of their right to male privilege and power, that it had prevented them from fully actualizing "masculinity." Narratives of castrated black men, humble Stepin Fetchits who followed white men as though they were little pets, was to my mind the stuff of white fantasy, of racist imagination. In the real world of my growing up I had seen black males in positions of patriarchal authority, exercising forms of male power, supporting institutionalized sexism.

Given this experiential reality, when I attended a predominantly white university, I was shocked to read scholarly work on black life from various disciplines like sociology and psychology written from a critical standpoint which assumed no gender distinctions characterized black social relations. Engaged in my undergraduate years with emergent feminist movement, I took Women's Studies classes the moment they were offered. Yet, I was again surprised by the overwhelming ignorance about black experience. I was disturbed that the white female professors and students were ignorant of gender differences in black life—that they talked about the status and experiences of "women" when they were only referring to white women. That surprise changed to anger. I found my efforts ignored when I attempted to share information and knowledge about how, despite racism, black gender relations were constructed to maintain black male authority even if they did not mirror white paradigms, or about the way white female identity and status was different from that of black women.

In search of scholarly material to document the evidence of my lived experience, I was stunned by either the complete lack of any focus on gender difference in black life or the tacit assumption that because many black females worked outside the home, gender roles were inverted. Scholars usually talked about black experience when they were really speaking solely about black male experience. Significantly, I found that when "women" were talked about, the experience of white women was universalized to stand for all female experience and that when "black people" were talked about, the experience of black men was the point of reference. Frustrated, I begin to interrogate the ways in which racist and sexist biases shaped and informed all scholarship dealing with black experience, with female experience. It was clear that these biases had created a circumstance where there was little or no information about the distinct experiences of black women. It was this critical gap that motivated me to research and write *Ain't I a Woman*. It was published years later, after publishers of feminist work accepted that "race" was both an appropriate and marketable subject within the field of feminist scholarship. This acceptance came only when white women began to show an interest in issues of race and gender.

When contemporary feminist movement first began, feminist writings and scholarship by black women was groundbreaking. The writings of black women like Cellestine Ware, Toni Cade Bambara, Michele Wallace, Barbara Smith, and Angela Davis, to name a few, were all works that sought to articulate, define, speak to and against the glaring omissions in feminist work, the erasure of black female presence. During these early years, white women were zealously encouraging the growth and development of feminist scholarship that specifically addressed their reality, the recovery of buried white women's history, documentary evidence that would demonstrate the myriad ways gender differences were socially constructed, the institutionalization of inequality. Yet there was no concurrent collective zeal to create a body of feminist scholarship that would address the specific realities of black women. Again and again black female activists, scholars, and writers found ourselves isolated within feminist movement and often the targets of misguided white women who were threatened by all attempts to deconstruct the category "woman" or to bring a discourse on race into feminist scholarship. In those days, I imagined that my work and that of other black women would serve as a catalyst generating greater engagement by black people, and certainly black females, in the production of feminist scholarship. But that was not the case. For the most part, black folks, along with many white women, were suspicious of black women who were committed to feminist politics.

Black discourse on feminism was often confined to endless debates about whether or not black women should involve ourselves in "white feminist" movement. Were we black or women first? The few black women academics who were seeking to make critical interventions in the development of feminist theory were compelled to first "prove" to white feminists that we were on target when we called attention to racist biases that distorted feminist scholarship, that failed to consider the realities of women who were not white or from privileged classes. Though this strategy was necessary for us to gain a hearing, an audience, it meant that we were not concentrating our energies on creating a climate where we could focus intensively on creating a body of scholarship that would look at black experience from a feminist standpoint. By focusing so much attention on racism within feminist movement, or proving to black audiences that a system of gender inequality permeated black life, we did not always direct our energies towards inviting other black folks to see feminist thinking as a standpoint that could illuminate and enhance our intellectual understanding of black experience. It seemed that individual black women active in feminist politics were often caught between a rock and a hard place. The vast majority of white feminists did not welcome our questioning of feminist paradigms that they were seeking to institutionalize; so too, many black people simply saw our involvement with feminist politics as a gesture of betrayal, and dismissed our work.

Despite the racism we confronted within feminist circles, black women who embraced feminist thinking and practice remained committed and engaged because we experienced new forms of self-improvement. We understood and understand now how much a critique of sexism and organized efforts to affirm feminist politics in black communities could be liberatory for women and men. Black women thinkers and writers like Michele Wallace and Ntozake Shange, who initially had huge black audiences responding to the emphasis in their work on sexism, on gender differences in black life, faced hostile black audiences who were not willing to dialogue. Many black female writers witnessing the black public's response to their work were fearful that engagement with feminist thinking would forever alienate them from black communities. Responding to the idea that black women should become involved with feminist movement, many black people insisted that we were already "free," that the sign of our freedom was that we worked outside the home. Of course, this line of thinking completely ignores issues of sexism and male domination. Since the ruling rhetoric at the time insisted on the complete "victimization" of black men within white supremacist patriarchy, few black folks were willing to engage that dimension of feminist thought that insisted that sexism and institutionalized patriarchy indeed provide black men with forms of power, however relative, that remained intact despite racist oppression. In such a cultural climate, black women interested in creating feminist theory and scholarship wisely focused their attention on those progressive folks, white women among them, who were open to interrogating critically issues of gender in black life from a feminist standpoint.

Significantly, as feminist movement progressed, black women and women of color who dared to challenge the universalization of the category "woman" created a revolution in feminist scholarship. Many white women who had previously resisted rethinking the ways feminist scholars talked about the status of women now responded to critiques and worked to create a critical climate where we could talk about gender in a more complex way, and where we could acknowledge differences in female status that were overdetermined by race and class. Ironically, this major intervention did not serve as a catalyst compelling more black women to do feminist work. Currently, many more white women than black women do scholarship from a feminist standpoint that includes race. This is so because many academic black women remain ambivalent about feminist politics and the feminist standpoints. In her essay, "Toward a Phenomenology of Feminist Consciousness," Sandra Bartky makes the point that "to be a feminist, one has first to become one." She reminds us that just thinking about gender or lamenting the female condition "need not be an expression of feminist consciousness." Indeed, many black women academics chose to focus attention on gender even as they very deliberately disavowed engagement with feminist thinking. Uncertain about whether feminist movement would really change the lives of black females in a meaningful way, they were not willing to assume and assert a feminist standpoint.

Another factor that restricted black female participation in the production of feminist scholarship was and is the lack of institutional rewards. While many academic white women active in feminist movement became a part of a network of folks who shared resources, publications, jobs and so on, black females were often out of this loop. This was especially the case for individual black women creating feminist scholarship that was not well received. In the early stages of my work, white women scholars were often threatened by its focus on race and racism. Far from being rewarded or valued (as is the case now), in those days I was perceived as a threat to feminism. It was even more threatening when I dared to speak from a feminist standpoint on issues other than race. Overall, black female scholars, already seriously marginalized by the institutionalized racism and sexism of the academy, have never been fully convinced that it is advantageous for them to declare publicly a commitment to feminist politics, either for reasons of career mobility or personal well-being. Many of us have relied on networks with black male scholars to help further our careers. Some of us have felt and still feel that claiming a feminist standpoint will alienate these allies.

Despite many factors that have discouraged black women from producing feminist scholarship, the system of rewards for such work has recently expanded. Work in feminist theory is seen as academically legitimate. More black women scholars than ever before are doing work that looks at gender. Gradually, more of us are doing feminist scholarship. Literary criticism has been the location that has most allowed black female academics to claim a feminist voice. Much feminist literary criticism responded to the work of black women fiction writers which exposed forms of gender exploitation and oppression in black life; this literature was receiving unprecedented attention, and speaking critically about it was not a risky act. These works spoke to feminist concerns. Black women writing about such concerns could address them, often without having to claim a feminist standpoint. More than any nonfiction feminist writing by black women, fiction by writers like Alice Walker and Ntozake Shange served as a catalyst, stimulating fierce critical debate in diverse black communities about gender, about feminism. At that time, nonfiction feminist writing was most often ignored by black audiences. (Michele Wallace's *Black Macho and the Myth of the Superwoman* was a unique exception.) White women academics were usually accepting of black females doing literary criticism that focused on gender or made reference to feminism, but they still saw the realm of feminist theory as their critical domain. Not surprisingly, work by black literary critics received attention and at times acclaim. Black women scholars like Hazel Carby, Hortense Spillers, Beverly Guy-Sheftall, Valerie Smith, and Mae Henderson used a feminist standpoint in the production of literary scholarship.

Despite a burgeoning body of literary criticism by black women from a feminist standpoint, more often than not black women academics focused attention on issues of gender without specifically placing their work within a feminist context. Historians like Rosalyn Terborg Penn, Deborah White, and Paula Giddings chose critical projects that were aimed at restoring buried knowledge of black female experience. Their work—and that of many other black female historians—has expanded and continues to expand our understanding of the gendered nature of black experience, even though it does not overtly insist on a relationship to feminist thinking. A similar pattern developed in other disciplines. What this means is that we have an incredible work built around the issue of gender-enhancing feminist scholarship without explicitly naming itself as feminist.

Clearly, contemporary feminist movement created the necessary cultural frame-work for an academic legitimation of gender-based scholarship: the hope was that this work would always emerge from a feminist standpoint. Conversely, work on gender that does not emerge from such a standpoint situates itself in an ambivalent, even problem-atic, relationship to feminism. A good example of such a work is Deborah White's *Ar'n't I a Woman*. Published after *Ain't I a Woman*, this work, whether intentionally or not, mirrored my work's concern with re-thinking the position of black women in slavery. (White makes no reference to my work—a fact which is only important because it coin-cides with the absence of any mention of feminist politics.) Indeed, one can read White's work as a corrective to interdisciplinary nontraditional academic work that frames the study of women within a feminist context. She presents her work as politically neutral scholarship. Yet, the absence of feminist standpoint or references pointedly acts to dele-gitimize and invalidate such work even as it appropriates the issues and the audience feminist movement and feminist scholarship creates. Given that so little solid academic factual work is done to document our history, White's work is a crucial contribution even though it exposes the ambiguous relationship many black women scholars have to feminist thought.

When that ambiguity converged with the blatant antifeminism characteristic of many black male thinkers, there was no positive climate for black scholars collectively to embrace and support sustained production of feminist work. Even though individual black scholars still choose to do this work, and more recent graduate students dare to place their work in a feminist context, the lack of collective support has resulted in a failure to create the very education for critical consciousness that would teach unknow-ing black folks why it is important to examine black life from a feminist standpoint. The current antifeminist backlash in the culture as a whole undermines support for feminist scholarship. Since black feminist scholarship has always been marginalized in the academy, marginal to the existing academic hegemony as well as to the feminist mainstream, those of us who believe such work is crucial to any unbiased discussion of black experience must intensify our efforts to educate for critical consciousness. Those black women scholars who began working on gender issues while still ambivalent about feminist politics and who have now grown in both their awareness and commitment must be willing to discuss publicly the shifts in their thinking.

Toward a Critical Race Theory of Education

Gloria Ladson-Billings and William F. Tate IV

The presentation of truth in new forms provokes resistance, confounding those committed to accepted measures for determining the quality and validity of statements made and conclusions reached, and making it difficult for them to respond and adjudge what is acceptable.

—DERRICK BELL, *FACES AT THE BOTTOM OF THE WELL*

I am not included within the pale of this glorious anniversary! Your high independence only reveals the immeasurable distance between us. The blessings in which you this day, rejoice, are not enjoyed in common. The rich inheritance of justice, liberty, prosperity and independence bequeathed by your fathers, not by me . . .

—FREDERICK DOUGLASS, *MY BONDAGE AND MY FREEDOM*

IN 1991 SOCIAL activist and education critic Jonathan Kozol delineated the great inequities that exist between the schooling experiences of white middle-class students and those of poor African American and Latino students. And, while Kozol's graphic descriptions may prompt some to question how it is possible that we allow these "savage inequalities," this article suggests that these inequalities are a logical and predictable result of a racialized society in which discussions of race and racism continue to be muted and marginalized.[1]

In this article we attempt to theorize race and use it as an analytic tool for understanding school inequity.[2] We begin with a set of propositions about race and property and their intersections. We situate our discussion in an explication of critical race theory and attempt to move beyond the boundaries of the educational research literature to include arguments and new perspectives from law and the social sciences. In doing so, we acknowledge and are indebted to a number of scholars whose work crosses disciplinary boundaries.[3] We conclude by exploring the tensions between our conceptualization of a critical race theory in education and the educational reform movement identified as multicultural education.

UNDERSTANDING RACE AND PROPERTY

Our discussion of social inequity in general, and school inequity in particular, is based on three central propositions:[4]

1. Race continues to be a significant factor in determining inequity in the United States.

2. U.S. society is based on property rights.

3. The intersection of race and property creates an analytic tool through which we can understand social (and, consequently, school) inequity.

In this section we expand on these propositions and provide supporting "meta-propositions" to make clear our line of reasoning and relevant application to educational or school settings.

RACE AS FACTOR IN INEQUITY

The first proposition—that race continues to be a significant factor in determining inequity in the United States—is easily documented in the statistical and demographic data. Hacker's look at educational and life chances such as high school dropout rates, suspension rates, and incarceration rates echoes earlier statistics of the Children's Defense Fund.[5] However, in what we now call the postmodern era, some scholars question the usefulness of race as a category.

Omi and Winant argue that popular notions of race as either an ideological construct or an objective condition have epistemological limitations.[6] Thinking of race strictly as an ideological construct denies the reality of a racialized society and its impact on "raced" people in their everyday lives. On the other hand, thinking of race solely as an objective condition denies the problematic aspects of race—how do we decide who fits into which racial classifications? How do we categorize racial mixtures? Indeed, the world of biology has found the concept of race virtually useless. Geneticist Cavalli-Sforza asserts that "human populations are sometimes known as ethnic groups, or 'races.' . . . They are hard to define in a way that is both rigorous and useful because human beings group themselves in a bewildering array of sets, some of them overlapping, all of them in a state of flux."[7]

Nonetheless, even when the concept of race fails to "make sense," we continue to employ it. According to Nobel Laureate Toni Morrison:

> Race has become metaphorical—a way of referring to and disguising forces, events, classes, and expressions of social decay and economic division far more threatening to the body politic than biological "race" ever was.

> Expensively kept, economically unsound, a spurious and useless political asset in election campaigns, racism is as healthy today as it was during the Enlightenment. It seems that is has a utility far beyond economy, beyond the sequestering of classes from one another, and has assumed a metaphorical life so completely embedded in daily discourse that it is perhaps more necessary and more on display than ever before.[8]

Despite the problematic nature of race, we offer as a first meta-proposition that race, unlike gender and class, remains untheorized.[9] Over the past few decades theoretical and epistemological considerations of gender have proliferated.[10] Though the field continues to struggle for legitimacy in academe, interest in and publications about feminist theories abound. At the same time, Marxist and Neo-Marxist formulations about class continue to merit consideration as theoretical models for understanding social inequity.[11] We recognize the importance of both gender- and class-based analyses while at the same time pointing to their shortcomings vis-a-vis race. Roediger points out that "the main body of writing by White Marxists in the United States has both 'naturalized' whiteness and oversimplified race."[12]

Omi and Winant have done significant work in providing a sociological explanation of race in the United States. They argue that the paradigms of race have been conflated with notions of ethnicity, class, and nation because

> theories of race—of its meaning, its transformations, the significance of racial events—have never been a top priority in social science. In the U.S., although the "founding fathers" of American sociology . . . were explicitly concerned with the state of domestic race relations, racial theory remained one of the least developed fields of sociological inquiry.[13]

To mount a viable challenge to the dominant paradigm of ethnicity (i.e., we are all ethnic and, consequently, must assimilate and rise socially the same way European Americans have), Omi and Winant offer a racial formation theory that they define as "the sociohistorical process by which racial categories are created, inhabited, transformed and destroyed. . . [It] is a process of historically situated *projects* in which human bodies and social structures are represented and organized." Further, they link "racial formation to the evolution of hegemony, the way in which society is organized and ruled." Their analysis suggests that "race is a matter of both social structure and cultural representation."[14]

By arguing that race remains untheorized, we are not suggesting that other scholars have not looked carefully at race as a powerful tool for explaining social inequity, but that the intellectual salience of this theorizing has not been systematically employed in the analysis of educational inequality. Thus, like Omi and Winant, we are attempting to uncover or decipher the social-structural and cultural significance of race in education. Our work owes an intellectual debt to both Carter G. Woodson and W. E. B. Du Bois, who, although marginalized by the mainstream academic community, used race as a theoretical lens for assessing social inequity.[15]

Both Woodson and Du Bois presented cogent arguments for considering race as *the* central construct for understanding inequality. In many ways our work is an attempt to build on the foundation laid by these scholars:[16] Briefly, Woodson, as far back as 1916, began to establish the legitimacy of race (and, in particular, African Americans) as a subject of scholarly inquiry.[17] As founder of the Association for the Study of Negro Life and History and editor of its *Journal of Negro History,* Woodson revolutionized the thinking about African Americans from that of pathology and inferiority to a multitextured analysis of the uniqueness of African Americans and their situation in the United States. His most notable publication, *The Miseducation of the Negro,* identified the school's role in structuring inequality and demotivating African-American students:

> The same educational process which inspires and stimulates the oppressor with the thought that he is everything and has accomplished everything worthwhile, depresses and crushes at the same time the spark of genius in the Negro by making him feel that his race does not amount to much and never will measure up to the standards of other peoples.[18]

Du Bois, perhaps better known among mainstream scholars, profoundly impacted the thinking of many identified as "other" by naming a "double consciousness" felt by African Americans. According to Du Bois, the African American "ever feels his two-ness—an American, A Negro; two souls, two thoughts, two unreconciled strivings.[19] In a current biography of Du Bois, Lewis details the intellectual impact of this concept:

> It was a revolutionary concept. It was not just revolutionary; the concept of the divided self was profoundly mystical, for Du Bois invested this double consciousness with a capacity to see incomparably further and deeper. The African-American—seventh son after the Egyptian and Indian, the Greek and Roman, the Teuton and Mongolian—possessed the gift of "second sight in this American world," an intuitive faculty (prelogical, in a sense) enabling him/her to see and say things about American society that possessed a heightened moral validity. Because he dwelt equally in the mind and heart

of his oppressor as in his own beset psyche, the African American embraced a vision of the commonweal at its best.[20]

As a prophetic foreshadowing of the centrality of race in U.S. society, Du Bois reminded us that "the problem of the twentieth century is the problem of the color line."[21]

The second meta-proposition that we use to support the proposition that race continues to be significant in explaining inequity in the United States is that class- and gender-based explanations are not powerful enough to explain all of the difference (or variance) in school experience and performance. Although both class and gender can and do intersect race, as stand-alone variables they do not explain all of the educational achievement differences apparent between whites and students of color. Indeed, there is some evidence to suggest that even when we hold constant for class, middle-class African-American students do not achieve at the same level as their white counterparts.[22] Although Oakes reports that "in academic tracking, . . . poor and minority students are most likely to be placed at the lowest levels of the school's sorting system,"[23] we are less clear as to which factor—race or class—is causal. Perhaps the larger question of the impact of race on social class is the more relevant one. Space limitations do not permit us to examine that question.

Issues of gender bias also figure in inequitable schooling.[24] Females receive less attention from teachers, are counseled away from or out of advanced mathematics and science courses, and although they receive better grades than their male counterparts, their grades do not translate into advantages in college admission and/or the workplace.[25]

But examination of class and gender, taken alone or together, do not account for the extraordinarily high rates of school dropout, suspension, explusion, and failure among African-American and Latino males.[26] In the case of suspension, Majors and Billson argue that many African-American males are suspended or expelled from school for what they termed "non-contact violations"—wearing banned items of clothing such as hats and jackets, or wearing these items in an "unauthorized" manner, such as backwards or inside out.[27]

The point we strive to make with this meta-proposition is not that class and gender are insignificant, but rather, as West suggests, that "race matters," and, as Smith insists, "blackness matters in more detailed ways.[28]

THE PROPERTY ISSUE

Our second proposition, that U.S. society is based on property rights, is best explicated by examining legal scholarship and interpretations of rights. To develop this proposition it is important to situate it in the context of critical race theory. Monaghan reports that "critical race legal scholarship developed in the 1970s, in part because minority scholars thought they were being overlooked in critical legal studies, a better-known movement that examines the way law encodes cultural norms."[29] However, Delgado argues that despite the diversity contained within the critical race movement, there are some shared features:

an assumption that racism is not a series of isolated acts, but is endemic in American life, deeply ingrained legally, culturally, and even psychologically;

a call for a reinterpretation of civil-rights law "in light of its ineffectuality, showing that laws to remedy racial injustices are often undermined before they can fulfill their promise";

a challenge to the "traditional claims of legal neutrality, objectivity, color-blindness, and meritocracy as camouflages for the self-interest of dominant groups in American society";

an insistence on subjectivity and the reformulation of legal doctrine to reflect the perspectives of those who have experienced and been victimized by racism firsthand;

the use of stories or first-person accounts.[30]

In our analysis we add another aspect to this critical paradigm that disentangles democracy and capitalism. Many discussions of democracy conflate it with capitalism despite the fact that it is possible to have a democratic government with an economic system other than capitalism. Discussing the two ideologies as if they were one masks the pernicious effects of capitalism on those who are relegated to its lowest ranks. Traditional civil rights approaches to solving inequality have depended on the "rightness" of democracy while ignoring the structural inequality of capitalism.[31] However, democracy in the U.S. context was built on capitalism.

In the early years of the republic *only* capitalists enjoyed the franchise. Two hundred years later when civil rights leaders of the 1950s and 1960s built their pleas for social justice on an appeal to the civil and human rights, they were ignoring the fact that the society was based on *property rights*.[32] An example from the 1600s undescores the centrality of property in the Americas from the beginning of European settlement:

> When the Pilgrims came to New England they too were coming not to vacant land but to territory inhabited by tribes of Indians. The governor of the Massachusetts Bay Colony, John Winthrop, created the excuse to take Indian land by declaring the area legally a "vacuum." The Indians, he said, had not "subdued" the land, and therefore had only a "natural" right to it, but not a "civil right." A "natural right" did not have legal standing.[33]

Bell examined the events leading up to the Constitution's development and concluded that there exists a tension between property rights and human rights.[34] This tension was greatly exacerbated by the presence of African peoples as slaves in America. The purpose of the government was to protect the main object of society—property. The slave status of most African Americans (as well as women and children) resulted in their being objectified as property. And, a government constructed to protect the rights of property owners lacked the incentive to secure human rights for the African American.[35]

According to Bell "the concept of individual rights, unconnected to property rights, was totally foreign to these men of property; and thus, despite two decades of civil rights gains, most Blacks remain disadvantaged and deprived because of their race.[36]

The grand narrative of U.S. history is replete with tensions and struggles over property—in its various forms. From the removal of Indians (and later Japanese Americans) from the land, to military conquest of the Mexicans,[37] to the construction of Africans as property,[38] the ability to define, possess, and own property has been a central feature of power in America. We do not suggest that other nations have not fought over and defined themselves by property and landownership.[39] However, the contradiction of a reified symbolic individual juxtaposed to the reality of "real estate" means that emphasis on the centrality of property can be disguised. Thus, we talk about the importance of the individual, individual rights, and civil rights while social benefits accrue largely to property owners.[40]

Property relates to education in explicit and implicit ways. Recurring discussions about property tax relief indicate that more affluent communities (which have higher property values, hence higher tax assessments) resent paying for a public school system whose clientele is largely nonwhite and poor.[41] In the simplest of equations, those with "better" property are entitled to "better" schools. Kozol illustrates the disparities: "Average expenditures per pupil in the city of New York in 1987 were some $5,500. In the highest spending suburbs of New York (Great Neck or Manhasset, for example, on Long Island) funding levels rose above $11,000, with the highest districts in the state at $15,000."[42]

But the property differences manifest themselves in other ways. For example, curriculum represents a form of "intellectual property."[43] The quality and quantity of the curriculum varies with the "property values" of the school. The use of a critical race story[44] appropriately represents this notion:

> The teenage son of one of the authors of this article was preparing to attend high school. A friend had a youngster of similar age who also was preparing to enter high school. The boys excitedly poured over course offerings in their respective schools' catalogues. One boy was planning on attending school in an upper-middle-class white community. The other would be attending school in an urban, largely African-American district. The difference between the course offerings as specified in the catalogues was striking. The boy attending the white, middle-class school had his choice of many foreign languages—Spanish, French, German, Latin, Greek, Italian, Chinese, and Japanese. His mathematics offerings included algebra, geometry, trigonometry, calculus, statistics, general math, and business math. The science department at this school offered biology, chemistry, physics,

geology, science in society, biochemistry, and general science. The other boy's curriculum choices were not nearly as broad. His foreign language choices were Spanish and French. His mathematics choices were general math, business math, and algebra (there were no geometry or trig classes offered). His science choices were general science, life science, biology, and physical science. The differences in electives were even more pronounced, with the affluent school offering courses such as Film as Literature, Asian Studies, computer programming, and journalism. Very few elective courses were offered at the African American school, which had no band, orchestra, or school newspaper.

The availability of "rich" (or enriched) intellectual property delimits what is now called "opportunity to learn"[45]—the presumption that along with providing educational "standards"[46] that detail what students should know and be able to do, they must have the material resources that support their learning. Thus, intellectual property must be undergirded by "real" property, that is, science labs, computers and other state-of-the-art technologies, appropriately certified and prepared teachers. Of course, Kozol demonstrated that schools that serve poor students of color are unlikely to have access to these resources and, consequently, students will have little or no opportunity to learn despite the attempt to mandate educational standards.[47]

CRITICAL RACE THEORY AND EDUCATION

With this notion of property rights as a defining feature of the society, we proceed to describe the ways that the features of critical race theory mentioned in the previous section can be applied to our understanding of educational inequity.

Racism as Endemic and Deeply Ingrained in American Life
If racism were merely isolated, unrelated, individual acts, we would expect to see at least a few examples of educational excellence and equity together in the nation's public schools. Instead, those places where African Americans do experience educational success tend to be outside of the public schools.[48] While some might argue that poor children, regardless of race, do worse in school, and that the high proportion of African-American poor contributes to their dismal school performance, we argue that the cause of their poverty in conjunction with the condition of their schools and schooling is institutional and structural racism. Thus, when we speak of racism we refer to Wellman's definition of "culturally sanctioned beliefs which, regardless of the intentions involved, defend the advantages Whites have because of the subordinated positions of racial minorities." We must therefore contend with the "problem facing White people [of coming] to grips with the demands made by Blacks and Whites while at the same time *avoiding* the possibility of institutional change and reorganization that might affect them.[49]

A Reinterpretation of Ineffective Civil Rights Law

In the case of education, the civil rights decision that best exemplifies our position is the landmark *Brown v. Board of Education of Topeka, Kansas.* While having the utmost respect for the work of Thurgood Marshall and the National Association for the Advancement of Colored People (NAACP) legal defense team in arguing the *Brown* decision, with forty years of hindsight we recognize some serious shortcomings in that strategy. Today, students of color are more segregated than ever before.[50] Although African Americans represent 12 percent of the national population, they are the majority in twenty-one of the twenty-two largest (urban) school districts.[51] Instead of providing more and better educational opportunities, school desegregation has meant increased white flight along with a loss of African-American teaching and administrative positions.[52] In explaining the double-edge sword of civil rights legislation, Crenshaw argued that

> the civil rights community ... must come to terms with the fact that antidis-
> crimination discourse is fundamentally ambiguous and can accommodate
> conservative as well as liberal views of race and equality. This dilemma
> suggests that the civil rights constituency cannot afford to view antidiscrim-
> ination doctrine as a permanent pronouncement of society's commitment to
> ending racial subordination. Rather, antidiscrimination law represents an
> ongoing ideological struggle in which occasional winners harness the moral,
> coercive, consensual power of law. Nonetheless, the victories it offers can be
> ephemeral and the risks of engagement substantial.[53]

An example of Crenshaw's point about the ambiguity of civil rights legislation was demonstrated in a high school district in Northern California.[54] Of the five high schools in the district, one was located in a predominantly African-American community. To entice white students to attend that school, the district funded a number of induce-ments including free camping and skiing trips. While the trips were available to all of the students, they were attended largely by the white students, who already owned the expensive camping and skiing equipment. However, these inducements were not enough to continuously attract white students. As enrollment began to fall, the district decided to close a school. Not surprisingly, the school in the African-American community was closed and all of its students had to be (and continue to be) bused to the four white schools in the district.

Lomotey and Staley's examination of Buffalo's "model" desegregation program re-vealed that African-American and Latino students continued to be poorly served by the school system. The academic achievement of African-American and Latino students failed to improve while their suspension, expulsion, and dropout rates continued to rise. On the other hand, the desegregation plan provided special magnet programs and ex-tended day care of which whites were able to take advantage. What, then, made Buffalo a model school desegregation program? In short, the benefits that whites derived from school desegregation and their seeming support of the district's desegregation program.[55] Thus, a model desegregation program becomes defined as one that ensures that whites are happy (and do not leave the system altogether) regardless of whether African-American and other students of color achieve or remain.

Challenging Claims of Neutrality, Objectivity, Color-blindness, and Meritocracy

A theme of "naming one's own reality" or "voice" is entrenched in the work of critical race theorists. Many critical race theorists argue that the form and substance of scholarship are closely connected.[56] These scholars use parables, chronicles, stories, counterstories, poetry, fiction, and revisionist histories to illustrate the false necessity and irony of much of current civil rights doctrine. Delgado suggests that there are at least three reasons for naming one's own reality in legal discourse:

1. Much of reality is socially constructed.

2. Stories provide members of outgroups a vehicle for psychic self-preservation.

3. The exchange of stories from teller to listener can help overcome ethnocentrism and the dysconscious conviction of viewing the world in one way.[57]

The first reason for naming one's own reality is to demonstrate how political and moral analysis is conducted in legal scholarship. Many main-stream legal scholars embrace universalism over particularity.[58] According to Williams, "theoretical legal understanding" is characterized, in Anglo-American jurisprudence, by the acceptance of transcendent, acontextual, universal legal truths or procedures.[59] For instance, some legal scholars might contend that the tort of fraud has always existed and that it is a component belonging to the universal system of right and wrong. This view tends to discount anything that is non-transcendent (historical), or contextual (socially constructed), or nonuniversal (specific) with the unscholarly labels of "emotional," "literary," "personal," or "false."

In contrast, critical race theorists argue that political and moral analysis is situational—"truths only exist for this person in this predicament at this time in history."[60] For the critical race theorist, social reality is constructed by the formulation and the exchange of stories about individual situations.[61] These stories serve as interpretive structures by which we impose order on experience and it on us."[62]

A second reason for the naming-one's-own-reality theme of critical race theory is the psychic preservation of marginalized groups. A factor contributing to the demoralization of marginalized groups is self-condemnation.[63] Members of minority groups internalize the stereotypic images that certain elements of society have constructed in order to maintain their power.[64] Historically, storytelling has been a kind of medicine to heal the wounds of pain caused by racial oppression.[65] The story of one's condition leads to the realization of how one came to be oppressed and subjugated and allows one to stop inflicting mental violence on oneself.

Finally, naming one's own reality with stories can affect the oppressor. Most oppression does not seem like oppression to the perpetrator.[66] Delgado argues that the
dominant group justifies its power with stories—stock explanations—that construct
reality in ways to maintain their privilege.[67] Thus, oppression is rationalized, causing
little self-examination by the oppressor. Stories by people of color can catalyze the necessary cognitive conflict to jar dysconscious racism.

The "voice" component of critical race theory provides a way to communicate the
experience and realities of the oppressed, a first step on the road to justice. As we attempt
to make linkages between critical race theory and education, we contend that the voice
of people of color is required for a complete analysis of the educational system. Delpit
argues that one of the tragedies of education is the way in which the dialogue of people
of color has been silenced. An example from her conversation with an African-American
graduate student illustrates this point:

> There comes a moment in every class when we have to discuss "The Black
> Issue" and what's appropriate education for Black children. I tell you, I'm
> tired of arguing with those White people, because they won't listen. Well,
> I don't know if they really don't listen or if they just don't believe you. It
> seems like if you can't quote Vygotsky or something, then you don't have
> any validity to speak about your own kids. Anyway, I'm not bothering with
> it anymore, now I'm just in it for a grade.[68]

A growing number of education scholars of color are raising critical questions about the
way that research is being conducted in communities of color.[69] Thus, without authentic
voices of people of color (as teachers, parents, administrators, students, and community
members) it is doubtful that we can say or know anything useful about education in
their communities.

THE INTERSECTION OF RACE AND PROPERTY

In the previous sections of this article we argued that race is still a significant factor
in determining inequity in the United States and that the society is based on property
rights rather than on human rights. In this section we discuss the intersection of race
and property as a central construct in understanding a critical race theoretical approach
to education.

Harris argues that "slavery linked the privilege of Whites to the subordination
of Blacks through a legal regime that attempted the conversion of Blacks into objects
of property. Similarly, the settlement and seizure of Native American land supported
White privilege through a system of property rights in land in which the 'race' of the
Native Americans rendered their first possession right invisible and justified conquest."
But, more pernicious and long lasting then the victimization of people of color is the

construction of whiteness as the ultimate property. "Possession—the act necessary to lay the basis for rights in property—was defined to include only the cultural practices of Whites. This definition laid the foundation for the idea that whiteness—that which Whites alone possess—is valuable and is property.[70]

Because of space constraints, it is not possible to fully explicate Harris's thorough analysis of whiteness as property. However, it is important to delineate what she terms the "property functions of whiteness," which include: (1) rights of disposition; (2) rights to use and enjoyment; (3) reputation and status property; and (4) the absolute right to exclude. How these rights apply to education is germane to our discussion.

Rights of disposition. Because property rights are described as fully alienable, that is, transferable, it is difficult to see how whiteness can be construed as property.[71] However, alienability of certain property is limited (e.g., entitlements, government licenses, professional degrees or licenses held by one party and financed by the labor of the other in the context of divorce). Thus, whiteness when conferred on certain student performances is alienable.[72] When students are rewarded only for conformity to perceived "white norms" or sanctioned for cultural practices (e.g., dress, speech patterns, unauthorized conceptions of knowledge), white property is being rendered alienable.

Rights to use and enjoyment. Legally, whites can use and enjoy the privileges of whiteness. As McIntosh has explicitly demonstrated, whiteness allows for specific social, cultural, and economic privileges.[73] Fuller further asserts that whiteness is both performative and pleasurable.[74] In the school setting, whiteness allows for extensive use of school property. Kozol's description of the material differences in two New York City schools can be interpreted as the difference between those who possess the right to use and enjoy what schools can offer and those who do not:

> The [white] school serves 825 children in the kindergarten through sixth grade. This is approximately half the student population crowded into [black] P.S. 79, where 1,550 children fill a space intended for 1,000, and a great deal smaller than the 1,300 children packed into the former skating rink.[75]

This right of use and enjoyment is also reflected in the structure of the curriculum, also described by Kozol:

> The curriculum [the white school] follows "emphasizes critical thinking, reasoning and logic." The planetarium, for instance, is employed not simply for the study of the universe as it exists. "Children also are designing their own galaxies," the teacher says.

> In my [Kozol's] notes: "Six girls, four boys. Nine White, one Chinese. I am glad they have this class. But what about the others? Aren't there ten Black children in the school who could *enjoy* this also?[76]

Reputation and status property. The concept of reputation as property is regularly demonstrated in legal cases of libel and slander. Thus, to damage someone's reputation is to damage some aspect of his or her personal property. In the case of race, to call a white person "black" is to defame him or her.[77] In the case of schooling, to identify a school or program as nonwhite in any way is to diminish its reputation or status. For example, despite the prestige of foreign language learning, bilingual education as practiced in the United States as a nonwhite form of second language learning has lower status.[78] The term *urban*, the root word of *urbane*, has come to mean black. Thus, urban schools (located in the urbane, sophisticated cities) lack the status and reputation of suburban (white) schools and when urban students move to or are bused to suburban schools, these schools lose their reputation.[79]

The absolute right to exclude. Whiteness is constructed in this society as the absence of the "contaminating" influence of blackness. Thus, "one drop of black blood" constructs one as black, regardless of phenotypic markers.[80] In schooling, the absolute right to exclude was demonstrated initially by denying blacks access to schooling altogether. Later, it was demonstrated by the creation and maintenance of separate schools. More recently it has been demonstrated by white flight and the growing insistence on vouchers, public funding of private schools, and schools of choice.[81] Within schools, absolute right to exclude is demonstrated by resegregation via tracking,[82] the institution of "gifted" programs, honors programs, and advanced placement classes. So complete is this exclusion that black students often come to the university in the role of intruders—who have been granted special permission to be there.

In this section we have attempted to draw parallels between the critical race legal theory notion of whiteness as property and educational inequity. In the final section we relate some of the intellectual/theoretical tensions that exist between critical race theory and multicultural education.

THE LIMITS OF THE MULTICULTURAL PARADIGM

Throughout this article we have argued the need for a critical race theoretical perspective to cast a new gaze on the persistent problems of racism in schooling. We have argued the need for this perspective because of the failure of scholars to theorize race. We have drawn parallels between the way critical race legal scholars understand their position vis-à-vis traditional legal scholarship and the ways critical race theory applied to education offers a way to rethink traditional educational scholarship. We also have referred to the tensions that exist between traditional civil rights legislation and critical race legal theory. In this section we identify a necessary tension between critical race theory in education and what we term the multicultural paradigm.

Multicultural education has been conceptualized as a reform movement designed to effect change in the "school and other educational institutions so that students from diverse racial, ethnic, and other social-class groups will experience educational equality."[83]

In more recent years, multicultural education has expanded to include issues of gender, ability, and sexual orientation. Although one could argue for an early history of the "multicultural education movement" as far back as the 1880s when George Washington Williams wrote his history of African Americans, much of the current multicultural education practice seems more appropriately rooted in the intergroup education movement of the 1950s, which was designed to help African Americans and other "unmeltable" ethnics become a part of America's melting pot.[84] Their goals were primarily assimilationist through the reduction of prejudice. However, after the civil rights unrest and growing self-awareness of African Americans in the 1960s, the desire to assimilate was supplanted by the reclamation of an "authentic black personality" that did not rely on the acceptance by or standards of white America. This new vision was evidenced in the academy in the form of first, black studies and later, when other groups made similar liberating moves, ethnic studies.[85]

Current practical demonstrations of multicultural education in schools often reduce it to trivial examples and artifacts of cultures such as eating ethnic or cultural foods, singing songs or dancing, reading folktales, and other less than scholarly pursuits of the fundamentally different conceptions of knowledge or quests for social justice.[86] At the university level, much of the concern over multicultural education has been over curriculum inclusion.[87] However, another level of debate emerged over what became known as "multiculturalism."

Somewhat different from multicultural education in that it does not represent a particular educational reform or scholarly tradition, multiculturalism came to be viewed as a political philosophy of "many cultures" existing together in an atmosphere of respect and tolerance.[88] Thus, outside of the classroom multiculturalism represented the attempt to bring both students and faculty from a variety of cultures into the school (or academy) environment. Today, the term is used interchangeably with the ever-expanding "diversity," a term used to explain all types of "difference"—racial, ethnic, cultural, linguistic, ability, gender, sexual orientation. Thus, popular music, clothes, media, books, and so forth, reflect a growing awareness of diversity and/or multiculturalism. Less often discussed are the growing tensions that exist between and among various groups that gather under the umbrella of multiculturalism—that is, the interests of groups can be competing or their perspectives can be at odds.[89] We assert that the ever-expanding multicultural paradigm follows the traditions of liberalism—allowing a proliferation of difference. Unfortunately, the tensions between and among these differences is rarely interrogated, presuming a "unity of difference"—that is, that all difference is both analogous and equivalent.[90]

To make parallel the analogy between critical race legal theory and traditional civil rights law with that of critical race theory in education and multicultural education we need to restate the point that critical race legal theorists have "doubts about the foundation of moderate/incremental civil rights law."[91] The foundation of civil rights law has been in human rights rather than in property rights. Thus, without disrespect to the pioneers of civil rights law, critical race legal scholars document the ways in which civil rights law is regularly subverted to benefit whites.[92]

We argue that the current multicultural paradigm functions in a manner similar to civil rights law. Instead of creating radically new paradigms that ensure justice, multicultural reforms are routinely "sucked back into the system" and just as traditional civil rights law is based on a foundation of human rights, the current multicultural paradigm is mired in liberal ideology that offers no radical change in the current order.[93] Thus, critical race theory in education, like its antecedent in legal scholarship, is a radical critique of both the status quo and the purported reforms.

We make this observation of the limits of the current multicultural paradigm not to disparage the scholarly efforts and sacrifices of many of its proponents, but to underscore the difficulty (indeed, impossibility) of maintaining the spirit and intent of justice for the oppressed while simultaneously permitting the hegemonic rule of the oppressor.[94] Thus, as critical race theory scholars we unabashedly reject a paradigm that attempts to be everything to everyone and consequently becomes nothing for anyone, allowing the status quo to prevail. Instead, we align our scholarship and activism with the philosophy of Marcus Garvey, who believed that the black man was universally oppressed on racial grounds, and that any program of emancipation would have to be built around the question of race first.[95] In his own words, Garvey speaks to us clearly and unequivocally:

> In a world of wolves one should go armed, and one of the most powerful defensive weapons within the reach of Negroes is the practice of race first in all parts of the world.[96]

Endnotes

1   Jonathan Kozol, *Savage Inequalities* (New York: Crown Publishers, 1991). For further discussion of our inability to articulate issues of race and racism see Toni Morrison, *Playing in the Dark: Whiteness and the Literary Imagination* (Cambridge: Harvard University Press, 1992); Gomel West, "Learning to Talk of Race," *New York Times Magazine,* August 2, 1992, pp. 24, 26; and Beverly Daniel Tatum, "Talking about Race, Learning about Racism: The Application of Racial Identity Development Theory in the Classroom," *Harvard Educational Review* 62 (1992): 1-24.

2   Throughout this article the term *race* is used to define the polar opposites of "conceptual whiteness" and "conceptual blackness" (Joyce King, "Perceiving Reality in a New Way: Rethinking the Black/white Duality of our Time [Paper presented at the annual meeting of the American Educational Research Association, New Orleans, April 1994]). We do not mean to reserve the sense of "otherness" for African Americans; rather, our discussion attempts to illuminate how discussions of race in the United States positions *everyone as* either "white" or "nonwhite." Thus, despite the use of African-American legal and educational exemplars, we include other groups who have been constructed at various time in their history as nonwhite or black. Readers should note that some of the leading legal

scholars in the critical race legal theory movement are of Latino and Asian-American as well as African-American heritage.

3   See, for example, Patricia Hill Collins, *Black Feminist Thought* (New York: Routledge, 1991); Joyce King and Carolyn Mitchell, *Black Mothers to Sons: Juxtaposing African American Literature and Social Practice* (New York: Peter Lang, 1990); and Patricia Williams, *The Alchemy of Rare and Rights: Diary of a Law Professor* (Cambridge: Harvard University Press, 1991)

4   These propositions are not hierarchical. Rather, they can be envisioned as sides of an equilateral triangle, each equal and each central to the construction of the overall theory.

5   Andrew Hacker, *Two Nations: Black and White, Separate, Hostile, Unequal* (New York: Ballantine Books, 1992); and Marian Wright Edelman, *Families in Peril: An Agenda for Social Change* (Cambridge: Harvard University Press, 1987).

6   Michael Omi and Howard Winant, "On the Theoretical Concept of Race," in *Race, Identity and Representation in Education,* edited by C. McCarthy and W. Crichlow (New York: Routledge, 1993), pp. 3-10.

7   Luigi Luca Cavalli-Sforza, "Genes, People and Languages," *Scientific American,* November 1991, p. 104.

8   Morrison, *Playing in the Dark,* p. 63.

9   This assertion was made forcefully by the participants of the Institute NHI (No Humans Involved) at a symposium entitled "The Two Reservations: Western Thought, the Color Line, and the Crisis of the Negro Intellectual Revisited," sponsored by the Department of African and Afro-American Studies at Stanford University, Stanford, Calif., March 3-5,1994.

10 See, for example, Nancy Chodorow, *The Reproduction of Mothering* (Berkeley: University of California Press, 1978); Simone DeBeauvoir, *The Second Sex* (New York: Bantam Books, 1961); Vivian Gornick, "Women as Outsiders," in *Women in Sexist Society,* edited by V. Gornick and B. Moran (New York: Basic Books, 1971), pp. 70-84; Nancy Hartsock, "Feminist Theory and the Development of Revolutionary Strategy," *Capitalist Patriarch and the Case for Socialist Feminism,* edited by Z. Eisenstein (London and New York: Monthly Review Press, 1979); and Alison Jagger, *Feminist Theory and Human Nature* (Sussex, England: Harvester Press, 1983).

11 See, for example, Samuel Bowles and Herbert Gintis, *Schooling in Capitalist America* (New York: Basic Books, 1976); Martin Carnoy, *Education and Cultural Imperialism* (New York: McKay, 1974); Michael W. Apple, "Redefining Inequality: Authoritarian Populism and the Conservative Restoration," *Teachers College Record* 90 (1988): 167-84; and Philip Wexler. *Social Analysis and Education: After the New Sociology* (New York: Routledge & Kegan Paul, 1987).

12 David Roediger, *The Wages of Whiteness* (London: Verso, 1991), p. 6.

13 Michael Omi and Howard Winant, *Racial Formation in the United States from the 1960s to the 1990s,* 2nd ed. (New York: Routledge, 1994), p. 9.

14 Ibid., p. 56.

15 Carter G. Woodson, *The Miseducation of the Negro* (Washington, D.C.: Association Press. 1933): and W. E. B. Du Bois, *The Souls of Black Folks* (New York: Penguin Books, 1989; firm published in 1903).

16 Our decision to focus on Woodson and Du Bois is not intended to diminish the import of the scores of African-American scholars who also emerged during their time such as George E. Haynes. Charles S. Johnson, E. Franklin Frazier, Abram Harris, Sadie T. Alexander, Robert C. *Weaver.* Rayford Logan. Allison Davis. Dorothy Porter. and Benjamin Quarles. We highlight Woodson and Du Bois as early seminal thinkers about issues of race and racism.

17 See John Hope Franklin. *From Slavery to Freedom,* 6th ed. (New York: Alfred A. Knopf. 1988).

18 Woodson, *The Miseducation of the Negro.* p. xiii.

19 Du Bois, *The Souls of Black Folks,* p. 5. Other people of color, feminists, and gay lesbian theorists all have appropriated Du Bois's notion of double consciousness to explain their estrangement from mainstream patriarchal, masculinist U.S. culture.

20 David Levering Lewis, W *E. B. Du Bois: Biography of a Rare, 1868-1919* (New York: Henry Holt. 1993), p. 281.

21 Du Bois, *The Souls of Black,* p.1

22 See, for example, Lorene *Cary. Black Ice* (New York: Alfred A. Knopf. 1991); and Jeannie Oakes. *Keeping Track: How Schools Structure Inequality* (New Haven: Yale University·Press, 1985).

23 Oakes. *Keeping Track,* p, 67.

24 American Association of University Women. *How Schools Shortchange Girls: A Study of Mayor Findings on Gender and Education* (Washington, D.C.: Author and National Education Association. 1992).

25 Myra Sadker, David Sadker, and Susan Klein. The Issue of Gender in Elementary and Secondary Education," *in Review of Educational Research in Education, vol. 19,* edited by G. Cerant (Washington. D.C.: American Educational Research Association, 1991), pp. 269-334.

26 Hacker, *Two Nations,* puts the dropout rate For African-American males in some large cities at close to 50 percent.

27 Robert Majors and Janet Billson. *Cool Pose: The Dilemmas of Black Manhood in America* (New York: Lexington Books, 1992).

28 Corneal West. *Rare Matters* (Boston: Beacon Press, 1993): and David Lionel Smith, "Let Our People Go," *Black Scholar* 23 (1993): 75-76.

29 Peter Monaghan, " 'Critical Race Theory' Questions the Role of Legal Doctrine in Racial inequity," *Chronicle of Higher Education,* June 23,1993, pp. A7. A9.

30 Delgado, cited in Monaghan. "Critical Race Theory." Quotations are from p. A7. For a more detailed explication of the first item in the list. see *Bell. Faces at the Bottom of the Well.*

31 Manning Marable, *How Capitalism Underdeveloped Black America* (Boston: South End Press. 1983).

32 Derrick Bell, *And We Are Not Saved: The Elusive Quest for Racial Justice* (New York: Basic Books, 1987).

33 Howard Zinn, *A Peoples History of the United States* (New York: Harper & Row. 1980), p. 13.

34 Bell, *And We Are Not Saved.*

35 William Tate, Gloria Ladson-Billings, and Carl Grant, The *Brown* Decision Revisited: Mathematizing Social Problems," *Educational Policy* 7 (1993) 255-75.

36 Bell, *And We Are Not Saved*, p. 239.

37 Ronald Takaki, A *Different* Mirror: A *History of Multicultural America* (Boston: Little Brown, 1993).

38 Franklin, *From Slavery to Freedom.*

39 Clearly, an analysis of worldwide tensions reinforces the importance of land to a people— Israel and the Palestinians, Iraq and Kuwait, the former Soviet bloc, Hitler and the Third Reich, all represent some of the struggles over land.

40 Even at a time when there is increased public sentiment for reducing the federal deficit, the one source of tax relief that no president or member of Congress would ever consider is that of denying home (property) owners their tax benefits.

41 See, for example, Howard Wainer, "Does Spending Money on Education Help?" *Educational Researcher* 22 (1993): 22-24; or Paul Houston, "School Vouchers: The Latest California Joke," *Phi Delta Kappan* 75 (1993): 61-66.

42 Kozol, *Savage Inequalities,* pp. 83-84.

43 This notion of "Intellectual property" came into popular use when television talk show host David Letterman moved from NBC to CBS. NBC claimed that certain routines and jokes used by Letterman were the intellectual property of the network and, as such, could not be used by Letterman without permission.

44 Richard Delgado, "When a Story Is Just a Story: Does Voice Really *Matter?" Virginia Law Review* 76 (1990): 95-111.

45 See, for example, Floraline Stevens, *Opportunity to Learn: Issues of Equity for Poor and Minority Students* (Washington, D.C.: National Center for Education Statistics, 1993); idem, "Applying an Opportunity-to-learn Conceptual Framework to the Investigation of the Effects of Teaching Practices via Secondary Analyses of Multiple-case-study Summary Data," *The Journal of Negro Education* 62 (1993): 232-48; and Linda Winfield and Michael D. Woodard, "Assessment, Equity, Diversity in Reforming America's Schools," *Educational Policy* 8 (1994): 3-27.

46 The standards debate is too long and detailed to be discussed here. For a more detailed discussion of standards see, for example, Michael W. Apple, "Do the Standards Go Far Enough? Power, Policy, and Practices in Mathematics Education," *Journal for Research in Mathematics Education* 23 (1992): 412-31; and National Council of Education Standards and Testing, *Raising Standards for American Education: A Report to Congress, the Secretary of Education, the National Goals Panel, and the American People* (Washington, D.C.: Government Printing Office, 1992).

47 Kozol, *Savage Inequalities.*

48 Some urban Catholic schools, black independent schools, and historically black colleges and universities have demonstrated the educability of African-American students. As of this writing we have no data on the success of urban districts such as Detroit or Milwaukee that are attempting what is termed "African Centered" or Africentric education. See also Mwalimu J. Shujaa, Editor, *Too Much Schooling, Too little Education: A Paradox of Black Life in White Societies* (Trenton, N.J.: Africa World Press. 1994).

49 David Wellman, *Portraits of White Racism* (Cambridge, England: Cambridge University Press, 1977). Quotations are from pp. xviii and 42.

50 See, for example, Gary Orfield, "School Desegregation in the 1980s," *Equity and Choice,* February 1988, p. 25; Derrick Bell, "Learning from Our Losses: Is School Desegregation Still Feasible in the 1980s? *Phi Delta Kappan* 64 (April 1983): 575; Willis D. Hawley, "Why It Is Hard to Believe in Desegregation," *Equity and Choice,* February 1988, pp. 9-15; and Janet Ward Schofield, *Black and White in School: Trust, Tension, or Tolerance?* (New York: Teachers College Press, 1989).

51 James Banks, "Teaching Multicultural Literacy to Teachers," *Teaching Education* 4 (1991): 135-44.

52 See Karl Taeuber, "Desegregation of Public School Districts: Persistence and Change," *Phi Delta Kappan* 72 (1990): 18-24; and H. L. Bisinger, "When Whites Flee," *New York Times Magazine,* May 29, 1994, pp. 26-33, 43, 50, 53-54, 56. On loss of professional positions, see Sabrina King, "The Limited Presence of African American Teachers," *Review of Educational Research* 63 (1993): 115-49; and Jacqueline Irvine, "An Analysis of the Problem of Disappearing Black Educators," *Elementary School Journal* 88 (1988): 503-13.

53 Kimberle Williams Crenshaw, "Race Reform, and Retrenchment: Transformation and Legitimation in Antidiscrimination Law," *Harvard Law Review* 101 (1988): 1331-87.

54 Ibid., p. 1335.

55 Kofi Lomotey and John Statley, "The Education of African Americans in Buffalo Public Schools" (Paper presented at the annual meeting of the American Educational Research Association, Boston, 1990).

56 Richard Delgado, "Storytelling for Oppositionists and Others: A Plea for Narrative," *Michigan Law Review* 87 (1989): 2411-41.

57 See Richard Delgado et al., "Symposium: Legal Storytelling," *Michigan Law Review* 87 (1989): 2073. On dysconsciousness, see Joyce E. King, "Dysconscious Racism: Ideology, Identity and the Miseducation of Teachers," *Journal of Negro Education* 60 (1991): 135. King defines dysconsciousness as "an uncritical habit of mind (including perceptions, attitudes, assumptions, and beliefs) that justifies inequity and exploitation by accepting the existing order of things as given . . . Dysconscious racism is a form of racism that tacitly accepts dominant White norms and privileges. It is not the *absence* of consciousness (that is, not unconsciousness) but an *impaired* consciousness or distorted way of thinking about race as compared to, for example, critical consciousness."

58 These notions of universalism prevail in much of social science research, including educational research.

59 Williams, *Alchemy of Race and Rights*

60 Richard Delgado. "Brewer's Plea: Critical Thoughts on Common Cause," *Vanderbilt Law Review* 44 (1991): 11.

61 For example. see Williams, *Alchemy of Rare and Rights*; Bell, *Faces at the Bottom of the Well*: and Mari Matsuda, "Public Response to Racist Speech: Considering the Victim's Story," *Michigan Law Review* 87 (1989): 2320-81.

62 Delgado, "Storytelling."

63 Ibid.

64 For example, see Crenshaw, "Race, Reform, and Retrenchment."

65 Delgado, "Storytelling."

66 Charles Lawrence, "The Id, the Ego, and Equal Protection: Reckoning with Unconscious Racism," *Stanford Law Review* 39 (1987): 317-88.

67 Delgado et al., "Symposium."

68 Lisa Delpit, "The Silenced Dialogue: Power and Pedagogy in Educating Other People's Children," *Harvard Educational Review* 58 (1988): 280.

69 At the 1994 annual meeting of the American Educational Research Association in New Orleans, two sessions entitled "Private Lives, Public Voices: Ethics of Research in Communities of Color" were convened to discuss the continued exploitation of people of color. According to one scholar of color, our communities have become "data plantations."

70 Cheryl I. Harris, "Whiteness as Property," *Harvard Law Review* 106 (1993): 1721.

71 See Margaret Radin, "Market-Inalienability," Harvard *Law Review* 100 (1987): 1849-906.

72 See Signithia Fordham and John Ogbu, "Black Student School Success: Coping with the Burden of 'Acting White,'" *The Urban Review* 18 (1986): 1-31.

73 Peggy McIntosh, "White Privilege: Unpacking the Invisible Knapsack," *Independent School,* Winter, 1990, pp. 31-36.

74 Laurie Fuller, "Whiteness as Performance" (Unpublished preliminary examination paper, University of Wisconsin—Madison, 1994).

75 Kozol, *Savage Inequalities,* p. 93

76 Ibid., p. 96; emphasis added.

77 Harris, "Whiteness as Property," p. 1735.

78 David Spener, "Transitional Bilingual Education and the Socialization of Immigrants," *Harvard Educational Review* 58 (1988): 133-53.

79 H. G. Bissinger, "When Whites Flee," *New York Times Magazine,* May 29,1994, pp. 26-33, 43,50,53-54,56.

80 Derrick Bell, *Race, Racism, and American Law* (Boston: Little, Brown, 1980).

81 We assert that the current movement toward African-centered (or Africentric) schools is not equivalent to the racial exclusion of vouchers, or choice programs. Indeed, African-centeredness has become a logical response of a community to schools that have been abandoned by whites, have been stripped of material resources, and have demonstrated a lack of commitment to African-American academic achievement.

82 Oakes, *Keeping Track.*

83 James A. Banks, "Multicultural Education: Historical Development, Dimensions, and Practice," *in Review of Research in Education,* vol. 19, edited by L. Darling-Hammond (Washington, D.C.: American Educational Research Association, 1993). p. 3.

84 George Washington Williams, *History of the Negro Race in America from 1619-1880: Negroes as Slaves, as Soldiers, and as Citizens* (2 vols.) (New York: G. P. Putnam & Sons, 1882-1883). On the intergroup education movement, see, for example, L. A. Cook and E. Cook, *Intergroup*

Education (New York: McGraw-Hill, 1954); and H. G. Traeger and M. R. Yarrow, *They Learn What They Live: Prejudice in Young Children* (New York: Harper and Brothers, 1952).

85 See, for example, Vincent Harding, *Beyond Chaos: Black History and the Search for a New Land* (Black Paper No. 2) (Atlanta: Institute of the Black World, August 1970); J. Blassingame, editor, *New Perspectives in Black Studies* (Urbana: University of Illinois Press, 1971); James A. Banks, ed., *Teaching Ethnic Studies* (Washington, D.C.: National Council for the Social Studies, 1973); and Geneva Gay, "Ethnic Minority Studies: How Widespread? How Successful?" *Educational Leadership* 29 (1971): 108-12.

86 Banks, "Multicultural Education."

87 In 1988 at Stanford University the inclusion of literature from women and people of color in the Western Civilization core course resulted in a heated debate. The university's faculty senate approved this inclusion in a course called Cultures, Ideas, and Values. The controversy was further heightened when then Secretary of Education William Bennett came to the campus to denounce this decision.

88 In the "Book Notes" section of the *Harvard Educational Review* 64 (1994): 345-47, Jane Davagian Tchaicha reviews Donaldo Macedo's *Literacies of Power* (Boulder: Westview Press, 1994) and includes two quotes, one from noted conservative Patrick Buchanan and another from Macedo on multiculturalism. According to Buchanan, "Our Judeo-Christian values are going to be preserved, and our Western heritage is going to be handed down to future generations, not dumped into some landfill called multiculturalism" (quoted in Tchaicha, p. 345). Macedo asserts that "the real issue isn't Western culture versus multiculturalism, the fundamental issue is the recognition of humanity in us and in others" (quoted in Tchaicha, p. 347).

89 In New York City, controversy over the inclusion of gay and lesbian issues in the curriculum caused vitriolic debate among racial and ethnic groups who opposed their issues being linked to or compared with homosexuals. Some ethnic group members asserted that homosexuals were not a "culture" while gay and lesbian spokespeople argued that these group members were homophobic.

90 Shirley Torres-Medina, "Issues of Power. Constructing the Meaning of Linguistic Difference in First Grade Classrooms" (Ph.D. dissertation, University of Wisconsin-Madison, 1994).

91 Richard Delgado, "Enormous Anomaly? Left-Right Parallels in Recent Writing about Race," *Columbia Law Review* 91 (1991): 1547-60

92 See Bell, *And We Are Not Saved.*

93 See Cameron McCarthy, "After the Canon: Knowledge and Ideological Representation in the Multicultural Discourse on Curriculum Reform," in *Race, Identity and Representation,* edited by C. McCarthy and W. Crichlow (New York: Routledge, 1994), pp. 290; and Michael Olneck, "Terms of Inclusion: Has Multiculturalism Redefined Equality in American Education" *American Journal of Education* 101 (1993): 234-60.

94 We are particularly cognizant of the hard-fought battles in the academy waged and won by scholars such as James Banks, Carlos Cortez, Geneva Gay, Carl Grant, and others.

95 Tony Martin, *Race First: The Ideological and Organizational Struggles of Marcus Garvey and the Universal Negro Improvement Association* (Dover, Mass.: The Majority Press, 1976).

96 Marcus Garvey, cited in ibid., p. 22.

Early Schooling and Academic Achievement of African American Males

James Earl Davis, Temple University

ONE FACTOR THAT has been consistently associated with the achievement gap is school disengagement by African American males (Carter, 2003; Polite, 2000). Despite the prevalent view that achievement matters, research studies provide only modest evidence about the effects of disengagement among Black boys[1] in the early grades. Little evidence is available on the antecedents of underachievement for young males—the exception being the negative effects of some family and schooling background variables (Ferguson, 2000; Polite & Davis, 1999). This is due, in part, to the sparse data available on the experiences and outcomes of African American males in the early grades. However, the negative consequences of the achievement gap are more widely known and accepted. In general, we know that for these students, lower levels of achievement appear to have the most significant consequences for future development of social identity, cognitive ability, emotional capacity, and social competence—each negatively influenced by poor schooling experiences (Heath & MacKinnon, 1988). Similarly, the inherent social and economic limitations associated with underachievement are also supported by research across the disciplines (Anderson, 2000; Jencks & Phillips, 1998; Mincy, 1994; Murnane, Willett, & Levy, 1995; O'Connor, 1999). Thus, rather than ask questions about known negative effects of the achievement gap for African American males, one might pose the following question: What are the mechanisms at work that are responsible for African American males' achievement lags and apparent disengagement in early years of schooling?

This article centers on African American males in the early years of their formal schooling (kindergarten through 3rd grade), specifically their experience and achievement outcomes. Research on African American boys' achievement, performance, and school behavior will serve as the core of this article. Initially, I provide an overview of the current achievement status of African American males coupled with attention to the gender and racial context, particularly at school, in which these boys develop academically and socially. Published research from a variety of sources grounds the article in the most useful and reliable data that substantiate the achievement gap between African American males and their school peers, as well as provide direction to addressing lags in educational achievement. In doing so, I identify variables and factors that are needed to fully understand the achievement gap for African American males in early education. I try to situate current achievement status and disengagement experience as well as anchor the discussion about explanations within a larger argument about the role of schools and teachers as gender socializing agents for African American males.

Some assumptions are apparent in this article. I assume that African American males need to be cared for and nurtured in responsive schools; that these schools and teachers need to be supported in meeting the needs of Black males; and a critical component of sup- port includes increasing the ability of schools to contribute to Black males' social, cognitive, gender, and academic development. Based on these assumptions, I focus on findings from the research literature on Black male achievement and factors such as school organization that are associated with achievement outcomes. Second, I explore the degree to which schooling and gender identity help to explain possible disengagement and opposition to schooling experienced by Black boys in the early years. Throughout the article, I critique current research efforts and recommend a research agenda for understanding disparities in achievement and attitudes toward schooling among African American boys.

GENDER AND RACIAL CONTEXT OF ACHIEVEMENT

Considerable attention has been directed toward understanding gender differences in education. Central to this effort has been the investigation of the effects of gender on schooling experiences and achievement. In most of this work, gender is viewed from a social constructivist perspective, where qualities of masculinity are culturally attributed and defined (Connell, 1995; Ferguson, 2000; Thomas, 1990). Schooling contexts are often cited as important sources for gender construction and development (Thorne, 1986). Likewise, school experiences and opportunities are also circumscribed by race and ethnicity. Yet the intersection between gender and race in these contexts is often overlooked in educational research. In particular, the current plight of young African American males in schools demands much more focus, both theoretically and methodologically. Namely, issues of race and gender are central to any discussion about African American males and achievement (Delpit, 1988; Fine, 1991; Fordham, 1996; Mickelson, 1991; Williams, 1996).

Whether related to background and family resources (Corcoran & Adams, 1997) or opportunities to learn and develop that are influenced by gender relations (Adler, Kless, & Adler, 1992; Best, 1983), Black males are too often disadvantaged by this perplexing and misunderstood intersection of race and gender.

Although research on the schooling experiences of African Americans has a long history, recent discussions, particularly those presented by popular media about the unique plight of Black males and the racial achievement gap, have captured the interest of many. These discussions surrounding the educational status of Black males and the nature of their precarious educational position are infused with compelling descriptors such as worlds apart, epidemic of failure, and left behind. From this discourse has emerged an urgency to address the education achievement problems of Black males. Given this urgency, it seems ironic that scant attention has been given to the educational experiences and perspectives of Black boys in early schooling. In particular, little is known about the processes and experiences of early schooling, particularly issues of masculinity and how it influence schooling. To be fair, the idea of Black masculine identity and underachievement has gained currency in some literature and popular press (Boyd-Franklin & Franklin, 2000), yet the main of education research remains silent.

To be Black and male in American schools places one at risk for a variety of negative consequences: school failure, special education assignment, suspensions, expulsions, and violence (Ferguson, 2000; Polite & Davis, 1999). Rates of Black male school attrition, relatively poor academic performance, and college enrollment and persistence are seen, in part, as a function of Black males' inability or disinterest in fulfilling their roles as conventional learners in school settings. These negative school experiences and outcomes are viewed, to varying degrees, as products of structural factors, results of cultural adaptations to systemic pressures and maladaptive definitions of masculinity (Boykin & Bailey, 2000; Hare & Hare, 1985; Majors & Mancini Billson, 1992). What has emerged from this focus on the educational problems of Black males is an archetype of masculine behavior that is either deficient or distorted under the weight of racism, economic marginality, and cultural pathology (Hunter & Davis, 1992). Although masculinity is generally seen as being important (Akbar, 1991; Connell, 1995), it is regarded, however, as unidimensional and implicitly universal. Thus, this framework obscures the diversity and complexity of the constructions of so-called masculinities and how they are played out for African American males in schools.

Contrary to the generally accepted objectives of schooling, the current thinking of many researchers and educators is that schools are not meeting the particular social and developmental needs of African American males (Brown & Davis, 2000). In response, gender-exclusive school environments are being suggested as a measure to reverse disproportionate rates of school failure experienced by Black males (Span, 2000). It is argued that consistent and positive males in educational settings provide models for young Black males to emulate. These positive role models are believed to counter inappropriate sex-role socialization and maladaptive masculine identity (Cunningham,

1993). In turn, conceptions of masculinity are developed that are not antithetical to expected behaviors, roles, and expectations in school settings.

Broader sociological and economic forces are seen as undermining both the development and the appropriate expressions of masculinity among African American boys, particularly among the inner-city poor. In contrast, alternative models of masculinity (Akbar, 1991; Winbush, 2001) are being prescribed. However, its image of masculinity as either evasive or arrested still dominates the discourse. The ties between the meaning of masculinity and schooling objectives are believed to be incongruent and often diametrically opposed. One reason commonly mentioned for the disengagement, alienation, and poor academic performance of Black males is that they perceive most educational activities as feminine and irrelevant to their masculine identity and development. Furthermore, it is also believed that schools, specifically teachers, impose a feminine culture on males that induce oppositional behaviors. Given the reactions to these school contexts and gender expectations, many Black boys are seen as both victims and participants in their own educational demise.

RESEARCHING BLACK BOYS AT SCHOOL

During the past decade, a corpus of journal articles, reports, and scholarly and popular books have detailed the precarious nature of Black males in school and society (Boyd-Franklin & Franklin, 2000; Brown & Davis, 2000; Garibaldi, 1992; Majors & Gordon, 1994; McCall, 1994; Mincy, 1994; Polite & Davis, 1999; Williams, 1996). Although the current plight of young Black males in school is the focus of some of this work, very little is known about how early schooling contexts and experiences affect achievement outcomes. This interaction of school context, identity, and socialization is important to consider.

In the midst of trying to get a handle on the education crisis of Black boys, we have unfortunately learned too little about how boys construct personal meaning for their social and academic lives. We do know that Black boys are both loved and loathed at school. They set the standards for hip-hop culture and athleticism while experiencing disproportionate levels of punishment and academic failure. This juxtaposition leads to a range of behaviors and strategies within school that set the tone for the overall problematic educational experience of Black boys (Sewell, 1997). The response of these boys to a context that defines them as both sexy and as sexually threatening is often problematic. The spaces they create in response offer a sanctuary for the development of a set of relational and performance patterns that are unique to this group. These masculine spaces are erected, consciously or subconsciously, in schools that construct them as alien and undesirable. Clearly, schools are critical sites for young Black males as they make meaning of who they are, what they are supposed to do, and how others perceive them.

Although Black boys as well as Black girls are negatively affected by schooling, some research suggests that the problems facing Black boys are more chronic and extreme, thus deserving special policy and programmatic attention (Garibaldi, 1991, 1992; Polite, 1993; Watson & Smitherman, 1991). Others cite cultural messages about Black males and how they are negatively constructed in the media and perceived in everyday life (Belton, 1995; Blount & Cunningham, 1996; Harper, 1996). These images portray the Black male as violent, disrespectful, unintelligent, hyper-sexualized, and threatening. These cultural messages, without a doubt, carry over into schools and negatively influence the ways young Black male students are treated, positioned, and distributed opportunities to learn. For instance, Black boys' demeanors are misunderstood by White middle-class teachers and seen as defiant, aggressive, and intimidating (Majors, Tyler, Peden, & Hall, 1994; Slaughter-Defoe & Richards, 1994). Furthermore, in almost every category of academic failure, Black boys are disproportionately represented (Entwisle, Alexander, & Olson, 1997). One study documents that only 2% of African American males enrolled in the public school system of a large midwestern U.S. city achieved a cumulative grade point average of at least a 3 on a 4-point scale. At the same time, three fourths of Black males in that system were performing below average (Leake & Leake, 1992). In addition, a report on academic performance comparing Black males in a large urban and suburban school district found that fewer than 3% of Black males were enrolled in advanced classes (Wright, 1996). Clearly, by all measures of school attainment and achievement, Black males are consistently placed at risk for academic failure. In addition to lags in test score performance and grades, African American males are referred for special education placement at a much higher rate than all other students and they are much more likely to be suspended or expelled from school (Harry & Anderson, 1999). There is growing evidence that Black male disengagement with schooling develops in the early grades and continues to intensify as they progress through school (Carter, 2003). By all indicators, Black males consistently fall behind other students in early school performance and lead their peers in school infractions and other negative outcomes. The direction of the relationship between these negative educational experiences and school disengagement are surprisingly unclear. From the current literature, it is difficult to establish whether disengagement or achievement is the antecedent. Although the body of research on Black boys in the early grades is limited, it provides some useful insights. Much of this work, comparative in nature, examines the academic experiences and outcomes of Black boys relative to other students. Slaughter-Defoe and Richards (1994) suggested that as early as kindergarten, Black males are treated differently than other male and female students. Throughout elementary and middle school, Black boys consistently receive lower ratings by teachers for social behavior and academic expectations (Rong, 1996). In their study of factors related to school outcomes for Black males, Davis and Jordan (1994) found that boys' school engagement reflected in study habits and attendance were positively related to achievement and grades. Black boys who spend more time on homework and attend school regularly also perform better academically and are more engaged in their schooling. They also found that remediation, grade retention, and suspensions induce academic failure among Black boys. A longitudinal qualitative study of young African

American males from their preschool years into late adolescence is informative concerning parental involvement. Rashid (1989) found that the extent of parental involvement in the early years of schooling was critical, including the preschool program in which the boys were initially enrolled. Likewise, parental mediation of peer contacts and the availability of positive adult male role models was important in the lives of these boys.

Although recent attention has been paid to the relative poor academic performance of African American boys in school, its scope and focus are clearly not enough. Much of this work, I contend, is not really about understanding the achievement gap among Black boys and their peers. Rather, the field has been concerned about documenting poor performance and achievement deficits of Black males throughout their schooling years. Therefore, despite research attention directed toward Black males in school, insights about effective ways of countering the achievement gap and reversing high levels of disengagement go wanting. One research area that has been neglected deals with issues of Black boys' early child- hood schooling and home experiences, such as school readiness. This area of investigation would provide potentially useful information on Black males' trajectory of achievement and differences in school engagement over time.

Indeed, the early educational experiences of African American boys are by far the most important in the developmental trajectory of achievement throughout school (Best, 1983; Entwisle et al., 1997). Data on early schooling is spare and is usually limited to test scores and other measures of achievement. The large national data sets that are available, such as Children of the National Longitudinal Survey of Youth (prekindergarten–5th grade), Prospects (1st and 3rd grades), and the National Assessment of Educational Progress (4th grade), although potentially useful, have been underutilized. Specifically, achievement and personal background information about African American boys from these data sources may be helpful in establishing achievement patterns and explanatory factors during the early years of schooling. On the other hand, qualitative and ethnographic studies of early childhood and schooling of Black boys are more rare. When these studies are published, they are usually focused on issues of socialization, attitudes, and peer relations without much linkage to achievement outcomes (Tyson, 2002). Using a developmental perspective to study changes in African American boys' achievement and performance from kindergarten to 3rd grade and beyond should frame both quantitative and qualitative research on achievement. Research questions that pay attention to specific changes in achievement with respect to grade level, subject area, school culture, and student characteristics (e.g., socioeconomic background, attitudes, and identity) would benefit from longitudinal studies in this area.

For preschool Black boys, three common criteria often used as indicators of school readiness include student academic skill development, attitude, and behaviors (U.S. Department of Education, National Center for Education Statistics, 1993). Using data from the National Longitudinal Survey of Youth, some interesting patterns of Black boys' academic readiness skills appear (Nettles & Perna, 1997). Boys have lower test scores relative to girls on motor and social development tests. Similarly, boys score lower on verbal memory test. However, there are no differences in scores on the Peabody Picture Vocabulary Test, a language-independent measure, between the two groups. Furthermore, Black boys fidget more, begin speaking much later than girls, and are more likely to have a verbal stuttering or stammering problem. These indicators of early literacy for Black boys should prompt a research and intervention agenda that seeks to uncover meaningful explanations for achievement outcomes.

EXPLAINING BLACK MALE SCHOOL ACHIEVEMENT AND DISENGAGEMENT

Reasons cited for African American boys' academic achievement and disengagement in the early years of schooling are numerous. Although many of the theories and explanations are attractive and popular, particularly among some policy makers and social activists, they tend to lack substantial research support. In general, macro- and micro-explanations about the declining performance of African American boys relative to their White and female peers need more empirical study.

The most influential theories currently proposed to account for the relatively low academic performance of African American boys center on three areas: (a) student attitudes, (b) social organization of schools, and (c) masculine identity. Much research about student attitudes focus on student resistance and cultural opposition to schooling and achievement (Cook & Ludwig, 1998; Fordham, 1996; MacLeod, 1995). The notion that attitudes of Black students are the results of negative cultural orientation toward schooling is most closely associated with Fordham (1996). The idea of a cultural orientation implies that negative school attitudes can be found among Black students because it is learned behavior that is community enforced. The assumption that young children in school, especially Black boys, are participants and victims in this anti-achievement milieu guides this work. Data from the Early Childhood Education Component of the National Household Education Survey (U.S. Department of Education, National Center for Education Statistics, 1993) revealed some early patterns concerning school engagement for Black boys. For instance, 5-year-old Black boys are more likely to lack confidence about their abilities in school compared to Black girls (23.5% vs. 9.7%), and boys are less likely to speak out in class compared to girls. However, parents report no differences in their reading levels. But parents indicate they played more with Black girls (e.g., arts, crafts, toys, and games). In general, African American boys have very positive experiences in early schooling. Almost all of them (98%) report looking forward to going to kindergarten each day, and the vast majority of them like their teacher and say good things about their school. These findings are supported by an ethnographic study that found Black boys to be achievement oriented and very engaged in the process of learning in elementary school. Interestingly, only boys who were struggling academically expressed negative attitudes toward school (Tyson, 2002).

From the evidence reported here, although limited, the picture about disengagement of Black boys in the early school years becomes less clear. I posit that the inconsistency of findings of disengagement of Black boys in school is due to differences in the developmental experiences and attitudes of young boys relative to older students in middle and high school. Most of the research on schooling opposition and attitudes focus on adolescents and not during the early years of school (Ainsworth-Darnell & Downey, 1998; Fordham, 1996; Solomon, 1991; Welch & Hodges, 1997). The research that exists on Black males' attitudes in the early grades is relatively recent and typically focuses on peer relations. Little attention is given to how young Black males construct personal meaning of education and achievement inside and outside school. Particularly, discussions about how young Black males make sense of their own gender/race identity connected with achievement and engagement attitudes have been noticeably absent from research studies.

Explanations of the achievement gap relating to how schools are organized have concentrated on curriculum issues, teaching strategies, school achievement climate, and expectations. How schools structure students' opportunities to learn has been shown to influence academic achievement (Epstein & MacIver, 1992; Lee & Bryk, 1988). Access to academic experiences and achievement through the curriculum, teachers, and other school activities are of particular importance for African American males who may be already marginalized at school (Finn & Cox, 1992; Sanders & Reed, 1995). Elementary schools, particularly those in low-income inner-city and rural areas, traditionally have been neglected, underfunded, and burdened with limited parental and community support. Because of complex social and economic reasons, young Black males in these schools setting are acutely at risk for limited achievement and school disengagement. For instance, classrooms that require a tremendous amount of disciplinary attention may produce limited learning environments that shortchange Black boys in terms of academic instruction and learning activities. If school and classroom climate are negatively affected by discipline problems, academic engagement and instructional focus will surely suffer. This link between school climate and student achievement is documented (Irvine, 1990; Polite, 2000) but requires much more research specifically focused on African American boys.

Ability grouping of Black boys in elementary schools also appears to have negative consequences on their achievement levels. Although much evidence on Black boys is not readily available, a few studies point in this direction. Simmons and Grady (1992) reported that Black boys in the early grades were overenrolled in lower level courses. For instance, throughout the 3rd grade, Black boys perform equally well as their peers on districtwide assessment in reading and math. Beginning in the 4th grade, however, Black boys experience a sharp decline in their test scores. The percentage of Black males in the top reading group dropped from 23% in Grades 1 and 4 to 12% in Grade 6. These declines correspond to the ability grouping of Black boys in which they only have access to lower level courses. When elementary Black boys have unequal access to the curriculum, achievement inequalities in the later grades are not surprising. Other school organization efforts such as magnet schools, charter schools, after-school programming, block scheduling, looping, extended, and year-round schooling are important areas for study to determine if specific achievement effects of these strategies occur for Black boys in the lower grades.

The need for early school-based intervention for African American boys who are placed at risk for school disengagement is supported by findings from research on schooling success. Interventions such as Success for All (Madden, Slavin, Karweit, Dolan, & Wasik, 1993), where implementation generally begins in kindergarten through the 3rd grade or preschool through the 3rd grade and then continue up to Grades 4 and 5, appear appropriate and effective. Although evidence suggests that substantial reading effects typically occur in the first year of implementing the program at kindergarten and 1st grade, some large effects are found in the 2nd and 3rd grades after the initial year of implementation. To ensure academic success for African American boys, curriculum improvement, instruction, and support for teachers should begin in preschool and earlier before boys begin to underachieve. It is clear that program interventions are less effective if they are implemented after boys have fallen too far behind. Although early intervention strategies for Black boys are necessary, they are not always sufficient. The effects of early interventions alone generally fade over time, particularly for cognitive outcomes (Wasik & Slavin, 1993). Thus, more research on early and sustained interventions, particularly whole-school reform initiatives such as Success for All, Comer, Title I, and Reading Recovery, is needed to accurately map achievement during the early schooling years of African American males.

Another explanation for Black male underachievement centers on gender identity. One reason commonly mentioned for the alienation and poor academic performance of Black males is that they perceive schooling activities as feminine and irrelevant to their masculine sense of self (Noguera, 2003). Others contend that the increased presence of committed and successful Black male adults in educational environments is essential for enhancing Black boys' academic and social identity development. An array of program initiatives has captured the attention of school administrators, local communities, and parents as possible solutions to school-related problems associated with Black males. Some of these programs are school-affiliated with local groups and organization teaming with school districts to offer support services and mentoring for Black boys. Others are community-based that operate independent from schools in their efforts to mobilize proactive community resources to improve the academic chances of Black boys (Hopson, 1997). All these programs seek to support current school activities by providing a positive presence of adult Black men. Mentoring programs that assign professional Black men as role models for young boys, typically in elementary and middle schools, have been established in many school districts. Professional Black men serve as teachers' aides, tutors, and reading partners for Black boys needing academic support and guidance. The justification for these initiatives points to the need for consistent and positive Black men in educational set- tings who provide models for young Black males to emulate. It is no surprise that Black male organizations such as Concerned Black Men, Inc., Black men's church groups, Black fraternities, and Million Man March chapters are at the forefront of these school-based programs.

Others contend that the increased presence of committed and successful Black male adults in educational environments is essential for enhancing Black boys' academic and social development (Jeff, 1994; Span, 2000). This positive male presence is meant to diffuse traditional masculine behaviors and counters negative gender role socialization of Black boys. The development of conceptions and expressions of masculinity that match positive behaviors and deportment in school settings is the primary objective of these interventions.

Approaches such as organizing all-male schools and classrooms take a more radical approach to current schooling conditions. Given the severity of problems associated with Black boys in schools, advocates for race- and gender-exclusive schooling defend these strategies that attempt reorganize the gendered nature of schools and classrooms as the best approach (Watson & Smitherman, 1991). Many advocates for Black boys see teachers as responsible for imposing feminine standards of behavioral expectations that induce school disengagement attitudes and behaviors (Holland, 1992). These all-male academies serve as compensatory devices aimed at restoring a normative masculinity to the center of Black boys schooling experiences.

Alternative Afrocentric models of masculinity are also being proposed (Akbar, 1991; Jeff, 1994; Kunjufu, 2001) and used in manhood development programs and curricula for younger males. These models call for an overthrow of Western models of male socialization and a regrounding of Black boys and men in a new cultural awareness. African American immersion schools and curricula that stress African and African American history and culture are viewed as positive strategies in building self-esteem and self-confidence and promoting dispositions for learning (Brown, 1995; Murrell, 1994, 2002; Pollard & Ajirotutu, 2000). These schools embrace a new conception of masculinity that shifts from dominate ideas of male socialization to a cultural awareness grounded in the positive experiences and history of African people, particularly Black men. The intent of these models are transformative; however, images of a normative masculinity being either unfulfilled or misdirected still dominate and limit policy and practice solutions.

There has been much controversy on the development of all-male public schools (Span, 2000). A few of these schools, located primarily in large urban areas, exist in theory as all-male because their enrollment also includes African American girls (Watson & Smitherman, 1991). Another area of so-called gender tracking that experiences less political and legal resistance is the single-sex classroom. A number of school districts have experimented with within-school single-sex instruction. The Baltimore City public schools and Washington, D.C., public schools are two large urban systems that successfully implemented single-sex classes (Ascher, 1992). These classes, particularly aimed at Black boys, were designed to help boys catch up to the achievement and performance levels of girls. Unfortunately, very little is known about the effectiveness of these gender-tracked classrooms as well as all-male academies and school-based and community interventions. Recent studies on the effectiveness of culturally themed and African-centered schooling experiences for Black boys have been mixed. Fifth-grade Black boys enrolled in a cultural immersion school were found to take more personal responsibility for their intellectual and academic achievement than their peers in a traditional school. The immersion school, however, appears to account for no other achievement or identity differences (Sanders & Reed, 1995). In addition, Hudley (1995, 1997) identified potential effects on academic self-concept for Black males enrolled in separate Afrocentric classrooms but little effects on achievement.

PROMOTING RESEARCH ON ACHIEVEMENT IN EARLY SCHOOLING

Much of the attention paid to highlighting and understanding Black male underachievement has ironically hindered our understanding of why some African American boys actually achieve and perform well in school. Too often, our research efforts have focused on failure instead of profiling Black boys who are high achievers in elementary school (Ford & Harris, 1996). Studying high achievers also acknowledges teaching strategies, school structures, and student attitudes that are effective in producing achievement results. There is a need to rethink how African American boys with similar demographic backgrounds and shared schooling environments produce differential achievement outcomes. Lessons to be learned from this research approach would be incredibly insightful.

Not all Black boys are the same. This simple point is not an obvious one given most of the discussions about the so-called Black boy problem in American schools. But where are the high-achieving African American boys? It is apparent from the national conversation on troubled boyhood that the inclusion of high-achieving Black boys' experiences muddles the discussion. In essence, we have created a separate conversation and agenda that removes Black boys with competitive test scores and positive school experiences from an important national debate. Racism, stereotypes, lower expectations, and pervasive peer and popular culture define the "other" boyhood crisis that many Black boys face daily (Kimmel, 2000). African American boys create major problems and challenges for schools: These challenges are cultural and gender based. The difficulty for schools, in part, rests in their inability to deal with where these Black boys are coming from and their authentic experiences of being young, Black, and male in U.S. public schools. Although educational institutions acknowledge that these students often bring diverse backgrounds and perspectives, little is understood about the complex lives African American boys lead inside and outside school.

The dismal statistics of the achievement gap and behavioral problems are compelling, but understanding the so-called Black male achievement problem calls for a solutions-oriented research agenda. This includes a research focus on the active role African American boys themselves play in creating their own school experience and opportunities for achievement. This is not to say that how schools structure students'

opportunities to learn is not important. For sure, inequalities in schooling have potentially lifelong consequences for Black male educational attainment, employment, and
family relations. Access to quality academic programs, curricula, and teacher quality are
extremely important (Ferguson, 1991, 2003) for these Black boys who bring to school
many skills, dispositions, and behaviors that marginalize. But to always cast these young
males as victims strips them of any agency in how they make meaning of who they are
at school. New gender centric research project in the schooling of Black boys are also
required—ones that seek to capture the complexity and variations in the voices and
experiences of Black boys at school. Understanding the role of peers, in addition to
teachers and families, in the social construction of masculinity for Black boys in early
education would constitute a major research effort in addressing issue of disengagement
and achievement. Studying Black boys' constructions of masculinity and framing how
they link these constructions to achievement motivation and performance will be extremely important in unpacking the achievement gap problem.

Also, a new research agenda on the role of teachers in increasing the achievement levels of Black boys is being called for. Teacher accountability is a dominant theme in school
reform efforts across the United States. Much of this concern for accountability centers on
student learning and achievement outcomes (Boykin, 1994). But should teachers be held
responsible for the social outcomes and experiences of Black boys? It goes without saying
that teachers play a very significant role in the school lives of students. Because most of the
school day is spent in classrooms under the supervision and guidance of teachers, their
influence on Black boys should never be taken for granted. Although teachers are blamed
for many problems Black boys face, ironically, most of the proposed solutions aimed at
remedying the educational plight of African American boys have excluded teachers. The
rationale for this position is that teachers are blamed for students' poor levels of academic
performance and engagement (Holland, 1992). Teachers' influence on Black boys is too
important, however, to silence them and reduce their contribution to this national conversation. Black males in general share this desire for a more personal connection with
teachers (Davis, 1999). They feel they are often misunderstood and wrongly judged because of how they look and act. Teachers bear a disproportionate role in monitoring social
relationships not only in their classrooms but also in other social settings at the school.
Traditionally, teachers have felt that their student social networks and relationships were
off-limits to them. As teachers are being held accountable for structuring student's learning opportunities, so must teachers take a more active role in understanding Black boys
and intervening when necessary with social lessons that cultivate an appreciation for the
importance of school and achievement.

CONCLUSIONS

As I have tried to illustrate in this article, research on early schooling for African American boys is crucial in mapping achievement trajectories as well as understanding the

reasons for underachievement and school engagement. Unfortunately, studies in the field have been limited in their ability to reasonably account for the achievement gap problem. Given the strengths and weaknesses of these studies, both theoretically and methodologically, the range and focus of research in the field of Black male educational studies can be strengthened. Research findings about effective program and policy intervention outcomes that appear to be robust and consistent over time should be the goal of a progressive research agenda in the study of Black boys in early education. With the zeal to improve the educational and life chances for Black males should also come a renewed interest and urgency in doing outcome- based research that informs policy and practice.

I have suggested three explanatory areas (student attitudes, social organization of schools and curriculum, and masculine identity) that have the greatest potential for structuring a broad research agenda on Black boys' achievement outcomes in the early years of schooling. Related to these research areas is the pressing need to effectively utilize national databases in which data on Black boys are analyzed both comparatively and independently. Furthermore, research and program evaluation efforts need to be more deliberately focused on Black boys' experiences and achievement outcome in national early interventions such as Head Start, Early Head Start, and Healthy Start.

Early schooling is a place in which Black boys begin to make sense about their various identities at school. In the process, counter identities are created inside and outside school that feed on a traditional masculine hegemony of behaviors and attitudes. I am well aware that the development of Black boys' social identity is complicated by the heavy dosages they get from immediate and distance sources, such as family, community, church, and the media. Indeed, these social messages provide young males with information about their place and purpose. Schools, for sure, are contested sites in which Black boys learn to negotiate the endorsement and participation in a variety of gendered identities that could enhance or restrict their achievement possibilities. Sadly, too many schooling experiences of Black boys represent yet another disappointing aspect of their young lives. For many of them, schools ignore their aspirations, disrespect their ability to learn, fail to access and cultivate their many talents, and impose a restrictive range of their options. Within this overwhelming oppressive schooling context, too many Black boys simple give up—beaten by school systems that place little value on who they are and what they offer.

Certainly, a concerted research program and research-based interventions aimed at disentangling the achievement quagmire hold the possibility for ensuring that African American males reach their highest achievement potential. The nation's social and economic stability are dependent on these efforts.

Endnotes

1 The terms *boys* and *males* are used interchangeably throughout the article. However, *boys* denotes a more developmentally appropriate description of early childhood students.

References

Adler, P. A., Kless, S. J., & Adler, P. (1992). Socialization to gender roles: Popularity among elementary school boys and girls. *Sociology of Education, 65,* 169-187.

Ainsworth-Darnell, J. W., & Downey, D. B. (1998). Assessing the appositional culture explanation for racial/ethnic differences in school performance. *American Sociological Review, 63,* 536-553.

Akbar, N. (1991). *Visions of black men.* Nashville, TN: Winston-Derek.

Anderson, E. (2000). *The code of the streets.* Chicago: University of Chicago Press.

Ascher, C. (1992, June). School programs for African-American males . . . and females. *Phi Delta Kappan,* pp. 777-782.

Belton, D. (1995). *Speak my name: Black men on masculinity and the American dream.* Boston: Beacon.

Best, R. (1983). *We've all got scars: What boys and girls learn in elementary school.* Bloomington: Indiana University Press.

Blount, M., & Cunningham, G. P. (Eds.). (1996). *Representing Black men.* New York: Routledge.

Boyd-Franklin, N. B., & Franklin, A. J. (2000). *Boys into men: Raising our African American teenage sons.* New York: E. P. Dutton.

Boykin, A. W. (1994). Reformulating educational reform. Toward the proactive schooling of African American children. In R. J. Rossi (Ed.), *Educational reforms and students at risk.* New York: Teachers College Press.

Boykin, A. W., & Bailey, C. T. (2000). *The role of cultural factors in school relevant cognitive functioning: Synthesis of finding on cultural context, cultural orientation, and individual differences* (Report no. 42). Washington, DC: Center for Research on the Education of Students Placed at Risk, Johns Hopkins and Howard Universities.

Brown, K. (1995). African American immersion schools: Paradoxes of race and public education. In R. Delgado (Ed.), *Critical race theory: The cutting edge* (pp. 373-386). Philadelphia: Temple University Press.

Brown, M. C., & Davis, J. E. (Eds.). (2000). *Black sons to mothers: Compliments, critiques, and challenges for cultural workers in education.* New York: Peter Lang.

Carter, P. L. (2003). Black cultural capital, status positioning, and the conflict of schooling for low-income African American youth. *Social Problems, 50,* 136-155.

Connell, R. W. (1995). *Masculinities.* Berkeley: University of California Press.

Cook, P. J., & Ludwig, J. (1998). The burden of "acting White": Do Black adolescents disparage academic achievement? In C. Jencks & M. Phillips (Eds.), *The Black-White test score gap* (pp. 375-400). Washington, DC: Brookings Institution.

Corcoran, M., & Adams, T. (1997). Race, sex and intergenerational poverty. In G. Duncan & J. Brooks-Gunn (Eds.), *Consequences of growing up poor.* New York: Russell Sage.

Cunningham, M. (1993). Sex role influence on African American males. *Journal of African American Males Studies, 1,* 30-37.

Davis, J. E. (1999). Forbidden fruit: Black males' constructions of transgressive sexualities in middle school. In W. J. Letts & J. T. Sears (Eds.), *Queering elementary education: Advancing the dialogue about sexualities and schooling*. Lanham, MD: Rowman & Littlefield.

Davis, J. E., & Jordan, W. J. (1994). The effects of school context, structure, and experience on African American males in middle and high school. *Journal of Negro Education, 63,* 570-587.

Delpit, L. (1988). The silenced dialogue: Power and pedagogy in educating other people's children. *Harvard Educational Review, 58,* 280-298.

Entwisle, D. R., Alexander, K. L., & Olson, L. S. (1997). *Children, schools, and inequality.* Boulder, CO: Westview.

Epstein, J., & MacIver, D. (1992). *Opportunities to learn: Effects of eighth graders' curriculum offerings and instructional approaches* (Report no. 34). Baltimore, MD: Center for Research on Effective Schooling for Disadvantaged Students, Johns Hopkins University.

Ferguson, A. A. (2000). *Bad boys: Public schools in the making of Black masculinity (law, meaning and violence).* Ann Arbor: University of Michigan Press.

Ferguson, R. F. (1991). Racial patterns in how school and teacher quality affect achievement and earnings. *Challenge: A Journal of Research on Black Men, 2,* 1-35.

Ferguson, R. F. (2003). Teachers' perception and expectations and the Black-White test score gap. *Urban Education, 38,* 460-507.

Fine, M. (1991). *Framing dropouts: Notes on the politics of an urban high school.* Albany: State University of New York Press.

Finn, J. D., & Cox, D. (1992). Participation and withdrawal among fourth-grade pupils. *American Educational Research Journal, 29,* 141-162.

Ford, D., & Harris, J. (1996). Perceptions and attitudes of Black students toward school, achievement, and other educational variables. *Child Development, 67,* 1141-1152.

Fordham, S. (1996). *Blacked out.* Chicago: University of Chicago Press.

Garibaldi, A. M. (1991). The educational experiences of Black males: The early years. *Challenge: A Journal of Research on Black Men, 2,* 36-49.

Garibaldi, A. M. (1992). Educating and motivating African American males to succeed. *Journal of Negro Education, 61,* 12-18.

Hare, N., & Hare, J. (1985). *Bringing the Black boy to manhood: The passage.* San Francisco: Black Think Tank.

Harper, P. M. (1996). *Are we not men? Masculine anxiety and the problem of African-American identity.* New York: Oxford University Press.

Harry, B., & Anderson, M. G. (1999). The social construction of high-incidence disabilities: The effects on African American males. In V. C. Polite & J. E. Davis (Eds.), *African American males in school and society: Policy and practice for effective education.* New York: Teachers College Press.

Heath, P. A., & MacKinnon, C. (1988). Factors related to the social competence of children in single-parent families. *Journal of Divorce, 11,* 49-65.

Holland, S. (1992). Same-gender classes in Baltimore: How to avoid the problems faced in Detroit/Milwaukee. *Equity and Excellence, 25,* 2-4.

Hopson, R. (1997). *Educating Black males: Critical lessons in schooling, community, and power.* Albany: State University of New York Press.

Hudley, C. A. (1995). Assessing the impact of separate schooling for African American male adolescents. *Journal of Early Adolescence, 15,* 38-57.

Hudley, C. A. (1997). Teacher practices and student motivation in middle school program for African American males. *Urban Education, 32,* 304-319.

Hunter, A., & Davis, J. (1992). Constructing gender: Afro-American men's conceptualization of manhood. *Gender & Society, 6,* 464-479.

Irvine, J. J. (1990). *Black students and school failure: Policies, practices, and prescriptions.* Westport, CT: Greenwood.

Jeff, M. F. X. (1994). Afrocentrism and African-American male youth. In R. Mincy (Ed.), *Nurturing young Black males: Challenges to agencies, programs and social policy.* Washington, DC: Urban Institute.

Jencks, C., & Phillips, M. (Eds.). (1998). *The Black-White test score gap.* Washington, DC: Brookings Institution.

Kunjufu, J. (2001). *State of emergency: We must save African American males.* Chicago: African American Images.

Leake, D. O., & Leake, B. L. (1992). Islands of hope: Milwaukee's African American immersion schools. *Journal of Negro Education, 61,* 4-11.

Lee, V., & Bryk, A. (1988). Curriculum tracking as mediating the social distribution of high school achievement. *Sociology of Education, 61,* 78-94.

MacLeod, J. (1995). *Ain't no making it: Leveled aspirations in a low income neighborhood.* Boulder, CO: Westview.

Madden, N. A., Slavin, R. E., Karweit, N. L., Dolan, L. J., & Wasik, B. A. (1993). Success for all: Longitudinal effects of a restructuring program for inner-city elementary school. *American Educational Research Journal, 30,* 123-148.

Majors, R. (2001). *Educating our Black children: New directions and radical approaches.* London: Routlege Falmer.

Majors, R. G., & Gordon, J. U. (1994). *The American Black male: His present status and his future.* Chicago: Nelson-Hall.

Majors, R. G., & Mancini Billson, J. (1992). *Cool pose: The dilemmas of Black manhood in America.* New York: Lexington.

Majors, R. G., Tyler, R., Peden, B., & Hall, R. E. (1994). Cool pose: A symbolic mechanism for masculine role enactment and copying by Black males. In R. G. Majors & J. U. Gordan (Eds.), *The American Black male: His present status and his future* (pp. 245- 259). Chicago: Nelson-Hall.

McCall, N. (1994). *Makes me want to holler: A young Black man in America.* New York: Vintage Books.

Mincy, R. B. (Ed.). (1994). *Nurturing young Black males: Challenges to agencies, programs, and social policy.* Washington, DC: Urban Institute.

Murnane, R., Willett, J., & Levy, F. (1995). The growing importance of cognitive skills in wage determination. *Review of Economics and Statistics,* pp. 251-266.

Murrell, P. C. (1994). In search of responsive teaching for African American males: An investigation of students' experiences of middle school mathematics curriculum. *Journal of Negro Education, 63*(4), 556-569.

Murrell, P. (2002). African-centered pedagogy: Developing schools of achievement for African American children. Albany, NY: State University of New York Press.

Nettles, M., & Perna, L. (1997). *The African American data book: Higher and adult education* (Vol. 2). Fairfax, VA: Frederick D. Patterson Research Institute.

Noguera, P. (2003). The trouble with Black boys: The role and influence of environmental and cultural factors on the academic performance of African American males. *Urban Education, 38,* 431-459.

Polite, V. (1993). Educating African-American males in suburbia: Quality education? Caring environment? *Journal of African American Male Studies, 1,* 92-105.

Polite, V. C. (2000). When "at promise" Black males meet the "at risk" school system: Chaos! In M. C. Brown & J. E. Davis (Eds.), *Black sons to mothers: Compliments, critiques, and challenges for cultural workers in education*. New York: Peter Lang.

Polite, V., & Davis, J. E. (Eds.). (1999). *African American males in school and society: Policy and practice for effective education*. New York: Teachers College Press.

Pollard, D., & Ajirotutu, C. (2000). *African-centered schooling in theory and practice*. Westport, CT: Bergin & Garvey.

Rashid, H. (1989). Divergent paths in the development of African-American males: A qualitative perspective. *Urban Research Review, 12*, 12-13.

Rong, X. L. (1996). Effects of race and gender on teachers' perception of the social behavior of elementary students. *Urban Education, 31*, 261-290.

Sanders, E. T., & Reed, P. L. (1995). An investigation of the possible effects of an immersion as compared to a traditional program for African-American males. *Urban Education, 30*, 93-112.

Sewell, T. (1997). *Black masculinities and schooling: How Black boys survive modern schooling*. London: Trentham.

Simmons, W., & Grady, M. (1992). *Black male achievement: From peril to promise* (Report of the Superintendent's Advisory Committee on Black Male Achievement). Upper Marlboro, MD: Prince George's County Public Schools.

Slaughter-Defoe, D. T., & Richards, H. (1994). Literacy as empowerment: The case for African American males. In V. L. Gadsden & D. A. Wagner (Eds.), *Literacy among African American youth: Issues in learning, teaching, and schooling* (pp. 125-147). Cresskill, NJ: Hampton.

Solomon, R. P. (1991). *Black resistance in high school*. Albany: State University of New York Press.

Span, C. (2000). "Black schools for Black children": Black males, Milwaukee, and immersion schools. In M. C. Brown & J. E. Davis (Eds.), *Black sons to mothers: Compliments, critiques, and challenges for cultural workers in education*. New York: Peter Lang.

Thomas, K. (1990). *Gender and the subject of higher education*. London: Open University Press.

Thorne, B. (1986). Girls and boys together, but mostly apart: Gender arrangements in elementary schools. In W. Hartup & Z. Rubin (Eds.), *Relationships and development*. Hillsdale, NJ: Lawrence Erlbaum.

Tyson, K. (2002). Weighing in: Elementary-aged students and the debate on attitude toward school. *Social Forces, 80*, 1156-1190.

U.S. Department of Education, National Center for Education Statistics. (1993). *National household education survey*. Washington, DC: Office of Educational Research and Improvement.

Wasik, B. A., & Slavin, R. E. (1993). Preventing early reading failure with one-to-one tutoring: A review of five programs. *Reading Research Quarterly, 28*, 179-200.

Watson, C., & Smitherman, G. (1991). Educational equity and Detroit's male academies. *Equity and Excellence, 25*, 90-105.

Welch, O., & Hodges, C. (1997). *Standing outside on the inside: Black adolescents and the construction of academic identity*. Albany: State University of New York Press.

Williams, B. (Ed.). (1996). *Closing the achievement gap: A vision for changing beliefs and practices*. Washington, DC: Association for Supervision and Curriculum Development.

Wright, D. L. (1996). *Concrete and abstract attitudes, mainstream orientation, and academic achievement of adolescent African-American males* [unpublished doctoral dissertation]. Howard University, Washington, DC.

"Those Loud Black Girls": (Black) Women, Silence, and Gender "Passing" in the Academy

Signithia Fordham, Rutgers University

This article explores the impact of gender diversity on school achievement. Using data obtained from an ethnographic study of academic success in an urban high school, this analysis examines how the normalized definition of femaleness-white middle-class womanhood—juxtaposed with a two-tiered dominating patriarchy, propels African-American females to resist consuming images that assert their "nothingness." "Loudness,"[1] thus becomes a metaphor for African-American women's contrariness, embodying their resistance to this proclaimed "nothingness." How "loudness" reflects their efforts to subvert the repercussions of these prevailing images is examined along with an assessment of its impact on academic achievement. GENDER DIVERSITY, BLACK FEMALES, RESISTANCE, ACADEMIC SUCCESS, GENDER "PASSING"

I. Introduction

IN THE ACADEMY[2] women are compelled to "pass"[3] as the male dominant "Other" if they desire to achieve a modicum of academic success (Pagano 1990:13; K. Scott 1991:150; White 1985:36). "Passing" implies impersonation, acting as if one is someone or something one is not. Hence, gender "passing," or impersonation—the coexistence of a prescription and proscription to imitate white American males and females—suggests masquerading or presenting a persona or some personae that contradict the literal image of the marginalized or doubly refracted "Other." For example, Patricia Williams (1988), an African American who is also a Harvard Law School graduate, describes the seemingly contradictory strategies her mother encouraged her to use to succeed in the academy. These strategies were intended to negate her identification with her mother—a dubious role model for success in the academy and the larger society. These same strategies were also supposed to motivate her to reclaim the disinherited white components of her identity.[4]

> My Mother was [constantly] asking me not to look to her as a role model. She was devaluing that part of herself that was not Harvard and refocusing my vision to that part of herself that was hard-edged, proficient, and Western. She hid the lonely, black, defiled-female part of herself and pushed me forward as the projection of a competent self, a cool rather than despairing self, *a masculine rather than a feminine self.* [P. Williams 1988:20, emphasis added]

Likewise, Pagano describes how the academy compels female teachers to hide their femaleness to obtain the desired academic approval of their male peers and superiors. She notes that female teachers often

> present [themselves] as the genderless "author," "artist," or "scientist" . . . (in order] to quell any doubts [they] may have about [their] right to so present [themselves], to speak in the voice of authority—the tradition—and to compete with [their] male colleagues for scarce academic resources . . . hunch [their] bodies in shameful secrecy as [they] walked the corridors of [their] departments for fear that someone would notice [they] were in drag. [Pagano 1990:13]

Gender "passing" is thus a reality for both African-American women and white women. Indeed, it could be debated that the first and some would argue the only-commandment for women in the academy is "Thou must be taken seriously." "Thou must be taken seriously" is a euphemism for "thou must not appear as woman." Therefore, for women to be taken seriously in the academy, they must not only receive a form of schooling the contents of which prepares them to survive and prosper in a world organized by and for men (not women) (Rich 1979:238), but in addition they must transform their identity in such a way that the resulting persona makes the female ap pear not to be female. This evolving persona reflects and highlights socially defined maleness. "Being taken seriously," then, implies discarding or at least minimizing a female identity in a self-conscious effort to consume, or at least present the appearance of being, the male dominant "Other." It also suggests avoiding the traditional dichotomous definition of womanhood: good girl-bad girl, virgin-seductress, angel-whore. The problem, however, is much larger than a common or universal definition of womanhood; it is also the larger society's "acceptance of and complicity in a hierarchy of female goodness that imputes moral superiority to some women's lives and immorality to others" (Palmer 1989:151).

In America, white womanhood is often defined as a cultural universal.[5] Yet, the moral superiority of white womanhood is rarely explicitly verbalized in the academy. Indeed, it is most often labeled "femaleness" minus the white referent. Nonetheless, *white* and middle class are the "hidden transcript[s]" (Scott 1990) of femaleness, the womanhood invariably and historically celebrated in academe. In striking contrast, black womanhood is often presented as the antithesis of white women's lives, the slur or "the nothingness" (see Christian 1990; Walker 1982) that men and other women use to perpetuate and control the image of the "good girl" and by extension the good woman. Hence, the academy's penchant for universalizing and normalizing white middle-class women's lives compels black women and other women of color to seek to appropriate the image and attempt to consume the lives of the female "Other."[6]

Ironically, gender "passing" is rarely identified as a factor in the differentiated academic performance of African-American and white American students. It is also seldom identified as a factor producing asymmetrical outcomes in African-American males' and African-American females' school performance. This response persists despite widespread acknowledgment that (1) African-American students' school performance is gender-differentiated at all levels of the academy (Fleming 1978, 1982, 1983, 1984; Fordham 1988, 1990; Fordham and Ogbu 1986; Garret-Vital 1989; Gurin and Epps 1975; Lewis 1988; Meisenheimer 1990; Sexton 1969; Smith 1982); (2) America's patriarchal system is stratified, with some males having more power and privileges than other males in the patriarchy; and (3) African-American females are doubly victimized by the existence of a two-tiered patriarchy.

A central goal of the analysis presented in this article is to identify and describe how the existence of a subversive, diverse womanhood among African-American women, juxtaposed with a two-tiered dominating patriarchy, influences and often adversely affects academic achievement. An ancillary goal is to document how the absence of "official" recognition of gender diversity in a predominantly African-American high school in Washington, D.C., mutilates the academic achievement of large numbers of female African-American students. I begin the analysis by briefly describing the research site: Capital High and Capital Community. In the next section of the analysis I present the conceptual context, offering both a narrative of how gender is repeatedly constructed and negated in culturally and racially stratified social systems and a discussion of the repetitious construction of an egalitarian ideal within the African-American community. My goal here is to delineate a culturally distinct route to womanhood among African-American women. Specifically, I discuss issues involving the symbolic transformation of African-American women's gendered "Self."[7] Included in this section is a somewhat detailed discussion of the theoretical frame, highlighting anthropological discussions of egalitarianism and how the existence of this process within the

African-American community creates pockets of "safe cultural space" for the promotion of African-American women's self-definition (see Collins 1991). I end this section by fusing these arguments *to* claims regarding the black fictive kinship system,[8] highlighting improvisation or the ad hoc[9] construction of the African-American gendered "Self." In the fourth section of the article I present a somewhat general discussion of how the desire for academic success combined with the negation or suppression of gender diversity among African-American females at Capital High compels them to silence and/or emulate the male dominant "Other." I also include in this section documentation of African-American females' resistance to this silence and imitation mandate. Although acknowledging the common features of the high achieving female students—they work hard, they are silent; when they vocalize, they speak "in a different voice" (Gilligan 1982). I focus my analysis on Rita, a high-achieving female who symbolizes this composite image. Rita, I argue, epitomizes black women's struggle to commingle or fuse two divergent lives concurrently. I postulate that she is both unwilling and unable to be silent. She is also irrevocably committed to the retention of her female, African-American gendered "Self." Moreover, I argue, her speech is masked and disguised in ways that nullify and negate the perception of her femaleness. I try to show how her speech, thinking, voice, and writing styles emulate the dominant male "Other" while embracing her largely unconscious perceptions of African-American womanhood. I also cite several examples of how the child-rearing practices of the parents and teachers of the high-achieving females unwittingly cremate these young African American women's efforts to flee the African-American community and, in the process, paradoxically enhance their affiliation with the larger American society. The concluding section of the article focuses on some of the possible implications of constructing an African-American female for success in the academy and the excessive price she pays for transforming her gendered "Self."

II. The Social Context of the School

Capital High School (a pseudonym) is located in a predominantly African-American section of the city of Washington, D.C. Essentially, it is a school within a school. As a school within a school, Capital at tracts students from all socioeconomic segments of the city of Washington. Indeed, its recruitment efforts are very successful. More than a fourth of the students are non-community residents who travel from various parts of the city to participate in the school's advanced placement and humanities programs.[10] Hence, Capital High is not a school that can be accurately labeled low-income or inner-city, euphemisms for slums and the "underclass." The school's complex student body and diverse, rudimentary class structure[11] do not lend themselves readily to such uncomplicated labeling. It is far more accurate to label Capital a "magnet school," because through its multilevel, multi-rigorous curriculum it accurately reflects the diverse population of the entire city.

The first two years of the study were the most intense. During the first year, 33 11th grade students whose parents had consented to their participation in the study served as key informants. As key informants, these students' were self-consciously interrogated. They were interviewed, observed, and analyzed for more than a year. These students formed a varied group, representing both high-achieving and underachieving students-male and female-and the diverse population described above. My interactions with these students included classroom observations, home visitations, observations of before- and after-school activities, and formal and informal interviews. I also observed and interviewed their parents, teachers, and other school officials. Following a year of interrogating the key informants, the second year of the study included administering an in situ survey to 600 students in grades nine through twelve. For the analysis presented here, data from twelve of the high-achieving students-six males and six females-and twelve of the underachieving students-six males and six females-were examined and interpreted.

In the tradition of sociocultural anthropology, I spent virtually every school day from September to June—and most weekends—in the field, collecting data and trying to understand why, how, and at what cost African-American adolescents achieve school success. To protect the identity of the community and its residents, I gave the school the fictitious name Capital High; the community in which it is located was labeled Capital Community. A large number of the students come from one-parent homes; some of them live in public or low-income housing. Of the nearly 2000 students, almost 500, about one-fourth of the student body, are eligible for the reduced lunch program.

The school's population (students and teachers) is predominantly black. However, virtually every department has at least one white teacher, with the English Department having the largest number four females. In addition, the teachers who teach the more advanced or "difficult" classes (i.e., Advanced Placement English, Advanced Placement Physics, Chemistry, Advanced Placement Mathematics, Government, etc.) are white. They are also the teachers who serve as sponsors for the JETS Club, It's Academic, the Chess Club, and so on. Hence, there is virtually no relationship between the white teachers' power and influence in the academic learning, achievement, and emerging perceptions of the students and their numbers at the school. Further, there is in place at the school a four-tier curriculum: two special programs (Advanced Placement and Humanities); the regular curriculum, where most of the nearly 2000 students are centered; and a program for those students in need of special education. In addition, where there are areas of overlap in the regular curriculum and the two special academic programs, students are grouped according to their performance on standardized examination. And, based on test results, they are permitted and/or required to take the appropriate courses for their skill levels.

III. The Conceptual Context

Constructing and Nullifying Cultural-Specific Femaleness

In a socially, culturally, and racially stratified society like the United States, cultural-specific routes to womanhood are inevitable. Indeed, the stratified nature of state systems suggests the following: (1) gender construction is not universal and (2) status inequity vis-a-vis gender is a sine qua non in such contexts. Hence, femaleness in such contexts is not the same for all women, just as maleness is not the same for all men. Gender diversity (i.e., what it means to be male or female in different social classes and social groups) is rarely officially acknowledged in the academies of contemporary nation-states. Therefore, like most other women of color, African-American women are compelled to consume the universalized images of white American women, including body image, linguistic patterns, styles of interacting, and so forth. Because womanhood or femaleness is norm referenced to one group-white middle-class Americans-women from social groups who do not share this racial, ethnic, or cultural legacy are compelled to silence or gender "passing." Although all women born and reared in America are "educated in romance," in Holland and Eisenhart's (1990) term, and victimized by sexism, not all American women take the same train to a common sexist station. Therefore, as Evans suggests:

> [Anthropologists] need to examine the ways by which the Women's Movement has perpetrated a type of cultural imperialism that takes the oppression of white women as its norm and develops its theory from the experience of a small minority of women in global terms. (1988:189]

"Those loud Black girls"[12] is an example of both the diversity of gender construction in Euro-American contexts and the efforts to sup press that diversity. It is also a quintessential example of African American women's commitment to being visible as culturally specific women. Curiously, these young women appear to be motivated to highlight the practices of gender-specific constructions in contexts that compel male impersonation or, at the very least, the adoption of a male voice.[13] "Those loud Black girls" is also an example of how a people's history is reflected in their daily lives. As Davis (1971) argues so convincingly, African-American women bring to the academy broadly defined—a history of womanhood that differs from that of white or any other American women. African-American women's history stands in striking contrast to that generally associated with white womanhood and includes (1) more than 200 years in which their status as women was annulled, compelling them to function in ways that were virtually indistinguishable from their male slave counterparts; (2) systemic absence of protection by African-American and all other American men; (3) construction of a new definition of what it means to be female out of the stigma associated with the black experience and the virtue and purity affiliated with white womanhood; and (4) hard work[14] (including slave and domestic labor), perseverance, assertiveness, and self-reliance. In other words, the history of African-American males and females includes an extended period when gender differences were minimized, resulting in a kind of "deformed equality" (Davis 1971) or, as Cary (1991) describes it, a period when African American females were "officially" classified as the "neutered 'Other.'"

These images flooded my psyche the day I discovered Grace Evans's (1980) article entitled "Those Loud Black Girls." At long last, I thought, someone has accurately captured what I learned about black womanhood at Capital High and what I personally experienced growing up African and American. Since the word *anecdotal* is almost always preceded by the word *merely*, prior to reading Evans's essay, I never quite trusted the validity of my personal experiences. Growing up female and African-American in American society, I learned early on to discount the validity of my experiences. Evans, an African American social studies teacher in the public school system in several inner-city schools in London, locates "those loud Black girls" in the following setting":

> In staff rooms [of the schools] a common cry to be heard from white teach-
> ers—usually women, for male teachers seldom revealed that everything for
> them was not firmly under control—was, "Oh, those loud Black girls!" This
> exclamation was usually followed by the slamming of a pile of folders on to
> a table and the speaker collapsing into a chair or storming off to get a cup
> of coffee. The words were usually uttered in response to a confrontation in
> which the teacher's sense of authority had been threatened by an attitude
> of defiance on the part of a group of Black girls in a classroom or corridor.
> The girls' use of patois and their stubborn refusal to conform to standards of
> "good behavior," without actually entering the realm of "bad behavior" by
> breaking any school rules, was exasperating for many teachers. The behavior
> of the girls could be located in the outer limits of tolerable behavior, and they
> patrolled this territory with much skill, sending a distinct message of being
> in and for themselves. [Evans 1988:183]

Evans goes on to admit that, as an African-American student in a predominantly white high school in the northeastern United States, she was *not* one of "those loud Black girls." Indeed, she acknowledges that it was her invisibility, her silence, as well as her link to a successful male, her brother, that enabled her to become the "successful" student she was in high school. She asserts:

> I was not a loud Black girl myself; I was one of the quiet, almost to the point of
> silent, Black or "coloured" girls who did her homework, worked hard, seldom
> spoke unless spoken to and was usually to be found standing on the margin
> of activities. I demanded no attention and got none. In the early years of my
> schooling I was considered by most of my teachers to be at best an average

or just above average student, certainly not a particularly promising one. If it
had not been for an elder brother whose academic excellence was noted at an
early age, I probably would have remained ignored by teachers, but word got
around in the schools I attended that I was his sister, and teachers began to
expect more from me. Looking back, I believe that my silence stemmed from
two things: a perception on my part of minority status and a very deliberate
priming for the professions that my parents began when I was very young.
[Evans 1988:184]

Elsewhere I described the black girls who were academically successful at Capital High
as "phantoms in the opera" (Fordham 1990). I made this assertion because the academically successful black girls achieved academic success in the following ways: (1)
becoming and remaining voiceless or silent or, alternatively, (2) impersonating a male
image-symbolically-in self-presentation, including voice, thinking, speech pattern, and
writing style, in the formal school con text when formally interacting with their teachers in classrooms, assemblies, club meetings, and so forth. At the same time, however,
I noted that silence for the African-American female is not to be interpreted as acqui-
escence. Rather, I argued that silence among the high achieving females at the school
is an act of defiance, a refusal on the part of the high-achieving females to consume the
image of "nothingness" (see Christian 1990) so essential to the conception of African
American women. This intentional silence is also critical to the rejection and deflection
of the attendant downward expectations so pervasive among school officials.

Pagano acknowledges and describes women's forced emigration toward silence and
maleness in the academy. She declares:

The more successful [women] have been as students, scholars, and teachers,
the greater has been [their] active participation in [their] own exclusion.
[Pagano 1990:12]

She goes on to document how women pawn their collective voice in exchange for success
in the existing patriarchic structure. By engaging in such practices, she argues, women
ensure the continued existence of authority in the male image and their (women's) complicity in the lie that asserts that they are naturally silent. She concludes by asserting
that women who either remain or become silent are instrumental in maintaining female
dependency and invisibility in the academy. Hence, "those loud Black girls" are doomed
not necessarily because they cannot handle the academy's subject matter, but because
they resist "active participation in [their] own exclusion" (Pagano 1990:12).

In analyzing a small portion of the Capital High ethnographic data, Pagano's claim
is verified in a predominantly African-American context. The following general patterns
emerge among the high-achieving females: (1) resistance as a tenuous, ghostlike existence and status at the school; (2) the coexistence of excellent grades and the appearance

of an erasable persona; (3) parenting, teaching, and child-rearing practices that reward their silence and obedience with good grades, as well as the assertive suppression and denial of physicality and sexuality; (4) alienation and isolation from the black fictive kinship system's ad hoc orientation; and (5) the assiduous commingling and maintaining of an academically successful persona *and* a "nice girl" persona with very little external reward or remuneration from parents or guardians, especially mothers. Such parental child-rearing practices suggest that nurturing a black female for success—as defined by the larger society-is far more disruptive of indigenous cultural conventions and practices than previously thought. Evans acknowledges some of the costs involved:

> The prize of a good education [is often] attained at the cost of great sacrifice on the part of one's parents, sometimes the entire family. Aside from this cost, another price is paid by the recipient of an education, and this is the personal cost of the process of deculturalisation, or de-Africanisation, whereby all personal expressions of one's original African culture are eliminated and [Euro-American] codes established instead. The mastery of standard English to replace West Indian patois is only one aspect of this trans formation. It includes training the body to adopt European body language and gesture, and the voice to adopt European tones of speech and non-verbal expression The price of a good education, a [Euro-American] education, in short, was, and still is, the denial of one's Black cultural identity. This is the price of entry to the middle-class. It is this legacy of education as a double-edged sword that creates a similar suspicion towards Black teachers on the part of Black students as exists on the part of the Black community towards Black members of the police force. The presence of Black faces does not change the essential nature of an institution, nor does it alter its ethos. [Evans 1988:185]

In stark contrast, the following salient patterns are common among the underachieving females in the study: (1) striking visibility and presence-(these young women were known by everyone at the school and did not try to minimize the disruption that their visibility implied); (2) lack of congruency between grades and standardized test scores, with standardized test scores frequently dwarfing Grade Point Average (GPA); (3) parenting and child-rearing practices that suggest unconditional support for their daughters' self-defined academic plans and other espoused goals; (4) encapsulation and immersion in the black egalitarian (i.e., fictive kinship) system (see Fordham 1987, 1988, 1991a, 1991b; Fordham and Ogbu 1986); and (5) obtaining and maintaining support and nurturing from peers and the significant adults in their lives. In the next section I discuss how anthropologists have traditionally framed egalitarianism and how it appears to operate in the contemporary African-American community. I end this discussion by fusing these arguments to the black fictive kinship system, including its improvisation or ad hoc orientation.

Ad-Hocing and Evoking an Egalitarian Ideal

The existence of an egalitarian ideal within the African-American community does not imply the absence of hierarchy. Hierarchy and hierarchies exist in contemporary African-American communities. Individuals are categorized and ranked. Age, sex, and individual characteristics are the usual distinguishing elements. However, as Flanagan (1989:248) points out, anthropologists' historical claims regarding the existence of egalitarian societies do not eliminate the hierarchy between individuals. Like all anthropologically described egalitarian societies, universally employed criteria are visible: "age, sex, and personal characteristics." Like other groups that anthropologists have identified as practicing an egalitarian ideology, members of the African-American community negotiate areas of dominance and status and the contexts in which they will mark these characteristics.

Anthropologists have consistently attributed to societies labeled egalitarian principles of reciprocity—including the sharing of food and power—an undifferentiated economy, and, in some instances, the control of productive as well as reproductive resources (Flanagan 1989:247). Egalitarianism in the African-American community embraces all of these elements. In fact, this approach to life appears to have emerged in response to their American enslavement. To survive, enslaved Africans learned to "live with" the lack of differentiation externally imposed upon them as slaves and, ironically, to make use of the lack of differentiation in ways that not only assured their survival (as individuals), but also promoted the growth and well-being of the entire group.

The idealization of an egalitarian ethos within the African-American community also does not imply the absence of "historical tensions . . . and the interpersonal power struggles that form a part of daily existence" (Flanagan 1989:247). There are tensions and power struggles within African-American communities. Indeed, some people would argue that these features are everywhere, even more rampant than they are in the dominant society. The presence of these tensions and power struggles does not, however, negate the centrality of the claim I am making in this analysis: In African-American communities, an egalitarian ideal or ethos influences the behaviors and responses of African-American peoples. Self-actualization is thus fully realized only in so far as the individual becomes validated through other people. Achieving human status means perceiving oneself as being intimately connected to other people. Consequently, the most highly valued group strategies are those that enable the individual to be seen as embodying those qualities and characteristics that will enhance the status of the group. In this way, he or she is seen as personifying the egalitarian ideal.

In the African-American community, ad-hocing or improvising one's life is what comes to mind when I attempt to capture the torturous relationship between the individual and the group.[15] Ad-hocing or improvising one's life suggests constructing an identity that, on the one hand, does not violate one's sense of "Self," while, on the other hand, enhancing one's sense of fit within a given context. Improvisation is the term used most frequently in describing African-Americans' constructions of music, especially jazz (see

Keil 1966) and, more recently, rap (see Powell 1991; Rose 1991). It also captures the patterns found in other aspects of the material and nonmaterial culture of African-Americans, including dance, quilting (Wahlman and Scully 1983), speech practices (Baugh 1983), and so forth. In each of these very different areas, symmetry is obtained not through uniformity, but through diversity.

At Capital High, the effects of the idealization of the egalitarian ethos are manifestly obvious. They are most visible in the kind of orientation that makes it unnecessary for everyone to possess the same level of expertise in the same subject areas. They are also evident in the various ways the students respond to this process. Leveling behaviors are not difficult to detect. They are manifested in many aspects of the actors' interactions. This egalitarian approach to life coexists with a static, individually competitive, non-leveling curriculum and course of study in the high school context. Further, because the curriculum is what really matters, it is juxtaposed with the widespread lack of individual competition and individual improvisations among the students at the school. The egalitarian ethos is also evident in Capital High students' tendency to seek unity in race and group solidarity rather than individualism and socioeconomic class.

Coexisting with this egalitarian ethos, however, is a not too subtle African-American gender hierarchy embedded in both the African origins of the group and the dominant Euro-American patriarchy. This gender hierarchy is less conspicuous and in some ways barely visible to the unskilled observer. Nevertheless, it exerts an extremely powerful influence on the behavior and expectations of the students male and female—at the school.

Because African-Americans' gender hierarchy both parallels and diverges from the organizational structure in place in the dominant segment of American society—that is, because it is a synthesis of that which is both African and American-black males are in the power (or is it more accurate to say, the most visible?) positions at Capital High. It is they who manipulate the formal school rules. For example, class schedules at the school are planned and prepared by these men with the tacit support of the women. Also, although rules regarding when school will begin and end, what holidays will be celebrated, when football games and other athletic events will be scheduled, are made by several bureaucrats downtown in the administrative offices, Capital's principal often takes it upon himself to modify these official rules to meet the academic needs of Capital students, as he perceives them.

The gender hierarchy at Capital is also pregnant with tensions, conflicts, traditions, and subtle internal meanings. Black females are conversant with black patriarchy, with its refracted African-American origin as well as its subordinate status vis-à-vis the dominant society's patriarchy. They also are familiar with how that authority is expressed and how they are expected to respond to it. It is, however, the splicing and grafting of the dominant Euro-American patriarchal system onto the preexisting black patriarchy, with its vastly different authority base, that is implicated in how black females learn to seek and, in some instances, achieve school success. Regrettably, space limitations do not permit a discussion here of how men of African ancestry in America fuse and seek to replicate the dominant male role.

As I have already indicated, the distinctively constructed gender roles of African peoples in American society are frequently ignored, disparaged, or ridiculed in the larger American society. For example, Elsa Barkley Brown insists that, more than virtually any other people, "African-American women have indeed created their own lives, shaped their own meanings, and are the voices of authority on their own experience" (1988:15). This is their reality, she argues, because, as noted above, for more than 200 years women of African ancestry were not allowed to construct their identity as they had done in the various African countries from which they had come. Nor were they permitted to impersonate womanhood as constructed and practiced by Euro-American women. Hence, womanhood as remembered, and femaleness as observed, were not available to them; they had no choice but to improvise a new definition of femaleness that would be a synthesis of the bicultural worlds they remembered and inherited.

Against this background, African-American women are not seen as the archetypal symbol of womanhood, as is the case for white American women. Indeed, role ambiguity has always haunted the life of the African-American woman. Sojourner Truth is said to have lamented "Ar'n't I a Woman?" (White 1985); Zora Neale Hurston (1969) described black women as "mules," suggesting the existence of strength and endurance. Hurston's image conflicts with that of the white American female for whom idleness—until the feminist movement of the '70s—was the quintessential symbol (Sacks 1976). Indeed, according to Palmer, for the white American woman to transform the unconscious link of women with "sex, dirt, housework, and badness," she [the white woman] "needed another woman to do the hard and dirty physical labor. She needed a woman different from herself, one whose work and very identity confirmed [her] daintiness and perfection" (1989:138). In other words, she needed a black woman.

IV. Learning Silence and Gender "Passing"

Gender "Passing": The Female High Achievers

As Rich (1979) and Pagano (1990) suggest, gender "passing" in the academy is unavoidable. Also, as I have already indicated, during the schooling process women receive a form of schooling the contents of which prepare them to survive and prosper in a world organized by and for men, not women (Rich 1979:238). Consequently, "being taken seriously," that is, becoming a good student, implies certifying male knowledge, conferring the names of the father and contradicting (women's) own biology (Pagano 1990:37-38).

The high-achieving female students at Capital High are living by the first academic commandment for women: "thou must be taken seriously." At the same time, each of them is guilty of seeking a "safe cultural space"[16] to retain their varied perceptions of the gendered African-American "Self." Virtually all of them—Alice, Sia, Lisa, Katrina, and Maggie—are thought of as serious young women, headed for the fast track and a life away from the ghetto. Each of these women is somehow able to walk the tightrope that living two divergent lives mandates. In striking contrast, Rita presents a less balanced persona. Like the other high-achieving female members of the sample, she is compelled to commingle two divergent lives. The important distinction, however, is that she is far less willing than her high-achieving female counterparts to camouflage, in the school context, her perceptions of the gendered African-American female "Self."

Rita is acknowledged to be a brilliant student, but all her teachers and many of her peers worry about her because she presents a "polyrhythmic, nonsymmetrical, nonlinear" persona. She is bold and sassy, creative, complex, and indeflatable. She frequently challenges the values and rules of the school with conviction, vacillating between demanding total adherence to the dominant ideology of the larger society on the part of her teachers and other school administrators and discounting and disparaging these same values and rules in her personal life. Her actions suggest a "contradictory unity"—an attempt to suture that which is socially defined as incompatible, both in terms of her perceptions of what it means to be black and female and in masking the mastering aspects of the school curriculum. For example, Rita identifies math as her weakest subject in the core curriculum. At the same time, however, she is quite knowledgeable of how computers function and is able to decipher and manipulate computer hardware and a bevy of software quite well.

It was the possession of these computer skills that inspired her math teacher, Ms. Costen, to pay her $40.00 to develop a program for one of her friends who was failing a computer course. Partly as a sick joke, and partly because Rita is convinced that Ms. Costen was acting inappropriately when she asked her to perform what she perceived to be an intellectually dishonest task, she deliberately sabotaged the computer program. She also did not return the $40.00. Her reasoning was that Ms. Costen is a teacher and teachers are supposed to be paragons of virtue, modeling behaviors and attitudes sanctioned by the larger society. In general, although Rita expects teachers to rigorously adhere to the norms, values, and rules of the educational establishment, she feels that it is acceptable and even admirable for her and her peers to blatantly flaunt these same ideals by resisting and outsmarting the teachers at their own game. As she perceives it, her efforts and those of her peers are to be labeled subtle, ongoing resistance to the celebration of the dominant "Other" endemic at Capital High. As students, she and her peers are free to subvert the existing dominating system. On the other hand, as a teacher, Ms. Costen—despite her blackness—does not have the same options available to her. As Rita perceives it, Ms. Costen's role as teacher takes precedence over her connectedness to the black community. Also, according to Rita's perception, her teacher's desire to create a "safe cultural space" is a contested concept.

Hence, like those "loud Black girls" discussed in Evans's essay (1988), Rita refuses to "conform to standards of 'good behavior' . . . without actually entering the realm of 'bad behavior' by breaking any school rules." Rather, she lives on the edge, self-consciously stretching legitimate school rules to help her retrieve a safe cultural space. She is a master craftsperson, baffling her teachers, decertifying the sanity of her mother and most other family members, and ultimately assuring officials at St. Elizabeth's[17] that their beds will be occupied. The following description of Rita's behavior resonates in this analysis.

As I have already indicated, all 33 key informants were 11th graders. During the spring of the academic year, those students who had performed well on the PSAT were strongly encouraged by their teachers and other school officials to apply for admission to the colleges that they were interested in or that had indicated an interest in them. Since Rita had the highest score on the verbal component of the exam, she had received letters from numerous colleges inviting her to apply. Responding to these letters was no problem. Her dilemma emerged when her English teacher, Ms. Apropos, asked all the students in her English class to share their essays so that she could help them make a good impression on the various admissions committees. She advised them to write strong, upbeat essays that reflected a positive outlook on life. The other students followed her advice unequivocally. They created positive, upbeat essays.

Rita was the only exception. She decided not to write an essay in this genre. She chose, instead, to write about the value of death and dying. Ms. Apropos was speechless. She could not believe that a teenager whose life is on the uptake would even be capable of thinking such morbid, melancholy thoughts. Ms. Apropos had secretly harbored doubts about Rita's sanity for a long time.[18] These fears grew by leaps and bounds when she assigned the class *The Crucible* and Rita refused to read it, claiming that it violated her religious beliefs.[19] When she later asserted that she was going to write about death and dying in her college admission essay, all doubts regarding her mental stability were removed. Ms. Apropos was absolutely sure that "girlfriend" was crazy. This initial impression was reinforced when she tried and failed to get Rita to change her mind.

Rita's willingness to display these dialectic characteristics at school appear to make her an unfeeling and thoughtless person. She is not. Admittedly, she has learned the ideology of the society well. And, at some level, she believes that American society is truly democratic and that the individual makes it or fails based solely on ability. In the school context she is committed to the meritocratic ideals promulgated there and does not want to have any information around her that might suggest that what she has learned, and perhaps is learning, in school is misleading or even untrue. She is definitely a child of the post-civil rights era, in that, like many nonblack persons, she wants to believe that African-Americans have achieved socioeconomic parity with the dominating group: white Americans.

> Some—a lot of times I have people ask me "Do you think you are a white person?" But I don't know, maybe it's me. Maybe I don't carry myself like a black person. I don't know. But I'm black. And I can't go painting myself white or some other color, it's something that I have to live with. So it's the *way it is, and it's not like having herpes or something—it's not bad*. It's—I think

it's just the same as being white, as far as I'm concerned—everybody's equal.
[Interview with author, 4 May 1983]

At the same time, Rita's consistent practice of breaching the cultural assumptions so valued in the school context often leads her teachers to erase their perception of her as a bright, intelligent person. Also, the "slam dunking" part of her persona that propels her to the margins of good behavior, without actually forcing her into the realm of "bad behavior," makes "shrinking lilies" out of most adults who interact with her or, alternatively, motivates them to avoid contact with her, if that is an option. Needless to say, Rita submitted her essay on the value of death and dying. She was also accepted at her chosen institution.

As noted above, the most salient characteristic of the academically successful females at Capital High is a deliberate silence, a controlled response to their evolving, ambiguous status as academically successful students. Consequently, silence as a strategy for academic success at Capital is largely unconscious. Developing and using this strategy at the high school level enables high-achieving African-American females to deflect the latent and not too latent hostility and anger that might be directed at them were they to be both highly visible and academically successful. Invisibility is a highly valued prerequisite for academic success. This is particularly true for these young teenage girls whose evolving sexuality and reproductive capabilities actually undermine their chances of success in the public domain. Learning silence, then, is an obligatory component of Capital's high-achieving females' academic success. They are taught to be silent by their parents, teachers and other school officials, and male peers—both explicitly and implicitly—in order to allay the perception that they are just women, that is, that they will behave in ways typically associated with women and femaleness. Gilligan (1982) has described women as being preoccupied with "relationships." Further, she asserts that this "way of knowing" (relating) is not loudly applauded in the academy. With only a couple of exceptions, the high-achieving females at Capital High are invisible in the highly visible arenas at the school (e.g., class rooms, assemblies in the auditorium, and so forth). Females are encouraged to be "seen rather than heard," to be passive rather than assertive.

Like Evans (1988), prior to her teachers' realization that she was genetically connected to an academically successful male, the high achieving females at Capital High are not central; they are more liminal and marginal than their high-achieving male cohorts. These women's voices are heard primarily through what they write and their pithy responses to questions asked in the classroom and other formal school contexts. They rarely speak extemporaneously in the classroom context. When called upon by their teachers, they are able to answer correctly and politely, but they generally do not announce or celebrate their presence by speaking or in some way making themselves visible. Curiously, the female exceptions—principally Rita—use the voice of a comedian or clown to convey their visibility, a persona used almost exclusively by the high-achieving male students. Rita's high-achieving female cohorts refuse to join her in her impersonation of the "Other." The high-achieving females appear to be afraid to speak because speech will bring attention to their female "Selves." It also may be that, intuitively, as Lewis and Simon point out, these "women know that being allowed to speak can be a form of tyranny" (Lewis and Simon 1986:461). As young African-American women, the high-achieving females at Capital High are intimately conversant with feelings surrounding dissonance and place.

Most of the academically successful girls acknowledge that this newfound silence represents a change from the way they once behaved in school. Each of them can recall when her female voice was not a deterrent to academic success. Some of them attribute their growing, evolving silence to parental controls that are increasingly directed toward limiting both their extrafamilial activities and the fulfillment of their female sexuality. Others are unable to articulate why they have come to be silent. They only know that, for some reason, they are learning or have learned not to speak, not to be visible.

At Capital High, most parentally supported limitations are intended to minimize their daughters' femaleness, especially their emerging sexuality. Paradoxically, the female high achievers interpret their parents' seeming lack of support as having the unintended consequence of unmasking their evolving invisibility. For example, Rita's mother made her quit the track team because she feared that Rita would get involved in some undesired activities, including a sexual relationship with some "little boy." Rita indicated that her mother's demand had the unintended consequence of putting a spotlight on her, making her more visible and subjecting her to ridicule.

It is important to acknowledge that a common, relentless theme in the child-rearing practices of virtually all of the mothers of the high achieving females is an absolute insistence that their daughters be "taken seriously." In addition, these mothers demand control of their daughters' lives and even the options they seriously consider for their futures. The mothers' conditional support for their daughters' voiced academic aspirations confuses them, making their enormous efforts in school appear less valuable. For example, Rita's mother was ambivalent about her daughter's desire to go to college. Indeed, it is probably more accurate to say that she was fearful of Rita's school achievement and what it meant in terms of options for her.

> I'm going to tell you like this, Ms. Fordham: I am really happy that Rita's doing what she's doing [in school], and I'm not going to be hypocritical about it. But if Rita didn't go to college, it would not make me a bit of difference No, it would not. Because, like I said, you know, education is good. And I think that Rita—she says that she wants to go into neurology, or something to that effect. And from studying the Bible and looking at the events the way that they are today, the Bible shows that this system is not going to be here that long. Whenever it is that it's going to come to an end well, not the system, it is not going to end, but the end of wickedness, we don't know. See, the Bible says there's going to be people that's going to survive the destruction of the system of things. But from looking at the way that things are going on the world

scene, and looking at your colleges and things today, I mean, they have-the individual, when they're going *to* college and things, they go there for the right purpose-because there's a lot of kids that go there and—for the right purpose, but a lot of things happen in college. See? And . . . I mean kids that get hung up with drugs, and these sororities and things now, the things that they—[I] was reading some article in the paper about these sororities [fraternities] initiating these young guys, and they died from drinking all this—over-drinking and stuff like that, the things they make them do. And, basically, I just—you know, I'm just not that enthused. [Interview with author, 5 May 1983]

The intensity of this mother's ambivalence about her daughter's desire to go to college, as well as Rita's prior assertions regarding her mother's lack of support for her academic efforts, led me to ask her if she would be happier if Rita did not go to college.

I think I would. Yeah. Because I'm not looking forward to a future, you see, because the system is crumbling, basically. I know education and every—I'm not against learning, now, don't misunderstand me, I'm not against learning. I'm happy that Rita has the qualifications and things to go to college. I mean, were things different, and we were living at a different period of time, I mean, it would be all right. Now her father's all for it, you know, and I'm not totally against it, but I'm saying—looking at—for people now to plan a career—and I mean, I've seen people with college degrees and everything, they [black people] cannot even get a job. [Interview with author, 5 May 1983)

At this point in their young lives, the high-achieving females read their parents' insistence on silence and invisibility in the school con text and strict extrafamilial limitations-no dating, no after-school activities, and so forth-as well as uncertainty and/or ambivalence about their academic goals, as a lack of support for what they dream of doing: going to college immediately after high school and living their lives in ways that parallel their white American peers.

The silence attendant to female academic excellence is exacerbated in the school context where, again, the high-achieving females are given episodic, rather than contin-uous, unlimited support for their academic achievement and their voiced future dreams. This is the reality, despite the fact that the teaching staff and other adult members of the school are primarily African-American and female.[20] The following example of a coun-selor's response to Katrina's-another high achiever-excellent performance on a required District of Columbia public school system exam is illuminating.

Ms. Yanmon is Katrina's counselor. In fact, she is the counselor of all the students who participate in the advanced placement program at the school. They are virtually her only counselees, even though they make up less than a fourth of the school's student population.

Like every other student at the school, Katrina took the LSE (Life Skills Examination). This is a District of Columbia Public School requirement. Every student must pass it before he or she is eligible for graduation. When I went to Ms. Yanmon's office to ask her if I might look at the scores of her other counselees who were participating in my study, she readily agreed. As I sat in her office looking at the test results, I mentioned that I had an extremely interesting interview with Katrina the day before. This is how I recorded our interaction in my field notes (4-8 February 1983):

> [Ms. Yanmon] does not talk about Katrina unless I [allude to] her [first]. When I mentioned . . . that Katrina made a perfect score on the LSE, her response startled me. She [lamented the fact] that although Paul want[s] to be the valedictorian [of their class], her guess is that Katrina will be the valedictorian . . . , and Paul will be the salutatorian . . . . "Capital has not had a male [valedictorian] in about 10 years," [she mourned] . . . . "The girls do better." . . . She then asked to see the copy of [Katrina's] performance on the Life Skills Examination. I told her that [Katrina's] perfect score was the only one I had seen so far . . . . I was flabbergasted! This counselor had not talked with [Katrina] about her outstanding performance. [Ms. Yanmon acknowledged that she had not talked with Katrina about her exam results] and said, after looking at her performance sheet, . . . "I must talk with her about [this]."

Silence around female achievement was not unusual. In some ways, this silence suggested that school officials took their ability and willingness to do the work for granted; in other ways, the silence could be—and was—perceived by the students as discounting and/or disparaging their academic effort and achievement. At the same time, however, these girls were learning an important lesson for survival in the academy: the most efficient way to intersect the patriarchic system at the school is to perform all assigned tasks while remaining silent, to respond as if absent rather than present. In my field notes I recorded my response to Ms. Yanmon's seeming lack of interest in Katrina's LSE scores (4-8 February 1983):

> I could not help but wonder if [Ms. Yanmon] would have been so nonchalant about [Katrina's] perfect [exam] score if it had been made by either Paul or Norris.[21] I don't think so. All of the minute details began to return, [including] her reluctance to allow me to talk with Katrina as I was contemplating whom to include in the study.

Katrina admits that her higher grades in school have had all kinds of undesired, and sometimes unexpected, consequences in her life. For example, she has never had a lot of friends, so it would be a mistake to label her popular. She was quick to point out, however, that she did not mean to suggest that she is without friends. That was and still is not the case. It simply means that she has always been able to count on one hand the number of persons she could label "friend." She attributes some of this to her ability to perform well in school. *Ironically, her higher academic performance has cost her a sense of voice.*

Lisa, another high-achieving member of the sample, has a similar tale to tell. When her classmates teased her or pulled her hair, for example, she managed always to ignore them. As did Katrina, she re fused to let them bait her into physical or verbal confrontations. Both Katrina and Lisa ignored their detractors, remaining silent when they were expected to (1) cry, (2) report their detractors to the principal or their classroom teachers, or (3) take some action that suggested a violation of their person or space. Regardless of the nature or source of the abuse they received, these high-achieving females' general re action was to not respond; they refused to retaliate or show pain. Curiously, their silence promoted, and is implicated in, their subsequent academic success.

There is also the problem of the male high achievers who acknowledge fear of female academic success. For example, Paul, who would ultimately graduate salutatorian of the class, was extremely concerned about Katrina's higher grade point average. He and Norris, the student who would graduate third in the class, constantly joked about how to get rid of Katrina prior to graduation, with throwing her from the subway train being the most frequently mentioned method. Most of their conversations about Katrina's higher GPA were ensconced in the "ritualized insult" pattern characteristic of "Black street speech" (see Baugh 1983), but the fear and anxiety they experienced, especially Paul, because of Katrina's higher grade point average were unmistakable. These responses are most often seen as problematic. Let me now turn to a brief discussion of the cultural meaning and some possible social implications of these findings.

V. Conclusions and Implications

I began this analysis by asserting that gender "passing" is a sine qua non for women in the academy if they desire to achieve a modicum of academic success (Pagano 1990:13). I followed this observation by emphasizing that the first commandment for women in the academy is "Thou must be taken seriously." Further, I argued, for women to be seen as being serious about the work of the academy, they must receive (as opposed to claim) a form of schooling the contents of which prepares them to survive and prosper in a world organized by and for men, not women (Rich 1979:238). I went on to point out that, for African-American women in the academy, being taken seriously also means dissociating oneself from the image of "those loud Black girls," whose "refusal to conform to standards of 'good behavior,' without actually entering the realm of 'bad behavior' by breaking . . . school rules," severely undermines their limited possibilities for academic success. Moreover, I documented, with data from the Capital High research site, how "those loud Black girls" are doomed, how their reluctance to engage in "active participation in [their] own exclusion" (Pagano 1990:12) from the academy strips them of a sense of power. N. Scott (1985) has described responses of this nature on the part of those who have been historically excluded as the "weapons of the weak." Audre Lorde asserts that responses in this genre on the part of African-Americans and other peoples of color indicate that they know they cannot use "the master's tools . . . to dismantle the master's house" (1990:287).

The distinctive history of people of African ancestry and their current social conditions, I argue, are implicated in the structure and configuration of their gender roles. African-Americans' continuous, ongoing lack of dominance and power in the Euro-American patriarchic structure has had, and continues to have, severe implications for African-American women (and men). Still further, I indicate that, in the case of the academically successful females at Capital High, silence and invisibility are the strategies they feel compelled to use to gain entry into the dominating patriarchy.

The findings presented here certify that at Capital High black females are the more successful students. Ironically, they are also the least visible. They are the people "passing" for someone they are not: the white American female and, ultimately, the white American male. Silence is implicated in their greater school success because it conceals their female voice and the resulting gender expectations.

For African-American women, socialization to silence and invisibility is not without pain. It is painful because, as I documented in the above analysis, black females pay an inordinate price for academic success: it leads to an "ignorance of connections," an uncertain "fork in the road." Although I have talked about black girls' school achievement in one particular context (Capital High), it is important to acknowledge that parental ambivalence about the value of academic learning is not limited to the parents of the students at Capital High. The disheartening, unintended consequences associated with the uncertainty of academic excellence are frequently recorded in the research literature. For example, in her book *Talking Black* (1989), bell hooks describes how her parents' ambivalence about her preoccupation with school-related learning robbed her of her confidence, threatening her pursuit of academic excellence. At the same time, she acknowledges that it was her parents' ambivalence about the value of school and schooling that forever welded her to the African-American community.

> My parents' ambivalence about my love for reading led to intense conflict. They (especially my mother) would work to ensure that I had access to books, but would threaten to burn the books or throw them away if I did not conform to her other expectations. Or they would insist that reading too much would drive me insane. Their ambivalence nurtured in me a like certainty about the value and significance of intellectual endeavor which took years for me to unlearn. While this aspect of our [race] reality was one that wounded and diminished, their vigilant insistence that being smart did not make me a "better" or "superior" person (which often got on my nerves because I think I wanted to have that sense that it did indeed set me apart,

> make me better) made a profound impression. From them I learned to value
> and respect various skills and talents folk might have, not just to value people
> who read books and talk about ideas. They and my grandparents might say
> about somebody, "Now he don't read nor write a lick, but he can tell a story,"
> or as my grandmother would say, [he can] "call out the hell in words." [hooks
> 1989:79]

Socialization to silence and invisibility is also distressing because it isolates and alienates
black girls from their more communal and popular underachieving female cohorts. Still
further, learning to be silent can be so distressful that it sometimes results in a decision
to abandon the effort to succeed in school because, in part at least, it evokes "ignorance
of connections." This occurs because many of the high achieving girls do not understand
why their parents—particularly their mothers—and many of their female teachers do
not appear to be supportive of their academic achievements.

However, lack of adult female support is a misperception. As hooks's analysis suggests, the seeming lack of support solders the African-American female to the black
community forever. It is also a mis-perception to see parental support as universally
constructed. As this analysis suggests, parental support is not a universal construction.
Indeed, this analysis documents that the existence of gender diversity and what it means
to nurture are pervasive. Hence, for the African American female to achieve school success, all of the usual symbols of nurturing are turned upside down and/or inside out.
These data clearly suggest that what can be labeled nurturing is cultural-specific. The
academically successful females at Capital High are using a Euro American definition of
power and nurture in concluding that the significant adults in their lives are not supportive of their academic goals. They come to this enormous conclusion because they view
their underachieving friends' parents' drastically different interactional patterns as the
more appropriate model. The academically successful girls also study the Euro-American
model via television and other media sources, including their textbooks. These sources
strongly influence what they come to value and define as nurturing and supportive.

Regrettably, the high-achieving females at Capital High do not discern that their mothers and their seemingly unsupportive teachers are often unconsciously preparing them
for a life away from the black community, a life in which they are the "doubly-refracted
'Other.'"[22] As the "doubly-refracted 'Other,'" "the African-American female's survival "out
there" is largely dependent upon her ability to live a life saturated with conflict, confusion,
estrangement, isolation, and a plethora of unmarked beginnings and endings, jump starts,
and failures. It is also likely to be a life in which a family of procreation[23] and connections
takes a back seat to "makin' it."

Therefore, the central questions haunting this entire analysis and smoldering in
the lives of all African-American females are the following: Is gender diversity something to celebrate? Should we seek its fragmentation? If so, how? Should our goal be to
transform "those loud Black girls"? Should success for African-American women be so

expensive? Finally, should the African-American female seek to reconstruct her life to become successful, pawning her identity as a "loud Black girl" for an identity in which she is the "doubly-refracted [African-American] Other"?

Acknowledgments

The research on which this analysis is based was funded initially by grants from the National Institutes of Education (NIE-G-82-0037), the Spencer Foundation, and a dissertation fellow-ship from the American University in Washington, D.C. More recently, a National Science Foundation training grant has afforded me time away from the classroom and the opportu-nity to consider and develop the analysis presented here. An earlier version of this article was presented at the Anthropology Bag Lunch Symposium in the Department of Anthropology, Rutgers University, New Brunswick, New Jersey, 20 February 1991. I wish to thank my col-leagues in the Department of Anthropology at Rutgers for helpful comments and suggestions. I would especially like to thank the faculty, staff, and students at Capital High, their parents, and all other adults in Capital Community for allowing me to intrude in their lives. In ad-dition, I wish to express a special note of thanks to Linda Chalfant and Professors Gerald Davis and Brett Williams for helpful comments and suggestions on successive drafts of this manuscript. I am solely responsible for this final version.

Endnotes

1   Loudness, as I am using it here, is not meant to convey the usual meanings, including noisiness, shrillness, flashiness, ostentatiousness, and so on. Rather, it is meant as one of the ways by which African-American women seek to deny the society's efforts to assign them to a stigmatized status that Christian (1990) has described as "nothingness." There-fore, "those loud Black girls" is here used as a metaphor proclaiming African-American women's existence, their collective denial of, and resistance to, their socially proclaimed powerlessness, or "nothingness."

2   As I am using the term, the academy includes all levels of schooling, but especially that aspect of schooling that begins at the secondary level, that is, junior high or middle school and beyond. I am including precollegiate schooling in my definition of the academy be-cause this is where notions of adult gender-differentiated behaviors—including possible mate selection—are initially nurtured and practiced

3   Historically, in the African-American community, "passing" meant appropriating the body of the "Other" (i.e., the mulatto would pretend to be white and essentially assume a gen-der-appropriate white body) (see Brown 1972; C. Green 1967; Ione 1991; Montgomery 1907; Washington 1987; What It Means to Be Colored in the Capital of the United States 1907 [author and publisher not listed]). Today, while blackness or African-ness is still a stigma, it is no longer the stigma it was. Therefore, in post-civil rights America, not very many people of African ancestry feel the need to assume a white persona to escape a stigmatized

identity. Nonetheless, despite the wholesale acceptance of blackness by contemporary African-Americans, blackness as a cultural symbol is still loaded with many social and cultural stigmata. Because it continues to be a stigma in many contexts, for example, "Dressed as Death in a black, hooded shroud" (Grove 1991:B1), some people of African ancestry resort to "passing" in a figurative rather than a literal sense. Hence, although the African-American values his or her African ancestry and is secure with his or her identity as a person of African ancestry, he or she is compelled to this figurative "passing" because he or she cannot represent black and blackness and also appropriate the white [whiteness of the "Other" while retaining an idealized perception of an uncontaminated, nonhybridized "Other." Against this backdrop, I am postulating that in the contemporary context some physically identifiable African-Americans often feel obliged to engage in a kind of identity plagiarism (see Fordham 1993a) in which the racially identifiable African American body takes on the cognitive map of the racially and culturally dominant "Other." In their construction of an idealized "Otherness," these con temporary African-Americans unwittingly lose that which invokes and fuels their creativity, that which gives voice to their African-American humanness. Unable to speak or even think in their native voice, these individuals become a "sort of surrogate and even [subversive] [S]elf" (Said 1989:3). Meanwhile, because they are compelled to assume the identity of the "Other"—in exchange for academic success—they cannot represent themselves; they are forced to masquerade as the authentic, idealized "Other."

4   P. Williams's (1988) maternal grandfather is racially identified as white.

5   I am sensitive to the possibility that I will be accused of making essentialist claims (Fuss 1989) regarding race as well as white and black womanhood. It is currently fashionable to argue that much of what is written related to these issues can be dismissed because the writer is likely to be accused of making claims regarding some "true essence—that which is most irreducible, unchanging, and therefore constitutive of a given person or thing" (Fuss 1989:2). This is not my intention. What I hope to show in this analysis is how African American women are compelled to construct an ad hoc identity in a context where, for much of their history in this country, they have not only been barred from its "hallowed halls," but have also, at the same time, been defined and represented by those who repeatedly defined them as "nothingness." I am not positing that there is some "pure or original [race or] femininity, a [race or] female essence, outside the boundaries of the social and thereby untainted . . . by a [racist or] patriarchal order" (Fuss 1989:2). Indeed, I realize that there is more than one of each of these, including white womanhood within the dominant community. Nevertheless, I am positing that when the issue is black and white womanhood, white womanhood in all its various forms is usually elevated.

6   It is important to point out that both black and white women "are objectified, albeit in different ways, . . . [in order to] dehumanize and control both groups" (Collins 1991:106).

7   See Fordham (1993c) for a detailed discussion of some of the implications affiliated with the transformation of the gendered "Self."

8   See Fordham (1987, 1988) and Fordham and Ogbu (1986) for a detailed discussion of the emergence and development of the fictive kinship system in the African-American community.

9   Elsewhere (Fordham 1993b) I offer a detailed discussion of how female students at Capital High create an African-American female identity in a con text that does not sanction gender diversity.

10   This is the fictitious name I gave the flagship academic program at Capital High.

11   As many researchers have suggested (see, for example, Cox 1948; Dollard 1957; Frazier 1969; Landry 1987; Ogbu 1978), race undercuts class in the African-American community. Hence, class phenomena do not have the same meaning in the black and white communities. For example, Obgu (1978) argues quite convincingly that there is a lack of congruency among the various classes in the African-American and white communities. As he describes it, middle class in the white community is not analogous to middle class in the black community. The same is true of the designations: working class, lower class, upper-middle class, and so forth. Furthermore, as I am beginning to analyze the quantitative data collected during the Capital High study, I am overwhelmed by the unanimity of the response to the following question: "Would you say that socially your family belongs to the upper class? Middle class? The lower class?" Would you describe your neighborhood as mainly up per class? Middle class? Lower class? Almost invariably, the students chose "middle class" as the appropriate response.

12   I am indebted to Grace Evans (1988) for this characterization of African American females.

13   Payne (1988) supports Evans's (1988) analysis of gender diversity by noting that the school context is impregnated with male norms and values. These features are so pervasive, she argues, that for some women existence is tantamount to "suffocat[ing] in comfort" (see Emerson, cited in Hendrickson 1991). Payne highlights resistance as a primary female response to this construction of the academic context, even postulating that for some young women in the academy pregnancy is an attempt to validate and affirm their female "Self" in this male-dominated institution.

14   Hard work is probably best described as work outside the home (i.e., paid labor). It is also accurate to describe hard work as laborious and intense. As enslaved females, African-American women received no, or virtually no, remuneration for their labor outside the home. Once manumission occurred, they were further victimized in that they were not adequately compensated for their labor.

15   It may appear that I am making some essentialist or timeless claims about the African-American community. That is not my intention. Indeed, I want to emphasize that I am not claiming that there exists out there some "true essence" (see Fuss 1989). Obviously, each African-American constructs the world differently. The point I am making here is that, in spite of their differential understanding and perception, African-Americans also share "socially acquired knowledge." In some contexts this is known as culture (see Bohannan 1992; Spradley and McCurdy 1989).

16   Following Collins (1991), I am defining a "safe cultural space" as a site where African-American women are able to celebrate and applaud their varied sense of "Self." Elsewhere (Fordham 1993b) I have indicated that the academy neither encourages nor promotes gender diversity. Further, I argue, because the African-American female "Self" is seen primarily as an illegitimate form, these women's quest for a safe cultural space is often pursued surreptitiously. Hence, finding a "safe cultural space" is a challenge for all African-American females at Capital, regardless of level of achievement or academic effort.

17   A federally funded hospital for the mentally ill in Washington, D.C.

18   I am able to make this assertion because I was at the school for more than two years. During that time, I had numerous conversations with Ms. Apropos about Rita (she was only one of several students in the sample that Ms. Apropos taught) and many other students. I was able

to observe many of these students in Ms. Apropos's English classes. She was one of several teachers who was willing to share with me information that went beyond the rudimentary, about the students, their parents, and the administrators. Ms. Apropos was frequently baffled and buoyed by Rita's contradictory behaviors, her concurrent acceptance and rejection of school norms and values.

19 For a more detailed discussion of Rita's ambivalent religious beliefs, see chapter 6 of my forthcoming book, tentatively titled: *Acting White and Book Black Blacks: An Ethnography of the Dilemma of School Success at Capital High* (1993a).

20 I am not suggesting that this fact is unimportant. It is. However, as Lorde notes, "the master's tools will never dismantle the master's house" (1990:287). Her argument indicates a need for an African-American education that is not at the same time a "miseducation" (Woodson 1933).

21 Paul and Norris would graduate numbers second and third, respectively, in the shadow of Katrina, who would graduate first.

22 See Fordham (1993b).

23 A family of procreation suggests the active involvement of ego in producing a family.

References

Baugh, John. (1983). *Black Street Speech: Its History, Structure and Survival.* Austin: University of Texas Press.

Bohannan, Paul. (1992). *We, The Alien: An Introduction to Cultural Anthropology.* Prospect Heights, Ill.: Waveland Press.

Brown, Elsa Barkley. (1988). "African-American Women's Quilting: A Framework for Conceptualizing and Teaching African-American Women's History." In *Black Women in America: Social Science Perspectives.* Micheline R. Malson, Elizabeth Mudimbe-Boyi, Jean F. O'Barr, and Mary Wyer, editors. Pp. 9-18. Chicago: University of Chicago Press.

Brown, Letitia Woods. (1972). *Free Negroes in the District of Columbia, 1790-1846.* New York: Oxford University Press.

Cary, Lorene. (1991). *Black Ice.* New York: Knopf.

Christian, Barbara. (1990). "What Celie Knows That You Should Know." In *Anatomy of Racism.* David T. Goldberg, ed. Minneapolis: University of Minnesota Press.

Collins, Patricia Hill. (1991). *Black Feminist Thought: Knowledge, Consciousness, and the Politics of Empowerment.* New York: Routledge.

Cox, Oliver C. (1948). *Caste, Class and Race: A Study in Social Dynamics.* New York: Modern Reader.

Davis, Angela. (1971). *Reflections on the Black Woman's Role in the Community of Slaves.* The Black Scholar.

Dollard, John. (1957[1937]). *Caste and Class in a Southern Town.* Garden City, N.Y.: Doubleday.

Evans, Grace. (1988). "Those Loud Black Girls." In *Learning to Lose: Sexism and Education.* London: The Women's Press.

Flanagan, James G. (1989). "Hierarchy in Simple 'Egalitarian' Societies." *Annual Review of Anthropology* 18:245-266.

Fleming, Jacqueline. (1978). "Fear of Success, Achievement Related Motives and Behavior in
     Black College Women." *Journal of Personality* 46:694-716.

—. (1982). "Sex Differences in the Impact of Colleges on Black Students." In *The Undergraduate
     Woman: Issues in Educational Equity.* P. J. Perun, editor. Lexington, Mass.: Lexington
     Books.

—. (1983). "Sex Differences in the Educational and Occupational Goals of Black College
     Students: Continued Inquiry into the Black Matriarchy Theory." In *The Challenge of
     Change.* M. S. Horner, C. Nadelson, and M. Notman, editors. New York: Plenum.

—. (1984). *Blacks in College: A Comparative Study of Students' Success in Black and in White
     Institutions.* San Francisco: Jossey-Bass Publishers.

Fordham, Signithia. (1987). *Black Students' School Success as Related to Fictive Kinship: An
     Ethnographic Study in the District of Columbia Public School System, 2 vols.* Washington,
     D.C.: American University Press.

—. (1988). "Racelessness as a Factor in Black Students' School Success: Pragmatic Strategy or
     Pyrrhic Victory?" *Harvard Educational Review* 58(1):54-84.

—. (1990). "Phantoms in the Opera: Black Girls' Academic Achievement at Capital High.
     Symposium: New American Women." Paper presented at the Annual Meeting of the
     American Anthropological Association, November, New Orleans.

—. (1991a). "Peer-Proofing Academic Competition Among Black Adolescents: 'Acting White'
     Black American Style." In *Empowerment Through Multicultural Education.* Christine
     Sleeter, ed. Pp. 69-90. New York: SUNY.

—. (1991b) "Racelessness in Private Schools: Should We Deconstruct the Racial and Cultural
     Identity of African-American Adolescents?" *Teachers College Record* 92(3):470-484.

—. (1993a). *Acting White and Book-Black Blacks: An Ethnography of Academic Success at Capital
     High* (working title) (in press).

—. (1993b). *Spawning the "Doubly-Refracted Other": African-American Women's School Success
     at Capital High* (in press).

—. (1993c). *Transforming the Gendered Self: The Construction of a Plagiaristic Identity and Ac-
     ademic Success* (in press).

Fordham, Signithia, and John U. Ogbu. (1986). "Black Students' School Success: Coping with
     the 'Burden of 'Acting White.'" *The Urban Review* 18(3):176-206.

Frazier, E. Franklin. (1969(1957]). *The Black Bourgeoisie.* New York: The Free Press.

Fuss, Diane. (1989). *Essentially Speaking: Feminism, Nature and Difference.* New York: Routledge.

Garret-Vital, Michelle R. (1989). "African-American Women in Higher Education: Struggling
     to Gain Identity." *Journal of Black Studies* 20(2):180-191.

Gilligan, Carol. (1982) *In a Different Voice: Psychological Theory and Women's Development.*
     Cambridge, Mass.: Harvard University Press.

Green, Constance M. (1967). *The Secret City: A History of Race Relations in the Nation's Capital.*
     Princeton: Princeton University Press

Grove, Lloyd. (1991). "Marching In a Different Parade: For Desert Storm Protesters, The Trail
     of Victory." *The Washington Post,* August 2: B1.

Gurin, Patricia, and Edgar Epps. (1975). *Black Consciousness, Identity and Achievement.* New
     York: John Wiley & Sons.

Hendrickson, Paul. (1991). "Reporter Out of No Woman's Land: Gloria Emerson, Taking Sides
     From Vietnam to Gaza." *The Washington Post,* June 5: B1, B8, B9.

Hochschild, Arlie Russell. (1975). "Inside the Clockwork of Male Careers." In *Women and the
     Power to Change.* Florence Howe, editor. New York: McGraw-Hill.

Holland, Dorothy C., and Margaret A. Eisenhart. (1990). *Educated in Romance: Women, Achieve-ment, and College Culture*. Chicago: University of Chicago Press.

hooks, bell. (1989). *Talking Black*. Boston, Mass.: South End Press.

Hurston, Zora Neale. (1969). *Mules and Men*. New York: Negro Universities Press.

Ione, Carole. (1991). *Pride of Family: Four Generations of American Women of Color*. New York: Summit.

Keil, Charles. (1966). *Urban Blues*. Chicago: University of Chicago Press.

Landry, Bart. (1987). *The New Black Middle Class*. Berkeley: University of California Press.

Lewis, Diane. (1988). "A Response to Inequality: Black Women, Racism and Sexism." In *Black Women in America: Social Science Perspectives*. Micheline R. Malson, Elizabeth Mudimbe-Boyi, Jean F. O'Barr, and Mary Wyer, editors. Pp. 41-63. Chicago: University of Chicago Press.

Lewis, Magda, and Roger I. Simon. (1986). "A Discourse Not Intended for Her: Learning and Teaching Within Patriarchy." *Harvard Educational Review* 56(4):457-472

Lorde, Audre. (1990). "Age, Race, Class, and Sex: Women Redefining Difference." In *Out There: Marginalization and Contemporary Cultures*. Russell Ferguson, Martha Gever, Trinh T. Minh-Ha, and Cornel West, editors. Pp. 281-288. Cambridge, Mass.: MIT Press.

Montgomery, Winfield S. (1907). *Historical Sketch of Education for the Colored Race in the District of Columbia, 1807-1905*. Washington, D.C.: Smith Brothers.

Ogbu, John U. (1978). *Minority Education and Caste: The American System in Cross-Cultural Perspective*. New York: Academic Press.

Pagano, Jo Anne. (1990). *Exiles and Communities: Teaching in the Patriarchal Wilderness*. Albany: State University of New York Press.

Palmer, Phyllis. (1989). *Domesticity and Dirt: Housewives and Domestic Servants in the United States, 1920-1945*. Philadelphia, Penn.: Temple University Press.

Payne, Irene. (1988). "A Working-Class Girl in a Grammar School." In *Learning to Lose: Sex ism and Education*. London: The Women's Press.

Powell, Catherine Tabb. (1991). "Rap Music: An Education with a Beat From the Street." *Journal of Negro Education* 60(3):245-259.

Rich, Adrienne. (1979). *On Lies, Secrets, and Silence: Selected Prose 1966-1978*. New York: W.W. Norton.

Rose, Patricia. (1991). "Fear of a Black Janet": Rap Music and Black Cultural Politics in the 1990s." *The Journal of Negro Education* 60(3):276-290.

Sacks, Karen. (1976). *The Rockefeller Gang Created Ladies*. Unpublished MS.

Said, Edward W. (1989). "Representing the Colonized: Anthropology's Interlocutors." *Critical Inquiry* 15:205-225.

Scott, James. (1985). *Weapons of the Weak: Everyday Forms of Peasant Resistance*. New Haven, Conn.: Yale University Press.

—. (1990). *Domination and the Arts of Resistance*. New Haven, Conn.: Yale University Press.

Scott, Kesho Y. (1991). *The Habit of Surviving: Black Women's Strategies for Life*. New Brunswick, N.J.: Rutgers University Press.

Sexton, Patricia Cayo. (1969). *The Feminized Male: Classrooms, White Collars and the Decline of Manliness*. New York: Random House.

Smith, Elsie. (1982). "Black Female Adolescent: A Review of the Educational, Career, and Psychological Literature." *Psychology of Women Quarterly* 6 (Spring).

Spradley, James P., and David W. Mccurdy. (1989). *Anthropology: The Cultural Perspective*. 2nd ed. Prospect Heights, Ill.: Waveland Press.

Wahlman, Maude Southwell, and John Scully. (1983). "Aesthetic Principles of Afro-American Quilts." In *Afro-American Folk Art and Crafts.* William Ferris, editor. Pp. 79-97. Boston, Mass.: G. K. Hall

Walker, Alice. (1982). *The Color Purple*: New York: Harcourt Brace Jovanich

Washington, Mary Louise. (1987). *Invented Lives: Narratives of Black Women 1860-1960.* Garden City, N.Y.: Anchor Press.

White, Deborah Gray. (1985). *Ar'n't I a Woman? Female Slaves in the Plantation South.* New York: Norton.

Williams, Patricia J. (1988). "On Being the Object of Property." In *Black Women in America: Social Science Perspectives.* Micheline. R. Malson, Elizabeth Mudimbe-Boyi, Jean F. O'Barr, and Mary Wyer, editors. Chicago: University of Chicago Press.

Woodson, Carter G. (1933). *The Miseducation of the Negro.* Washington, D.C.: Associated Publishers.

Framing and Reviewing Hip-Hop Educational Research

Emery Petchauer, Lincoln University

HIP-HOP (CULTURE) WAS created in the postindustrial Bronx of the early 1970s as a source of identity formation and social status by and for Black and Latino young people (Chang, 2005; Rose, 1994).[1] It was in this crumbling physical and social context because of post industrialization that youth and young adults sampled earlier Black and Latino cultural forms such as mambo, funk, and Jamaican *soundclash*—music, dance, and creative spirits included—to create a rich, complex, and interwoven set of expression that gang-leader-turned-social-organizer Afrika Bambaataa termed *hip-hop* (Chang, 2005; Thompson, 1996). These expressions of hip-hop, known as the *four elements,* include *emceeing* (i.e., rapping), *DJing* (i.e., *turntablism*), forms of dance such as *breaking* (i.e., breakdancing), and writing graffiti (Chang, 2006; Perkins, 1996; Rose, 1994; see Appendix A for a glossary). Recently, the expressions of hip-hop have expanded to include other creative activities such as spoken word poetry, theater, clothing styles, language, and some forms of activism (Chang, 2006).

Because of the commodification and exploitation of cultural forms such as hip-hop in the mid-1980s, today most commercial media representations of hip-hop portray it as a narrow musical genre synonymous with rap music.[2] Hence, celebrities such as Kanye West, Jay-Z, and Lil Kim whose public personas are shaped largely by corporate media connote the totality of hip-hop in the public eye, and these eclipse the variety of hip-hop musical and thematic genres past and present and other hip-hop practices that still flourish in local scenes around the world. Much controversy has surrounded hip-hop in large part because of the menacing images that some rappers intentionally cultivate, how record labels selectively produce and market them to specific demographics (e.g., suburban adolescents), the violence depicted in hip-hop that is both real and exaggerated, and (most recently) hip-hop-themed pornography (Miller-Young, 2008). Consequently, scholars such as Kilson (2003) and McWhorter (2003) have labeled hip-hop as nihilistic and destructive, whereas others such as Boyd (2003) and Ginwright (2004) have praised hip-hop as prophetic, empowering, and full of educational potential.[3]

Much confusion also has surrounded hip-hop. This has been the case because there is little translation between the (mis)representations in the commercial media and the grounded expressions that are created in local spaces. Confusion also exists because of the different perspectives on hip-hop as an expression of racial identity and affiliation in the 21st century. Treatments of hip-hop consistently acknowledge the African (American) roots of hip-hop, but Black aesthetic perspectives situate hip-hop as a distinct subset of African American culture (e.g., Alim, 2004b; Clay, 2003; Perkins, 1996; Richardson, 2006, 2007; Smitherman, 1997), and civic-participatory perspectives acknowledge the Black aesthetics of hip-hop but more often emphasize the ways it has been adopted, localized, and (re)created by different groups around the world (e.g., Chang, 2006; Kitwana, 2005; Mitchell, 2001; Pardue, 2004, 2007; Pennycook, 2007a, 2007b).[4] These different assumptions contribute to some of the confusion and controversy surrounding hip-hop and shape how scholars interpret their research, as I discuss below.

Hip-hop has become relevant to the field of education and educational research in at least three distinct ways. First, at an increasing rate, teachers are centering rap music texts in urban high school curricula, often in the name of culturally responsive teaching and critical pedagogy, to empower marginalized groups, teach academic skills, and educate students about how aspects of their lives are subject to manipulation and control by capitalist demands. Second, hip-hop exists as more than a musical genre. The creative practices of hip-hop and the messages constructed in the music are woven into the processes of identity formation by which youth and young adults conceive of themselves, others, and the world around them (Chang, 2006; Dimitriadis, 2001; Ginwright, 2004; Petchauer, 2007a). This includes not only Black and Latino youth in the United States but other ethnicities as well (Iwamoto, Creswell, & Caldwell, 2007), including White youth (Kitwana, 2005). Processes of identity formation have the potential to be intricately woven into teaching, learning, and nearly all things educational. Finally, more and more higher education institutions around the world, particularly in North America, are engaging hip-hop in an academically rigorous manner through courses, research, conferences, and symposia. Currently, more than 100 institutions offer courses on hip-hop, with many universities offering multiple courses in various departments (Walker, 2006).

The overall purpose of this integrated review is twofold. First, I aim to make the burgeoning and discursive body of hip-hop scholarship more accessible to educational researchers and practitioners by briefly framing it into three categories and identifying

Figure 16.1.

Three categories of hip-hop scholarship and three strands to be reviewed.

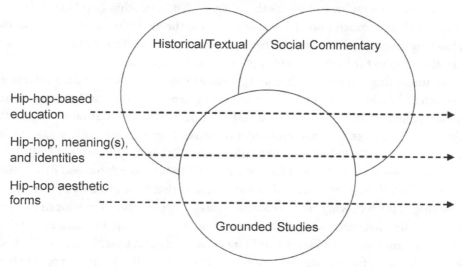

the strengths and weaknesses of hip-hop scholarship in these categories with respect to educational research. These categories are *historical and textual, social commentary,* and *grounded studies*. Such a framing also lends some necessary historical perspective to the development of hip-hop scholarship in and beyond the field of education. Second, according to the criteria described in the following section, I identify and critically review three major strands of literature relevant to educational research that exist across the above three categories. I identify these strands as *hip-hop-based education; hip-hop, meaning(s), and identities;* and *hip-hop aesthetic forms*. Figure 16.1 depicts the relationship among these three categories and strands of literature. Finally, I outline some directions for future research and some theoretical and methodological avenues to get there. With this twofold purpose, this review is intended to be relevant to researchers who might be unfamiliar with hip-hop in the field of education and scholars who have centered hip-hop in their research agendas.

Search Method

A topic such as hip-hop that exists across traditional disciplinary boundaries and venues of publication presents some challenges to a coherent and useful review. This is the case foremost because many findings from scholarship on hip-hop completed outside the field of education are useful in educational contexts (e.g., Pennycook, 2007a), as is illustrated below. Also, theoretical lenses such as discourse (e.g., Jaworski & Coupland, 2006) that have been traditionally situated in other disciplines often hold explanatory power in education. Consequently, while reviewing and evaluating literature on a transverse topic such as hip-hop, it is helpful to apply one of Marcus's (1998) tenets of multi-sited ethnography: "follow the thing" (p. 91). To "follow hip-hop," a useful review must take place through a broad lens not limited to the field of education or respective publishing venues, and scholarship that is strictly in the field of education must be seen in relationship to the broader body of scholarship on hip-hop.

In attempting to follow hip-hop and generate a coherent review, an iterative process of search and evaluation was used. The review began by searching for the terms *rap* and *hip-hop* (and alternate spellings) in abstracts of peer-reviewed journal articles in the Education Resources Information Center database, Sage journals database, and Project Muse, with no limitations on publication years.[5] Other key journals not included in these databases such as *Teachers College Record* and *Harvard Educational Review* were also searched. This search resulted in 203 abstracts that were evaluated for inclusion according to the following criteria: studies taking place in schools or educational programs, studies that centered students' interpretations of hip-hop, and studies that dealt with topics such as youth identity or literacy narrowly and broadly defined that had clear implications for educational contexts and processes. These criteria apply to literature both inside and outside of the United States. Empirical and nonempirical studies were included, as were two relevant doctoral dissertations. References in these works were surveyed for additional relevant citations, which were then obtained from a variety of disciplinary publications and evaluated. Identical criteria of relevance were used to evaluate books or book chapters on hip-hop, rap, and education. In total, 26 articles, chapters, and books are reviewed in the three majors strands of this article (designated by an asterisk in the references section; see Appendix B).

According to these criteria, several genres of research and scholarship on hip-hop are excluded from this review. For example, many examples of journalistic literature such as Shaw's (2000) *West Side: Young Men and Hip-Hop in L.A.* that deal with African American males navigating the music industry and urban environments were excluded because they were only marginally relevant to education. Analyses that are wholly textual and deconstruct rap lyrics to illustrate, for example, how Black female emcees represent themselves in their rap lyrics (Guillory, 2005) were excluded because they deal solely with the researchers' analysis of texts and products rather than, for example, how students and listeners mobilize texts or how teachers use them in school curricula. Similarly, literature that addresses specific hip-hop icons such as Tupac Shakur (e.g., Wells-Wilbon, Jackson, & Schiele, 2008) were also excluded, but studies that deal with how students mobilize and use these popular images in their daily lives (e.g., Dimitriadis, 2001) were reviewed because of their implications on pedagogy and curriculum.

The intent of these search methods and criteria was not to garner every scholarly and relevant work on hip-hop. Because hip-hop scholarship exists in many academic disciplines and outside of traditional academe venues,[6] some relevant works were surely not caught by this search method and these criteria. The reviewed works, however, were sufficient to provide a framework into which these uncaptured works could most likely be categorized and to illustrate trends and future avenues for hip-hop educational research.

Three Kinds of Literature That Engage Hip-Hop

The scholarly work on hip-hop resides in numerous disciplines and specializations such as philosophy (e.g., Darby & Shelby, 2005), sociology (e.g., Rose, 1994), psychology and counseling (e.g., Brown, 2006), communications (e.g., Dimitriadis, 2001), higher education (e.g., Petchauer, 2007a), Black studies (Smitherman, 1997), cultural studies (e.g., McLaren, 1997), women's studies (e.g., Pough, 2004), spirituality (e.g., Pinn, 2003), ethnomusicology (e.g., Krims, 2001), critical literacy (e.g., Morrell, 2004), curriculum studies (Ibrahim, 2004), sociolinguistics (e.g., Alim, 2004b), and more. Forman and Neal's (2004) *That's the Joint! The Hip Hop Studies Reader* alone demonstrates the diversity of approaches to hip- hop, their necessity, and the burgeoning field of Hip-Hop studies.

This interdisciplinary and discursive body of literature can be framed according to three heuristic categories: historical and textual, social commentary, and grounded studies. Central to these categories are notions of text, the "groundedness" and privilege of interpretation, and research methods (or absence thereof). Although these categories are not completely separate and at times draw on one another, they create a useful heuristic to frame hip-hop scholarship. This section defines and illustrates each of these categories through a brief review of the strengths and weakness of some key contributions to educational research.

Historical and Textual Literature

The earliest and most prevalent approaches used to analyze hip-hop have been historical and textual in nature. These scholarly works generally completed by academicians for an academic audience apply discipline-specific analytical tools and frameworks to historical, narrative, and textual manifestation of hip-hop (e.g., lyrics, movies, magazines, videos). Often praised as the touchstone academic text on hip-hop, Rose's (1994) foundational *Black Noise: Rap Music and Black Culture in Contemporary America* was a sociohistorical analysis of hip-hop and the postindustrial context that surrounded its genesis in the Bronx. Other works within this category have traced hip-hop to its African and African American roots. For example, Smitherman (1997) connected the communicative practices of rap to African American Language features such as the *aspectual be, zero copula,* narrativizing, and signifying. Thompson (1996) made clear some of the African origins of hip- hop such as similarities between moves in breaking and Kongo dances. Roediger (1998) traces the very term *hip-hop* to African origins through the word *hipi* (i.e., to be aware or have one's eyes open) derived from Wolof speakers. The literature in this category that is more textual rather than historic also generates from the field of cultural studies (Giroux, 1994). From this approach, for example, violent and nihilistic rap lyrics within the subgenre of *gangsta rap* are products that students and teachers can analyze to understand knowledge, social identities, oppositional and oppressive practices, and (counter)hegemonic structures (McLaren, 1997), including the role of the music industry.

Historical and textual approaches have made a significant impact on the field of education in the past 15 years. Broadly, they have helped to establish hip-hop as an essential domain of inquiry and identified some of the complex and contradictory ways that these texts could function as both oppressive and empowering. Despite the valuable and creative contributions, they are often limited to researchers' explanations of how hip-hop might function in the lives of those who create it in local contexts. This limitation is because of the production of scholarly works separate from the lived experiences of people who identify with and create hip-hop. Scholarly works are separate when they focus on products such as rap songs more than the groups, processes, and contexts that create them. Studies such as these often lack empirical substantiation that these texts contain the same meanings in the hermeneutical estimation of actors in local spaces. Thus, these approaches seldom capture the grounded and local meanings that cultural expressions, metaphors, rituals, and readings hold for groups and the complex processes through which they coconstruct meaning in and beyond educational settings.

Social Commentary Literature

Emerging during the mid-1990s during the same time as the historical and textual literature, the social commentary literature often maintains some of the characteristics of historical and textual approaches, but most of this body of literature has been generated outside of academe and for a broader audience. Works of this nature by George (1998), Kitwana (2002, 2005), and Chang (2005, 2006) have made invaluable contributions to understanding hip-hop because they have often built on an author's privileged insider status to capture lost voices and generate new questions and insights about the complex origins and expansion of hip-hop since its genesis. For example, Chang's (2005) *Can't Stop Won't Stop: A History of the Hip Hop Generation*, based on extensive interviews, included a detailed chronicle of the transition in youth culture from the gangs of the Bronx in the late 1960s and early 1970s into hip-hop.[7] This not only filled a considerable void in more completely understanding one social context that led to hip-hop but also projected the voices of some of hip-hop's earliest participants to spaces beyond their current neighborhoods—literally and figuratively.

Despite these laudable contributions, journalistic and social commentaries pose a number of obstacles to academicians exploring hip-hop and its educational uses and implications. Kitwana's (2005) work concerning new and emerging racialized identities in hip-hop, especially different kinds of White consumers, illustrated the common limitation of journalistic methods. While introducing the text, Kitwana stated it was a product of "[interviewing] numerous industry insiders and everyday fans about white kids and hip-hop" (p. 6) during 10 years of traveling the country documenting and engaging in hip-hop. Aside from anecdotal descriptions of the circumstances in which some specific conversations took place, this is the most detailed methodological explanation that is provided for one reading with a research lens. Similar criticisms apply to other texts (e.g., George, 1998; Shaw, 2000). Consequently, although social commentary works are vital contributions to documenting and understanding hip-hop, they do not allow one to evaluate conclusions through a critique of chosen techniques of data collection and analysis, all of which are necessary for replication and evaluation of the validity of the arguments and interpretations presented. Most works of social commentary also do not connect results to theories that increase explanatory power, connect findings to other bodies of research, and help synthesize an otherwise discursive body of research.

Grounded Literature

Grounded studies of hip-hop move away from researchers' and commentators' privileged interpretations of hip-hop texts and focus on the meaning-making processes between hip-hop and the people who create, encounter, and practice it. These approaches focus on how students mobilize hip-hop or rap music in local contexts (e.g., Dimitriadis, 2001), how teachers use it in school curricula (e.g., Morrell & Duncan-Andrade, 2002), how knowledge and performances of hip-hop identity can function as cultural capital among Black youth (Clay, 2003), or how the practices of hip-hop contain particular "ways of doing" for hip-hop-identified students of all different ethnicities (e.g., Petchauer, 2007b). Grounded studies fill the void created by historical and textual approaches because they are derived from local participants and creators of hip-hop rather than from products or texts. They focus on processes more than products, often through research designs (e.g., ethnography, portraiture, grounded theory) despite similar theoretical orientations of textual approaches.

Because grounded explorations are normally directed toward an academic audience, a reader is often afforded enough methodological specificity on which to make a critical evaluation of the research findings and attempt to replicate studies, unlike social commentary approaches. In addition, results that are framed by relevant theory incorporate many strengths offered by historical or textual studies. Hence, by bridging the gap between local practice and theory, studies classified within this category serve as valuable contributions to educational research. These studies comprise a significant number of studies critically reviewed in the subsequent sections, so I discuss some of their specific limitations below.

Three Strands of Scholarly Work Relevant to Education

The three categories above serve as a heuristic to organize the burgeoning field of hip-hop scholarship with important educational implications. In each of these above categories is work relevant to the narrower field of education. In this section, I transverse across these categories to give a critical review of three major strands of work relevant to the field of education: (a) hip-hop-based education—studies that use hip-hop, especially rap songs and lyrics, as curricular and pedagogical resources; (b) hip-hop, meaning(s), and iden-tities—studies that focus on how students mobilize these texts and how they intersect with identities; and (c) hip-hop aesthetic forms—studies that conceptualize the ways of doing or habits of mind produced by hip-hop practices.

Hip-Hop-Based Education

A current trend concerning hip-hop within educational research and practice involves utilizing hip-hop (in most cases rap lyrics or songs) in classrooms for a variety of purposes. These purposes range from teaching academic and critical literacies (e.g., Al-exander-Smith, 2004; Alim, 2007; Duncan-Andrade & Morrell, 2005; Ginwright, 2004; Hill, 2006; Morrell, 2004; Morrell & Duncan-Andrade, 2002; Stovall, 2006) or citizen-ship more broadly through hip-hop as an educational program itself (e.g., Pardue, 2004, 2007). These trends are evident not only in the United States but also in other countries such as Brazil, which is further discussed below.

Educational initiatives such as these often generate from culturally responsive (Gay, 2000; Ladson-Billings, 1994) and critical pedagogies (Freire, 1970; Giroux, 1996) as well as cultural modeling approaches (Lee, 1995, 2007) more generally. According to these ap-proaches, there is educational benefit to centering in curricula and pedagogical practice the cultures, realities, and ways of learning that students bring with them into class-rooms. The fundamental assumptions within new literacy studies (e.g., Hull & Schultz, 2002; Street, 1993) that students create and engage in literacy practices in out-of-school contexts and that literacy includes ways of "behaving, interacting, valuing, thinking, be-lieving, speaking, and often reading and writing" (i.e., discourse; Gee, 1996, p. viii) also frequently underlie this body of scholarship (also see Kirkland, 2008). The most laudable works within this category maintain clear connections to these theoretical tenets, and the more questionable works generate from a pragmatic "what works" orientation and look to utilize rap texts as an initial lure into learning without any reflexive or serious engagement with them (Paul, 2000).

Rap texts for academic and critical literacy. Morrell and Duncan-Andrade (2002; Mor-rell, 2004) used an ethnographic approach to study a curricular unit that was designed to use rap texts as a bridge to canonical works of literature in an urban English and lan-guage arts classroom of ethnic minority students. The goals of the unit were (a) to utilize students' involvement with hip-hop to scaffold their critical and analytical skills, (b) to provide students with the awareness and confidence needed to transfer these skills onto canonical texts, and (c) to enable students to critique messages of popular culture media. The researchers concluded that students were able to make meaningful connections be-tween the rap texts and Romantic and Elizabethan poetry as well as make connections between the poems and the larger social contexts. Though the unit was designed and im-plemented for a high school senior AP-level course, it can be seen as emblematic of similar rap- based units at various levels of education designed to teach literary concepts such as tone (Alexander-Smith, 2004), research skills and citations (Wakefield, 2006), and critical literacy (Hill, 2006) in which teacher-researchers have made similar, favorable evaluations of their units and lessons in urban school contexts through ethnographic methods.

Though outside of the English and language arts classroom, Stovall (2006) used ethnography to explore a use of rap lyrics similar to the above studies. While facilitating a thematic unit within an urban high school social studies class consisting of 19 African American and Latino students, Stovall utilized rap lyrics from socially conscious and progressive artists such as Black Star, OutKast, and Talib Kweli as prompts to discuss social issues relevant to the students' lives. After playing a song he selected from the above artists, Stovall would facilitate a discussion that connected to issues such as the meaning of a just society, the misrepresentations of celebrity lives in the media, and how schools promote deception. Writing activities often followed after discussions.

Stovall's (2006) evaluations of the unit are important to note because they also apply to the other curricular projects referenced above. He recognized that the texts centered in the curriculum were chosen by the facilitator and not the students. Although one could argue that the lived realities of the students were centered because rap was integrated into the curriculum, the students still did not select the texts. The artists included in curricula are often those cherished by many hip-hop- inspired teachers and scholars who came of age in the "golden era" of 1990s hip- hop.[8] Kitwana (2002) suggested that there are now micro generations within the category *hip-hop generation,* and this point requires critical and culturally responsive pedagogues to reconsider if simply including their preferred version of hip- hop in the curriculum constitutes centering student realities.

Similar to Stovall's (2006) study, Williams's (2007) critical ethnography used critical social theory (e.g., Leonardo, 2004) to study a series of Freirean, hip-hop-based discussions (i.e., critical cultural cyphers) with eight high school seniors in a large, metropolitan high school. These students, five males and three females, were Asian, Mexican, Iranian, Caucasian, and African American—an accurate, diverse representation of students who identify with hip-hop. The overall goals of the discussions were to enable students to develop counternarratives, use language of critique and transcendence, and develop critical consciousness (Freire, 2002). Over the course of one semester, the students were to define hip-hop, identify problems in hip-hop, and develop actions in response to the problems. Unlike other studies such as Stovall's, the discussions were based on hip-hop-derived topics such as violence, misogyny, and drugs as decided by the students and rarely based on any specific rap texts.

Through descriptions of the meetings and exit interview with the participants, Williams (2007) illustrated that the critical cultural cyphers were spaces that enabled the students to revise and reconstruct their thought processes about the above topics and their own lives, which is a form of critical consciousness as outlined by Freire (2002). Participants had the most difficulty formulating specific actions for change based on their critiques of hip-hop. What is missing from Williams's analysis, however, is how any of the students' racial identities or critical understandings of race among one another intersected with their development of critical consciousness. Also, it is interesting to note that one of the participants who attended only one discussion meeting and was expelled from school also demonstrated characteristics of the same critical consciousness while reflecting on his poor decisions during his exit interview. This suggests that the exit interviews may have been an agent of critical consciousness as well as (or in the place of) the critical cultural cyphers and that research with similar intent must clearly demonstrate causal links between hip-hop-based interventions and observed outcomes.

It is important to note and that the studies above are typically more concerned with what seems to work rather than how it works, why it works, or what may be some of the unintended implications. Primarily because of research design, no reviewed studies controlled for mediating or moderating variables such as race, gender, or students' engagements with hip-hop outside of the classroom. Researchers have not considered teacher's familiarity with hip-hop and how it may affect such educational programs. Also, there is a tendency in such studies as these for *success* or *improved academic achievement* to be conflated with academic engagement or ambiguous altogether. Studies often imply that hip-hop-based education is successful if students enjoy or are engaged in the process. Although these outcomes should not be overlooked, many studies have simultaneously ignored measurable out- comes such as GPA, course grades, number of behavioral infractions, and learning. These oversights are understandable when considering some of these venues of publication (e.g., *English Journal*) that may be less concerned about research designs or methods and that are typically directed toward practitioners. Ultimately, these areas should be addressed by subsequent iterations of hip-hop educational research.

Newman's (2007) ethnographic and genre analysis study also highlights some of the overlooked issues in hip-hop-based education, mainly that students sometimes prefer the genres of rap music more often eschewed by teachers. This study looked at how a class of Black and Latino high school students in a creative rap course in Queens, New York, responded to conscious and hardcore genres of rap music. By *conscious* rap, Newman referred to music by artists such as dead prez or Talib Kweli that often identifies systemic causes of violence, poverty, and racism experienced by ethnic minorities, generally critiques capitalism, and affirms a Black identity. In the category of *hardcore* rap,[9] Newman included more commercially successful rap artists such as 50 Cent and Jay-Z, whose music and entrepreneurial successes (e.g., clothing lines) affirm free market capitalism, which in some instances could be seen as materialistic, and contain no direct affirmation of Black identity.

Newman (2007) concluded that the students favored the hardcore rap over the conscious rap because the latter was understood by students as containing little desire for economic mobility or stability—things these working-class students desired. By contrast, the hardcore, capitalist-affirming rap offered students a form of hope for individuals who are skilled enough to overcome their environments. Artists such as Jay-Z are often seen as heroes to young people because their narratives frequently describe skill-fully navigating dangerous social contexts that students also experience (Hill, 2009), and some artists' real lives demonstrate entrepreneurial successes and shrewd business investments. Overall, Newman's study illustrated that boasts of success (however ma-terialistic they may be) can be more desirable to working-class students than a critique of capitalism or affirmation of racial identity and solidarity.

Hip-hop as educational program. The use of hip-hop as a curricular resource is not limited to the United States but also occurs in international contexts. Pardue's (2004, 2007) critical ethnographic work that explored hip-hop-based, government- and state-funded educational programs in Sao Paulo, Brazil, focused on broader educational uses of hip-hop compared to the examples of rap-based curricula discussed above. In Sao Paulo, uses were broader because hip-hop activities such as DJing, street dancing, rapping, and graffiti art were the educational methods used to develop citizenship, self-esteem, and some transferable skills such as graphic and artistic design among poor and working-class youth on the social periphery (*periferia*). It is important that the participants included not only youth or students but also adult hip-hoppers who were employed by the state to teach in these programs in state-built cultural activity centers.

Pardue (2004) argued that employing hip-hop practitioners as worker–educators of the state was neither a case of the state completely co-opting hip-hop nor a case of mar-ginalized citizens creating a coherent movement of social change. One emphasis that is largely missing from Pardue's study, however, is a cogent analysis of race in this hip-hop and educational context. Pardue (2007) touched on hip-hop's function to affirm a Black identity among youth and young adults in the Sao Paulo periphery and how non-hip-hop-identified organizers judged this as radical and dangerous, but hip-hop's influence on racial formation is largely overlooked in favor of a general class-based analysis.

In a working-class suburban school in the United States, Alim (2007) gave an over-view of critical Hip-Hop language pedagogies focused on increasing students' awareness of their own Black and Hip-Hop linguistic practices,[10] the power structures and "official" language ideologies in which such practices are situated, and how students' communica-tive practices can be used against them through discrimination and linguistic profiling (Baugh, 2003). Toward these goals, groups of "linguistically profiled and marginalized youth" (p. 162) were introduced to speech variations through their school curricula and became ethnographers of their own speech communities and generators of knowledge.[11] Though Alim gave no clear details as to the number of students involved or the success of such programs, it is a useful example of a non-rap, hip-hop-based educational program designed to empower ethnic minority students.

Summary. Hip-hop has been used in schools as a curricular resource to teach ac-ademic and critical literacies. Efforts such as these most frequently involve teachers centering rap texts for students to analyze and deconstruct but also include programs that use the wider expressive elements of hip-hop as educational means themselves. These latter programs occur mostly outside of the United States in Brazil. Among these programs, researchers have paid little attention to differences in student engagement by gender or, more specifically, to the fact that adolescent girls are less likely to participate in music and hip-hop-based community programs compared to adolescent boys (Baker & Cohen, 2008).

In studies such as those by Pardue (2004, 2007) and Williams (2007) that generate from a critical studies approach, the primacy given to the socioeconomic class of participants often precludes any focus specifically on racial identity and formation through hip-hop. Though race is a social construct, this is a clear shortcoming in the scholarly literature because, as a powerfully determinant social category, race is still a source of identification, group solidarity, and stability or a burden for students (King, 2007; T. Perry, Steele, & Hilliard, 2004) with related structural and economic implications (Lipman, 2003). Because of this class-based focus, research in this strand has not explored in detail how hip-hop-based curricula establish racial(ized) contexts of such programs or how they might shape racial identity, awareness, or development of students. The potentially problematic issue here—how students use and interpret hip-hop in ways that may be unexpected or even undesirable to educators—is central to the next thread of research.

Hip-Hop, Meaning(s), and Identities

Another significant strand of scholarly work deals with the active relationship(s) between youth or young adults and the rap texts they encounter in school curricula and in their own social and cultural practice. Such scholarship has argued that knowledge of rap music and videos functions as cultural capital (Clay, 2003; Dimitriadis, 2001), a resource for racial and generational identity formation among African American students (Dimitriadis, 2001; Hill, 2009) and racial identity formation among Black immigrant students in Canada (Forman, 2001; Ibrahim, 1999, 2004). This scholarly work can be situated within poststructuralist perspectives of identity performance (Butler, 1990) and of texts in which they "contain no essential or inherent meaning but are always given meaning by people, in particular times and in particular places" (Dimitriadis, 2001, p. 11; also see Bakhtin, 1981). These assumptions problematize the body of work discussed in the previous section: Although educators utilized these texts for particular educational purposes, students can mobilize them for others.

Racial and generational identity. Dimitriadis's (2001) 4-year ethnographic study of how African American youth at a midwestern community center used rap texts and popular movies to construct notions of place, self, and history is a foundational contribution to this area of scholarship. Drawing on poststructuralist and feminist notions of identity (Butler, 1990), the study illustrated that the works of Southern rap by artists such as Eightball & MJG and Master P allowed the two main participants to construct a Southern heritage and experience "stability and feelings of invulnerability in the face of intense anxiety" (p. 61). Similarly, constructing a myth that rap artist Tupac Shakur survived his fatal 1996 shooting helped youth in this study transcend feelings of vulnerability in their local spaces. Other participants drew on knowledge of and interaction with the movies *Panther* and *Malcolm X* to cope with uncertainties in their lives such as the possibility of a Ku Klux Klan march in their town.

Building on Dimitriadis's (2001) study, Hill's (2009) one-year ethnography of students' interpretations of texts in a rap-centered English course at an urban high school placed the concerns of Dimitriadis's study into a classroom context. Hill concluded that the 20 ethnically diverse students made meaning of rap texts in ways that competed with and at times undermined the course goals to allow students to create a community of (counter)storytelling and challenge hegemonic conceptions of realty. For example, in studying the song "Things Done Changed" by The Notorious B.I.G., a nostalgic rap text that Hill believed might illustrate the structural and social forces behind neighborhood violence and drug economy,[12] students interpreted the text to suggest that their generation was an exception compared to previous ones and more morally corrupt in comparison. These student interpretations held despite Hill's challenges for an alternate and less self-depreciating one.[13] Similarly, the study made clear some of the limits of the ability of hip-hop-based culturally responsive curricula to empower students. For example, students reported feeling empowered by participating in a community of personal storytelling through interpreting rap texts, but one student in particular became silenced and academically disengaged through discussing rap texts that centered on the topic of abortion. Related, students of all ethnicities constructed the hip-hop-centered classroom environment as a "Black thing," which made different performances of Blackness (e.g., African American vernacular English [AAVE], Black cultural references) among students central to "authentic" classroom membership. White students performing and experimenting with these aspects of their identities felt as outsiders to the class but were accepted by other students when they demonstrated awareness of the limits of their identification with Black culture. Hill concluded that even some African American students from middle-class backgrounds felt excluded by the hip-hop (i.e., Black in this case) curriculum, and thus it "produced new cultural margins and, thus, new forms of marginalization" (p. 64).

Clay's (2003) ethnographic study of Black youth and hip-hop focused more specifically on Black racial identity through the lens of cultural capital (Bourdieu, 1987). The study explored how hip-hop functioned as cultural capital among Black youth at a northern California community center. Clay concluded that performing language, dress, and gestures associated with hip-hop functioned as cultural capital used to authenticate a Black identity based on traditional gender roles. According to Clay's observations, students who wore popular clothing styles, demonstrated knowledge of popular rap lyrics, and replicated the gender(ed) relationship in rap videos were seen by their peers as more popular.

Clay's (2003) focus on popular fashion among the youth suggested that it was the most prominent performance of cultural capital at the youth center, but she did not acknowledge that, consequently, financial capital was thus an important variable in the youths' ability to perform a Black identity. Most important, unlike in Hill's (2009)

ethnography, there was no evidence in the study that the youth racialized the performances of hip-hop cultural capital as Black. Youth did not place one another on a
continuum of Blackness or make any judgments about the "authentic" racial identity
of their peers because of their performances of hip-hop cultural capital. Youth at the
center acted on judgments about who was popular vis-à-vis hip-hop fashion, not about
who was Black. Because Clay defined hip-hop as the Blackest cultural form (Gilroy,
1997), inherent to her analysis was that performances of hip-hop cultural capital were
simultaneously performances of Blackness.

Apart from research on high-school age youth, one study in this thread explored
hip-hop among college students. Iwamoto et al.'s (2007) study of the meanings of rap
music differed significantly from these other studies because of its phenomenological
design, precise methodological details, and eight ethnically diverse college student participants. The participants included one Caucasian, two Asian Americans, two African
Americans, and three Latinos, with four males and four females. The researchers sought
to understand the meanings of rap music in general (opposed to any specific texts) for
these students.

The researchers concluded that "rap music elicits powerful emotions and significant
meanings across ethnic and racial groups" (Iwamoto et al., 2007, p. 346). Specifically,
students became avid rather than casual listeners when they developed empathy with
the music by relating to themes such as overcoming hardships, living in violent environments, experiencing racism, being exposed to drugs, and being in and out of love.
Social contexts in which students experienced these themes were listening to the music
in the car, at home, among friends, while walking on campus, and at dance clubs. Rap
music also had psychological and emotional effects on the students because of the diversity of content listed above to match listeners' moods. Rap music was also experienced
as educational because it shared new experiences, realities, and topics with listeners,
resulting in some instances in which listeners sought additional information on topics
because they were mentioned in a rap song (though these were not specified). Though
the researchers identified these effects across the ethnicities in the study, they paid no
attention to any differences across ethnicities or genders in relation to how students
experienced the music.

Racial identity in global contexts. Key characteristics of Dimitriadis's (2001) study
such as its performance and poststructuralist assumptions about identity are also evident
in studies that explored the intersection of youth identities and hip-hop texts in global
contexts. By *global contexts,* I refer not only to locations outside of the United States but
also to *transcultural flows* around the world, "ways in which cultural forms move, change
and are reused to fashion new identities in diverse contexts" (Pennycook, 2007a, p. 6).
Ibrahim's (1999, 2004) critical ethnographic work on 16 French-speaking immigrant
and refugee teens in Canada looked at how the students (10 male and 6 female) grew to
construct themselves as Black through contact with popular culture resources, mainly
rap music. Ibrahim (1999) contended that once in a North American context and faced

with the social imaginary (Anderson, 1983) of already being Black, the Francophone African youth then "became" Black by investing themselves in rap music, characteristics of Black stylized English (Ibrahim, 1999), and hip-hop clothing (Ibrahim, 2004). Ibrahim (1999) saw this process as emblematic of African youth's "desire to belong to a location, a politics, a memory, a history, and hence a representation" (p. 353).

In the English as a second language (ESL) context, Ibrahim (1999, 2004) concluded that because his participants were attracted to and invested in a marginal topic such as hip-hop, it should be centered in ESL curricula. Ibrahim clearly demonstrated that identification with rap and hip-hop and the process of becoming Black affected what students chose to learn, but it was not made clear how the claim that the identification and process affect how these students learned. Though Ibrahim's claim of investment where one sees oneself mirrored is substantiated in his study, it does not explain the attraction to hip-hop that exists across so many racial groups in the United States, including White youth.

Forman (2001) made similar conclusions in an ethnographic study about how Somali immigrant and refugee students in two North American high schools negotiated Somaliness and Blackness through symbolic creativity (Willis, 1990). Some students adopted the camouflage styles of hip-hop clothing as ways to claim a new Blackness yet maintain connections to the military fighting men in the Somalia capital of Mogadishu. Others attempted to perform AAVE and hip-hop language that they encountered in the music and videos. Forman assessed that these acts were influenced by "several overlapping elements of teen identity and youth rebellion that meet in the cultural conjunctions of the Somali immigrant and refuge experience" (p. 53).[14]

Hip-hop literacies and discourse. A small body of work has explored literacy in relation to hip-hop; however, there is a fundamental difference in this body between exploring literacy practices that take place *with* hip-hop texts (e.g., Jocson, 2006) and literacy practices that might be produced *by* hip-hop activities and hip-hop-identified folks. Richardson (2006, 2007), in the latter of these categories, has examined Hiphop literacies and Hiphop discourse from sociolinguistic (e.g., Smitherman, 1994) and new literacy studies (Gee, 1996; Street, 1993) theoretical perspectives. Richardson (2007) defined Hiphop literacies as "ways in which people who are socialized into Hiphop discourse manipulate as well as read language, gestures, images, material possessions, and people, to position themselves against or within discourse in order to advance and protect themselves" (p. 792). Important to this definition is that she situated both Hiphop discourse and literacies within the larger category of Black discourse. This is a point I return to below.

Richardson's research was both textual and grounded. To illustrate Hiphop literacies, Richardson (2006) analyzed rap texts such as OutKast's "The Whole World" video and rap artist Lil Kim's criminal trial to identify AAVE characteristics (e.g., Southern pronunciation, diction, signifying) and the trickster and badman or badwoman figures. The grounded aspect of Richardson's (2006, 2007) work derives from an exploration of how three African American women in college negotiated the meanings of rap texts and videos that contained stereotypical and sexist themes. By viewing rap videos and conducting semistructured interviews with the women in her home, Richardson concluded that the women attempted to redefine traditional sexual and gender performances often by focusing on the "video chicks" and rappers' agencies. Richardson noted that the participants struggled to overcome or speak beyond the "dominant discursive sphere" because the ways they made sense out of the rap videos were clearly related to prevalent stereotypes of Black women, men, and sexuality.

These characteristics of Richardson's research underscore two important points. The first deals with the different perspectives on hip-hop as an expression of Blackness in the 21st century, as was discussed at the start of this review. Richardson's work clearly illustrates how conceptualizing hip-hop as a Black aesthetic (i.e., locating Hiphop discourse within Black discourse) leads one to situate young African Americans as part of hip-hop regardless of any particular activities (e.g., rapping) or hip-hop community in which they participate. This is likely why Richardson (2006) implied that participants were practitioners of Hiphop or had the "lived experience" of Hiphop but gave no clear details regarding their activities as practitioners, their lived experiences, or how they were socialized into Hiphop discourse. From the perspective of hip-hop as a Black aesthetic, the literacy practices were considered "hip-hop" either because the participants were African Americans or because the literacy practices occurred while interpreting rap texts. From a civic-participatory perspective that acknowledges the clear Black roots of hip-hop but also emphasizes its adaptations, localizations, and (re)creations (Chang, 2006; Mitchell, 2001), it is unclear what is decidedly "hip-hop" and thus new about the literacy practices Richardson identified. Second, and related, the research illustrates the difference between looking into rap songs and videos to contain literacy or discourse practices rather than looking into the lives of hip-hop practitioners, their creative activities such as emceeing and DJing, and the local hip-hop communities of practice (Wilson, 2007). Essentially, this is the fundamental difference between what I identify as hip-hop content and hip-hop form. The final strand of scholarly work explores this difference.

Summary. Research in the hip-hop, meaning(s), and identities thread generally has focused on the active relationships between hip-hop texts and youth in and out of schools. Two empirical studies have considered college students in this manner. Specifically, studies have illustrated how these groups of listeners, especially African Americans from urban locations, make meaning of rap texts in ways that can be unexpected and even undesirable to teachers. These are important considerations in light of the research in the hip-hop-based education thread because they illustrate that culturally responsive curricula can undermine some of its own goals. Little research of this intent in the United States has put at the center of analysis how youth and young adults use hip-hop text to shape racial identity. This topic has received more attention in global contexts outside of the United States in which global capitalism has fueled the spread of commodified cultures such as hip-hop and made it an available resource for students to use to (re)construct racial identity. In this global context, however, no identified research has made connections to important areas such as learning and achievement in schools.

Hip-Hop Aesthetic Forms

The previous section reviewed research that examined the active relationship between listeners and rap music lyrics. In these studies, researchers theorize hip-hop and rap music as texts to be mobilized, used, and made meaningful by students. In contrast, conceptualizing hip-hop not as a text to be analyzed or included in a curriculum but rather as a set of aesthetic practices containing and producing situated ways of doing (and being) constitutes a third strand in the literature. Some of these ways of doing may be ideological such as a critical wariness toward formal institutions of learning (Wilson, 2007), and some of these may be more technical such as transferring memorization skills into the classroom that were developed through performing as an emcee (Petchauer, 2007b). This section examines scholarship that has identified some of these situated ways of doing or theorized them by using hip-hop aesthetics as conceptual starting points. Scholarship in this burgeoning area does not present a coherent set of hip-hop aesthetic forms but instead presents some tentative ideas with implications for education.

Hip-hop pedagogies. Pennycook's (2007a, 2007b) ethnographic work examined how English (or Englishes) became "authentically" localized via the creative practices of emcees in Senegal, Tanzania, and Malaysia. This process occurred when artists stopped imitating themes in American rap music and took up local themes or when artists fused local languages into rap. In discussing the implications of this research, Pennycook (2007a) moved from a focus on content to a focus on form by concluding, "Hip-hop both produces and is produced by a cultural context that often thinks differently about questions of language, writing, identity, and ownership from the mainstream discourses of the academy" (p. 150). He argued for allowing the flows by which hip-hop language(s) have traveled among rappers (i.e., transmodal and transtextual characteristics) to "open up new ways of thinking about education" (p. 154) called hip-hop pedagogies. More specifically, he argued, "The verbal performance of rap," such as the conscious mixing of linguistic traditions and styles, "is in itself an explicit engagement with language awareness" (p. 147).

These ways of doing within hip-hop are not derived only from performance rap. Christen (2003) used primary and secondary source interviews with graffiti writers to illustrate that there are distinct processes of mentoring and apprenticeship within hip-hop graffiti crews according to which new members develop new skills and are socialized into the group. This process of socialization often includes developing independence, collaboration, responsibility, and citizenship to one's group. Graffiti writers often keep a *blackbook,* which is a type of working sketchbook portfolio where a writer cultivates a personal style of drawing letters, sketches designs for potential pieces, and competes with others. Thus, forms of instruction, learning, assessment, correction, revision, and other educational processes are imbedded within these communities and activities.

Rice (2003) theorized hip-hop pedagogies by writing about how the practice of *sampling* in hip-hop can guide pedagogues to consider new ways of teaching argumentation in college composition classes. Sampling is the practice by which a DJ or hip-hop music producer takes any snippet of previously recorded music and uses it to create new music

THINKING ABOUT BLACK EDUCATION

in a new context (Schloss, 2004). Similar to Pennycook (2007a), this approach considers "the way hip-hop constructs dis- course, the way it produces rhetorical meaning through its complex method of digital sampling, and how such a rhetoric functions within the scope of argumentation" (Rice, 2003, p. 454). Rice demonstrated this approach by sampling and juxtaposing descriptions from important events or artifacts from 1963 (e.g., a Leonard Freed photograph, a Freddie Roach album cover) against one another. With these sources,

> the student writer looks as the various distinct moments she has collected and figures out how these moments together produce knowledge. Just as DJs often search for [drum] breaks and cuts in the music that reveal patterns, so, too, does the student writer look for a pattern as a way to unite these moments into a new alternate argument and critique. (p. 465)

Rice's artifacts that were sampled through this hip-hop approach produced the argument that "information technology informs power relations at the levels of race and class" (p. 465).

Rice's exploration of this hip-hop pedagogy was unavoidably vague because of the limitations of the written word to clearly represent an epistemology that is rooted in hip-hop turntablism and digital media. However, this idea is made clearer by the findings of Petchauer's (2007b) portraiture study of *hip-hop collegians*: college students whose educational interests, motivations, and practices have been shaped by involvement in hip-hop. The study employed the notion of worldview (Kearney, 1984) to look at how participation in hip-hop at and around three different higher education institutions in different parts of the United States implicated eight students' educational experiences, approaches, and lives. Participants included students who identified as Filipino/a, Dominican, Caucasian, and African American as well as hip-hoppers who occupied overlapping roles of emcees, DJs, graffiti writers, event promoters, music producers, activists, and educators.

As in Rice's (2003) discussion, the idea of hip-hop sampling was evident in Petchauer's (2007b) study, but through how some participants conceptualized hip-hop as an approach to education. For one participant, sampling from various news sources and different classes to complete assignments was "in the spirit of hip-hop." Other participants consciously sampled the experiences of other students and friends to conceptualize education and navigate institutions, which is a form of *sampled consciousness* (karimi, 2006). The study also illustrated how some hip-hop collegians navigated educational institutions that they saw as part of a hegemonic system that could compromise some of their ideals that were derived from hip-hop. These ideals included a graffiti-derived belief that one should not have to spend money to create art and a rap-derived critical consciousness (Freire, 2002) according to which participants questioned metanarratives and viewed institutions of higher education as containing insufficient representations of knowledge and the world.

As in Iwamoto et al.'s (2007) study, hip-hop collegians perceived and experienced hip-hop as an educator, exposing them to counternarratives of protest and snippets of information (e.g., the names of political prisoners) that some students took the liberty to explore on their own. More technically, the study also illustrated how for one student pursuing a career as an emcee, the habit of memorizing songs for biweekly performances and the daily ritual of shorthanding raps in his personal rhyme book carried over into the classroom by allowing him to commit material to memory through rhyme and take notes in an abbreviated way. Though the portraits of this study lent face, place, and space to the general label *hip-hop generation*, the portraits presented discursive findings rather than a coherent hip-hop worldview among participants at different institutions.

Hip-hop forms as pedagogical resources. A small body of work within classrooms also touches on how hip-hop aesthetic forms can be used in school curricula. Cooks (2004) attempted to teach the writing process in school by drawing on the process of writing raps that some of his students already possessed outside of school. Cooks observed that for one African American middle school student in particular who wrote raps, the process of writing essays and the process of writing raps held common features that enhanced both genres of writing. These common features were narrative perspective and organization. Also, there were clear differences between the genres as performed by the focal student. For example, essays typically had a clear pronouncement of the objective of the piece at the start and featured more repetition of important points. Raps had superior use of analogies and dialogue. Cooks concluded that students can improve their writing skills by drawing on the strengths of different forms such as rap.

Mahiri's (2006) ethnographic study of the technology-based projects created by students in an eighth-grade class within a high poverty school identified the presence of the hip-hop aesthetic form of sampling, as defined above. Informed by the notion of semiotic domains (Gee, 2003), Mahiri focused on one award-winning student project that was "characterized by 're-mixing' multimodal texts of images, animations, print, and sound" (p. 55). In the project, the students sampled the cultural resources most immediate to them such as the popular R&B singer Aaliyah and gospel singer Kirk Franklin. Mahiri summarized that the projects "[utilized] technological resources to sample, cut and paste, and re-mix multimedia texts for replay in new configurations, just as hip-hop DJs reconfigure images, words, and sounds, and play them anew" (p. 58).

Summary. Scholarship that has focused on the aesthetic forms of hip-hop and their implications on education has argued that there are particular was of learning and being imbedded within and produced by hip-hop practices. As researchers initiate more empirical work in this more recent area, one important consideration is how habits of body and mind in hip-hop may undermine educational goals and practice. This is largely overlooked in this area of research, except for Petchauer's (2007b) recognition that one participant's refusal to purchase art supplies for her art major and her ideas that art was a communal practice (both ideas derived from writing graffiti) may have contributed to her disillusionment with the art program at her college and her ultimate change of major.

Future Directions and How to Get There

In forging new directions for hip-hop educational research, I amplify many of Dimitriadis's (2008) general ideas for studying youth culture in the 21st century, particularly the recommendation to move beyond (or eliminate) the dichotomous language of *urban* and *suburban* because the terms do not capture the widespread status of hip-hop and the transcultural sites where people (re)construct it. This move beyond the lingua franca also applies to the term *youth*. Hip-hop remains a power influence in the lives of college students and middle-aged adults (Chang, 2006; Iwamoto et al., 2007; Petchauer, 2007b), yet comparatively few studies have looked at how this influence changes (or doesn't) as hip-hop-identified folks navigate educational and labor institutions after high school. Considering that the collegiate experience is often a formative season of independence and intellectual, political, and moral change, the different ways that hip-hop may be woven into these processes is an important and ripe area of future work. In the rest of this section, I offer some specific new directions and questions for each of the three strands of reviewed literature.

Hip-Hop-Based Education

Research has demonstrated that hip-hop-based education can help develop critical literacy and academic skills in students. However, and perhaps ironically, the reviewed literature demonstrates that many uses of hip-hop in school curricula are uncritical themselves and have not taken into consideration if these programs help students learn course material, improve their motivation to learn, or increase graduation rates. These are areas for further research.

Aside from the teacher–researchers who study their own hip-hop-based curricula, researchers in this area know very little about other (i.e., nonresearching) teachers who use hip-hop in classrooms. Even general descriptive statistics are not known. To understand hip-hop-based pedagogy and curricula in greater detail, it would be helpful to know who is using hip-hop in the curriculum, their motivations for doing so, their prior experiences (if any) in hip-hop or resistance movements, and how successful they are at using hip-hop to accomplish various educational goals. Findings in these areas would help substantiate or call into question the tacit assumption that a teacher must be young(er) and keep up with popular trends to successfully use hip-hop in the classroom.

Frequently, teacher–researchers using hip-hop in classrooms suggest an abiding appreciation and affection for hip-hop themselves and membership in the real and imagined community of the hip-hop nation. Recalling the notion that there are multiple micro generations who identify with hip-hop, most researchers have neither acknowledged nor interrogated the intergenerationalness of the hip-hop nation in the classroom. How do teachers' common or different tastes of rap music and dispositions compared to those of students implicate hip-hop-based education? Related, how do hip-hop-identified teachers navigate formal school systems, and has their pedagogy been shaped in ways that are more complex and subtle than bringing rap explicitly into curricula?

Hip-Hop, Meaning(s), and Identities

Research outside of the United States has shown that rap texts and hip-hop activities are sets of expressions available to Black students to construct Black racial identities in schools and educational programs. Yet most research in the United States has only acknowledged and not centered the potential for hip-hop to do this when used in curricula and the subsequent opportunity to critically educate African American students about their power and influence connected to global, corporate media. In terms of hip-hop and constructions of racial identity, this applies to African American youth and the wide range of ethnicities that identify with hip-hop, Blackness through hip-hop, or hip-hop originators and contributors of other ethnic backgrounds (e.g., Latino, Filipino). These are additional areas of exploration.

In expanding as such, particularly in the area of race and ethnicity, it is helpful to foreground the interrelatedness of Blackness and Whiteness in the United States (Fishkin, 1995) and of ethnicities more generally in the complex, globalized development of hip-hop during the past 30 years. For example, it is clear that Puerto Rican Americans in the Bronx have shaped and made steady the development of breaking (Hazzard-Donald, 1996; Israel, 2002) and that Filipino Americans particularly in the western United States have done the same with DJing and turntablism (Pray, 2001; Wang, 2004). However, these were not racially isolated processes but occurred—as Toni Morrison said of American literature—"in contemplation of . . . black presence" (see Fishkin, 1995, p. 430). Consequently, as researchers explore "non-Black" groups within hip-hop, they should keep in mind the interrelatedness of these ethnic groups even in defining themselves vis-à-vis Blackness or other racial constructs.

As research expands in these and other ways, one very useful distinction to make is between directors and receptors of hip-hop (Williams, 2007). Directors take active roles to integrate hip-hip into their lives often through participating in its expressive elements and (re)defining its position in their lives. They might subscribe to the maxim *I am Hip-Hop.* Receptors come in contact with hip-hop but less intentionally. They might enjoy the music and even own some of it but do not consciously cultivate hip-hop as part of their lives. These distinctions or variations thereof could help researchers nuance the broad(ening) category of the hip-hip nation.

Hip-Hop Aesthetic Forms

As the most recent thread of scholarship on hip-hop, the aesthetic forms of hip-hop and their implications on learning and learning environments are ripe areas of research. Specifically, how can the habits of body and mind within hip-hop support or harm educational goals and processes? Strangely, many researchers who recognize the damaging role that corporate media has had on hip-hop have been culturally irresponsive through the same practice: separating rap from the rest of hip-hop for the sake of analysis. Because hip-hop is conceptualized as a set of interrelated practices with common aesthetics such as sampling (Hoch, 2006; Potter, 1995; Shusterman, 2000), this line of research will hold more promise if researchers look at hip-hop holistically with practices in connection with one another rather than divorce them from one another. Studies that hold to this principle are better equipped to pinpoint the kinds of hip-hop pedagogies discussed above and the habits that educators might desire to cultivate in students.

New directions often require applying different theoretical perspectives. Discourse (Gee, 1996) and other ideas within new literacy studies (Street, 1993) have been employed as helpful theoretical constructs to explain how language, behaviors, and ways of doing are connected to situated identities. However, the helpful breadth of discourse as it is used in these studies also has a weakness. Specifically, what *isn't* discourse? It is critical that researchers make unambiguous the causal and attributional links between hip-hop and their findings, something that has not been accomplished thus far through discourse. The presence of a particular set of values, practice, or habit of mind among youth and young adults involved in hip-hop does not mean that it is derived from or connected to hip-hop in any way. Researchers must work to demonstrate the ways that these variables might be inter- woven with hip-hop and what findings can be rightfully attributed to it.

One theoretical resource that has thus far been underutilized in hip-hop scholarship and that would enable more work in these areas and supplement discourse is sociocultural theory as concisely reviewed by Nasir and Hand (2006). From this perspective, contextualized hip-hop practices would be units of analysis and direct researchers to identify the "cultural norms and expectations, artifacts and conventions, and com- munity-level organization" (p. 465). It is important that Nasir and Hand argued that such an approach allows for considerations of how race affects such practices—a focus that is generally limited in hip-hop educational research. According to these theoretical perspectives, the symbolic tools and ideational artifacts present within hip-hop activities are also important foci of future work. Conceptualizing hip-hop as a community of practice and social network (Wilson, 2007) with localized language ideologies and epistemologies also complements these sociocultural theories.

Multisited qualitative studies (Marcus, 1998; also see Dimitriadis, 2008) are one approach equipped to help explore many of these new directions. Marcus (1998) explained,

> the idea is that any cultural identity or activity is constructed by multiple agents in varying contexts, or places, and that ethnography must be strategically conceived to represent this sort of multiplicity, and to specify both intended and unintended consequences in the network of complex connections within a system of places. (p. 52)

In these ways, researchers must be ready to follow the people, thing, metaphor, plot, story, allegory, or life (Marcus, 1998, pp. 90–94). The directions and theoretical recommendations require researchers to both think and act less in physically defined sites and instead design research around "chains, paths, threads, conjunctions, or juxtapositions of locations" (Marcus, 1998, p. 90), just as this review of literature did. Multisited work is also more equipped to make contextualized, qualitative research more broadly relevant through theoretical generalizability (Dimitriadis, 2008; Fine, 2006). Multisited work on hip-hop conceptualizes it as a process more than product (Alim, 2006) and entails deep, extended immersion in the underground spaces of hip-hop: bedroom and dorm room music studios, cherished local events, impromptu moments of inspiration, an emcee's rhyme book, a graffiti writer's blackbook, and the local manifestations of the communal spaces that hip-hoppers around the world call the *cipher* (Spady, Alim, & Meghelli, 2006).

APPENDIX A
Glossary of hip-hop terms

Breaking:	The quintessential form of hip-hop dance that is still practiced around the world. Also called *b-boying, b-girling,* and *breakdancing,* though the latter term is eschewed by many local practitioners (see Israel, 2002).
Cipher/cypher:	The communal, circular space were hip-hoppers often express themselves individually and collectively through dancing, rapping, or competing (i.e., *battling*) to music often played by an accompanying DJ. The term is also used symbolically to represent an extend community of hip-hoppers (Spady, Alim, & Meghelli, 2006).
Conscious rap:	Subgenre of rap music that more prominently identifies systemic causes of oppression and affirms a critical consciousness and Black identity.
DJing:	Playing and manipulating vinyl records through a variety of techniques on two turntables and a mixer instrument (see Pray, 2001).
Emceeing:	Speaking with rhyme, cadence, and Black stylistic features over hip-hop instrumentals. Also called *rapping* or *rhyming.*
Gangsta rap:	Subgenre of rap music that more prominently centers or glorifies narratives of violence, illegal activities, materialism, misogyny, or "street" life.
Graffiti writing:	Legal and illegal visual art through spray paint and custom modified markers. Variations include *tagging, bombing,* and *getting-up.*
Hip-hop (culture):	Expressive practices created in the postindustrial United States and that draw from Black and Latino cultural forms.
Hip-hop elements:	Emceeing, DJing, breaking, and graffiti writing. Knowledge (i.e., *overstanding*) is often included too.
Hip-hop generation:	African American and other groups born after 1965 for whom hip-hop has been a defining cultural influence.
Hip-hop nation:	The real and imagined community of people whose lives have been shaped and influenced by hip-hop in various ways.

Hip-hopper: One who is part of hip-hop.

Party rap: Subgenre of rap music that is generally enjoyed for entertainment purposes because of its danceable beat and musicality rather than for the meanings of the lyrics.

Reality rap: Subgenre of rap music that often features narratives of violence, illegal activities, or "street" life but as cautionary tales for critical evaluation.

Sampling: Practice by which a DJ or hip-hop music producer takes any part of previously recorded material and uses it to create new music in a new context and composition (Schloss, 2004).

Turntablism: Art that involves creating musical compositions by manipulating prerecorded music on vinyl records with at least one turntable and a mixer instrument (see Pray, 2001).

APPENDIX B
Summary of reviewed articles

Study	Research Context	N	Sample Characteristics	General Findings
Alexander-Smith (2004)	7th grade language arts classroom in the United States		Classroom of African American students	Teachers can successfully use rap texts to teach literary devices
Alim (2007)	Working-class, suburban high school in United States			Teaching students to be ethnographers of their own speech can enable them to develop critical awareness of language ideologies and linguistic profiling
Christen (2003)			Graffiti writers (primary and secondary sources)	There are particular processes of mentoring and apprenticeship within the communities and activities of hip-hop graffiti

Clay (2003)	Low-income community center in Northern California		Group of Black teenagers	Hip-hop dress, language, and gesture functioned as cultural capital to authenticate Black identity based on traditional gender roles
Cooks (2004)	8th-grade language arts classroom in the United States		Classroom of African American students (one focal student)	Teachers can draw on the process of writing raps to teach the academic writing process
Dimitriadis (2001)	Midwestern community center		Group of African American working-class youth (two focal students)	Participants used texts such as rap to construct notions of place, self, and history
Forman (2001)	One U.S. and one Canadian high school		Somali immigrant and refugee teenagers	Participants used hip-hop clothing and African American vernacular English and hip-hop language to claim Blackness yet maintain connections to Somaliness
Hill (2006)	Language arts high school classroom in Philadelphia	20	Classroom of male ($n = 8$) and female ($n = 12$) ethnically diverse students	Rap texts can be used to develop critical perspectives on race relations
Hill (2009)	Language arts high school classroom in Philadelphia	20	Classroom of male ($n = 8$) and female ($n = 12$) ethnically diverse students	Rap-based curricula can both empower and silence student voices as they are used to teach academic skills construct identity
Ibrahim (1999, 2004)	High school in Canada	16	Francophone male ($n = 10$) and female ($n = 6$) African immigrant and refugee teenagers	Participants constructed themselves as "Black" by adopting Black stylized English, rap, and hip-hop clothing

Iwamoto, Creswell, and Caldwell (2007)	U.S. college campus	8	Ethnically diverse male ($n = 4$) and female ($n = 4$) college students	Rap music elicits powerful emotions and significant meanings across racial groups; it was also experienced as educational as it exposed students to new experiences, topics, and realities
Mahiri (2006)	High-poverty 8th-grade classroom in Northern California	25	Classroom of African American students	Student projects resembled the multimodal, hip-hop aesthetic of sampling
Morrell and Duncan-Andrade (2002)	12th-grade, urban, language arts classroom in United States		Classroom of ethnic minority students	Rap texts can be used to scaffold literary interpretation and interpretation
Newman (2007)	Urban creative rap high school classroom in Queens, NY	20	Black and Latino, working-class, and low-income students	Students favored hardcore rap over socially or politically conscious rap because the former offered hope for economic mobility
Pardue (2004, 2007)	State-supported, hip-hop-based citizenship program in Brazil		Poor and working-class youth; hip-hop instructors	Programs were neither full co-option of hip-hop by government or a coherent movement of social change
Pennycook (2007a, 2007b)	Senegal, Tanzania, Malaysia		Local rappers and lyrics	English language practices became localized when rappers fused local themes and languages with the music; these transglobal flows open up new ways of thinking about education

Petchauer (2007b)	Three U.S. universities	8	Ethnically diverse male ($n = 6$) and female ($n = 2$) hip-hop collegians	Participants demonstrated hip-hop as an approach to education, experienced hip-hop as an educator, and navigated respective institutions based on hip-hop ideals
Rice (2003)				Hip-hop aesthetic practices such as sampling create new ways to conceive and teach argumentations in college composition
Richardson (2006, 2007)	United States; private location viewing rap videos	3	African American women	Participants attempted to redefine traditional gender and sexual performances by focusing on agency
Stovall (2006)	Social studies high school classroom in Chicago	16	Black and Latino students	Rap texts can be used to discuss social issues affecting students' lives
Wakefield (2006)				Rap texts can be used to teach research skills and citations
Williams (2007)	Urban high school in California	8	Ethnically diverse male ($n = 5$) and female ($n = 3$) high school	Hip-hop-based discussions can promote the development of critical consciousness

APPENDIX C
Selected list of artists, descriptors, and songs used in curricula

Artist	Party	Conscious	Reality	Gangsta	Entrepreneur	Sample Song
50 Cent	X		X	X	X	"I Get Money"
Common		X				"A Retrospect for Life"
dead prez		X				"They Schools"
Eightball & MJG	X		X			"Memphis City Blues"
Jay Z	X	X	X	X	X	"Ballad for a Fallen Soldier"
Kanye West	X	X				"All Falls Down"
KRS-ONE/ Boogie Down Productions	X	X				"Love's Gonna Get'cha"
Lil' Kim	X		X	X		"No Matter What They Say"
Master P	X		X		X	"Ride 4 You"
Eve	X		X			"Love is Blind"
Nas	X	X	X	X		"If I Ruled the World"
OutKast	X	X	X			"Ms. Jackson"
Public Enemy		X				"Fight the Power"
Talib Kweli		X				"Get By"
The Notorious B.I.G.	X		X	X		"Things Done Changed"
T. I.	X		X	X		"Rubberband Man"

Note. Categorizing and attaching descriptors to rap artists is tenuous because interpretations of lyrics vary, many artists' work evolve over long careers (e.g., Jay-Z), artists have eschewed such ostensibly simplistic labels, and hip-hop resists dichotomous framing (Shusterman, 2000). Consequently, this table and its categories should be read as a tentative heuristic and not a definitive framework.

Endnotes

1   In this review, I omit the word *culture* after hip-hop to avoid a needless debate about if hip-hop fits definitions of culture. I do this because varying definitions of culture abound and because the significance of hip-hop to educational research and people who create and enjoy hip-hop is not dependent on any definition of culture.

2   Regarding terminology, I use the terms *hip-hop music* and *rap music* separately, wherein the former includes rap music but also live and recorded productions such as mix tapes, beat tapes, and scratch or turntablism albums—all of which are unique artistic creations with their own nuanced hip-hop aesthetics.

3   Alridge (2005) is one of the few exceptions to this polarized discourse as his historical and textual analysis identified the common ideals of self-determination, liberatory education and pedagogy, economic solidarity, and pan-Africanism among the civil rights movement, Black freedom struggle, and conscious hip-hop.

4   Part of the difference in how researchers frame hip-hop can be explained by the aspect they examine. Studies that focus on rap more frequently locate hip-hop firmly within African American culture because rap contains rich examples of African American vernacular English and Black-stylized English. Studies that focus on other hip-hop expressions and activities such as DJing less frequently center Black aesthetics because such activities have been significantly shaped by other groups (e.g., Filipino Americans in turntablism). See I. Perry (2004, pp. 9–37) for a nuanced treatment.

5   The term *hip-hop* is subject to a few different spellings (e.g., Hiphop, Hip-Hop, hip-hop) for reasons that are often very specific. Consequently, in this review I alternate spelling in instances to remain consistent with the authors whose work I am reviewing and to honor their intents. Because these spellings are not arbitrary, this alternation also serves as ongoing illustration of different assumptions and positions taken up by researchers about hip-hop.

6   Work on hip-hop that exists outside of the traditional definition of the academy is at times relevant. Among other reasons, this is because scholarship on hip-hop has blurred the lines between academic and nonacademic work because of many academically trained and hip-hop-identified scholars producing work outside of academe (e.g., Jeff Chang) or producing work both inside and outside of academe (e.g., Oliver Wang) and because of accomplished journalists now producing work within academe (e.g., Bakari Kitwana). Also, it is important to acknowledge that influential hip-hop artist intellectuals such as KRS-ONE (Parker, 2003) and Chuck D (1998) who are invited to lecture on college campuses have also written critical texts.

7   Hip-hop was not a panacea for gang violence, though Chang (2005) and others have illustrated that it did at times function as a nonviolent alternative as the gangs of the late 1960s dissipated in the early 1970s. Most important in this alternative was the social gatherings and parties promoted and DJed by former Black Spades gang leader Afrika Bambaataa and the creation of the Universal Zulu Nation.

8   Some of these golden era artists are A Tribe Called Quest, Common, De La Soul, Gang Starr, Jeru tha Damaja, KRS-ONE, Main Source, Pete Rock & C. L. Smooth, Showbiz & A. G., Souls of Mischief, Public Enemy, and the Wu-Tang Clan.

9   Categories of rap music such as conscious and hardcore are both helpful and harmful. They
    are helpful because, like all categories, they provide a useful lexicon; they are harmful, how-
    ever, because ignoring creative contexts or the linguistic practices of rap can enable one to
    categorize an artist in virtually any category. See Appendix C for further descriptions.

10 Regarding the relationship between Hip-Hop and Black linguistic practices, Alim (2004a,
    pp. 393–394) notes that hip-hop nation language (HHNL) is rooted in African American
    language and yet expands on it. Among other characteristics, HHNL is used, adapted,
    borrowed, and transformed by different groups and ethnicities in and outside of the United
    States and has regional variations.

11 Alim (2007) did not specifically identify the students as Black, though it is suggested
    through the focus on Black linguistic practices and a wider discussion of Black communities

12 For example, the artist raps, "Back in the days our parents used to take care of us / Look at
    'em now they even fuckin' scared of us / Callin' the city for help because they can't maintain
    / Damn, shit done changed."

13 Mahiri and Conner (2003) provided a contrast to such findings by empirically illustrating
    that Black adolescents can critique violence in rap music when it is one aspect of a larger
    curriculum

14 It is a noteworthy paradox that representations of African Americans as nihilistic, un-
    predictable, and dangerous and as despised in society are often the chosen frameworks
    for Black identity formation or resistance in some global contexts. See Elam and Jackson
    (2005) for a wider discussion of this topic.

References

*Alexander-Smith, A. C. (2004). Feeling the rhythm of the critically conscious mind. *English Journal, 93*(3), 58–63.

Alim, H. S. (2004a). Hip-hop nation language. In C. A. Ferguson, E. Finegan, S. B. Heath, & J. R. Rickford (Eds.), *Language in the USA: Themes for the twenty first century* (pp. 387–406). Cambridge, UK: Cambridge University Press.

Alim, H. S. (2004b). *You know my steez: An ethnographic and sociolinguistic study of styleshifting in a Black speech community.* Durham, NC: Duke University Press.

Alim, H. S. (2006). "The Natti ain't no punk city": Emic views of hip-hip cultures. *Callaloo, 29*(6), 969–990.

*Alim, H. S. (2007). Critical hip-hop language pedagogies: Combat, consciousness, and the cultural politics of communication. *Journal of Language, Identity, and Education, 6*(2), 161–176.

Alridge, D. P. (2005). From civil rights to hip hop: Toward a nexus of ideas. *Journal of African American History, 90*(3), 226–252.

Anderson, B. (1983). *Imagined communities: Reflections on the origin and spread of nationalism.* London: Verso.

Baker, S., & Cohen, B. Z. (2008). From snuggling and snogging to sampling and scratching: Girls' non-participation in community-based music activities. *Youth & Society, 39*(3), 316–339.

Bakhtin, M. M. (1981). *The dialogic imagination: Four essays by M. M. Bakhtin.* (C. Emerson & M. Holquist, Trans.). Austin: University of Texas Press.

Baugh, J. (2003). Linguistic profiling. In S. Makoni, G. Smitherman, A. F. Ball, & A. K. Spears (Eds.), *Black linguistics: Language, politics and society in Africa and the Americas* (pp. 155–168). London: Routledge.

Bourdieu, P. (1987). *Distinction: A social critique of the judgment of taste.* Cambridge, MA: Harvard University Press.

Boyd, T. (2003). *The new H.N.I.C.: The death of civil rights and the reign of hip-hop.* New York: New York University Press.

Brown, V. (2006). Guiding the influence of hip-hop music on middle-school students' feelings, thinking, and behaving. *Negro Educational Review, 57*(1–2), 49–68.

Butler, J. (1990). *Gender trouble: Feminism and the subversion of identity.* New York: Routledge.

Chang, J. (2005). *Can't stop won't stop: A history of the hip hop generation.* New York: St. Martin's.

Chang, J. (2006). *Total chaos: The art and aesthetics of hip-hop.* New York: Basic Books.

*Christen, R. S. (2003). Hip-hop learning: Graffiti as an educator of urban teenagers. *Educational Foundations, 17*(4), 57–82.

Chuck D. (1998). *Fight the power: Rap, race, and reality.* New York: Delta Books.

*Clay, A. (2003). Keepin' it real: Black youth, hip-hop culture, and Black identity. *American Behavioral Scientist, 46*(10), 1346–1358.

*Cooks, J. A. (2004). Writing for something: Essays, raps, and writing preferences. *English Journal, 94*(1), 72–76.

Darby, D., & Shelby, T. (2005). *Hip-hop and philosophy: Rhyme 2 reason.* Peru, IL: Open Court.

*Dimitriadis, G. (2001). *Performing identity/performing text: Hip hop as text, pedagogy, and lived practice.* New York: Peter Lang.

Dimitriadis, G. (2008). *Studying urban youth culture.* New York: Peter Lang.

Duncan-Andrade, J. M. R., & Morrell, E. (2005). Turn up that radio, teacher: Popular culture pedagogy in new century urban schools. *Journal of School Leadership, 15*(3), 284-304.

Elam, H., & Jackson, K. (Eds.). (2005). *Black cultural traffic: Crossroads in global performance and popular culture.* Ann Arbor: University of Michigan Press.

Fine, M. (2006). Bearing witness: Methods for researching oppression and resistance. A textbook for critical research methods. *Social Justice Research, 19*(1), 83–108.

Fishkin, S. F. (1995). Interrogating "Whiteness," complicating "Blackness": Remapping American culture. *American Quarterly, 47*(3), 428–466.

*Forman, M. (2001). "Straight outta Mogadishu": Prescribed identities and performative practices among Somali youth in North American high schools. *Topia, 5,* 33–60.

Forman, M., & Neil, M. A. (Eds.). (2004). *That's the joint! The hip hop studies reader.* New York: Routledge.

Freire, P. (1970). *Pedagogy of the oppressed.* New York: Continuum.

Freire, P. (2002). *Education for critical consciousness.* New York: Continuum.

Gay, G. (2000). *Culturally responsive teaching: Theory, research, and practice.* New York: Teachers College Press.

Gee, J. P. (1996). *Social linguistics and literacies: Ideology in discourses.* London: Taylor and Francis.

Gee, J. P. (2003). *What video games have to teach us about learning and literacy.* New York: Palgrave.

George, N. (1998). *Hip hop America: Hip hop and the molding of Black generation x.* New York: Viking.

Gilroy, P. (1997). "After the love has gone": Bio-politics and etho-poetics in the Black public sphere. In A. McRobbie (Ed.), *Back to reality: Social experience and cultural studies* (pp. 83–115). Manchester, UK: Manchester University Press.

Ginwright, S. (2004). *Black in school: Afrocentric reform, urban youth, and the promise of hip-hop culture.* New York: Teachers College Press.

Giroux, H. A. (1994). Doing cultural studies: Youth and the challenge of pedagogy. *Harvard Educational Review, 63*(3), 278–308.

Giroux, H. A. (1996). *Fugitive cultures: Race, violence, and youth.* New York: Routledge.

Guillory, N. A. (2005). Schoolin' women: Hip-hop pedagogies of Black women rappers. *Dissertation Abstracts International, 66*(03). (UMI No. 3167093).

Hazzard-Donald, K. (1996). Dance in hip hop culture. In W. E. Perkins (Ed.), *Droppin' science: Critical essays on rap music and hip-hop culture* (pp. 220–235). Philadelphia: Temple University Press.

*Hill, M. L. (2006). Using Jay-Z to reflect on post-9/11 race relations. *English Journal, 96*(2), 23–27.

*Hill, M. L. (2009). *Beats, rhymes, and classroom life: Hip-hop, pedagogy, and the politics of identity.* New York: Teachers College Press.

Hoch, D. (2006). Toward a hip-hop aesthetic: A manifesto for the hip-hop arts movement. In J. Chang (Ed.), *Total chaos: The art and aesthetic of hip-hop* (pp. 349–363). New York: Basic Books.

Hull, G., & Schultz, K. (Eds.). (2002). *School's out! Bridging out-of-school literacies with classroom practice.* New York: Teachers College Press.

*Ibrahim, A. (1999). Becoming Black: Rap and hip-hop, race, gender, identity, and the politics of ESL learning. *TESOL Quarterly, 33*(3), 349–369.

*Ibrahim, A. (2004). Operation under erasure: Hip-hop and the pedagogy of affective. *Journal of Curriculum Theorizing, 20*(1), 113–133.

Israel (Director). (2002). *The freshest kids: A history of the b-boy* [Motion picture]. United States: Image Entertainment.

*Iwamoto, D. K., Creswell, J., & Caldwell, L. (2007). Feeling the beat: The meaning of rap music for ethnically diverse midwestern college students—A phenomenological study. *Adolescents, 43*(166), 337–351.

Jaworski, A., & Coupland, N. (2006). *The discourse reader.* London: Routledge.

Jocson, K. M. (2006). "Bob Dylan and hip-hop": Intersecting literacy practices in youth poetry communities. *Written Communication, 23*(3), 231–259.

karimi, r. (2006). how i found my inner dj. In J. Chang (Ed.), *Total chaos: The art and aesthetics of hip-hop* (pp. 219–232). New York: Basic Books.

Kearney, M. (1984). *World view.* Novato, CA: Chandler and Sharp.

Kilson, M. (2003, July 17). The pretense of hip-hop Black leadership. *Black Commentator, 50.* Retrieved July 20, 2003, from http://www.blackcommentator.com/50/50_kilson.html

King, J. E. (2007). Critical and qualitative research in teacher education: A blues epistemology for cultural well-being and a reason for knowing. In M. Cochran-Smith, S. Feima-Nemser, K. E. Demers, & J. D. McIntyre (Eds.), *Third handbook of research for teacher education: Enduring questions and changing context* (pp. 1094–1136). New York: Routledge.

Kirkland, D. E. (2008). "The rose that grew from concrete": Postmodern Blackness and new English education. *English Journal, 97*(5), 69–76.

Kitwana, B. (2002). *The hip-hop generation: Young Blacks and the crisis of African American culture.* New York: HarperCollins.

Kitwana, B. (2005). *Why White kids love hip-hop: Wankstas, wiggers, wannabes, and the new reality of race in America.* New York: Basic Books.

Krims, A. (2001). *Rap music and the poetics of identity.* Cambridge, UK: Cambridge University Press.

Ladson-Billings, G. (1994). *The dreamkeepers: Successful teachers of African American children.* San Francisco: Jossey-Bass.

Lee, C. (1995). The use of signifying as a scaffold for literary interpretation. *Journal of Black Psychology, 21*(4), 357–381.

Lee, C. (2007). *Culture, literacy, and learning: Taking bloom in the midst of the whirlwind.* New York: Teachers College Press.

Leonardo, Z. (2004). Critical social theory and transformative knowledge: The functions of criticism in quality education. *Educational Researcher, 33*(6), 11–18.

Lipman, P. (2003). *High stakes education: Inequality, globalization, and urban school reform.* New York: Routledge.

*Mahiri, J. (2006). Digital DJ-ing: Rhythms of learning in an urban school. *Language Arts, 84*(1), 55–62.

Mahiri, J., & Conner, E. (2003). Black youth violence has a bad rap. *Journal of Social Issues, 59*(1), 121–140.

Marcus, G. E. (1998). *Ethnography through thick & thin.* Princeton, NJ: Princeton University Press.

McLaren, P. (1997). Gangsta pedagogy and ghettocentricity: The hip-hop nation as counter-public space. In P. McLaren (Ed.), *Revolutionary multiculturalism: Pedagogies of dissent for the new millennium* (pp. 150–192). Boulder, CO: Westview.

McWhorter, J. H. (2003, Summer). How hip-hop holds Blacks back. *City Journal.* Retrieved September 10, 2003, from http://www.city-journal.org/html/13_3_how_hip_hop.html

Miller-Young, M. (2008). Hip-hop honeys and da hustlaz: Black sexualities in the new hip-hop pornography. *Meridians: Feminism, Race, Transnationalism, 8*(1), 261–291.

Mitchell, T. (Ed.). (2001). *Global noise: Rap and hip-hop outside the USA.* Hanover, CT: Wesleyan University Press.

Morrell, E. (2004). *Linking literacy and popular culture: Finding connections for lifelong learning.* Norwood, MA: Christopher-Gordon.

*Morrell, E., & Duncan-Andrade, J. M. R. (2002). Promoting academic literacy with urban youth through engaging hip-hop culture. *English Journal, 91*(6), 88–92.

Nasir, N. S., & Hand, V. M. (2006). Exploring sociocultural perspectives on race, class, and learning. *Review of Educational Research, 74*(4), 449–475.

*Newman, M. (2007). "I don't want my ends to just meet; I want my ends overlappin'": Personal aspiration and the rejection of progressive rap. *Journal of Language, Identity, and Education, 6*(2), 131–145.

*Pardue, D. (2004). "Writing in the margins": Brazilian hip-hop as an educational project. *Anthropology and Education Quarterly, 35*(1), 411–432.

*Pardue, D. (2007). Hip-hop as pedagogy: A look into "heaven" and "soul" in Sao Paulo, Brazil. *Anthropological Quarterly, 80*(3), 673–709.

Parker, K. (2003). *Ruminations.* New York: Welcome Rain.

Paul, G. P. (2000). Rap and orality: Critical media literacy, pedagogy, and cultural synchronization. *Journal of Adolescent & Adult Literacy, 44*(3), 346–251.

*Pennycook, A. (2007a). *Global Englishes and transcultural flows.* London: Routledge.

*Pennycook, A. (2007b). Language, localization, and the real: Hip-hop and the global spread of authenticity. *Journal of Language, Identity, and Education, 6*(2), 101–115.

Perkins, W. E. (Ed.). (1996). *Droppin' science: Critical essays on rap music and hip-hop culture.* Philadelphia: Temple University Press.

Perry, I. (2004). *Profits of the hood: Politics and poetics in hip-hop.* Durham, NC: Duke University Press.

Perry, T., Steele, C., & Hilliard, A. (2004). *Young, gifted, and Black: Promoting high achievement among African American students.* Boston: Beacon.

Petchauer, E. (2007a). African American and hip-hop cultural influences. In A. P. Rovai, L. B. Gallien, & H. Stiff-Williams (Eds.), *Closing the African American achievement gap in higher education* (pp. 20–38). New York: Teachers College Press.

Petchauer, E. (2007b). "Welcome to the underground": Portraits of worldview and education among hip-hop collegians. *Dissertation Abstracts International, 68*(06). (UMI No. 3271452).

Pinn, A. B. (2003). *Noise and spirit: The religious and spiritual sensibilities of rap music.* New York: New York University Press.

Potter, R. A. (1995). *Spectacular vernaculars: Hip-hop and the politics of Postmodernism.* Albany: State University of New York.

Pough, G. D. (2004). *Check it while I wreck it: Black womanhood, hip-hop culture, and the public sphere.* Boston: Northeastern University Press.

Pray, D. (Director). (2001). *Scratch* [Motion picture]. United States: Palm Pictures.

*Rice, J. (2003). The 1963 hip-hop machine: Hip-hop pedagogy as composition. *College Composition and Communication, 54*(3), 453–471.

*Richardson, E. (2006). *Hiphop literacies.* New York: Routledge.

*Richardson, E. (2007). "She was workin it like foreal": Critical literacy and discourse practices of African American females in the age of hip hop. *Discourse and Society, 18*, 789–809.

Roediger, D. (1998). What to make of wiggers: A work in progress. In J. Austin & M. N. Willard (Eds.), *Generations of youth: Youth cultures and history in Twentieth- Century America* (pp. 358-366). New York: New York University Press.

Rose, T. (1994). *Black noise: Rap music and Black culture in contemporary America.* Hanover, CT: Wesleyan University Press.

Schloss, J. G. (2004). *Making beats: The art of sample-based hip-hop.* Hanover, CT: Wesleyan University Press.

Shaw, W. (2000). *West side: Young men & hip hop in L.A.* New York: Simon & Schuster.

Shusterman, R. (2000). *Pragmatist aesthetics: Living beauty, rethinking art* (2nd ed.). Lanham, MD: Rowman & Littlefield.

Smitherman, G. (1994). *Black talk: Words and phrases from the hood to the amen corner.* Boston: Houghton Mifflin.

Smitherman, G. (1997). "The chain remains the same": Communicative practices in the hip-hop nation. *Journal of Black Studies, 28*(1), 3–25.

Spady, J. G., Alim, H. S., & Meghelli, S. (2006). *The global cipha: Hip-hop culture and consciousness.* Philadelphia: Black History Museum Press.

*Stovall, D. (2006). We can relate: Hip-hop culture, critical pedagogy, and the secondary classroom. *Urban Education, 41*(6), 585–602.

Street, B. V. (1993). The new literacy studies: Guest editorial. *Journal of Research in Reading, 16*(2), 81–97.

Thompson, R. F. (1996). Hip-hop 101. In W. E. Perkins (Ed.), *Droppin' science: Critical essays on rap music and hip-hop culture* (pp. 211–219). Philadelphia: Temple University Press.

*Wakefield, S. R. (2006). Using music sampling to teach research skills. *Teaching English in the Two-Year College, 33*(4), 357–360.

Walker, M. A. (2006, October 19). Enrolling in hip-hop 101 [Electronic version]. *Diverse Issues in Higher Education.* Retrieved April 15, 2008, from http://www.diverseeducation.com/artman/publish/article_6539.shtml

Wang, O. (2004). Spinning identities: A social history of Filipino American DJs in the San Francisco Bay(1975 -1995). *Dissertation Abstracts International, 66*(03). (UMI No. 3167226).

Wells-Wilbon, R., Jackson, N. D., & Schiele, J. H. (2008). Lessons from Maafa: Rethinking the legacy of slain hip-hop icon Tupac Amaru Shakur [Electronic version]. *Journal of Black Studies.* Retrieved October 13, 2008, from http://jbs.sagepub.com/pap.dtl

Williams, A. D. (2007). The critical cultural cypher: Hip-hop's role in engaging students in a discourse of enlightenment. *Dissertation Abstracts International, 68*(08). (UMI No. 3260489).

Willis, P. (1990). *Common culture: Symbolic work at play in the everyday cultures of the young.* Boulder, CO: Westview.

Wilson, J. (2007). *Outkast'd and claimin' true: The language of schooling and education in the southern hip-hop community of practice.* Unpublished doctoral dissertation, University of Georgia, Athens.

"Be Real Black for Me": Imagining BlackCrit in Education

Michael J. Dumas and kihana miraya ross[1]

You don't have to search and roam,'
Cause I got your love at home.

—CHARLES MANN, DONNY HATHAWAY, AND ROBERTA FLACK (1972)

IN INTRODUCING CRITICAL Race Theory (CRT) to the field of education, Gloria Ladson-Billings and William Tate (1995) invoke Carter G. Woodson and W.E.B. Du Bois as two foundational intellectual progenitors of analyses that use race as a theoretical lens to understand and explain social inequities. Woodson is perhaps known best for advancing the study of Black history, and for his critical exploration of both Black education and *miseducation* in the United States (Woodson, 1919, 1933). Du Bois, of course, is the preeminent sociologist, activist, and Pan-Africanist scholar who authored *The Philadelphia Negro* (Du Bois & Eaton, 1899), the first major study of a Black community, and *The Souls of Black Folk* (Du Bois, 1903), which articulates the Black experience of "double consciousness," which Du Bois describes as the "sense of always looking at one's self through the eyes of others, of measuring one's soul by the tape of a world that looks on in amused contempt and pity" (p. 2). Inspired by Woodson and Du Bois, and drawing on the explication of CRT in legal studies, Ladson-Billings and Tate

---

1   University of California, Berkeley, USA

offer an extended explanation of how schooling becomes a site in which Whites exercise their "absolute right to exclude" (p. 60) Black children. They conclude by echoing Black liberationist Marcus Garvey's pronouncement that "in a world of wolves," anti-Black oppression requires a defensiveness in which Black people commit to "the practice of race first in all parts of the world" (quoted in Ladson-Billings & Tate, 1995, p. 62).

Thus, CRT enters the field of education as a decidedly *Black* theorization of race. That is, even as CRT is offered as a tool to analyze race and racism in general, it is, at its inception in education (and arguably, in legal studies as well), an attempt to make sense of and respond to institutionalized racism, as this racism is experienced and endured by Black people. It is not that Ladson-Billings and Tate (1995) understood the applicability of CRT as limited to Black people; rather, it is that their explication of CRT centers most decidedly on anti-Black racism. Therefore, one might be tempted to argue that CRT is—inherently—a Black Critical Theory. But it is not a theorization of blackness or even the Black condition; it is a theory of race, or more precisely, racism, based on analysis of the curious administration of laws and policies intended to subjugate Black people in the United States. Although heavily imbued with concern for the psychic and material condition of Black subjects, individually and collectively, CRT in education functions much more as a critique of White supremacy and the limits of the hegemonic liberal multiculturalism (McLaren, 1995; Melamed, 2011), which guides policy, practice, and research in the field. Understanding this distinction between a theory of racism and a theory of blackness (in an anti-Black world) is key: whereas the former may invoke Black examples, and even rely on Black experience of racism in the formation of its tenets, only critical theorization of blackness confronts the specificity of *anti-blackness*, as a social construction, as an embodied lived experience of social suffering and resistance, and perhaps most importantly, as an antagonism, in which the Black is a despised thing-in-itself (but not person for herself or himself) in opposition to all that is pure, human(e), and White (Gordon, 1997; Wilderson, 2010).

Here, we want to take what seems to us implicit in Ladson-Billings' and Tate's advancement of CRT analysis in education, and make it explicit in a call to revisit and articulate the foundations of a Black Critical Theory, or what we might call *BlackCrit*, within, and in response to CRT. Of course, this brings to mind the number of other racialized "crits" that proliferated in response to CRT's initial formulation—namely, LatCrit, AsianCrit, and TribalCrit. In some sense, all these emerged as critiques of the perceived "Black–White binary" of CRT, and as efforts to more precisely name and address the racial oppression of Latino/as, Asians and Pacific Islanders, and Indigenous peoples (Brayboy, 2005; Chang, 1993; Hernandez-Truyol, 1997). At their best, these "crits" deepen and complicate our understanding of how race is employed ideologically and materially, and extend the theoretical and empirical utility of CRT. However, their existence either presumes that CRT functions in the main as a BlackCrit, or suggests that "race" critique accomplishes all that Black people need; Black people become situated as (just) "race," whereas other groups, through these more specifically named crits, offer and benefit from more detailed, nuanced, historicized, and embodied theorizations of their lived racial conditions under specific formations of racial oppression.

BlackCrit becomes necessary precisely because CRT, as a general theory of racism, is limited in its ability to adequately interrogate what we call "the specificity of the Black" (Wynter, 1989). That is, CRT is not intended to pointedly address how antiblackness—which is something different than White supremacy—informs and facilitates racist ideology and institutional practice. More, it cannot fully employ the counterstories of Black experiences of structural and cultural racisms, because it does not, on its own, have language to richly capture how antiblackness constructs Black subjects, and positions them in and against law, policy, and everyday (civic) life. As Ladson-Billings and Tate (1995) insisted 20 years ago, citing the title of Cornel West's (1993) book, *Race Matters, and,* they quickly add, citing David Lionel Smith (1993), "blackness matters in more detailed ways" (cited in Ladson-Billings & Tate, 1995, p. 52). Advancing BlackCrit helps us to more incisively analyze these "more detailed ways" that blackness continues to matter, and in relation to CRT, how blackness matters in our understanding of key tenets related to, for example, the permanence of racism and whiteness as property. And, in conversation with the critique of multiculturalism offered by Ladson-Billings and Tate, BlackCrit helps to explain precisely how Black bodies become marginalized, disregarded, and disdained, even in their highly visible place within celebratory discourses on race and diversity.

In their 1972 duet, "Be Real Black For Me," Roberta Flack and Donny Hathaway offer what historian Waldo Martin (2008) describes as "an invocation" that invites listeners—Black listeners, most of all—to "embrace blackness [as] 'an interrelated and empowering emotional psychology and liberation politics'" (p. 245). What sounds, on first listen, to be an exchange between lovers, is, in fact, a love song to and for a collective Black "we" grappling with the liberal aims of the Civil Rights Movement amid a new, more defiant nationalism with a cultural politics, which proclaimed that Black is Beautiful. "'Be Real Black for Me,'" in Martin's (2008) analysis, "engaged and thus signifies an audacious and inspiring historical moment of black imagining, re-imagining and nation building" (p. 247). The song does not presume what it means to "be real Black"; rather, it invites a broader (re) imagining of the significance of blackness in our everyday lives. The only truth advanced is that it is important to love being Black, to embrace it as a conscious act of care, power, and healing. We read hints of this same proposition throughout Ladson-Billings' and Tate's article as well, as the authors explore the moral and political potentiality of CRT in education.

In our own historical moment, an insurgent #BlackLivesMatter movement demands a renewed critical imagining and praxis of blackness. As activist and community organizer Alicia Garza (2014), one of the creators of #BlackLivesMatter, explains,

> When we say Black Lives Matter, we are talking about the ways in which Black people are deprived of our basic human rights and dignity. It is an acknowledgement [that] Black poverty and genocide is state violence. It

is an acknowledgement that 1 million Black people are locked in cages in this country—one half of all people in prisons or jails—is an act of state violence. It is an acknowledgement that Black women continue to bear the burden of a relentless assault on our children and our families and that assault is an act of state violence. Black queer and trans folks bearing a unique burden in a hetero-patriarchal society that disposes of us like garbage and simultaneously fetishizes us and profits off of us is state violence.

In the field of education, we have countless examples of the dehumanization of Black bodies, from the long legacy of federal, state, and district policies and practices designed to deprive Black communities and children of educational resources (Anderson, 1988; Anyon, 1997; Rothstein, 2014; Watkins, 2001), to the absence of culturally relevant and sustaining pedagogies (Ladson-Billings, 1995; Paris, 2012), and to the *maladministration* of school discipline policies (Crenshaw, 1991; Ferguson, 2000; Noguera, 2003; Skiba, Michael, Nardo, & Peterson, 2002). Specific recent incidents attest to antiblackness in schools (Dumas, 2016): A teacher in Illinois repeatedly referred to two Black students as "nigger," even after they asked him not to (Malm, 2014). In Florida, school officials ordered a young Black girl to either straighten or cut off her naturally curly hair, or face expulsion (Munzenrieder, 2013). And in New York, a school principal described Black teachers as "gorillas" and derided their "big lips" and "nappy hair" (Klein, 2013). Black-Crit in education promises to help us more incisively analyze how social and educa- tion policy are informed by antiblackness, and serve as forms of anti-Black violence, and following from this, how these policies facilitate and legitimize Black suffering in the everyday life of schools (Dumas, 2014). Of course, BlackCrit is not the only critical theory of blackness, just as CRT is not the only way to critically theorize race. That is to say, we do not intend to propose BlackCrit as something altogether new, or as the superlative approach to analysis of Black experience or racial discrimination. We simply wish to offer BlackCrit as a way to enrich our understanding of concepts already developed in CRT, and to suggest ways to move forward the conversation about CRT in education begun by Ladson-Billings and Tate two decades ago.

We begin by exploring the ways that CRT engages blackness and anti- blackness, emphasizing how it speaks to a BlackCrit without explicitly naming or theorizing it. We then discuss the minimal literature that has emerged on BlackCrit (all outside of education), and explain how formations of BlackCrit not only take into account, but also complicate, critiques of the "Black/white paradigm." Bringing all these ideas together, we suggest some key concepts that might emerge in a more robust BlackCrit, and how these might be useful in critical race analysis in education.

CRT and the Specificity of Blackness

Although CRT is useful for a general analysis of race and racism, particularly as these "do their work" in law and policy, we read in some of the key readings a specific concern with the experience of Black people on the receiving end of racial constructions and racist practice. Our aim here is to highlight explorations of blackness and antiblackness in foundational CRT texts to move toward an articulation of BlackCrit that is consistent with honors and extends work that has already begun.

Trading Away the Black

In Derrick Bell's (1993) allegorical tale, "The Space Traders," aliens come to Earth and promise the United States gold and a sustainable solution to the nation's energy and fuel shortage, all in exchange for the entire Black population. The aliens insist that the decision is entirely up to the U.S. government; they will not take the nation's Black citizens by force. The news of the aliens' offer provokes a nationwide debate, with the White House and most U.S. citizens heavily in favor of forcing the removal of Black citizens.

Opponents of the trade included some corporate interests, liberal political groups, and of course, Black people themselves, represented primarily by Black civil rights and church leaders. Although corporate executives emphasized lost revenues from Black consumers, and the loss of cheap labor provided by Black workers, liberal activists warned of a slippery slope, in which the aliens might return for other maligned groups. In the end, the decision was put to a "democratic" vote, and Black people lost. Bell's story ends, "There was no escape, no alternative. Heads bowed, arms now linked by slender chains, black people left the New World as their forebears had arrived" (p. 194).

We highlight "The Space Traders" here because it exemplifies much of the theoretical imagination of CRT. Key concepts such as interest-convergence and whiteness as property are explored as racial allegiances are formed and broken, and the nation claimed as the inherent entitlement of White citizens. And, foundational to Bell's future-world is a nation in which the social and economic condition of Black people has drastically declined, laws to address the legacy of slavery and Jim Crow eviscerated, and White commitment to racial equity and justice all but gone. But, what we want to emphasize here is that "The Space Traders," this classic CRT allegory, is not about White supremacy or racism in general, but in relation to Black people and Black experience of racial suffering in the United States quite specifically. It draws on the history of anti-Black animus and disregard to depict a society quite eager to be rid of Black people, and able to craft justifications based not simply on broad ideas about prejudice or opposition to diversity, but a pointed antipathy to Black existence. The story is an exploration of how Whites, across temporal space, participate—here quite literally—in the fungibility of Black bodies (Hartman, 1997), the easy market exchange of Black *things* for other desired goods.

Whites as Propertied

This leads us to Cheryl Harris's (1993) seminal essay, "Whiteness as Property," which traces how whiteness evolved from a racial identity to a form of protected property. Harris argues that whiteness was first constructed to secure for Whites specific entitlement to domination over Black and Indigenous peoples, and then, after the end of formal racial segregation, continued to preserve for Whites certain benefits in social status, material resources, and political power. Because whiteness as property is so rarely acknowledged, however, claims for redress become powerfully imagined as unwarranted and unequal taking from Whites, even as they operationalize their whiteness to maintain and increase advantage. Harris concludes her essay with a discussion of how, in the United States, the legal and popular conceptualization of affirmative action as "equal treatment" occludes the necessity for "equalizing treatment" (p. 1788)—that is, redistributive policies and practices that might follow from an ideological challenge to the right to exclusivity that is inherent in the social construction of whiteness.

In education research, "whiteness as property" is often invoked in analyses of educational policies and practices that maintain educational disproportionalities in such areas as school discipline, testing and tracking policies, and access to culturally relevant curricula (Leonardo & Broderick, 2011; Matias, 2015; Matias, Mitchell, Wade-Garrison, Tandon, & Galindo, 2014). In general, the argument is that whiteness accords to White students, parents, and communities a sense of entitlement to educational opportunities, privileged spaces, and structural advantages (Dumas, 2015; Leonardo, 2009). This is all valuable work, in its own right. At the same time, Harris is clear that whiteness is constructed as property based on two related notions: one, that Black people are, in fact, not people at all, but a form of property to which Whites are entitled; and two, that all land is White property as well, Indigenous peoples are not entitled to property, or to even be on property. Thus, whiteness puts Black people to work as exploited labor, or more accurately, Black property works to maintain and expand the property of Whites (Smith, 2014). At the same time, whiteness makes necessary the dispossession and extermination of Indigenous peoples, as there is no land upon which they could rightfully stand that is not always already the property of Whites.

Slavery in particular, Harris contends, was both justified by and furthered the need for the construction of whiteness as property. She notes,

> The construction of white identity and the ideology of racial hierarchy . . .
> were intimately tied to the evolution and expansion of the system of chattel
> slavery. The further entrenchment of plantation slavery was in part an an-
> swer to a social crisis produced by the eroding capacity of the landed class
> to control the white labor population. (p. 1716)

Whiteness, then, as a form of entitlement, a birthright that can be enjoyed and repeatedly cashed in, becomes especially important as a possession of poor Whites who will never have much actual cash. Placated by this fictive property, poor Whites imagine themselves as always worth more than Black beings, and as connected to propertied Whites with whom they otherwise have no shared interests. Because slavery was based solely on race, "it became crucial to be 'white,' to be identified as white, to have the property of being white," Harris explains. "Whiteness was the characteristic, the attribute, the property of free human beings" (p. 1721).

Our point here is to insist that implicit in the construction of whiteness as property, and in Harris' theorizing, is an understanding of the foundational importance of Black people as the property of Whites, and, we should say, the lands of Indigenous peoples as always also the property of Whites. Although we may now theorize and identify instances of whiteness as property in CRT scholarship, without actually taking into account Black and Indigenous exploitation and removal, we believe a renascent BlackCrit might more fully explore what it means to take a historical account of being owned by propertied Whites, and then, even in this historical moment, owing an ongoing debt of deference—dare we say, servitude?—to all Whites, regardless of class.

Intersecting Blackness

Within CRT, intersectionality offers an opportunity to analyze the confluence of race and other dimensions of difference, most notably gender, sexuality, and social class (Crenshaw, 1989, 1991; Delgado, 2010). Although it has been broadly applied to a full range of intersections, the initial formulation of intersectionality in the work of Kimberlé Crenshaw was intended to address the peculiar position of Black women with relation to race and sex discrimination law. In short, Crenshaw argued, Black women could find themselves without a valid claim of sex discrimination, if it were possible that race was a factor in their unequal treatment, and similarly, could be denied a race discrimination claim if it were not clear that it was race *alone* that was the basis of the behavior they suffered. Crenshaw (1989) explains,

> Consider an analogy to traffic in an intersection, coming and going in all four directions. Discrimination, like traffic through an intersection, may flow in one direction, and it may flow in another. If an accident happens in an intersection, it can be caused by cars traveling from any number of directions and, sometimes, from all of them. Similarly, if a Black woman is harmed because she is in the intersection, her injury could result from sex discrimination or race discrimination. (p. 149)

More than simply a question of law, Crenshaw critiques White feminist scholars for racializing gender as White, and race scholars—particularly Black scholars—for constructing racial grievances in terms of the experiences and needs of Black men. In public discourse and cultural politics, Black women then become either invisible, marginalized, or without an adequate framework to make sense of and explain their everyday experiences of multidimensional (or multidirectional, to use Crenshaw's traffic analogy) oppression. For example, Black women who suffer domestic violence at the hands of Black men may be less likely to report their abusers, given their own concerns about police violence against Black men. Thus, some Black women may not heed calls by feminists to more severely punish violence against women, because these feminist discourses fail to express any concern about police violence, not only against Black men but also against Black women, who are inevitably, also, racialized by police. At the same time, within Black cultural and political spaces, Black women may face pressure to set aside issues of sexual violence for the good of "the race," even as Black public discourse leaves little room for consideration of violence against (Black) women as a race issue. Black women are thus "theoretically erased" (Crenshaw, 1989, p. 2), but perhaps existentially erased as well.

In this regard, intersectionality, as Crenshaw (1991) introduces it, is an attempt to capture the complexity of Black experience, for Black women, first of all, and also for Black men. "I am Black," she contends, is "not simply a statement of resistance but also a positive discourse of self-identification" (p. 1297). She argues that at this historical moment, "to occupy and defend a politics of social location" becomes an important strategy for collective mobilization and identity. Thus, she insists on the salience of race and racial identification. What intersectionality offers is a way to "[reconceptualize] race as a coalition between men and women of color" (p. 1299). That is, Black struggle is inherently and always a coalition of Black people with different social location, across boundaries of gender, but also social class, sexuality, and other differences. BlackCrit finds its meaning not in insisting on a unitary racial location, asserting an essential Black counterstory or political project. Rather, its criticality necessitates an acknowledgment of, and a wrestling with difference, and interdependence across difference.

Our point here is not to debate the issue of the inclusion of Black women and girls—which has emerged more recently in critique of the White House My Brother's Keeper initiative (see, for example, Crenshaw, 2014, 2015)— but to emphasize that, once again, attention to blackness and antiblackness is at the core of key CRT texts and theoretical formulations. To be clear, we are not suggesting that CRT itself is intended to be a Black theory. Rather, we want to demonstrate that much of the early work is motivated by, and seeks to respond to the Black experience of racial oppression. This, of course, raised critiques—some of them valid—of a "Black/White binary," which we turn to in the next section. However, as we want to suggest throughout this article, any limitations of the Black/White binary (or paradigm) only further underscore the need for BlackCrit as a theoretical construct to attend specifically to the Black experience of anti-Black racism and White supremacy, without attempting to generalize to all racialized subjects.

The Black/White Paradigm

From its inception, CRT sought to demystify racism and racial oppression. CRT scholars seek to understand and challenge the ways race and racial power are constructed and reproduced in U.S. society (Crenshaw, 1995), question the very foundation of the liberal order (Delgado & Stefancic, 2000), and articulate their critiques and challenges through specific insights and principles. Specifically, the acceptance that racism is not an anomaly but rather the norm in U.S. society (Delgado, 1995) where everyday acts of racial inequality and discrimination are firmly rooted in White hegemony (Taylor, Gillborn, & Ladson-Billings, 2009), allows CRT scholars to interrogate domination from a standpoint that acknowledges race as the organizing principle of society (Leonardo, 2004) and privileges the racialized experiences of people of color.

Although the original tenets of CRT refer to people of color en masse, Phillips (1998) argues that the original CRT workshops, held annually between 1989 and 1997, may have privileged the experiences of African Americans and heterosexuals. Although the workshops were originally conceived of by Kimberlé Crenshaw and organized by scholars with leftist orientations, in the early 1990s, non-Black scholars of color began to critique CRT for its "Afrocentrism," or the centering of the Black experience to the extent that the experiences of other peoples of color were ignored (Phillips, 1998). At the CRT workshop in 1992, non-Black CRT scholars of color formed a caucus and challenged the workshop's Black scholars for "[overemphasizing] the history and present circumstances of black people, with an unprincipled neglect of the conditions of non-black peoples of color" (p. 1252). These scholars argued that

> the scholarship and discourse produced under the rubric of "Critical Race Theory" generally and effectively has equated African American "blackness" with "race" and measured that experience against Euro-American "whiteness" without examining how Asian American, Latina/o and Native American experiences or identities figure in the race/power calculus of this society and its legal culture. (Valdez as quoted in Phillips, 1998, pp. 1252-1253)

In short, non-Black CRT scholars critiqued Black CRT scholars' conflating "race" with "Black" to the exclusion of other "outgroups."

Much of this critique was contextualized within the notion of a Black/White paradigm. Perea (1997) for example, sets out to identify and critique what has been called the Black/White binary or Black/White paradigm of race and the ways it excludes Latinos and Latinas from full participation in racial discourse, diminishes Latino/a history, and perpetuates negative stereo- types of Latina/os in the United States. Perea points to the robust scholarship on race that focuses solely on African Americans and Whites to illuminate how the Black/White binary shapes race thinking and reifies the Black/White binary paradigm. Perea (1997) notes, "The mere recognition that 'other people of color' exist, without careful attention to their voices, their histories, and their real presence, is merely a reassertion of the Black/White paradigm" (p. 1219). Perea painstakingly evaluates the work of scholars such as Andrew Hacker, Toni Morrison, and Cornel West, and suggests that as a result of focusing almost exclusively on whiteness and blackness, they marginalize other outgroups, ignore the ways non-Black people of color are racialized in the United States, and reify the Black/White binary.

Farley (1998), however, argues that the use of the phrase "Black/White paradigm" is a serious flaw in LatCrit theory and risks alienating Black people. Farley contends there is in fact no such thing as a Black/White paradigm except as a "tool for the master" (p. 171) and that discussions of moving beyond the Black/White paradigm may be heard by Whites "as a way to relieve themselves of the burden of having to speak of their former slaves" (p. 172). While Farley points to the importance of examining the ways White supremacy injures non-Black people of color, he suggests reframing the language in a way that forces White supremacy center stage. Hence, rather than moving beyond the Black/White paradigm, discussions that focus on moving "beyond the white supremacist language of black-or-white" (p. 172) or "White Over Black paradigm" (Phillips, 1998) nestle the responsibility within dominant racial ideology.

Furthermore, given the significance of African American ethnicity to U.S. political and social contexts and the "centrality of anti-black racism to the patterns of domination we call white supremacy" (Espinoza & Harris, 1997, p. 1596), attention to antiblackness is a critical component in resisting White supremacy. In fact, Nakagawa (2012) argues, "anti-black racism is the *fulcrum* of white supremacy" (emphasis added). While acknowledging that focusing on Black and White may reify a false racial binary that disregards the experiences of non-Black people of color, Nakagawa points to a real binary in which White people occupy one side—"the side with force and intention" and "the way they mostly assert that force and intention is through the fulcrum of anti-black racism." Nakagawa notes that the very structure of the U.S. economy has its roots in race slavery and numerous other structures such as the U.S. concept of ownership rights, the federal election system, criminal codes, and federal penitentiaries, are fueled by anti-Black racism and in the case of national politics, a fear of Black people.

Still, all race scholars agreed on the necessity of interrogating the specific oppressions of non-Black outgroups within a White supremacist society. In other words, regardless of the problematic notion of moving beyond the so-called Black/White binary, the need for CRT focused explicitly on non-Black people of color, was indisputable. Hence, these early critiques of the "Black/White paradigm" or "Black/White binary" in CRT lay the foundation for the proliferation of other "racecrits," namely, LatCrit, AsianCrit, and TribalCrit. These racecrits sought to address the experiences of Latinas/os, Asians, and Indigenous people in ways CRT had failed to do. These "crits" worked to advance our understanding of the ways non-Black people are raced and draw our attention to issues such as language, nativistic racism, and colonialism (Brayboy, 2001, 2005; Castagno & Lee, 2007; Cerecer,

2013; Chae, 2004; Chang, 1993; Haynes Writer, 2008; Solorzano & Bernal, 2001; Solorzano & Yosso, 2002; Valdes, 1996; Yosso, 2006).

BlackCrit

Still, as other racecrits began to emerge, some Black scholars began to question whether it was necessary to have a line of CRT that explicitly focused on the Black experience. In other words, the proliferation of these other racecrits either meant that CRT was considered the same thing as a critical Black theory, or that a theory of race and racism was enough to encompass the experiences of Blacks in the United States. Although CRT may have privileged the experiences of African Americans at its inception, the notion that it could (or should) suffice for theorizing blackness, became increasingly problematic—both ideologically and practically.

Although the emergence of other racecrits served to deepen our understanding of the racialization of non-Black "outgroups," it also effectively shifted the focus away from the Black experience. Phillips (1998) notes that Black history and politics were further decentered in the eighth and ninth CRT workshops and suggests that the only attention given to Black folks at this time were "critiques of black homophobia and chastisement of blacks for our role in enforcing repressive aspects of the Black/White paradigm" (p. 1253). Furthermore, Phillips notes that at the conclusion of its first decade, CRT had completely aligned itself with what LatCrit was at its inception. Where the experiences of Blacks are decentered (or pushed out), Phillips questions,

> What institutional arrangements are suited to our articulation of the particular culture and needs of African Americans, which may or may not come to be called "BlackCrit," but which should definitely take into account the convergence between the politics of the Critical Race Theory Workshop and LatCrit theory? (p. 1254)

Although Phillips does not articulate what a potential BlackCrit may involve, the notion that its development had become necessary was clear.

Indeed, some scholars began to consider the potential of its explanatory power for underscoring the specific forms of racial oppression Black people experience, both in the United States and abroad. For example, Lewis (2000) notes, "The strand of Critical Race scholarship that I am labeling 'BlackCrit' addresses the significance of racial attitudes toward Africans and peoples of African descent in the structure and operation of the international human rights system" (p. 1076). Lewis was concerned with expanding iterations of the racialization of Black folks to include Black people outside the U.S. con- text. In other words, just as violence and material racism against Black people in the United States has been effectively muted, so have these forms of oppression been ignored against Black people in Africa and the Caribbean for example. Lewis argues that BlackCrit human rights theorists have created or built upon at least three significant critiques of human rights law including a deeper recognition of the role of race in human rights law, or the problems with so-called race-neutral laws, the ways race and gender intersect with human rights, and the primary role of United States in human rights violations both in the United States and abroad.

Still, other scholars' discussion of the development of a BlackCrit situates it within the context of anticipated (or actual) objections. While Phillips (1998) understands why there may be a need to carve space to articulate the specific culture and needs of African Americans, she argues for its development within the CRT workshop rather than as a separate entity or organization. Phillips points to concerns about a regressive Black nationalism that may deny sexism in the Black community, legitimate homophobia, and deny the possibility of African Americans being racist toward non-Black people of color and whites. Another potential danger in constructing a BlackCrit theory is the notion that it would necessarily be essentialist. Roberts (1998) notes,

> BlackCrit could erroneously imply that Blacks share a common, essential identity; it could erroneously attribute to all people of color the experiences of Black people; and it could reinforce the white-black paradigm as the only lens through which to view racial oppression. (p. 855)

Still, Roberts cautions against allowing such fears to prevent scholars from developing a theory that is Black specific. In other words, "writing about Black people is not essentialist in and of itself. It only becomes essentialist when the experiences discussed are taken to portray a uniform Black experience or a universal experience that applies to every other group" (p. 857). Citing the usefulness of a BlackCrit, Roberts notes that studying the relation- ship between reproductive policies and Black women would have been impossible outside of a Black-specific theory:

> I could not have adequately described these policies without focusing on black- white relationships and on the particular meaning of blackness. These repressive reproductive policies arose out of the history of the enslavement of Africans in America. The institution of slavery gave whites a unique economic and political interest in controlling Black women's reproductive capacity. This form of subjugation made Black women's wombs and the fetuses they carried chattel property. The process of making a human being's very reproductive capacity the property of someone else is not replicated in other relationships of power in the United States. (p. 858)

Ultimately Roberts warns about the dangers in advocating an antiessentialism that becomes a detaching from Blackness. Roberts notes, "We should be concerned about avoiding blackness when so many people still feel uneasy about 'loving blackness'" (p. 862).

Still, more than 15 years later, the notion of a BlackCrit remains woefully under-theorized. Particularly in an age where technology often renders brutal antiblackness visible as public spectacle, and calls of "Black lives matter" echo in the streets, we must ask, what are the theoretical tools that will assist us in an examination of the specificity of the Black. More importantly, for the purposes of this article, what does a BlackCrit in education do for us? Surely Ladson-Billings and Tate's introduction of CRT into education 20 years ago raised significant questions about the ways structural racism excludes Black children specifically from equitable educational opportunities. Still, how can we build on this initial focus on blackness, and conceptualize a Black theoretical framework that distinguishes racism from blackness, and expands CRT's ability to illuminate the specificity of blackness in an anti-Black world?

Toward a Conceptualization of a Black Critical Theory

In the first verse of "Be Real Black for Me," Donny Hathaway tells his lover, "You don't have to wear false charms." If indeed this song is, as historian Waldo Martin suggests, a love song to and for Black people, we can read Hathaway as cautioning against a false or grandiose front, a posturing of certainty where there is no need, and where what matters is the ability to hold blackness gently in one's arms. Part of the "false charm" we want to avoid here is the suggestion that BlackCrit is a theoretical formulation entirely of our own making, or even that we are ready to present it as a coherent theory. Given that CRT, and even some of the other racecrits are often explained through the enumeration of "tenets," there is a temptation to do the same here for BlackCrit. But two things are true: First, there are a number of critical Black theories that inform our thinking (which we will credit below), and second, we are not convinced that BlackCrit is best served by the kind of fixedness implied by the notion of *tenets*, a term most commonly associated with religious statements of faith, or rigid ideological schools of thought. We want to resist that here, at least for now, to leave space for further scholarship and collective deliberation. Instead, what we hope to offer here are some framing ideas that might inspire and serve us well in conceptualizing BlackCrit, and then help us move from initial conceptualization to an ever richer theorization.

We begin with a foundational idea that is probably inherent to any possible formulation of BlackCrit: Antiblackness is endemic to, and is central to how all of us make sense of the social, economic, historical, and cultural dimensions of human life. Of course, this is a more specific iteration of the CRT tenet that asserts that racism is normal and permanent in U.S. society (Bell, 1993; Delgado, 1995). But, antiblackness is not simply racism against Black people. Rather, antiblackness refers to a broader antagonistic relationship between blackness and (the possibility of) humanity. The concept is most developed in an intellectual project called Afro-pessimism (although not everyone who writes in, or in relation to, this project would define themselves as Afro-pessimists). Afro-pessimism

posits that Black people exist in the social imagination as (still) Slave, a thing to be possessed as property, and therefore with little right to live for herself, to move and breathe
for himself (Gordon, 1997; Hartman, 1997, 2007; Sexton, 2008; Wilderson, 2010). In fact,
there is no Black Self that is not already suspect, that is not already targeted for death,
in the literal sense and in terms of what Orlando Patterson (1982) calls "social death," in
which the participation of Black people in civic life, as citizens, is made unintelligible by
the continual reinscribing and re-justification of violence on and against Black bodies.
A full explication of antiblackness is beyond the scope of this article, but the essence of
antiblackness is that Black people are living in what Saidiya Hartman (2007) calls "the
afterlife of slavery," in which Black humanity and human possibility are threatened and
disdained "by a racial calculus and a political arithmetic that were entrenched centuries
ago" (p. 6). To insist that antiblackness is endemic and permanent means that BlackCrit
intervenes at the point of detailing how policies and everyday practices find their logic in,
and reproduce Black suffering; it is also to imagine the futurity of Black people against
the devaluation of Black life and skepticism about (the worth of) letting Black people
go on (see, for example, Moten, 2013, who posits a Black optimism, not so much against
Afro-pessimism, but certainly in necessary tension with it).

    We offer a second framing idea for BlackCrit: *Blackness exists in tension with the neo-
liberal-multicultural imagination.* After World War II, the United States began to slowly
dismantle laws that overtly inscribed racial discrimination. By the mid- to late-1960s,
with the signing of various federal and state civil rights measures, and the end of Jim
Crow, the nation came to assert itself as officially antiracist (Melamed, 2011). In this new
embrace of multiculturalism, the state first took an active role in the establishment and
enforcement of antidiscrimination laws, and even implemented a number of programs
(e.g., affirmative action, Head Start) intended to correct generations of racist policies
and practices. With the rise of neoliberalism in the 1980s, the state began to retreat from
an active role in addressing racism, and instead entrusted the market with advancing
diversity and opportunity for all. An emergent neoliberal multiculturalism celebrated
the opening of various markets to a broader range of racially diverse consumers. It is
presumed that racism is no longer a barrier to equal opportunity; thus, those groups
that do not experience upward mobility and greater civic (and buying) power are presumed to have failed on their own, as a result of their own choices in the marketplace
and/or their own inability to internalize national values of competition, and individual
determination and hard work.

    In this context, Black people become—or rather, remain—a problem, as the least as-
similable to this multicultural imagination. The relative successes of some other groups
of color are offered as evidence of the end of racism. Persistent joblessness, disparities
in educational achievement, and high rates of incarceration are all seen as problems
created by Black people, and problems of blackness itself. Here, then, Black people are
seen to stand in the way of multicultural progress, which is collapsed here with the advancement of the market, which in turn, under neoliberalism, is presumed to represent

the interests of civil society and the nation-state. In our view, then, BlackCrit proceeds with a wariness about multiculturalism (and its more current iteration, diversity) as an ideology that is increasingly complicit with neoliberalism in explaining away the material conditions of Black people as a problem created by Black people who are unwilling or unable to embrace the nation's "officially anti-racist" multicultural future. We do not mean to suggest opposition to coalitions among and between groups of people of color, or even to endorse a kind of essentialist racial separatism. However, we want to recognize that the trouble with (liberal and neoliberal) multiculturalism and diversity, both in ideology and practice, is that they are often positioned against the lives of Black people (Dumas, 2016; Sexton, 2008).

Third, we offer that BlackCrit should create space for Black liberatory fantasy, and resist a revisionist history that supports dangerous majoritarian stories that disappear Whites from a history of racial dominance (Leonardo, 2004), rape, mutilation, brutality, and murder (Bell, 1987). Fanon (1963) notes, "You do not disorganize a society . . . if you are not determined from the very start to smash every obstacle encountered" (p. 3). In the wake of the brutal killings of Eric Garner or Natasha McKenna, for example, we may understand Tupac Shakur's (1991) call for "every nigga on my block [to] drop two cops" as a manifestation of Fanon's theory in a way that makes sense in the lived reality of people raced as Black today—people who navigate the constant threat (and reality) of police terror. Still, in reflecting upon this, we understand it is not (as it may appear) a fantasy of murder or the destruction of human beings. We do not see this as a desire on Shakur's part to witness the death of police officers or to know their families' grief. Rather, it is a fantasy of the eradication of a prison and the beginning of a necessary chaos. It represents the beginning of the end. It is the first taste of freedom.

This glimpse of freedom stems from the potential of attacking the army of whiteness and the wondrous possibilities of the ensuing pandemonium. Fanon notes, "Decolonization, which sets out to change the order of the world, is clearly an agenda for total disorder" (p. 2). Although Shakur's suggestion is not an end-all solution to racial oppression, it is the disruption of a power dynamic that becomes the ray of hope for larger systemic change. Hence, as we celebrate the "peaceful protests" against the numerous recent police murders of Black men, women, and children, we must also acknowledge the place of Black liberatory fantasy in collective Black struggle. Fanon writes,

> The work of the colonist is to make even dreams of liberty impossible for the colonized. The work of the colonized is to imagine every possible method for annihilating the colonist . . . for the colonized, life can only materialize from the rotting cadaver of the colonist. (p. 50)

Hence, BlackCrit should also make space for the notion of chants becoming battle cries, tears becoming stones in clenched fists, and the hand-written signs machine guns—for the idea that the blood of whiteness must flow in the streets.

Toward BlackCrit in Education

BlackCrit encourages policy analysis and advocacy that attend to the significance of blackness in the social construction of White supremacy, and then in education specifi-cally, how antiblackness serves to reinforce the ideological and material "infrastructure" of educational inequity—the misrecognition of students and communities of color, and the (racialized) maldistribution of educational resources. Such work neither is meant to displace a broader theorization of critical race policy analysis nor is it intended to reify a Black–White binary. For us, BlackCrit takes its place within the broader critical race project, and at the same time, necessarily occupies a location of its own, similar to the other racecrits, in a way that provides space for further development and imagination.

We conclude this article by briefly offering some explanation of how we might apply BlackCrit in analysis of education policy and practice. We chose to highlight school desegregation and school discipline, because these are two areas where Black students, and Black families and communities figure quite prominently, and where the discourses are so heavily informed by (anti) blackness.

School Desegregation: On Carelessly Moving Black Bodies Around

School desegregation research tends to assess effectiveness in terms of legal victories and policy compliance, the willingness of Whites to participate in busing programs rather than flee public schools, and the extent to which desegregation contributes to cross-cultural learning and the reduction of prejudice (Orfield & Eaton, 1996; Orfield & Lee, 2004; Wells, 1995; Wells, Duran, & White, 2008). CRT scholars have rightly criticized school desegregation policies, and the aims of integration more broadly, as efforts which have done more to maintain White material advantage than extend oppor-tunities for Black children (Dumas, 2011, 2014, 2015; Horsford, Sampson, & Forletta, 2013; Ladson-Billings, 1998; Tillman, 2004). White resistance to school desegregation has always been fierce, and opponents have used the courts and the legislative process to undermine integration altogether, or implement policies that provide special ed-ucational benefits for White children, and create more segregated spaces within and across schools, in which White children will not have to be in the same classrooms as Black children.

Perhaps most significantly for BlackCrit, critical race theorists have also called attention to the myriad ways that school desegregation has been deleterious to the stability of Black communities and families, the development of healthy Black racial identities, and the emotional and social well-being of Black children placed at risk in what Ladson-Billings (2014) has called "a deal with the devil." Derrick Bell (2004) in reflecting critically on his own experience championing school desegregation, notes the damage done to Black children:

In these white schools, black children all too often met naked race-hatred and a curriculum blind to their needs. Black parents, who often lived far from the schools where their children were sent, had no input into the school policies and little opportunity to involve themselves in school life. (p. 112)

BlackCrit follows CRT in interrogating the White supremacy inherent in the formation of, and White resistance to, school desegregation, and embraces CRT's reliance on the lived experiences of Black children, parents, and communities as counter stories to the liberal hegemonic frame used in assessing the effectiveness of integration policies and practices. Where BlackCrit goes further is in analyzing the specific formations of anti-blackness that serve as the foundation for opposition to school desegregation, but which are also embedded in various attempts to implement policies intended to bring racial balance. For example, to convince White families to send their children to predominantly Black schools, district leaders often placed attractive magnet programs in these schools, which had often been long deprived of resources. Although these specialized programs were ostensibly open to all students, the overwhelming number of spaces were occupied by White students. The very fact that such programs were not offered to Black students prior to integration is a clear case of disregard for Black bodies, and is informed by a deep belief that Black people are undeserving of strong academic programs, and worse, simply would not have the capacity to succeed in more rigorous courses of study. The antiblackness is only compounded when Black students—children all—had to endure seeing their White peers offered higher status and greater resources in schools that had historically been places of Black pride and community uplift.

More broadly, BlackCrit helps us think about desegregating schools as spaces in which Black children and their families are the objects of education policy that has other aims besides the defense of Black humanity. These other aims—racial balance, preju-dice reduction, cultural pluralism—ultimately displace analytical frames that highlight Black well-being and futurity, and thus place Black lives at further risk. Here, BlackCrit might envision a liberatory fantasy in which Black subjects respond to integrationist policy proposals with a decided, "Hell naw" and then "I *said*, 'Hell naw!' with the same decided defiance that *The Color Purple*'s Miss Sophia rejected Miss Millie's offer to serve as her maid. And, we might throw in a direct punch to Miss Millie's husband's face as well, regardless of the cost: "Hell naw!" to going where we are hated and beaten down.

School Discipline: Control of Black Bodies, Already Subhuman, Already Despised
Scholars have argued that school discipline has become the new equity issue as many wrestle with the disproportionate number of incidents of school discipline involving Black students (Bireda, 2002; Gordon, Piana, Keleher, 2000; Gregory, Skiba, & Noguera, 2010; Gregory & Weinstein, 2008; Monroe, 2005; Skiba & Peterson, 2003). Even when controlling for socio-economic status, Black students outnumber all other groups in every aspect of the disciplinary system (Gregory et al., 2010; Skiba et al., 2002). BlackCrit

promises to address racialized school discipline and the ways that Black children's bod-ies, clothing choices, and spoken and body language represent the "outer limits in a field of comparison in which the desired norm is a docile bodily presence and the intonation and homogeneous syntax of Standard English" (Ferguson, 2000, p. 72). BlackCrit may also forward our under- standing of the symbolic role of discipline in schools. Noguera (1995) asserts,

> The disciplining event, whether it occurs in public or private, serves as one of the primary means through which school officials "send a message" to perpetrators of violence, and to the community generally, that the authority vested in them by the state is still secure. (p. 198)

Where Black children's bodies can represent the ultimate threat to authority, the disci-plining of Black children can be understood as the definitive reinforcement of security and order.

Still, BlackCrit may offer a more robust theorizing of exactly what Black students are resisting (Nasir, Ross, McKinney de Royston, Givens, & Bryant, 2013). Black students are subjected to the harshest disciplinary actions, such as corporal punishment (Greg-ory, 1997), zero tolerance policies (Skiba, 2000), the criminalization of student behavior (Hirschfield, 2008), and the school to prison pipeline (Toldson, 2008; Wald & Losen, 2003). Certainly, this "discriminatory disciplining" mirrors racialized state repression within the larger society. As Alexander (2012) notes, "lynch mobs may be gone, but the threat of police violence is ever present" (p. 141). The threat of police violence is real, par-ticularly when there are increasing examples of law enforcement officers' ability to abuse, sometimes fatally, with total impunity. In a song specifically about police terrorism in Black communities and police murders of young Black men, Tupac Shakur famously commented, "tell me what a Black life's worth . . . the truth hurts" (T. Shakur, 1997). If in fact, #Blacklivesmatter in the educational context, BlackCrit should interrogate the dissonance between the hashtag and racialized disciplinary policies and practices in U.S. public schools. If the demand for recognition of the worth of Black lives is muted by institutionalized repression of Black students, Shakur's question (and answer) becomes painfully salient.

Although scholars tend to focus on the discipline gap itself, or on the connection between discipline and prison rates, the disciplining of Black children must be under-stood in the context of larger systems of repression. This is necessary to begin thinking about strategies to combat the failure of public schools to effectively educate Black chil-dren, and their success in reproducing dominant racial ideology and the repression of the Black body. Referring to the current state of affairs as a "discipline gap" or as "dis-proportionate rates of discipline" may serve to obfuscate the egregiousness and exact substance of antiblackness.

Love at Home: Carrying It On

As part of refusing to make peace with the war on Black people, Assata Shakur (1987) ends her autobiography with a poem titled, "The Tradition." While this poem is a recognition and celebration of the trajectory of Black resistance, it also serves as a call to action. She writes,

> . . . In tales told to the children
> In chants and cantatas.
> In poems and blues songs
> and saxophone screams,
> We carried it on.
>
> In classrooms. In churches
> In courtrooms. In prisons
> We carried it on
>
> On soapboxes and picket lines.
> Welfare lines, unemployment lines.
> Our lives on the line,
> We carried it on . . .
>
> On cold Missouri midnights
> Pitting shotguns against lynch mobs.
> On burning Brooklyn streets.
> Pitting rocks against rifles,
> We carried it on . . .
>
> Carried on the tradition
> Carried a strong tradition
> Carried a proud tradition
> Carried a Black tradition.
>
> Carry it on.
> Pass it down to the children.
> Pass it down.
>> Carry it on.
>> Carry it on now.
>
> Carry it on
> To Freedom! (pp. 264-265)

Ultimately we offer that BlackCrit *carry it on*. Carry it on from a place of love. Not just a love for the Harlem Renaissance or the Civil Rights Movement, but love for loud colors and loud voices. Love for sagging pants, hoodies, and corner store candies. Love for gold grills and belly laughs on hot summer porches. Carry it on as a site of struggle—as engaging with the historical and contemporary yearning to be at peace. As forging refuge from the gaze of White supremacy—where Black children dream weightless, unracialized, and human. Where language flows freely and existence is nurtured and resistance is breath. Where the Black educational imagination dances wildly into the night—quenching the thirst of yearning and giving birth to becoming.

Declaration of Conflicting Interests

The author(s) declared no potential conflicts of interest with respect to the research, authorship, and/or publication of this article.

Funding

The author(s) received no financial support for the research, authorship, and/or publication of this article.

References

Alexander, M. (2012). *The new Jim Crow*. New York, NY: The New Press.

Anderson, J. D. (1988). *The education of Blacks in the South, 1860-1935*. Chapel Hill: University of North Carolina.

Anyon, J. (1997). *Ghetto schooling*. New York, NY: Teachers College.

Bell, D. (1987). *And we are not saved: The elusive quest for racial justice*. New York, NY: Basic Books.

Bell, D. (1993). *Faces at the bottom of the well*. New York, NY: Basic Books.

Bell, D. (2004). *Silent covenants*. New York, NY: Oxford University Press.

Bireda, M. R. (2002). *Eliminating racial profiling in school discipline: Cultures in conflict*. Lanham, MD: Rowman & Littlefield.

Brayboy, B. M. J. (2001, November). *Toward a Tribal Critical Theory in higher education*. Paper presented at the Association for the Study of Higher Education, Richmond, VA.

Brayboy, B. M. J. (2005). Toward a tribal critical race theory in education. *The Urban Review*, 37, 425-446.

Castagno, A. E., & Lee, S. J. (2007). Native mascots and ethnic fraud in higher education: Using tribal critical race theory and the interest convergence principle as an analytic tool. *Equity & Excellence in Education*, 40, 3-13.

Cerecer, P. D. Q. (2013). The policing of native bodies and minds: Perspectives on schooling from American Indian youth. *American Journal of Education*, 119, 591-616.

Chae, H. S. (2004). *Using Critical Asian Theory (AsianCrit) to explore Korean-origin, working-class/poor youth's experiences in high school* (Unpublished doctoral dissertation). Teachers College Columbia University, New York, NY.

Chang, R. S. (1993). Toward an Asian American legal scholarship: Critical race theory, post-structuralism, and narrative space. *California Law Review, 81*, 1241-1323.

Crenshaw, K. (1989). Demarginalizing the intersection of race and sex: A black feminist critique of antidiscrimination doctrine, feminist theory and antiracist politics. *University of Chicago Legal Forum, 1989*, 139-167.

Crenshaw, K. (1991). Mapping the margins: Intersectionality, identity politics, and violence against women of color. *Stanford Law Review, 43*, 1241-1299.

Crenshaw, K. (Ed.). (1995). *Critical race theory: The key writings that formed the movement.* New York, NY: The New Press.

Crenshaw, K. (2014, July 29). The girls Obama forgot. *The New York Times.* Available from http://www.nytimes.com

Crenshaw, K. (2015). *Black girls matter: Pushed out, overpoliced and underprotected.* New York, NY: African American Policy Forum.

Delgado, R. (1995). *Critical race theory: The cutting edge.* Philadelphia, PA: Temple University.

Delgado, R. (2010). Rodrigo's reconsideration: Intersectionality and the future of critical race theory. *Iowa Law Review, 96*, 1247-1288.

Delgado, R., & Stefancic, J. (Eds.). (2000). *Critical race theory: The cutting edge.* Philadelphia, PA: Temple University.

Du Bois, W. E. B. (1903). *The souls of black folk.* Chicago, IL: A.C. McClurg.

Du Bois, W. E. B., & Eaton, I. (1899). *The Philadelphia Negro: A social study* (No. 14). Philadelphia: University of Pennsylvania Press.

Dumas, M. J. (2011). A cultural political economy of school desegregation in Seattle. *Teachers College Record, 113*, 703-734.

Dumas, M. J. (2014). Losing an arm: Schooling as a site of Black suffering. *Race, Ethnicity and Education, 17*, 1-29.

Dumas, M. J. (2015). Contesting White accumulation: Toward a materialist anti-racist analysis of school desegregation. In K. Bowman (Ed.), *The pursuit of racial and ethnic equality in American public schools: Mendez, Brown, and beyond* (pp. 291-313). Lansing, MI: Michigan State University.

Dumas, M. J. (2016). Against the dark: Antiblackness in education policy and discourse. *Theory Into Practice, 55*, 11-19.

Espinoza, L., & Harris, A. P. (1997). Afterword: Embracing the tar-baby. LatCrit theory and the sticky mess of race. *California Law Review, 85*(5), 1585-1645.

Fanon, F. (1963). *The wretched of the earth* (Vol. 149). New York, NY: Grove Press.

Farley, A. P. (1998). All flesh shall see it together. *Chicano-Latino Law Review, 19*, 163-176.

Ferguson, A. A. (2000). *Bad boys.* Ann Arbor: University of Michigan.

Garza, A. (2014). A herstory of the #BlackLivesMatter Movement [Web Log Post]. Retrieved from http://thefeministwire.com/2014/10/blacklivesmatter-2/

Gordon, L. R. (Ed.). (1997). *Existence in Black.* New York, NY: Routledge.

Gordon, R., Piana, L. D., & Keleher, T. (2000). *Facing the consequences: An exami-nation of racial discrimination in US public schools.* Oakland, CA: Applied Research Center.

Gregory, A., Skiba, R., & Noguera, P. (2010). The achievement gap and the discipline gap: Two sides of the same coin? *Educational Researcher, 39*, 59-68.

Gregory, A., & Weinstein, R. S. (2008). The discipline gap and African Americans: Defiance or cooperation in the high school classroom. *Journal of School Psychology, 46*, 455-475.

Gregory, J. F. (1997). Three strikes and they're out: African American boys and American schools' responses to misbehavior. *International Journal of Adolescence and Youth, 7*, 25-34.

Harris, C. I. (1993). Whiteness as property. *Harvard Law Review, 106*, 1707-1791.

Hartman, S. V. (1997). *Scenes of subjection*. New York, NY: Oxford University Press.

Hartman, S. V. (2007). *Lose your mother*. New York, NY: Farrar.

Haynes Writer, J. (2008). Unmasking, exposing, and confronting: Critical race theory, tribal critical race theory and multicultural education. *International Journal of Multicultural Education, 10*(2) 1-15.

Hernandez-Truyol, B. E. (1997). Indivisible identities: Culture clashes, confused constructs and reality checks. *Harvard Latino Law Review, 2*, 199-230.

Hirschfield, P. J. (2008). Preparing for prison? The criminalization of school discipline in the USA. *Theoretical Criminology, 12*, 79-101.

Horsford, S. D., Sampson, C., & Forletta, F. M. (2013). School resegregation in the Mississippi of the West: Community counternarratives on the return to neighborhood schools in Las Vegas, Nevada, 1968–1994. *Teachers College Record, 115*(11), 1-28.

Klein, R. (2013, July 10). NYC principal accused of making racist remarks, calling black teachers "gorillas." *Huffington Post*. Retrieved from http://www.africanamerica.org/topic/nyc-principal-accused-of-making-racist-remarks-calling-black- teachers-gorillas

Ladson-Billings, G. (1995). Toward a theory of culturally relevant pedagogy. *American Educational Research Journal, 32*, 465-491.

Ladson-Billings, G. (1998). Just what is Critical Race Theory and what's it doing in a nice field like education? *Qualitative Studies in Education, 11*(1), 7-24.

Ladson-Billings, G. (2014, April 7). *Discussant remarks*. In B. Baldridge (Chair), *Lessons lost in six decades since Brown: Resurrecting the sociocultural dimen- sions of race and education*. Symposium conducted at the meeting of the American Educational Research Association, Philadelphia, PA.

Ladson-Billings, G., & Tate, W. F., IV. (1995). Toward a critical race theory of education. *The Teachers College Record, 97*(1), 47-68.

Leonardo, Z. (2004). The color of supremacy: Beyond the discourse of "white privilege." *Educational Philosophy and Theory, 36*, 137-152.

Leonardo, Z. (2009). *Race, whiteness and education*. New York, NY: Routledge.

Leonardo, Z., & Broderick, A. (2011). Smartness as property: A critical exploration of intersections between whiteness and disability studies. *Teachers College Record, 113*(10), 2206-2232.

Lewis, H. (2000). Reflections on "BlackCrit Theory": Human Rights. *Villanova Law Review, 45*(1075), Article 9.

Malm, S. (2014, October 30). Teacher who called students the "N-word" and "slaves" when they objected to term African-American is fired after outrage. *The Daily Mail*. Available from http://www.dailymail.co.uk

Mann, C., Hathaway, D., & Flack, R. (1972). Be Real Black For Me [Recorded by Roberta Flack and Donny Hathaway]. On the album *Roberta Flack and Donny Hathaway* [LP]. Los Angeles, CA: Atlantic.

Martin, W. E. (2008). Representation, authenticity and the cultural politics of Black power. In J. W. Cook, L. B. Glickman, & M. O'Malley (Eds.), *The cultural turn in US history* (pp. 243-266). Chicago, IL: University of Chicago.

Matias, C. E. (2014). White face, Black friend: A Fanonian application to theorize racial fetish in teacher education. *Journal of Educational Philosophy and Theory, 48*(3), 221-236.

Matias, C. E., Mitchell, K. V., Wade-Garrison, D., Tandon, M., & Galindo, R. (2014). What is critical whiteness doing in OUR nice field like Critical Race Theory? *Equity & Excellence, 47*, 289-304.

McLaren, P. L. (1995). White terror and oppositional agency: Towards a critical multicultural-ism. In C. E. Sleeter & P. L. McLaren (Eds.), *Multicultural education, critical pedagogy, and the politics of difference* (Vol. 4, pp. 33-70). New York, NY: State University of New York Press.

Melamed, J. (2011). *Represent and destroy*. Minneapolis: University of Minnesota.

Monroe, C. R. (2005). Why are "bad boys" always Black? Causes of disproportionality in school discipline and recommendations for change. *Clearing House: A Journal of Educational Strategies, Issues and Ideas, 79*(1), 45-50.

Moten, F. (2013). Blackness and nothingness (Mysticism in the flesh). *The South Atlantic Quarterly, 112*, 737-780.

Munzenrieder, K. (2013, November 26). Orlando-area Christian school threatens to kick out black girl over her natural hair. *Miami New Times*. Retrieved from http://www.miaminewtimes.com/news/orlando-area-christian-school-threatens-to-kick-out-black-girl-over-her-natural-hair-6526104

Nakagawa, S. (2012, May 12). Blackness is the fulcrum [Web log post]. Retrieved from http://www.racefiles.com/2012/05/04/blackness-is-the-fulcrum/

Nasir, N. I. S., Ross, K. M., Mckinney de Royston, M., Givens, J., & Bryant, J. N. (2013). Dirt on my record: Rethinking disciplinary practices in an all-Black, all-male alternative class. *Harvard Educational Review, 83*, 489-512.

Noguera, P. A. (1995). Preventing and producing violence: A critical analysis of responses to school violence. *Harvard Educational Review, 65*, 189-212.

Noguera, P. A. (2003). The trouble with Black boys: The role and influence of environmental and cultural factors on the academic performance of African American males. *Urban Education, 38*, 431-459.

Orfield, G., & Eaton, S. E. (1996). *Dismantling desegregation*. New York, NY: The New Press.

Orfield, G., & Lee, C. (2004). *Brown at 50: King's dream or Plessy's nightmare?* Cambridge, MA: Harvard University Civil Rights Project.

Paris, D. (2012). Culturally sustaining pedagogy a needed change in stance, terminology, and practice. *Educational Researcher, 41*, 93-97.

Patterson, O. (1982). *Slavery and social death*. Cambridge, MA: Harvard University Press.

Perea, J. F. (1997). The black/white binary paradigm of race: The "normal science" of American racial thought. *California Law Review*, 1213-1258.

Phillips, S. L. (1998). *Convergence of the critical race theory workshop with LatCrit theory: A history. University of Miami Law Review, 53*(4), 1247-1256.

Roberts, D. E. (1998). BlackCrit theory and the problem of essentialism. *University of Miami Law Review, 53*(4), 855-862.

Rothstein, R. (2014). *The making of Ferguson: Public policies at the root of its troubles*. Washington, DC: Economic Policy Institute.

Sexton, J. (2008). *Amalgamation schemes: Antiblackness and the critique of multiracialism*. Minneapolis: University of Minnesota.

Shakur, A. (1987). *Assata: An autobiography*. Westport, Conn: Lawrence Hill. Shakur, T. (1991). Trapped. On *2Pacalypse Now* [CD]. Santa Monica, CA: Interscope.

Shakur, T. (1997). I wonder if heaven got a ghetto. On *R u still down? (remember me)*. [CD] Santa Monica, CA: Interscope; New York, NY: Jive. Atlanta, GA: Amaru Entertainment.

Skiba, R. (2000). *Zero tolerance, zero evidence: An analysis of school disciplinary practice* (Policy Research No. SRS2). Bloomington, IN: Indiana Education Policy Center.

Skiba, R. J., Michael, R. S., Nardo, A. C., & Peterson, R. L. (2002). The color of discipline: Sources of racial and gender disproportionality in school punishment. *The Urban Review*, *34*, 317-342.

Skiba, R., & Peterson, R. (2003). Teaching the social curriculum: School discipline as instruction. *Preventing School Failure: Alternative Education for Children and Youth*, *47*, 66-73.

Smith, A. (2014, June 20). The colonialism that is settled and the colonialism that never happened [Web log post]. Retrieved from https://decolonization.wordpress.com/2014/06/20/the-colonialism-that-is-settled-and-the-colonialism-that-never-happened

Smith, D. L. (1993). Let our people go. *The Black Scholar*, *23*(3/4), 74-76.

Solorzano, D. G., & Bernal, D. D. (2001). Examining transformational resistance through a critical race and LatCrit theory framework: Chicana/o students in an urban context. *Urban Education*, *36*, 308-342.

Solorzano, D. G., & Yosso, T. J. (2002). Critical race methodology: Counter- storytelling as an analytical framework for education research. *Qualitative Inquiry*, *8*, 23-44.

Taylor, E., Gillborn, D., & Ladson-Billings, G. (Eds.). (2009). *Foundations of critical race theory in education*. New York, NY: Routledge.

Tillman, L. C. (2004). (Un)intended consequences? The impact of the Brown v. Board of Education decision on the employment status of black educators. *Education and Urban Society*, *36*, 280-303.

Toldson, I. A. (2008). *Breaking barriers*. Washington, DC: Congressional Black Caucus Foundation.

Valdes, F. (1996). Latina/o ethnicities, critical race theory, and post-identity politics in postmodern legal culture: From practices to possibilities. *La Raza LJ*, *9*(1), Article 1.

Wald, J., & Losen, D. (2003). Defining and redirecting a school-to-prison pipeline. *New Directions for Youth Development*, *99*, 9-15.

Watkins, W. H. (2001). *The white architects of Black education*. New York, NY: Teachers College.

Wells, A. S. (1995). Reexamining social science research on school desegregation: Long- versus short-term effects. *Teachers College Record*, *96*, 691-706.

Wells, A. S., Duran, J., & White, T. (2008). Refusing to leave desegregation behind: From graduates of racial diverse schools to the Supreme Court. *Teachers College Record*, *110*, 2532-2570.

West, C. (1993). *Race matters*. New York, NY: Vintage.

Wilderson, F. B., III. (2010). *Red, white & black*. Durham, NC: Duke University Press.

Woodson, C. G. (1919). *The education of the Negro prior to 1861*. Washington, DC: Associated Publishers.

Woodson, C. G. (1933). *The miseducation of the Negro*. Washington, DC: Associated Publishers, Inc.

Wynter, S. (1989). Beyond the word of man: Glissant and the new discourse of the Antilles. *World Literature Today*, *63*, 637-648.

Yosso, T. J. (2006). *Critical race counterstories along the Chicana/Chicano educational pipeline*. New York, NY: Routledge.

Contributors

Antwi A. Akom is Founding Director of the Social Innovation and Urban Opportunity Lab—a joint research lab between the University of California at San Francisco (UCSF) and San Francisco State University. His research lies at the intersection of science, technology, spatial epidemiology, community development, health communications, medical sociology, ethnic studies, African American studies, culturally responsive human-centered design, big data, and public health. He is also a faculty affiliate with UCSF's Center for Vulnerable Populations at Zuckerberg San Francisco General Hospital and Trauma Center. He holds a PhD in urban sociology from the University of Pennsylvania. Dr. Akom is currently Professor in Africana Studies, specializing in health, medicine, nutrition, social and spatial epidemiology, urban planning, and climate justice.

James A. Anderson is Dean of the College of Education and the Edward William and Jane Marr Gutgsell Professor of Education at the University of Illinois Urbana–Champaign. He has written a seminal text in the field of Black Education, *The Education of Blacks in the South, 1860–1935*, for which he won the 1990 American Educational Research Association Outstanding Book Award. Anderson's scholarship focuses broadly on the history of U.S. higher education, with a specialty in Black education. Anderson has served as senior editor of the *History of Education Quarterly* and has participated in the production and filming of PBS documentaries *School: The Story of American Public Education* (2001), *The Rise and Fall of Jim Crow* (2002), *Forgotten Genius: The Percy Julian Story* (2007), and *Tell Them We Are Rising: The Story of Black Colleges and Universities* (2018).

James Earl Davis is the Bernard C. Watson Endowed Chair in Urban Education and Professor of Higher Education and Educational Leadership. His research focuses on gender and schooling outcomes; men, boys, and masculinity; the sociology of higher education; and applied research methods. He is particularly interested in issues of access and equity in the educational pipeline as they are informed by gender, race, class, and the intersection of these social locations. His research agenda has been driven by recurring questions related to what we know about the social context of identity and how institutions and policy are implicated in academic and social outcomes. He has received a National Science Foundation grant for "STEMing the Tide: Exploring Factors Related to Males of Color Interest, Engagement and Achievement in Mathematics and Science," a research project that investigates identity and its relationship to science and mathematics achievement for boys and young men of color.

Davison M. Douglas is an American historian, law professor, and former Dean of the oldest law school in the United States, William & Mary Law School in Williamsburg, Virginia. He is the author or editor of several books, including *Jim Crow Moves North: The Battle Over Northern School Segregation, 1865–1954* (2005) and *Reading, Writing and Race: The Desegregation of the Charlotte Schools* (1995), and has had numerous articles published in journals such as the *Michigan*,

Northwestern, Texas, UCLA, Wake Forest, and *William and Mary* law reviews. He has lectured on American constitutional law and history at various universities in the United States, Africa, Asia, Australia, and Europe.

Michael J. Dumas taught at the University of California, Berkeley in the Graduate School of Education and the Department of African American Studies. He earned a PhD in urban education with an emphasis in social and educational policy studies from the Graduate Center of the City University of New York. His work centers on the cultural politics of Black education, the cultural political economy of urban education, and fugitive possibilities in and against education research. His work has appeared in the *Harvard Educational Review, Teachers College Record, Race Ethnicity and Education, Discourse: The Cultural Politics of Education,* and *Educational Policy.* He is primarily interested in how schools become sites of Black material and psychic suffering and anti-Black violence, how disgust with and disdain for Blackness inform defenses of inequitable distribution of educational resources, and ways that anti-Blackness persists in education policy discourses and in broader public discourses on the worth of economic and educational investment in Black children.

Signithia Fordham is a prominent anthropologist and Distinguished Professor at the University of Rochester. She received her BA with honors in social science education at Morris Brown College, her MA from St. John's College in liberal education, and her PhD from the American University. Her pioneering research has been funded by the Spencer Foundation, National Science Foundation, and Open Educational Research Initiative. A force in the field of anthropology of education, she has produced high-impact research books and articles, namely, *Blacked Out: Dilemmas of Race, Identity and Success at Capital High* (University of Chicago Press, 1996); *Downed by Friendly Fire: Black Girls, White Girls, and Suburban Schooling* (University of Minnesota Press, 2016); "Black Students' School Success: Coping with the Burden of 'Acting White'" (with John Ogbu, 1986); "Why Can't Sonya (and Kwame) Fail Math?" (2000); "Speaking Standard English from Nine to Three: Language Usage as Guerrilla Warfare at Capital High" (1998); and "Those Loud Black Girls: (Black) Women, Silence, and Gender 'Passing' in the Academy" (1993). In 2019, she received the Legacy Award from the Association of Black Anthropologists.

Trudier Harris is a celebrated American literary historian and the University Distinguished Research Professor at the University of Alabama at Tuscaloosa. In 2009, she retired from the English Department at the University of North Carolina at Chapel Hill as the J. Carlyle Sitterson Distinguished Professor. Harris has published more than 20 authored and edited books, such as *Exorcising Blackness: Historical and Literary Lynching and Burning Rituals* (1984); *Fiction and Folklore: The Novels of Toni Morrison* (1991); *Saints, Sinners, Saviors: Strong Black Women in African American Literature* (2001); *The Oxford Companion to African American Literature* (1997); *Reading Contemporary African American Drama: Fragments of History, Fragments of Self* (2007); and *The Scary Mason-Dixon Line: African American Writers and the South* (2009). Her memoir, *Summer Snow: Reflections from a Black Daughter of the South,* appeared in 2003. Notably, Harris was the first African American to be hired in a tenure-eligible position and to earn tenure at the College of William & Mary, where she also received an honorary degree in 2018.

bell hooks was an award-winning cultural critic, critical pedagogue, and celebrated Black feminist author. She returned home to Kentucky some years before her death to become the Distinguished Professor in Residence in Appalachian Studies at Berea College. hooks was the author of more than 30 books, including *We Real Cool: Black Men and Masculinity* (2004), *Teaching Community: A Pedagogy of Hope* (2003), and *Ain't I a Woman? Black Women and Feminism* (1981). As an interdisciplinary scholar, her work provided commentaries on race, gender, and place. hooks was involved in running the bell hooks Institute, which opened in 2021 to celebrate the life and work of acclaimed intellectual, feminist theorist, cultural critic, artist and writer.

Gloria Ladson-Billings is a distinguished educational theorist of race, culture, and pedagogy. She is the former Kellner Family Distinguished Professor of Urban Education in the Department of Curriculum and Instruction at the University of Wisconsin–Madison, where she also served as the assistant vice chancellor of academic affairs. Ladson-Billings is known for her work in the fields of culturally relevant pedagogy and critical race theory. Ladson-Billings's *The Dreamkeepers: Successful Teachers of African-American Children* is a significant text in the field of education. Her entire body of work is essential reading across many subfields in education. She was born in Philadelphia, PA, and was educated in the Philadelphia public school system. Ladson-Billings served as President of the American Educational Research Association (AERA) in 2005–2006. During the 2005 AERA annual meeting in San Francisco, Ladson-Billings delivered her presidential address, "From the Achievement Gap to the Education Debt: Understanding Achievement in U.S. Schools," in which she outlined what she called the "education debt," highlighting the combination of historical, moral, sociopolitical, and economic factors that have disproportionately affected African American, Latino, Asian, and other non-White students.

Elizabeth McHenry is Professor of English at New York University and author of *Forgotten Readers: Recovering the Lost History of African American Literary Societies* (2002). Her research focuses on African American literature and the various histories of Black print culture. *Forgotten Readers* has made a major contribution to Black education by uncovering the history of Black readers and their literary practices. McHenry has received many accolades for her work: the Hurston/Wright Legacy Award for Nonfiction (2003); Lora Romero First Book Publication Prize, American Studies Association (Honorable Mention, 2003); Society for the History of Authorship, Reading and Publishing Book History Award, 2003; Black Caucus of the American Library Association Award for Nonfiction (2003); and John Hope Franklin Center Book Award (2002).

John Ogbu was Professor of Anthropology at the University of California, Berkeley at the time of his death in 2003. Ogbu was best known for his work on voluntary, involuntary, and autonomous minorities. He was the author of many texts, including *Minority Education and Caste: The American System in Cross-Cultural Perspective* (1978). He was one of four intellectuals of focus in *Eminent Educators: Studies in Intellectual Influence* (2000). He was posthumously awarded the George Spindler Award for Distinction in the Anthropology of Education from the American Anthropological Association. Ogbu was a major figure in the application of anthropological theories and methods to problems related to minority education in the United States and abroad.

Emery Petchauer is Associate Professor in the Department of English with a faculty appointment in the Department of Teacher Education at Michigan State University. His research has focused on the aesthetic practices of urban arts, particularly hip-hop culture, and their connections to teaching, learning, and living. He is the author of *Hip-Hop Culture in College Students' Lives* (2012), the first scholarly study of hip-hop culture on college campuses, and the coeditor of *Schooling Hip-Hop: Expanding Hip-Hop Based Education Across the Curriculum* (2013).

His scholarship is informed by many decades of organizing and sustaining urban arts spaces across the United States. Dr. Petchauer also studies high-stakes teacher licensure exams and their relationship to the racial diversity of the teaching profession.

kihana miraya ross is Assistant Professor of African American Studies at the University of California, Berkeley. Her groundbreaking research draws on critical ethnographic and participatory design methodologies to examine the multiplicity of ways that antiblackness is lived by Black students in what she calls the "afterlife of school segregation," a phrase she coined to introduce a framework that illuminates the ways in which, despite the end of legal segregation of schooling, Black students remain systematically dehumanized and positioned as uneducable. Her work also explores how Black educators and students collectively imagine and resist anti-Blackness, and racialization processes. Her current book project explores the ways Black girls and Black woman educators create a fugitive space within a Black women's studies elective class at a public high school in an urban district in Northern California.

Mano Singham is the former director of the University Center for Innovation and Teaching and Education and Adjunct Associate Professor of Physics at Case Western Reserve University. Originally from Sri Lanka, he is the author of four books: *Quest for Truth: Scientific Progress and Religious Beliefs* (2000), *The Achievement Gap in US Education: Canaries in the Mine* (2005), *God vs. Darwin: The War Between Creationism and Evolution in the Classroom* (2009), and *The Great Paradox of Science: Why Its Conclusions Can Be Relied Upon Even Though They Cannot Be Proven* (2019). His research interests are located within the fields of education, theories of knowledge, and physics and philosophy.

Thomas Sowell is the Rose and Milton Friedman Senior Fellow on Public Policy at the Hoover Institution. Trained as an economist and social theorist, he is known for his published work in economics, history, social policy, ethnicity, and the history of ideas. Writing from a libertarian conservative perspective, Sowell has written more than 30 books, and his work has been widely anthologized. He is a 2002 National Humanities Medal recipient for his innovative scholarship incorporating history, economics, and political science. He has published numerous books, articles, and editorials. His most recent book, *Discrimination and Disparities* (2018), gathers a wide array of empirical evidence to challenge the idea that different economic outcomes can be explained by any one factor, be it discrimination, exploitation, or genetics.

William F. Tate, IV is Provost and Executive Vice President of Academic Affairs at the University of South Carolina (USC). He holds the USC Education Foundation Distinguished Professorship with appointments in Sociology and Family and Preventive Medicine (secondary appointment). Prior to joining the University of South Carolina faculty, he served as Dean and Vice Provost for Graduate Education at Washington University in St. Louis, where he held the Edward Mallinckrodt Distinguished University Professorship in Arts & Sciences. Tate is a past president of the American Educational Research Association, where he was awarded fellow status. In addition, he was elected to the National Academy of Education. Tate earned his PhD at the University of Maryland, College Park, where he was a Patricia Roberts Harris Fellow. He completed a second postdoctoral training program in the Department of Psychiatry-Epidemiology and Prevention Group at the Washington University School of Medicine, where he earned a master's degree in psychiatric epidemiology.

Vanessa Siddle Walker is professor and Winship Distinguished Research Professor at Emory University. For 15 years, her research has focused on the segregated schooling of African American children in the South, considering both portraits of individual school communities (*Their Highest Potential*, University of North Carolina Press) and, more recently, the network of educational activity that undergirded the development of these schools throughout the South. The latter results are reported in the *American Educational Research Association Journal*, the *Review of Educational Re- search*, and a book forthcoming (*Principal Leaders*, University of North Carolina Press).

Heather Andrea Williams is the Geraldine R. Segal Professor of American Social Thought and Professor of Africana Studies at the University of Pennsylvania. She is the author of *Self-Taught: African American Education in Slavery and Freedom* (2005) and *Help Me to Find My People: The African American Search for Family Lost in Slavery* (2012), both published by University of North Carolina Press, as well as *American Slavery: A Very Short Introduction* (2014), published by Oxford University Press. Williams has received fellowships from the Ford Foundation, Spencer Foundation, Woodrow Wilson Foundation, and Andrew W. Mellon Foundation.

Editors

Hilton Kelly became the Dean of the College of Liberal Arts and Education at the University of Wisconsin at Platteville in 2022. For most of his career, Kelly has been a Professor of Educational Studies and Africana Studies, and Chair of the Educational Studies Department at Davidson College. He received his BA in history from the University of North Carolina at Charlotte and both his MS in labor studies and PhD in sociology from the University of Massachusetts at Amherst. His research and teaching interests include sociology of education, critical race theory, the Age of Jim Crow, the lives, work, and careers of African-American educators, and social memory studies. In 2010, he published Race, Remembering, and Jim Crow's Teachers in the Routledge Studies in African-American History and Culture Series. His articles have appeared in Urban Education, Educational Studies, The Urban Review, The Journal of Negro Education, The American Sociologist, and Vitae Scholasticae: The Journal of Educational Biography. In 2018, he served as the President of the American Educational Studies Association.

Heather Moore Roberson, PhD is Dean of Diversity, Equity, and Inclusion and Associate Professor of Community & Justice Studies and Black Studies at Allegheny College. She received her BA in Educational Studies and American Studies from Trinity College and her MA and PhD in American Studies from Purdue University. Moore Roberson conducts research in the fields of critical race theory, boyhood studies, and justice learning. She has published several book chapters and select articles in various interdisciplinary journals like Radical Teacher and Professing Education.

Index

#BlackLivesMatter, 465–66, 480

A

Abdul-Jabbar, K., 242, 264
absolute right to exclude, 371
academic achievement, African American males and, 381–82
achievement gap, Black and white students and, 303–4, 381–82
    Chinese students' behavior and, 310–11
    culturally relevant pedagogy and, 327
    economic disparities and, 304–5
    education statistics and, 304
    explaining achievement and disengagement, 387–91
    favored explanations for, 304–10
    gender and racial context of, 382–84, 399–402, 402–3, 404–10, 410–17
    problems with delivery of education, 312–14
    promoting research on, 391–92
    sociopathological model and, 305
    victim status and, 309
    Also see Shaker Heights
acting white, 241–43, 247, 248, 250–58, 264–66, 268–69, 306, 307
    American Indians, Mexican Americans and, 266
    honor of being Black and, 284–86
    minorities outside the U.S., 266–67
active learning, 312
Adams, J.Q., 11
ad-hocing, 408–10
African American literary societies, 84
African American press, cultural work of, 65
    development of literary character in, 99–100
    new political strategy for, 69–70

African Methodist Episcopal church (AME), 46, 100
African Repository, 69
afro-pessimism, 475–76
Ain't I a Woman, 353, 354
all-male public schools, 390
Alvord, J.W., 39–40, 42, 44–46, 49, 51, 53, 55
American Colonization Society, 69
American Missionary Association, 59
American Negro Academy, 173
American Race Problem, The, 150
American Teachers Association (ATA), 165, 173–75
Anderson, B., 67
Anderson, J., 166, 177
Andrews, C.C., 71
Andrews, W., 93
Anglo-African Magazine, 67, 98, 99, 102, 103
anti-blackness, 464
antiliteracy laws, slaves and, 9–10, 14–15
    in Alabama, 17
    in Connecticut, 17–18
    covert literacy lessons and, 20–21
    Frederick Douglass and, 24–26
    in Georgia, 15–16
    motivation for, 22
    in North Carolina, 16
    "pit schools" and, 21
    Sabbath and, 12–22
    slave masters' wives and, 20
    slave schools and, 17–18
    in Virginia, 16–17
    Also see slavery/slaves
Anti-Slavery Examiner, 91
Appeal to the Colored Citizens of the World, 15–16
Armstrong, S., 60
Ar'n't I a Woman, 357
Aronson, J., 307

Ashe, A., 306
Atlanta Race Riot of 1906, 171
Atlanta University Conferences, 173
Auld, H., 25
autonomous minorities, 243
avoidance, 252–54

B

Bambara, T.C., 354
Bartky, S., 355
Bass, N., 18
Bechtold, A.L., 212
Bell Aircraft Corporation, 152
Bell Curve, The, 305
Bibb, H., 11, 90–92
Birth of a Nation, 171
Black achievement ideology. *See* Nation of
    Islam
Black critical theory. *See* BlackCrit
Black educators, school equality and, 163–67
    American Teachers Association
        (ATA), 165
Black teacher organizations and, 164–65, 166
    educational leadership (1921-1938)
        and, 179–86
    Elders-Carswell Bill and, 178
    early resistance (1878-1894) and,
        167–71
    Georgia Education Association and,
        176
    Georgia Teachers and Education Asso-
        ciation (GTEA), 165, 167, 180–86
    interracial interaction and, 168–70
    national collaborations and, 173–75
    new beginnings (1917-1921) and,
        175–79
    shields for teachers, 176
    shifting attitudes (1894-1916) and,
        171–75
    use of professional organizations, 176
Black Equal Rights Association, 49
Black feminist thought, 323
Black Georgia Teachers Association, 169
Black liberatory fantasy, 477
Black literary arts, 75
Black Macho and the Myth of the Superwoman,
    356

Black press. *See* African American press
Black scholars, feminist scholarship and,
    353–57
Black students' school success, 241–43
    ambivalence, affective dissonance and,
        242–43
    collective identity, cultural frame and,
        246–48
    cultural-ecological influences on,
        243–45
    explaining achievement and disengage-
        ment, 387–91
    fictive kinship and, 248–50
    group loyalty and, 250–51
    job ceilings and, 244
    researching Black boys at school,
        384–87
    schooling as a subtractive process, 248
    substandard schooling and, 244
    Also see achievement gap, acting white
Black teacher organizations, 164–65, 166
Black/white paradigm, 471–75
BlackCrit, 463, 464–66, 471–75
    conceptualization of, 475–77
    in education, 478–80
    school discipline and, 479–80
    school segregation and, 478–79
Blake: or the Huts of America, 100
Bleak House, 95–97
Bond, H.M., 54, 148, 149, 167, 198, 199, 206,
    208
Booker T. Washington High School
    Charles Lincoln Harper and, 200–2
    principalship of, 201
*Brief Historical Sketch of Negro Education in
    Georgia, A,* 167
Brigham, C., 149
Brown, E.B., 409
Brown, H.B., 92–93
Brown v. Board of Education, 150, 233, 367
Buffalo Urban League, 152
Bullock, H.A., 49, 53
Bunche, R., 306
Butchart, R.E., 44

C

Capital High School (Washington, D.C.),

250–58, 259–63, 268
  avoidance and, 252–54
  Black students "acting white" at,
    250–58
  fictive kinship and, 250
  high-achieving students and, 259–63
  lunching and, 259
  underachieving Black students at,
    251–58
  Also see acting white
Carby, H., 356
Carver, G.W., 228
castelike minorities, 243
Christian Recorder, 67, 99, 100–1, 104
Civil War, 12, 14
Cohen, W., 54
Colored American, The, 66, 68, 105
  cultural literacy and, 83–84
  David Ruggles and, 81
  as a lasting text, 86–87
  literacy societies and, 79–81
  literary character and, 81
  promotion of literacy in, 79
  "proper reading" and, 80
  public speaking and, 86
  purpose of publication, 82
  typical content of, 81–82
  as *Weekly Advocate,* 82
Commission of Enrollment, 41–42
conceptions of knowledge, 333–35
Convention of Colored men of the United
    States, 17–18
Cooper, F., 68
Cornish, S., 68, 70, 78, 82
Crandall, P., 18
Creole, 97
critical pedagogy, 348
critical race theory, education and, 359–60,
    366–69, 463–66
  Black/white paradigm and, 471–75
  intersecting Blackness, 469–70
  multicultural paradigm and, 371–73
  specificity of race and, 467–70
  whites as propertied and, 468–69
  Also see BlackCrit, race
Cuffe, P., 70–71
cultural competence, 327–28
cultural critique, 328–29

cultural literacy, 83–84
cultural synchronization, 320
culturally relevant pedagogy, 317–18, 335–36
  conceptions of knowledge, 333–35
  conceptions of self and others, 330-32
  concrete experiences as a criterion of
    meaning and, 324–25
  context and methodology for studying,
    323–24
  cultural competence and, 327–28
  cultural critique and, 328–29
  cultural synchronization and, 320
  dialogue in assessing knowledge claims
    and, 325
  ethic of caring and, 325–26
  ethic of personal accountability and,
    326
  illusion of atheoretical inquiry and,
    321–22
  participant-observer role for researchers
    and, 322–23
  social relations and, 332–33
  student achievement and, 327
  teaching, culture and, 318–20
  theoretical underpinnings of, 329–30
Curry, J., 22, 23–24
Curtiss-Wright, 152

D

Daniel, P., 54
Davis, A., 354, 404–5
Delany, M., 96–98, 100
desegregation, price of, 225–30
difference, 372
diversity, 372
Division of Negro Education, 182, 184
Dixon, J.C., 184, 185
dominant paradigm of ethnicity, 361
Dorsey, H., 175
Douglass, F, 10, 24–26, 65, 88, 89, 90, 99
  as an antislavery lecturer, 91
  decision to publish *Bleak House,* 95–97
  Martin Delany and, 96–98
  split with early supporters, 92
Douglass, M., 27–28
Douglass' Monthly, 88
Dred Scott, 98

Druid High School, 226–27
Du Bois, W.E.B., 39, 50, 94, 124, 131, 171, 172–73, 362–63, 463
Dunbar High School, 216–18
    principalship of, 216
    William Syphax and, 216

E

Eaton, J., 52–53
eaves-dropping, 11–12
educational achievement, Black students and, 197–200
    alumni of successful high schools, 198
    Book T. Washington High School and, 200–2
    discipline problems and, 219
    Dunbar High School and, 216–18
    Frederick Douglass High School, 204–6
    I.Q. scores and, 198, 219, 221
    law and order, 220
    McDonough 35 High School, 206–9
    political milestones and, 197
    principals of, 221
    P.S. 91 (Brooklyn) and, 213–16
    St. Paul of the Cross and, 202–4
    successful high schools and, 198
    test scores and, 219
    Xavier Prep and, 212–13
egalitarian ideal, 408–10
Elders-Carswell Bill, 178, 179
Emerson, R.W., 93
enticement laws, 54
equality, 233
eugenics, 126
Evans, G., 405–6

F

Fard, W.D., 276
Federal Bureau of Education, 52–53
feminist scholarship. *See* Black scholars
fictive kinship, 241, 248–50, 267, 401
Fire Next Time, The, 306
Fordham, S., 306, 307
Forten, J., 18
Foster, F.S., 103
Frederick Douglass High School, 204–6

curriculum of, 205
Edna Campbell and, 205, 206
I.Q. scores and, 205–6
Frederick Douglass' Paper, 67, 88, 92
    American writers of European descent in, 94–95
    creative parity of Black and white writers in, 94–95
    decision to publish *Bleak House*, 95–97
    intended readership of, 88
    literary objectives of, 88–89
    Martin Delany and, 96–98
    place of Black literature and, 92
    slave narratives and, 93–94, 97
Freedmen's Bureau, 39–40, 42, 44, 48, 53
Freedom's Journal, 66, 68, 105
    adult reading instructions in, 73
    Black literary arts and, 75
    content of, 70–71
    educational programs and, 72
    ending publication of, 78–79
    establishment of, 79
    George Moses Horton and, 75–76
    initial readership of, 68
    literary character and, 77, 79
    as a makeshift textbook, 71–72
    quest for racial equality, 77
    representation of the Black community, 71
    representation of wealth in, 74
    self-improvement and, 76
Freire, P., 348–49
Fugitive Slave Act, 98
Fultz, M., 165

G

Gannett, W.C., 38
Garrison, W.L., 18, 92
Gates, H.L.G., Jr., 65–66
gender inequity, 353
gendered passing, Black girls and, 399–402, 417–20
    ad-hocing and, 408–10
    case study of, 402–3
    conceptual context of, 404–7
    egalitarian ideal and, 408–10
    learning silence and, 410–17

gendered Self, 400, 401
Georgia Association of Educators, 180
Georgia Educational Association, 43, 167,
    176, 177, 185
Georgia Equal Rights Association, 167
Georgia Teachers and Education Association
    (GTEA), 165, 167, 180–86
Georgia Teachers Association, 170, 176, 178,
    180
Gerry, A., 101
gerrymandering of school districts, 138–41
Giddings, P., 356
Gilliam, D., 241, 242
Gloucester, J., 72
Grant, D., 168, 169
Grant, R.H., 210–11, 221
Grossman, J., 130–31
group loyalty, 250
Gutman, H., 38, 41, 47
Guy-Sheftall, B., 356

H
Hall, C.H., 24
Hall, G.S., 126
Hamilton, T., 98, 99
Hampton Normal and Agricultural Institute,
    60
Harper, C.L., 200–2
Harper, F.E.W., 99–100, 103
Harris, C.I., 369–70
Harris, V.H., 184, 185
Hayes Compromise of 1876, 168
Henderson, M., 356
Herald, The, 181, 183, 184, 185
Heroic Slave, The, 97
Herrnstein, R., 305
high-achieving females, 406–7, 410–17,
    417–20
hip hop, educational research and, 427–29
    confusion about, 428
    four elements of, 427
    future directions of research on,
        446–49
    grounded literature about, 433
    hip-hop aesthetic forms, 443–45,
        447–49
    hip-hop as educational program,
        437–38

hip-hop-based education and, 434–38,
    446
hip-hop forms as pedagogical resources,
    445
hip-hop literacies and discourse,
    441–42
hip-hop pedagogies, 443–45
historical and textual literature about,
    431–32
meanings, identity and, 438–42, 447
racial and generational identity,
    438–40
racial identity in global contexts,
    440–41
rap texts for academic and critical
    literacy, 434–37
research method for research on,
    429–31
social commentary literature about,
    432–33
three kinds of literature on, 431–33
three strands of scholarly work about,
    433–45
Hoffman, F., 125–26
hooks, b., 418–19
Hope, J., 174
Horton, G.M., 75–76
Hughes, M., 226
Hunt, H.A., 176, 177, 180, 181, 182, 183
Hurston, Z.N., 225–26
Hyde Park Improvement Protective Club, 127,
    135

I
immigrant minorities, 243
Industrial High School, 226
Intelligence Can Be Taught, 312
intelligence testing, 148–49, 150, 198, 202–3,
    205–6, 208, 210, 212, 304
intersectionality, 470
involuntary minority, 309

J
Jackson, M., 10–14, 28–29
Jacobs, H., 13
job ceilings, 244
Jocelyn, S., 18
Johnson, C., 144, 148–49

Johnson, J.W., 180, 228
Johnson, L.A., 211
Jones, A.T., 22–23
Jones, J., 44
Jones, M.A., 181
Journal of Negro History, 362

K

Keith Elementary School, 140
King, M.L., Jr., 225, 228
Kleinberg, O., 150
Kluger, R., 163–64
Kozol, J., 359, 365, 370
Ku Klux Klan, 147–48, 200

L

Ladies Literary Society, 85
Ladson-Billings, G., 463–64, 465
Life of Josiah Henson, The, 93
literary character, 66, 67, 77, 79, 81, 99
literary community, 66
Liverpool Mercury, 71
Lofton, C., 218
Logan, T.M., 56–57
Lomotey, K., 367–68
loud Black girls. *See* gendered passing
loudness, 399
Louisiana Educational Relief Association,
    42–43
lunching, 259
Lusher, R.M., 56

M

Malcolm X., 306–7
March 1917 Workers Conference, 176
Marrs, E., 24
Marshall, T., 165, 200, 306, 367
McDonough 35 High School, 206–9
    I.Q. scores and, 208
    principalship of, 207
    racial diversity of, 206
    Mack Spears and, 207, 208, 209
McDonough, J., 207
McPherson, J.M., 45
Measurement of Intelligence, The, 148
Menard, J.W., 42–43
Military Reconstruction Acts, 50

Miller, K., 135
minority/dominant relationships, 308
minority groups, three types, 243–44
Miseducation of the Negro, The, 362
Mohraz, J., 125
Morrison, T., 227, 361
Muhammad, E., 276
Muhammad, L.F., 281
Muhammad, W.F., 276
multicultural paradigm, 371–73
multiculturalism, 233, 372, 464, 477
Murray, C., 305

N

Narrative of the Life of Frederick Douglass, an
    American Slave, 93
Narrative of the Life of Henry Bibb, 90–92
Narrative of William W Brown, a Fugitive Slave,
    93
Nat Turner's rebellion, 14, 249
Nation at Risk, A, 233
Nation of Islam (NOI), Black achievement
    ideology and, 273–75, 293–96
    comparison of achievement ideologies,
    277
    dysfunctional schools and, 289–90
    historical origins of, 275–76
    honor of being Black, 284–86
    membership requirements, 281–84
    NOI students studying together,
    288–89
    NIO women, academic performance
    and, 287–88
    non-NOI attitudes toward NOI stu-
    dents, 286–87
    research methodology of study of,
    276–80, 280–81
    Also see oppositional behavior
National Association for the Advancement of
    Colored People (NAACP), 164, 165,
    175, 178, 179, 186, 200, 367
National Association of Teachers in Colored
    Schools (NATCS), 173–74
National Education Association (NEA), 185
National Educational Association and the Black
    Teacher, The, 164
National Era, 95

National Housing Act of 1934, 133
National Urban League, 148
native anthropologists, 322
native schools, 39
Negro Common School Conference, 173
neutered Other, 405
New Negro, 175
New York Commercial, 124
New York Times, 124
New York Weekly Advocate, 83
Nordhoff, C., 38
North Star, 88, 92
    American writers of European descent
    in, 94–95
    creative parity of Black and white
    writers in, 94
    intended readership of, 88
    literary objectives of, 88–89
    place of Black literature and, 92
    slave narratives and, 93–94
northern school segregation, 123
    curricular variations for Black and
    white students, 150–53
    defense of Black intelligence and,
    149–50
    examples of, 134–38
    Indiana and, 143
    intelligence testing and, 148–49
    Ku Klux Klan and, 147–48
    migration of southern Blacks and,
    124–29
    New Jersey and, 132, 134, 138, 141,
    145–46
    New York City and, 142–43
    Ohio and, 137–38, 139, 141, 146
    Pennsylvania and, 136–37
    racially gerrymandered school district
    lines and, 138–41
    reasons for, 144–50
    tracking of Black students, 151
    vocational schools and, 151
    white parents opposition to, 146–47
    Also see southern black migrants
nothingness, 399

O
Oberlin College, 128–29

Opportunity, 148–49
oppositional behavior, resistance to, 273–75,
    290–93
    organizational habitus and, 274–75
    Also see Nation of Islam
oppositional collective of social identity,
    246–48, 273, 274
oppositional cultural frame of reference,
    246–48
organizational habitus, 274–75, 284, 285
O'Rourke, M., 109
Orr, G., 169
Other, 399–402

P
Pagano, J.A., 400, 406
Partridge, G.E., 126
passing. *See* gendered passing
pauper education, 37
Peabody, E., 93
Peake, Mary (Black teacher), 40–41
Peake, Mary (daughter), 19
Peake, Mary (wife), 19
Peake, T., 19
Pechstein, L.A., 145–46
Penn, R.T., 356
Perlman, J., 151
Perry, T., 174
Phoenixonian Literary Society, 85
Pierce, E.L., 38
Pioneer School of Freedom, 41
"pit schools," 21
Plessy v. Ferguson, 126, 171, 172
Poems on Miscellaneous Subjects, 89–90, 92
property, Whiteness as, 468
property rights, 360, 363–66
    human rights and, 364–65
    race and, 369–71
P.S. 91 (Brooklyn, NY), 213–16
    Martin Shor and, 214, 215
    student grades and, 214–15
public speaking, 86

R
race
    American life and, 366
    as factor in inequity, 360–63

feminist scholarship and, 354
    as a metaphor, 361
    multicultural paradigm of, 371–73
    neutrality, objectivity, color-blindness,
        meritocracy and, 368–69
    performative dimension of, 294
    property and, 360–66, 369–71
Race Differences, 150
race riots, 133–34
racelessness, 307
Ransom, R.L., 51
Ray, C., 85
reading circles, 102
reading rooms and, 81
*Repository of Religion and Literature, and of
    Science and Art*, 67, 99, 101, 104, 105
reputation and status property, 371
Reuter, E., 149–50
rights of disposition, 370
rights to use and enjoyment, 370
Riles, W., 207
Rising in the Sun, 167, 172, 181
Rosenwald Foundation, 183, 184
Ruggles, D., 81
Russworth, J., 68, 70, 78

S
Sabbath school system, 44, 56
Sargent, E., 264
Savannah Education Association, 167
school equality. *See* Black educators, school
    equality and
Schultz, M.J., 164
Shaker Heights, Ohio, 303–4, 304–5
    population statistics, 303–4
Shange, N., 355
Shor, M., 214, 215
Shujaa, M., 233
Shakur, A., 481
silence, 399, 410–17
slavery/slaves
    abolition movement and, 16
    acquiring literacy, 9–29
    Civil War and, 12, 14
    narratives, 93–94, 97
    political significance of slave literacy,
        48–49
    punishment for reading, 47–48

    violence and, 13
Smith, B., 354
Smith, G., 90–92
Smith, H., 171
Smith-Hughes Act, 175–76
Smith, V., 356
social relations, 323–33
sociopathological model, 305
Song of Solomon, 227
Souls of Black Folk, The, 94, 463
southern black migrants to the north, 124–29,
        129–31, 131–34, 134–44
    competition for jobs, housing and
        political influence, 126
    employment discrimination and, 128,
        134
    impact on southern farmers, 175
    northern Black newspapers and, 130
    public accommodations discrimina-
        tion and, 131
    race riots and, 133–34
    residential segregation and, 127, 132–33
    statistics about, 124, 129
    vigilante violence and, 133
    white supremacy and, 125
Space Traders, The, 467
Spears, M., 207, 208, 209
Spillers, H., 356
State and County Educational Reorganization,
        143–44
status mobility system, 245
St. Augustine High School, 209–11
    Father Robert H. Grant and, 210
    Father Matthew O'Rourke and, 209
    I.Q. scores and, 210
    Leo A. Johnson and, 211
Statley, 367–68
Steele, C., 307, 311
stereotype threat, 307
Stono Rebellion, 14, 21
Stowe, H.B., 38, 95
St. Paul of the Cross, 202–4
    I.Q. scores and, 202–3
Stuckey, S., 166
Study of American Intelligence, The, 149
subordinate minorities, 243
Sutch, R., 51
Syphax, W., 216

T

Talking Black, 418–19
Talmadge, E., 185
Tappan, A., 18
Tappin, E., 178
Tate, H., 186
Tate, W., 463–64, 465
Taylor, S.K., 19–20
Terman, L., 148
Terrell, M.C., 129
Thomas, J.O., 176
tracking, 151, 208, 213, 363
Treisman, U., 309
Turner, E., 11
Turner, H.M., 176
Turner, N., 17

U

Uncle Tom's Cabin, 95–97
underachieving females, 407
universal education, ex-slaves and, 37–60
    Black labor power and, 51–52
    Black motivation for, 46–47
    Commission of Enrollment and, 41–42
    early Black schools, 40–41
    early enrollment statistics, 43–44
    educational clauses, labor contracts and, 52
    farmer class opinion of, 50–55
    Georgia and, 43
    industrial Northeast and, 50–51
    long-range purpose of, 59
    Louisiana Educational Relief Association, 42–43
    missionary societies and, 59
    New England classical liberal curriculum and, 57–58
    Richard Wright and, 58–59
    short-term purpose of, 59
    slave punishment for reading, 47–48
    southern state constitutional law and, 50
    statistics about, 49
    support by prominent southern whites, 56–57
    vagrancy laws and, 54
urban, definition of, 371

V

vagrancy laws, 54
vocational schools, 151
voluntary-immigrant minorities, 273–74

W

Walker, D., 15, 17, 79
Wallace, M., 354, 355, 356
Walling, W.E., 126–27
Walsh, E., 265
Ware, C., 354
Washington, B.T., 11, 38, 46, 170, 177, 228
Washington, M., 97
Washington Post, 241, 264
Watkins, F.E., 89–90, 92
Watson, T., 171
Weekly Advocate, 82
Weekly Anglo-African, 67, 99, 101, 102–3
Weinberg, M., 45
Wheatley, P., 75
Whimbey, A., 312
White, D., 356, 357
white feminist movement, 354
White Georgia Educational Association, 177
White Marxists, 361
white supremacism, 125, 171, 464
White, W., 178
white womanhood, 401
whiteness, 468–69
Whittier, J.G., 91
Wiener, J., 50, 54
Williams, G.W., 372
Williams, J., 91
Williams, P., 18, 400
Woodson, C.G., 217, 362, 463
Wright, R., 58–59
Wright, R.R., Sr., 167–70, 173, 174
Wright, T., 18

X

Xavier Prep, 212–13
    I.Q. scores and, 212
    Sister Anne Louise Bechtold and, 212
    tracking and, 213

Y

Young, K., 148